The Italian Renaissance

Blackwell Essential Readings in History

This series comprises concise collections of key articles on important historical topics. Designed as a complement to standard survey histories, the volumes are intended to help introduce students to the range of scholarly debate in a subject area. Each collection includes a general introduction and brief contextual headnotes to each article, offering a coherent, critical framework for study.

Published

The German Reformation: The Essential Readings
C. Scott Dixon

The English Civil War: The Essential Readings
Peter Gaunt

The Italian Renaissance: The Essential Readings
Paula Findlen

The Scientific Revolution: The Essential Readings
Marcus Hellyer

Stalinism: The Essential Readings
David L. Hoffmann

The Cold War: The Essential Readings
Klaus Larres and Ann Lane

The Third Reich: The Essential Readings
Christian Leitz

The Counter-Reformation: The Essential Readings
David M. Luebke

The Crusades: The Essential Readings
Thomas F. Madden

The Russian Revolution: The Essential Readings
Martin Miller

The French Revolution: The Essential Readings
Ronald Schechter

Cromwell and the Interregnum: The Essential Readings
David L. Smith

The Italian Renaissance

The Essential Readings

Edited by Paula Findlen

Blackwell
Publishing

Editorial material and organization © 2002 Paula Findlen

BLACKWELL PUBLISHING
350 Main Street, Malden, MA 02148-5020, USA
9600 Garsington Road, Oxford OX4 2DQ, UK
550 Swanston Street, Carlton, Victoria 3053, Australia

First published 2002 by Blackwell Publishing Ltd

Library of Congress Cataloging-in-Publication Data

The Italian Renaissance : the essential readings / edited by Paula Findlen.
      p. cm. — (Blackwell essential readings in history)
   Includes bibliographical references and index.
   ISBN 978-0-631-22282-8 (hbk) — ISBN 978-0-631-22283-5 (pbk)
    1. Italy—Civilization—1268–1559—Historiography. 2.
Renaissance—Italy—Historiography. I. Findlen, Paula. II. Series.

   DG445 .I78 2002
   945'.05—dc21

                      2002022982

A catalogue record for this title is available from the British Library.

Set in 10 on 12 Photina
by SNP Best-set Typesetter Ltd, Hong Kong

For further information on
Blackwell Publishing, visit our website:
www.blackwellpublishing.com

Contents

Cover Illustration   vii

List of Illustrations   viii

Acknowledgments   x

Part I   Introduction   1

    1 Understanding the Italian Renaissance   4
    Paula Findlen

Part II   Was There a Renaissance State?   41

    2 Civic Traditions in Premodern Italy   47
    Gene Brucker

    3 Cosimo de' Medici: *Pater Patriae* or *Padrino?*   64
    Anthony Molho

Part III   Urban Life and Values   91

    4 "Kin, Friends, and Neighbors": The Urban
    Territory of a Merchant Family in 1400   97
    Christiane Klapisch-Zuber

    5 Sumptuary Law and Social Relations in
    Renaissance Italy   124
    Diane Owen Hughes

    6 The Virgin on the Street Corner: The Place
    of the Sacred in Italian Cities   151
    Edward Muir

Part IV Gender and Society   167

7 "The Most Serious Duty": Motherhood, Gender,
   and Patrician Culture in Renaissance Venice   173
   Stanley Chojnacki
8 Gender and Sexual Culture in Renaissance Italy   192
   Michael Rocke

Part V The Power of Knowledge   213

9 Petrarch's Conception of the "Dark Ages"   219
   Theodor E. Mommsen
10 Commerce with the Classics   237
   Anthony Grafton
11 Isotta Nogarola: Women Humanists – Education
   for What?   273
   Lisa Jardine

Part VI Patronage, Art, and Culture   293

12 Heroes and Their Workshops: Medici Patronage
   and the Problem of Shared Agency   299
   Melissa Meriam Bullard
13 The Court Lady's Dilemma: Isabella d'Este and
   Art Collecting in the Renaissance   317
   Rose Marie San Juan

Index   341

Cover Illustration

Andrea Mantegna (1431–1506)
Camera degli Sposi, Meeting Scene, west wall, 1465–74
Palazzo Ducale, Mantua

Mantegna depicted the duke of Mantua, Ludovico Gonzaga, meeting his sons, cardinal Francesco and prince Federico, on the border between Mantua and Milan as the duke of Milan, Francesco Sforza, lay ill. Mantegna included King Christian I of Denmark, related by marriage to duke Ludovico, and Emperor Frederick III, Mantua's overlord, in this imaginary scene, though there is no record of their actual presence, to convey Mantua's powerful connections outside their tiny state. Ludovico reportedly hosted ambassadors visiting Mantua in the Camera degli Sposi. Mantegna's paintings were designed to impress them with his skills as a ruler and his taste as a patron of the arts; the north wall additionally served the practical purpose of advertising the beauty of the duke's daughters for potential suitors by depicting them in a family scene at court.

Illustrations

Plates

1 Ambrogio Lorenzetti, *The Good City-Republic* (1338–40)
Source: Sala dei Nove, Palazzo Pubblico, Siena (partial view
of east wall). Copyright Scala / Art Resource, NY.   9

2 Vittore Carpaccio, *Two Venetian Ladies on a Terrace* (ca. 1495)
Source: Museo Civico Correr, Venice. Copyright Alinari /
Art Resource, NY.   18

3 Anonymous, *The Execution of Savonarola* (1498 or after)
Source: Museo di San Marco, Florence. Copyright Alinari /
Art Resource, NY.   28

4 Agnolo Bronzino, *Portrait of Ugolino Martelli* (ca. 1535–8)
Source: Staatliche Museen, Berlin. Copyright Alinari /
Art Resource, NY.   36

5 Raphael, *Pope Leo X with Two Cardinals* (1517/18)
Source: Uffizi Gallery. Copyright Alinari / Art Resource, NY.   46

6 Vittore Carpaccio, *The Healing of the Possessed Man* (1494)
Source: Accademia, Venice. Copyright Cameraphoto /
Art Resource, NY.   96

7 Lavinia Fontana, *Portrait of a Family* (ca. 1600)
Source: Pinacoteca Nazionale di Brera, Milan.
Copyright Scala / Art Resource, NY.   172

8   Pedro Berruguete (?), *Portrait of Federico da Montefeltro and His Son Guidobaldo* (1480–1)
    Source: Galleria Nazionale delle Marche, Urbino.
    Copyright Alinari / Art Resource, NY.   218

9   Sandro Botticelli, *Adoration of the Magi* (ca. 1470–5)
    Source: Uffizi Gallery, Florence. Copyright Alinari /
    Art Resource, NY.   298

10 Titian, *Portrait of Isabella d'Este* (ca. 1536)
    Source: Kunsthistorische Museum, Vienna. Copyright
    Erich Lessing / Art Resource, NY.   331

11 Andrea Mantegna, *Mars and Venus* (ca. 1497)
    Source: Musée du Louvre, Paris. Copyright Giraudon /
    Art Resource, NY.   335

12 Andrea Mantegna, *Pallas Expelling the Vices from the Garden of Virtue* (ca. 1502)
    Source: Musée du Louvre, Paris. Copyright Alinari / Art
    Resource, NY.   336

Maps

1   Renaissance Italy   12
2   Italy ca. 1600   30

Acknowledgments

The publication of a volume intended for a general readership is, more than any research project, the work of many hands. I especially thank Tessa Harvey, Tamsin Smith, Louise Spencely, and Angela Cohen at Blackwell Publishing for inviting me to do this and encouraging the project to completion. I also am appreciative of their desire to solicit many opinions as to what a good volume on Renaissance Italy might include. Thanks to all the anonymous readers who told me what they liked and didn't like, and reminded me not to reinvent the wheel when many of the spokes were good and strong. And thanks to Bill Bowsky, Michelle Fontaine, Anthony Grafton, Duane Osheim, Maureen Miller, Laurie Nussdorfer, Katharine Park, and Randolph Starn for their helpful suggestions about readings. William Nelson created the maps for this book and Anthony Grahame copy-edited the manuscript. I owe Ken Gouwens a special debt on this project. This is the second time that we have collaborated on presenting aspects of Renaissance Italy to a wider audience. Ken read all the parts of this volume with great care, saved me from many infelicities, and has worked closely with me to ensure that readers will find our two volumes of critical essays and source readings complementary introductions to Italian Renaissance society and culture.

I am especially appreciative of the student input I received in the course of preparing this volume. Tara Nummedal, now a professor teaching her own classes on the Renaissance, helped me to compile a bibliography from which these readings were selected. Charles McVicker kindly did some last minute xeroxing when I was far from home. But my biggest thanks goes to all the students who have taken my seminar on "Power, Art, and Knowledge in Renaissance Italy" at Stanford University during the last few years. They have been the victims of earlier versions of the Reader and have offered honest opinions so to what interests students today about the Renaissance. The students in our Overseas Studies Program in Florence asked good questions on field trips to the "real thing" when I taught this class there in Fall 2000. All of them have inspired me with their continued enthusiasm not just for the Leonardos and Machiavellis of this world but for someone like Sienese peasant Benedetto di Massarizia, who knew that the red stockings and shiny silver buckle that he purchased with hard-earned money were simply too important in his life not to be written down.

The authors and publishers gratefully acknowledge the following for permission to reproduce copyright material:

Extract, "Civic Traditions in Premodern Italy," by Gene Brucker, in *Journal of Interdisciplinary History* 29:3, Winter 1999, pp. 357–77, © 1999 by the Massachusetts Institute of Technology and the editors of the *Journal of Interdisciplinary History*. Reprinted by permission of MIT Press, USA;

Extract, "Cosimo de' Medici: Pater Patriae or Padrino" by Anthony Molho, in *Stanford Italian Review* 1, 1979, pp. 5–33. Reprinted by permission of Anma Libri, Saratoga, California;

Extract, "Kins, Friends and Neighbors: The Urban Territory of a Merchant Family in 1400," by Christiane Klapisch-Zuber, in *Women, Family and Ritual in Renaissance Italy*, translated by Lydia G. Cochrane, pp. 68–93, © 1985. Reprinted by permission of The University of Chicago Press;

Extract, "Sumptuary Law and Social Relations in Renaissance Italy" by Diane Owen Hughes, in *Disputes and Settlements*, edited by John Bossy, pp. 69–99, published by Cambridge University Press in 1983. Used with permission;

Extract, "The Virgin on the Street Corner: The Place of the Sacred in Italian Cities," by Edward Muir, in *Religion and Culture in the Renaissance and Reformation*, edited by Steven Ozment, pp. 25–40, © 1989. Reprinted by permission of Copyright Clearance Centre inc.;

Extract, " 'The Most Serious Duty': Motherhood, Gender, and Patrician Culture in Renaissance Venice," by Stanley Chojnacki, in *Refiguring Woman: Perspectives on Gender and the Italian Renaissance*, edited by Marilyn Migiel and Juliana Schiesari. © 1991 Cornell University. Used by permission of the publisher, Cornell University Press;

Extract, "Gender and Sexual Culture in Renaissance Italy," by Michael Rocke, in *Gender and Society in Renaissance Italy*, edited by Judith C. Brown and Robert C. Davis, published by Longman, pp. 150–70, © 1998. Reprinted by permission of Pearson Education;

Extract, *Commerce with the Classics: Ancient Books and Renaissance Readers*, by Anthony Grafton, pp. 11–52, published by University of Michigan Press in 1997. Reprinted with permission;

Extract, "Isotta Nogarola: Women Humanists – Education for What?" by Lisa Jardine, in *History of Education*, 1983, vol. 12, no. 4, pp. 231–44. Reprinted by permission of Taylor & Francis Ltd., PO Box 25, Abingdon, Oxfordshire OX14 3UE;

Extract, "Heroes and Their Workshops: Medici Patronage and the Problem of Shared Agency," by Melissa Meriam Bullard in *Journal of Medieval and Renaissance Studies* 24, 1994, pp. 179–98. Copyright 1994, Duke University Press. All rights reserved. Reprinted with permission;

Extract, "The Court Lady's Dilemma: Isabella d'Este and Art Collecting in the Renaissance," by Rose Marie San Juan, in *Oxford Art Journal* 14, 1991, pp. 67–78. Reprinted by permission of Oxford University Press.

The publishers apologize for any errors or omissions in the above list and would be grateful to be notified of any corrections that should be incorporated in the next edition or reprint of this book.

Part I

Introduction

Introduction to Part I

The Italian Renaissance is an interesting and complex moment in the history of politics, society and culture. This volume contains thirteen essays designed to introduce readers to some of the most fundamental aspects of the period in question. I have organized these readings thematically because I still agree with the Swiss German historian Jacob Burckhardt, whose *The Civilization of the Renaissance in Italy* (1860) remains the classic study of this subject, that the Renaissance was not an event that unfolded in a series of neat chronological steps but a subject that emerged episodically. Part I offers an introductory overview to the Italian Renaissance and extensive, though by no means comprehensive, bibliography of some of the important work on this period in English. Part II examines politics and the Renaissance city-state. Part III introduces readers to crucial aspects of behavior in the cities, the physical location in which many activities that define the Renaissance occurred. Part IV examines the nature of marriage and motherhood and attitudes towards sexuality. Part V discusses the intellectual life of Renaissance Italy, offering three different perspectives on humanism. Finally, Part VI turns to the problem of patronage in relationship to the production of art and culture in the fifteenth and early sixteenth centuries.

These different themes by no means exhaust the variety of subjects that an introductory volume on Renaissance Italy might cover. But they are all essential for a better understanding of why this society continues to fascinate us. Each of the essays in this volume demonstrates some of the best work in political, social, and cultural history done in the past few decades. I have supplemented them with introductory essays, designed to raise general questions about the theme as a whole, and with images that reflect directly the themes of each section. Looking at art is a fundamental aspect of understanding Italian Renaissance history, not simply for the pleasure it affords but because it offers us crucial pieces of evidence about how this society envisioned itself.

Historical inquiry should be a process that yields multiple interpretations of a single subject. This volume is not designed to describe Renaissance Italy in any definitive sense, because there are many aspects of this world that a single book cannot cover in adequate detail. Rather its goal is to inform readers about key attributes of this world and to invite you to participate in the process of understanding and imagining this particular past. Since the modern idea of history – understanding the past in its own terms – was, in part, a creation of Renaissance humanism, this makes it all the more fitting that historians continue to exercise their skills on grappling with the problems and pleasures of a society that truly appreciated the value of a historical perspective.

1

Understanding the Italian Renaissance

Paula Findlen

> No enterprise, no matter how small, can begin or end without these three things: power, knowledge, and love. Fourteenth-century Tuscan saying[1]

I How Petrarch Rediscovered Italy

In 1337, the son of a Florentine merchant who had spent most of his life in the papal city of Avignon in southern France, made his first trip to Rome. Gazing upon the city that had once been the center of the Roman Empire and the heart of Christendom until the papacy moved to Avignon in 1309, Francesco Petrarca (1304–74) lamented the sorry condition of "the remains of a broken city." Already in his writings he anticipated a moment when future generations would emerge from "this slumber of forgetfulness into the pure radiance of the past."[2]

Petrarch's profound sense of displacement from his own times and his fierce desire to recapture the glories of a neglected past lay at the heart of the cultural movement we know as the Renaissance. He belonged to the earliest generations of humanists who had begun to re-examine the ancient

---

1 Vittore Branca, ed., *Merchant Writers of the Italian Renaissance*, trans. Murtha Baca (New York: Marsilio Publishers, 1999), p. ix. Readers wishing to consult other surveys of Renaissance Italy might start with Lauro Martines, *Power and Imagination: City-States in Renaissance Italy* (New York: Vintage, 1980, 1979), Peter Burke, *The Italian Renaissance: Culture and Society in Italy* (Princeton: Princeton University Press, 1986; 1972); and Lisa Jardine, *Wordly Goods: A New History of the Renaissance* (London: Macmillan, 1996). The most fundamental account remains Jacob Burckhardt, *The Civilization of the Renaissance in Italy*, trans. S. G. C. Middlemore (London: Penguin, 1990).

2 Petrarch, *Rerum familiarium libri I–VIII*, p. 294 (*Fam.* VI, 2): "Et euntibus per menia fracte urbis et illic sedentibus, ruinarum fragmenta sub oculis erant." In Petrarca, *Opere* (Florence: Sansoni, 1975), p. 484; and Petrarch, *Africa* (1336), in John T. Paoletti and Gary M. Radke, *Art in Renaissance Italy* (London: Laurence King, 1997), p. 26.

past in the study of law and literature and, in Petrarch's case, use the lessons he learned from antiquity to examine the spiritual malaise of the mid-fourteenth century.[3] By the end of his life, he surrounded himself with the artifacts that evoked the world he wished to inhabit: manuscripts written by ancient Romans such as his beloved Cicero, to whom Petrarch composed imaginary letters in an effort to converse with the dead; ancient coins and medals; books of modern authors such as Dante Alighieri (1265–1322) and Giovanni Boccaccio (1313–75) who transformed Tuscan prose into a celebrated literary style; a painting by Giotto that was among his dearest possessions; and Greek manuscripts that he found himself unable to read because there was no one fully capable of unlocking their ancient grammar.

A Tuscan who spent most of his life outside of Italy, Petrarch exhibited a passionate craving for the best things that his society could offer him, ancient as well as modern. He attempted to perfect his Latin in imitation of Cicero in his letters, dialogues, and treatises, and celebrated the resurgence of his native Tuscan by writing poetry in this vernacular. He wrote dialogues between himself and Augustine, his favorite Christian writer, in order to explore the problems of a moral existence in a world rife with temptations, among them, the pleasure of knowledge itself. After numerous trips to Italy during which he collected manuscripts and met admirers such as Boccaccio, Petrarch finally returned to his native land. He initially settled in Milan in 1353, later moving to the small town of Arquà, south of Padua, in 1370 to enjoy his final years in proximity to one of the great centers of learning.

In retrospect, it might seem obvious to us that such cities as Florence, Venice, and Rome should be the centerpiece of the Italian Renaissance, because their leading historians and artists engaged so actively in their myth-making in the fifteenth and sixteenth centuries, but this was not immediately evident to contemporary observers. The Italy to which Petrarch returned was not Tuscany, but Milan, center of a thriving court culture, Verona, home of rich monastic libraries, Padua, a great center for law and scholarship, and of course Rome, a ghost of the past. His friend Boccaccio, another Tuscan who spent years away from Florence working for his family's business in Naples, felt a similar ambivalence towards Florence, though he returned there in 1341. Angevin Naples, he wrote with great nostalgia, had been "happy, peaceful, abounding in good things, magnificent, and ruled by a single king." Instead he found Florence filled with "as many opinions as there are men, and always under arms, and at war as much at home as abroad." Boccaccio eventually retreated to his

---

3   Ronald G. Witt, *In the Footsteps of the Ancients: The Origins of Humanism from Lovato to Bruni* (Leiden: Brill, 2000); and Charles Trinkhaus, *The Poet as Philosopher: Petrarch and the Formation of Renaissance Consciousness* (New Haven: Yale University Press, 1979).

birthplace of Certaldo in 1361, where he celebrated "the absence of the ambitions and the unpleasantness and annoyances of our town-dwellers."[4] He had no special love for fourteenth-century Florence nor any particular allegiance to its politics.

Following his death in 1374, Petrarch's home and tomb in Arquà became pilgrimage sites for his admirers who saw him as the embodiment of the cultural movement that another Tuscan, the painter and historian Giorgio Vasari (1511–74), would describe in 1550 as a *rinascita* – a rebirth. Boccaccio, too, would be celebrated as the embodiment of all that was great about Florence. However, Vasari did not have either writer in mind when he wrote these words. He referred specifically to the transformation of the arts between the fourteenth and the sixteenth centuries, beginning with Cimabue (ca. 1240–1302) and Giotto (1266/67–1337) and culminating in Michelangelo Buonarotti (1475–1564) who was still alive when Vasari completed his first edition. Sixteenth-century French humanists translated *rinascita* into *renaissance* to describe the general revival of learning and culture that they had witnessed. As French culture extended its influence throughout Europe in the seventeenth and eighteenth centuries, this foreign word stuck. In 1764 no less a figure than the great English historian Edward Gibbon described himself as seeing the "renaissance" of art as he gazed at the paintings in the Uffizi galleries and contemplated writing a history of the Medici. By the mid-nineteenth century historians such as Jules Michelet and Jacob Burckhardt used this concept to define the period as a whole.[5] Burckhardt, in particular, insisted that it was not simply the revival of antiquity that constituted the Renaissance. If Petrarch wished to think and write like a Roman, it was a reflection of a much more fundamental transformation of his society.

In *The Civilization of the Renaissance in Italy* (1860), Burckhardt famously remarked: "The Renaissance would not have been the process of world-wide significance which it is, if its elements could be so easily separated from one

---

4   Giovanni Boccaccio, *Fiametta*, as quoted in Vittore Branca, *Boccaccio: The Man and His Works*, trans. Richard Monges and Dennis J. McAulifee (New York: New York University Press, 1976), p. 58; idem, *Epistola consolatoria a Pino de' Rossi*, in Branca, *Boccaccio*, p. 129. For a fine account of why Naples was appealing, see Jerry H. Bentley, *Politics and Culture in Renaissance Naples* (Princeton: Princeton University Press, 1987).

5   Vasari alluded to the "progress of art's rebirth" in the preface to his *Lives of the Most Eminent Italian Architects, Painters, and Sculptors from Cimabue to Our Times*, first published in 1550 and reissued with important modifications in 1568. See Giorgio Vasari, *The Lives of the Artists*, ed. and trans. Julia Conaway Bondanella and Peter Bondanella (Oxford: Oxford University Press, 1991), p. 6. On the idea of the Renaissance, see especially Wallace K. Ferguson, *The Renaissance in Historical Thought: Five Centuries of Interpretation* (New York: Houghton Mifflin, 1948); and Paula Findlen, *A Fragmentary Past: The Making of Museums and the Making of the Renaissance* (forthcoming).

another."[6] While we may no longer agree with Burckhardt on the precise meaning of the Italian Renaissance, which he defined as the birth of the modern western world and modern man, his idea of the interconnectedness of Italian Renaissance society still stands. If today most of us primarily experience the Italian Renaissance through viewing its great works of art in museums and in countless reproductions of paintings such as Sandro Botticelli's *Birth of Venus* (ca. 1485) and Leonardo da Vinci's *Mona Lisa* (1503–6), and by reading a handful of its most important books such as Boccaccio's *Decameron* (ca. 1350) and Machiavelli's *The Prince* (1513), we need to remember that these things are not timeless and isolated artifacts but were products of a specific historical moment. Understanding the Italian Renaissance allows us to appreciate how the cultural traces of the Renaissance that have survived emerged from its social, political, economic, and religious fabric. This context is well worth studying because Italy played a fundamental role in shaping the politics and culture of western Europe from antiquity through the seventeenth century.

Just as Petrarch's vision of the past is part of a more complicated story about the growth of humanist learning, which looked to ancient Greece and Rome for models of good politics and culture, the emergence of Florence, Venice, and Rome as Renaissance cities filled with great artists and generous patrons cannot be told in isolation from developments throughout the Italian peninsula in this crucial period of its history. No single individual or city gave birth to the Italian Renaissance or fully contained its achievements. Instead we might think of the Italian Renaissance as a Shakespearean drama in which the minor characters and the settings themselves were often the hinge of the entire story. In the past two decades, social and cultural history has given us a richer portrait of Renaissance Italy than we previously enjoyed. Many of the articles in this volume reflect this new understanding of the Renaissance. We now have a much better comprehension of how such issues as family and sexuality, friendship and patronage, knowledge and faith defined the parameters of behavior in this world in relationship to our continued appreciation of the great politics, art, and literature of the time. The chapters in this volume invite readers to explore the dynamic among these different dimensions of the Italian Renaissance.

2   The Italy that Petrarch Saw

But let us return to the beginning of the Italian Renaissance – the moment of Petrarch's great nostalgia. The world that Petrarch inhabited was a study in contrasts, and this was surely part of his disaffection from it. The poverty

6   Burckhardt, *Civilization*, p. 120.

of Rome, the only major city of this period whose walls were not constantly being rebuilt to accommodate a population bursting at the seams, appeared all the more incongruous in a landscape defined by urban growth and prosperity. Florence, already a city of over 100,000 inhabitants before the great plague pandemic of 1348 killed somewhere between one-third to one-half its population, typified this other face of Italy that Petrarch certainly knew well. It was a thriving commercial society that expressed its pride through great civic commissions such as the building of the Duomo, initiated in 1296 and halfway towards completion when Petrarch visited Florence, and the decoration of the south Baptistery doors that Andrea Pisano completed in 1336. To the south of Florence, the government of Siena commissioned Ambrogio Lorenzetti to paint his *Allegory of Good and Bad Government* (1338–40), a subtle account of the many forces that shaped a city, on the walls of the Palazzo Pubblico (Plate 1). To the north, noble families such as the d'Este in Ferrara, the Gonzaga in Mantua, and the Visconti in Milan had just begun to establish their rule over their respective cities. In Venice, artisans laid the foundation stones of the Doge's Palace in 1340. The growth of many Italian towns in the face of the papacy's abandonment of Italy, and despite the intermittent struggles between ruling families who used their allegiance to the pope or the emperor as a pretext for attacking their enemies, was one of the many paradoxes that troubled witnesses to Italy's fourteenth century.

In contrast to the nation-states that emerged in Spain, France, and England during the Renaissance, Italy would not become a nation until 1860, the year Burckhardt completed his great study of Renaissance Italy, and this new Italy did not include the Papal States until 1869. Although Renaissance Italy lacked any prospect for unified political leadership and seemed to have temporarily ceded its religious primacy to the French, it surpassed all other parts of Europe, with the possible exception of Flanders, in its commercial economy. "Money is the vital heat of a city," observed the Franciscan preacher Bernardino da Siena (1380–1444). A steady stream of transactions involving florins, ducats, and bills of exchange, all neatly recorded in account books that survive from this period, defined the world in which the majority of city-dwellers lived. Boccaccio vividly captured this world in his tales of greedy and gullible merchants who betrayed and were betrayed by their wives while engaging in commerce far from home. He had direct experience of such things working as a banker's apprentice in Naples. "Make me this calculation," a fourteenth-century Venetian merchant wrote repeatedly in his notebook.[7] The connections among cities – linked by trade, immigration, and politics – made Italian society thrive.

---

7   John E. Dotson, ed. and trans., *Merchant Culture in Fourteenth Century Venice: The Zibaldone da Canal* (Binghamton, NY: Medieval and Renaissance Texts and Studies, 1994), p. 29 and *passim*.

Plate I Ambrogio Lorenzetti, *The Good City-Republic* (1338–40). *Source:* Sala dei Nove, Palazzo Pubblico, Siena (partial view of east wall).

This panel is part of Ambrogio Lorenzetti's (ca. 1295–1348) famous fresco cycle, most commonly known as the *Allegory of Good and Bad Government*. Commissioned by the Nine who ruled Siena from 1287 to 1355, it offers an idealized portrait of the virtues of republican government. Lorenzetti's fresco transforms details of an Italian city-state into a utopian image of a harmonious and prosperous society. The fact that Lorenzetti's fresco cycle was located in the Room of the Nine in the Palazzo Pubblico, the seat of government in Siena, suggests its importance as a work of public art. City officials and visitors who entered the room were first confronted with an image of a violent and chaotic city ruled by Fear, "The City-State Under Tyranny" (west wall). Looking at the north wall, they saw "The Virtues of Good Government," a fresco depicting how communal government dispensed justice, maintained peace, and preserved the common good. Finally they turned to the image of "The Good City-Republic," where Security maintains peace by guarding the city gates that open into the countryside. Inside the walls, the social and economic life of the city thrives. Note the depiction of Siena's Duomo in the upper-left corner as well as the presence of aristocratic family towers that suggest the kind of oligarchical power that controlled the city. Building projects, a lively market, and a marriage procession (lower-left corner) offer a snapshot of an Italian city on the eve of the Black Death.

The merchant community in Avignon, for example, was filled with all manner of Italians, trading goods, opening branches of their banks, and offering services to an international clientele. When Francesco Datini (ca. 1335–1410) decided to become a merchant, he opened his first shop in Avignon, followed by branches in Pisa, Genoa, Valencia, and Majorca. But he also made sure to become a Florentine citizen after returning to Italy in 1382, and eventually left all of his wealth to his native city of Prato upon his death.[8] Like Petrarch, he could not spend his entire life outside Italy without eventually seeking recognition at home.

More often than not, citizenship in the Italian Renaissance cities was defined by long absences for its male members, who stayed away from home so that their family businesses might prosper and, at times, because the vicissitudes of politics had forced them into exile. In July 1449, for instance, Alessandra Strozzi lamented the fact that her youngest son, thirteen-year-old Matteo, was about to depart for Naples to learn his trade, following his two elder brothers who also had left Florence in pursuit of honor and profit.[9] The mobility of Italian merchants and patricians brought the values and practices of the Italian cities into contact with many parts of the world. For all these reasons, Petrarch could experience Italy even from the distance of Avignon, because so much of Italy had migrated to southern France with the papacy's abandonment of Rome.

The commercial economy of northern and central Italy produced forms of governance that reflected the emergence of a wealthy urban elite and a society in need of revenue to fund the costs of intermittent warfare. Communal government shaped the politics of many Italian city-states as early as the twelfth century, though there were other cities ruled by hereditary princes with feudal land holdings. The cities of Tuscany, principally Florence, Siena, and Pisa, were ruled by an elected citizen elite who levied public taxes to support the enterprise of the state. Machiavelli would later observe with pride that Tuscany contained three republics and "no baronial castles."[10] Their merchants and bankers traveled all over the Mediterranean, Levant, and northern Europe. The maritime republics of Genoa and Venice, both as large as Florence, rested their prosperity on trading empires

---

8 Bernardino da Siena's sermons are quoted in Robert Bonfil, *Jewish Life in Renaissance Italy*, trans. Anthony Oldcorn (Berkeley: University of California Press, 1994), p. 24. On Datini, see Iris Origo, *The Merchant of Prato: Daily Life in a Medieval City* (Harmondsworth: Penguin, 1986; 1957).

9 Alessandra Strozzi, *Selected Letters of Alessandra Strozzi*, ed. and trans. Heather Gregory (Berkeley: University of California Press, 1997), p. 45.

10 Niccolò Machiavelli, *The Discourses*, ed. Bernard Crick, trans. Leslie J. Walker, S. J. and Brian Richardson (London: Penguin, 1983; 1970), p. 243. This work seems to have been written between 1516 and 1519, though it was already in gestation when Machiavelli completed *The Prince*.

that competed with each other for control of transport and commerce between East and West. *Januensis ergo mercator*, "Genoese therefore a merchant," went a saying of the time. Venice's fifteenth-century chroniclers noted with pride that Venetian patricians "continue to trade." They praised their elected head of government, the doge, for having the appearance of a prince, the virtues of a citizen, and the temperament of a merchant.[11]

City-states increasingly were territorial states whose geography reflected the ambitions of their leading citizens. In Petrarch's time, the expansion of various states had just begun and would be completed in the fifteenth and early sixteenth centuries. The Florentines, for example, annexed Pisa in 1406 and Livorno in 1421 with the specific goal of acquiring access to the sea, as the culmination of a territorial state that had begun with the submission of Prato to Florentine rule in 1350. The Venetians declared their primacy over the Genoese by establishing an overseas empire in the Eastern Mediterranean that included much of Istria, Dalmatia, Crete, and colonies scattered between Venice and Constantinople. The size of their territorial state within Italy, beginning with the capture of Treviso in 1389 and culminating in the acquisition of Bergamo by 1428, deeply alarmed neighboring states such as Milan and Ferrara (see Map 1). Pope Pius II would write of the Venetians in 1459 that "they aim at the dominion of Italy and all but dare to aspire to the mastery of the world." But he was quick to add that if the Florentine state grew as strong, "they would also have an equal ambition for empire."[12] To a certain extent, the logic of the city-state reflected the dynamics of trade in which the wealthiest cities and rulers had the resources to secure their position within a region. Subject cities might occasionally rebel when they sensed weakness at the center, or when external threats from other rulers forced them to reconsider their allegiances, but they came to accept the idea that Italy would be a land of many would-be princes but few actual rulers.[13]

At the beginning of the Renaissance, Italy was a crossroads between northern Europe and the Levant.[14] Tuscan gradually emerged as a com-

11   Steven Epstein, *Genoa and the Genoese, 958–1528* (Chapel Hill: University of North Carolina Press, 1996), p. xvi; and Marin Sanudo, *Praise of the City of Venice* (1493), in *Venice: A Documentary History 1450–1630*, ed. David Chambers and Brian Pullan (Oxford: Blackwell, 1992), p. 11. It was said of the Venetian doge: "He has the bearing of a prince, but in the Senate he is a senator, and in the marketplace a citizen." In Edward Muir, *Civic Ritual in Renaissance Venice* (Princeton: Princeton University Press, 1981).

12   Aenius Sylvius Piccolomini, *Memoirs of a Renaissance Pope: The Commentaries of Pius II (An Abridgment)*, ed. Leona C. Gabel, trans. Florence A. Gragg (New York: Capricorn Books, 1962; 1959), p. 352.

13   Two exemplary studies of subject cities are Judith C. Brown, *In the Shadow of Florence: Provincial Society in Renaissance Pescia* (Oxford: Oxford University Press, 1982); and James S. Grubb, *Firstborn of Venice: Vicenza in the Early Renaissance State*. Baltimore: Johns Hopkins University Press, 1988).

14   The classic study of this subject remains Fernand Braudel, *The Mediterranean and the*

Map 1 Renaissance Italy.

mercial language across the Mediterranean before becoming the literary language of educated Italians in the sixteenth century. Genoese and Venetian dialects helped to create the international language of seafarers. Societies in proximity to Italy also shaped its culture. In parts of northern Italy, French and German were the lingua franca, just as Arabic and Greek continued to be spoken in parts of southern Italy – vestiges of centuries of foreign rule and a reflection of the constantly shifting boundaries between Italy, France, and the Holy Roman Empire. The economic opportunities in Italy also attracted foreigners. When the French diplomat Philippe de Commynes visited Venice in 1495, he alluded to the prominence of Greek, German, and Turkish colonies in the city, when he remarked that "most of the people are foreigners."[15] Slaves, mostly of Slavic and eastern European origin, were yet another foreign population who entered the households of wealthy patricians as servants – the ultimate example of how a commercial society connected different peoples.[16] From this perspective, Italy seemed utterly lacking in a single unifying identity – an entrepôt more than a state – save for a lingering sense that all parts of the Italian peninsula had inherited a legacy and a language from the Roman empire and had vested interests that loosely bound them together.

The emphasis on local interests shaped Italy as a region of multiple identities, roughly unified by language, customs, and culture. If the idea of communal government distinguished Italy from the rest of Europe, it was by no means uniform or evident in every part of Italy. The Florentines, Venetians, and Genoese, for example, all considered themselves citizens of great republics. But the nature of republican rule expressed itself differently in each instance. While all cities restricted active citizenship to the population of adult males who paid taxes, some cities such as Florence made membership in a guild (organizations which regulated entry into the major professions within a city) a crucial factor. Other cities made the question of lineage a primary criterion for political participation. The most famous case is Venice, whose "Golden Book" (*Libro d'oro*) recorded the names of all descendants of the city's ruling families since 1297, defining for the next five hundred years who could hold office. In 1377 the Visconti rulers of Milan created a similar book to distinguish their nobility, though it did not

Mediterranean World in the Age of Philip II, trans. Siân Reynolds (New York: Harper and Row, 1972–3), 2 vols. See also David Abulafia, *The Two Italies: Economic Relations between the Norman Kingdom of Sicily and the Northern Communes* (Cambridge: Cambridge University Press, 1977).
15   John Martin and Dennis Romano, ed., *Venice Reconsidered: The History and Civilization of an Italian City-State 1297–1797* (Baltimore: Johns Hopkins University Press, 2000), p. 20.
16   This important subject is only just beginning to receive more attention. See Iris Origo, "The Domestic Enemy: Eastern Slaves in Tuscany in the Fourteenth and Fifteenth Centuries," *Speculum* 30 (1955): 321-66; and Robert C. Davis, "Slave Redemption in Venice, 1585–1797," in Martin and Romano, *Venice Reconsidered*, pp. 454–87.

have the same sort of lasting impact on the city's politics.[17] Both in the northern and southern-most parts of Italy, lineage mattered in ways that seemed less apparent in Tuscany.

The Florentines were suspicious of their city's nobility. They excluded magnates from holding office in 1293, out of fear that they would abuse their power. Their towers, that defined the political divisions of the medieval city, were slowly being toppled to make way for new civic buildings and, with them, a new style of politics.[18] "I am not a prince," Cosimo de' Medici (1389–1464) explained to pope Pius II (1458–64), carefully underscoring the distinction between the basis of his unofficial control of Florentine politics and hereditary rule. Cosimo also distinguished the legitimacy of his position, as unofficial ruler of Florence (1434–69), from rule by force. "A republic cannot be run in the same way as a despotic regime," he told Francesco Sforza, who had wrested the duchy of Milan from the hands of the Visconti in 1450.[19] He was acutely sensitive to the political differences within the Italian city-states and to the importance of communal traditions in his own city, as were the Venetians who declared that because they were a republic "everything must be done by ballot."[20] The Venetian doge, elected as head of state for life in a process as complex and embattled as the election of a new pope by a cardinals' conclave, was decidedly not a prince who could act without the consent of the Great Council.[21] Rather, he was their first citizen, a prince when the republic needed a princely figurehead but always a citizen constrained by the rules of citizenship in a Renaissance republic.

17   The best starting point for understanding Venetian history is still Frederic C. Lane, *Venice: A Maritime Republic* (Baltimore: Johns Hopkins University Press, 1973). For a recent reassessment, see Martin and Romano, *Venice Reconsidered*; and Gary Wills, *Venice, Lion City: The Religion of Empire* (New York: Simon & Schuster, 2001). The Venetian and Milanese registers are discussed in Stanley Chojnacki, *Women and Men in Renaissance Venice: Twelve Essays on Patrician Society* (Baltimore: Johns Hopkins University Press, 2000), p. 30 and *passim*. The most accessible study of Milanese court culture is Gregory Lubkin, *A Renaissance Court: Milan under Galeazzo Maria Sforza* (Berkeley: University of California Press, 1994).

18   Gene Brucker, *Renaissance Florence* (Berkeley: University of California Press, 1983; 1969), p. 133; and Carol Lansing, *The Florentine Magnates: Lineage and Faction in a Medieval Commune* (Princeton: Princeton University Press, 1991). Around 1200, Florence had more than 150 towers, and even today cities such as Bologna and San Gimignano contain a few of the aristocratic family towers. "Magnate" is a term for the older ruling families of Florence, in contrast to newer families such as the Medici who came to rule the city.

19   Dale Kent, *Cosimo de' Medici and the Florentine Renaissance: The Patron's Oeuvre* (New Haven: Yale University Press, 2000), p. 348.

20   Lunardo Emo to doge Andrea Gritti, ca. 1528–29, in Martin and Romano, *Venice Reconsidered*, p. 170.

21   The Great Council of Venice consisted of all the adult males of patrician families (approximately 3,000). The real decision-making bodies were the Senate and the Council of Ten. See Robert Finlay, *Politics in Renaissance Venice* (New Brunswick: Rutgers University Press, 1980).

It is a mistake to think of the Italian republics and their claims to reinvent Roman traditions of liberty as the dominant approach to Renaissance
politics, when it was one of several viable alternatives. Numerous other
Italian states were ruled by dukes, marquises, and aristocratic lords who
built fortresses and castles to dominate the lands they held. Giovanni
Antonio di Blazo Orsini, prince of Otranto, duke of Bari, and count of Lecce
and Conversano reputedly commanded four hundred castles, according to
one chronicler in 1444, and could ride from Naples to Taranto entirely on
his own lands.[22] Other states thrived under the leadership of mercenary
soldiers (*condottieri*), who commanded powerful armies and maintained
strategic allegiances with neighboring city-states. The Sforza in Milan, the
Montefeltro in Urbino, the Malatesta in Rimini, Cesare Borgia in Romagna,
and many lesser-known princes of this period were cut from this cloth. Such
changes led pope Pius II to declare famously that in Italy "a servant can
easily become a king."[23] As a Sienese aristocrat, Pius II disliked the ease with
which merchants and soldiers could become heads of state. And yet
Machiavelli would complain what a socially closed world a city like Florence
could be for the son of a poor country gentleman, rendering it difficult
for a man without status, money, and connections to get a decent post in
government. So we must not take Pius's assessment to mean that anyone
could aspire to rule.

Italy, in other words, was a region of many different kinds of governments, elective and hereditary, communal and despotic, secular and religious, local and foreign. At the beginning of the thirteenth century there
were over two hundred city-states in the Italian peninsula, perhaps as many
as three hundred. The majority of them were in northern and central Italy,
where approximately one-third of the population lived in towns or cities.[24]
Southern Italy was more rural, often ruled by foreign monarchs (both
French and Spanish), and dominated by aristocratic, land-holding families
whose castles still mark the terrain of such regions as Lazio, Campania, Calabria, and Puglia.[25] The number of city-states was considerably diminished

22   Denys Hay and John Law, *Italy in the Age of the Renaissance 1380–1530* (New York:
Longman, 1989), pp. 186–7.
23   Burckhardt, *Civilization*, p. 33.
24   Burke, *Italian Renaissance*, p. 209; and Benjamin G. Kohl and Alison Andrews Smith,
Major Problems in the History of the Italian Renaissance (Lexington, MA: D.C. Heath, 1995),
p. 56. See Philip Jones, *The Italian City-State: From Commune to Signoria* (Oxford: Clarendon
Press, 1997).
25   The feudal aspects of Renaissance Italy were not confined to the Kingdom of Naples and
Sicily, however, but could also be found in parts of northern Italy such as the regions sur-
rounding cities such as Ferrara and Mantua, and the Friuli region north of Venice. See Trevor
Dean, *Land and Power in Late Medieval Ferrara: The Rule of the Este, 1350–1450* (Cambridge:
Cambridge University Press, 1988); Edward Muir, *Mad Blood Stirring: Vendetta and Factions in*

by Petrarch's time and would decline further in the next two centuries, as powerful rulers and cities absorbed smaller communes into their territorial states. To take one example, Siena, the great medieval banking center, had become a shadow of its former self by the fifteenth century, a small town of about fifteen thousand depopulated by plague, besieged by mercenary companies, and coveted by ambitious rulers who hoped to acquire it, as the Medici finally did in 1557.[26]

Machiavelli would later complain that the problem with Italy was that everyone aspired to be a prince and, as result, each one impeded the other from ever realizing this goal. But he did not cease to dream of Italy as a cultural ideal that might be realized from its Roman inheritance. The last lines of *The Prince* came from a poem by Petrarch: "the ancient valor is not yet dead in Italian hearts."[27] Almost two hundred years after Petrarch lamented the condition of Rome, Machiavelli continued to see Italy as a region whose antiquity might inspire a new modernity. He had experienced the cultural transformation of Italy that occurred in the fifteenth century as well as the political turbulence of the period between 1492 and 1527, when internal quarrels among Italian rulers and foreign invasions had thrown the Italian peninsula into chaos, once again. Yet he still believed in the greatness of Italy's cities and the innovations they produced, because he had lived in an age in which they had been the marvel of Europe. Florence, "the heart of Italy," Venice, "a terrestrial paradise," Rome, "the head of the world" (*caput mundi*).[28] This was the Italy that emerged in the century following Petrarch's return home.

3 Cities of Wood Become Marble

Even as the vitality of the late medieval cities gave way to the emergence of a smaller number of territorial states, dominated by the largest cities (Florence, Venice, Milan, Rome, and Naples), what remained was a thriving urban culture. The population of the Italian cities, though greatly dimin-

Friuli during the Renaissance (Baltimore: Johns Hopkins University Press, 1993); and Tommaso Astarita, *The Continuity of Feudal Power: The Carracciolo di Brienza in Naples* (Cambridge: Cambridge University Press, 1992).

26 William Caferro, *Mercenary Companies and the Decline of Siena* (Baltimore: Johns Hopkins University Press, 1998).

27 Niccolò Machiavelli, *The Prince*, trans. George Bull (London: Penguin, 1961), p. 138. The full stanza in Petrarch is: "Virtù contro a furore/Prenderà l'arme, e fia el combatter corto;/ Che l'antico valor/Nell'italici cor non è ancor morto."

28 Felix Gilbert, *Machiavelli and Guicciardini: Politics and History in Sixteenth Century Florence* (New York: Norton, 1984; 1965), p. 30; Finlay, *Politics*, p. 17; and Stinger, *The Renaissance in Rome*.

ished after the arrival of plague, gradually increased during the fifteenth and early sixteenth centuries to the levels prior to 1348. Such a demographically challenged age offered great scope for moralists who argued that marriage, as one fifteenth-century humanist put it, was "the fundamental union, which by its multiplication makes the city."[29] For cities to thrive, families had to flourish. Public dowry funds (*Monte delle doti*), established in many cities in the fifteenth century, offered a good example of intersections between public and private interests. Citizens provided the government with income to spend on maintaining the state in war and peace. In return, a modest investment at the time of birth was supposed to yield a healthy dowry by the time a daughter was of marriageable age, though the expenditures of state often exceeded the promised returns (Plate 2).[30]

The size of the population not only influenced the marriage market and economic opportunities for urban residents but also played a role in determining the power of different groups. A city, after all, was a microcosm of human ambition. Nobles, patricians, scholars, clerics, artists, and artisans lived and worked cheek to jowl in the streets and piazzas, while the inhabitants of the surrounding countryside routinely traveled through the city gates, bringing the fruits of the countryside into the marketplace and exporting aspects of urban life into their own world. A large portion of the population did not enjoy the benefits of citizenship as part of living in the city. Yet each sector of Renaissance society found a means to turn the dynamic between patricians and *popolani* (ordinary city-dwellers), and the city and the countryside, to his or her own advantage. "Never trust anyone to the point where he can unmake you," wrote one merchant in a diary written for his heirs. "Try to stay close to whoever is in power."[31] Such advice about how to survive life in a Renaissance city indicates how the politics of the Italian city-states left urban inhabitants calculating to what degree their relationships with each other furthered their own interests.

However wary urban residents were of each other, they were not indifferent to the collective effect of their activities on the image of the city itself.

---

29   David Herlihy and Christiane Klapisch-Zuber, *Tuscans and Their Families: A Study of the Florentine Catasto of 1427* (New Haven: Yale University Press, 1985), p. 230. This statement was made by Leonardo Bruni in 1436.

30   Anthony Molho and Julius Kirshner, "The Dowry Fund and the Marriage Market in Quattrocento Florence," *Journal of Modern History* 50 (1978): 403–38.

31   Giovanni di Pagolo Moretti, *Ricordi* (early fifteenth century), in Branca, *Merchant Writers*, pp. 68, 71. The dynamics of urban behavior have been especially well explored in Richard Trexler, *Public Life in Renaissance Florence* (New York: Academic Press, 1980); and Ronald F. E. Weissman, *Ritual Brotherhood in Renaissance Florence* (New York: Academic Press, 1982); and Dennis Romano, *Patricians and Popolani: The Social Foundations of the Venetian Renaissance State* (Baltimore: Johns Hopkins University Press, 1987).

Italian Renaissance cities were celebrated throughout western Europe as marvels of architectural design and urban planning. During the fifteenth century, as the Florentine humanist and architect Leon Battista Alberti (1404–72) eloquently observed, cities of wood became cities of marble. If the quintessential building projects of the late Middle Ages had been churches, communal palaces, and merchant halls, Italian Renaissance building was defined by the urban palace. In his *Panegyric to the City of Florence* (1403–4), the humanist Leonardo Bruni (1370–1444), who became chancellor of the city in 1427, praised Florence's "wealth of build-

Plate 2   Vittore Carpaccio, *Two Venetian Ladies on a Terrace* (ca. 1495). *Source:* Museo Civico Correr, Venice.

Vittore Carpaccio (ca. 1465–1526) was known for his ability to capture the ordinary fabric of everyday life in his adopted city of Venice. His portrait of two Venetian women has sometimes been interpreted as a portrait of high-class courtesans in a city famous for its prostitutes. More likely, it is an image of the forced leisure of Venetian patrician women, increasingly confined to their homes to preserve their family's honor. Such an image brings to mind the crucial advice offered by the Venetian humanist Francesco Barbaro (1390–1454) in *On Wifely Duties* (1416): "I would have wives be seen in public with their husbands, but when their husbands are away wives should stay at home." The ambiguity of Carpaccio's painting also captures one of the fundamental debates in Renaissance society at this time: how to distinguish between class and wealth. The growth of sumptuary laws in many Italian cities reflected an effort on the part of the urban elite to maintain their place in the order of things by specifying the use of clothing, jewelry, and dowries according to social status, religion, and occupation. The *zoccoli* (platform shoes) the women are wearing made it virtually impossible for them to walk without being attended by servants.

◀——————————————————————————————————

ings," including "the homes of the private citizens."[32] Merchant families, hereditary princes, and despots all contributed to the material transformation of various cities. Private family palaces and chapels became a measure of one's status in the city and often defined the territory that a family controlled. By the late fifteenth century Renaissance Italy was gripped with a building fever that transformed small towns as well as major cities. Duke Federico da Montefeltro (1420–82) took such a personal interest in designing the ducal palace that formed the nucleus of Urbino in the 1460s that many considered him to be its architect. Lorenzo de' Medici (1449–92) was sufficiently intrigued by reports of its splendor that he had an architect send him copies of the plans. Under duke Ercole I d'Este's rule in Ferrara (1471–1505), new palaces, streets, and fortresses transformed this small city into one of the greatest Renaissance courts in Europe.[33] The act of building expressed well the competitive spirit of the Italian city-states that looked to each other in establishing their reputations.

32   Leon Battista Alberti, *On the Art of Building* (written ca. 1450, published 1485), in Alison Cole, *Virtue and Magnificence: Art of the Italian Renaissance Courts* (New York: Harry N. Abrams, 1995), p. 21; and Leonardo Bruni, *Panegyric to the City of Florence* (1403–4), in *The Earthly Republic: Italian Humanists on Government and Society* ed. Benjamin G. Kohl and Ronald G. Witt with Elizabeth B. Welles (Philadelphia: University of Pennsylvania, 1978), pp. 139–40.
33   Thomas Tuohy, *Herculean Ferrara: Erco d'Este (1471–1505) and the Invention of a Ducal Capital* (Cambridge: Cambridge University Press, 1996).

Wealthy citizens also expressed their civic pride and piety through sponsorship of monasteries, churches, hospitals, and other buildings that contributed to the public good. The Florentine patrician Giovanni Rucellai, an important patron of Alberti, felt that he had "given myself more honor, and my soul more satisfaction by having spent money than by having earned it." He was not alone in this belief. Adding up the staggering sums that his predecessors had spend on building, charity and taxes, a youthful Lorenzo de" Medici observed in 1472 that "although many people might think it would be better to have something in your purse, I think that it brings honor to our State, and I believe the money was well spent, and I am well content with this."[34] Both understood that public munificence was a direct expression of economic capital and political power.

The effect of this new kind of urban patronage on many cities was quite visible to a new generation of pilgrims and tourists who came to Italy. Rome, a city where cows wandered through the muddy ruins of the Colosseum in the fourteenth century, emerged as a splendid center, thanks to the building projects of various popes from Nicholas V (1446–55) to Sixtus V (1585–90). Only after the papacy returned from Avignon in 1377, and survived the turbulent era of the Great Schism (1378–1417) when different factions recognized different popes, did Rome become the nucleus of the Papal States. In the same era when the Medici controlled Florence and the Sforza ruled Milan, the papacy extended its territorial claims to encompass much of central Italy. Rome emerged as an urban center to rival any of the other Italian cities, as Roman nobles and cardinals rushed to build palaces that incorporated pieces of Roman ruins into the design to cater to the new taste for the antique. By the early sixteenth century artists and humanists flocked to the Eternal City to associate themselves with the papal court under Julius II (1503–13) and Leo X (1513–21), just as they migrated to other cities such as Florence, Ferrara, Mantua, and Urbino where the ruling elite invested in culture.[35] If Renaissance Italy appeared in retrospect to be a cultural unity, it was because so many Italian rulers employed the same individuals at different moments in their careers, due to the reputations they had developed elsewhere.

The building culture of the Italian Renaissance cities demanded a wide array of specialized skills from its ordinary citizens whose labor realized

---

34   Richard Goldthwaite, *The Building of Renaissance Florence: An Economic and Social History* (Baltimore: Johns Hopkins University Press, 1980), p. 85; Branca, *Merchant Writers*, p. 157 (March 15, 1472).

35   Ingrid D. Rowland, *The Culture of the High Renaissance: Ancients and Moderns in Sixteenth-Century Rome* (Cambridge: Cambridge University Press, 1998); Charles L. Stinger, *The Renaissance in Rome* (Bloomington: Indiana University Press, 1985); and Peter Partner, *Renaissance Rome 1500–1559: A Portrait of a Society* (Berkeley: University of California Press, 1976).

dreams of great buildings filled with magnificent art.[36] This raises a fundamental point about our image of the Italian Renaissance: the books, paintings, sculptures, and buildings that give shape to the Italian Renaissance were all products of manual labor, as were the fine clothes, jewelry, wedding chests, mirrors, and furniture which adorned the bodies and homes of Renaissance Italians. Italian cities thrived because of the presence of skilled labor. The increased amount of legislation dealing with sumptuary laws, for instance, not only reflected anxieties about religion and social status – as expressed through attempts to regulate expenditures on clothes, jewelry, and dowries – but also underscored the essential fact that there was a wide variety of goods and services that one could acquire in a city and a population ready to expend their florins and ducats in acts of conspicuous consumption.

Knowledge in a Renaissance city also had its artisanal component. Prior to the advent of the printing press, which first appeared in Europe around 1450 and arrived in Italy in 1465, making books was a physical act that required skilled copyists. One of the most knowledgeable men in fifteenth-century Italy was a Florentine bookseller, Vespasiano da Bisticci (1421–98), who thoroughly disdained the printed book as a poor substitute for a handmade copy. Famed throughout northern Italy for his work, he knew everyone in power because he provided the labor that made Renaissance libraries come into existence, just as the Venetian printer Aldus Manutius (ca. 1449–1515) would do for the next generation that sat in his printing house to assist him in the task of creating the ideal Renaissance library in print. When Cosimo de' Medici requested a library of 200 books, Vespasiano employed forty-five scribes for twenty-two months to fill this order.[37] The ability of booksellers to mediate between literate patrons and the artisanal world of book production gave them unique insights into the place of knowledge in Renaissance society. In this respect, Vespasiano was not unlike a younger Tuscan, Leonardo da Vinci (1452–1519), whose success with a number of his patrons rested on his ability to translate his skills into practical expertise in architecture, engineering, and armaments in addition to his abilities as a painter. Thus, on many levels, Renaissance Italy was a world of skilled artisans who worked in cities, served princes at court and on the battlefield, and found ways to enrich their families by making their particular expertise essential to their society.[38]

36   Goldthwaite, *Building of Renaissance Florence*.
37   Brian Richardson, *Printing, Writers and Readers in Renaissance Italy* (Cambridge: Cambridge University Press, 1999), p. 3. By contrast, Alberti claimed in 1466 that the same number of books could be printed in one hundred days.
38   On Italian artisans, see Samuel K. Cohn, Jr., *Laboring Classes in Renaissance Florence* (New York: Academic Press, 1980); and Robert C. Davis, *Shipbuilders of the Venetian Arsenal: Workers and Workplace in the Preindustrial City* (Baltimore: Johns Hopkins University Press, 1991).

Written words were among the most valuable commodities in Renaissance society. The inhabitants of the Italian cities were unusually literate because writing, like counting, was a practical skill. Approximately one-third of urban males and a smaller percentage of women were literate.[39] One of the most important figures in an Italian city was the notary whose ability to read and write allowed him to memorialize a wide variety of ordinary human interactions concerning marriage, dowries, property, business, taxes, and inheritance. The written word was the third party to virtually every transaction of significance that occurred in an Italian city. Those who possessed the ability to read and write had access to an entirely different level of society.

Writing was not simply a skill of the elite but a manifestation of a society that documented all of its activities. The Sienese cloth-cutter Benedetto di Bartolomeo, who transcribed the forty-five sermons that Bernardino da Siena gave in his native city in the summer of 1427, understood well that his literacy was a special gift. He described himself as a man with "a wife and several children, few possessions, and much virtue."[40] Benedetto might have appreciated the decision of a merchant's wife, Margherita Datini, to have the family notary, Ser Lapo Mazzei, teach her how to read and write in her thirties. Her husband Francesco worried that some of these skills were not entirely useful. "Do not pay so much heed to reading that you do all other things ill," he counseled. Datini did not equate literacy with the cultivation of learning but saw it as a necessary part of business. Reading, of the sort Petrarch had in mind when he talked about his desire to know Cicero, was not exactly the kind of literacy that Datini valued. He was not unlike wealthy peasants who, unable to read or write themselves, nonetheless understood the power of words when they asked others to record their important transactions for them.[41]

We should not assume, however, that the two kinds of literacy were mutually exclusive. Just as the busy commercial life of the city produced a new building aesthetic, it also encouraged new attitudes towards learning. One Florentine merchant recorded how he copied favorite passages from Boccaccio in his notebooks "during the plague epidemic of 1449 for my own pleasure."[42] Copying Petrarch's vernacular poems was also a favorite

---

39 Paul F. Grendler, *Schooling in Renaissance Italy: Literacy and Learning 1300–1600* (Baltimore: Johns Hopkins University Press, 1989), p. 77.
40 Franco Mormando, *The Preacher's Demons: Bernardino of Siena and the Social Underworld of Early Renaissance Italy* (Chicago: University of Chicago Press, 1999), p. 43.
41 Origo, *Merchant of Prato*, p. 213. For a fascinating discussion of peasant literacy, see Duccio Balestracci, *The Renaissance in the Fields: Family Memoirs of a Fifteenth-Century Peasant*, trans. Paolo Squatriti and Betsy Merideth (University Park, PA: Pennsylvania State University Press, 1999).
42 Kent, *Cosimo de' Medici*, p. 71.

pastime of those who could read and write. Literature, history, advice, and finance appeared together indiscriminately in the merchant diaries and account books of the Italian Renaissance.

The Florentine merchant Giovanni di Pagolo Morelli expressed his own sense of Petrarch's values when he noted that behaving like the Romans was generally not useful in everyday life, "especially in the things with which we have to deal, which are more material than the great events of Rome." But he made an exception for politics as an arena in which one should think and behave like a Roman. "For as we are descended from them in essence we should show this in virtue and substance as well."[43] Such comments, inscribed in notebooks as lessons for sons to learn from their fathers, suggest the ways in which ordinary citizens were able to translate Petrarch's high-minded ideals into practical results. "Books ring with the voices of the wise," observed cardinal Bessarion in 1468 as he donated his great library to the city of Venice. "They are full of the lessons of history, full of life, law, and piety. The live, speak, and debate with us; they teach, advise, and comfort us; they reveal matters which are furthest from our memories, and set them, as it were, before our eyes."[44] The learning of the schools helped to shape the discourse of public life, but reading a tale from Boccaccio could be the consolation of a merchant in an hour of despair.

In the same period in which cities of wood became marble, their citizens found a new voice in the sort of public eloquence that Petrarch hoped to inspire. Humanist learning was primarily the domain of educated patricians – lawyers, doctors, theologians, notaries, and scholars who made a living either teaching or working in the service of the state as secretaries – and princes who knew their Cicero, Livy, Virgil, Aristotle, and other ancient writers so well that they could cite them line and verse. They had studied with famous masters like Guarino of Verona (1374–1460), who had skills that Petrarch only dreamed of and provided his pupils with a thorough grounding in the *studia humanitatis*. This term, borrowed from Cicero, encompassed grammar, rhetoric, poetry, history, and moral philosophy. Guarino's reputation rested on his association with the famous Greek scholar Manuel Chrysoloras. He traveled with him to Constantinople before 1403 and 1408, returning laden with Greek manuscripts that promised to unlock further the secrets of antiquity. By the 1430s his school was flourishing in Ferrara, as was the school of Vittorino da Feltre (ca. 1378–ca. 1446) in Mantua and many others of this kind in different Italian cities.[45]

43   Giovanni di Pagolo Morelli, *Ricordi*, in Branca, *Merchant Writers*, p. 75.
44   Chambers and Pullan, *Venice*, p. 357.
45   Charles G. Nauert, *Humanism and the Culture of the Renaissance* (Cambridge: Cambridge University Press, 1995), pp. 35, 46–8. See also Anthony Grafton and Lisa Jardine, *From Humanism to the Humanities* (Cambridge, MA: Harvard University Press, 1986); and Grendler, *Schooling*.

Young princes and patricians studied Greek and Latin with famous humanist teachers who taught them to see history and the manifest destiny of Italy in new ways.

By the mid-fifteenth century humanist learning far surpassed Petrarch's relatively modest ambitions to converse with Cicero and read an occasional Greek manuscript. Renaissance humanists readily critiqued Petrarch's medieval Latin and wrote in an Italic script that was supposed to simulate how the Romans had written. One particularly apt pupil of Guarino's, Lorenzo Valla (1407–57), became so skilled in the historical evolution of Latin as a language that he wrote a *Declamation on the Forged Donation of Constantine* (1440), using his philological skills to prove that the evidence for the emperor Constantine's donation of political authority to pope Sylvester I rested on an eighth-century forgery purporting to be a fourth-century document. The results of the new learning were not always so controversial. The vast majority of humanists devoted themselves to perfecting the rules of grammar, and to historical projects that celebrated the Roman art of historical narrative as a framework within which to interpret the events of Renaissance Italy. Leonardo Bruni, for instance, famously argued that his research proved that Florence was a city of Roman origin rather than one founded by the emperor Charlemagne. The Renaissance city visibly changed with the diffusion of humanist values in society. Albert's neoclassical buildings in Florence and Mantua, for example, reflected his reading of ancient architectural treatises. What lay inside many new palaces also mattered, for many of them now contained private studies, filled with books, coins, paintings, and other artifacts associated with humanist learning.[46] Buildings specifically made to hold libraries also appeared, most notably, the Vatican Library conceived by pope Nicholas V in 1451 and inaugurated by Sixtus IV in 1475.[47]

Just as learning embellished the inner spaces of the city, it also played a powerful role in its politics. Coluccio Salutati (1331–1406), the first humanist to become chancellor of the Florentine republic in 1375, in essence the state's chief bureaucrat, expressed well the social and political aspirations of the new learning when he wrote: "Since it is characteristic of man to be taught and the learned are more human than the unlearned, the

---

46 Dora Thornton, *The Scholar in His Study: Ownership and Experience in Renaisance Italy* (New Haven: Yale University Press, 1997); and Findlen, *A Fragmentary Past*. For a discussion of how humanism intersected with art and material culture, see Patricia Fortini Brown, *Venice and Antiquity: The Venetian Sense of the Past* (New Haven: Yale University Press, 1996); and Leonard Barkan, *Unearthing the Past: Archeology and Aesthetics in the Making of Renaissance Culture* (New Haven: Yale University Press, 1999).

47 Anthony Grafton, ed., *Rome Reborn: The Vatican Library and Renaissance Culture* (Washington, D.C.: Library of Congress in Association with the Biblioteca Apostolica Vaticana, 1993).

ancients appropriately referred to learning as *humanitas*."[48] Learning was implicitly a criterion for active membership in the community. The sense of the past that humanists cultivated not only allowed them to reconstruct gloriously Roman histories of their cities, but also provided them with practical skills in great demand in the Italian city-states. The cities of marble, after all, were also cities of paper. Their bureaucracy generated mountains of documents that recorded the daily activities of state – councils, elections, diplomatic relations, and taxes all required the skills of a good humanist education. Sforza's Milan, for example, had so much paperwork that it employed several secretaries in the chancery to organize an archive of state papers and the origins of the Uffizi galleries, which we today think of as a great art museum, lay in the urgent need for more offices (*uffizi*) to house the Florentine bureaucracy and its papers. Humanists filled an important need in Renaissance politics. They not only espoused the high-minded ideals of Rome with great eloquence, but they also knew how to put their talents to use in writing letters for their rulers and in representing their state abroad, while at home their scholarly skills made them ideal candidates to organize state archives and to examine and authenticate ancient documents of state.

The public uses of learning, however, never entirely precluded alternative interpretations of the importance of a humanist education. "Even though the study of letters promises and offers no reward for women and no dignity," declared the Venetian Cassandra Fedele (1465–1558), "every woman ought to seek and embrace these studies."[49] Fedele was one of a handful of women who pursued a humanist education in the fifteenth and sixteenth centuries. Her literacy vastly exceeded the rudimentary knowledge of letters that Margherita Datini acquired from the family notary. Women such as Fedele implicitly challenged the idea that women could not participate fully in all aspects of humanism learning. Fedele publicly demonstrated her eloquence and her mastery of Greek, Latin, history, and rhetoric by giving orations at the University of Padua, to the Venetian people and even before the Venetian doge. Much like the marchesa of Mantua, Isabella d'Este (1474–1539), who was one of many noblewomen who ruled Renaissance states while their husbands were absent from home, Fedele's unusual accomplishments bring into relief the general expectations of learning at this time. More typical was a woman like Alessandra Strozzi who complained to her sons about having to send so many letters to elicit

---

48   Peter Burke, *The European Renaissance: Centres and Peripheries* (Oxford: Blackwell, 1998), p. 29.

49   Cassandra Fedele, "Oration in Praise of Letters," in *Her Immaculate Hand: Selected Works by and about the Woman Humanists of Quattrocento Italy*, ed. Margaret L. King and Albert Rabil, Jr. (Binghamton, NY: Medieval and Renaissance Texts and Studies, 1992; 1983), p. 77.

a response from them because "writing seems like hard work."[50] The vast majority of humanist secretaries, laboring to produce and organize reams of paper for the expanding apparatus of state, would have agreed wholeheartedly with her assessment.

At the end of the fifteenth century, the ideal citizen of an Italian city-state was an educated male patrician willing to put his learning to public use, not simply to entertain courtiers (though this was surely what many scholars found themselves doing, writing plays, poems, and histories for public occasions) but to enhance the glory and reputation of his city. He had, of course, excellent taste since in his spare time he read works such as Alberti's *On Painting* (1434/5) and *On the Art of Building* (ca. 1450). He could recite poetry spontaneously in the manner of Petrarch and tell a lusty tale worthy of Boccaccio. He was conversant with the leading artists and artisans of the day. He knew the history of Rome and had connected it to the history of whatever city he considered home. One possible candidate for ideal citizenship was the son of an impoverished scholar who so loved Livy's *Decades* that he made the index for them for a Florentine publisher and sent his seventeen-year-old son to deliver a barrel of good red wine to seal the agreement.[51] This young son not only imbibed the lessons of Livy in his family library, inheriting his father's love of history, but coupled it with an unparalleled thirst for politics. He was the Florentine Niccolò Machiavelli (1469–1527).

4   What Machiavelli Knew About His World

A few months before his death in June 1527, a dispirited Machiavelli told a friend, "I love my native city more than my own soul."[52] Niccolò Machiavelli's love of Florence was not simple hyperbole but the result of extended reflection on the state of the Italian peninsula during the period of the Italian Wars (1494–1530). A brief sketch of what transpired between Petrarch's rediscovery of Rome and Machiavelli's lament for Florence helps us to understand the evolution of Renaissance Italy. Machiavelli had spent his youth in the Florence of Lorenzo de' Medici and had come of age in a city set ablaze by the fiery sermons of the Dominican preacher Girolamo Savonarola (1452–98) who publicly exhorted the Florentines to expel the Medici and rejuvenate their republic. When the Florentines

---

50   Strozzi, *Selected Letters*, p. 59.
51   Sebastian de Grazia, *Machiavelli in Hell* (Princeton: Princeton University Press, 1989), p. 6.
52   Machiavelli to Francesco Vettori, April 16, 1527, in Maurizio Viroli, *Niccolò's Smile: A Biography of Machiavelli*, trans. Anthony Shugaar (New York: Farrar Straus and Giroux, 2000), p. 254.

answered his call, barring Piero de' Medici's entry to the Palazzo Vecchio in 1494, Savonarola worked with the city leaders to develop a republican government modeled on that of Venice. He expanded membership in the Great Council to approximately 3,000 adult males and laid the groundwork for transforming the position of Standard-Bearer of Justice (*gonfaloniere*) from an elected position that rotated every two months into a position for life, like the office of the doge. Unfortunately Savonarola's aspirations to make Florence the new Jerusalem, purged of errors of faith as well as politics, forced his Florentine allies to choose between Savonarola and the papacy. On May 24, 1498, Savonarola and two associates were burned in Piazza della Signoria[53] (Plate 3). Four days later, a twenty-nine year-old Machiavelli learned that he had finally gotten a coveted government post as secretary to the Second Chancery, an office dealing with Florentine territories and foreign relations with other states.

Machiavelli"s entry into Italian politics occurred at a particularly chaotic moment. The death of Lorenzo in 1492 cemented growing discontent with the Medici's oligarchical rule of their city. But the unsettled situation in Florence was simply one of many problems in the Italian peninsula. In the late fifteenth century growing fears about the strength and reach of the Ottoman Empire, beginning with its conquest of Constantinople in 1453, finally reached Italian soil. Popes Nicholas V and Pius II tried to rally the Italian states for a crusade, but found only lackluster support for this initiative, especially on the part of the Venetians whom Pius II accused of preferring a good trading relationship with the Turks to matters of faith. In July 1480 a Turkish fleet of 18,000 men landed near the southern coastal city of Otranto and held it for more than a year until Aragonese troops in the Kingdom of Naples recaptured the city. Such episodes reminded the Italian city-states that their borders were more vulnerable than they had previously thought.

A great deal of this vulnerability, however, came from within. Despite attempts to create a diplomatic accord among the Italian city-states, through the formation of the Italian League in 1455, such agreements were quickly overshadowed by the ambitions of various rulers. The death of Ferrante of Aragon (1458–94) provided a perfect opportunity for the French and Spanish monarchs to claim the Kingdom of Naples as their lawful inheritance, since rule of Naples had passed from the French Angevins to the Spanish Aragonese by force in 1435. The Angevin line being extinct by 1494, it fell to their nearest relatives to claim their inheritance.

---

53 Donald Weinstein, *Savonarola and Florence: Prophecy and Patriotism in the Renaissance* (Princeton: Princeton University Press, 1970). For an interesting general portrait of the apocalyptic tone of this period, see Ottavia Niccoli, *Prophecy and People in Renaissance Italy*, trans. Lydia G. Cochrane (Princeton: Princeton University Press, 1990).

Plate 3 Anonymous, *The Execution of Savonarola* (1498 or after). *Source*: Museo di San Marco, Florence.

This anonymous painting in the convent of San Marco depicts one of the famous events in Florentine history: the burning of the Dominican preacher Girolamo Savonarola (1452–98) and two associates on May 24, 1498 in Piazza della Signoria. After becoming Prior of San Marco in 1491, Savonarola preached publicly of the vanities, excess, and corruption in Medicean Florence at the end of Lorenzo de' Medici's regime and promised his listeners that a new Jerusalem would emerge from the ruins of the city. He famously persuaded Botticelli to give up the pagan themes of his earlier work in favor of a more spiritual kind of painting. The political chaos after Lorenzo's death in 1492 transformed Savonarola from a preacher into a prophet. In an unusual marriage of church and state, he became the guiding force of the Florentine Republic from 1494 until 1497, to such a degree that he even wrote its constitution before his increasingly vitriolic attacks on the papacy and growing divisions within the Florentine government led to his imprisonment, torture, and death. Machiavelli would count him among those "unarmed prophets" who were unable to maintain their power. This painting depicts the most important public piazza, with the medieval symbols of communal government, the Palazzo della Signoria and the Loggia della Mercanzia prominently displayed, and Brunelleschi's cupola to the Duomo also in view.

At the same time, other rulers attempted to use the contest over Naples to their advantage, with unfortunate results. At the end of the fifteenth century, the alliances between various Italian city-states and foreign powers became a pretext for direct involvement in Italian politics. The duke of Milan, Ludovico Sforza, insecure in his own position in Lombardy, invited the French into Italy to destabilize the Aragonese. Charles VIII's army moved swiftly from Milan to Naples, capturing the city by February 1495. Other states allied with the Spanish to expel the French. In 1498 a new French king, Louis XII (1498–1515), began to consider the possibility of deposing his one-time ally Sforza so that he might lay claim to both Lombardy, which he ruled from 1499 until 1513, and Naples. One of the reasons that Leonardo eventually migrated to France was due to his contact with French patrons in Milan in the early sixteenth century.

Around the same time, Ferdinand of Aragon started to contemplate the role that Italy might play in an expanded vision of a Spanish empire that crossed both the Atlantic and the Mediterranean. The years of the Italian Wars were also a crucial period in which explorers and conquistadors such as Columbus and Cortèz made the "Indies" a part of Spain. King Ferdinand's vision proved to be more powerful and better supported within Italy than that of his French rival. By 1504 Spain held Naples, ruling over it until 1707. Ferdinand acquired Milan in 1513. The Spanish temporarily allowed Ludovico Sforza to rule his city again from 1530 until his death in 1535, and subsequently controlled Lombardy until 1713. In 1563, king Philip II established his Supreme Council of Italy to oversee Spain's Italian posses- sion. By 1600 approximately five million of Italy's thirteen million inhabi- tants were under Spanish rule (see Map 2).[54] The failure of the Italian states to prevent large portions of the peninsula from coming under foreign rule was one of the pressing questions that Machiavelli contemplated as he wrote *The Prince*.

The papacy, which played an important role in maintaining the Italian League at mid-century, had also become part of the problem. "It is the Church that has kept, and keeps, Italy divided," concluded Machiavelli in *The Discourses on the First Ten Books of Titus Livy* (1516–19).[55] Machiavelli's well-known fascination with Cesare Borgia (ca. 1476–1507) reflected the emergence of the illegitimate son of pope Alexander VI (1492–1503) as a major force in Italian politics in the late 1490s. The year Machiavelli got his job was the year Borgia renounced his cardinalate in order to pursue his ambition to rule Romagna. Machiavelli did not meet Borgia until 1502, when he had conquered much of central Italy. But he had heard of his

---

54   Gregory Hanlon, *Early Modern Italy. 1550–1800* (New York: St. Martin's Press, 2000), p. 74.
55   Machiavellli, *The Discourses*, p. 145.

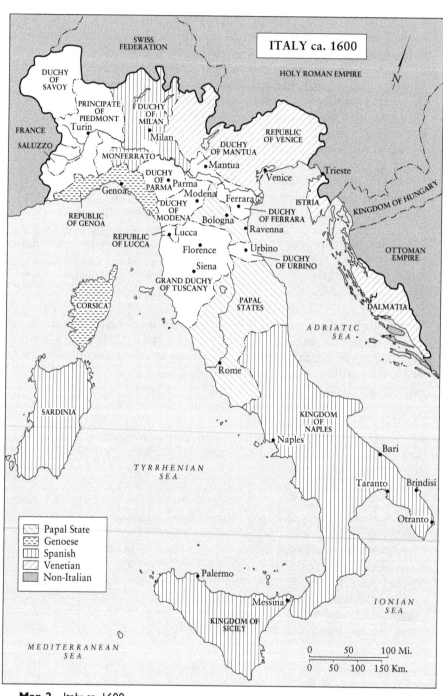

Map 2   Italy ca. 1600.

talent and his aspirations. When he came to know Borgia, he admired his skill in creating and maintaining a state by force.

The Venetians also faltered at this crucial moment in Italy's history. Having largely used their wealth and geographic isolation to insulate themselves from the problems facing many other Italian states, they found themselves with few allies. On May 14, 1509, French troops defeated the Venetians at Agnadello. Most of their mainland territories surrendered to their enemies (king Francis I, emperor Maximilian I, pope Julius II, and the duke of Ferrara) within a few weeks. While the Venetians eventually regained their possessions by 1517, their political standing within Italy was considerably weakened by the 1530s.[56] Machiavelli would later observe that the lack of a strong army and their historic unwillingness to work with the papacy had left Venice vulnerable to such an attack.

It was an auspicious moment, in other words, to be well-versed in politics. Machiavelli, the offspring of an illegitimate member of a respectable Florentine family, felt that his position as secretary offered him unique opportunities to rub shoulders with the leading figures of his time – Cesare Borgia, Leonardo da Vinci, Isabella d'Este were but a few of the people he encountered in his travels on behalf of the troubled Florentine Republic. Years later, after the fall of the Florentine Republic in 1512 which forced Machiavelli into a life of leisure because his services were not wanted by the new Medici government, he reflected on the possibilities that lay before him. He was no merchant, he confessed. He had little land, few books, good Latin, and a gift with words. What should such a person do? He concluded: "Not knowing how to reason about the art of silk or about the art of wool, or about profits and losses, it is necessary that I reason about the state."[57] Thinking about politics might be a poor substitute for being in the thick of things, but he hoped that the fruits of his reflection might earn him a new office in Medicean Florence and assist Florence's rulers in avoiding the mistakes of the past.

There is no doubt that Machiavelli felt somewhat disaffected from his world. He had been forced out of government, one of few to lose their posts with the return of the Medici, and spent most of his days at his country villa in Sant'Andrea in Percussina, reading, writing, and thinking. In the spring of 1513, as he completed *The Prince* and filled his leisure hours in exile reading the poetry of Dante, Petrarch, and Ovid when he felt playful, and

---

56 Robert Finlay, "Fabius Maximus in Venice: Doge Andrea Gritti, the War of Cambrai, and the Rise of Habsburg Hegemony, 1509–1530," *Renaissance Quarterly* 53 (2000): 988–1031. These events are often described as the War of the League of Cambrai (1509–17), referring to the League made by Venice's enemies to defeat and partition the Venetian Republic.

57 De Grazia, *Machiavelli in Hell.* p. 132. This passage comes from a letter to Francesco Vettori, Florentine ambassador to the pope, written April 9, 1513.

Cicero and Livy when he wished to contemplate weighty affairs, he had only recently returned from months of imprisonment in the Bargello where he had been tortured on suspicion of conspiring against the Medici who had returned to Florence precisely because they allied themselves with the Spanish and now sat on the papal throne (Leo X, 1513–21 and Clement VII, 1523–34). In the coming years, Machiavelli's literary production mitigated his sense of disaffection. Works such as his *Discourses* and *The Art of War* (1521) reflected conversations he had with young men in the Orti Oricellari, the gardens of Bernardo Rucellai's palace where leading citizens gathered to discuss politics and culture. They reflected Machiavelli's growing ambition to get his Renaissance readers to see how history might offer a vital resources for understanding the modern problems of state, not to mention the peculiarities of Italian politics that looked increasingly dated in a world subject to the growing power of France and Spain.

Machiavelli's reemergence in society also manifested itself in his plays, which only tangentially referred to politics and instead offered sharp observations about life in a Renaissance city. The city of Florence after 1512 seemed curiously empty of its leading artists and writers because so many, like Michelangelo and Leonardo, had immigrated to Rome with the election of Leo X in 1513, making Machiavelli's occasional presence in the city even more welcome. Audiences laughed heartily at *The Mandrake* (1518), a tale of lust and deceit that subtly dissected the Florentine obsession with wealth and lineage, presenting the city as a world teeming with middlemen who knew how to close a deal. "This is your Florence," he declared in the Prologue.[58] The Florentines also appreciated his poetry, though not everyone would have agreed with Machiavelli's own opinion that his verses were so good that he deserved a place in Ludovico Ariosto's list of great poets in *Orlando Furioso* (1516).[59] A great prose writer surely, however, since all of Machiavelli's works were written in Tuscan rather than Latin, reflecting the growing trend towards using the vernacular in the sixteenth century.

Machiavelli's *Florentine Histories* (1520–5) represented the culmination of his efforts to present his version of the past. It was also the only work that Machiavelli wrote under the patronage of the Medici. While he dedicated *The Prince* to Leo X's nephew, Lorenzo de' Medici (1492–1519), it was cardinal Giulio de' Medici, appointed by his cousin Leo X to rule Florence after Lorenzo's death, who specifically commissioned Machiavelli's history of Florence. Giulio, the future Clement VII, seems to have been the only Medici who decided to put Machiavelli's talents to use. He asked his advice on how to rule the city in 1519. When Clement VII became pope in 1523,

58   Niccolò Machiavelli, *Mandragola*, ed. and trans. Mera J. Flaumenhaft (Prospect Heights, IL: Waveland Press, 1981), p. 9.
59   De Grazia, *Machiavelli in Hell*, p. 48.

Machiavelli must have felt that times were auspicious for his return to public service. And skilled men were urgently needed as Florence prepared itself for the renewal of war. In spring 1526, shortly before Machiavelli's death, he was sent out to inspect public buildings and fortifications – a small job perhaps but well suited to the author of *The Art of War*.

In the 1520s, as the artist Benevenuto Cellini (1500–71) observed, "The whole world was now at war."[60] Machiavelli did not live to see the emperor Charles V's German and Spanish troops sack the papal city on 6 May 1527, an event which left its mark not only in the decimation of the populace but also in more whimsical ways such as the graffiti of a German soldier who carved the name "Luther" into one of Raphael's frescoes in the Vatican.[61] Clement VII was held virtual prisoner in Castel Sant'Angelo and subsequently fled Rome for refuge in Orvieto until 1528. Subsequent agreements between the pope and the emperor made it clear who had the upper hand in Italy. On February 24, 1530, Clement VII crowned Charles V emperor in Bologna. Imperial troops were then in the process of besieging the city of Florence, which had once again rejected the Medici with the establishment of the Second Florentine Republic in 1527. Spanish troops entered a starving and beleaguered city in August 1530. The following year, Charles V forced the Florentines to accept the hereditary rule of the Medici and forced the Medici to accept his sovereign authority. On May 1, 1532, the old *signoria* that had shaped communal rule in Florence since the late thirteenth century, was abolished. The Medici proclaimed their new status by making the Palazzo della Signoria their residence as well as the center of the new state. They were now truly princes, reflecting a growing preference for this form of governance in sixteenth-century Italy, despite the continuation of republics such as Venice and Lucca.

5   Ending the Renaissance

The end of republican rule in Florence certainly did not signal the end of the Renaissance, because there were too many different aspects to the Italian Renaissance for the conclusion of a single episode to determine the outcome. Instead, the transformation of Florence from a republic to the capital city of the Grand Duchy of Tuscany might well be the logical culmination of certain tendencies already inherent in Italian society throughout fifteenth century such as the consolidation of states under hereditary rulers. Comparing Lorenzo "Il Magnifico" with his grandson Lorenzo de' Medici in 1516, Lodovico Alamanni noted that he could not

---

60   Benevenuto Cellini, *Autobiography*, trans. George Bull (London: Penguin, 1956), p. 69.
61   André Chastel, *The Sack of Rome, 1527*. trans. Beth Archer (Princeton: Princeton University Press, 1983), p. 92. See also Kenneth Gouwens, *Remembering the Renaissance: Humanist Narratives of the Sack of Rome* (Leiden: Brill, 1998).

mingle informally with citizens as his illustrious grandfather had done "because being in such a grand position, it would be improper for him to act like a private citizen." If Florentines initially were "unfamiliar with the ways of courts," as Alamanni observed, they soon learned to treat the Medici as rulers rather than first citizens.[62]

Politics was a different sort of preoccupation by the end of the sixteenth century, when the former Jesuit Giovanni Botero (1544–1617) composed *The Reason of State* (1589), based on his experiences in Spanish Milan, the duchy of Savoy, and papal Rome. Botero took for granted some of the issues that Machiavelli had begun to explore such as the image of Italy shaped by an accord between the Spanish and the pope. He dismissed Machiavelli's perceptive comments about the attractions of rule by ability and force (what Machiavelli called *virtù*), preferring instead to underscore the importance of the right to rule and the effects of just rule. He downplayed the idea that the papacy had played an unfortunate role in Italy's troubles, as the pinnacle of princely ambition in the Renaissance game of politics, by underscoring the union between politics and faith as the basis for legitimate rule. Botero, in other words, reflected the results of Italian politics after the Spanish conquest of Italy and the difficult period of the Reformation, when the emergence of Protestantism redrew the political and religious map of Europe and led Catholics to define more precisely what it mean to be a good Catholic in the decrees of the Council of Trent (1545–63). He wrote in light of a renewed and expanded papacy and a flourishing of Catholicism not just in Italy and Catholic Europe, but throughout the world in the era of the Jesuit and Franciscan missions that Christianized parts of Asia and the Americas.[63] He wrote of politics in light of Machiavelli and in recognition of the transformation of Italy in his own century.

The first decades of the sixteenth century were a moment of profound nostalgia. Machiavelli's close friend Francesco Guicciardini (1483–1540), who had successfully worked both for the Florentine republic and for the Medici, found himself unexpectedly out of favor in 1537. His spent the last years of his life composing *The History of Italy* (1540) so that posterity would understand how "the misfortunes of Italy" (*le calamità d'Italia*) between 1492 and 1530 had occurred. The underlying premise of Guicciardini's tragic narrative was the idea of a golden age, culminating in the rule of Lorenzo de' Medici. Italy in 1490, he informed his readers, had seemed equal to the best moments that history recorded of the Roman empire. Such nostalgia led later generations of scholars, reading

---

62   Kohl and Smith, *Major Problems*, p. 443. This was the same Lorenzo to whom Machiavelli dedicated *The Prince*.

63   John M. Headley, "Geography and Empire in the Late Renaissance: Botero's Assignment, Western Universalism, and the Civilizing Process," *Renaissance Quarterly* 53 (2000): 1119–55.

Guicciardini's words, to imagine the unraveling of Italian politics in these decades as the end of the Renaissance.

Less than ten years before Guicciardini began his history, a Mantuan aristocrat who spent the majority of his life in the service of the dukes of Urbino put the finishing touches on a portrait of Renaissance court life under the rule of Guidobaldo da Montefeltro (1472–1508) and Elisabetta Gonzaga (1471–1526). Baldassare Castiglione (1478–1529) wrote *The Book of the Courtier* (1528) as a description of the qualities of a perfect courtier that emerged in four evenings of imaginary conversation at the court of Urbino. In discussions monitored by Elisabetta Gonzaga and her noblewomen, male courtiers defined the best attributes of male and female courtiers and described how their skillful display of *sprezzatura* – the ability to make difficult things look easy – would win them praise and honor (Plate 4). In the same period, the satirist Pietro Aretino (1492–1556) dissected the values that Castiglione celebrated by offering up bawdy portraits of Roman courtesans and prostitutes who perpetuated the illusions of their noble clientele that paying for their attentions was not all about sex, simply because they could recite Petrarchan verse.[64] Several decades later, the Florentine Giovanni della Casa (1503–56), who spent his youth at the papal court and later served as archbishop of Benevento and papal *nuncio* (ambassador) in Venice, composed a short response to Castligione's *Book of the Courtier* in the form of his *Galateo* (1558). Delia Casa astutely observed that the first lesson of courtiership concerned the regulation of the body, its appetites, and its embarrassing intrusions into the heady world of politics and culture. No conversation about the virtues of the ancients would matter, he intoned, if one did not know how to eat gracefully, defecate discreetly, and avoiding showing one's companions snotty and crumpled handkerchiefs.[65]

Like Guicciardini, Castiglione wrote of Urbino as if it were in the past. True, the principal inhabitants of this version of Urbino were dead by the time he finished the book, though a number of its key protagonists – pope Leo X's secretary Pietro Bembo (1470–1547), a Venetian who argued that Tuscan should be the basis for good Italian prose regardless of one's region of origin and became a cardinal in 1539, and the poet Bernardo Accolti (1458–1535) – still lived. Many had read drafts of the book during the late 1510s, participating in the collective burnishing of the mirror of their

64 Paula Findlen, "Humanism, Politics, and Pornography in Renaissance Italy," in *The Invention of Pornography*, ed. Lynn Hunt (New York: Zone, 1993), pp. 49–108; and Bette Talvacchia, *Taking Positions: On the Erotic in Renaissance Culture* (Princeton, NJ: Princeton University Press, 1999).

65 Antonio Santosuosso, "Giovanni Della Casa and his *Galateo*: On Life and Success in the Late Italian Renaissance," *Renaissance and Reformation* 11 (1975): 1–13.

Plate 4 Agnolo Bronzino, *Portrait of Ugolino Martelli* (ca. 1535–8). *Source:* Staatliche Museen, Berlin.

Agnolo di Cosimo di Mariano Tori, known as Bronzino (1503–72) was one of the leading court painters in Florence during the sixteenth century and also a poet. Bronzino first came to the attention of the Medici when he arrived in Florence to work on decorations for the 1539 marriage of duke Cosimo I and Eleonora of Toledo, daughter of the viceroy of Naples. He soon became the leading portrait painter of the Medici court, producing numerous images of idealized courtiers as well as the official portraits of the Medici family as they established themselves as the hereditary grand dukes of Tuscany. Bronzino's portrait of Ugolino Martelli was completed after he spent two years (1530–32) in Urbino, the setting for Baldassare Castiglione's *Book of the Courtier* (1528). His painting captures visually many of the attributes of a good courtier described by Castiglione. Martelli was a young Florentine scholar who is presented as the embodiment of the virtues of learning and art. His hand rests on the ninth book of Homer's *Iliad*. Behind him is a miniature reproduction of Michelangelo's *David* (1504). His black garments reflect the new taste for dressing in emulation of Spanish courtiers.

society. But the activities that they described did not disappear in the next century. The cultural pursuits such as poetry, music, and painting that Castiglione celebrated formed the basis for court life in the sixteenth and seventeenth centuries. The wide circulation of his book – some fifty-eight editions in Italy alone in the sixteenth century – ensured that many literate residents of the Italian cities also strove to emulate the virtues of the courtier, reciting poems, discussing paintings, joking with Boccaccio, and carefully managing their appearance to make a good impression on others. Such popularity suggests how humanist values enjoyed a significantly broader audience in late Renaissance Italy than they had during the inception of this intellectual movement. A half-century later, when the poet Torquato Tasso (1544–95) composed *Malpiglio, or On the Court* (1585), he could talk about a young man who "has read Castiglione's *Courtier* and has also memorized it."[66]

By the time Tasso wrote of a young courtier who knew Castiglione better than Cicero, one important change had taken place that directly affected the reading of many classics of Italian Renaissance literature. The reformed Catholicism that emerged from the Council of Trent led to the establishment of the Index of Prohibited Books in 1557. While primarily concerned with banning writings by heretical authors, the Index also identified authors whose writings were morally questionable. The works of Machiavelli and Aretino were banned outright. Lorenzo Valla's critical comments on the church's dubious temporal authority also ended up on the Index. Boccaccio's *Decameron* and Castiglione's *Book of the Courtier* were carefully expurgated to remove offending passages about the sex lives of clerics, the political ambitions of popes, and of course pagan concepts such as Machiavelli's idea of fortune (*fortuna*) that did not give due authority to God as the agent who shaped the world. As a result, late sixteenth-century readers saw these works in light of the potential conflict their ideas posed with the current teachings of the Catholic Church. But they did not cease to read the books of the Renaissance. Putting works on the Index virtually ensured them an audience. Since the majority of Italian books were published in Venice, a city that openly defied the pope on more than one occasion, no one could really complain that it was hard to get a copy of *The Prince*.[67]

66   Torquato Tasso, *Tasso's Dialogues*, ed. and trans. Garnes Lord and Dain A. Trafton (Berkeley: University of California Press, 1982), p. 155. Peter Burke, *The Fortunes of the Courtier* (University Park, PA: Pennsylvania State University Press, 1996; 1995).
67   Paul Grendler, *The Roman Inquisition and the Venetian Press, 1540–1605* (Princeton: Princeton University Press, 1977). The classic study of heretical reading in this period remains Carlo Ginzburg, *The Cheese and the Worms: The Cosmos of a Sixteenth-Century Miller*, trans. John and Anne Tedeschi (Baltimore: Johns Hopkins University Press, 1980). Heresy in general in this period is well discussed in John Martin, *Venice's Hidden Enemies: Italian Heretics in a Renaissance City* (Berkeley: University of California Press, 1993).

While the post-Tridentine Catholic Church may have taken a dim view of the excessive paganism of some Renaissance humanists, whose love affair with antiquity was not always easily reconciled with Christianity, they assisted the institutionalization of Renaissance learning in other ways. It was one of the new religious orders, the Society of Jesus (founded in 1540), that made humanist learning the centerpiece of their educational system, building on the tradition of Christian humanism that had already been a strong part of Roman intellectual life since the late fourteenth century.[68] The first Jesuit college opened in Messina in 1548. By 1600 there were forty-nine Jesuit colleges in Italy, and that number more than doubled in the seventeenth century.[69] The Jesuits educated the sons of many prosperous Italian families as well as their own novices. Their colleges formalized the humanist study of ancient languages and rhetoric in ways that the fifteenth-century academies and universities largely had been unable to do. In this respect, the Catholic Church fully embraced the idea of humanism as the foundation for Catholic education.

The arts as well as learning continued to thrive in late Renaissance Italy. When Giorgio Vasari wrote his *Lives of the Artists*, he did not do this because the age of great painting and sculpture had ended but because he considered himself to be living at its pinnacle. Michelangelo was still alive and working in Rome when Vasari published his first edition of 1550. He had only been dead four years when the second edition appeared in 1568. Vasari's narratives of the growth and perfection of the arts in Italy diverged from Guicciardini's dismal account of the tragedy of Italy in many important ways. The political breaks that Guicciardini saw in 1492, 1494, and 1527 hardly mattered to Vasari, because art had not disappeared as a result of the death of Lorenzo de' Medici, the invasion of the French king Charles VIII, or the Sack of Rome. Quite the opposite since the Rome of the Farnese pope, Paul III (1534–49), enjoyed the presence of Michelangelo and many other talented painters and sculptors, while the artistic programs in many other cities – Mantua, Florence, and Venice, to name a few – were flourishing. In many respects, the true heyday of Renaissance Rome lay not in the fifteenth century but at the end of the sixteenth century when many of the haphazard building projects of a succession of popes and cardinals made way for a more systematic approach to urban planning.

Such activities easily contradict the prevalent view that the political and religious disasters of the early sixteenth century effectively brought the Renaissance to a close. Both the sixteenth-century courts and church

---

68 John W. O' Malley, *Praise and Blame in Renaissance Rome* (Durham, NC: Duke University Press, 1979).
69 Grendler, *Schooling*, p. 371; and John W. O'Malley, *The First Jesuits* (Cambridge, MA: Harvard University Press, 1993).

increased their support for many of the activities that we associate with the idea of the Renaissance. If there is one major change that we can point to, it is perhaps the economy. Renaissance Italy had emerged as a result of the commercial vitality of the Mediterranean and of the unique goods and services that various Italian city-states offered to the rest of Europe. Despite the warfare and changes of government in the early sixteenth century, much of this economy remained in place for the next century. A wide array of Italian cities continued to offer unique goods and services. Venice continued to be an important port of call, while the Tuscan city of Livorno (Leghorn) emerged as one of the new ports connecting the Atlantic and Mediterranean economies. In the course of the seventeenth century, however, Italy's overall economic prosperity seems to have eroded.[70] In part, this was because of new international upheavals such as the Thirty Years' War (1618–48), but it also reflected the emergence of the Atlantic world economy which made cities such as Seville, London, and Amsterdam strong competitors with the Italian ports, and produced new and cheaper goods that competed successfully with many of the high quality products that Italian artisans continued to produce. Some have argued that the strength of the guild system in many Italian cities was ultimately a liability in relation to newer economic initiatives that favored a larger scale production over more careful regulation of different industries.

Yet even the transformation of the Italian economy was too slow and uneven for us to conclude that it triggered the end of the Renaissance. So we are left with a puzzling question: how exactly should we describe the transformation of Renaissance Italy into something different, something *beyond* the Renaissance, in the course of the sixteenth and seventeenth centuries? Most recently, William Bouwsma has suggested that we see the period from 1550 to 1640 as a "waning of the Renaissance" – a gradual cessation of the values, practices, and beliefs that characterized the idea of a rebirth of society.[71] Such an image holds a great deal of appeal because it presents the Renaissance as a general cultural ideal that manifested itself in many different forms before fading into the background to allow room for new political ideas, religious practices, and intellectual initiatives.

---

70   Carlo Cipolla, "The Economic Decline of Italy," *Economic History Review* ser. 2, 5 (1952–53): 176–87; and Judith Brown, "Prosperity or Hard Times in Renaissance Italy?" *Renaissance Quarterly* 42 (1989): 761–80. For a more general account, see Domenico Sella, *Italy in the Seventeenth Century* (New York: Longman, 1997), pp. 19–49.
71   William J. Bouwsma, *The Waning of the Renaissance 1550–1640* (New Haven: Yale University Press, 2000). For other discussions of the end of the Italian Renaissance, see especially Eric Cochrane, ed., *The Late Italian Renaissance* (New York: Harper Torchbooks, 1970); idem, *Italy 1530–1630*, ed. Julius Kirshner (New York: Longman, 1988); Peter Burke, *The European Renaissance: Centres and Peripheries* (Oxford: Blackwell, 1988); and Hanlon, *Early Modern Italy*.

The Italian Renaissance did not simply end, in some definitive sense. If this were true, we would not be studying the humanities in our own universities, nor would we place such a premium on historical thought as a fundamental aspect of the human experience. We continue to find Petrarch's reflections on the problems of living in one's own time, Machiavelli's astute comments on how to maintain power, and Castiglione's arguments about the virtues of self-presentation relevant to our own concerns. Italy ceased to be the epicenter of western Europe by the late seventeenth and eighteenth centuries, when France and England came to dominate discussions of politics, economy, and culture, and when their trans-Atlantic empires became as large and influential as the one the Spanish created in the sixteenth century. But Italy did not cease to capture the imagination of foreigners, who traveled to Italy in greater numbers after the Renaissance than they had done in the era when it seemed to be the center of the world.

Foreigners increasingly came to Italy on the Grand Tour not only to see its Roman antiquities but also to admire the tangible accomplishments of Italian Renaissance society. In 1620, for example, Michelangelo's descendants opened the *Casa Michelangelo* so that art connoisseurs could see examples of the work that Vasari celebrated.[72] By the late seventeenth century the great Florentine astronomer Galileo Galilei's telescope was on display in the grand ducal galleries of the Uffizi next to images such as Raphael's *Pope Leo X with Two Cardinals* (1517). Guidebooks took visitors through the piazzas, churches, and palaces of Italy, offering learned commentary on what was worth seeing of Italy's past. Vasari's *rinascita* became more than simply a word describing the process by which a new vision of the arts emerged between the fourteenth and sixteenth centuries. It became a historical label for an age that was increasingly removed from the present. Time allowed the idea of the Renaissance to take shape and give coherence to the diversity of activities that defined Italian society in this period. In this respect, the Italian Renaissance is a direct product of our own engagement with Petrarch. He polemically labeled the period since the fall of the Roman empire to his own time the "Dark Ages." We have responded by agreeing with Vasari that the subsequent age should be called the "Renaissance." As the argument for the Renaissance as the birth of the modern world has receded, this label itself has been subject to inspection.[73] But the fascination with the society that produced this word remains.

---

72   Burke, *European Renaissance*, p. 200.
73   Randolph Starn, "Who's Afraid of the Renaissance?" In *The Past and Future of Medieval Studies*, ed. John van Engen (Notre Dame: University of Notre Dame Press, 1994), pp. 129–47; and Anthony Molho, "The Italian Renaissance, Made in the USA," in *Imagined Histories: American Historians Interpret the Past*, ed. Anthony Molho and Gordon S. Wood (Princeton: Princeton University Press, 1998), pp. 263–94.

Part II
Was There a Renaissance State?

Introduction to Part II

In *The Civilization of the Renaissance in Italy*, Jacob Burckhardt famously described the Italian Renaissance state as "a work of art." By this phrase, he signified the elaborate and self-conscious process by which the Italian city-states developed their forms of governance in the late fourteenth and fifteenth centuries. The state was a constantly evolving entity. There was also no single version of the "state" in the Renaissance – indeed we may well question whether we should even use this term for the kind of politics practiced in this period because it implies a kind of stability, permanency, and degree of institutionalization that most Renaissance states did not have. But Burckhardt was surely right to suggest that the state was artfully rendered by those who held power in many regions of Italy. Like a Renaissance painting, it was the work of many hands – some more visible than others in the brushstrokes they applied to the canvas.

The structures of governance in Renaissance Italy varied significantly from one region to another. During the late eleventh and twelfth centuries the urban centers of northern and central Italy gave birth to the "commune" – collective governance based on the election of prominent citizens to key offices, normally for a term of two to three months, who governed a city-state with the help of a Great Council that authorized various executive councils to create law, maintain social order, levy taxes, and defend the city in times of war. Cities such as Florence, Siena, Pisa, Genoa, Bologna, and Venice exemplified the emergence of a kind of government that suited a prosperous mercantile society in which families rose to power through wealth and enterprise as well as through lineage. Communal government contrasted notably with feudal aristocratic rule that concentrated power in the hands of a single family that, by force or by imperial and papal privileges, had a hereditary right to rule. Regions such as the Romagna, the Marches, Lazio, and the Kingdom of Naples, and those surrounding northern cities such as Ferrara, Mantua, and Verona gave birth to this other form of governance. Both images of the state shaped politics and society in Renaissance Italy. The limitations of each also helped to foster new kinds of government in the late fourteenth and fifteenth centuries.

The problems with communal government rested in what political representation really meant in a society in which wealth and power was concentrated in the hands of the few. In many cities, the idea of "citizenship" was restricted only to prominent adult males, significantly limiting who could participate in government and fostering the formation of a *signoria* (a select governing body). Important offices rotated most frequently among a small group of leading families and those whom they patronized. Even the guild system that organized the major professions of a late medieval and early Renaissance city made a distinction between the *Arti Maggiori* (Major

Guilds) and the *Arti Minori* (Minor Guilds), and allowed wealthy guilds such as the bankers, lawyers, and cloth and wool merchants to enjoy disproportionate representation, making it highly unlikely that a butcher would become head of government – unless the bankers wanted it to happen. Who, then, represented the *popolo*? During the 1370s through the 1410s revolts of workers and artisans occurred in many cities, the most famous one being the revolt of the *Ciompi* (woolworkers) in Florence in 1378 that briefly produced a more representative government. By and large, however, efforts to expand the idea of communal government failed.

In the case of Florence, the aftermath of the Ciompi revolt produced a renewed consensus among the city's elite that rule of the few was preferable to rule of the many. But which few? Communal government had partly emerged in response to concerns over the factionalism among urban elites. As Gene Brucker describes in his essay, the mercantile elites of many Italian cities had a high level of civic consciousness. They filled their cities with beautiful churches, dramatic piazzas, public palaces to house communal government, and splendid works of charity sponsored by organizations such as the religious confraternities. They also strove to secure their cities by controlling the territory around them. Yet men of new wealth were not immune to old ambitions. Factionalism among those who held office increasingly made the government a weapon in the hands of the majority. The Venetian Republic adeptly managed this problem through its elaborate balloting system that reflected an emerging consensus, after political unrest in the fourteenth century threatened their ideal of communal rule, that elected office was not a place for charismatic or impetuously youthful leadership. As a result, the most important Venetian offices were held by patricians in their late fifties or older.

Cosimo de' Medici's exile in 1433, for example, offers a typical instance of how changes in government came to directly affect the fortunes of leading citizens. As Anthony Molho argues in his essay, Cosimo's political astuteness allowed him to understand better than any of his contemporaries how he might manipulate this system upon his return to Florence in 1434 in order to create an oligarchy within a republic, a structure of power that would last well beyond his death in 1464. While Florence would continue to maintain the mechanisms of communal rule, the system increasingly worked in the favor of his family. Their financial fortunes declined steadily through the late fifteenth and early sixteenth centuries, and the family often seemed on the verge of extinction. But Cosimo's legacy lived on not only in his grandson Lorenzo, but also in the papacies of Leo X and Clement VII and ultimately in the creation of the hereditary Grand Duchy of Tuscany in 1569 after the return of the Medici to Florence in 1530.

The trajectory of the Medici family is well known among Renaissance rulers because it endured so much longer than many others who aspired to power and survived the many changes of government in Florence. While families such as the d'Este in Ferrara and the Gonzaga in Mantua maintained their duchies for centuries with relatively tranquility, many Renaissance despots were upstart rulers with only a tenuous legal claim to power. They made and remade states with great rapidity in the second half of the fifteenth century. Francesco Sforza used his army and tenuous connections to the Visconti family by marriage as the basis for establishing himself as ruler of Milan in 1450 – thanks to the support of enough Milanese who had been discontent under the previous duke and unable or unwilling to maintain Milan's brief flirtation with republic governance. But his own family lost the reins of power within a half-century, and helped to precipitate the disastrous entry of the French into Italy in 1494. The success of men like Cosimo de' Medici and Francesco Sforza also helped to shape a new image of papal politics. In the same period in which they asserted their control over Florence and Milan, powerful families came to see the election of one of their male relatives to the papal throne as the means to secure and expand the territory under their control, and the premise for establishing a state for themselves if they did not already have one.

It is little wonder that Machiavelli could not stop talking about politics, because he lived in an era in which politics was a constant experiment. *The Prince* (1513) provides one of the most cogent statements of the failure of the Italian states to prevent outsiders from ruling Italy better than the Italians. Yet, at the same time that Machiavelli criticized Italy's rulers for their inability to halt foreign invasions, he could not help but admire the talent and potential of many of the men who had made Italy such a dynamic political environment in the course of the fifteenth century. The two essays by Gene Brucker and Anthony Molho underscore different aspects of the traditions Machiavelli inherited and helped to transform.

Plate 5 Raphael, *Pope Leo X with Two Cardinals* (1517/18). *Source:* Uffizi Gallery.

Raphael (1483–1520) painted this image near the end of a short but distinguished career that began in his home of Urbino, a city famous for its artists and musicians, and ended in Rome. His portrait of Leo X (1513–21), the first of the Medici popes, captures the Renaissance papacy at its height, as does his equally famous portrait of Julius II (1503–13), who reputedly told Michelangelo in 1506, when the artist asked him if he wanted to be portrayed with a book in hand: "Better show me with a sword, because I'm no scholar." By contrast, Leo X appears with his hand resting on a fourteenth-century Bible opened to the first lines of John (undoubtedly in reference to his own name Giovanni). Behind him is his cousin, cardinal Giulio de' Medici, who became Clement VII (1523–34) and cardinal Luigi de' Rossi. Raphael captured the emerging power of cardinals, who had begun to build palaces all over the city to accommodate their growing households as the wealth and magnificence of the papal court grew. By the early sixteenth century the Papal States had expanded to encompass most of central Italy. Martin Luther felt that the papacy had corrupted faith itself, and loudly voiced his criticisms the year Raphael completed this portrait.

2

Civic Traditions in Premodern Italy

Gene Brucker

The character of Italy's communal experience, and its role in its historical evolution, has been one of the most controversial themes in recent historiography. The traditional interpretation, formulated initially by the chroniclers and historians of Italian towns and accepted by (among others) Jacob Burckhardt in his classic work, *The Civilization of the Renaissance in Italy* (New York, 1929), stressed the progressive, innovative and "modern" qualities of that civic world. The institutions and values fostered by those urban governments were seen as the solvent that destroyed the old feudal system, with its hierarchical social structure, its land-based economy, and its fragmented political order. The towns were the dynamic engines that created a new capitalist economy; a social order based on wealth; a political system that stressed cooperation, equality, and freedom; and a culture that embodied secular rather than religious values.

Lane, the distinguished historian of Venice, articulated this vision: "My thesis here is that republicanism . . . is the most distinctive and significant aspect of these Italian city-states, that republicanism gave to the civilization of Italy its distinctive quality . . . and contributed mightily to its triumph later in modern nations and primarily in our own."[1]

Since World War II, however, this view of the communes and their historical significance has been challenged by scholars who have emphasized the weaknesses, limitations, and failures of these urban regimes. Some critics have stressed their instability, their failure to overcome factional discord, and their tendency to rely upon powerful lords (*signori*) from feudal backgrounds to resolve their recurrent crises. By the end of the thirteenth

---

1 Frederic C. Lane, *Venice and History* (Baltimore, 1966), 520.

century, independent communal regimes had been replaced by *signorie* in those regions of northern Italy where feudal nobilities were powerful. Communal regimes in Lombardy, the Veneto, and Emilia-Romagna were viewed as aberrant phenomena with brief life spans in a world that remained overwhelmingly feudal. Independent communes did survive longer in central Italy – Tuscany and Umbria – where rural nobilities were weaker, but these regions witnessed the gradual demise of these republics, which were either absorbed by their more powerful neighbors, like Florence, or (like Siena and Perugia) were taken over by local *signori*.[2]

Since World War II, an international cadre of scholars has studied the history of Florentine republicanism intensively, particularly its mature phase in the fifteenth century, and its demise in the sixteenth. Florence's past is too exceptional and idiosyncratic to serve as a model for the Italian city-state experience, but no Italian city has left a richer documentary record, nor a more fully articulated civic ideology. In his treatise on Florence's constitution, written c. 1440, Bruni, the civic humanist, focused on the exercise of public power by the magistrates, and the limits imposed on their authority by the statutes. The executive bodies (the Signoria and their two advisory colleges) could initiate legislation, but their proposals had to be ratified by a two-thirds vote of the councils of the *popolo* and the Commune. To prevent an excessive concentration of authority in the hands of a few, the tenure of all civic offices was brief (between two and six months), and eligibility to those positions was carefully regulated.[3]

Florence's constitution was a mixture of the aristocratic and the democratic. In Bruni's world, those citizens (magnates) "with too great a power of numbers and of force at their command" were excluded from the chief executive offices, while "mechanics and members of the lowest class" were not allowed any role in the state. "Thus, avoiding the extremes, the city look[ed] to the mean, or rather to the best and the wealthy but not overpowerful." That middling mass of politically active citizens comprised artisans and shopkeepers from the lower guilds and merchants, cloth manufacturers, bankers, and professionals (lawyers, notaries, physicians) from the greater guilds.[4]

2   Daniel Waley, *The Italian City-Republics* (London, 1969), 221–39; Philip Jones, "Economia e società nell'Italia medievale: la leggenda della borghesia," in Ruggiero Romano and Corrado Vivanti (eds.), *Einaudi Storia d'Italia* (Turin, 1978), I, 185–372; Romano, "Una tipologia economia," and Vivanti, "Lacerazioni e contrasti," in *idem* (eds.), *Einaudi Storia d'Italia* (Turin, 1973), I, 253–304, 867–948, respectively.
3   For recent surveys of the literature, see Brucker, *The Civic World of Early Renaissance Florence* (Princeton, 1977), 3–13; John Najemy, "Linguaggi storiografici sulla Firenze rinascimentale." *Rivista storica italiana*, XCVII (1985), 102–59. Leonardo Bruni, "On The Florentine Constitution," in Gordon Griffiths, James Hankins, and David Thompson (eds.), *The Humanism of Leonardo Bruni* (Binghamton, 1987), 171–4.
4   Bruni, "Florentine Constitution," 171.

Every year, more than a thousand citizens participated directly in the political process as members of the supreme executive and as officials who staffed the forty-odd commissions responsible for the administration of the dominion, the collection of taxes, and the enforcement of sumptuary laws. More than a thousand citizens assembled regularly each year as members of the legislative councils. They also participated in the administration of their guilds, as consuls and councillors. They attended meetings of their electoral districts (*gonfaloni*) and assemblies of their parish churches.

Thousands of Florentines also participated in the meetings and rituals of their confraternities and in the processions that commemorated civic and religious holidays. The anniversary (June 24) of John the Baptist, the city's patron saint, was celebrated by a procession that included the secular and religious authorities, representatives of subject communities, and a large contingent of guildsmen. This annual ritual symbolized most dramatically the civic community and the bonds that united its members.[5]

The political agenda of this large and heterogenous mass of middling Florentines, which constituted the *popolo*, was quite straightforward. These citizens wanted their traditional place and voice in the government, based upon their guild memberships. The essence of republicanism for these men was its corporate and collegiate quality, in which decisions were made and policies formulated by citizens chosen to represent the whole community. As Najemy wrote, they believed in the principles "of consent and representation as the foundation of legitimate republican government, of officeholding as a public trust, of the supremacy of law, and of the delegated quality of all formal power." They felt that the common good (*ben comune*) was best served by the firm and equitable administration of justice, which would protect their persons and their property, regulate their business affairs, and adjudicate their private disputes. They also favored rigorous scrutiny of the conduct of civic officials and severe punishment for malfeasance.[6]

In the interest of a fiscal system that was fair, they supported the famous law of the *catasto* (1427), which allocated the tax burden according to the declared wealth of individual households. Appended to their tax returns were statements that articulated with clarity and eloquence their perception of an ideal civic polity. Giovanni Corbinelli informed the catasto officials that he prayed to God "to give [them] grace to do justice to each [taxpayer], and if [they did] so, [they would give] health to this city in perpetuity and . . . be the instrument to maintain this *popolo* in liberty forever."

5   Gregorio Dati, *Istoria di Firenze dall'anno MCCCLXXX all'anno MCCCCV* (Florence, 1735), in Brucker (ed.), *The Society of Renaissance Florence* (New York, 1971), 75–8.

6   Najemy, "The Dialogue of Power in Florentine Politics," in Anthony Molho, Kurt Raaflaub, and Julia Emlen (eds.), *City States in Classical Antiquity and Medieval Italy* (Stuttgart, 1991), 278.

Giovanni Vettori wrote, "If you act according to your honor, you will maintain and strengthen this glorious city in triumph and virtue." A belt maker named Luca di Cino appended to his tax report, "I, Luca, have compiled this document with my own hand, and I believe that what I have declared is the whole truth. . . . So that the commune will have what it is owed, and you will have done your duty and [preserved] your honor, and we will be treated fairly, may Christ keep you in peace."[7]

The tenor of these statements reveals another dimension of the popolo's agenda: the desire for strong, active, and even intrusive government. These citizens were convinced that their turbulent and violence-prone society required a heavy measure of discipline and regulation. This was not a community that trusted its members to live together in peace and harmony (*vivere civile*) without coercion. Florentines had no conception of a private realm immune from public scrutiny and intervention. No intimation is evident in either public or private records that the citizenry resented this close surveillance and regulation of their private lives.

By large majorities, they voted in favor of special magistracies to regulate (among other matters) their weddings and funerals, their clothing and jewelry, their relations with the Jewish community, and their sexual behavior. These officials hired informers to spy on their fellow citizens, and they established boxes (*tamburi*) into which secret denunciations could be deposited. Florentine statutory law gave broad powers to the Signoria and its colleges to elect certain officials, to cancel or alter judicial penalties, to issue safe conducts and grants of immunity from persecution, and to force individuals and corporate bodies to obey their decrees. These magistrates did not hesitate to intervene in privates affairs – for example, to prohibit a mother described as "quarrelsome and prone to scandalous behavior" from living with her two nubile daughters.[8]

Two cases will illustrate the extent of this arbitrary executive authority. In April 1429, on the occasion of a tournament in honor of a visiting member of the Portuguese royal family, the Signoria issued an executive order that a penalty of 1,000 florins would be levied against five citizens unless they appeared with horses and armor to participate in the joust. Eleven years later, the Signoria threatened to impose a fine of 1,000 florins on Uguccione de' Ricci unless he could persuade his cousin, the archbishop of Pisa, to abandon a judicial process against an alleged usurer in his ecclesiastical, court.[9]

7 Catasto, 17, fol. 749r; 18, fol. 806r; 21, fol. 88r, Archivio di Stato di Firenze (hereinafter ASF).

8 For examples of regulatory legislation and its enforcement, see Brucker (ed.), *Society of Renaissance Florence*, 179–212. Deliberazioni dei Signori e Collegi (ordinaria autorità), 99, unpaginated, February 25, 1498, ASF.

9 Giudice degli Appelli, 75, fols. 201r–201v, 80, fol. 282r, ASF.

Within this republican polity, that men from the city's most prominent wealthy lineages wielded more power and influence than did citizens of lesser rank was a perennial fact of political life, as valid for the fifteenth century as for that pristine age when Dante's ancestor, Cacciaguida, lived. These men of high social status (*ottomati*) viewed their political system from a somewhat different perspective than did the popolo. They, too, favored a strong, activist government, accepting the principle that the general welfare of the community took precedence over private interests. But they resented the political role of the popolo in the regime, and after the Ciompi revolution, they succeeded in limiting their access to civic office, and their influence on policy.

Even though the ottomati had gained a dominant role in the regime by the early fifteenth century, they were unable to control the bitter rivalries and factional quarrels that periodically threatened the stability of the regime. The primary source of these partisan conflicts was not political or ideological but personal and familial – the struggle among individuals and families for civic office, and the benefits and perquisites that accrued to those who held it. These conflicts intensified during times of crisis, particularly during the years of warfare (1391 to 1402, 1411 to 1414, and 1423 to 1431) that drained the city's wealth, sparked widespread unrest in Florence and throughout the dominion, and inspired bitter quarrels and recriminations within the leadership. An especially intense crisis in the early 1430s culminated in the emergence of one family, the Medici, which was able to create a party or faction composed of kinfolk, neighbors, friends, and clients that governed Florence for sixty years (1434 to 1494).[10]

The ability of the Medici to seize and maintain control of the republic was due not only to their political skills but also to the vast wealth that they could use to buy allegiance. They immobilized their rivals by exiling them and by excluding the rank and file from office, while restoring the political rights of old magnate families. They preserved many of the republican institutions inherited from the past, though they did replace the old legislative councils (in which the influence of the popolo was strong) by smaller and more tractable bodies of their adherents.

When the regime was threatened by internal discord and popular unrest, it created commissions (*balie*) with extraordinary powers to reform the state. The Medici developed complex electoral strategies to ensure that their allies would control the major electoral offices, while excluding any current or potential rivals. They gradually dismantled the old judicial system administered by foreign (and supposedly impartial) judges, substituting magistra-

---

10   The main themes in this paragraph, and the one preceding, are discussed in detail in Brucker, *Civic World*, 248–507; Dale Kent, *The Rise of the Medici: Faction in Florence 1426–1434* (Oxford, 1978).

cies staffed by citizens from the ranks of their partisans. Even though the statutes guaranteed the right "of citizens to be free to give counsel and to judge public affairs," the regime was prepared to silence its critics by accusing them of fomenting discord and engaging in treasonous activity. As had been true throughout the republic's history, the distinction between legitimate criticism and sedition was always a fine line.[11]

To the more equitable system of tax assessments embodied in the catasto, they favored the older method of *arbitrio*, by which tax commissions in each electoral district decided levies to be imposed on their neighbors. As the Medici had long recognized, this was a powerful weapon for rewarding friends and punishing enemies.

The Medicean system of government reached its apogee under Lorenzo, who, following in his grandfather Cosimo's footsteps, built a polity that retained its formal republican facade while enabling its *maestro* to control the levers of power. Lorenzo's authority derived primarily from the elaborate network of patron–client relations that Cosimo had developed and that he and his father Piero had fostered and expanded. Lorenzo's network extended from the city throughout the dominion, even beyond Florentine territory to include the whole Italian peninsula.[12]

Lorenzo was the supreme patron of the Florentine state, and letters came to him from individuals, corporations, ecclesiastical foundations, and political authorities inside and outside the state's territorial boundaries. Petitioners appealed to Lorenzo for support and favor – for civic office, ecclesiastical benefices, tax exemptions, cancellation of criminal sentences, arranging marriages, and letters of recommendation. Lorenzo's influence was considered to be decisive in the operations of the Florentine government, and personal appeals for his help more useful than requests to the civic magistracies.

Writing to Lorenzo in 1478, Giovanni Capponi noted that Medicean support for his family "[was] the reason why . . . we have with assurance had recourse to you and to your ancestors, by whom graciously we have been exalted." In 1488, Piero Buondelmonti wrote to a close associate of Lorenzo "that everything proceeds from God by the virtue, merits and

---

11   On Medicean electoral strategies, see Nicolai Rubinstein, *The Government of Florence Under the Medici 1434–1494* (Oxford, 1966); on the fisc, Elio Conti, *L'imposta diretta a Firenze nel Quattrocento 1427–1494* (Rome, 1984); on the judicial system, Lauro Martines, *Lawyers and Statecraft in Renaissance Florence* (Princeton, 1968), 387–404; on the issue of "free speech," Rubinstein, *Government of Florence*, 156–7.

12   For descriptions of Lorenzo's network, see Lorenzo de' Medici (ed. Riccardo Fubini et al), *Lettere* (Florence, 1977–). 6 v. to date. For a succinct summary, see Francis W. Kent. "Patron–Client Networks in Renaissance Florence and the Emergence of Lorenzo as 'Maestro della Bottega,'" in Bernard Toscani (ed.), *Lorenzo de' Medici: New Perspectives* (New York, 1993), 279–313.

dignity of our God on earth, the Magnificent Lorenzo, to. whom I beg you to recommend me as his creature."[13]

Friends in high places were critical in this highly competitive and ago-nistic society. Giovanni Rucellai, the wealthy merchant, once wrote that he needed a large circle of *amici* to protect himself from his enemies. Alberti commented that "there is really nothing more difficult in the world than distinguishing true friends amid the obscurity of so many lies, the darkness of people's motives and the shadowy errors and vices that lie about us on all sides." Even close friends were capable of betrayal; discord within fami-lies over inheritances, marriages, and business transactions were common. Florence was a veritable cauldron of suspicion, mistrust, and envy, fuelled by the struggle for wealth, status, and reputation, which in concrete terms signified the ability to obtain civic office and to arrange honorable marriages for daughters and lucrative careers for sons.[14]

In this "paradise inhabited by devils," the achievement of these objectives was an arduous enterprise. The attainment of high civic office could be thwarted by the machinations of one's enemies. A family's prosperity could be destroyed by business failures or confiscatory taxation. The competition for appropriate marriage partners led to the escalation of dowries and the inability of impoverished fathers from prominent lineages to contract "honorable" liaisons. The penalties exacted upon these losers included imprisonment for debt, withdrawal from the city to a mar-ginal life in the *contado*, and unemployable sons and unmarriageable daughters.[15]

These unpalatable scenarios explain the desperate tone of the appeals to Lorenzo and other prominent figures in the regime – for instance, that of Bernardo di Nicola, who pleaded for a reduction of his tax bill, which would be "the cause of [his] coming again to life," and that of Bernardo Cambini, who, seeking to obtain a seat in the Signoria that his ancestors had occupied, "did not wish by comparison [with them] to appear 'a wooden man.'" Cambini added that his selection to the supreme executive "would be useful in enabling [him] to marry [his] daughters."[16]

13   *Idem, Household and Lineage in Renaissance Florence* (Princeton, 1977), 212; *idem*, "Lorenzo and Oligarchy," in Gian Carlo Garfagnini (ed.), *Lorenzo il Magnifico e il suo mondo* (Florence, 1994), 46.

14   Alessandro Perosa (ed.), *Giovanni Rucellai ed il suo Zibaldone* (London, 1960), 9. Leon Battista Alberti, quoted in Ronald Weissman, *Ritual Brotherhood m Renaissance Florence* (New York, 1982), 29. Weissman's first chapter, "Judas the Florentine," 1–41, describes the agonis-tic character of Florentine society.

15   F. W. Kent, "Un paradiso habitato da diavoli": Ties of Loyalty and Patronage in the Society of Medicean Florence," in Anna Benvenuti (ed.), *Le radici cristiane di Firenze* (Florence, 1994), 198; Brucker, "Florentine Voices from the *Catasto*," *I Tatti Studies*, V (1993), 22–32.

16   F. W. Kent, *Household and Lineage*, 83; *idem*, "Patron–Client Networks," 294.

In addition to manipulating the political system and promoting a city-wide network of patron–client bonds, Lorenzo also developed a strategy to limit the autonomy of the city's corporate bodies and make them more responsive to the regime's agenda. Florence's major guilds – Lana, Calimala, and Cambio – had long since been taken over by Medici partisans, as had been the Merchant's Court (*Mercanzia*), which regulated commercial and financial affairs. Lorenzo's influence within the Florentine church was solidified by the appointment of Rinaldo Orsini, his brother-in-law, as archbishop. He intervened directly in the administration of San Lorenzo, his family's parish church, and in monastic and conventual foundations that had been subsidized by Medici largesse. The Medici also funded and governed the city's charitable foundations – hospitals, foundling homes, and hostels for plague victims.

Confraternities – approximately 100 of them – constituted one of the most important segments of the city's associative life. These societies were an obvious target for Medicean penetration. Since their memberships comprised as much as one-fifth of the adult male population, they were potential sources of either support for or resistance to the regime. By joining these sodalities, Lorenzo was able to control their ritual and charitable activities and to exert a decisive influence on their internal administrations. After becoming a member of the confraternity of Sant' Agnese, for example, Lorenzo was recognized as its chief benefactor and patron. He also supervised the society's transformation from an egalitarian association of neighbors into "a more aristocratic organization, whose councils promoted Medicean political interests and whose rituals worshipped and magnified the aura surrounding the lineage."[17]

The Florentines never wholly accepted Medicean hegemony. Opposition to the regime came initially from those families whose members had been exiled, excluded from office, and penalized by the judicial and fiscal systems. But even the Medicis' close allies and associates came to resent the dominant and often domineering roles of first Cosimo and, later, Piero and Lorenzo. Playing subversive roles in the crises of 1458 and 1466, which threatened the regime's stability, they adopted republican slogans, calling for the restoration of "liberty," "freedom," and "good government" and the abolition of the Medici's self-aggrandizing electoral and fiscal strategies. Echoes of these sentiments are found in council debates throughout the 1450s and 1460s, testifying to the tenacious survival of republican ideology in the city.

No public criticism of Lorenzo and his authoritarian regime, however, was ever voiced; it would have invited "immediate imprisonment, exile or

---

17   Weissman, *Ritual Brotherhood*; John Henderson, *Piety and Charity in Late Medieval Florence* (Oxford, 1994); Nicholas Eckstein, *The District of the Green Dragon: Neighborhood Life and Social Change in Renaissance Florence* (Florence, 1995), 217.

even death." Opposition took the form of conspiracies, which were inevitably crushed; of anonymous placards posted in the city squares; of negative gossip and rumors that circulated in public places; and of critical comments recorded in private diaries and account books. Although many of Lorenzo's detractors were motivated by a sense of personal mistreatment, they justified their opposition by appealing to the republican tradition, which (so they claimed) the Medici had destroyed. When Lorenzo died in 1492, the entire city participated in his funeral rites with expressions of grief and loss. Yet, according to one witness, many of these mourners "instead rejoiced, thinking that the republic would recover its liberty and they would escape from servitude."[18]

Two years after Lorenzo's death, a French invasion precipitated the expulsion of the Medici, and the city was given the opportunity to "recover its liberty." A makeshift republican regime restored most of the institutional structures that the Medici had dismantled. One significant innovation was the creation of the Great Council, whose members included all of the citizens whose fathers and/or grandfathers had qualified for the highest executive offices – the Signoria and its two colleges. The Great Council voted on all legislative proposals and selected the officials who filled the civic magistracies and those who governed the dominion. This "fundamental law of the republican period" shifted the balance of power from the elite back to the popolo. Given the large number of citizens newly integrated into the government, the reformers expected this revived commitment to the *vivere popolare* (republican government) to enable the regime to survive and prosper.[19]

The establishment of this republican polity could not have occurred at a more difficult time than in the wake of the French invasion. By maintaining its traditional alliance with the French monarchy, the republic incurred the enmity of those states and interests (Venice, Naples, and the papacy) that had fought to keep the French out. The arduous military effort to rescue the rebel city of Pisa drained hundreds of thousands of florins from the city's treasury, and imposed heavy burdens upon the citizenry. These fiscal problems were compounded by a series of poor harvests that threatened the urban poor with starvation, and by the disruption of trade routes that resulted in unemployment among the workers in the cloth industry.

These crises exacerbated the deep and pervasive divisions within the government. A hard core of Medici supporters sought to weaken the new

18   Alison Brown, "Lorenzo and Public Opinion in Florence," in Garfagnini (ed.), *Lorenzo il Magnifico e il suo mondo*, 61–85.
19   Felix Gilbert, *Machiavelli and Guicciardini* (Princeton, 1965), 19. The phrase, *vivere popolare* was commonly used by contemporaries, for example, Luca Landucci, *Diario fiorentino del 1450 al 1516* (Florence, 1883), 97, 110.

regime and to prepare for the Medici's resumption of power. Furthermore, the conflict that had resulted from Savonarola's brief and tumultuous career as a religious leader with a political agenda still persisted after his execution in 1498. But the issue that ultimately doomed the republic concerned the balance of power between the elite and the popolo. Members of the old and prominent lineages attempted to monopolize the major offices and to formulate civic policy by curtailing the authority of the Great Council, with its guild constituency, and enacting institutional reforms that would give them a greater voice in fiscal matters and foreign policy. The popolo strongly resisted these efforts, consistently voting against proposals to levy taxes for military operations. During this period, the regime was periodically threatened by Medicean conspiracies, rebellions in the dominion, and military incursions by foreign troops. Instead of uniting the citizenry in defense of the regime, these perils intensified the factional quarrels and divisions.[20]

The republican regime that governed Florence from 1494 to 1512 was the city's most "democratic" polity since the late fourteenth century. Some 3,000 citizens – one-fourth of the adult male were population – belonged to the Great Council. Not since the 1460s were Florentines so free to express their opinions in council deliberations. But this unaccustomed freedom to discuss the *res publica* did not result in coherent and constructive policies, but, rather, in lengthy and inconclusive debates that revealed the deep fissures within the city and the regime's inability to respond effectively to crises.

The civic mood throughout these years was one of pervasive anxiety: "We are in such a state that our demise appears to be imminent. . . . To live in this manner is the height of insanity. . . . It is not necessary to describe the dangers and disorders that confront the city; they are so great that one can speak of chaos." Speakers repeatedly criticized every facet of government – the fisc, the administration of justice, the selection of officials, and the conduct of military affairs and foreign policy. They also speculated about the sources of "disorder" and the failure of the citizenry to unite in defense of the liberty that their ancestors "had acquired with so much bloodshed." One popular explanation was that private interest had become more important than the general welfare. An ominous sign of civic alienation was the frequent absence of a quorum at sessions of the Great Council, leading to the postponement of legislative action and a halt to the selection of magistrates.[21]

---

20   Gilbert, *Machiavelli and Guicciardini*, 7–104, Humfrey Butters, *Governors and Government in Early Sixteenth Century Florence 1502–1519* (Oxford, 1985), 1–165.

21   The quotations in this paragraph are from Denis Fachard (ed.), *Consulte e pratiche della Republica fiorentini 1498–1505* (Geneva, 1993), 1–9.

Civic debates exposed all of the systemic weaknesses of republican government throughout the communal era. From city to city, the scenario varied only in the details: beleaguered regimes plagued by internal divisions, weak and indecisive leadership, the erosion of civic institutions and values, and the transfer of power from the community to an individual or a family. In Florence, this process was more prolonged than elsewhere; republican ideals there were stronger and more deeply rooted in the urban culture. The Medici were finally successful in regaining control of the state, with the assistance of their two popes, Leo X (1513–21) and Clement VII (1523–34). The transformation was solidified with the selection of Cosimo de' Medici as Duke of Florence in 1537, establishing a dynasty that ruled the city and its territory for two centuries.

The Florentine elite accepted the Medicean *principato*, in exchange for the recognition of its privileged position in government and in society. Francesco Guicciardini, a historian and a prominent figure among the ottomati, preferred that the regime be controlled by the city's leading families, but he accepted a high office under the Medici that brought him *onore e utile*, honor and profit.

The educational process by which upper-class Florentines were converted from citizens to courtiers was described by Alamanni, a Medici partisan, in 1516:

> Florentines are not accustomed to be deferential to anyone except their magistrates and then only with some pressure and effort. They felt that it was beneath their dignity to doff their hats, and this ancient practice became embedded in their customs. . . . The older generation will never abandon this habit, but being wise, these men will not revolt (*non fanno mai novità*). But the younger generation is more flexible, more malleable, and the prince can win their support and loyalty by inviting them to join his court, and by granting them offices and benefits.[22]

The construction of an authoritarian government and a hierarchical social order, begun by the Medici in the fifteenth century, was completed in the sixteenth. The popolo were too weakened and demoralized by successive crises (plagues, famines, the depredations of military forces, heavy taxation, and conspiracies) to challenge their exclusion from the polity. Under the Medici, the *popolani* (citizenry) had become accustomed to a political and social order based on patronage and clientage, which offered them more support than did their civic institutions and their guilds. After the expulsion of the Medici in 1494, a merchant named Piero Vaglienti expressed the view

---

22   Lodovico Alamanni, quoted in Rudolf von Albertini, *Das Florentinische Staatsbeunisstsein im Übergang von der Republik zum Prinzipat* (Bern, 1955), 370.

of many citizens of middling rank: "Now one does not know to whom to turn for help. . . . With a prince [*signore*] there is only one [leader], but now in Florence there are a hundred, and some pull you in one direction, and others in another."[23]

Within the ranks of the popolo, too, were hundreds, perhaps thousands, who had benefitted from Medicean favors and welcomed their return to power. In the dominion, the peasantry, which comprised some 70 percent of the total population, were largely indifferent; they could not distinguish between rulers and exploiters, whether republican or Medicean. As for the residents in the subject towns, who were governed by officials sent from Florence, the words "liberty" and "freedom," so often articulated in council deliberations, had little meaning for them.[24]

The demise of the republic at the hands of Medici rule did not signal a revolutionary change in the lives of the Florentine populace. It brought no abatement to the plagues, famines, and marauding armies that afflicted every urban community in Italy at the time. Nonetheless, the establishment of the principato produced a degree of political stability that the city had not experienced for decades. Medici princes continued the tradition of a strong and intrusive government. The implementation of its policy was the task of the granducal bureaucracy, the upper echelons of which were recruited from the city's elite families. To bolster their status and reinforce the principle of hierarchy, members of these lineages also received tides of nobility when they enrolled in the exclusive knightly order of Santo Stefano. The Medici also utilized the city's traditional rites and ceremonies, both secular and religious, to enhance their reputation and curry favor with the populace.[25]

The Medici grand dukes gradually eradicated all traces of the *vivere popolare* and civil society. Although Cosimo I once asserted that he was bound "by the laws, the order and the magistrates of our city," in reality he was the sole fount of power. "Our advice is our will," he once wrote to a councillor, "and we consider as adversaries all those who oppose it." Varchi, the historian, told his readers not to marvel "that [he spoke] only of Cosimo, and never of the state nor the magistracies, since . . . Cosimo alone govern[ed] everything, and nothing [was] said or done, however great or small, concerning which he [did not say] either 'yes' or 'no.'" Early in his

23 F. W. Kent, "Patron–Client Networks," 302.

24 George Bull (trans.), *The Autobiography of Benvenuto Cellini* (Baltimore, 1956; orig. pub. 1538–63), 21–2.

25 The impact of a devastating plague in the early 1630s is described by Giulia Calvi, *Histories of a Plague Year* (Berkeley, 1989). Political stability ensued not only in the city but also in the territory; See Giorgio Spini, *Cosimo I de' Medici e la indipendenza del principato mediceo* (Florence, 1945), 178–87. The elaborate celebration of a Medici marriage is described by James Saslow, *The Medici Wedding of 1589: Florentine Festival as Theatrum Mundi* (New Haven, 1996).

rule, Cosimo had published a decree that prohibited "any kind of assembly, congregation or conventicle," since such gatherings were viewed as potential sources of dissent and conspiracy.[26]

Under the Medici grand dukes, guilds lost their autonomy and became state agencies for the regulation of commerce, industry, the retail trades, and the crafts. The confraternities were also radically transformed:

> In contrast to traditional confraternities of republican Florence, sixteenth-century confraternities reveal major departures in ideology, ritual and social organization, introducing principles of hierarchy into confraternal membership, localizing new confraternities in parishes, bringing city-wide confraternities under the control of the duke, stressing a new ethic of obedience, and replacing older rituals that emphasized community, equality and the suspension of social differentiation and hierarchy with ritual celebrations of status, honor and rank.

For example, when a group of Florentine intellectuals spontaneously formed a cultural society in the early 1540s, Cosimo first disbanded and then reconstituted the association as the Academia Florentina, its membership and its constitution strictly controlled by the prince.[29]

The establishment of the Medici principato brought Florence and its territory into the larger Italian world dominated by autocratic rulers and landed nobles, in which, as Machiavelli asserted, "no republics nor any *vivere politico* had ever existed, since those men are totally hostile to civic life." Members of Florence's of leading families adapted easily to this milieu, changing their mode of dress to conform to courtly fashion, and intermarrying with noble lineages from other Italian provinces. Some acquired fiefs in Tuscany and elsewhere; those with military training found employment in the armies of Italian and foreign princes. The church provided career opportunities for the younger sons of these families, and convents became a convenient depository for their unmarried sisters.[28]

---

26 Eric Cochrane, *Florence in the Forgotten Centuries* (Chicago, 1973), 43, 64; Benedetto Varchi, quoted in Furio Diaz, *Il Granducato di Toscana: I Medici* (Turin, 1987), 74; Cochrane, *Florence*, 40.

27 Weissman, *Ritual Brotherhood*, 198. See also Konrad Eisenbichler, "Italian Scholarship on Pre-Modern Confraternities in Italy," *Renaissance Quarterly*, L (1997), 567–80. Diaz, *Granducato*, 201.

28 Niccolò Machiavelli, *Discorsi*, I, chap. 55, in Guido Mazzoni and Mario Casella (eds.), *Tutte le opere di Niccolò Machiavelli* (Florence, 1929), 127. Machiavelli mistakenly included Lombardy and the papal states in his catalogue of regions that had never experienced republican government. Landucci, *Diario fiorentino*, 371: "Si cominciò a lasciare la portatura de' capucci, e nel 1532 non se ne vedeva pure uno, che fu spenta l'usanza, e scanbio di capuccio si porta berrette e cappegli . . . e or cominciossi a portare la barba" ([Florentines] no longer wore hoods on their cloaks, and by 1532, there were none to be seen. Instead of hoods, they wore caps, and they also began to grow beards).

The Medici recruited substantial numbers of aristocrats into their bureaucracy; the economic benefits of state service were an important source of revenue for these noble houses. The ottomati, whose ancestors had once proudly governed their free city and its territory, had become loyal subjects and servants of the prince, competing with their rivals for his favor and largesse.[29]

Certain distinctive features of post-invasion Italy were inherited from city-state republics. The concept of individual rights and liberties, and of a private realm immune from state intervention, had never been a part of the communal legacy. Nor did it emerge, either in theory or practice, during this age of autocratic government. The impulse toward scrutiny, surveillance, and control was no less present in republican than in despotic regimes, or, for that matter, than in the feudal governments of Piedmont and Sicily. This intrusive and invasive mentality was manifest in the flood of legislation emanating from these governments, and in the publication of edicts (*bandi*), the repetition of which testified to their limited efficacy.[30]

The responsibility for enforcing this thicket of legislation was entrusted to a large, expensive, and burdensome bureaucracy, which was trained to execute the ruler's will, and to regard his subjects with suspicion and condescension. For example, to implement Cosimo I's prohibition against the export of grain from the duchy, the Medici government employed a veritable army of "functionaries, agents, rectors, notaries, police officials, spies and informers." These officials inspected all goods in transit at the borders; they examined the account books and the storage facilities of grain merchants; and they invaded the cottages of villagers and peasants to search for hidden food supplies. Their methods were as arbitrary and ruthless as those of the tax officials who collected the gabelles and the levies that subsidized the regimes' administrative and military structures.[31]

These tactics, employed by every regime from Sicily to Piedmont to enforce obedience and raise revenue, created a pernicious legacy for the future – a pervasive and deeply rooted distrust of, and hostility to, the state, its institutions, its operations, and its personnel. Subjects did not perceive the state as a protector and defender but as an exploiter and predator. It is as true today, as it was in the seventeenth and eighteenth centuries, that "by and large, the state bureaucracy has oppressed rather than served the

---

29   The definitive study of these ottomati is Burr Litchfield, *Emergence of a Bureaucracy: The Florentine Patricians, 1530–1790* (Princeton, 1986).

30   Diaz, *Granducato*, 3: "La libertà civile, in quanto tutela dei diritti individuali, è sempre state . . . ignorata dalle 'democrazie' communali" (civil liberty, in the sense of protecting individual rights, had always been ignored by communal "democracies"). For the legislation that flooded granducal Tuscany, see *Legislazione toscana raccolta e illustrata da Lorenzo Cantini* (Florence, 1800–7), 30v.

31   Diaz, *Granducato*, 133.

Italian citizen. . . . Far from exercising over time a pedagogic role in Italian society, the state has rather itself been shaped by those patron–client and kinship relations which are so deeply rooted in Mediterranean culture." From the highest to the lowest level of the bureaucracy, officials were commonly viewed as arrogant, inefficient, and corrupt.[32]

An Austrian diplomat in the 1730s sent this report on the Tuscan bureaucracy back to his master in Vienna: "Theft is everywhere in the military and civil administration, in the finances: there is no tribunal, no receivership where the prince is not deceived and the people oppressed. . . . [The officials] all *eat*, to use the local term, they eat off everything, off the vilest things, off the most miserable people." Since the state was not a reliable source of protection and justice, the majority of Italians instead depended upon kinship ties and the support of powerful patrons. As Delille has noted, the truly poor in early modern society "are not those who have nothing whatsoever, but those who are outside any network of solidarity."[33]

The post-Tridentine Catholic church supported the efforts of secular rulers to discipline and control their recalcitrant subjects. The church's ideology was, in most respects, identical to that of Italy's princes, and it defended the principle of hierarchical organization, which it exemplified, as it applied to Italy's "society of orders." While insisting upon its own autonomy, and its immunity from secular control, the church advocated the doctrine of submission to both lay and ecclesiastical authority, developing strategies to instruct the laity in doctrinal matters and to persuade laymen to perform their Christian obligations.[34]

Priests were required to keep records of their parishioners' vital statistics (births, marriages, and deaths) and to threaten those who violated the church's rules with excommunication. More effectively than in the past, the parish clergy established tighter controls over marriage, sexual behavior, and social life and brought the confraternities under their surveillance. The clergy also tried to weaken kinship ties in their communities, but with only limited success.[35]

32   Paul Ginsborg "The Italian Republic in the Face of the Future," *Italian History and Culture* (Florence, 1966), II, 4.

33   Jean Claude Waquet (trans. Linda McCall), *Corruption: Ethics and Power in Florence, 1600–1770* (University Park, 1991), 17. Gerard Delille, quoted in Domenico Sella, *Italy in the Seventeenth Century* (New York, 1997), 83.

34   Sella, *Italy in the Seventeenth Century*, 80–1.

35   John Bossy, "The Counter-Reformation and the People of Catholic Europe," *Past & Present*, 47 (1970), 51–70; William Hudon, "Religion and Society in Early Modern Italy – Old Questions, New Insights," *American Historical Review*, CI (1996), 783–804. The plight of confraternities is a major theme in Bossy's seminal article, "Counter-Reformation," 54–9, but his statement that confraternities were no longer an obstacle to uniform parochial observance "because they ceased to exist" is too extreme. See Sella, *Italy in the Seventeenth Century*, 137–42.

Behind all of these strategies were the revitalized coercive powers of the Roman church: excommunication, the Index, and the Inquisition. The Medici grand dukes were more receptive to the operation of these mechanisms than were most other Italian rulers. Civic life in the Tuscan duchy was vitiated by Cosimo's subservience to the Roman papacy: "The persecutions of the Inquisition . . . against any citizen suspected of heresy, the vigilance of the clergy in scrutinizing the behavior and thoughts of Tuscans . . . created a climate of heavy, bigoted conformism."[36]

The most potent and influential legacy received by postrevolutionary Italy was not a civic tradition inherited from the communal era but the structures and patterns developed during the "age of absolutism" – authoritarian government, both secular and religious, and a hierarchical social order in which patron–client networks flourished, in both the north and the south. Only a few urban communities – Venice, Genoa, Lucca, and San Marino – retained some degree of political autonomy. The primary objective of urban elites in those cities was the preservation of their privileged status. In towns governed by princes or viceroys, elites (both secular and ecclesiastical) were able to minimize their tax burdens and maintain their property and influence in the countryside.[37]

No associations of any kind could be established without the approval of secular and religious authorities. Unlike the European authorities across the Alps, those in Italy effectively stifled religious dissent in their territories, with the sole exception of the Waldensian community in Piedmont. The absence of any serious challenge to religious orthodoxy was, and long remained, a significant deterrent to the revival of civic values and traditions. The popularity of Italy's most celebrated novel – Alessandro Manzoni's *I promessi sposi* (Milan, 1827) – was due primarily to the familiarity of nineteenth-, and even twentieth-century Italians with its depiction of seventeenth-century Lombardy as overwhelmingly "feudal," with its lawless and arrogant nobles and their *bravi* (hired thugs), its dependent and deferential lower orders, its autocratic but fundamentally weak government, and its religious culture of submission and obedience."[38]

---

36 Diaz, *Granducato*, 194.
37 Sella, *Italy in the Seventeenth Century*, 52–62; Stuart Woolf, *A History of Italy 1700–1860: The Social Constraints of Political Change* (New York, 1991), 21–6.
38 Sella, *Italy in the Seventeenth Century*, 154–5. An illustration of the survival of this mentality in the nineteenth century involved Bettino Ricasoli, the "enlightened" Tuscan statesman and landowner:

Whenever there was the least hesitant attempt to change customary relationships, with the peasants hinting at the existence of wishes diverging from those of their master, Ricasoli reacted swiftly, conveying to his factor [steward or manager] at Brolio that he was the master, that the property was his, that he alone could decide how to manage

If the definition of *civil society* includes as a central feature "a complex tissue of voluntary associations which occupy a public space and have a public voice," then it is difficult to find evidence for this phenomenon in pre-revolutionary Italy. The academies and fledgling masonic lodges that were formed in the eighteenth century did not have a political agenda, nor any significant influence on princes and their administrators. Italy's elites were united Only in their determination to preserve their traditional privileges.[39]

Not until the revolutionary era, which witnessed the radical overhaul of Italy's political and socioeconomic structures, were conditions ripe for the first tentative efforts to establish a civil society. This process was painfully slow and halting in a country whose citizens viewed the state as "a hostile presence . . . not merely in terms of the identification of the state with the land-owner, the tax-collector, and the *carabiniere*, but because of the paucity of intermediary strata attached to the values of the state." Even though the associations established before and after unification helped to contribute to this fledgling form of civil society, the assumption of "any simple correlation among voluntary associations, civil society and liberal democracy" is hardly warranted. As Nolan recently suggested, scholars "should pay less attention to quantifying civil society and more to understanding the qualitatively different meanings of associational life in different contexts. Societies can be, and since the nineteenth century have been, bourgeois without necessarily being liberal."[40]

it, and the first peasant that dared to speak ill of him would be dismissed. (Federico Chabod [trans. William McCuaig], *Italian Foreign Policy. The Statecraft of the Founders* [Princeton, 1996], 293).

39   Raymond Carr, *Times Literary Supplement*, 15 Oct. 1993, 4. See also Ernest Gellner, *Civil Society and Its Rivals* (New York, 1996). Woolf, *History of Italy*, 69–74, 95–111; Aldo Mola, *La massoneria nella storia d'Italia* (Rome, 1981), 21–57; Cochrane, *Tradition and Enlightenment in the Tuscan Academies, 1600–1800* (Chicago, 1961), 3–47.

40   Woolf, *History of Italy*, 476; Mary Nolan, "Against Exceptionalism," *American Historical Review*, CII (1997). 772–3.

3

Cosimo de' Medici: *Pater Patriae* or *Padrino?*

Anthony Molho

Cosimo de' Medici's political biography, at least in its basic outlines, has been well known for centuries.[1] The son of Giovanni di Bicci de' Medici, himself the founder of his family's famous bank, Cosimo was born in 1389 and was first drawn into politics during the 1410s. In the following decade he became the leader of a political faction, which, during the years of the war against Lucca (1429–33), clashed with older factions, led by Rinaldo degli Albizzi, Niccolò da Uzzano, and other patricians whose families had become politically entrenched after 1382. Cosimo's increasing power, based as it was on his great financial resources, his astuteness, and the successful organization of his relatives, friends, and clients (*parenti ed amici*) into an effective political force, led to his banishment from the city in 1433, shortly after the ignominious conclusion of the first Florentine war against Lucca. But, as most historians know, not quite one year later his opponents were themselves forced into exile and Cosimo was recalled from Venice. Thus was initiated the long era of Medicean domination which, except for two relatively short intervals totalling twenty-one years, lasted nearly three centuries. Cosimo, the founder of his family's extraordinary fortunes, savoured his success for thirty years until his death in 1464. During that period not only

1 Angelo Fabroni, *Magni Cosmi Medicei Vita*, 2 Vols. (Pisa, 1789); Curt Gutkind, *Cosimo de' Medici il Vecchio* (Florence, 1940); E. F. Gombrich, "The Early Medici as Patrons of Art," in E. F. Jacob, ed., *Italian Renaissance Studies – A tribute to Cecilia M. Ady* (London, 1960), pp. 279–311; Alison M. Brown, "The Humanist Portrait of Cosimo de' Medici, Pater Patriae," *Journal of the Warburg and Courtauld Institutes*, 24, Nos. 3–4 (1961), 186–221; Raymond de Roover, *The Rise and Decline of the Medici Bank* (Cambridge, Mass., 1963); Nicolai Rubinstein, *The Government of Florence under the Medici (1434–1494)* (Oxford, 1966); Dale Kent, *The Rise of the Medici-Faction in Florence 1426–1434* (Oxford–New York, 1978).

did he consolidate his family's primacy in Florence and administer his bank's affairs, but he also distinguished himself as the prime Florentine patron of the arts. In the interval, he brought about a volte-face in the conduct of Florentine diplomacy by abandoning the Florentine–Venetian alliance, traditionally directed against the proverbial Florentine enemy, Milan, and helping to install at the helm of the Milanese state an old and trusted friend of his, the mercenary Francesco Sforza. Architect of the *Lega Italica* of 1454, friend and associate of popes, princes, and *signori*, so universal was the esteem in which he was held, so great his success that, shortly after his death, the Florentine government bestowed upon him the title *pater patriae*, father of the fatherland.

If, indeed, enough facts are known about Cosimo with which to write a reasonably detailed chronicle of his life, it is also true that the work of recent historians has provided important analytical tools with which to understand particular aspects of his experience. Raymond de Roover's splendid history of the Medici bank offers numerous insights into the financial infrastructures of the Medici family in the Quattrocento and of Cosimo's remarkable capacities as manager of his clan's vast fortunes. Perhaps even more relevant to the political historian is the work of two other scholars: Nicolai Rubinstein and Gene Brucker. The first has unravelled, in a punctilliously precise analysis, the complicated mechanisms used by Cosimo and his descendants to control the commune's electoral councils and by so doing to ensure the screening of possible opponents from important offices, while concurrently preserving virtually intact the facade of communal, republican institutions. Gene Brucker's contribution, though less direct in the sense that he has not explicitly analyzed the political history of Florence after 1434, is equally important, for in his various studies Brucker has advanced a theoretical framework within which to interpret the social and political history of Florence in the late Trecento and the Quattrocento.[2] Very briefly, Brucker's thesis is that following the defeat of the Florentine proletariat in 1378, and the establishment of an aristocratic regime in 1382, the corporate structure of Florentine politics was emptied of its significance and that during this era, which begins in the late fourteenth century and spans the years of the Medicean regime in the fifteenth, aristocratic and individualistic institutions and values dominated the social and political structures of the city. Where before 1378 collectivist impulses had prevailed (albeit, Brucker would insist, in the most tenuous and fragile of ways), in the subsequent period personal ties of friendship and particularly of cliental relations determined the conduct of politics. More recently Dale Kent, who though she is not a student of Brucker's can nevertheless be considered his

---

2   Gene A. Brucker's *Renaissance Florence* (New York, 1969) contains a concise presentation of the author's views.

ablest disciple, has written the history of the Medici party in the years immediately preceding Cosimo's exile in 1433 and his subsequent repatriation one year later by applying rigorously prosopographic standards in her reconstruction of Florentine politics of those years.[3]

The Medicean manipulations of electoral processes and the cliental structure of Florentine society throughout the Quattrocento are, then, the two prevalent explanations currently available to help one assess the impact which the Medici had on the politics of their city. An attempt to understand Cosimo's contribution to the creation and consolidation of the Medicean regime must start by acknowledging the considerable value of Rubinstein's and Brucker's contributions, even if in the end one will need to alter not only details but also certain important aspects of the current generalizations. In this brief, programmatic essay I shall touch upon three specific aspects of Florentine political realities which may help one understand the nature and limits of Cosimo's power. These aspects I have labelled: class, political fragmentation, and patronage. I shall deal with each in turn, trying in the process to specify what I mean by them.

One can start by referring to a term which, for the past five centuries, has served as a pendant to Cosimo's name. For, only a few months after his death on 1 August 1464, the Florentine government granted Cosimo the title *pater patriae*, an honor never until then earned by any Florentine. This posthumous acclamation, as Allison Brown has elegantly shown, codified sentiments existing in his life, for Cosimo never lacked a number of sycophants ready to extol his virtues and accomplishments.[4] If Quattrocento

3   In addition to her book, mentioned in note 1, see her: "The Florentine *reggimento* in the Fifteenth Century," *Renaissance Quarterly*, 28 (1975), 575–638; and "I Medici in esilio: una vittoria di famiglia ed una disfatta personale," *Archivio storico italiano*, 132 (1976), 3–63.
4   Brown, "The Humanist Portrait," see note 1. See, also, Benedetto Dei's *Cronaca* in *Archivio di Stato di Firenze* (hereinafter ASFi.), *Manoscritti*, 119, f. 14v, commenting on Cosimo's exile in 1433: "Somma delle somme pella novità e chaciata d'un tanto groriosissimo cittadino quanto era Chosimo de' Medici, colona, fontana e stendardo di tutta Italia e padre de' poveri. . . ." No sooner had the Medici been recalled to Florence than overly flattering letters from friends began reaching them. An example: ASFi., *Mediceo Avanti il Principato* (hereinafter *MAP.*), V, 653, Malpiglio d'Antonio di Malpiglio Cicioni to Giovanni di Cosimo de' Medici in Venice, 20 November 1434: "Vegho la nostra patria, la nostra città medichata e ata a prosperare durante el buon ghoverno principiato." A number of panegyrics for Cosimo and other members of the Medici family can be found in *Biblioteca Nazionale di Firenze* (hereinafter BNFi.), *Manoscritti Palatini* 215, especially ff. 90r, 91r, 92v–93r. Typical of the tone of these poems is the one addressed to Cosimo and his brother Lorenzo (therefore composed before the latter's death in November, 1440) by Anselmo Calderoni: "Sonetto di messer Anselmo Chalderoni, mandato a Chosimo de' Medici in laude della virtù di lui e di Lorenzo, a onta de' Malivoli invidiosi. O lume de' terrestri ciptadini, o chiaro specchio d'ogni merchatante, o vero amicho a tutte hopere sancte, ho onor degli illustri fiorentini, o speranza de' grandi e de' piccini, o socchorso d'ogniun ch'è bisogniante, o de' pupilli et vedove ajutante, o forte schudo de' Toschan

Florentines would have had little difficulty understanding the courtly ambience in which such extravagant praise was born, as is suggested by certain sardonic asides found in contemporary sources, it is true that subsequent historians have tended to be more generous to Cosimo.[5] Some have argued, many more have assumed, that not only was he a benevolent, paternalistic figure, forever eager to have commerce with Florentines of all stations of life, exchanging pleasantries with *contadini* and *artigiani*, forsaking the formalities and rigors which his position in society bestowed upon him, but also that through his extraordinary largesse he provided employment for masons, carpenters, smiths, scribes, and craftsmen of all kinds, so that in the end the interpretive tradition seems fully to have justified the first half of his title. As for the second half, particularly in the nineteenth and twentieth centuries, it has been accepted even more unquestioningly than the first. For *patria* often has been equated with *stato*, and one is well aware of the layers of meaning with which this term has been endowed: the state as a work of art, an abstract notion, an ideal encompassing and transcending particularistic institutions and traditions, such as the *Parte Guelfa*, tower societies, guilds, confraternities, the extended family, even the relics of those social classes which had existed in the thirteenth and fourteenth centuries. Thus, Cosimo, it has been suggested, was *pater* of just this type of centralizing organism; he was the astute political leader (a condition not precluding either his benevolence or paternalism) of a government which encompassed and dominated all of society. Political historians, the argument runs, must focus their attention on communal institutions centered on the Palazzo de' Signori, on the men who most frequently and successfully served the government in its major magistracies, and on their relations with Cosimo and his lieutenants.

Elsewhere I have argued that this emphasis on prosopography, on the identification of ruling elites and the exposition of their internal histories, has often resulted in a distortion of our perception of political processes in the Tre- and Quattrocento by eliminating any trace of that intense class consciousness and of class conflict which are clearly evident in contempo-

---

confini, o sopr' ogni altro a' dDio charitativo, o prudente o temperato, giusto e forte, o padre al buono e patrignio al chattivo, o di somma pietate larghe porte, o aversario d'ogni atto lascivo, o tu che rendi per mal buone sorte, dobbian fino alla morte, per Chosmo e Lorenzo tutti noi, poveri preghar senpre Iddio per voi." A somewhat altered version of this poem was recently published by Antonio Lanza, ed., *Lirici toscani del Quattrocento* (Rome, 1973), p. 344.

5   See, for example, Filippo di Cino Rinuccini's comment, written two years after Cosimo's death: Filippo di Cino Rinuccini, *Riccordi Storici*, ed. G. Aiazzi (Florence, 1840), pp. c–cv, referring to Cosimo's son, Piero, but with clear enough reference to the position inherited by Piero from his father: "sicché si vide chiaro lui esser manifesto tiranno nella città nostra; che così adviene dove si lascia fare uno troppo grande sopra gli altri, che è cosa perniziosissima nelle repubbliche, e sempre poi riesce a questo fine."

rary documents.[6] This consideration is directly relevant to an interpretation of Cosimo's political career and of his title *pater patriae*. For the title itself, by positing an abstract notion of the state, would seem nicely to reinforce nineteenth- and twentieth-century idealist conceptions, which have been at the heart of recent interpretations of Italian politics.

Modern historians readily acknowledge that Florentine society was divided between a majority of poverty stricken and politically oppressed inhabitants and those few who, by virtue of birth and of economic success, belonged to the ruling class. Statistics of an increasingly elaborate nature have been adduced to document the phenomenon. But seldom have the political and cultural consequences of this division been sufficiently investigated. I would suggest that the principal characteristic of Florentine life throughout the Quattrocento, during and following Cosimo's career, was the cleavage which rent political and cultural manifestations into experiences perceived and assimilated differently by the rich and the poor.

The rich, of course, knew that they were different. Their entire style of life, from their palaces[7] and shops to their country villas and their clothing, set them apart from their social inferiors. Their very use of language, throughout the Quattrocento increasingly allusive, synoptic, esoteric – in their correspondence and, as much as one can reconstruct it, in their conversations – was strikingly different from the concrete, direct, almost earthy language used by the common folk. And, more pertinently, their attitude toward the poor as a class brimmed with contempt often translating itself into a hatred which barely concealed their fear of them. The *volghata* desires peace, apprehensively commented his brother to Cosimo while the Florentine rulers were desperately attempting in the mid-1430s to defeat Lucca.[8] The plague is not too bad, wrote Cosimo's factotum, Matteo di ser Giovanni de' Rossi; it claims its victims only among *gente di bassa mano*.[9] Better to die than to live the life of the poor, remarked that other famous contemporary of Cosimo's, and his relative by marriage, Giovanni Rucellai.[10] Even preach-

---

6 "Politics in the Italian Communes: The View from America," a lecture delivered at Boston University, before the annual meeting of the New England Renaissance Conference, October, 1975.

7 Rinuccini, in his *Ricordi*, p. xc refers to a government decree passed in February 1462/63 (dates from 1 January through 24 March are given both in the Florentine and the common styles) to encourage the construction of houses "perocchè per la grande moltitudine, e per lo assai murare di belle e grandi case dagli uomini nobili e potenti, pativa il popolo disagio di abitazioni."

8 *MAP.*, XI, 608, Lorenzo di Giovanni de' Medici in Castelluccio to Cosimo in Ferrara or Venice, 3 February 1437/38.

9 *MAP.*, CXXXVIII, 22, Matteo di ser Giovanni de' Rossi in Florence to Giovanni di Cosimo de' Medici in Trebbio, 7 September 1437: ". . . ci fa danno, ma in giente di bassa mano, fanciulli et fanciulle il più forte . . . la terra è molto vota di gente da bene."

10 *Giovanni Rucellai ed il suo Zibaldone*, ed. A. Perosa (London, 1960), p. 16: "Chi non observa

ers and religious figures were often contemptuous of the poor. San Bernardino of Siena, one of the most popular preachers of the 1420s, in a sermon delivered in Florence, explained to his listeners that wealth was the prize conferred by God on those who were obedient to their parents, while those dishonoring their families would suffer seven penalties, the first of which would be a life of poverty.[11] Nearly half a century later, Piovano Arlotto, a country priest on cordial terms with the Medici, when visiting a friend who offered him a meal of coarse and tough salad leaves, exclaimed indignantly to his host: "Surely, I cannot believe that you intended this salad for us. These leaves must have been intended for your workers and masons."[12] Finally, the *Canzona del Popolo*, composed by a Giovambattista dell'Ottonaio and sung during the annual festivities of the carnival, portrays the populace as a fickle, vengeful, irrational mass which "burns and destroys itself and those who govern it."[13]

But how did the poor view their social superiors? Can one posit the existence of a deferential, symbiotic relationship in which the poor, knowing their station in life, had developed a resigned, if vaguely hopeful, attitude about their condition? Had the workers and the poor lost the consciousness, which they had clearly possessed in the Trecento that they shared "an identity of interests as between themselves and as against their rulers and employers"?[14] Was Florence in the Quattrocento, as France was to be in the

misura nello spendere suole presto impoverire, et chi vive povero in questo mondo, patisce molte necessità et soffera molti stremi bisogni, et meglio gli sarebbe morire che stentando vivere in miseria." See also his comments on p. 12 about the sufferings and tribulations of the rich, who are envied and hated by the poor: "Et conoscendo il povero secondo natura che' [1] richo atiene alcuna cosa di suo ragione, se gli porta molto aschio et invidia, onde i richi sono molto perseguitati et molestati." By being generous a rich man "scema molto la' nvidia e la malivolenza che i richi portono per ie richezze loro. . . ."

11 S. Bernardino da Siena, *Le prediche volgari inedite – Firenze 1424–1425 – Siena 1425*, ed. P. Dionisio Pacetti, O. F. M. (Siena, 1935), pp. 71–2: Children who obey their parents will have seven rewards: "Il primo Messer Domenedio ti farà ricco di roba e di senno naturale. . . . Chi fa il contrario, che disonori il padre e la madre, sette cose in contrario arà: Prima, povertà contro a ricchezze."

12 Piovanno Arlotto, *Motti e facezie*, ed. Gianfranco Folena (Milan, 1953), p. 107: "Postisi a tavola fu dato loro uno vino non molto egregio ed ebono una insalata di borrana e cicerbita, la quale pugneva le mani a chi la lavò, che quasi non si poteva toccare; pensa chi l'aveva in bocca come faceva! . . . in modo che 'l Piovano non si poté contenere che non dicessi a messere Giovanni: – Voi avete questa sera iscambiate le vivande; per certo non posso credere questa sia quella avete ordinato per noi: dovevano essere queste di questi vostri operai e muratori." See also his contrast between "uomini regali, giusti e buoni" and the "uomini poveri" on pp. 64–5.

13 *Canti carnascialeschi del rinascimento*, ed. Charles S. Singleton (Bari, 1936), pp. 302–3: ". . . vago di mutazion, con suo faville / arde e ruina sé e chi lo regge; / è d'un linguaggio e parla più di mille; / varia nel vero e mai non si coregge; / spesso il suo peggio elegge; / trema a un cenno o non teme niente; / sempre nel fin si pente: / e più variando più resta ingannato. . . ."

14 A phrase borrowed from E. P. Thompson, *The Making of the English Working Class* (London, 1963; rev. ed., Penguin, 1968), p. 12.

seventeenth century, "a society of orders, not one of classes," a suggestion recently made by Gene Brucker? Unfortunately, neither the evidence is abundant nor has the surviving documentation been carefully studied. The police deliberations for the period preceding 1465 consist of a mere three fragments, while the judicial records, massive and forbidding in their detail and badly damaged in the flood of 1966, can be studied only with great difficulty. Hopefully, in a few years' time, after the work of some extremely able young American scholars has progressed beyond the stage it has now reached, we may be able to answer these questions more confidently.[15] For lack of any statistical evidence on criminality, on forms of sociability, on residence patterns, on town–country relations, not to speak of economic and political perceptions, one has to rely on impressions, collected, one fears, in a less systematic and scientific method than one might otherwise wish.

Contemporary documents, particularly Quattrocento letters, suggest that Florentine entrepreneurs with substantial landholdings in the *contado* often took an interest in the well-being of their farmworkers. Wealthy landlords assumed responsibility for extending small favors to their *mezzadri* (sharecroppers): they might fund dowries for young girls; intervene with political or judicial authorities when their workers ran afoul of the law; grant small loans or extend the deadlines for the repayment of old ones. Cosimo de' Medici, his brother, and their sons often addressed themselves to problems of this sort in their correspondence with their agents.[16] Cosimo's reputation as a generous and accessible patron rests in part on this relationship which he, together with other contemporaries of his social standing, cultivated. Indeed, it is interesting to observe that Angelo Poliziano's collection of vignettes about Quattrocento Florence contains several stories in which Cosimo, while sojourning in his various estates, entertained his workers in his private residence. Cosimo's rapport with his farm workers, which Poliziano sketches in these stories, is based on a sense of deference, almost of awe, which the wealthy townsman evoked among his farmhands. And though occasionally a studied jocularity insinuates itself in these exchanges, often the stories end either with Cosimo reprimanding his visitor

---

15 Four young American scholars are currently working on questions directly relevant to the themes of this essay. I have profited greatly from my conversations with them, and as I specifically acknowledge in later sections of this paper, I have learned much from their work. They are: Samuel Cohn (Harvard University) writing a thesis on marriage patterns among the poor in Trecento and Quattrocento Florence; Yoram Milo (Stanford University) working on the activities of Jewish moneylenders in mid-fifteenth-century Florence; Jeffrey Newton (Brown University) writing on hospitals and the poor from the late thirteenth century to the Ciompi Revolution; Ronald Weissman (University of California at Berkeley) completing a thesis on confraternities in the fifteenth and early sixteenth centuries.

16 Numerous letters in *MAP.*, XI, to Matteo di ser Giovanni de' Rossi, the principal agent of the Medici, as well as to Giovanni da Volterra contain information of this sort.

for inadvertently committing a gaffe, or with the peasant puzzling over his host's habits and behavior.[17] Even so, private and literary documents suggest that in the countryside, at a time of acute labor shortages, landlords did exert an effort to cultivate ties of dependence with their workers. This relationship, at least as it was perceived by the landlords themselves, is nicely summarized by Giovanni Rucellai in a passage which he inserted in his diary in 1480, when he was already an old man. The men of the rural parish of San Piero a Quarachi, gathering of their own free will, had decided, records Rucellai, to assume the responsibility of maintaining his beautiful garden in Quarachi. This they did because the men of the parish were grateful for the many benefits conferred on them by Rucellai and also because, he continued in a hopeful vein, it seemed to them that the beauties of the garden brought fame to their village.[18]

Relations between employers and workers seem very different in the city. When looking at this situation, one's first impression, shared by many scholars, is that in the Quattrocento there was no recurrence of the Ciompi Revolution. Workers did not take to the streets to protest their working conditions and their wages. The collectivist impulses channelled through the guilds in the Trecento and nurtured during the course of that tumultuous century were undermined in the Quattrocento. But what is one to make of these generalizations? Perhaps one can begin to assess their validity by referring to some specific incidents, well documented in contemporary sources.

The first is described in great detail by Francesco di Tommaso Giovanni, a minor politician but astute observer of his times, in his private diary.[19] On 18 June 1458 Francesco became an official of the *Otto di Guardia*, the internal police. On 7 July, while the *Capitano* of the *Otto* was sending Antonio di Piero Boccino da Verçaia, a thief, to be executed, the condemned man's mother, seeing her son led away, began wailing in the Piazza della Signoria. No sooner had she started than a tumult (*romore*) began, the armed escort

17 *Angelo Polizianos Tagebuch (1477–79)*, ed. A. Wesselski (Jena, 1929), p. 28, n. 45: "Facendo dar Cosmo collattione a un contadino, gli fe' mettere pere moscatelle dinanzi. Hora essendo colui avvezzo a peruzze salvatiche, disse: Oh, noi le diamo a' porci. Al-l'hora Cosmo, volto a un famiglio, disse: Non già noi; levale via!" Also, p. 161, no. 307: "Confortando Cosmo un povero contadino che si accostasse al fuoco, essendo gran freddo, gli rispose: Cosmo, e' non fa freddo. E Cosmo: Io vorrei che tu m'insegnassi come tu fai. Rispose: Se voi vi metteste tutti e panni vostri adosso, come fo io e miei, e' non vi farebbe freddo." Also, the incident referring to Cosimo's father, Giovanni, who after having entertained at dinner one of his numerous friends who were "contadini delle alpi," asked his wife, Nonnina, "dicesse non so che sonetti; e dimandato poi quel che gne ne paresse, la lodò, dicendo però che vorrebbe più tosto che le sue nuore sapessero fare di due cioppe vecchie una nuova, che dire queste favole" (p. 81, n. 169).

18 Rucellai, *Zibaldone*, p. 23: "parendo agli uomini del popolo . . . avere riceuti molti benefici da me, et anchora . . . che le bellezze . . . del giardino mio . . . desse loro fama."

19 *ASFi., Carte Strozziane*, II, 16 bis. ff. 24v–25r.

was assaulted by the onlookers, the thief freed, led to the Church of San Firenze, and then taken to Santa Croce where he was hidden in the church's roof. (I maintain here the passive voice used by the narrator.) The *Otto* were immediately mobilized, especially because "the people had risen in a tumult" (*levandosi il popolo a romore*). Clearing the crowd from the Piazza de' Signori, they made their way toward Santa Croce, amid a hostile crowd which pelted the passing officials with rocks. Finally gaining access to the church, with the aid of four *maestri* sent over by the priors, they found the thief hiding behind a beam in the roof, brought him down, and dragged him back to the Piazza de' Signori, which was *piena di popolo*. Summarily condemned for his new crime, he was decapitated, in front of the *Porta del Capitano* before a "huge crowd" (*infinito popolo*). "And in this way," Francesco concludes his description of the execution, "we disabused the people of their bad habits" (*isgannamo il popolo perchè non s'avezzi*). But the story does not end here, for a few days later the *Otto* discovered that what had seemed only a spontaneous and accidental series of events was nothing of the sort. Indeed, on the day preceding the incident, a conspiracy had been spawned by the thief's *vicini ed amici* who gathered by the church of the Camaldoli, carefully planned the operation and preordained that the mother's wailing was to be the sign to charge the *Capitano* and free the prisoner. Eighteen men were arrested as promoters of the conspiracy, and "because they were poor people" it was decided to punish them not by the imposition of a fine, but by exiling them from Florence. All eighteen received sentences, which varied from one to ten years.

The sad fate of Antonio di Piero Boccino and of his would-be helpers is not terribly significant in the unfolding of Florentine public events in the 1450s. After all, no Florentine chronicle or contemporary history contains a reference to this series of events. Francesco di Tommaso Giovanni probably recorded it in his diary only because he had been so intimately involved in Antonio's capture and execution. But the importance of these events may lie precisely in their typicality, their almost quotidian normality.[20] They represented, it seems, a routine manifestation of tensions ubiquitous to the

---

20 Rucellai, in his *Zibaldone*, p. 50, records what must have been a near riot in 1440, on the eve of the battle of Anghiari: "Era dentro divisioni cipttadinesche; stettesi più dì sanza sonare ore; fessi uno bargiello che stava per istanza da Santa Trinita nel palagio de' Gianfigliazzi che facieva giustizia di fatto sanza avere a stare a sindachato, così nel contado come nella cipttà, e inpicchone molti sanza confessione o chomunione alle finestre del detto palagio e alle sponde del ponte a Santa Trinita." Pietro Pietribuoni, in his *priorista*, BNFi., *Conventi Soppressi*, C. 4. 895, f. 171r, recounts a series of incidents in May 1456 strikingly similar to those described by Francesco di Tommaso Giovanni. Two strangers, unjustly arrested by the *Otto*, were being led to the Palazzo de' Signori. The crowd began yelling: "Campa, campa. El popolo ad furia tolgono i detti prigioni alla famiglia, dove un di questi saccomanni entrò nella chiesa di *Sancta Croce*. Et i frati lo salvorono, l'altro per uno maççieri fu menato in palagio."

unfolding of Florentine life, and were therefore unworthy of recording by chroniclers or historians. An analysis of Francesco di Tomasso Giovanni's detailed description leads to certain important – if admittedly tentative – conclusions. To begin with, at least eighteen men, gathering in one place, decided to assault the communal officials. Moreover, their meeting place, the church of the Camaldoli, was situated in the parish of Santa Maria alla Verzaia, from which hailed the friend they were seeking to help. Of the eighteen, six are identified by *popolo* (i.e., parish of their residence) and all six lived either in that parish or in an adjoining one. Moreover, all eighteen seem to have been members of the working class. Eleven are identified by profession, and they consisted of a carpenter, a painter, two weavers, a wine seller, a messenger, a cook, one who lived (or else worked) in the communal brothel, a goldsmith's assistant, a cobbler, and a broker (*sensale*). One witnesses, in a most tenuous way, therefore, the existence of a local, working-class community, surrounding the church of the Camaldoli, a community which offered its members the possibility of socializing with each other and of taking common action. Finally, what strikes one about this incident is the severity of the punishments – one death penalty and eighteen banishments – and the diarist's inflexibly sententious and arrogant comment about this whole affair: "We disabused the people of their bad habits."

These two facts – on the one hand the existence of local working-class communities, and on the other hand the severity and singlemindedness of upper-class repression – are tentatively confirmed in a series of other documents. Samuel Cohn, in a ground-breaking essay, concluded that, in the fifteenth century, working-class communities in Florence were characterized by a striking incidence of geographic endogamy.[21] Workers tended overwhelmingly to marry in the *popolo* of their residence, a fact reinforcing the impression that the parish was the focal point of their lives. A cursory examination of criminal records of the courts of the *Otto*, the *Podestà* and the *Capitano* reveals that a large percentage of cases involved plaintiffs and culprits who shared residence in the same or in contiguous parishes, or else common origins in the *contado* or in foreign countries, or, just as frequently, who exercised the same occupation.[22] This pattern, though tenuous, based

---

21 "Marriage Relations and Class Formation in Primitive Capitalism: Florence during the High Renaissance," unpublished typescript.
22 This statement is based on an analysis of the following sources: *Otto di Guardia e Balia* 14, *Capitano del Popolo* 3826, *Podestà* 4847. Some examples, all taken from the sentences given by the *Otto*: f. 7v, 7 January 1460: Five "tessitori drapporum de Allamania" condemned for assault; f. 7v, same date: Three inhabitants of the popolo of San Piero Maggiore, one from popolo of San Simone, and one from an unspecified popolo condemned "pro ludo"; f. 12r, 13 January 1460/61: Two "portatores" condemned for assaulting another "portatorem"; same folio and date: Niccolò Niccolai de Alamania condemned for having falsely accused Federigo Curradi de Alamania; f. 12v, 18 January 1460/61: Two "tessitori drapporum" and a "Maniscalco" condemned for gambling; f. 20r, 9 February 1460/61: Two "Lombardi" condemned for

as it is on an analysis of fewer than two-hundred cases, if confirmed by subsequent research, would begin to answer the question of what happened to the working class in the Quattrocento. Neither did it disappear, nor did its members acquiesce to the rule of the upper classes. Rather, as Cohn was first to suggest, the workers had become fragmented and been repressed. While in the Trecento workers actively and realistically could aspire to a share of the city's political control, in the Quattrocento their field of action seems to have been restricted to neighborhoods or parishes. How and why this fragmentation took place, and what role the upper classes played in bringing about this phenomenon, are questions which research currently in progress may illuminate in the near future.

Nor does it seem that the same bonds of dependence between employers and workers which prevailed in the countryside – farmworkers receiving small benefits and enjoying the protection of their powerful and wealthy lords, the landowners hoping to maintain a supply of reasonably content and docile laborers – also prevailed in the city. Poliziano's nearly four-hundred vignettes drawn from Florentine life during Cosimo's and Lorenzo's days do not once portray a harmonious or pleasant relationship between a well-to-do Florentine and a city worker. These exchanges are almost invariably characterized by a sharp tension, often breaking into verbal abuse or physical violence.[23] Those wealthy Florentines who populate Poliziano's stories were all too well aware that the city's workers were not satisfied with their lot and that many of them could conceive of a different way in which to govern the city. In one of a handful of stories dealing with fourteenth-century events which Poliziano included in his collection, a *ciompo* (woolworker) was confronted by a member of the Albizzi family and asked how the workers expected to rule the city when they lacked political experience. The worker's response was simple: "We shall do exactly the opposite of what you have done, and by so doing we shall maintain the state."[24] And Poliziano's inclusion of a one-line proverb betrays an aware-

asaulting a passer-by; f. 23v, 20 February 1460/61: Four "tessitori drapporum" condemned for unspecified cause. The three volumes consulted contain many other such cases.
23 *Polizianos Tagebuch*, p. 24, n. 38: "Ser Piero Lotti passava per la Vigna, onde un ciompo mostrò gli un votacessi col piombion e disse: Ser Piero togliete quell'anguilla, et egli: To' quel intingol tu." P. 63, n. 135: "Essendo de' Dieci Cosmo, e con esso un Giuliano di Particino artefice, huomo audace, advenne che detto Giuliano molto caricava Cosmo in dire che queste famiglie fanno poco conto de' popolani"; Angelo Acciaioli, incensed by this behavior, tried to hit the "artefice" but was prevented from doing so by Cosimo who said: "Egl'era qui fra noi un pazzo, e sarebbesi poi detto che e' ve ne fussero stati due."
24 Ibid., pp. 95–6, n. 199: ". . . Come credete voi potere mantenere lo stato, i quali non siete usi, conciosia cosa noi, usi sempre al governo, non l' habbiamo potuto mantenere. Rispose il clientulo: Noi faremo a punto il contrario di quello che havette fatto voi, e così lo verremo a mantenere."

ness of the existing relations between those who ruled and those excluded from the city's government: "Violence, that is arms, is the judge of appeals of the powerful."[25] Piovano Arlotto, composing the *Facezie* at about the same time, wondered aloud once why it was that "the poor, so much more numerous, did not pillage the goods of the rich."[26] Neither Cosimo's correspondence, nor that of any other prominent contemporary Florentine examined in the preparation of this essay, contains the solicitations for help by urban workers, or the offers of assistance preferred by the rich which, as we noticed, commonly characterized the relations of workers and employers in the countryside. The evidence seems to suggest that in the city there was a neat separation between the rich and the poor and that the bonds of patronage and of clientage did not extend from the upper echelons to the bottom rungs of the social hierarchy. Politics in Quattrocento Florence depended on the maintenance of such a relationship of force between employers as a class and their workers.

Before concluding this section, it may be interesting to dwell on another specific incident, one in which Cosimo played a protagonist's role. On 16 March 1446, in his capacity as convener (*proposto*) of the *ufficiali del monte*, Cosimo introduced a resolution which led to the reorganization of the sales tax on wine (*gabella del vino*). With one exception, this provision does not deal with wine consumption by private individuals; rather, it outlines procedures for collecting the tax, identifies the gates through which wine could be imported into the city, describes the manner in which wine barrels were to be sealed, and so forth. The one exception deals with the consumption of wine by workers employed in the wool and silk industries, the overwhelming majority of the city's working class. These workers were prohibited from taking to work more than one small fiasco of wine; the penalty on offenders was 20 *soldi*, a sum larger than the daily wage of most workers.[27] The law does not offer a reason for the imposition of this restriction, but its enactment offers a glimpse of the caution, fear, and firmness with which the rulers of Florence dealt with their workers. This divide, between workers – as a class fragmented and oppressed, yet capable of creating new bonds

25 Ibid., p. 201, n. 384: "La violenza, overo l'armi sono il giudice dell'appellagioni de' potenti."
26 Arlotto, *Facezie*, p. 90, n. 55: "Come i poveri non saccheggiano i ricchi, sendo maggior immero."
27 *Monte Comune–Periodo repubblicano, no. provvisorio 1121* (*Deliberazioni degli ufficiali del Monte*), f. 7v where it is indicated that on 16 March 1445/46 Cosimo was appointed *proposto* of the *Monte*: f. 8r, same date: ". . . da qui inançi nelle botteghe de' lanaiuoli, e tintori e purgatori e setaioli, tintori di seta non possa entrare vino in barile ne in mezo barile sotto pena di lire venti. . . . Possano i lavoranti sopra detti mestieri portare nelle botteghe ove lavorano ogni dì per loro here u' fiascho di tenuta di due metadelle e non più delle lor case overo d'altro luogho, e portando magior fiascho chaggia in pena di s. 20 il fiascho."

of sociability in neighborhoods and parishes – and employers – dominant, aware of their preeminence, and ever vigilant of class insubordination – may well have represented the basic influence in the formation of Quattrocento Florentine politics.

Faced by their employers' systematic oppression after 1382, the workers in Florence seem to have had no choice but to redefine the cultural focus of their lives at the parish and neighborhood levels through which they maintained a sense of their collective identity. Their employers, triumphant after 1382, consolidated their domination of the city by relying upon the system of patronage which, to a very large extent, had enabled them to impose their hegemony in the past. Clienteles, and the bases which they offered to powerful politicians, had been traditional fixtures in the history of Florence. Chroniclers and contemporary observers, from Compagni through the two Villani to Stefani, often refer to the *amici* and *seguaci* who formed the rank-and-file membership of cliental groups. Unfortunately, one knows little about the composition of these clienteles. How did someone like Manetto Scali very early in the Trecento, Carlo Strozzi in the aftermath of the expulsion of the Duke of Athens in 1343, or Piero degli Albizzi before the Ciompi Revolution in 1378, form his political base? Manetto Scali, according to Compagni, was trusted by the Whites in 1301 precisely because *era potente di amici e di seguito*.[28] Similarly vague references are found in other contemporary accounts, to which modern historians have been prevented by the paucity of the sources from adding much concrete detail.

If the history of clientele groups in the Duecento and early Trecento remains largely unknown, it is true that when one reaches the very late fourteenth and fifteenth centuries, one begins to perceive patterns explaining both the norms and traditions which Cosimo respected during his long political career and those which, because of his success and longevity, he managed to alter.

Perhaps it might be simplest to start with a brief definition of patronage, one offered a decade ago by the American anthropologist Jeremy Boissevain: "Patronage is founded on the reciprocal relations between patrons and clients. By patron I mean a person who uses his influence to assist and protect some other person, who then becomes his 'client', and in return provides certain services to his patron. The relationship is assymetrical, for the nature of the services exchanged may differ considerably."[29] Inherent in this

---

28 *Dino Compagni e la sua cronica*, ed. I. del Lungo (Florence, 1879), pp. 182–3, II, XVI: "M. Manetto Scali (nel quale la parte Bianca aveva gran fidanza, perchè era potente di amici e di seguito) cominciò aforzare il suo palagio. . . ."

29 Jeremy Boissevain, "Patronage in Sicily," *Man*, I (1966), 19–33; the quotation comes from p. 19.

definition of patronage is the assumption that the patron possesses goods, "things," which he can distribute to his clients. This view, postulating a fixed relationship between patron and client, has more recently been considerably revised by Boissevain and by a number of political anthropologists, among whom it strikes me that Paul Littlewood has advanced a most subtle and interesting interpretation. According to this revised view, a patron's position may not at all depend on his possession of goods, but rather on his ability to bring his clients in contact with other individuals capable of honoring their requests.[30] Thus, in the network of social relations, a patron tends to maintain his privileged position precisely because he acts as a broker, a go-between, serving as a source of information for those offering and those seeking certain goods or services. In return, clients could provide their patrons with a variety of services. "Clients protect a patron's good name and report the activities of his enemies. It is in their interest to do this, for the stronger their patron is, the better he is able to protect them. . . . In a society where social prestige is measured by the resources a person can command to protect and advance the position of his family, a clientele of persons who owe services of various types is a considerable asset."[31]

This definition of patronage seems to me appropriate to the Florentine political situation. Before and after 1434, bosses such as Donato Acciaioli, Maso degli Albizzi, Cosimo de' Medici, and his contemporary Tommaso Soderini led clienteles whose members expected of their *capo* favors and services which in the overwhelming number of cases they could not deliver directly. More often than not the patron could honor the request only by addressing himself to yet another individual, an officeholder, a member of a tax commission, or a Florentine magistrate in the *contado* or *distretto*. Examples of this practice abound in the extant letters of these political bosses, though it is quite evident that only fragments of their correspondence have survived, and that these fragments, more often than not, contain letters received rather than those written by them. Thus, for example, Donato Bellandi, who, in early 1389, was serving as *potestà* of Vinci, wrote to Donato Acciaioli that an unspecified *ingiuria* had been com-

30 Paul Littlewood, "Strings and Kingdoms – The Activities of a Political Mediator in Southern Italy," *Archives européennes de sociologie*, 15 (1974), 33–51. The bibliography on patronage is quite vast. Here I cite the following few works which have helped me to clarify my thinking: J. K. Campbell, *Honour, Family and Patronage* (Oxford, 1964); C. Geertz, "The Changing Role of the Cultural Broker: The Javanese Kijaji," *Comparative Studies in Society and History*, 2 (1960), 228–49; Adrian C. Mayer, "Patrons and Brokers: Rural Leadership in Four Overseas Indian Communities," in M. Freedman, ed., *Social Organization – Essays Presented to Raymond Firth* (Chicago, 1967), pp. 167–88; E. R. Wolf, "Kinship, Friendship and Patron–Client Relations in Complex Societies," in M. Banton, ed., *The Social Anthropology of Complex Societies* (London, 1966), pp. 1–22.
31 Boissevain, "Patronage," p. 23.

mitted against one of his notaries. Having taken personal offense, Bellandi now was pressing the case in the court of the *Esecutore* "as you advised me to do." Therefore, "if friendship or family ties mean something, this is the time that you must help me," he pleaded with Donato.[32] Or, again, in June 1394 Cola di Jacopo from Ascoli, who was then chancellor of Pistoia, wrote to Donato asking that he in turn write to Messer Giovanni Panciatichi who was then in a position to extend Cola's term of office.[33] Or, finally, Niccolò Gherardini of Arezzo asked that Donato intercede with his brother, Cardinal Agnolo Acciaioli, so that the latter might confer an ecclesiastical benefice to a friend of his.[34]

Indeed, the overwhelming bulk of personal letters from that period deal with rather trivial requests of this sort. And just as was the case with Donato Bellandi whose notary had been offended, but who personally assumed responsibility for settling this matter and in turn sought to involve his social and political superior Donato Acciaioli in this affair, these letters also convey the strong impression that at all levels of political society these ties of dependence, to which Brucker first alluded more than a decade ago,[35] offered the only possibility, short of insurrectionary and rebellious attempts to which disenfranchised and oppressed workers periodically recurred, of obtaining some of the advantages and emoluments of the existing social and economic system. Such a web of personal ties of mutual interdependence, more often than not referred to by contemporaries as *amicizia*, created in the city a series of parallel hierarchies which conditioned the response and limited the options for political action of those men who comprised the Florentine political class.

It appears that each of these hierarchies or clienteles tended to recruit its members primarily within a restricted geographic area in the city, most often within the gonfalon in which resided its most powerful members. By the late Trecento the gonfalons offered a convenient and rather obvious focus for the political activities of important Florentine politicians. Sixteen in number, gonfalons were originally assigned responsibility of organizing

---

32 *Biblioteca Laurenziana, Ashburnham,* 1830, *cassetta* 3, no. 275: Donato Bellandi, *potestà* of Vinci, to Donato Acciaioli in Florence, 22 February 1388/89: "la quale ingiuria reputo essere stata fatta nella mia persona," and he is pressing the case in the court of the Esecutore "chome voi mi chonsigliaste ch'io faciessi. Per tanto io vi priegho quanto più posso, se amistà o parentado dee valere, che ora franchamente m'atiate."

33 Ibid., no. 242, Cola Jacobi de Esculo, cancellarius Pistorii to Donato Acciaioli in Florence, 11 June 1394.

34 Ibid., no. 155, Niccolò di Niccolò Gherardini in Arezzo to Donato Acciaioli in Florence, 24 November 1385.

35 "The Structure of Patrician Society in Renaissance Florence," *Colloquium – A Journal of Historical and Social Thought,* 1 (1964), 2–11. Since then Brucker expanded his views in his *Renaissance Florence.*

the citizen militia, each bringing under its flag its able-bodied men in times of military or political crisis. With the passage of time in the fourteenth century, however, the gonfalons retained only vestiges of that responsibility, while concurrently acquiring considerable jurisdiction over two important governmental activities: the distribution of forced loans among the gonfalon's inhabitants, and the certification of political eligibility of local residents during the periodic redactions of electoral lists.[36]

Juridically, the authority of each gonfalon was vested in its politically eligible inhabitants, with the gonfalon's affairs administered by the district's chief officer, the *gonfaloniere di compagnia*, who was often assisted by two or three *pennonieri*. Periodic meetings of a gonfalon's members took place in a prominent church located within its boundaries. Thus, for example, gonfalon Drago of Santo Spirito met in the church of San Frediano, Ferza in the church of San Felice in Piazza, Vaio in Santa Maria sopra Porta, Lion Rosso in San Pancrazio, Lion d'Oro in San Lorenzo, and so forth.[37] Although only

---

36   Historians of Florence have not given much attention to the institution of the gonfalon and its importance in the city's political and social history. Passing references are found in Robert Davidsohn, *Storia di Firenze* (Florence, 1973; original German edition Berlin, 1896–1908), V, ch. 2, particularly 276–96. Primarily, however, one must look in the Commune's Statutes, of which the most easily accessible, and most obvious starting point is the redaction of 1322–5, edited and published by Romolo Caggese, *Statuti della repubblica fiorentina*, 2 Vols. (Florence, 1909–10), I, *liber quintus, rub.* LXXIII, LXXXIII–CXI. In this context I should point out that an uncatalogued collection of documents in *ASFi.* entitled *Ufficiali del Fuoco*, and comprising more than one hundred volumes, deal entirely with the activities of gonfalon officials who, it emerges from these documents, were charged with organizing neighborhood fire brigades, and appointing officials to assess damage caused by fires.

37   Except for gonfalon *Lion Rosso* whose account books were recently discovered in the archive of the Vallombrosan monastery of San Pancrazio by Prof. William Kent, the history of the various gonfalons must be reconstructed by examining the cartularies of notaries who, on occasion, were appointed as official notaries of various gonfalons. Thus, for example, the cartularies of ser Paolo di Piero di Bartolomeo Banderai (*ASFi., Notarile Anticosimiano,* B 740–767, years 1391–1423) contain numerous records of gonfalon Lion d'Oro; ser Tommaso di Domenico Carondini Bambelli Pacini (Ibid., C 187–190, years 1409–36) deal with the gonfalon Lion d'Oro; ser Francesco di Piero Giacomini da Castro Fiorentino (ibid., G 209–212, years 1398–1431) with gonfalon Scala; ser Bartolomeo di Giovanni Lapini (ibid., L 54, years 1410–17) gonfalon Vaio; ser Francesco di ser Tommaso Masi (ibid., M 265–268, years 1404–98) with gonfalon Lion d'Oro; ser Bartolomeo di ser Piero di ser Riccomanno de' Migliorati da Coiano (ibid., M 546, years 1411–46) with gonfalon Lion d'Oro; ser Piero di Jacopo Migliorelli (ibid., M 568–572, years 1434–77) with the same gonfalon; ser Amerigo Vespucci (Ibid., V 292–294, years 1429–72) gonfalon Unicorno and gonfalon Drago, quarter of Santo Spirito; ser Tommaso di ser Piero di Angelo Cioni (ibid., T 565–566, years 1450–53) gonfalon Lion d'Oro. But the task of systematically exploring the *Archivio notarile* is almost impossible: about 4,000 volumes for the fifteenth century alone have survived, only a tiny fraction of which have indexes. The references in this note, that is, are not by any means exhaustive; they simply identify some cartularies in which such records can be found.

fragmentary records of these meetings have survived, it is clear that one issue dominated most gonfalons's deliberations: the distribution of taxes among all the district's inhabitants. Frequently, at the conclusion of these meetings, syndics were appointed, charged with imposing individual assessments, and often empowered to confiscate and sell at auction property belonging to tax delinquents.[38] Thus, often even after the imposition of the *Catasto* in 1427, the gonfalon, as a corporation, assumed collective responsibility before the communal exchequer (*Camera del Comune*) for paying the global assessment of a forced loan levied on all its inhabitants.

Given the nature of this responsibility, those who controlled each gonfalon exerted real influence in the distribution of taxes, thus being able to command the following of less powerful men, and to damage the interests of their opponents. Indeed, an examination of the surviving deliberations of various gonfalons reveals that within each district there existed a clearly articulated elite consisting of two or three dozen families which consistently were represented in their gonfalon's meetings. Of the nearly three dozen records of such deliberations discovered in registers of the notarial archive, the largest number of participants was seventy-one, but this was an unusual occasion, the only one on which more than fifty men gathered to participate in such meetings.

An examination of the electoral lists prepared in the late Trecento and first half of the Quattrocento reinforces the impression that each gonfalon was dominated by a small number of men, whose names prevail in the scrutiny lists of those years. Based upon the figures recently presented by Dale Kent in her study of the *scrutinio* of 1433, it is possible to calculate that, for example, in the gonfalon Vipera in the eight different redactions of the scrutiny for the three major offices prepared between 1382 and 1453 four families (not consistently the same four during these seventy years) controlled from a minimum of 59.8 percent to a maximum of slightly more than 71 percent of that gonfalon's lists of approved candidates for those three most prestigious offices.[39]

This same picture also emerges from the 1452 scrutiny for the gonfalonierate of justice, the single highest Florentine magistracy. A tabulation of the results of that scrutiny neatly identifies some of the city's major political bosses: the Soderini, for example, controlled 56.52 percent of the eligibilities in their gonfalon (Drago–Santo Spirito); between the two of them, the Canigiani and the da Quarata more than 58 percent in the gonfalon

---

38   Thus, for example, see *Notarile anticosimiano*, M 267, ff. 194r–v, 21 February 1443/44, and ff. 287r–v, 15 May 1451 when the syndics of gonfalon Lion d'Oro deliberate on the confiscation of goods of tax delinquents.

39   Kent, "The Florentine *Reggimento*," Appendix. An analysis of the electoral lists for the other gonfalons for which statistics were presented by Kent yields very much the same results.

Scala; the Nardi alone controlled nearly 55 percent of the eligibilities in Carro of Santa Croce; the Acciaioli more than 43 percent in Vipera.[40]

The existence of this small number of extremely powerful families within each gonfalon was clearly recognized by contemporaries, some of whom in their diaries and *ricordanze* explicitly referred to the phenomenon. Giovanni di Pagolo Morelli, for example, writing sometime between 1390 and 1410, urged his sons to become friendly with men in their gonfalon who might be able to help them.[41] Giovanni Rucellai, sometime after the middle of the fifteenth century, echoed this piece of advice, congratulating himself on his ability to maintain good relations with the men of his gonfalon, who had always helped him with his tax assessments.[42] The private correspondence of many fifteenth-century Florentines, dealing as it does with tax problems, also reinforces the view that the traditional structure of Florentine political

---

40   ASFi., *Tratte* 16: Deliberations of the Accoppiatori of 1452. For a discussion of this document, which contains the *borsa* for the gonfalonierate of justice, see: Rubinstein, *The Government*, pp. 45–8. In the following tables are listed all those families whose members controlled a minimum of 20 percent of the *polizze* of their gonfalon. It should be pointed out that all *casate* bearing the same last name have been grouped together.

Quarter of Santo Spirito,	Gonfalon Scala:	Canigiani	27.58%
		Quarata	31.03%
	Gonfalon Ferze:	Ridolfi	28.94%
	Gonfalon Drago:	Soderini	56.52%
Quarter of Santa Croce,	Gonfalon Carro:	Nardi	54.54%
	Gonfalon Ruote:	Niccolini	22.97%
	Gonfalon Bue:	Cocchi Donati	35.48%
	Gonfalon Lion Nero:	Morelli	25.53%
Quarter of S. Maria Novella,	Gonfalon Unicorno:	Bartoli	30.30%
	Gonfalon Lion Bianco:	Ventura	22.50%
		Malengonelle	22.50%
	Gonfalon Lion Rosso:	Rucellai	28.98%
	Gonfalon Vipera:	Acciaioli	43.75%
Quarter of San Giovanni,	Gonfalon Drago:	Carnesecchi	25.00%
	Gonfalon Chiavi:	Pandolfini	25.00%
	Gonfalon L. d'Oro:	Medici	20.21%
		Dietisalvi	20.21%
		Della Stufa	20.21%
	Gonfalon Vaio:	Pucci	22.22%
		Medici	22.22%

41   Giovanni di Pagolo Morelli, *Ricordi*, ed. V. Branca (Florence, 1956), p. 253: "Appresso, sia cortese: Ingegnati d'acquistare uno amico o più nel tuo gonfalone. . . ."
42   Rucellai, *Zibaldone*, p. 9: "Non ci ò trovato migliore rimedio a difendersi quanto a guardarsi da non avere nimici . . . appresso, d'essere in gratia et in benivolentia de' consorti et de' parenti et de' vicini et del resto degl'uomini del tuo gonfalone, de' quali io m' ò molto da lodare, perchè sempre ne li sgravi che si sono fatti per 'l gonfalone m'anno servito et aiutato et avuto compassione di me."

patronage was based primarily on favors which prominent men could deliver on the basis of the authority and prestige which they enjoyed within their gonfalons. This structure fragmented Florence into a series of patronal enclaves, each of which was dominated by the personality and influence of a very small number of men able to marshall the respect and cooperation of friends, clients, and relatives on those occasions when favors were asked of them.

One example graphically illustrates this system. Bartolomeo Cederni, a merchant of the mid-Quattrocento, is remembered today mostly because of his massive epistolary, numbering more than five hundred items. Having been a merchant, Cederni traveled a great deal in Naples, Venice, and, above all, Pisa. His principal contacts in Florence during his long absences were members of the Boni and Pandolfini families, as well as the notary ser Piero di ser Marianno Cecchi. In his numerous letters to them Bartolomeo constantly bombarded them with entreaties to be sollicitous of his tax situation, by urging them to discuss his case with his gonfalon's tax officials. Cederni was legally a resident of gonfalon Drago of Santo Spirito, a district dominated by the Soderini family. Responding to one of Cederni's numerous sollicitations, on 21 November 1447 ser Piero wrote that he had discussed the matter of his friend's assessment with the appropriate officials, receiving from each assurances of good treatment. And, in any case, continued ser Piero, you ought not to worry about this matter because your *amici ti vogliono bene*.[43] Precisely who these *amici* were, is made clear in a letter written on the very next day to Bartolomeo, this one by Tommaso Soderini, the head of his clan and the undisputed boss of his gonfalon. Soderini's letter is laconic. "I have received your two letters," he informs Bartolomeo. "I understand your need and shall do whatever is possible, and I shall do this voluntarily even if you had not written. Now I shall say no more on this."[44] To the best of my knowledge, Soderini occupied no public office at the time, and in his response he offered simply to make available to Cederni the arsenal of his unofficial and yet tangible influence in his gonfalon's affairs. His name reappears on many occasions in these letters. In one, dated October 1453, this one to Bartolomeo who was then himself in Florence, another resident of the gonfalon, Domenico di Guasparre Simone, urged that Bartolomeo go to the piazza, wait for Tommaso, and if possible

---

43 ASFi., *Conventi Soppressi*, 78 (*Badia*), 312, no. 324: Ser Piero di ser Mariano Cechi in Florence to Bartolomeo Cederni in Pisa, 21 November 1447: "E farò jo cogli altri tuoi amici e miei quanto sarà possibile, chon quel pocho che jo posso. Ma rinchoromi che ne riuscirai bene mediante gli amici tuoi che ti vogliono bene. . . ."

44 Ibid., no. 331: Tommaso Soderini in Florence to Bartolomeo Cederni in Pisa, 22 November 1447: "J' ò auto 2 tua e ò'nteso il tuo bisogno, e ò ne fatto e farò quanto mi sarà possibile, e fo llo volentieri e da mme sanza tua lettera. Ora jo non dirò altro sopra ciò."

speak to him, urging him to please take an interest in a case, that he does not fully identify.[45]

In most important respects, the patronage of the Medici family conformed to this pattern. In *The Rise of the Medici: Faction in Florence, 1426–1434* (Oxford, 1978), Dale Kent has demonstrated that in the years immediately before 1434 the Medici had forged a political faction whose members, by and large, she has been able to identify. The *palleschi*, as the Medici faction was known, having succeeded where other political alliances before had failed, exerted their influence throughout Florence, enabling Cosimo to become a patron whose influence extended throughout the entire city. Even so, it is important to emphasize both the similarities and differences between the Medicean faction and other pre- and post-1434 similar alliances. In the concluding section of this essay, I briefly touch upon these two themes: the extent to which the Medici relied on traditional structures of political patronage in Florence; and the reasons which might help one explain Cosimo's success in creating a citywide network of patronage.

The association of the Medici family with the gonfalon Lion d'Oro can be traced to the mid-fourteenth century, when Cosimo's grandfather moved to the *popolo* of San Lorenzo from that of San Tommaso.[46] Quickly, the Medici distinguished themselves as leading members of their gonfalon, which was the largest, most populous, and probably the wealthiest of the city's sixteen administrative units. Of the thirteen meetings of the gonfalon, for which records have been found for the years 1399–1427, Giovanni di Bicci was present in nine, always listed among the very first in attendance. His standing among his neighbors is reflected in the fact that five of the six times during those years, when the gonfalon appointed syndics to supervise the collection of back taxes and the confiscation of goods belonging to tax delinquents, Giovanni was one of these officials.[47] Of the Medici clients whom Dale Kent has identified, even at the time when the Medicean faction had been fully articulated, no fewer than one-fourth lived in Lion d'Oro, and as many as another fourth in adjoining gonfalons.[48] That Cosimo cultivated

45 Ibid., no. 545: Domenicho di Guasparre Simoni in Terzano to Bartolomeo Cederni in Florence, 23 October 1453: ". . . dove jo ti priegho che quando Tomaso si sta in sulla piazza e chosì Francesco Masini e *se* fia chomodo el parlare che tu adoperi lui mi gli raghomandi. . . ."
46 For an overview of the history of the Medici family in the fourteenth century, see Gene Brucker, "The Medici in the Fourteenth Century," *Speculum*, 32 (1957), 1–26. ASFi., *Notarile Anticosimiano* M 569 (1458–60), ff. 106r–109v, 112r–113r, 114r–117v, 120r–121r includes a series of acts dated November–December 1459, which indicate that the Medici had retained their patronage in the church of San Tommaso.
47 ASFi., *Notarile Anticosimiano* B 742, ff. 11r–12r, 16 May 1399; M 265 (1404–17), 4th bundle, ff. 69r–70r, 20 November 1412; M 546 (1421–6), ff. 102r–v, 10 June 1425; ff. 137r–138r, 8 August 1426; B 748, ff. 133r–v, 23 March 1404/5.
48 Kent, *The Rise of the Medici*.

this network of associations with the *amici* of Lion d'Oro, and that, in turn, those wishing to curry favor with the Medici were aware of this situation are facts neatly reflected in a letter written by Piero da Gagliano to Cosimo's son, Piero, in June 1448. Like the Medici hailing from the Mugello, Piero da Gagliano was residing in Naples, and had recently decided to settle in Florence. He was now writing to the Medici asking that they purchase for him, for a price which he left to their discretion and which he promised immediately to repay them, the house of Baldassare di Luigi da Prato "because the proximity of the house to yours renders this a very advantageous location."[49]

The Medici patronage of the church of San Lorenzo, and Cosimo's sponsorship of the construction of the church's *cappella maggiore* after 1442 can be largely explained by the long-standing association between that church and the gonfalon Lion d'Oro. Traditionally, the gonfalon's syndics also assumed responsibility for appointing the church's overseers (*operai*), and supervising in a general way the church's finances. In March 1405, for example, Cosimo's father, Giovanni, had been one of the district's three syndics with responsibility to appoint the *operai* of San Lorenzo and the officials to collect back taxes.[50] In the 1410s, for reasons which are unclear to me, the church's prior and canons petitioned directly the Signoria of Florence to appoint such overseers, but, in this case as well, the *signori* selected as *operai* prominent residents of Lion d'Oro, Giovanni di Bicci among them.[51] But even after the fire which destroyed the old church, and the launching of the project to rebuild a new and more grandiose edifice, the gonfalon, as a corporation, assumed the responsibility of financing and overseeing the project. Thus, in 1427, syndics were appointed to collect the

49   *MAP.*, XI, 552, Piero da Gagliano in Naples to Piero di Cosimo de' Medici in Florence, 17 June 1448: ". . . perchè la chasa è in luogho molto chomodo per essere presso a voi . . . e del preggio tutto rimetto in voi che meglio chonosciete il mio bisognio di me."

50   *ASFi., Notarile Anticosimiano* B 748, ff. 133r–v, 13 March 1404/5: meeting of the gonfalon Lion d'Oro in the church of San Lorenzo. Matteo di Nuccio Solosmei, *gonfaloniere di compagnia*, Giovanni di Bicci de' Medici and Niccolao di Ugolino Martelli, members of the *dodici buonomini* appointed as syndics. The men of the gonfalon, "advertentes quod utile est pro dicta ecclesia Sancti Laurentii quod eligantur et constituantur certi operarii, maxime qui exigant omnes pecunie quantitatibus debitas ecclesie, etc., omni modo etc., eligerunt dictum Matteum, Johannem et Nicholaum, presentes etc., ad eligendum et nominandum tres vel quatuor syndicos et procuratores pro dicto vexillo qui possint pro dicto vexillo imponere residuum et exigere etc. et acquirere mutuo etc. circa duodecim prestantias presentis distributionis quinquinarum. Et qui habuerunt baliam etc. pro faciendo etc. circa dictos quatuor operarios. . . ."

51   *ASFi., Provvisioni-Registri*, 105, ff. 311r–312r, 20 February 1415/16: The following six inhabitants of the gonfalon, together with the prior of the church of San Lorenzo appointed *operarii* for the following three years: Vieri di Andrea Rondinelli, Giovanni di Bicci de' Medici, Ugo di Andrea della Sufa, Filippo di messer Biagio de' Guasconi, Neroni di Nigio di Neroni, and Lorenzo di Andrea, *beccarius*.

district's back taxes with which to defray, in part, the construction of the *capella maggiore*, a responsibility Lion d'Oro shared with the church's prior and canons.[52] And thirteen years later, after construction was interrupted because of the financial crisis of the 1430s, the prior of San Lorenzo appealed directly to the gonfalon for permission to seek out an individual willing to assume the financial responsibility of bringing the project to its conclusion.[53] When nearly two years later arrangements between the prior and Cosimo were completed, Cosimo was granted patronage rights over the church's *cappella maggiore* and the central nave, and in exchange he was granted exclusive rights of erecting his coat of arms in those parts of the church. He, in turn, promised to have this work completed within six years.[54] Thus, Cosimo officially took over a responsibility which had belonged to the collegiality of the gonfalon, and in an expressly tangible manner established his supremacy in the district of his residence.

If Cosimo's power base in his gonfalon resembled that of several other political bosses, it is undeniable that he wielded more power and influence than any contemporary Florentine. Even a casual examination of his epistolary reveals the range of his political patronage and the variety of clients appealing to him for the most diverse types of assistance. A systematic analysis of the more than 1230 extant letters addressed to him reveals that almost 70 percent contain appeals for favors of sorts, ranging from pleas for small loans to requests for his intercession with the Pope for the granting of lucrative ecclesiastical benefices.[55] The largest group of letters, almost one of every five (19.53 percent, to be precise), asked for favors which Cosimo could honor by addressing himself to a local magistracy: foreigners

---

52   ASFi., *Notarile anticosimiano*, M 546 (1427–46), ff. 7r–v, 27 November 1427: The men of the gonfalon of Lion d'Oro appoint syndics charged with collecting the gonfalon's debts and paying its obligations. "Residuo vero dictarum pecuniarum exigendarum ut supra per dictos sindicos et seu que ad eorum manibus pervenient in futuro, factis primo solutiones suprascriptis et restitutiones ut supra dictum est et non prius possint et debeant dicti sindici et operarii expendere et expendi facere in muramento et constructione maioris cappelle dicte ecclesie S. Laurentii et pro ipsius constructionis que cappella fit per populanos dicte ecclesie et eo modo et forma prout eis videbitur et placebit et in hoc eorum conscientias honerandum."

53   Piero Ginori Conti, in his *La basilica di S. Lorenzo di Firenze e la famiglia Ginori* (Florence, 1940), Appendix V, published the notarial document referring to this meeting, without realizing, however, that this was a deliberation of the gonfalon Lion d'Oro. The archival reference for the document is: ASFi., *Notarile Anticosimiano*, C525 (1437–55), ff. 60r–61r, 20 November 1440. Only a few days after this decision, Cosimo donated to the Church of San Lorenzo a piece of property valued at about 400 florins: Ibid., A 663, ff. 1r–2v, 2 December 1440.

54   Ginori Conti, *La basilica di S. Lorenzo*, Appendix VI; the original in: *Notarile Anticosimiano*, I 9 (1442–3), ff. 40r–42v, 13 August 1442.

55   Nearly 1,000 letters of Cosimo are found in *MAP.*, XI and XII. The rest of his correspondence is dispersed throughout other volumes of *MAP.*; in a very few cases I have been able to locate some of his letters in other documentary collections.

advancing their candidacy for one of the judicial posts in the communal or guild governments open only to non-Florentines; Florentines pleading that they be considered for an office in the *contado* or *distretto*, or that their tax assessments be diminished. Significantly, the second largest group contains requests for Cosimo's intercession with the Pope: nearly 15 percent of his correspondence falls in this category. An additional eighty-odd letters (ca. 6.5 percent of the total) appealed for Cosimo's help with other ecclesiastical officials, so that nearly a total of one-fifth of his correspondents wrote to him hoping to receive favors from important church bureaucrats. The third largest category, nearly one of ten letters, involved favors obtained either in the courts of *condottieri*, such as Francesco Sforza, the Duke of Urbino, and others, or in those of foreign governments, Venice, Naples, Ferrara, and after 1450, Milan. Two other substantial groups of letters include pleas for personal assistance (loans, cash grants with which to fund dowries of poor girls or subsidize ecclesiastical institutions, pleas to arrange marriages, to lend manuscripts from his library, etc.) and, finally, undefined requests, to be explained to Cosimo by the letter's bearer.

This most cursory analysis of the contents of Cosimo's correspondence offers a hint about the sources of his extraordinary power and influence. Cosimo's power in Florence, it appears, depended overwhelmingly on the contacts – friendships, acquaintances, and business relations – which through the years he had acquired outside of Florence. It is difficult to convey adequately in brief the extent to which Cosimo – and with time his two sons and his nephew as well – had become the clearing house, the center of an information network through which requests for all sorts of favors were channelled. Quite obviously, the influence which he was in a position to exert has been most frequently detected in his city's internal policies, in his ability to command the respect and arouse the fear of many of his compatriots. What, perhaps, has not been sufficiently emphasized, is the extent to which, unlike any of his powerful contemporaries, Cosimo enjoyed a range of patronage and influence which they simply could not hope to match. Cosimo's standing amongst the most powerful Italian personages of his age was well known in his day. The Doge Foscari, *io sento è molto vostro amico*, wrote Andrea Mapheo, a Veronese stranded in Budapest, wishing permission to settle in Venice.[56] Alamanno Salviati knew that Cosimo had influence (. . . *jo so quello che tu puoj in lui* . . .) with Giovanni Vitelleschi, cardinal of Florence,[57] while Savese di Francesco, writing from Perugia, asked for a favor with a well-known mercenary, Troylo, who, he knew, "is yours

56 *MAP.,* XI, 161, Andreas Mapheus, Veronese in Buda to Cosimo in Florence, 3 March 1438.
57 *MAP.,* XII, 159, Alamanno Salviati, *Capitano* of Pistoia to Cosimo, 24 October 1435.

and you can dispose of him as if he were in your household" (*è vostro e de luy desponete per senpre come de n'unno de caxa vostra*).[58] And Alexander Tagliamillo, wishing to bring to the Pope's attention as a candidate for the archbishopric of Salerno his relative, Messer Niccola Tagliamillo, wrote to Cosimo, knowing that he wielded much influence with the Pope (*siete assay cho lo nostro Signore Santto Padre*).[59] Examples such as these could be multiplied, for the bulk of Cosimo's correspondents wrote to him precisely because he wielded influence with the men of power in Italy.

This ability, the capacity to reach out into the major sources of Italian patronage, endowed Cosimo with prestige and power unrivalled by any Florentine political boss. The Soderini, the Pitti, the Capponi, the Rucellai, the Acciaioli, and other prominent Florentines of Cosimo's generation could exert their patronage within a fairly limited radius: the gonfalon and the region of the *contado*, where they had their landed possessions above all, while occasionally they enjoyed a certain standing with a prelate or a lord. But none could rival Cosimo, for none had available that formidable instrument of Medici power: the Medici bank. It would be difficult to exaggerate the political benefit derived by the Medici from their bank. While exiled in Venice, Cosimo and his brother offered to advance a huge loan (about 30,000 florins) to the Venetian government, an offer gratefully accepted by his hosts.[60] Francesco Sforza's fortunes depended to no small degree on

---

58   *MAP.*, XI, 83, Savese di Francesco in Perugia to Cosimo, 4 January 1436/37.

59   *MAP.*, XI, 315, Alexander Tagliamillo in Naples to Cosimo, 20 July 1439.

60   Shortly after his arrival in Venice, Cosimo was authorized by the Venetian government to negotiate with Niccolò de' Fortebracci, a leading mercenary of the day, on behalf of the Venetians. *Archivio di Stato di Venezia, Senato Segreta*, XIII, ff. 43r–v, 24 January 1433/34. The offer to advance a loan to the Venetian government was reported by one contemporary chronicler and is referred to in a letter sent by a Venetian to one of Cosimo's relatives. *MAP.*, IV, 331, Jacomo Donado fu di messer Polo in Venice to Francesco di Giuliano de' Medici in Florence, 11 September 1434: "Io son zertissimo che avanti el zionzer haverete sapudo de la magnificha oferta che fe' Choximo e Lorenzo a la nostra Signoria da doverili inprestar per quanto tenpo piaxese a la nostra Signoria e darli adesso ducati trenta milia. . . . La nostra Signoria l'à regraziadi e ha habudo per azeto la oferta sua. . . . Queste son gran chosse e magnifiche chose, et està molto azeta a tuta questa tera questa soa oferta. . . ." Sanuto refers to a 15,000 florin loan advanced by Cosimo to the Venetian government; cited in Gutkind, *Cosimo de' Medici*, p. 117. In this context it may be interesting to cite the judgement of two of Cosimo's contemporaries. Luca Landucci, in his *Diario fiorentino dal 1450 al 1516*, ed. Iodoco del Badia (Florence, 1883), p. 3, so described Cosimo: "Cosimo di Giovanni de' Medici, el quale si chiamava da tutto 'l mondo el gran mercante, ch'aveva le ragioni per tutto l'abitato; non si poteva fare maggiore comparazione che dire: e' ti par essere Cosimo de' Medici: quasi dicendo: che non si poteva trovare el maggiore ricco e più famoso. . . ." And Rucellai, in his *Zibaldone*, p. 54, says: "Cosimo de' Medici, ricchissimo più che messer Palla [de' Strozzi], valentissimo di naturale e d'ingegnio quanto niun altro che avessi mai la nostra cipttà. E aveva tal seguito e tale concorso nella cipttà che si dicie che mai non fu niuno cipttadino maggiore di lui, et della città e del governo disponeva chome era di suo piaciere."

Cosimo's willingness to finance him directly;[61] and the Medici position in the Roman court has been too well described by Raymond de Roover to require additional elaboration here.[62] The example of Roberto da Gagliano, an *amico* of the Medici, rather graphically shows how Cosimo's financial resources could be marshalled on his clients' behalf. In his Catasto return, amended around 1430, Roberto declared: "I began a bank . . . with 500 florins advanced to me by Cosimo, which he held and deposited for me. I now find myself a creditor in this bank for 2,713 florins and 6,633 *lire di piccioli*." Thus, Roberto, it seems, was given a line of credit in the Medici bank; with this credit he launched a series of financial operations from which he stood to gain, according to his own tax declaration, nearly 3,700 florins.[63] The point is, that because of the bank and the political power which they derived from it, the Medici range of patronage far exceeded that of any other Florentine. If their rivals and competitors were bosses of their neighborhoods, the Medici had become patrons on a much vaster scale, which encompassed Florence's domain and often other parts of Italy. Eminent politicians themselves had to rely on Cosimo's good favors when establishing their contacts with foreign powerful lords. Conversely, the rewards conferred on faithful Medici clients and followers far exceeded whatever recompense could be reaped by followers of other political leaders. Thus, for example, shortly after Cosimo financed Francesco Sforza's successful takeover, members of the Acciaioli and the Della Stufa families, old political allies of the Medici, made their appearance in the Milanese court, fast gaining the new *signore's* favor by obtaining choice positions in the Milanese provincial bureaucracy.[64]

---

61 Pietribuoni, *Priorista* (BNFi., *Conventi Soppressi*, C. 4.895, f. 151r): "Al tempo de' detti Signori [January–February 1448/49] si donò al conte Francesco Isforça f. venticinque migli-aia perchè potessi aquistare Milano, benchè da Chosimo de' Medici n'aveva auto f. 50 migliaia in presto, e da' genovesi fiorini dieci mila donatogli pelli sua bisogni."

62 Raymond de Roover, *The Rise and Decline of the Medici Bank*, Ch. 9.

63 ASFi., *Catasto* 296 (*Aggiunte di secondi e terzi ufficiali*), f. 137r: "Giovanni et Ruberto d' Antonio da Galiano, gonfalon Lion d'Oro). . . . Principiaj un banco jo Ruberto detto con f. 500 mi servì Cosimo de' Medici che per me li tenne et diposità, nel quale bancho mi truovo avere a riscuotere f. 2713 d'oro e lire 6,633 di piccioli." By converting the lire to florins at the rate of 4.2 lire/florin (for the current rate of conversion, see Anthony Molho, *Florentine Public Finances in the Early Renaissance, 1400–1433* [Cambridge, Mass., 1971], p. 213) one obtains the figure of 1,579 florins; 1,579 + 2,713 − 500 = 3,792.

64 *Storia di Milano*, ed. Fondazione Treccani degli Alfieri per la storia di Milano (Milano, 1956), VII: 20, n.l, for the Della Stufa; for the Acciaioli, Pietribuoni, *Priorista*, f. 152r. See also Benedetto Accolti's explicit letter to his patron Piero di messer Luigi Guicciardini, written on 3 September 1435. MAP., XII, 30, Benedetto d'Areço, dottore di leggie in Volterra to Piero Guicciardini in Florence: "Qua tutti ci áno disposti per la vostra lettera nella mia raferma per sei mesi, se non che Cosomo, a cui instantia fu eletto uno messer Thomaso da Castiglione, scrisse una lettera loro, tanto stretta, che il fatto mio rimase indietro. Anno mandata l'alec-tione a Cosomo che il detto messer Tomaso possa venire per tutto Ottobre et me vogliono rafer-

This short essay examined three aspects of Florentine political experience which cast some light upon Cosimo's extraordinary position after his return from exile. Starting with the title *pater patriae*, it was suggested that this term reinforces modern idealist conceptions of the state which are inadequate to explain the structure of Florentine politics. The honor posthumously granted to Cosimo has to be understood as the recognition bestowed upon him by his admiring peers whose social and political ideals, in most fundamental respects, Cosimo had shared. The title itself might be seen as part of a continuing effort to create a political mythology at whose center stood Cosimo's persona. Repeatedly, in the thirty years following his death, Cosimo's example was invoked as the paragon of those virtues of self-control, generosity, and strength of character, which members of the Florentine aristocracy ascribed to themselves. When Cosimo's great-grandson, Piero, was exiled in 1494 and a new political regime created in Florence, the priors of the city ordered that the title *pater patriae*, inscribed on Cosimo's tomb, be effaced for, so the decree states, he could better be described as a *tyrannus* than as the father of his fatherland.[65] A new regime, supported by new social forces and political alliances, was now in need of forging its own ideology.

On the basis of evidence that suggests rather than proves the point, I then argued, following Cohn, that the Florentine urban workers and the poor, crushed by the aristocratic regime installed in 1382, were forced in the Quattrocento to redefine the focus of their social experience, abandoning their collectivist impulses, and organizing themselves at the neighborhood and parish level. But this fragmentation does not appear to have produced those "vertical" ties of association between "upper and lower orders" of society which some historians detect in Quattrocento Florence. In this sense, the exploitation of Florentine workers by their employers was not attenuated either by ties of clientage, or by paternalistic behavior of their social superiors, for these attitudes are not reflected in the relations between the rich and the poor in Renaissance Florence. The constant employment

---

mare insino alla sua venuta; per questo pocho tempo non voglio acectare, salvo se non credessi stare insino a Ognisanti. Se vedete potere contentare Cosomo che faccia indusgiare per questi due mesi l'are' caro, avisandolo ch' io non so' meno suo servidore che messer Thomaso." The fact that this letter is now today in the Medici archives most probably indicates that Piero Guicciardini did try to intervene on his client's behalf with Cosimo.

65   E. Muntz, *Les collections des Medicis au XV siècle* (Paris, 1888), p. 104, where the deliberation of the priors and colleges of 22 November 1495 is quoted as follows: "Deliberaverunt quod inscriptio sepulchri Cosme de Medicis in ede Sancti Laurentii in pavimento prope altare majus, cujus talis est titulus: *Cosmae Medici patri patriae*: omnino deleatur, quia talis titulus non meruit sed potius tirannus."

I wish to thank Mrs. Janice Clearfield, doctoral candidate in Art History at Brown University, for having very kindly brought this document to my attention.

of force, the exemplary and frequent punishment of those tempted to violate the social order, perhaps even the regulation of wheat prices, ultimately these were the political instruments through which the workers and the poor were kept in their place.

Patronage, on the other hand, was an institution which regulated the relations of members of the political class: those men who could deliver small favors by serving in communal office, who could constantly convey useful information about events taking place in Florence or abroad, and who could constantly defend the good name, the reputation and honor of their patron. Patronage had to do with politics, a notion well expressed by Dietisalvi Neroni, himself one of Florence's great political bosses, in a letter to Cosimo's son Piero: *Amicitia*, he wrote, "is useful and necessary in all things, and, as you know, above all, in politics."[66] And in another letter, this one addressed to Cosimo, Franco di Rosso, writing from Naples, asked for a letter of presentation to a powerful figure in the Neapolitan court "for the greater a man is the greater his need of support and of *amici*."[67]

If the metaphor *pater patriae* conveys an inadequate and largely false picture of Cosimo's position in Florentine society, might his political role be reflected in another image more suitable to the interpretation advanced in the second half of this paper? The answer to this question has already been offered in this essay's title: Cosimo as *padrino*, as the political patron, the go-between whose contacts and friendships with his powerful contemporaries enabled him to honor the requests of his supplicants and by so doing earned their support and devotion. Power, in the end, belonged to him not because of force, nor because of his control of the electoral processes, but, rather, because he had created a political machine which made it possible for him to award those who cooperated with him and his associates much more generously than could any other Florentine of his day.

66   *MAP.*, CXXXVII, 596, Dietisalvi Neroni in Scarperia to Piero di Cosimo in Florence, 1 April no year: ". . . in qualunche cosa l'amicitia è utile et necessaria, et maxime ne gli stati, chome a tte è noto."

67   *MAP.*, XII, 52, Franco di Rosso in Naples to Cosimo in Florence, 13 September 1435: ". . . quanto l'uomo è magiore tanto à magiore bisongnio di sostengnio e d'amici." Arlotto, *Facezie*, p. 174, n. 113, seems to be saying much the same thing when he advises his listeners to amass only a moderate amount of wealth and not to aspire to great riches. Those whose yearly income exceeds 100 florins have many preoccupations, among which: "arete a stare sottoposto a maggiore numero di gente. . . ."

Part III
Urban Life and Values

Introduction to Part III

Like many pre-modern societies, Renaissance Italy was overwhelmingly rural. The vast majority of people lived in the countryside and traveled infrequently to cities. Yet what they saw in the cities amazed them, as it did many of their contemporaries who came to Italy from other parts of Europe. Travelers described with wonder the marvel of Venice, a city built on water whose outline seemed to shimmer in the sunset reflected off its lagoon. They spoke with awe about Brunelleschi's Duomo, which one could see for miles outside the walls of Florence; and they praised many other civic and religious monuments that made cities rise from the plains and the mountains, signs of human industry and ingenuity. The variety and number of cities gave Italy a distinctive appearance. One did not need to travel far to find the walls of another commune.

The Italian Renaissance city was a world made up of many different parts. Most of the city's inhabitants were artisans and small shopkeepers – people who participated only marginally in political life unless necessity forced them to contemplate the deficiencies of their system of governance, or their fortunes improved enough over the generations to elevate them to a different category of citizenship. Their names were rarely among those drawn from the pouch or in some manner selected to govern, nor in all likelihood did most of them aspire to hold office. They might inhabit the same districts – variously called *gonfaloni, contrade,* and *rioni* – as the great merchants and bankers and attend the same churches, but they expected different things from their society.

For the majority of city dwellers, the virtues of citizenship were primarily defined by the social and economic advantages of civic life. Living within the city walls gave its inhabitants a distinct sort of identity that came from collective association. A cobbler in fifteenth-century Florence might count himself lucky to be a member of his professional guild and of one of the confraternities (lay fraternal religious organizations) frequently associated with one's occupation or one's neighborhood. He contrasted his lot in life not only to the peasant in the *contado*, but also to the masses of unskilled workers who immigrated to wealthy Italian cities in search of employment, and to the slaves in domestic service to wealthy mercantile families, whose arrival in the Renaissance city was never by choice. He hoped for a decent apprenticeship, possibly some education, a well-arranged marriage, and good fortune for his business and his family. And he was proud to participate in the collective rituals that defined his society and invested each city, and each quarter within each city, with a special significance. As Edward Muir describes in his essay, urban identity was both a social and an economic fact, and an act of symbolic association. The ritual life of most Italian cities, still evident today in historical festivals that recall the age of the communes, skillfully combined sacred and secular meaning.

The experience of the city could be quite heterogeneous. In the close-knit communities of Renaissance Italy, rubbing shoulders with the great was indeed possible. Cosimo il Vecchio might stand as godfather to the son of a wine-maker in his district of San Lorenzo, or to the daughter of a mason who helped to build his family palace on Via Larga. Wealthy patricians were well aware that it was their Christian duty to invest in society on many different levels. We need only think of the famous case of Francesco di Marco Datini, a mid-fourteenth century merchant who wrote "For the love of God and profit" on the top of every one of his ledgers. When he died childless, he left the entirety of his fortune for the relief of the poor in his native city of Prato. Part of the reason why Cosimo became known as *pater patriae* was because of his munificence, not only in his own neighborhood but throughout the city of Florence. He understood that investing in the city by restoring and embellishing its ancient churches and monasteries was an act of piety that would be repaid in this life as well as in the afterlife. Among other things, he recognized that a godly and beautiful city fostered a stronger sense of pride and community among its inhabitants.

If merchants and artisans were divided by their ambitions and fortunes, they nonetheless shared certain assumptions about how society ought to work. Networks of kinship and friendship, discussed in some detail in Christiane Klapisch-Zuber's essay, shaped the social possibilities in one's life, just as the neighborhood created an intensely local sense of religious identity – the parish – for men and women, and bound its male inhabitants together to create the districts that defined the city as a political entity. Even merchants who spent most of their lives far away from their native cities often found many of their life choices dictated by these associations; they did business abroad through networks shaped by those at home, and often returned home to marry and participate in the governance of their society.

The urban culture of Renaissance Italy was not without its social tensions. A world shaped by wealth was also one in which privilege was highly contested. When Cosimo commenced building the Palazzo Medici, he knew that he had to finesse this display of conspicuous consumption so that it not be perceived as a statement of his authority over his city. But the watchful citizens of Renaissance cities knew that some of the most expensive gestures lay in the small but important acts of daily life: as Diane Owen Hughes outlines in her essay, the amount of a dowry, the expense of a trousseau, the clothes one wore in public, and other measures of social distinction. We might see the sumptuary laws that emerged at this time as attempts to clarify social relations within an arena in which outward appearances often confused the issue. New wealth *ought* to look different from old wealth; Jews ought to be easily identifiable from Christians; prostitutes should not resemble women of honor when they paraded themselves in the public piazzas. Renaissance Italy, in other words, was a society acutely concerned with appearances. Such concerns reflected the governing elite's view of a well-ordered city in which all of its members could be easily and appropriately distinguished from each other. Needless to say, it was only within the context of a city that these issues could be raised at all, since fancy clothing, ornate jewelry, expensive gifts, and large buildings were not common enough currency among peasants to manifest themselves in elaborate sumptuary legislation.

Understanding how men and women of the fourteenth through sixteenth centuries experienced daily life within an urban environment brings us somewhat closer to understanding the social conditions that made the distinctive world of Renaissance Italy possible. The communal nature of Italian Renaissance politics – participatory and yet restrictive – was a direct outcome of the delicate calculus of human relations that life in the city revealed. The persistent fears about trust within this society in matters of family and business help us to understand how difficult it must have been to allow anyone to govern for very long. At the same time, the densely interwoven fabric of human relations made Renaissance Italy a dynamic and productive society – capable of creating fine products like the finished cloth the Florentines sold throughout the world, but also able to develop a rich interpersonal life that was expressed in diaries and account books. The more positive aspects of Renaissance urban values found their best expression in private acts of family and devotion that deepened one's sense of self in more reflective ways, and in public acts that transformed the space of the city into an elaborate stage upon which they enacted ceremonies to bind themselves together. Civic culture, like politics, could not be created without a collective will to make it central to a society's image of its well-being. If Renaissance Italians looked critically at the social acts of their kin and neighbors, they largely agreed that the embellishment of cities was for the common good, and that the churches and piazzas were there for all the citizens to enjoy, even when factions among those who inhabited them might claim them for their own. The three essays by Christiane Klapisch-Zuber, Diane Owen Hughes, and Edward Muir explore some of the most distinctive forms of social behavior that we associate with the Italian Renaissance cities.

Plate 6 Vittore Carpaccio, *The Healing of the Possessed Man* (1494). *Source:* Accademia, Venice.

The Scuola Grande di S. Giovanni Evangelista, one of the main confraternities in Venice, commissioned this painting by Vittore Carpaccio (ca. 1465–1526) as part of a series of paintings commemorating the religious life of the city in the 1490s. This was one of a number of commissions they offered him. The painting was displayed in the meeting rooms of the confraternity as part of a serious commemorating important moments of religious ritual in Venice. The ostensible subject is an exorcism, performed in the palace of the Patriarch of Grado (upper left). But the painting uses this event to recapture Venetian public life in the vicinity of the Rialto bridge. Patricians, clerics, and foreigners fill the public spaces of the city. A female servant sticks her head out of a doorway. Merchants bargain and unload their wares. Gondolas jam the Grand Canal. Since no one seems to pay special attention to the healing underway, Carpaccio suggests to his viewers that miracles are simply part of the daily fabric of a thriving Renaissance city. His painting captures many aspects of the social life of Venice at this time: careful attention to dress as a form of social distinction, the relative absence of women in public, the presence of slaves and freed slaves in Italian Renaissance cities, and the careful attention to architecture and urban planning to create an urban aesthetic.

4

"Kin, Friends, and Neighbors": The Urban Territory of a Merchant Family in 1400

Christiane Klapisch-Zuber

Parenti, amici, vicini: these three words are constantly found closely associated in the thoughts of Tuscans of the fourteenth and fifteenth centuries. Around 1400 a man like Giovanni Morelli will often use them to express the many relatives and associates on which an individual could rely; to be betrayed or abandoned by them signified to him ruin and poverty.[1] With Morelli as with his contemporaries, kinship, friendship, and neighborliness are thus almost always evaluated in terms of their social utility. The same viewpoint will serve here to analyze the composition, the range, and the role of this "personal group" centered on a given individual; in particular, I shall try to determine whether the blood relationship is the dominant constituent of these ties. If we can define the criteria for the recruitment or exclusion of these persons – persons who permitted the individual to play his social role to the full – it should clarify the functions ideally assigned to kinship and to alliance, as well as the functions that these two sorts of ties (or their substitutes) really fulfilled. Some aspects of this problem may be clarified by examining one particular case.

A Florentine merchant, Lapo di Giovanni Niccolini de' Sirigatti, kept a *Libro degli affari proprii di casa* from 1379 to 1421.[2] Like other Florentine

---

1 Giovanni di Pagolo Morelli, *Ricordi*, ed. V. Branca (Florence, 1956), 232: "Cosi il povero pupillo è pelato da' parenti, dagli amici, da' vicini e dagli strani; e da oguno con chi s'impaccia egli e rubato, ingannato e tradito" (Thus the poor ward is skinned by his relatives, by his friends, by his neighbors, and by outsiders; and by all he encounters he is robbed, cheated, and betrayed). Similarly, ibid., 246–7.

2 *Il Libro degli affari di casa di Lapo di Giovanni Niccolini de' Sirigatti*, ed. C. Bec (Paris: SEVPEN, 1969). The Niccolini have also been the object of a series of studies by one of their descendants, G. Niccolini da Camugliano: "A Medieval Florentine, His Family and his Possessions,"

ricordanze, it evokes the pell-mell of daily life, notes the people Lapo encountered, and describes their dealings. In its conception and organization this book is by no means especially original; to the contrary, it is marked by the dryness of its observations and information. Lapo states his intention to record the "events of the house, . . . all notations and memoranda and every thing that pertains to me"[3] – all that regards him, then, and those close to him, members of his "chasa" (Lapo's spelling). As with so many other examples of this private literature, Lapo's book recounts day by day the events that affected the number or the status of the members of the household and the acquisitions, transfers, or exchanges of goods that influenced its wealth. In this way he records a great number of relatives, both consanguineal and affinal, and others connected with him in all sorts of ways.[4] A further interest of his book is that the author, like many of his contemporaries, indulges late in life in the preparation of an annotated genealogical introduction designed to prove the antiquity and reinforce the social status of his lineage.

The Niccolini were a family relatively new to Florence, distinguishing themselves, toward the beginning of the fourteenth century, from the older lineage of the Sirigatti from Passignano, certain members of which had already arrived in the city by that time. Lapo's immediate ancestors were soon honored with municipal offices. His grandfather, also named Lapo, was a prominent silk merchant (*grande mercatante*) and became a *priore* in 1334 *gonfaloniere di justicia* in 1341 – the highest civic magistracy in Florence. The father of our Lapo, Giovanni, was also active in city government, although he never became *gonfaloniere*. When Lapo wrote his genealogical introduction (between 1417 and 1421),[5] he had already held

American Historical Review 31 (1925): 1–19: "Libri di ricordanze dei Niccolini," *Rivista delle Biblioteche e degli Archivi* 2 (1924): 1–30, 88–91, 172–87, 243–52; *The Chronicles of a Florentine Family, 1200–1400* (London, 1933). The author has exploited and in part published the private archives of the Niccolini family, particularly a second book of Lapo's devoted to his landholdings and the books of his sons.

3 "Fatti proprii di chasa . . . tutte richordanze e memorie e [ognie] chose che s'appartenessono a me" (*Libro*, 55).

4 His *lavoratori* (peasant farmers) and his business relations, treated in his business account books, are almost totally absent. In order to verify the accuracy of the notes in his private *Libro*, I have checked the papers of one of his notaries and friends, ser Antonio dall'Ancisa, for the years 1408–13 (Archivio di Stato di Firenze, henceforth abbreviated ASF, *Notarile antecosmiano*, A 807). It is evident from this comparison that those absent from Lapo's secret book but present in the notarized acts recorded by his friend are, for the most part, witnesses, whom Lapo mentions very rarely. On the use of collections of notarial documents for the reconstitution of kinship networks, see Diane O. Hughes, "Toward Historical Ethnography: Notarial Records and Family History in the Middle Ages," *Historical Methods Newsletter* 7 (1974): 61–71.

5 In his introduction to his edition of the *Libro*, C. Bec dates this addition between 1409 and 1413, basing his interpretation on the number of male children Lapo has at the time (*Libro*, 22, 58). In my opinion, Lapo's genealogy was composed either (as Bec suggests) before 1413,

that position himself at least three times and had played an important role in Florentine politics.[6] Why, in these circumstances, should he still feel the need to consolidate the political and social position of the family by evoking the Guelf loyalties of his ancestors and their admission into the circle of "good citizens"? Honors had been concentrated in one branch of the Niccolini family, and the lineage as a whole seems still relatively humble around 1400, whether we consider the number of its members and the influence of the entire group or the few individuals among them, notably our Lapo, who monopolized political command and material success. The interchangeable responsibilities and roles that assured the strength of the great Florentine families were less secure among the Niccolini. A man like Lapo, who had achieved personal success, sought to deflect onto all those he considered his kin the prestige that his grandfather, his father, his older brother, and he himself had acquired. Naturally, he expected personal benefits in exchange, but his first concern seems to have been dynastic. *Parenti, amici,* and *vicini* were to play an important role in this attempt at consolidation. When he conforms to the traditional strategies of his circle – and when he occasionally abandons these strategies in order to hasten their effects – Lapo ingenuously reveals the accepted functions of those contacts.

"I nostri e quei di casa nostra"

The family was first and foremost those who shared a house, the domestic group that lived in common. It is significant that in his introduction Lapo emphasizes the geographical roots of his line. Two houses in via del Palagio del Podestà in the *quartiere* of Santa Croce, extending east along the Arno, gave tangible expression to the "Florentinity" of the Niccolini from the time they came to the city. Those who were admitted to or excluded from these houses provide some measure of who Lapo considered his intimates. But the "family," for a Florentine of the merchant aristocracy, also included the members of that spiritual *casa* that was the lineage – deceased family members whose last resting place the descendants provided and whose memory was kept alive by masses celebrated in the family chapel[7] – and

---

or between 1417 and 1421 – that is, between the death of his first son and that of his last son, another moment in his life when Lapo had eight sons. I lean toward the second hypothesis, for he attributes an age to his brother Filippo (67) that is incompatible with the first date, and his remarks on the repossession of several houses could have been made only after 1417.

6   See *Libro*, C. Bec, Introduction, 11.

7   Lapo's father stipulates in his will that a *sepoltura nuova* (new tomb) be created in the church of Santa Croce. His descendants were to be buried there, and the tomb can still be seen today. He also provided in his will for masses to be said for ten years in the parish church of San Simone, near his house (*Libro*, 60–61). The Niccolini in fact were to have a "chappella di

living members scattered in different households, who by misfortune and awareness of their lineage were sometimes forced to unite under one roof. Lapo's book permits us to survey a great number of these persons, and even his reticences are in themselves significant.

First of all, the book offers a series of images, spread over forty years or so, that serve as points of reference to show how the composition and the size of the domestic group varied with the age of the head of household and with the tribulations undergone by the population as a whole.

At the time of his death in 1381, Lapo's father, Giovanni, was living with his wife, his married older son and the latter's wife and children, and two younger, unmarried sons. Two other children, both daughters, were married and living elsewhere. The elder, Monna, was already widowed and may have lived for some time under the paternal roof, with her daughter, before remarrying, as Florentine law and even her father's will permitted her to do.[8] By its size (nine to eleven persons) as well as by its vertical structure, the household was quite typical of the merchant families of Florence.[9]

After Giovanni's death, the brothers' alliance (made up of the family of the elder brother and the two younger brothers) did not long survive. Niccolaio, the eldest, separated from his brothers and received the house next to the principal dwelling of the family in the division of the estate that took place in 1382.[10] The two younger brothers, our Lapo and his younger brother Filippo, continued to live with their mother in the first house. At the beginning of 1384 they each took a wife simultaneously and celebrated their weddings with "a single festivity in our house on the via del Palagio."[11] Their behavior, once again, is quite typical of the young members of their class. The elder brother died soon after the father,[12] and to consolidate their situation our two young men[13] found it imperative to enter into alliances as soon as possible so that they could manage their own affairs and assure the guardianship of their nephews.[14] But – and this too is a typically Florentine

Sancto Niccolaio, ch'è in San Simone dov'è dipinta e intalgliata l'arme nostra" (chapel [in honor] of Saint Nicholas, in [the church of] San Simone, where our crest is painted and carved) (ibid., 90) and they also supported a priest at San Simone.

8   *Libro*, 61–2.

9   See D. Herlihy, "Mapping Households in Medieval Italy," *Catholic Historical Review* 58 (1972): 1–24; D. Herlihy and C. Klapisch-Zuber, *Les Toscans et leurs familles: Une analyse du catasto de 1427* (Paris, 1978), chap. 17.

10   *Libro*, 63–7.

11   "Una ffesta nella nostra chasa della via del Palagio" (ibid., 71–2).

12   His testament in *Libro*, 69–70.

13   Lapo must have been about 28 years old and Filippo about 26.

14   All the more so since their brother-in-law Pierozzo di Ruberto Ghetti, Fia's husband, had just died also, leaving two orphans, for whom Lapo took on the guardianship (February 1384; *Libro*, 71).

trait – fraternal solidarity did not last long under a common roof. In September of 1385, less than one year after their marriages, the two couples moved apart and divided the goods that the 1382 agreement had left undivided. Since he was older, Lapo quite naturally became head of *casa* Niccolini and acquired the principal house on via del Palagio del Podestà, in which he was to live until his death in 1430.[15]

From this moment onward, births were to swell the household that occupied this dwelling. Lapo was prolific: he had seven children by his first wife, Ermellina da Mezzola, in less than sixteen years of marriage;[16] and six by the second, Caterina Melanesi, in the twelve first years of their union.[17] Around 1402 his roof sheltered ten persons, not counting the domestics, and around 1410, fifteen. He was at the time over 50. At the peak of his responsibilities as head of household, ten unmarried children lived at home, along with his old mother, who was at least 80, and his sister Monna, widowed for the second time and whom he had taken in with her daughter Nanna.[18] The plague of 1417 carried away his eldest son and his youngest daughter,[19] but these losses were made up for by taking in his three granddaughters – the daughters of his daughter Lena and his son-in-law Ugo Altoviti, orphaned when both parents also died of the plague[20] – and he was again responsible for at least twelve persons. According to his *catasto* declaration of 1427,[21] the household was at that time reduced to eight persons and one slave woman; Giovanni, now the eldest son, had married and left the house. At this point Lapo was living only with his wife, five children, and a grandnephew.

15   *Libro*, 76–9. See his declaration to the *catasto* of 1427, ASF, *Catasto* 73, fol. 141.

16   *Libro*, 72. Ermellina was *menata* (brought to her husband's house) 11 May 1384 and died 28 February 1400. Only one of her children died in infancy, at one year.

17   Ibid., 92. She was *menata* 11 September 1401; Lapo's last son, Battista, was born 25 June 1413.

18   Nanna left his roof in January 1411 to go to her husband Berto da Filicaia (ibid., 113); Monna died before 1415 (ibid., 124). His mother, Bartolomea Bagnesi, died in 1416 (ibid., 134). Lapo had married two of his daughters, who left home in 1405 and 1409.

19   Niccolaio, 31 years old (ibid., 136); Ermellina, 14 years old, whose death is noted with her birth, not at the corresponding date (ibid., 94).

20   He took in their mother, who died in his house, for six months, and then kept her children (ibid., 137). Niccolaio, his nephew Francesco's son, was the sole survivor of a family of six persons (ibid., 135). The four children of his other nephew, Giovanni, were abandoned by their mother after the death of her husband (ibid., 137). The book does not say clearly if they continued to live in the house next to Lapo's own, which fell to their grandfather Niccolaio in the division in 1382 and which Lapo had bought back, or if they too were taken in by their great-uncle.

21   ASF, *Catasto* 73, fols. 141ff. The *uficiali* of the *catasto* decided to allow as *suo nipote* (his nephew) Bartolomeo di Giovanni di Niccolaio, "nine or ten years old," who was in fact his great-nephew.

This reduction of his household late in life is also a characteristic that can be observed statistically in the households of city dwellers of his circle. Lapo's father had been able to continue to keep his married eldest son with him, with his wife and children, because his household did not have too many mouths to feed; but Lapo, at the same age, had a *famiglia grandissima*. On several occasions he made an effort to make more room by getting his grown sons established elsewhere. His efforts were in vain: Niccolaio, the eldest, "too big a spender of his own money and others'," preferred to shelter "his appetites and desires" within the familial cocoon. The plague of 1417 swept him away, eliminating the problem of a congested house in radical fashion.[22] Giovanni, the next son, seems to have been in no greater hurry to submit to the holy laws of matrimony, even when Lapo paved the way with gold in 1418. While still seeking out a wife for him, Lapo offered him more than his share of his inheritance if he would leave the house.[23] His efforts were crowned with success before the *catasto* of 1427, since Giovanni is listed on its books on his own, with a wife at last.[24]

In the final analysis, Lapo owed the fairly simple structure of his household toward the end of his life to the fertility of his wives and to the fact that ten of his thirteen children survived to adulthood.[25] People of his rank in Florence were happy to marry one or two of their sons without having them leave the flock, as his own father had done. But the variations in the composition of Lapo's household reveal the flexibility of rules of residence in

22   On Niccolaio: "Troppo grande gittatore del suo e dell'altrui." Lapo attempted an accounting with Niccolaio in October 1416 "perché io gli voleva dare molgle e dargli la sua parte e dividerlo da mme" (because I wanted to give him a wife and give him his inheritance and his independence from me). They were unable to reach a *compromesso*, he states, "perché ancora non eravamo venuti a perfetione di nostra intentione" (because we had not yet reached perfect agreement) (*Libro*, 134; for the death of Niccolaio, ibid., 136–7).

23   "E io Lapo volglendo dargli molgle, e io abbiendo la familgla grandissima, mi diliberai volerlo partire da mme e dargli delle mie sustanze quella parte gli tocchava e ancora molto più, e questo perch'era il magiore de' miei filgliuoli che m'erano rimasi" (and I, Lapo, desiring to give him a wife, and having a very large family, decided to emancipate him and give him of my substance the share he deserved and much more, and this because he was the eldest of my remaining sons) (ibid., 143, 7 November 1418).

24   ASF, *Catasto* 73, fols. 97ff. His wife Tita declares she is 28, and he himself 38, although he was born in 1395. On these exaggerations of age, see Herlihy and Klapisch-Zuber, *Les Toscans*, chap. 13. In 1427 Giovanni lived in a house his father had reacquired from a cousin; see below, notes 57–9. These long bachelorhoods found their solaces, which translated into additional crowding in merchant households. In this way, the slave Lucia, declared by Lapo as early as 1427, and aged 25 when Lapo died in 1430, gave three sons to Paolo di Lapo before 1434 and continued to live in the house with her children when Paolo brought in an official wife (see Niccolini, *The Chronicles*, 112ff).

25   His son Paolo was to have twenty children by two wives, a concubine, and a mistress. Of the sixteen legitimate children, only eight were to reach adulthood (ibid., 130–8).

Florence, which bent to the practical conditions of cohabitation. If Lapo's progeny had suffered a higher mortality rate, he very probably would have been encouraged to keep his married son at home.

We can also see that his house was on several occasions saturated by an influx of close relatives who were widowed or in need owing to the plague. As head of *casa* Niccolini, Lapo opened his doors wide to these relatives in difficulty, as familial ethics required. The solidarity of these *congiunti stretti* – blood relatives – is never better expressed than in the momentary reunions brought about by a death or a low blow of fortune. To belong to the same *casa* also meant to be able to take refuge or to gather under the same roof when danger threatened.

We would have to exclude wives from among these intimates – the *prossimani* that Lapo finds himself taking in – as they are never completely considered full-fledged members of the lineage into which they entered by marriage. Nothing could better reflect their floating status than a comment of Lapo's at the time of his mother's death in 1416. He remarks that she "came to [her] husband in the year of our Lord 1349, the first day of October 1349, so that she remained in our house 67 years, 2 months, and 26 days."[26] The meticulousness of the reckoning reveals rather than masks the son's real feelings: this woman, who came of the Bagnesi family, remained all of her long life a transitory visitor in the Niccolini house.

The return of Monna and Lena Niccolini, when widowed, to their brother's or their father's house shows that they, in contrast, remained a part of the ideal *casa*, or "house."[27] Despite the intermittence of their appearances they continue to be considered blood kin, members of a family whose center remained the paternal or fraternal dwelling. An aged aunt of Lapo's, his father's sister Simona, widowed before the Black Death, may also have lived out her last years in the house of her nephew Niccolaio, Lapo's brother.[28] This woman thus returned to her family of birth after more than thirty years. The return of these widows (who, under the law, had the right of *tornata* to their family of birth) seems to have occurred because they were alone and, in particular, because they had no male descendant who could

---

26   "Ne venne a marito nelgli anni di Christo 1349, a dì primo d'ottobre 1349, sicchè venne a stare in casa nostra anni lxvii mesi due e dì 26" (*Libro*, 134).

27   His sister Monna, at least between 1406 and her death (1411–15?) (ibid., 104, 111–15, 124). Lena, her daughter, between February and July 1418 (ibid., 137).

28   Niccolini, "Libri di ricordanze dei Niccolini." Widowed in 1345, she and her two daughters were taken in, after the death of her father-in-law Gieri Delli, by her brothers. The daughters were married in 1349 and 1353. Her brother Giovanni's will, written in 1377, allowed her to live "sopra i suoi beni e delle sue herede a bastamento della sua vita" (on his holdings and on his inheritance, sufficient to her needs) (*Libro*, 61). The division between the three brothers gave this responsibility to the eldest, Niccolaio (ibid., 64).

care for them – but who would also find it to his interest to avoid the loss of the mother's dowry should she leave his house.[29]

More surprising is the acceptance of relatives or descendants who were not born Niccolini. Thus in 1419 Lapo welcomes his three granddaughters, nées Altoviti, after the plague of 1417–18 had orphaned them. Their inclusion in the household seems contrary to the rule that dictates that the descendants of a couple belong to the father's lineage, whose name they bear and within which they remain even if the widowed mother leaves this lineage to remarry. Here again, however, Lapo suggests that his granddaughters' presence under his roof was somewhat exceptional: it was at the request of one of their Altoviti relatives and of the Ufficio de' Pupilli, the communal office responsible for wards, that he took them in (and was reimbursed for his trouble).[30] Similarly, he supported his niece Nanna Folchi when he took in her mother, his own sister Monna, because the Folchi family seems to have been undergoing financial difficulties, and his deceased brother-in-law had left his widow just enough to provide a dowry for the daughter.[31] In 1410 Nanna received her nuptial ring in the house of her uncle Lapo and brought her husband the 800 *fiorini* scraped together from her father's creditors and his movable goods. We should mention one final situation, just as exceptional, that linked *casa* Niccolini with a woman relative bearing another name. In the division of 1385, Lapo received, along with the dwelling on via del Palagio, the obligation of sheltering and maintaining a first cousin, Lena Aghinetti, the daughter of one of his father's sisters.[32] This woman was a *pinzochera* – a member of a third order and a noncloistered nun. When she retired from the world in 1396, perhaps under her cousin's roof, she bequeathed her estate (a farm in the Mugello) to the family chapel in the parish church, San Simone. She may have owed her welcome into the Niccolini house to her semi-cloistered state, which, in the best of cases,[33] would necessarily sanctify the roof under which her pious activities took place.

---

29   See for example the case of Fia, Lapo's sister, cited in note 34.

30   *Libro*, 137. In 1427, when his niece Ermellina took the veil, Lapo mentions another 70 *fiorini* owed to him "dalla redità d'Ugho Altoviti per abitamento della figliuola" (from the inheritance from Ugo Altoviti for the girl's lodging) (ASF, *Catasto* 73, fol. 142v).

31   For the recuperation of the dowry, *Libro* 104, 111–15. For the marriage of "Nanna" Folchi, ibid., 113: "E a dì vi [6] di lulglio 1410, il detto Berto le diede l'anello in casa di me Lapo, nella via del Palagio, dove io abito" (and on the sixth day of July, 1410, the said Berto gave her the ring in the house of myself, Lapo, in the via del Palagio, where I live).

32   Ibid., 77.

33   At least this was so in the best of cases, since many of these members of the third order – particularly the females – had a dreadful reputation as shameless bigots, "ispigolistri picchapetti, ipocriti che si cuoprono col mantello del religioso" (bigots, breast beaters, and hypocrites who hide under the friar's cloak) (Morelli, *Ricordi*, 227).

Aside from those to whom blood and the family name gave full rights of residence, the material house might shelter more distant blood relatives, forced by an extraordinary or temporary situation to turn to the head of family. Consciousness of the spiritual *casa* (what Lapo calls the "familglia") reaches beyond those living in the same dwelling, however, even considering temporary additions to the household. Of blood relatives of all degrees mentioned in his *Libro* – those with whom he has dealings or whom he notes as among his contemporaries – only one-half (twenty-three persons) at one time or another share Lapo's roof. The rest break down into two groups of quite unequal size.

The first of these groups, and the largest, is made up of the families descended from his elder brother, Niccolaio, who were hard hit by the plague of 1417, and those of his sister Fia, whose four children remain within the two lineages to which she was successively allied.[34] The second group is made up of more distant cousins. Lapo calls them *nostri consorti* (our consorts) and here they bear the name of Sirigatti alone. If we go back to their common ancestor, Arrigo, surnamed Sirigatto, who lived during the first half of the thirteenth century, these cousins are no less than five canonical degrees removed from Lapo. Aside from them, Lapo notes in his brief preliminary genealogy that his great-uncle Biagio Niccolini must have had at least six children, over whom, however, he casts a modest veil: "[they] were all wicked men – one more than the other – and [they] destroyed what their father had earned."[35] This "wretched family" had only one descendant "about in the world" around 1420.[36] The genealogy published by Passerini shows, furthermore, that Lapo passes over certain branches of the family in total silence, as well as certain individuals who bore the Niccolini name and lived not only during his lifetime but even in his neighborhood.[37] Thus

---

34   Fia Magalotti, widowed in 1402, lived alone and *povera* (poor) in 1427 and made out a declaration for the *catasto* in her own name (ASF, *Catasto* 80, fol. 342). She lived at the time in the *quartiere* San Giovanni, while her son Guido lived in Santa Croce like Lapo (ibid., 69, fol. 544).

35   "Che tutti furono huomini piu tristi [*l'uno*] che l'altro e distrussono ciò che il loro padre avea ghadangniato" (*Libro*, 57).

36   Ibid. It may be the same Piero di Biagio, *commissario di guerra al Corniolo* in 1389 mentioned in the genealogy of L. Passerini, *Genealogia e storia della famiglia Niccolini* (Florence, 1870), table 1.

37   The branch of Giovanni di Niccolino, whose great-grandsons Antonio and Niccolò di Piero were living at the time of Lapo's writing. In this connection see Passerini, *Genealogia*; and J. Plesner, *L'émigration de la campagne à la ville libre de Florence au XIIIᵉ siécle* (Copenhagen, 1934), 221, Généalogie G (ser Paganelli). In the *catasto* of 1427, as in other contemporary documents, *Tratte* or *Prestanze* (which I thank David Herlihy for having brought to my attention) there appear a Niccolò d'Andrea Niccolini and a Giovanni d'Andrea Niccolini, *lanaiolo*, whose shop was on Lapo's street. They bear the name Niccolini, but never "de' Niccolini" nor "de' Sirigatti" as do Lapo and his immediate family. Furthermore, toward the middle of the fifteenth century,

our author does not even mention a paternal great-uncle, Giovanni, and all his descendants, long settled in the *contado*. Men of war, businessmen who were unlucky or ran through their fortunes, men who tilled the earth – Lapo considers them marginal to society and better ignored.

When he cuts his ties with his cousins' descendants in this manner, Lapo greatly reduces the number of his useful blood relatives. His contemporaries – Giovanni Morelli, for example, and later Leon Battista Alberti – saw in immediate kin the persons whom it is natural, and thus logical, to trust in family or commercial affairs.[38] Lapo thus has only a few "natural" contacts – collaterals or adult cousins who could come to his aid.[39] In the family agreements noted in his *Libro*, few of the arbiters are recruited from among the Niccolini.[40] In contrast, ser Niccolò Sirigatti, a notary and the oldest of the three *consorti*, is called on to play this role on two occasions: in 1380 to settle a matter between Lapo and his sister Monna,[41] and in 1403 to draw up the accounts for the guardianship of Lapo's nephews.[42] This "savio huomo" (wise man), as Lapo calls him, enjoyed enormous prestige among the Niccolini and was certainly well informed of their affairs, since he acted as notary for Lapo's father from the mid-fourteenth century onward.[43] A respected man (and of respectable age around 1400), he held important communal offices.[44] His talents and his experience thus made him particularly well qualified to decide the affaires of his *consorti*. On the other hand,

---

the descendants and heirs of Giovanni d'Andrea were called Niccoli (ASF, *Catasto* 64, fol. 301v, marginal indications of transfers of goods occurring between 1427 and 1457 or 1469). It is probable that this family was not related to Lapo's; it attempts to emphasize its individuality after 1450 by using a name quite different from that of the Niccolini de' Sirigatti (although the last part of that name disappears about the same period).

38   With numerous reservations and precautions, however, which Morelli recounts morosely (*Ricordi*, 218–23). On the choice of guardians, see ibid., 246–7.

39   His nephews Francesco and Giovanni arrived at adulthood and marriage in 1404 and 1405, probably at the age of 25 to 28 years. Their mature years were short, and twelve or thirteen years after their marriage they succumbed to the plague (*Libro*, 75 and 85).

40   This seems normal, since they were party to the problems concerning the estate. Filippo, Lapo's brother, was arbiter three times, however; his nephews Francesco and Niccolaio once each, for a total of 5 occurrences out of the 44 accumulated by 27 different arbiters who appear in 22 family arbitrations and *compomessi* noted in the *Libro*.

41   Concerning a payment by the Buondelmonti of 352 *fiorini* to return Monna's dowry, a sum paid to "la cha nostra e in uso d'essa si spesono" (our house and spent for her) (*Libro*, 60).

42   Ibid., 96.

43   He drew up the marriage acts of Simona Delli's daughters in 1349 and 1353 (Niccolini, "Libri di ricordanze," 24–5). He may have had landholdings in common with the Niccolini in the region of Passignano, since in 1363 he countersigned an act concerning lands that the Niccolini owned in this region (Plesner, *L'émigration*, 143–4).

44   He was notary of the Signoria in 1390 and 1400; *priore* in 1383, *gonfaloniere di compagnia* in 1387, one of the twelve Buonomini in 1397, *capitain* of the Compagnia d'Orsanmichele in 1402 (Passerini, *Genealogia*, table 1).

his nephew, also a notary, and his son seem never to have been called on to fulfill similar functions.

Lapo's book shows us what questions generally obstructed the solidarity and confidence normal among close kin. Paradoxically, the very means that their mutual confidence prompted relatives to employ in dealing with one another ended up working against them. Oral agreements that spared them the use of legal formulas and notarization were easily broken or reinterpreted, thus arousing the rancor of the other party. Lapo saves his bad humor and his scorn for those closest to him, in proportion to what he considers their betrayal: for his brother, who "per poco suo senno" (through his lack of good sense) failed to be grateful to Lapo for services rendered;[45] for a female cousin who acts as if he, Lapo, were not going to keep his word;[46] for his niece's husband, who was sticking his nose into his mother-in-law's affairs;[47] also for his son, who had dragged him into a questionable affair and who died without amassing any fortune or showing any desire to perpetuate the family;[48] and for a nephew who went bankrupt and left a number of debts unpaid.[49] Because he had not taken the trouble to write things down (which, incidentally, characterized his daily behavior as a businessman), Lapo was forced on more than one occasion to admit his disappointment concerning his familial attachments.[50]

Traces of positive sentiments toward his close kin are hard to find in Lapo's book.[51] This does not mean to say that those sentiments did not exist, but simply that they are not expressed here. In fact, we can guess that the cohesion of this little group of blood kin is, minor accidents aside, so well maintained by its community of interests, by its shared sense of name and

---

45   *Libro*, 143.
46   Ibid., 146.
47   Ibid., 124–5. Lapo does not keep a written account of the funds destined for his sister that pass through his hands, "che mmi faceva co'llei come con serocchia non pensando avere a renderne regione a Berto da Filicaia ne ad altri. . . . E non avendo scritto alcuna cosa di ciò, ò fatta questa scrittura a ricordanza" (because I acted with her as with a sister not thinking I owed any explanation to Berto da Filicaia [his niece's husband] or to others . . . and not anything written on this, I have made this notation and memorandum). He declares that he has rendered these services "perchè le donne non possono andare, né intendere, né essercitarsi come gli huomini" (because women cannot go about, nor comprehend, nor act as men do).
48   Ibid., 125 and 136–7: "mi diede assai fatiche" (It put me to a good deal of trouble).
49   Ibid., 135.
50   Similarly, Morelli, *Ricordi*, 243: "Non ti fidare mai di persona, fa le cose chiare e piu col parente e coll'amico che cogli strani, come che con ognuno, fa con carte di notaio, con obbrighi liberi a un'arte, non ti affidare a scritta di libri, se non per terza persona" (Do not ever trust anyone; be clear in things and still more with a relative or friend than with outsiders, but [deal this way] with all, use notarial forms, with free obligations to a guild, do not trust what is written in books, except by third parties). See below, note 61.
51   Except with his mother, when she dies ("una valente e cara e buona donna" – a brave, dear, and good woman) (*Libro*, 134), as C. Bec rightly remarks in his introduction, ibid., 24.

of spiritual patrimony, and by the authority and prestige of its uncontested chief, Lapo, that the expression of feelings could remain in the background. One thing that gives a clear indication of feelings within the lineage, however, is their attitude toward ancestral houses.

All his life, Lapo fought a centrifugal tendency for dwellings constructed by his ancestors to be removed from the control of the head of the "house" of Niccolini. The changing fortunes of the second of the houses situated on the via del Palagio are a good illustration of the need for geographical stability in order to maintain familial group identity. This house had fallen to the elder of the brothers, Niccolaio, in 1382. One of his sons, Giovanni, went bankrupt in 1409. To release him from prison, Lapo guaranteed a loan of 500 *fiorini* to satisfy his creditors, putting up the house as security. But when Giovanni died in 1417 without having been able to pay back his debts, Lapo found himself obligated, much against his will, to put the dowry of the deceased's widow before his own interests, and had to buy back for 350 *fiorini* a house that he already considered his own.[52] Several years later, in writing the genealogical introduction to his book, he declares himself glad: "although in this way [the houses] were left to many institutions and to many persons and given by some people as a dowry, they have finally returned to us, and may it please God that it be so for long years to come."[53] These words speak to a desire for geographical roots, expressed by the urban family as forcefully as by the rural family.

On two occasions Lapo also exercised a right of repurchase of family houses granted him by relatives' wills. In 1403 a female first cousin bequeathed to the hospital of Santa Maria Novella a group of houses and shops that had belonged to Biagio Niccolini, Lapo's half-brother on his mother's side, which her husband had bought from Biagio's heirs – those "tristi huomini." She granted to Lapo and his heirs the right to buy back this group of buildings, which were situated a little further along the via del Palagio, at the price of 300 *fiorini*.[54] Lapo let eighteen years go by before he exercised his right and negotiated with the hospital for the transfer of his great-uncle's buildings.[55] Thus in spite of his scorn for Biagio's descendants, Lapo retained an evident attachment for the places where Biagio had been perhaps the first to lay the foundations of the Niccolini merchant fortune.[56]

---

52   Ibid., 132 and 148.
53   "Bene che in questo mezzo si sono lasciate [le case] a molti luoghi e persone e date per alchuni in dote, alla fine sono tornate a nnoi, e chosì piaccia a Ddio che sia per lunghi tempi" (ibid., 156).
54   Ibid., 97–8. In 1427 one of these houses belonged to his great-nephew Niccolaio di Francesco, who rented it to Fruosino di Luca da Panzano (ASF, *Catasto* 73 fol. 334).
55   *Libro*, 143–5 (1421).
56   Ibid., 57: "E fu il primo di loro che chominciò a fare merchatantie" (and was the first of them to go into business).

Reconstructing the original unity of the lineage by gathering its houses together appears here as one of the governing principles in Lapo's *affari proprii di casa*.

The second occasion on which he makes use of a similar right is offered by his *consorto*, ser Niccolò Sirigatti. Niccolò provided in his will for a circuitous destiny for the house in which he lived, contiguous to the two principal Niccolini houses on via del Palagio.[57] If his son and then his nephew were to die "without legitimate and natural heirs," Lapo and his own successors "in the male line" and, failing this, any other descendant of his own father, Giovanni di Lapo, could have the house on payment of 300 *fiorini* to compensate the other heirs.[58] The nephew died in 1417, ser Niccolò's son died in 1427. At that time, as Lapo notes with satisfaction, "we can carry out the testament of the afore-mentioned Niccolò Sirigatti according to our wishes, [concerning] our share."[59]

Ser Niccolò's nephew, ser Francesco Sirigatti, also owned a house in the neighborhood that he did not want to see leave the family.[60] Fearing for his life in the plague that was rampant in Florence in 1417, he entrusted Lapo with this house, which he had mortgaged to him several years earlier, asking him to transmit it to his cousin, ser Niccolò's son, and to keep it himself in the event of the latter's death.[61]

These parallel courses of action and our memorialist's efforts to gather his ancestors' houses into as homogeneous a group as possible clearly express their need to assure the physical cohesion and succession of *casa Niccolini*.[62] At the end of his life, Lapo obviously had not yet achieved the

57   His testament in ibid., 101–2. This house was perhaps the first residential nucleus of the Sirigatti before the houses built by Lapo's direct ancestors. One ser Paganello Sirigatti, "judex et notarius populi sancti Simonis civ. Florentie" (judge and notary of the *gonfalone* of San Simone in the city of Florence) lived in the neighborhood around 1280–96 (Plesner, *L'émigration*, 221, Généalogie G).

58   "Sanza rede legittimi e naturali; per linea masculina" (*Libro*, 102).

59   "Si può a nostra volontà accompiere il testamento del detto ser Niccolò Sirigatti, la parte toccha a noi" (ibid.).

60   "Non escha della nostra familglia" (should not leave our family) (ibid., 116–17 and 136–7). A register of this notary is preserved (ASF *Not. antecos.* S 813, a. 1406–14). He seems to have worked for the most part in the *contado*, and he died in December 1417 at Pescia, perhaps taken there by his business.

61   *Libro*, 136 and 149. In point of fact, as ser Francesco died intestate, Lapo was to have great difficulty in 1417 assuring that the wishes of the deceased, given orally before witnesses, were carried out. Ser Francesco's sister brought suit against him, and as Lapo considered himself the executor of the will of his *consorto*, he was irritated by the actions of this distant cousin, who was acting "a grandissimo torto . . . e danno della sua anima" (very wrongly . . . and at great harm to her soul). The house ended up back in his hands, since his son Giovanni was established in it and declares it in his name in the *catasto* of 1427 (ASF, *Catasto* 73, fol. 97).

62   Lapo also bought several houses to round off his real estate holdings, one to lodge "lo prete che uficerà la cappella nostra" (the priest who will serve our chapel). In *Libro*, 95–96; he

formation of a perfectly closed concentration of buildings grouped around a stronghold and its own church, like those that Florentine *consorterie* of a former age inhabited. His efforts, tinged with a certain archaism, at least must have afforded him the comforting sentiment that his family was as solidly planted as older lineages that were more secure in their rights and surer of their identity.[63]

"Imparentarsi"

Because the material and political bases of his family were as yet not solid, Lapo could afford even less than some others to ignore the need for support from a powerful circle of relatives. His *Libro* shows how, in the span of thirty years, the Niccolini acquired them.

For a Florentine of 1400, a *parente* designated above all a *congiunto di parentado*, an affine. The term included maternal kin as well, however, and sometimes also close blood relatives. We have a sample of what the term represented for Lapo in the arbiters he chose in 1416 to supervise the liquidation of a debt. The five names he put forth "come miei tutti parenti e amici fidati" (all as my relatives and trusted friends) were those of his son-in-law, the husband of his niece (his sister's daughter), an ally through his daughter, a first cousin (son of a maternal uncle), and one other person whose possible kinship with the Niccolini I have been unable to establish.[64]

The matrimonial strategy that Giovanni Morelli recommended to his descendants when the possibility loomed that they might remain orphans and have to administer their own affairs is well known. In substance, Morelli advises them to acquire a substitute father, through friendship as long as they were too young to marry, or by alliance when that moment came.[65] The geographical area in which friends and particularly affines should be recruited is the *gonfalone*, a subdivision of the *quartiere*, and, failing that, the *quartiere*.[66] To look beyond the immediate neighborhood, a truly exceptional opportunity would have to present itself in the shape of

records the purchase in 1402 from the company of Orsanmichele of a house in chiasso Riconte; in ibid., 98 and 147; the purchase of a house contiguous to the latter in 1403; and in ibid., 107; the purchase in 1408 of a house contiguous to those of Biagio Niccolini.

63　On the new tendencies that soon would arise in Florence, see R. A. Goldthwaitie, "The Florentine Palace as Domestic Architecture," *American Historical Review* 77 (1972): 977–1012.

64　*Libro*, 129. On this last personage, see below, note 106.

65　Morelli, *Ricordi*, 253, 263, 283.

66　Ibid., 253. Florence was at that time divided into four *quartieri*, each of which was divided into four *gonfaloni*.

"an excellent relative, able to give satisfaction in every way."[67] Lapo's book enables us to verify whether the Niccolini observed this neighborhood endogamy and whether, when they did not, they acted from conscious matrimonial policy.

When Giovanni, Lapo's father, married off his daughters, probably in the 1370s, he chose neighbors as their husbands. Lapo's eldest sister, Guiduccia, seems to have married a Magaldi, a family that included some members who lived in the *quartieri* of Santa Croce and San Giovanni in 1427.[68] Lapo's second sister, Monna, married Alessandro Buondelmonti, a family of prestigious name that had come from Passignano, like the Sirigatti (who had been their *clienti* – dependents – in the thirteenth century). The Buondelmonti lived in another *quartiere* of Florence, but their properties around Passignano bordered on more than one of the Niccolini's lands there. Monna's dowry, 975 *fiorini* – a large dowry for the end of the fourteenth century – shows that the Niccolini were paying for a good marriage, one that lent them some of the prestige enjoyed by this old, landed family.[69] Fia, the third of Lapo's sisters, married Pierozzo Ghetti (who died in 1383) while her father was still alive. Lapo does not record the dowry, but it is probable that it did not reach the same heights as her sister's, since the Ghetti, a family from *quartiere* Santa Croce, like the Niccolini, were less prosperous than they.[70] Finally, Giovanni married his son Niccolaio to a Bardi, a family that held solid control of the *quartiere* of Santo Spirito, on the other side of the Arno, and that counted some family members who were landowners in the same region of Passignano.[71]

In these first marriages contracted by members of Lapo's generation, it seems that the father wanted to strengthen existing ties with families that had traditionally been their *padroni*, like the Buondelmonti, but at the same time to reinforce his ties with the land. In conformity with practices later

67   "D'uno parente che fusse ottimo e avesse tutte le parti da piacere" Morelli, *Ricordi*, 263.

68   This first sister died after eighteen months of marriage, according to her brother (*Libro*, 58). Passerini, *Genealogia*, table 1, gives her husband as a Magaldi, but her brother, who had cut all relations with that family, does not mention Magaldi's name.

69   On the Buondelmonti of that time, see L. Martines, *The Social World of the Florentine Humanists, 1390–1460* (Princeton, 1963), 210–14.

70   Another branch of the family figures among the 150 major contributors to the *prestanza* of 1403 (Martines, *The Social World*, 353–65), but not the branch to which Fia's husband belonged.

71   Niccolaio Niccolini's two brothers-in-law, Gerozzo and Andrea di Francesco di messere Gerozzo Bardi, have a *prestanza* in 1403 that amounts to less than Lapo's. They rank 130th in their *quartiere* while Lapo ranks 72d in his. Jacopo di messere Agnolo Bardi owned lands bordering on those of the Niccolini at Santa Maria di Monte Macerata and at San Fabbiano (*Libro*, 74 and 115). A Bardi, Vieri di Bartolo di messere Bindo, worked as *cassiere* (cashier) for Lapo in 1405.

recommended by Morelli, however, he clearly was also seeking to enlarge the circle of his relatives in the neighborhood by allying himself to relatively more modest families. The first marriages concluded after the death of Giovanni show that the two brothers, Lapo and Filippo, continued the same policy: their exogamous marriages are more numerous and seem somewhat more upwardly mobile than their local alliances.

Monna, widowed by Alessandro Buondelmonti before 1377,[72] was the first sister to remarry. She married a jurist, messer Jacopo Folchi, whose family lived in the *quartiere* of Santo Spirito.[73] Messer Jacopo was to die in Venice before 1406, leaving his wife a great many books and very few goods under the sun.[74] The dowry of 800 *fiorini* that Monna brought him reveals that this second marriage was less prestigious than the alliance with the Buondelmonti.

Lapo's sister Fia remarried as well, and into a fairly influential but less wealthy family in *quartiere* Santa Croce. The choice of Bese di Guido Magalotti, who later played a fairly active role in politics, is in the direct tradition of these local alliances: modest but solid and politically useful both on the level of the neighborhood and on that of communal institutions.[75] This marriage, however, was the last to take place in the Niccolini's own neighborhood. When Lapo and Filippo took a wife themselves, in 1384, they both allied themselves with Santo Spirito families. Ermellina da Mezzola, the daughter of an "honorabile chavaliere" (honorable knight) brought Lapo 700 *fiorini*, and Giletta Spini brought 800 *fiorini* to Filippo.[76] These dowries are not excessively high, somewhat lower, in fact, than the sums with which the Niccolini themselves dowered the women they gave in marriage. The imbalance suggests that they were seeking to marry upward; to *innalzarsi*, as Morelli recommends and as much contemporary evidence demonstrates.[77] The females of their family, on the contrary, had to have greater dowries to maintain their rank.[78]

In 1394, with the marriage of a niece, Agnoletta (the daughter of their elder brother), for whom they assumed guardianship in 1383,[79] the

---

72   According to his father's will, written in 1377 (*Libro*, 61).

73   He appears in 1382 as one of the three arbiters charged with settling the division of goods between Niccolaio, Lapo, and Filippo (ibid., 63). In 1427 the average wealth of the five Folchi was 817 *fiorini* (without deductions for *bocche*) at a time when the Niccolini's wealth reached 2,219 *fiorini*.

74   *Libro*, 104, 112.

75   On Bese Magalotti see ibid., Bec, Introduction, 13. The *catasto* of 1427 lists only four Magalotti households: three widows and Bese and Fia's son Guido, who declares only 809 *fiorini*. Lapo does not give the amount of Fia's dowry.

76   *Libro*, 71–2.

77   See Herlihy and Klapisch-Zuber, *Les Toscans*, chap. 14.

78   See below, note 93.

79   *Libro*, 70.

Niccolini entered a new period in their matrimonial activities. "As it pleased God, we married off Agnoletta," Lapo says, to a member of the great family of the Rucellai, giving her a dowry of 950 *fiorini*.[80] Like the Buondelmonti and the Bardi, the Rucellai family had many branches, some members of which (Agnoletta's husband, for example, Luca di Giovanni di Bingieri) were hardly shining lights in the firmament of Florentine fortunes.[81] Nevertheless, this new exogamous alliance – the Rucellai lived in the *quartiere* of Santa Maria Novella – undoubtedly appeared as advantageous to the Niccolini brothers, since they decided to greatly increase the dowry that her father had stipulated for Agnoletta in his will.[82] The marriage of their niece set the Niccolini's course firmly toward the merchant oligarchy.

Now a widower, Lapo took a second wife, Caterina Melanesi, who came from a family of *lanaiuoli* (wool merchants) from the other side of the Arno.[83] Lapo probably owed the 1,000 *fiorini* she brought him in dowry to the prestige he had already acquired in government service and to his professional success. In 1402 a niece, Checca Magalotti, born of the second marriage of his sister Fia, was given in marriage to Giovanni di Bernardo Ardinghelli, who belonged to a Santa Maria Novella family listed in 1403 as being as wealthy as Lapo's.[84] The wives that Lapo's nephews, Angoletta's brothers, took in the following years were not from the *quartiere* of Santa Croce either. Lorenza Bischeri, whom Francesco married in 1404, came from a San Giovainni family much wealthier than Lapo and brought to her husband only 800 *fiorini*[85] in the most unequal marriage that the Niccolini managed to conclude during this period. As for Giovanni, he married a Tosinghi, Tancia, dowered with 900 *fiorini*.[86] On the other hand, when Lapo's daughter Lena married Ugo Altoviti in 1405, father and husband were of equal wealth and the dowry Lapo paid him was no greater than 700 *fiorini*.[87] The dowry of Lapo's second daughter, Giovanna, married in 1409 to Giovanni Albizzi, rose to 1,000 *fiorini*.[88] It is difficult to grasp these dif-

80   "Chome fu piacere d'Iddio, maritammo l'Angnioletta" (ibid., 88, 89).

81   Martines, *The Social World*, 361. With his brother Jacopo he ranks only 121st in his *quartiere*, Santa Maria Novella.

82   Her father provided 600 *fiorini* (*Libro*, 69); her uncles and guardians gave her 950 *fiorini* (ibid., 89). On the practice of testators who reduced the dowries bequeathed to their marriageable daughters by one-quarter, leaving it to the guardians or to the brothers and the mother to increase them *insino in fiorini dugento più oltre alla dota* (by up to 200 florins more than the dowry [stipulated]), see Morelli, *Ricordi*, 223.

83   *Libro.*, 92.

84   Ibid., 94. The dowry was 900 *fiorini*.

85   Ibid., 98.

86   Ibid. It is unclear whether she was of the rich family of the Del Toso, *quartiere* Santa Maria Novella, or the Della Tosa, *quartiere* San Giovanni.

87   Ibid., 99–100. The rank of Ugo Altoviti in 1403 is 84th in *quartiere* Santa Maria Novella.

88   Ibid., 108. The Albizzi lived in quartiere San Giovanni.

ferences between the amounts of the dowries accorded by the Niccolini otherwise than by a comparison of the fortune and the influence of the partners in the contract. Generally speaking, the Altoviti appear to be half as wealthy as the Albizzi.[89] A year later another of Lapo's nieces, Giovanna Folchi, Manna's daughter, married Berto da Filicaia, who came from a Santa Croce lineage that lived on its landholdings and had a favorable audience in political circles. The dowry, 800 *fiorini*, approaches the average for dowries given by the Niccolini.[90] The last union mentioned in Lapo's book, the second marriage of his son Filippo, brought Filippo only 500 *fiorini*, the smallest of all the dowries our family received during this period. Filippo married a Rucellai, Parte di Albizzo, taking a wife in the clan to which the Niccolini had given a wife in 1395 to the tune of many *fiorini*.[91] Another similar reinforcement of the chains of alliance can be seen some years later, when Lapo arranged the marriage of his son Giovanni to Tita Albizzi.[92]

The Niccolini's matrimonial strategy evidently depended on Lapo's personal achievement as the "strong man" of the lineage. Evidence of this can be seen by a comparison of the average sums given and received in dowry in the first period (until 1385) and in the second (1395–1410). While the dowries given by the Niccolini remain at the same level from the first to the second period (respectively 890 and 870 *fiorini* on the average), those they received increased notably, passing from 750 to 900 *fiorini* on the average.[93] This rise probably reflects the rise in Lapo's own fortunes, for he now received more than he gave in matrimonial exchanges.

The strategy pursued by Lapo and those close to him becomes clearest if we look at its geographical dimensions. The alliances concluded plainly go beyond the borders of the *quartiere*; thus, if we remember Morelli's advice, they imply an abundance of exceptional opportunities offered to Lapo. Only one sister and the daughter of a sister were given in marriage (in 1385 and in 1410) to families in Santa Croce. But no Niccolini man took a wife within the *quartiere* during this period. On the other hand, there were many more exchanges with the families of Santa Maria Novella, in the west part of the city, since three Niccolini chose wives from that area and the family also gave three wives to it. The *quartiere* of Santa Spirito – across the Arno on the road to the family landholdings – and the *quartiere* of San Giovanni to the north

89   In the *catasto* of 1427 the thirty Albizzi households have an average wealth of 2,514 *fiorini*; the twenty-four Altoviti households, 1,244 *fiorini*.
90   *Libro*, 113. On the De Filicaia, see Martines, *The Social World*, 176 and 218.
91   *Libro*, 139–40.
92   The amount of the dowry, unfortunately, is unknown. The marriage took place between 1421, when Lapo's book ends, and 1427, when Giovanni appears as married in the *catasto* (ASF, *Catasto*, 73 fol. 97).
93   A part of this increase was perhaps linked to the general upward movement of dowries at the time (see Herlihy and Klapisch-Zuber, *Les Toscans*, chap. 14).

gave two wives and took one each. The exchanges seem to be numerically equal with Santa Maria Novella, to show a profit with San Giovanni and Santo Spirito, and to show a debit with the home *quartiere* of Santa Croce. This balance suggests that the Niccolini were truly seeking out good matches outside their neighborhood and that they succeeded in making some major coups beyond its boundaries, to the detriment of local alliances. Alliance certainly appears to have contributed to their rise as it brought them closer, between 1400 and 1410, to the great commercial and banking families of the Ardinghelli, the Bischeri, Altoviti, the Rucellai, and the Albizzi.

Little appears of the practical relations involved in alliance in a book as schematic as Lapo's. Two-thirds of the fifty or so relatives by marriage who are mentioned – wives excluded – appear only once: they bring a dowry, witness or guarantee its payment, assure the guardianship of orphans born of the marriage that had allied their family to the Niccolini, or are named executors of the will of a deceased family member.[94] Some, however, were associated with the Niccolini in their commercial affairs.[95] One alone added spiritual relationship to affinal relationship by becoming godfather to one of Lapo's children.[96] A dozen of the affines appear to have the closest links to Lapo and his immediate family when they are chosen to settle family conflicts and problems by arbitration.

Blood relatives, as we have seen, are seldom seen as judges in the arbitration to which they are party. Affinal relatives, on the other hand, form the reserve troops from which Lapo calls up familial peacemakers: brothers-in-law first (his sisters' husbands[97] or his wife's brother[98]), then sons-in-law[99] or his nieces' husbands,[100] then relatives on the maternal

94   The notarial protocols show that certain of these appear more often as witnesses to acts important in the life of the family. Research in this direction would thus be desirable.

95   This was the case for Niccolò di Gentile Albizzi and his brother Giovanni, Lapo's son-in-law, who were both Lapo's associates in his "bottega di San Martino" in 1415 (*Libro*, 119, 139) or for Andrea di Pierozzo Ghetti, associated with his first cousin Giovanni di Niccolaio Niccolini in 1409 (ibid., 73–4). Lapo's commercial books obviously would tell us much more about these familial business associations had they been preserved.

96   See below, note 127.

97   Bese Magalotti, Fia's husband, was called in October 1385 as arbiter in the division between Lapo and Filippo (*Libro*, 77–9); messer Jacopo Folchi, Monna's husband, was arbiter in 1382 in the division between the three brothers (ibid., 63).

98   Domenico Melanesi was called on at least three times as arbiter: to set the dowry for Nanna di Lapo in 1409 (ibid., 108), to supervise the application of an agreement between Lapo and his son Giovanni in 1411 (ASF, *Not. antecos.* A 807, 13 February 1411), and to supervise another agreement between Lapo and some bankrupt creditors in 1416 (*Libro*, 132).

99   Giovanni di Gentile Albizzi is arbiter in 1411 (ASF, *Not. antecos.* A 807, 13 February 1411) and twice in 1416 (*Libro*, 130 and 132). Ugo Altoviti also appears in the act of 13 February 1411.

100 Giovanni di Bernardo Ardinghelli was one of the five arbiters retained 8 May 1416 (ibid., 129).

side,[101] and finally somewhat more distant affines.[102] The frequent participation of his *parenti* shows that Lapo and his immediate family judged them knowledgeable enough concerning their family affairs to be able to take part, with the necessary discretion, in the resolution of thorny problems – as long as they were not directly involved. There are few of these family affairs, settled out of court – the appraisal of dowries, the division of estates, the settling of quarrels between a father and an independently established son, the repayment of non-interest loans conceded to friends, etc. – in which we do not see at least one of the arbiters drawn from this circle of in-laws. Their appearance was all the more welcome since a man of Lapo's age could not count on many of his close blood relatives. His paternal uncles were likely to be dead, like his father, whose contemporaries they were, while the maternal uncles, whose sister married young, were less distant from their nephew both in age and by their activity. In a society in which city men of this class married girls considerably younger than they, it is difficult to find a simple definition of the "generations" where affinal relatives are concerned. Thus, the husbands of sisters are contemporaries of the brother and can soon back him up in his affairs, while the wives' brothers, younger than the husband, will enter the picture later, and perhaps in a somewhat subordinate situation.[103] A man of fifty, contemplating his approaching death, would do well to provide for paternal substitutes with sufficient life expectancy, choosing his wife's brothers rather than his own brothers or his sisters' husbands, who would be even older than he. Thus age gaps – one could almost say a generational gap – between spouses reinforced ties with the allied lineage from which the wife came, and also contributed to an early indifference toward the families into which the sisters had married.[104]

The least we can say is that these situations of unequal age wove a subtle network of relations spaced out in time, in which one man benefited from the experience and authority of his maternal relations and of persons allied to him through his sisters before he could offer his protection to his own

101 Bardo di Filippo Bagnesi, Lapo's maternal uncle and the executor of Lapo's father's will (ibid., 63) was arbiter in arranging the settlement of a debt to Lapo in 1383 (ibid., 68); Rinieri di Bardo Bagnesi, Lapo's mother's nephew, served as arbiter twice in 1416 (ibid., 129 and 132).

102 Antonio di Tedice Albizzi, arbiter in 1405 (ibid., 100), 1416 (ibid., 134), 1418 (ibid., 143); Giovanni di Simone Altoviti in 1405 (ibid., 100), 1416 (ibid., 129, 132, 134); Jacopo di Berto da Filicaia in 1410 (ibid., 113). This "useful" kinship by affinity extended less far than kinship by consanguinity, however, since it does not seem to go beyond the second degree.

103 This can be observed in Lapo, whose brothers-in-law Jacopo Folchi and Bese Magalotti were called on around 1382–5, while Domenico Melanesi appears only in 1409 and 1416.

104 As we have seen, Lapo has no apparent relations with the Magaldi, into whose family he married his sister Guiduccia (see note 68 above). Nor did he maintain relations with the lineages with which his first cousins were allied (da Barberino, Villani, Panichi), or with the Delli, Vigorosi, Aghinetti families, into which his paternal aunts had entered by marriage.

affines – his wife's brothers and his brothers' affines – and obtain their services and their advice. This spacing of ages helps us to understand how affines changed place so rapidly in family councils and why their participation in Niccolini affairs remained for the most part episodic. But the number and the diversity of these instances undeniably reveal Lapo's need to rely on a circle of relations much broader than the nucleus of blood relatives.

"Parentevolmente e amorevolmente"

In choosing his affines in other *quartiere*, Lapo created a sort of void between his blood relatives, crowded into their grouped houses, and *parenti* established farther away. This void was filled by the "allies of choice," the *amici* whose presence had the task of insuring the harmonious proximity of neighboring lineages.

In Florence, friendship or, as the Florentines of the fifteenth century said, *amore* is not to be confused with kinship. *Parenti* are often closely connected with *amici*, however. The text of 1416 cited at the head of this section strikingly juxtaposes the terms *parenti* and *amici fidati*.[105] The arbiters Lapo retained on the occasion described in the text included one man who seemed to be neither a close relative nor an ally of Lapo, although his father, a banker, had been active a quarter-century earlier in the affairs of the Niccolini family.[106] Still, this person does not permit us to say that Lapo established the same confusion between kin and "friends" that can be easily found in France of the same epoch.[107] Who, then, were Lapo's friends?

Lapo presents an extremely small number of people as friends. Whereas he could rely on forty or so blood relatives and at least fifty affines, the number of his "friends" can be counted on the fingers on one hand. Excluding the five arbiters in 1416 who have been mentioned, those he declares as friends include, above all, a neighborhood notary, ser Antonio di ser Niccolaio di ser Pierozzo dall'Ancisa, and his entire family;[108] Antonio di Bertone Mannelli, the beneficiary of a non-interest loan in 1383;[109] and an intermediary at the time of the sale of a parcel of land.[110] Lapo's son

---

105   *Libro*, 129. See above, note 64.

106   In 1416 "Simone di Bonarota Simoni," whose father "Bonarota," *tavoliere* (money changer), was arbiter in the division between the three brothers in 1382 (*Libro*, 63). A genealogy of the Niccolini family (founded essentially on Lapo's book and which appears in ASF, Strozziane 2d ser., 16, fol. 19 mod.) qualifies Bonarrota di Simone di Bonarrota as a *cugino di serrochia* (a cousin of/through my sister), without explaining this appellation, however.

107   See J. M. Turlan, "Amis et amis charnels d'après les actes du Parlement au XIVᵉ siècle," *Revue historique de droit français et étranger* 4th ser., 47 (1969): 645–98.

108   *Libro*, 129–31.

109   Ibid., 68.

110   Ibid., 121.

Niccolaio had a bond of friendship with a certain Geppo di Bartolomeo.[111] Ser Antonio dall'Ancisa, the notary Lapo turned to from 1407 on,[112] also appears as his representative in delicate affairs,[113] which is probably what earned him the title of "intimo amico." Lapo and he were tied by the godparental relatationship, as were his son Niccolaio and his friend Geppo.[114] The *amore* that Lapo claims to bear this ser Antonio and his family is expressed in the desire to render him services, and the occasions for doing so reveal something of the nature of friendship in the fifteenth century.

In 1416, soon after ser Antonio had helped Lapo to untangle a complicated affair, the notary, his brother, and his mother attempted to buy back their paternal house, which had been sold.[115] Lapo guaranteed the 400 *fiorini* loan needed for this reacquisition, and he did so – "with no profit to myself, but for the love I bear that family." Thus *amore* permitted him to understand a friend's pressing need to regain possession of an ancestral house and made him rise above his appropriate and natural love of gain and the custom that dictated that a *servigio*, a courtesy, must always be repaid. The exchange of free favors seems to characterize relations between "friends,"[116] and – in a society in which every penny was counted – *amore* introduced a certain freedom of action. Behind this exchange, when it was disinterested, we can divine a certain desire to leave accounts perpetually open between friends, not to hold friends to an exact accounting in the repayment of loans.

---

111   Ibid., 126.

112   Ibid., 105ff. Ser Antonio's mother was born a Castellani and remarried a Buondelmonti from Passignano (ibid., 129).

113   Lapo had given his guarantee "come semplice" (like a simpleton) for a loan of 500 *fiorini* given to a friend and *compare* of his son, Goppe di Bartolomeo, and his associate Luca da Panzano, both of whom "facevano i fatti de' soldati" (provided for soldiers). The deal turned sour for Lapo when these two army supply men went bankrupt, and it was probably to the skill of ser Antonio that Lapo owed the compromise arrived at with the bankers who had made the loan (ibid., 125–9). Other arbitrations of ser Antonio: in 1418 (ibid., 140 and 141–2) and in 1421 (ibid., 144).

114   Ibid., 130: "Mio compare e intimo amicho e benivolo" (my associate as godparent and intimate and kind friend). Ser Antonio does not figure among the godparents of Lapo's children, so Lapo must have been godfather to one of his. On the *comparaggio* of his son Niccolaio, see ibid., 126.

115   Ibid., 129–31. The notary lived in 1427 with his mother, his brother, his wife and his ten children (two of them *nati d'amore* – love children) in this house on via del Palagio (ASF, *Catasto*, 73, fol. 1). The 2,015 taxable *fiorini* that he declares, before deductions for family responsibilities, make him a relative wealthy man.

116   "Sanza niuno mio utile, ma per amore ch'i' ò a quella familglia." As early as 1383 Lapo lent 150 *fiorini*, without interest, to Antonio di Bertone Mannelli, "per amore chome fa l'uno amicho all'altro" (out of love, as is done between friends) (*Libro*, 68).

For Lapo, however, friendship usually involved important social functions.[117] Friends were a ready source of obliging intermediaries,[118] lenders or guarantors of non-interest loans, sometimes arbiters in amicable settlements, and godfathers to the children. These varied functions enable us to enlarge somewhat the circle of Lapo's "friends" to include persons who are not specifically designated as such.

It is, first of all, in the give and take of daily business that these privileged relations of *amore* and confidence, which contemporaries naturally associated with kinship but which also characterized friendship, seem to be initiated. One Cristofano del Bugliasso, for example, whose name appears constantly in the first pages of Lapo's book, was an associate of the Niccolini brothers, having been an associate of their father, in their wool, cloth, and wool products shop on the ground floor of the house.[119] The young Niccolini heirs often had recourse to his experience before 1407, and in drawing up several family agreements they cast him in the role of a *parente*.[120] The friendship born of doing business together, which sometimes relaxed the strict rules of the game, thus tended to take the place of kinship. Moreover, such feelings created bonds like those of kinship but on the spiritual plane. Morelli, once again, eloquently compares friendship among fellow citizens to kinship;[121] he cites, among means of acquiring or retaining friends, serving as godfather to children of "good men, [men] of substance and power."[122] We have seen, in fact, that ser Antonio chose Lapo as

---

117   Morelli indicates in many passages how to acquire and keep friends: *Ricordi*, 150, 237, 241, 253, 260–1, 274, and particularly 279: "Ma sopra tutto, se vuoi avere degli amici e de' parenti, fa di non n'avere bisogno. Ingegnati d'avere de' contanti e sappigli tenere e guardare cautamente, e que' sono i migliori amici si truovino e i migliori parenti" (But above all, if you wish to have friends and relatives, try not to have need of them. Put your mind to having ready money and learn to keep it and treat it cautiously, and this will be the best friends and the best relatives that can be found).

118   Agnolo di ser Domenico Salvestri, *lanaiolo*, is *mezzano* (middleman) in the sale of a farmholding by Lapo to another wool merchant, for he is "amico dell'uno e dell'altro" (friend to both) (*Libro*, 121).

119   "Bottegha di lana, panni, istami (ibid., 65; September 1382).

120   He arbitrates the division between the three brothers (ibid., 63) and the settlement of a debt owed to Lapo (ibid., 68; 26 May 1383); he assures the guardianship and trusteeship for the orphans left by Niccolaio di Giovanni, (ibid., 70 and 96; 2 August 1383); he takes possession of a house bought from a priest for Lapo (ibid., 98; 20 November 1403); and he arbitrates between Lapo and his mother in 1407 (ibid., 105–6).

121   "Usa parentevolmente con ogni tuo cittadino, amagli tutti e porta loro amore; e se puoi, usa verso di loro delle cortesie" (Treat all fellow citizens like relatives, love them all and show them your love; and if you can, show them every courtesy) (Morelli, *Ricordi*, 237).

122   "Buoni homini e da bene e potenti." Ibid., 150: "Riteneasi con loro, mostrando loro grande amore in servigli di quello avesse potuto, in consigliarsi con loro di suoi fatti, dove e' dimostrava fede e speranza in loro; onoralli in dare loro mangiare e in tutte altre cose: battez-

godfather to his children; in like fashion, the man who was so obliged to Lapo and to his son Niccolaio served as the latter's *compare* (associate through godparenting). The twenty-two godparents of Lapo's thirteen children permit us to clarify somewhat better our author's network of friends.

Of these persons who "make Christians" of Lapo's children, only six carried out their mission *per l'amore di Dio* (for the love of God). The others contract this spiritual alliance with Lapo at the cost of lavish gifts, thus showing to how great an extent Florentine godparenting was an opportunity to *far onore* to someone.[123] A good example of a godparent chosen in this spirit of charity is Giovanni di Michele del Buono, who sponsored three of Lapo's children at the baptismal font, and each time *per l'amore di Dio*.[124] He enjoyed Lapo's trust, acted as purchasing agent when Lapo bought a house next to his own,[125] and also seems to have directed the first steps in the business world of Lapo's son Giovanni.[126] A "friend" of this sort seems to occupy a position subordinate to Lapo's, like Cristofano del Bugliasso and even ser Antonio, or like the army supply man who was *compare* to Niccolaio di Lapo. Lapo and his immediate kin thus allow themselves to be bound by spiritual kinship to men who did not belong to their milieu and

---

zare loro figliuoli, e simile cose e maggiori, come accaggiono tutto giorno nell'usare e praticare con quelle persone a chi altri vuole bene" ([His father] visited with them often, showing them great love in serving them in all possible ways, in discussing his affairs with them, whereby he showed faith and confidence in them; honoring them by giving them to eat and in all other things, baptizing their children, and such and greater things as occur every day in the frequentation and company of persons whom one esteems).

123   Besides Giovanni del Buono (see note 124), these included priest of the Niccolini chapel in 1403 (*Libro*, 93), Filippo di Niccolò) Giugni in 1389 (ibid., 80), and Lapo's brother-in-law Bernardo da Mezzola (ibid., 80), Simone Salviati in 1390 (ibid., 81), and the *speziale* (druggist) Lionardo di Mannino in 1396 (ibid., 89). Later, in 1445, a granddaughter of Lapo's, born to Paolo, who was at the time *priore*, had all of his fellow *priori* for godfather *per l'amore di Dio* (Niccolini, *The Chronicles*, 129). The efforts of a friend in common often permitted the arrangement of a desirable *comparaggio*. Francesco di Tommaso Giovanni reports in his *ricordanze* that "intervenne per me Nichol mio fratello" (my brother Nichol acted as intermediary for me) to ask Stoldo di Lionardo Frescobaldi if Francesco could stand as godfather to one of Stoldo's children. It is probable that a godparental relationship of this type was not *per l'amore di Dio*. On the other hand, Francesco himself insists that the most frequent godparents of his children (monks, the midwife, or the nurse) act as such "per l'amore di Dio, e così facciono" (for the love of God, and so shall it be) (ASF, *Strozz*, 2d ser., 16, fols. 15, 20v; 3 December 1436 and 13 June 1440). See C. Klapisch-Zuber, "Le *comparatico* à Florence: Parenté spirituelle et relations familiales avant la Contre-Réforme (14c–16e siècles)," in preparation.

124   In 1409, 1410, and 1413 (*Libro*, 109).

125   Ibid., 107; 1 December 1408.

126   ASF, *Not. antecos*. A 807, 13 February 1411. He was an associate of Giovanni and declares himself *lanifex* (wool merchant). In the 1427 *catasto* there is a *sensale* (broker) of the same name in the *quartiere* Santo Spirito (ASF, *Catasto* 67, fol. 295). He owed Lapo 23 *fiorini*.

with whom the conclusion of a matrimonial alliance would have been going too far, even though they felt the necessity to express their closeness *parentevolmente* (like a relative). Thus spiritual alliances and matrimonial alliances coincided only exceptionally within the Niccolini clan: only one of Lapo's children had a maternal uncle for godfather.[127] None of the families from which Lapo's other *compari* were recruited were also his relatives.

The system of *compari* thus introduces us into a circle of relations of a much greater social heterogeneity than that of affines, since Lapo allied himself spiritually with persons with whom matrimonial exchanges were not possible. This circle consisted primarily of neighbors. The godfathers of Lapo's children are for the most part inhabitants of the *quartiere*: of the twenty Florentines[128] he chose as godfather, at least half lived in the neighboring streets of *quartiere* Santa Croce, and a third in the *Gonfalone delle Ruote* in which Lapo lived. Their tax rate in the *prestanza* of 1403 enables us to identify half of them as among the 150 most highly taxed in their quartiere, thus as belonging to the same social milieu as Lapo. Certain of them – the bankers in particular – were noticeably even richer than he.[129] The other half of these godfathers were of lower social status than Lapo. The fact that he chose them suggests that Lapo was using *comparaggio* to bolster his local sphere of influence.[130] Many of these *compari* disappear from Lapo's book after the one mention of the baptism to which they had been invited. The brevity of their appearance leaves the impression that the choice of a godfather was generally conceived as an opportunity to repay an obligation, to honor a debt, or to render on the spiritual plane a service received in the day-to-day business world. As the people chosen were for the most part neighbors, they entered into a whole network of exchanges that unfortunately is revealed in Lapo's book only in this familial aspect, but that other sources speak of with a wealth of detail.[131]

Friendship among the Niccolini tended toward kinship without ever – or hardly ever – reaching that point, except perhaps on the spiritual level. It

---

127   Bernardo di messer Zanobi da Mezzola, Lapo's brother-in-law for five years, godfather of Luca Rinaldo "per l'amore di Dio" on 20 April 1389 (*Libro*, 81). Morelli's family often chose godmothers, either grandmothers or nurses, while Lapo chose only men.

128   His son, Jacopo e Miniato, was born when he was on official business in San Miniato Fiorentino. His godparents were the city government of that town (which accounts for his second name) and Bartolomeo Gambacorti, from a Pisan family (ibid., 89; 25 July 1398).

129   Thus Francesco di Agnolo Malatesti-Cavalcanti, *tavoliere*, (money changer) in 1386; Domenico di Demenico Giugni in 1395; Filippo di Niccolò Giugni in 1386 and 1389.

130   Among these less splendid godparents were ser Simone, the priest of the family chapel; Giovanni di Michele del Buono, *lanaiolo* (wool merchant); a *ritagliatore* (woolens cutter) and former business associate of Lapo, Matteo di Francesco di ser Orlandino (1410); a *speziale* (druggist), Lionardo di Mannino; an *approvatore* (appraiser), Niccolò di Monmigliore.

131   Thus Morelli, *Ricordi*, 260–1, for example, on how to drink with one's neighbors and maintain courteous relations with them.

appears as a geographically limited complement to marriage alliance, filling in gaps and for the most part exercising its role in situations where kinship did not operate. Friendship generally engaged individuals only. The godparent relationship, one of its best expressions, offered a tested means to reinforce the bonds between persons of the same geographical or business community without going so far as to ally their families. Thus "friends" were first of all privileged neighbors, encountered in the crush of the *bottega* or of the parish church, at the notary's down the street, or in the *loggia* of a neighboring house. These close encounters introduced a greater freedom in social relations. While blood relatives customarily ate together under the same roof and made this sharing into a right, and while affinally related families participated in the ritual feasting that sanctioned events important to their lineages, neighbors were invited to drop in for a glass of cool wine on a hot day or to stop for a snack outside the doorstep in simple gatherings that sealed neighborhood good feelings.[132] When he drinks wine with the baker, Cisti, messer Geri Spina becomes his "friend."[133] Thus Lapo must have drunk with the simple people among whom he chose certain of his *compari*. The goodwill of friends thus acquired or, more cynically, *comperati* (bought) (the expression is once again Morelli's)[134] satisfied a sociability that could not find complete expression in the constraining setting of the family and the lineage, or in the more formal relations of affinity, while at the same time it provided a complementary and locally-based support network.[135]

It is difficult to say whether Lapo is representative of people of his class in his systematic search for exogamous relationships and his utilization of *comparaggio* (the godparent relationship) on the very local level. An analysis of his book leads us to think that the small number of blood relatives available to be called on and the personal prestige he enjoyed early in life placed him in the somewhat exceptional position of needing to strengthen his prestige by allying himself out of the neighborhood and to compensate

132   "Arai una botte di vermiglio brusco, oloroso e buono, e simile il dì pe' gran caldi ritruovati co' tuoi vicini e con altri, e dà loro bere lietamente e proferra la botte e ciò che tu hai a ogni huomo" (You will have a barrel of tart red wine, with good taste and fragrance, and in this way on very hot days you will meet with your neighbors and others, and give them to drink merrily and offer the barrel and whatever you have to every man) (ibid., 261).
133   See Boccaccio, *Decamerone*, sixth day, second novella.
134   "Appresso, sia cortese: ingenati d'acquistare uno amico o più nel tuo gonfalone e per lui fa ciò che tu puoi di buono, e non ti curare per mettervi del tuo. Se se' riccco, sia contento comperare degli amici co' tuoi danari, se non puoi avere per altra via" (Next, be courteous: put your mind to acquiring one or more friends in your immediate neighborhood and do all the good you can for him, without stinting. If you are rich, be satisfied to buy friends with your money if you cannot have them by other means) (Morelli, *Ricordi*, 253).
135   See the observations of E. R. Wolf, "Kinship, Friendship and Patron/Client Relations in Complex Societies," in M. Banton, ed., *The Social Anthropology of Complex Societies*, 3d ed. (London and New York, 1966), 1–22.

this exogamy by spiritual alliance in a more restricted area. His recourse to different forms of kinship shows that, at least around 1400, a successful man's opportunities for action were still largely founded on kinship – but there were also occasions on which matrimonial strategy and choice of *compari* might violate his contemporaries' principles of action.

5

Sumptuary Law and Social Relations in Renaissance Italy

Diane Owen Hughes

> History has proved that all sumptuary laws have been everywhere, after a brief time, abolished, evaded or ignored. Vanity will always invent more ways of distinguishing itself than the laws are able to forbid.[1]

Voltaire's dismissal, written when sumptuary laws were on the wane in his own country, prompts the question, why, then, were they enacted? We do not have to wait until the eighteenth century to find reference to their futility. The concept of legislating against consumption was ridiculed almost from its inception, often by those who favoured controlling it. Franco Sacchetti, writing in Florence during the first century of its legislative activity against consumption, went further even than Voltaire to suggest that the law itself promoted what it sought to control. As the defeated enforcement officer in one of his *Trecentonovelle* explains to his superiors, legal insistence on restraint bred linguistic and stylistic invention:

> My lords, all the days of my life have I studied to learn the rules of the law, and now, when I did believe myself to know somewhat, I find that I know nothing. For when, obeying the orders that you gave me, I went out to seek the forbidden ornaments of your women, they met me with arguments the like of which are not to be found in any book of laws; and some of these I will repeat to you. There comes a woman with the peak of her hood fringed out and twisted round her head. My notary says, "Tell me your name, for you have a peak with fringes". The the good woman takes this peak, which is fastened round her head with a pin, and, holding it in her hand, she declares that it is a wreath. Then going further, he finds one wearing many buttons in front of her dress, and he says to her, "You are not allowed to wear these buttons." But she answers, "Yes, Messer, but I may, for these are not buttons but studs, and if you do not believe me, look, they have no loops, and moreover there

1   Quoted by Etienne Giraudias, *Etude historique sur les lois somptuaires* (Poitiers, 1910), pp. 103–4.

are no buttonholes." Then the notary goes to another who is wearing ermine and says, "Now what can she say to this? You are wearing ermine." And he prepares to write down her name. But the woman answers, "Do not write me down, for this is not ermine, it is the fur of a suckling." Says the notary, "What is this suckling?" and the woman replies. "It is an animal."[2]

The laws themselves tried to respond to this inventiveness of language and style: by the fifteenth century, the outlawing of expensive buttons involved the listing of *bottoni, maspilli* and *pianetti*; of headdresses, *berretti, cuffie, balzi, cappuci* and *selli*; of head ornaments, *cerchielli, ghirlande, corone, fruscoli, guazzeroni, frenelli* and *vespaii*. When the Venetian Senate in 1443 forbade women to wear dresses cut from cloth of gold or silver, they and their tailors began to use it to line sleeves, which were slashed or lengthened to let it show. This practice was outlawed in 1472; and finally in 1488 the Venetian legislators instructed their enforcement officers to report all changes in fashion.[3] The Genoese, a century later, required the Tailors' Guild to register new designs for approval by the censors, the so-called *Ufficio delle Virtù*.[4]

If legislators recognized a certain defeat in their innumerable preambles lamenting that their statutes were not observed,[5] their usual solution was not to abandon but to increase their legislative activity. The repeal in 1339 by the *Maggior Consiglio* of the voluminous Venetian sumptuary regulations of 1334 on the grounds that "they lead to confusion and civic impediment, as is clear to all and as even the officials constituted for this assert", is a rare example of a drawing back. And it had taken Zer Ziani Baduario, who proposed the repeal, three years to gather sufficient votes to push it through.[6] He certainly had later followers. Five citizens of Padua, two of whom were knights, accused the sumptuary law of 1504 of infringing liberty, damaging the city, and destroying marriage and lineage. But its supporters, who carried the day, argued that far from removing true liberty the law merely tried to restrain feminine licence, and that if it had not been passed a more drastic one would have been required.[7] Both in Padua and in Venice, cities

---

2 Novella 137.

3 Margaret M. Newett, "The Sumptuary Laws of Venice in the Fourteenth and Fifteenth Centuries", in T. F. Tout and James Tait (eds.), *Historical Essays by Members of the Owen's College, Manchester* (London, 1902), p. 275; G. Bistort, *Il Magistrato alle Pompe nella Repubblica di Venezia* (Venice, 1912), p. 372.

4 L. T. Belgrano, *Della vita privata dei Genovesi*, 2nd edn (Genoa, 1875), p. 265.

5 E.g. Siena, 1433, ed. Eugenio Casanova, "La donna senese nel Quattrocento nella vita privata", *Bullettino senese di storia patria*, vii (1901), p. 79.

6 Archivio di Stato, Venice (A.S.V.), Maggior Consiglio, Delib. spiritus, Reg. xxiv, 97; Newett, "Sumptuary Laws of Venice", p. 276.

7 Antonio Bonardi, *Il lusso di altri tempi in Padova*, Miscellanea di storia veneta, ser. 3, ii (Venice, 1910), pp. 166–7.

which have preserved records of the votes on sumptuary legislation, such arguments in its favour seem heavily to have outweighed its recognized defects.

Most cities turned their sporadic medieval legislation into formal Renaissance codes, which were endlessly amended in response to criticism and fashion. It has been calculated that the Italian cities produced eighty-three substantial sumptuary laws in the fifteenth century and more than double that number in each of the following two centuries.[8] Both Venice and Genoa produced at least eight pieces of extensive sumptuary legislation between 1450 and 1500, and other cities did not lag far behind. The Venetian Senate, in particularly productive sessions of 15 October 1562, issued four separate pieces of sumptuary law, one of which it modified only a month later. Turkish inactivity in 1562, which one observer claimed had given Venice the time to dedicate itself to luxury and display, may arguably also have given senators the time to turn from military affairs to matters of morality, but this certainly had not been the case in 1512 during the crisis of the League of Cambrai, when the Senate also enacted a major sumptuary code. As Venice's enemies gathered for the attack, the Senate debated dress materials, the size and design of sleeves, fringes and ornaments, belts and headdresses, shoes and slippers, home furnishings and bed linens.[9]

What provoked such legislative zeal? It may well have been the shock of losing so much of its *terrafirma* in 1509 that drove Venetians to "placate the anger of our Lord" by establishing a permanent magistracy to control consumption in the city, guiding it back to its moral foundations. The linking of private extravagance, moral degeneration and political decline had been the theme of moralists from Isaiah to Savonarola, and it is hardly surprising that citizen legislators should have seized on it in their hours of need. Although one might argue that the organization of Venice's *Magistrato delle Pompe* with offices at the Rialto and permanent boxes to receive anonymous accusations and the legislation of 1512, which its first magistrates guided through the Senate, fits into the city's psychology of loss during the crisis of the League of Cambrai,[10] such correspondence is rare. Padua had organized its magistracy before the beginning of the crisis;[11] other cities managed to conceive their long and repeatedly promulgated sumptuary laws without the guiding hand of special magistracies, just as Padua and Venice had done before the sixteenth century. And the laws themselves do

8   Rosita Levi Pisetzky, *Il costume e la moda nella società italiana* (Turin, *c.* 1978), pp. 30–6.
9   A.S.V., Senato, Terra, Reg. 18, 8 May 1512; Marino Sanudo, *Diarii*, ed. Federico Stefano, Guglielmo Berchet and Nicolo Barozzi, 58 vols. (Venice, 1879–1903), xiv (Venice, 1886), coll. 114–17.
10   As suggested by Felix Gilbert, "Venice in the Crisis of the League of Cambrai", in J. R. Hale (ed.), *Renaissance Venice* (London, 1973), pp. 274–92.
11   Bonardi, *Il lusso di altri tempi*, p. 82.

not, on the whole, follow the curves of crisis. Most major cities, with the significant exceptions of Milan and Genoa, issued their first sumptuary laws before the Black Death, for example; nor did that plague or any other encourage particular legislative activity against extravagance. Nor is sumptuary legislation linked in a simple or satisfying way to contemporary economic opinion or conditions. Born in a climate of expansion, it was several centuries old before Italian decline had set in.

Historians have tended, with Voltaire, to mock sumptuary legislation and, by implication, its legislators. At the best their impulses are labelled paternalistic, a term for which it is hard to find a definition without pejorative overtones. This label does not do justice to the fanaticism of legislating zeal within Italian Renaissance cities, nor does it explain the developmental aspects of the legislation. Finally, it obscures the fundamental question of why some societies – but not others – develop a passion to legislate against consumption. These questions lie at the centre of this chapter.

I

The first Italian sumptuary law is probably that contained in Genoa's first law code, the so-called *Breve della Campagna* of 1157, which banned the use of rich furs; but this restriction was omitted in its re-issue in 1161.[12] During the law's short life, the citizens of Genoa may have had the distinction of being the first to suffer such restrictions on dress since the days of the Carolingian empire. The aristocratic governments of other developing medieval cities do not seem to have issued sumptuary laws. They first appear, in the middle of the thirteenth century, in communes which had admitted the "popolo" in at least a partial way into the government: Siena, whose government issued a law regulating trains on dresses in 1249, had admitted *popolani* to the government for almost a decade; Bologna's similar decree in 1260 was issued by a government in which non-nobles had sat for over a generation, and its more extensive laws of 1288 were the work of a government which would go on to issue severe restrictions on its aristocracy; Florence's first (now lost) sumptuary law of 1281 was part of a general legal code produced by a compromise government in which a popular presence is unmistakable.[13]

12   F. Niccolai, *Contributo allo studio dei piu antichi brevi della campagna genovese* (Milan, 1939).
13   Robert Davidsohn, *Geschichte von Florenz* (Berlin, 1927), iv, pt. 3, p. 67; Ludovico Frati, *La vita privata in Bologna dal secolo XIII al XVII*, 2nd edn (Bologna, 1928), pp. 235–45; Hermann Kantorowicz and N. Denholm-Young, "De Ornatu Mulierum: A Consilium of Antonius de Rosellis with an Introduction on Fifteenth Century Sumptuary Legislation", in Helmut Coing and Gerhard Immel (eds.), *Rechtshistorische Schriften von Dr. Hermann Kantorowicz* (Karlsruhe, 1970), p. 357.

By this time sumptuary controls were being applied at various levels of European society. The Council of Montpellier had forbidden churchmen in 1195 slashings at the hems of their robes, and King Louis VIII had begun in 1229 to control the wardrobes of his nobles.[14] The character of the urban legislation, issued both in Italy and in southern France from the mid-thirteenth century, is significantly different from the royal: it does not regulate dress according to social hierarchy. Hierarchical considerations, absent from the Carolingian laws, have a place in Louis VIII's ordinance and are finely worked out in Philip the Fair's ordinance of 1294, which regulated the dress and furnishings (though not the food) of his subjects according to a system based on social rank and income. It has been argued that the restrictions were forced on the king by a nobility anxious to preserve its privilege in the face of royal advancement of the bourgeoisie.[15] If so, urban legislation seems to have found different advocates. None seems to be seriously concerned with hierarchy, and the Italian may show signs of an anti-aristocratic bias.

The limitation of numbers at weddings and funerals, if a form of sumptuary control, also served as a control on noble gatherings and a means, as Heers has suggested,[16] of weakening the power of those noble "clans" that had dominated the cities' early political life. In Bologna, for example, a proclamation of 1276, repeated in the statutes of 1289, deprived mourning of its focus for manifestations of family power.[17] Weeping at or striking the doors of the dead was forbidden, bells might be rung only at the place and time of burial, and a death might not be announced through the city. Those in attendance were limited to ten men and eight priests and the mourners at home, to male relatives within the fifth degree and women within the third. If torches were forbidden, candles limited, and shrouds regulated, the proclamation as a whole seems less dedicated to sumptuary than social control. Early clothing regulations also have an anti-aristocratic flavour. Siena's early reduction of trains on women's dresses, if it saved cloth, also censored an aristocratic style, one which by a later law of 1277 was completely forbidden to servants; and the outlawing of golden, jewel-bedecked crowns had similar overtones.[18]

They were laws designed less to keep down the upstart than to fetter the aristocrat. If it is true in Bologna from 1289 that knights and doctors of law

---

14   Pierre Kraemer, *Le luxe et les lois somptuaires au moyen âge* (Paris, 1920), pp. 33–4.

15   *Ibid.*, p. 89.

16   Jacques Heers, *Family Clans in the Middle Ages*, trans. by Barry Herbert (Amsterdam/New York, c. 1977), pp. 75–7.

17   Frati, *La vita privata in Bologna*, pp. 236–8.

18   Curzio Mazzi, "Alcune leggi suntuarie senesi del XIII", *Archivio storico italiano*, ser. 4, v (1880), pp. 133–44.

might go to their graves in "scarlet" and if in most of Tuscany certain exceptions were made for knights or members of the legal and medical professions, these seem to have been privileges exacted by those whose style of life
was most directly challenged by the laws. Women certainly knew who was
on their side. The intercessor who won for the women of Siena in December 1291 a few days' relaxation of the sumptuary law that forbade them
crowns and garlands of gold and pearls was Count Robert of Arras; just as
the annuller of a Florentine law of 1324 was the duke of Calabria.[19]

The sumptuary law, seen in this way as a curb on aristocratic display,
becomes a symbol of republican virtue. Savonarola's reformed city comes
to mind as perhaps the most fervent mating of sumptuary controls with
republicanism; and the memory outlived a generation of Medici rule: one
of the first acts of the re-established Florentine Republic in 1527 was the
publication of a new sumptuary law.[20] Despots also sought to control consumption, of course, but with less enthusiasm. One of the least active cities
in legislating against extravagance was Milan, whose first sumptuary code
seems to have been that issued by Gian Galeazzo in 1396 after his assumption of the title of duke of Milan. The law was re-issued virtually untouched
in its 1480 edition.[21] Within the duchy, the' impulse to legislate was urban.
The Sforza issued a sumptuary code in 1498, but not before the duke had
received at least one petition urging such action from nineteen "zealots of
the city of Milan"; and those emanating from the viceroys of the Spanish
king in the following century were meagre and largely devoted to proper
behaviour in church.[22] City authorities finally countered aristocratic torpor
in 1565 with the publication of a full and severe law; and it was citizens
again who in 1581 petitioned the king to regulate excessive consumption
and extravagance. Yet it took the virtual collapse of Milan's industrial
economy in the seventeenth century to coax from the authorities some
slender sumptuary codices.

The commissioners entrusted in 1581 with the promulgation of a new
sumptuary law so designed "that excess might be removed, but the decorum
and proper splendour of the city still be maintained", solicited citizen
opinion. One of the three extant replies recommended the sartorial hum-
bling of the noble: it required nobles to dress modestly, leaving the others,
especially prostitutes, free. The recommendation, written in the sceptical
tones of a man experienced through his travels in the ways of the world, in

19   Ibid., p. 138; Davidsohn, Geschichte von Florenz, p. 352.

20   Agostino Zanelli, "Di alcune leggi suntuarie pistoiesi", Archivio storico italiano, ser. 5, xvi
(1895), p. 210.

21   Ettore Verga, "Le leggi suntuarie milanesi", Archivio storico lombardo, xxv (1898), pp. 7–8.

22   Ettore Verga, "Le leggi suntuarie e la decadenza dell'industria in Milano, 1565–1750",
Archivio storico lombardo, xxvii (1900), pp. 53–5.

laws and their evasions, was taken up again and received more sober attention a few months later in a pamphlet entitled "A Way of Returning the People of Milan to Modest Dress". Both were undoubtedly inspired by Diodorus Siculus' account of the solution (recently revived by Montaigne)[23] of Zaleucus, the law-giver of the Locri, who restricted the freeborn and gave licence to whores and pimps. The unwillingness of the great to stain their honour by copying the lowly and disreputable would keep them modest, and the desire of the others to appear noble and honourable would make them modest. The pamphlet's suggestion of black, unornamented clothes for the great and powerful anticipates later laws which clothed noble women in black.[24] But in its permission of one heron plume to mark nobility, it suggests a mocking of the aristocratic pretensions that the earliest sumptuary laws strove to contain. We may be surprised that the pamphlet's author was a citizen of Lucca; but the Milanese seem to have found it natural to seek advice from foreigners. Another reply to the commissioners argued that Milan, so little able or willing to restrain extravagance through legislation, should turn to the example of other cities, and especially to Venice, a republic whose sumptuary codes regulated everything. They would also, though the Milanese respondent could not have known it, continue to be issued and amended until the republic itself had ceased to exist.

One would also like to define the economic motives behind the sumptuary laws, but they are harder to discern. The early, medieval laws showed little awareness of the point made by the worldly Milanese who wickedly proposed imposing restrictions at the top – that it was not simply man's pride that defeated the law but the needs of artisans "who seek their living in new inventions". So great was the opposition of Florence's luxury crafts to its severe sumptuary law of 1330, that within three years the officer to enforce it had to be appointed not by the usual civic commission but by the bishop of Siena.[25] If it was believed that foreign markets could compensate for those lost at home, the laws nowhere stated this. And, in any case, citizens must have been aware that the sumptuary laws of others also limited their markets, in the fourteenth century, the *Maggior Consiglio* of Venice forbade its citizens the use of cloth of gold';[26] contemporary sumptuary law in Nuremberg denied its citizens "silver cloth from Venice".[27]

The earliest sumptuary laws offered no economic explanations. When, in the last half of the fourteenth century, the custom of preambles began, we find some differences of approach between the maritime trading cities

23   *Essais*, i, ch. 43.
24   Verga, "Le leggi suntuarie" (1900), pp. 64–6.
25   Davidsohn, *Geschichte von Florenz*, p. 353.
26   Newett, The Sumptuary Laws of Venice", p. 275.
27   Kent Roberts Greenfield, *Sumptuary Law in Nürnberg* (Baltimore, 1918), p. 107.

and the more artisanal cities of the interior. Both Venice and Genoa emphasized investment: "our state has become less strong because money that
should navigate and multiply . . . lies dead, converted into vanities", said a
Venetian law of 1360;[28] "a great quantity of money which is kept dead and
wrapped up in clothing and jewels, converted into trade might bring great
returns and profits", began the Genoese law of 1449.[29] The cities of the interior expressed the need for restraint in almost exclusively moral terms. The
Bolognese laws of 1398 and 1401 were issued so "that the state might be
strengthened by good and honest customs and those pleasing to God".[30]
That of Siena in 1412 indicated a clearer sense that "it is necessary to
provide for a restraint of superfluous outlays from the purses of citizens, the
rich as well as the poor, for the conservation and utility and honour of the
Commune", but later preambles became even more general and moralistic.[31] The Pistoia legislation of 1558 also referred to the ruin of citizens,
which led to urban decline, but the legislators were thinking in the personal
and often strictly demographic terms that became common throughout
Renaissance Italy.[32]

Economic protectionism can be detected in some laws from about the
middle of the fifteenth century. The government of Siena began to back a
local silk industry in 1438, and by 1440 the commune had decided to fine
and brand anyone who removed a silkworker from the city.[33] While in its
total banning of silk garments (except for one pair of sleeves) in 1433, the
Consiglio Generale seems not to have considered the effects on Siena's
setaiuoli, who were necessarily doing business with silk acquired elsewhere,
its legislation of 1460 was protective of the new and still fragile industry. It
allowed Sienese women a few silken garments as long as they had been
made from cloth manufactured in the city.[34] Milan began in the seventeenth
century, after its prosperous silk industry had dramatically declined, to issue
protectionist legislation.[35] Protectionist attempts are, however, both late

28   Bistort, *Il Magistrato alle Pompe*, p. 66, n. 2. The law is edited, without the preamble, by
S. Romanin, *Storia documentata di Venezia*, 10 vols. (Venice, 1853–61), iii, pp. 386–9.
29   Belgrano, *Della vita privata*, p. 394.
30   Frati, *La vita privata in Bologna*, p. 242; Umberto Dallari and Luigi Alberto Gandini,
"Lo statuto suntuario bolognese del 1401 e il registro delle vesti bollate", *Atti e memorie della
R. Deputazione di Storia Patria per le Provincie di Romagna*, ser. 3, vii, p. 8.
31   Mazzi, "Alcune leggi suntuarie", p. 143.
32   ". . . onde aviene che assai giovani recusano amogliarsi, se gia excessiva dote et donera
non si danno, a tale che bene spesso le dote superano la sostanza et patrimonio dei mariti, et
le padri o fratelli delle fanciulle ne divengono poveri e nudi . . .", Zanelli, "Di alcune leggi
suntuarie", p. 214.
33   Luciano Banchi, *L'arte della seta in Siena nei secoli XV e XVI. Statuti e documenti* (Siena,
1881).
34   Casanova, "La donna senese", pp. 82–6, 89–93.
35   Verga, "Le leggi suntuarie" (1900), pp. 75–82.

and sporadic. They should not encourage us to believe that protectionism was generally an object or provocation of the law.

Nor do the sumptuary laws show a developed economic interest in bullion. Gold and silver, along with pearls and certain furs, form a privileged list of restricted items throughout the whole period of sumptuary control. The Sienese legislation of 1277–82 had allowed to women only one unadorned garland of silver for their heads, which was to weigh no more than two ounces. In Bologna in 1289 circlets for the head made of silver and gold were outlawed, as was almost every other ornament made of the precious metals. The fourteenth- and fifteenth-century allowance in many Italian cities of three gold rings became, like the single strand of pearls, a cliché of both law and contemporary portraiture. The restrictions were real, and the fines could be steep – in Siena £100 (or about one-half the average dowry of the period) for exceeding the two-ounce limit. But the level of concern seems to have borne no relation to the shifting price or availability of precious metals. In Venice where precious metal was regarded, at least by the beginning of the seventeenth century, as "the sinews of all government . . . , the patron of all",[36] its regulation in sumptuary law remained remarkably regular in times of shortness and in times of relative plenty. A law of 1443 forbidding Venetian women all cloth of gold and silver and embroideries employing the two metals seems, if not unusually severe, at least unusually serious, for the penalty exacted from fathers or husbands whose daughters or wives disobeyed was a forced loan of £1,000 payable to the state. The law's explanatory preamble, while it may indicate a rising cost of gold and silver, does not suggest that the legislators' chief concern was the metal market. What disturbed them was at once more personal and more remote: the recent custom of a bridegroom's gift to the bride of a dress of cloth of gold had risen from 150 or 200 to 600 ducats, "and every year these expenses grow, so that [the custom] is a consumer of our citizens, and what is worse, provokes the wrath of our almighty Creator".[37] In Genoa, where the fluctuations in the gold market were probably better understood than elsewhere, a law of 1449 allowing women up to £1,000 of gold and silver jewellery – far more than Siena and many other inland cities permitted their wives and daughters – was left essentially unchanged for more than half a century of increased availability of gold; and the new law of 1512 seems, without comment, to have reduced this allowance.[38] It is true that three merchants whose wives wore golden chains worth 25 florins

36   A Venetian senator, quoted by Fernand Braudel, *The Mediterranean and the Mediterranean World in the Age of Philip II*, trans. by Sian Reynolds, 2 vols. (New York, 1973), i, p. 462.
37   A.S.V., Senato, Terra, Reg. 1, p. 91.
38   Belgrano, *Della vita privata*, pp. 393–404; Archivio di Stato, Genoa (A.S.G.), Cod. Diversorum, x, 114, ann. 1511–12.

apiece in contravention of the law were hauled before a magistrate in 1453, but they escaped conviction by arguing that since the jewellery had been hidden by their clothes, it had not set a bad example.[39] Public morality, not money, was the magistrate's concern.

II

The church came at sumptuary legislation through the same moralistic door. Suspicious of an economy whose health lay in expansion, dependent on the use and manipulation of money, churchmen worried not about the economic consequences of the withdrawal of wealth from productive enterprise, but about the personal and social consequences of the victory of *luxuria*. If civic governments spoke of public and private ruin, the church spoke of corruption. The friars, confessors of the medieval Italian cities, looked to sumptuary legislation as a weapon in the war against sin. Fra Paolino, in his *Government of the Family*, written in 1304, just five years after Venice had promulgated its first sumptuary law, recommended the law as perhaps the only protection against the pride of wives whose personal desire for extravagance was supported by prevailing custom and pandered to by husbands. He thought the matter should be "regulated by laws after the manner of the Romans".[40] It was the social aspects of the related sins of pride, avarice and *luxuria* that the friars stressed. St Thomas had allowed that female display, even if it enhanced natural beauty, was usually not a sin so long as it was employed in pursuit of a husband; it was, in any case, venial, not mortal.[41] The Franciscan Orpheus de Cancellariis rejected this argument. The sin was mortal, he argued, not only because it was in contempt of God, but because, by threatening to ruin the fathers or husbands who supplied the wherewithal for their finery, women were a peril to others. And when their dress or habits were provocative; when, for example, they bared their shoulders or even their breasts, they became a public scandal. Orpheus admitted that the measure of extravagance was tied to fortune and that a woman could wear rich clothes without evil intention, but such expenses became a mortal sin if the clothes were unsuited to her station or would impoverish her and hence reverse her station.[42] San Bernardino of Siena went even further to set the question of extravagant dress in the

---

39   A.S.G., Div. filze, no. 20, 23 Jan. 1453, cited by Jacques Heers, *Gênes au XVᵉ siècle* (Paris, 1969), p. 65, n. 5.
40   Quoted in Cesare Foucard, *Lo statuto inedito delle nozze venetiane nel 1299* (Venice, 1858), Appendix.
41   *Summa Theologiae, Secunda Secundae*, quaestio 169.
42   Kantorowicz and Denholm-Young, "*De Ornatu Mulierum*", p. 355.

context of social charity, condemning extravagant trousseaux as extracted from the blood of the poor.[43]

The influence of the church in the promotion and direction of sumptuary legislation was important. There was undoubtedly a connection, for example, between the presence of the Franciscan Cardinal Latino in Florence for the negotiations preliminary to the establishment of a new government, and that government's promulgation in 1281 of the city's first sumptuary regulations. The cardinal, Salimbene tells us, had upset all women with a law restricting the length of their trains.[44] Churchmen remained active in encouraging sumptuary controls throughout the Italian peninsula. Florence had countered opposition to the sumptuary controls of 1330 by bypassing citizen commissions and giving responsibility for its enforcement to the bishop of Siena. So, too, under a military threat from Milan, the Venetian Senate appealed in 1438 to the patriarch Lorenzo Zustinian, who had the year before outlawed silk, trains, long sleeves or sleeves ornamented with pearls and hair adorned with gold, silver, pearls, or false tresses, threatening with excommunication all who disobeyed.[45] The Senate wanted him to help *them* control extreme headdresses and excessive trains by the same ecclesiastical means. In neighbouring Padua, the Council, in 1460, sought from the bishop a definition of the length of trains the church would allow women, which they agreed to include and enforce as part of the sumptuary code they were then enacting.[46] The Council had, in any case, been goaded into action by the Franciscan Jacopo della Marca, whose influence on the city seems to be reflected in the record of the Council's votes. An attempt to limit the train of a woman's dress to one-quarter of a *brachia* had been passed in 1440 by 47 votes to 4; and a more general restriction on women's clothing in 1459, by 51 votes to 11.[47] These are fairly typical fifteenth-century figures; in the following century the number of votes cast was slightly higher, but the margin of victory somewhat narrower. In 1460, however, after Fra Jacopo had stirred the city, the long sumptuary code, voted in three sections, was passed by 114 to 0 (with three votes to amend), 121 to 6, 117 to 9.[48] The issue had risen to the level of popular concern.

Renewed episcopal activity under the influence of a strong papacy probably stimulated sumptuary legislation throughout Italy in this period. In some places, the church assumed full or substantial responsibility for the promulgation of the law. Citizens seem to have found episcopal legislation

43   *Le prediche volgari*, ed. L. Banchi (Siena, 1880), pp. 193–4.
44   *Cronica*, in *Monumenta Germaniae Historica, Scriptores*, xxxii, p. 169.
45   Newett, "Sumptuary Laws of Venice", p. 259.
46   Bonardi, *Il lusso di altri tempi*, p. 150.
47   *Ibid.*, pp. 141–6.
48   *Ibid.*, pp. 149–50.

particularly hard to bear, both because of its severity and because of its penalty – excommunication. When Ginevra Sforza married Sante Bentivoglio in 1454, clothed with twelve attendants in gold brocade, a cloth the sumptuary law of Cardinal Bessarion had just denied to all Bolognese women, the church of San Petronio closed its doors to the bridal party. It went on to San Giacomo, where the friars married the couple, but some of the party suffered excommunication for flouting the law.[49] Everyone knew, of course, that the church also dispensed. The noble Venetian Cristina Corner managed in 1438 to secure from the pope for four and a half ducats, "in honour of her parents and in respect of her own beauty", the right to contravene the sumptuary regulations of the patriarch.[50] In Perugia, where the bishop had taken over sumptuary concerns in the middle of the fifteenth century, the pope allowed, in 1468 and 1469, episcopal absolution of those who had incurred excommunication by flouting his legislation.[51] But the need for papal intervention is perhaps a measure of the effectiveness in this period of the combined force of mendicant preaching and episcopal legislation against extravagance.

It would be wrong to see sumptuary legislation as a simple response to ecclesiastical demands. Initially the aims of the church and those of city governments seem to have differed. Cardinal Latino, whose limitation of trains was in line with contemporary urban legislation, also ruled that women must cover their heads, an ordinance which, according to Salimbene – if no lover of women, an admirer of their abilities – encouraged the production of silken veils woven with gold, "which all the more encouraged lust in the eye of the beholder".[52] But this concern for female modesty did not find its way into contemporary civic codes, which on the contrary began to restrict first the sumptuousness of female head coverings and then the anonymity they might provide.[53] Yet ecclesiastical attempts to control seductiveness in female dress (and deportment) do seem to have made headway throughout Italy in the course of the fifteenth and sixteenth centuries. The Piacenzan chronicler De Mussis was commenting as early as 1388 on "shameful dresses . . . called *ciprianae* . . . which . . . have such a large neck that the breasts show: and it looks as if the said breasts want to burst from the bosom".[54] But only one commune, Perugia, whose legisla-

---

49 Frati, *La vita privata in Bologna*, p. 35.

50 Bistort, *Il Magistrato alle Pompe*, pp. 71–2 (and a similar petition of the same date, pp. 72–3).

51 Ariodante Fabretti, *Statuti e ordinamenti suntuarii . . . in Perugia dall'anno 1266 al 1536*, Memorie della R. Accademia de Scienze di Torino, ser. 2, xxxviii, pp. 137ff.

52 *Cronica*, p. 170.

53 Siena ruled against veils as early as 1342. They allowed the customary mantle, which might be held with the hands, but not fixed in some more permanent way; for a woman's face "should be open and clear". Casanova, "La donna senese", pp. 71–2.

54 *Placentinae urbis descriptio*, ed. Muratori, in *Rerum Italicarum Scriptores*, xvi, p. 579.

tion already reflected the influence of ecclesiastics, had acted (in 1342) to control *décolletage* "beneath the collarbone".[55] Milan, where the Dominican Galvano Fiamma had disapproved in the first half of the fourteenth century of the bare throats and necks of its women, seems to have waited for almost a century before legislating against such exposure, and then only in the mildest way: low-cut necklines were allowed as long as the shoulder bones were covered in some other way.[56] The law encouraged women to resort to those shoulder covers of transparent silk mousseline (often embroidered with gold) which formed a part of many contemporary trousseaux.[57] It was only at the end of the fifteenth century that Milan, in legislation of 1498, outlawed necklines lower than one finger – placed sideways, as they took care to specify – from the collar-bone.[58]

By then a movement to cover female flesh was under way. Florence had already, in a law of 1456, forbidden any "baring of the throat and neck" although in 1464 the government had relented and allowed a *décolletage* of about three centimetres from the collar-bone in front and twice that amount from the neckbone behind, measures which, as portraits of the period show, were not rigidly observed.[59] Savonarola, however, made of *décolletage* a major issue, insisting on a two-finger measure. Like the Franciscan Orpheus de Cancellariis, who reminded his readers that the baring of shoulders and breasts, by making the woman a public scandal, brought style to the level of mortal sin, Savonarola inquired whether such display was the sign of an honest woman.[60] By the sixteenth century, Venice and even Genoa, whose women had a reputation for daring display, had begun to regulate the amount of flesh they might expose. A Genoese law of 1506 insisted on lower hemlines, while one of 1511–12 decreed that women must cover completely their shoulders and the "two bones before the throat", regulations that neighbouring Savona copied in 1531.[61] A Venetian law of 1562 ruled more liberally, and certainly more realistically, that camisoles or other coverings of the shoulder must be "so closed in front that the breast is covered".[62] Whatever the details of the legislation, they had become persuaded that such rules were necessary to ensure "la honestà muliebre".

55   Fabretti, *Statuti e ordinamenti suntuarii*, p. 95.
56   Verga, "Le leggi suntuarie milanesi" (1898), p. 22.
57   *Archivio storico lombardo*, ii, p. 65.
58   Verga, "Le leggi suntuarie milanesi" (1898), p. 50.
59   E. Polidori Calamandrei, *Le vesti delle donne fiorentine nel Quattrocento* (Florence, 1924), pp. 64–6.
60   Quoted by Pisetzky, *Il costume e la moda*, p. 39.
61   Emilio Paniani, *Vita privata genovese nel Rinascimento*, Atti della Società Ligure di Storia Patria, xlvii (Genoa, 1915), pp. 154–63.
62   Bistort, *Il Magistrato alle Pompe*, pp. 388–9.

The records of prosecution for contravention of the sumptuary laws clearly suggest that fellow citizens failed to accuse and the authorities themselves were reluctant to pursue women who disobeyed such rules of modesty. In Venice and Padua, for example, records of prosecution and even conviction for extravagance exist for the sixteenth century; but there seems to be no mention of a woman cited for the plunge of her neckline.[63] This stands in clear contrast with prosecutions in Bern in the following century, where almost 65 per cent of the 133 cases of unlawful clothing in 1681 were concerned with exposure.[64]

The growing association in Italian cities of *décolletage* with shame should be seen in the context of a larger change in the direction of the law. Early sumptuary legislation can be divided fairly evenly into laws concerning clothes (often those of men as well as women), weddings and funerals. Although the expenses involved in the ceremonies and feasts accompanying marriage and burial rose steadily with their further elaboration and although new and extravagant customs surrounding parturition and baptism ate into household budgets, legislation directed against ceremony declined significantly in the fifteenth century in relation to that directed against clothing, particularly the clothing of women (see figure 5.1). While some of this can be accounted for by legislators' attempts to counter rapid changes in style or evasions in the law, like those Sacchetti relates, that alone cannot explain the change, which the preambles to the laws enshrine. The preambles to the Venetian sumptuary laws of 22 May and 9 June 1334 locate in both sexes the extravagance they intend to attack, but that of 1360 mentions only "vanities" which are directed towards "brides and other women and ladies".[65] Most fifteenth-century preambles state explicitly that women are the ruin of men.[66]

Both the rhetoric and the timing of the dramatic focus on women in the fifteenth century, when ecclesiastical sumptuary activity was at its height, point to the church's role. Although it sporadically regulated excesses in clerical dress, the church's interest in lay extravagance had a distinctly feminine focus. The code that Jacopo della Marca urged on the Paduan Council was designed to rectify the "superfluous apparel and wanton expense surrounding the women of the city and district", and all its clauses deal with this problem. So, too, the legislation of Cardinal Bessarion in Bologna in 1453 was devoted to feminine dress.[67] Even where the church role is less

---

63 *Ibid.*, pp. 20–60; Bonardi, *Il lusso di altri tempi*, pp. 97ff.

64 John Martin Vincent, *Costume and Conduct in the Laws of Basel, Bern, and Zurich, 1370–1800* (Baltimore, 1935), p. 104.

65 Bistort, *Il Magistrato alle Pompe*, p. 66, n. 2: 329–52.

66 E.g. Casanova, "La donna senese", pp. 80–2 (Siena, 1426–7).

67 Bonardi, *Il lusso di altri tempi*, p. 147; Archivio di Stato, Bologna, Comune, Libro Novarum provisionum, f. 132.

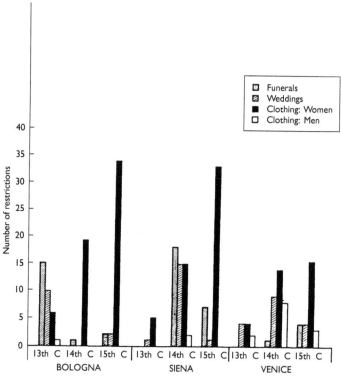

Figure 5.1 A comparison of sumptuary restrictions in three cities.

obvious, we often detect an association between ecclesiastical pressure and a narrowing of sumptuary interest to women. Bologna's laws of 1398 and 1401 were the first completely to exclude consideration of ceremonial extravagance and to focus on women; and while both were issued by urban authorities, their dating "in the time of the pontificate of Boniface IX" suggests ecclesiastical guidance. Padua's first two sumptuary laws of 1277 and 1398 regulated ceremony – weddings, baptisms and funerals. All of the fifteenth-century laws – issued in 1440, 1459, 1460, 1482 and 1488 – were devoted to female extravagance.[68]

But if the church's pressure both encouraged and directed sumptuary law in the fifteenth century, the legislation could count, as the votes in Padua show, on substantial popular support. Apart from generalities and clichés, it is hard to assess the response of women to their newly privileged

68   The early laws are cited by Bonardi, *Il lusso di altri tempi*, pp. 9–11; the later, edited by him, pp. 141–54.

sumptuary position. In Bologna, Cardinal Bessarion's law did provoke a female protest – from Sante Bentivoglio's learned and beautiful lover, Nicolosa Sanuti, whom Sabadino degli Arienti described on a hillside wearing a gown of purple silk and a rose-coloured cloak lined with the finest ermine.[69] She might have heard of events a year earlier in Siena, where the Emperor Frederick III had stopped with his fiancée Leonora of Portugal on the way to their coronation and marriage in Rome. Battista Petrucci, the daughter of a professor of rhetoric, had given a Latin recitation so appreciated by the couple that they asked her to select a reward. She chose release from all sumptuary regulations, a request which the city government reluctantly conceded.[70] Sanuti, however, argued not only for herself but for all the women of Bologna. Her elegant oration[71] reminded the cardinal that although Roman women had been limited in their use of gold and precious cloth during the rigours of the Second Punic War, freedom in finery was restored to them after the crisis had passed. That law, imposed by conditions of war, might be understandable, but it was hard to excuse the Bolognese restrictions, devised to feed the avarice of husbands who put money before dignity. They showed no concern for the domestic disruptions which would be a certain consequence of their restrictions, an argument that some Paduan nobles would use at the beginning of the next century in an attempt to defeat that city's sumptuary controls over women. The histories of women of the ancient world as well as the lives of many women of her own day proved, she argued, that feminine abilities could equal those of men: many resembled that "Amesia, whom, since she bore a manly spirit beneath a female form, they called Androgynos". Individual women of Bologna could rise, like some of their Greek and Roman predecessors, to heroic action; and collectively, she reminded the cardinal, they had within them the power of the Sabines – to save a civilization from demographic ruin. Women deserved freedom of choice in clothes because it was to clothes that they had been reduced. If one conceded (as surely the cardinal would) that "as patricians from the people, so should remarkable women differ from the obscure", then, she concluded, the sumptuary restrictions should be lifted.

> Magistracies are not conceded to women; they do not strive for priesthoods, triumphs, the spoils of war, because these are considered the honours of men. Ornament and apparel, because they are our insignia of worth, we cannot suffer to be taken from us.

69   Cecilia M. Ady, *The Bentivoglio of Bologna* (Oxford, 1936), pp. 141–54.
70   Orlando Malavolti, *Historia . . . de' Fatti e Guerie de' Sanesi, cosi esterne come Civili* (Venice, 1599), parte 3, b. 38b.
71   Ed. in Frati, *La vita privata in Bologna*, pp. 251–62.

In a letter to her lover on the eve of his marriage to Ginevra Sforza, a despairing Nicolosa Sanuti recanted.[72] But she had been right. Clothes were women's insignia, and the legislators knew it. They knew, too, that men had become implicated in them: they designed and made them, their money bought them, their status was reflected in them. In 1343 the rich women of Florence lined up before a notary to register the clothes they owned which were in contravention of the recently promulgated sumptuary law, which allowed that such clothes might continue to be worn as long as they were taxed and marked with a special lead seal bearing the Florentine lily on one side and a cross on the other. The clothes, recorded in an extant register,[73] show that same restless variety as the laws designed to control them: dresses (usually of silk) take the form of sleeved and sleeveless under-dresses and overdresses, often accompanied by cloaks and mantles, in various hues of red, blue and green, sometimes striped or pierced with white or contrasting colours, trimmed with fabric embroidered or woven with crowns, stars, rosettes, butterflies, birds and dragons. But from such sump-tuous riot some order emerges. Lady Guerriera, the wife of Jacopo di Antonio de Albizis, and her sisters-in-law Nera and Piera all registered gowns and matching tunics of green samite (a heavy silk often interwoven with gold). The same Guerriera and Nera registered mantles of white cloth embroidered with vines and grapes of blood-red and lined in cloth of shim-mering white. Their clothes appear just after those of their mother-in-law Joanna, who distinguished herself from them in counterpoint: a cloak of purple to their white and blood-red; a dress of scarlet with silken crowns, which reflected the green of the gowns of her daughters-in-law only in its lining. Dinga, the daughter of Sandro Altovito, and Lisabetta, the daughter of Gentile Altovito, came together to register their identical and elaborate tunics, which were divided into two spheres of red, then checked with silk, and trimmed with yet another fabric. Relationships can be as easily guessed from the clothing lists as from the names. Nor are we dealing here with simple thrift – some cloth and a tailor for all the women of a household. Lady Ginevra, the wife of Agnolo di Giani de Albizis, probably a distant relative of Joanna and her daughters-in-law, who lived in another district of the city, had earlier registered the single piece of her clothing which was in contravention of the law and on which she chose to pay the tax – a mantle of white cloth embroidered with vines and blood-red grapes, lined in cloth of shimmering white. Those brilliant and distinctive cloaks must have become Albizi insignia. Even the limited view of wardrobe that this register of outlawed clothes gives us provides a glimpse of a society that

---

72   Ady, *Bentivoglio*, p. 57.
73   Partly edited by Paolo d'Ancona, *Le vesti delle donne fiorentine nel secolo XIV* (Perugia, 1906).

described itself through clothes. Is it any wonder that the ordering of dress became for legislators a metaphorical way of talking about social distinction, a way of ordering human relations?

III

Fashion, in its delicate balancing of "the desire for imitation and differentiation", signifies, as Simmel observed, "the form of the social process".[74] Unlike more hierarchical societies, whose rules repressed such a process, or poorer ones, whose poverty forbade it, the urban society of medieval Italy measured progress in terms of its dynamic. For Riccobaldo of Ferrara, looking back at the end of the thirteenth century on the times of Frederick II, the past was simple and static, lacking both splendour and social movement. Clothes were plain, ornaments few, meals frugal, and dowries small.[75] More censorious critics like Dante looked back on such simplicity with nostalgia; and Villani even hoped that the sumptuary laws would restore it. But sumptuary law of the thirteenth and fourteenth centuries sought to restrain, not to re-order. Pistoia's extant sumptuary law of 1332 seems to be based on the Florentine law of 1330 which Villani applauded in his chronicle.[76] Of its twenty-seven sumptuary provisions, only two were arguably more concerned with style than with excess, regulating the wearing of bi-coloured garments. Most of the others regulated yardage, material and ornament. If this reflected the realities of dress, which was of simple cut, depending for its effect on the quality and amount of material and on accompanying ornament, it also reflected a society more attuned to excess than disorder.

By the middle of the fifteenth century, however, as women's costume, with the extraordinary development of ruffs, bodices and detachable sleeves, became a series of interchangeable parts, fashion and change became a new target of the law.[77] It sought to regulate the rapidly shifting parts of an unstable whole, which even Cesare Vecellio, in his popular book on fashion, found hard to grasp.[78] In Venice on the eve of the crisis of the League of Cambrai the Senate debated fashions in sleeves. The debate had begun in 1503 when the legislators outlawed "manege a comedo", those

---

74   Georg Simmel, *Philosophie der Mode* (Berlin, 1914), pp. 8–9.
75   *Historia Universalis*, in *Rerum Italicarum Scriptores*, ix, col. 128.
76   *Statuti suntuarii ricordati da Giovanni Villani . . . ordinati dal commune di Pistoia*, ed. Sebastiano Ciampi (Pisa, 1815).
77   On these costume developments, see *Abbiglamento e costume nella pittura italiana*, i: *Rinascimento* (Rome, *c.* 1962), pp. 103ff.
78   *Degli habiti antichi et moderni di diverse parte del mondo* (Venice, 1590), p. 141.

great leg-of-mutton sleeves which Lotto's subjects so favoured for their portraits and which the Senate found "an ugly fashion" requiring three or more
brachia of cloth of gold or silk for their execution.[79] By October 1504 the
senators recognized that that "dishonest fashion that is not appropriate to
women" had been replaced by "another fashion, larger and uglier than the
first", and they decided to ban all sleeves wider than one third of a *brachia*
at any point.[80] Within a year, they were outlawing "certain fashions and
new apparel, both offensive and dishonest, which were never before used in
this city" – namely, sleeves cut of many pieces of fabric of diverse colours.[81]
On 4 January 1507, the Senate complained that sleeves of the *investidure*
had grown larger every time the matter had been legislated about. "And if
[women] are granted the right to put six *brachia* [into the sleeves], in a few
months they will grow to an even larger size, so that they can be called not
sleeves of the *investidure* but sleeves of the gown itself and it will become
necessary to concede more."[82] They repeated the former limits and
restricted the sleeves of the gown, the so-called "manege ducali", to 32
brachia of silk or 28 of serge or another non-silken fabric. In the difficult
summer of 1509, the doge spoke before the *Maggior Consiglio* and
accounted for Venice's decline by the inordinate length of its sleeves.[83] The
concern for expense is, of course, ever present: every extra *brachia* was a
drain on the individual, and the point of the doge's speech was to encourage Venetian nobles to pay their state debts. But in the eyes of Renaissance
legislators, fashion changes bred worse than excess or extravagance, they
bred disorder. The *Consiglio Generale* of Siena spoke for more than that city
when, in 1426, it announced that fuller and more inclusive sumptuary legislation was needed in the city since laws against previous extravagances
had simply inspired worse ones.[84] The need to right the disorders of fashion
seems to have extended beyond mere expense. Comments and laws on the
disorder of clothes and the disruptiveness of fashion seem to have reflected
a growing, if less easily expressible sense of social disorder. And the endless
ordinances (*ordini*) to right the disorders (*desordini*) of dress seem to be ways
of talking about a society which had lost its right order, a society in which
(by Simmel's definition) differentiation had got out of hand.

Sumptuary law struck hardest at splendour and expense when they
encouraged unacceptable differentiation and withdrawal from the social

---

79   A.S.V., Senato, Terra, reg. 14, f. 197.
80   *Ibid.*, reg. 15, f. 37.
81   *Ibid.*, f. 77.
82   *Ibid.*, f. 190. The *investidura* seems to have been a full dress that might in fact come with
or without sleeves. See Bistort, *Il Magistrato alle Pompe*, p. 353, n. 4.
83   Sanudo, *Diarii*, viii, col. 497.
84   Casanova, "La donna senese", p. 80.

process. Sumptuary law was frequently lifted, on the other hand, to allow citizens properly to fulfil their civic (and highest social) function. Siena had allowed prohibited clothes to be worn for a short time in 1291 for the coming of Robert of Arras; and in 1459 the Venetian Senate, in order to welcome and impress the French ambassadors to the city, voted to require all women in attendance to appear in bright dresses and wear the jewels and ornament generally prohibited by the law.[85] Certain individual extravagance was actually encouraged when its effect was the fuller integration of the individual into the social fabric. Thus in Venice the Senate decided in 1433 to legislate in favour of more sumptuous dress for councillors of the doge, who had adopted the unfortunate practice of wearing sombre robes except during their hours of government service. A century later the *Maggior Consiglio* addressed itself to the same problem and registered a decree forcing councillors to wear their scarlet robes, which they seem to have given up doing.[86] Useful splendour was one thing, fashion another. Under the rule of fashion, clothing lost both its real function and its emblematic significance. Shoes that impeded walking, robes and accessories that confused or concealed rather than expressed identity – such perversions were the sign of a profoundly disordered society. The Milanese friar Pietro Casola remarked on the similarity between the Chinese custom of binding women's feet to make them smaller and the Venetian one of wearing shoes on platforms so that "they appear giants".[87] If such shoes kept feet from the mire, the legislators knew that women really wore them because "through the height of the shoes gowns can be made much longer".[88] The resulting "enormous and excessive expenses" were to be lamented, but the chief concern of the laws enacted against them was functional: these shoes, like bound feet, impeded walking to such an extent that, according to Casola, some women "are only kept upright by the support of slaves". Legislation against veils, which seems to have begun in Siena in 1343 and had little economic purpose, was concerned with the freedom from proper identification that such veils accorded their wearers. Officials of the commune were empowered to demand, on encountering a veiled woman, the name of her father and husband, her "terzo", "popolo" and

---

85   A.S.V., Senato, Terra, reg. 4, f. 126.

86   A.S.V., Misti, reg. 59, f. 12; Maggior Consiglio, Diana (33), f. 199; Newett, "Sumptuary Laws of Venice", p. 249.

87   He had visited Venice in 1494 on his way to and from the Holy Land. *Viaggio di Pietro Casola a Gerusalemme* (Milan, 1855), p. 14.

88   A.S.V., Maggior Consiglio, Ursa, f. 81, 2 March 1430; and see Bistort, *Il Magistrato alle Pompe*, pp. 168–71. In Genoa, such shoes were not outlawed, but the length of the skirt was fixed in 1449 at one *palma* whether they were worn or not: Belgrano, *Della vita privata*, p. 398. The association of platform shoes with prostitutes is clear not only in Sienese law but in contemporary costume books like Vecellio's.

"contrada".[89] This let them discover the names of those responsible for paying the fine if her clothing was in contravention of the sumptuary law but, more importantly, it restored an identity which clothes were meant to convey, not obscure. The perversion of purpose of the shoes and clothing perverted the wearer and society itself. Great platform shoes so impeded walking that "pregnant women walking on the road with these shoes [which are] so high that they cannot hold themselves up, fall and in the event destroy or abort their children, to the perdition of their body and soul".[90] Veils that masked perverted the function of normal headcoverings, which were commonly worn by women and had been endorsed by Cardinal Latino in the thirteenth century; their purpose was to protect the honour and modesty of the wearer. The mask, on the other hand, allowed a freedom akin to licence. In Siena, high platform shoes and veils fixed over the face to mask it were allowed only to one class of women – to prostitutes, women who lived outside the usual social categories.

The difference between *meretrix* and *matrona* stands at the heart of sumptuary distinction. Zaleucus' suggestion that only prostitutes be permitted rich dress as a means of shaming the virtuous into simplicity was taken up in the laws of some Italian cities: Siena allowed them not only platform shoes but also the dresses of cloth of gold and clothes painted or embroidered with trees, fruits, flowers and animals which it denied to other women; Brescia devised similar allowances.[91] In other cities, prostitutes were assigned more humiliating marks of distinction: in Venice, yellow scarves; in Milan, a cloak of common fustian, whose colour – white in the original law of 1412 – was changed to black in the new sumptuary code of 1498.[92] In most places prostitutes were increasingly segregated. In Genoa, for example, a city that did not identify them by either rich clothing or humiliating marks, a series of laws began at the end of the fourteenth century to confine prostitutes to a special district. This made it easier for communal officials to stand at the bordello door and collect the new tax imposed in 1418; but fiscal purposes were secondary.[93] Prostitutes were considered such outsiders in Ferrara by the end of the fifteenth century that

89   Casanova, "La donna senese", p. 70. In Venice in 1443 the Senate ruled that women could not cover their heads except to go to church, for veiling covered too many dishonourable acts: Terra, reg. 1, f. 105. A *crida* of the duke outlawed veils in Ferrara in 1476 for the same reason: Bernardino Zambotti, *Diario ferrarese dall'anno 1476 sino al 1504*, ed. Giuseppe Pardi, *Rerum Italicarum Scriptores*, 24–vii (Bologna, 1935), p. 6.
90   A.S.V., Maggior Consiglio, Ursa, f. 81.
91   Casanova, "La donna senese", pp. 53, 59, 61–2; A. Cassa, *Funerali, pompe, conviti* (Brescia, 1887), p. 100.
92   Bistort, *Il Magistrato alle Pompe*, pp. 264–6; Verga, "Le leggi suntuarie milanesi" (1898), pp. 68–9.
93   The tax was eventually transformed into a fixed monthly payment. Belgrano, *Della vita privata*, pp. 329–33.

responsibility for them was assigned to the same officials who collected the taxes on imported goods.[94]

Other women the sumptuary rules sought not to separate but to incorporate. Nicolosa Sanuti was right to notice that the legislation, by denying women clothing as an emblem of achievement, pushed them into a separate social category. And the legislators' frantic effort to deprive women of individual distinction or constant differentiation through fashion, certainly created for all women a kind of sumptuary ghetto. Nevertheless, at least part of the law's purpose was more positive than contemporary preaching and moralizing might seem to suggest. It sought to reconcile a woman's dual legal personality, as the daughter of one lineage and wife in another. The moment of reconciliation was marriage, when men's honour and position were most publicly displayed through their women, particularly through brides in whom the honour and position of the two houses merged. The bride, at that moment, dowered and arrayed in a trousseau, stood poised between the two sumptuary states – between childhood, when to a greater or lesser extent she might be indulged, and matronhood, when she would be struck by the full force of the sumptuary law.

Sumptuary restrictions in most cities were noticeably less severe for young, unmarried girls. In fourteenth-century Siena young women (*mulieres juvines*) were permitted a little additional jewellery, and in contemporary Lucca girls under the age of nine were allowed to wear more extravagant clothes.[95] Marriage signified almost everywhere the moment of passage from one sumptuary status to another: in Bologna in 1289, as in Lucca in 1337, that was when women lost the right to wear certain extravagant decorations.[96] The full refinement of the Genoese law of 1449[97] lets us explore the basis for such legal distinctions between children and married women. It explicitly established a period of sumptuary liminality which girls entered on the attainment of sexual maturity, or at least on becoming eligible to take a husband. At the age of twelve, the jewellery given them as children had to be put away. Although when she married, a trousseau pushed the Genoese bride towards sumptuary adulthood, the law demanded three further years of partial restraint when she could not receive from either her own family or her husband's any more than one silk dress, which could not, in any case, be dyed a fine red, and when all garments of silk pile were denied her. Three years from the day she crossed the threshold of her husband's house (the so-called *transductio*), she came of sumptuary age. Within this long period, the daughter was separated from

94   Zambotti, *Diario ferrarese*, p. 209, where the author reports his activities in this office.
95   Casanova, "La donna senese", p. 61; *Bandi lucchesi del secolo decimoquarto*, ed. Salvatore Bongi (Bologna, 1863), pp. 49–50.
96   Frati, *La vita privata in Bologna*, p. 239; *Bandi lucchesi*, pp. 47–53.
97   Ed. in Belgrano, *Della vita privata*, pp. 393–405.

her father's largesse, which was restored only on the day of her marriage, as trousseau; on this she had to live and dress while she was integrated into her new home. By the end of that period, it might well be understood that she would produce an heir and so move physically as well as legally from the status of *sponsa* to that of *matrona*. The period of greatest sumptuary restraint and special sumptuary status thus coincided with those years when her sexuality (and hence the honour of the man who was her legal guardian) was most at risk: when sexually mature, she had no husband; when married, she had borne no child.

No city found such distinctions totally satisfactory. By the beginning of the following century, Genoa had decided to allow girls to wear until they were taken into marriage golden headdresses that the law would deny them as wives.[98] The new approach may have been made necessary by the growing inability of fathers to arrange unaided the marriages of their daughters. Every city had come to feel by the fifteenth century that the institution of marriage itself had become a source of social disorder, from which fathers and daughters, not husbands, suffered most. The Venetian senator Giovanni Garzoni spoke in 1420 for more than himself or even his city, where dowries, trousseaux and other nuptial gifts had so increased that many nobles could not marry their daughters without ruining their heirs and estates; they were accordingly shut up in convents or kept at home unmarried.[99] The Senate's regulation of marital gifts and assigns was typical: a limit of 1,600 ducats for the dowry and trousseau, the latter set at no more than one-third of the whole. An attempt a few months later to repeal it was driven back, and the only exceptions eventually allowed were for the halt and the blind, the twisted and hunchbacked, whose deformities won them larger dowries.[100] Yet throughout Italy dowries went up, and laws to restrain them multiplied. The cry was everywhere the same: "our youth are no longer given to doing business in the city or at sea, or in other praiseworthy enterprise, placing all their hope in these excessive dowries";[101] "so many young men refuse to marry if they are not first given excessive dowries and gifts, with the result that the price of dowries exceeds the substance and patrimony of husbands, and the fathers or brothers of the brides become poor and are stripped bare by them".[102]

If demographic evidence suggests that men were marrying later and less frequently and that the convents were becoming fuller, the sumptuary evidence suggests that women who did marry were felt to have the whip hand over husbands whose livelihood seemed more and more to depend on their

---

98 A.S.G., Cod. Diversorum X, 114, ann. 1511–12.
99 A.S.V., Senato, Misti, reg. 53, f. 70.
100 Bistort, *Il Magistrato alle Pompe*, p. 108.
101 *Ibid.*, pp. 111–12: Venice, 1535.
102 Zanelli, "Di alcune leggi suntuarie", p. 214; Pistoia, 1558.

dowries. It is no wonder that such men lashed out at the changing fashions of their wives, which not only ate into the estate but also seemed to signify their loss of control. A series of new restrictions were passed overwhelmingly in Padua in 1555. Only one item was close: by a vote of 63 to 62 the Council barely agreed that the fines of 25 ducats would be paid by the fathers or husbands of the offenders.[103] Did they fear that by their inability to enforce the law at home, they would be called on publicly to pay up? It was certainly husbands who usually paid, since wives rather than daughters were called to account. In Siena, all the sumptuary cases which came before the court in the autumn months of 1438 concerned married women; and in 1475 the secret accusations that trickled into the office of the *Tre Segreti* assigned to sumptuary matters were also directed primarily against wives.[104] The later registers of Venice and Padua, cities whose laws show more varied sumptuary interests, record more contraventions by men, both at table and in their clothing. When the three censors of Padua heard in March 1554 that weddings in the city had been encouraging a sartorial splendour in contravention of the sumptuary laws, they visited the sites of the parties and ceremonies and prepared a list of the offenders: thirty-three men and thirteen women, only three of whom were unmarried.[105] The two extant Venetian registers, which begin in the last quarter of the seventeenth century, record a variety of sumptuary offences. One is devoted entirely to prostitutes; almost all the women in the other are married.[106]

Although most cities appointed special prosecutors and encouraged private accusation by awarding the accuser both secrecy and a portion of the fine, enforcement seems always to have been less important than the invention of the law itself. They expressed in it, or tried to, their fears for their society. On 8 May 1512, the Venetian sumptuary official Vetor Morexini rose to speak against Venetian women who "formerly would dance only with a scarf, and today will dance only with masks: they go into the fields to dance, they dance the *balla dil capello*".[107] He held their attention, and they voted against the dancers; for they all knew that his motion expressed more: a society led away by unknown women who danced the "balla dil capello", a French dance in which the women picked their partners.

Women were an object of fear, their power sufficient to ruin cities. Yet there was a gulf between most of the urban legislation and the ecclesiastical ranting of contemporary Isaiahs who sought to "smite with a scab the

103   Bonardi, *Il lusso di altri tempi*, pp. 186–92.
104   Casanova, "La donna senese", pp. 46–50, 86–9.
105   Bonardi, *Il lusso di altri tempi*, pp. 270–5.
106   Bistort. *Il Magistrato alle Pompe*, pp. 302–9.
107   Sanudo, *Diarii*, xiv, col. 200; Bistort, *Il Magistrato alle Pompe*, pp. 222–4.

crown of the head of the daughters of Zion" because they "are haughty, and walk with stretched forth necks and wanton eyes, walking and mincing as they go, and making a tinkling with their feet".[108] For it was issued by men who were fully implicated in female folly. They lived off the condemned dowries, they paid for the forbidden dresses, whose splendour reflected their status, and they generally appeared in court and paid the fines demanded for contravention of the law by their women. In talking about women, their dress and deportment, men were talking about themselves and about their often conflicting roles as fathers and husbands. But they did not just talk, they acted.

We must distinguish between *enforcement*, which failed, and *legislating*, which achieved objects of its own. The doge Andrea Gritti, on the way to the ceremonies marking his coronation in 1523, was being ostentatious in sending home a female relative to change out of her outlawed dress of cloth of gold; just as the earlier wedding festivities of a Corner and Loredan in the city in 1512 when "the women [were] obedient to the ordinance [because] they feared the *provedadori* would condemn them", are remembered for that concern.[109] Where prosecutions were undertaken, appeal and influence often let the guilty escape. And, of course, one could simply take the fines as a kind of luxury tax, an experiment which had been tried as early as 1299 in Florence and which finds a place in the Genoese and Sienese legislation of the fifteenth century – *pagar le pompe*, as the Venetians said.[110] The process of legislating had better success. The endless codes attest to it. So does the sense of development within them of, for example, the relations between fathers and daughters, husbands and wives.

It is striking in a society whose single most important transfer of personal assets had arguably become a woman's dowry (which even in marriage she continued to own) that so much legislation was designed to keep women from wearing their wealth. This infuriated women rich in their own right, as Nicolosa Sanuti's oration shows. Some communes came to allow women to display their dotal worth, "since all should not be equal to all", as the Genoese put it when they established jewellery limits based on the value of the dowry a woman took into her marriage.[111] But the wealth which determined what a woman might wear was always paternal wealth – what she had received as her father's daughter. When Siena toyed with this system, in 1424, it limited the gifts husbands might give to their wives at marriage and established the limit as a percentage of the dowry.[112] This

---

108   Is. iii. 16–17.

109   Sanudo, xix, col. 443; cols. 161–2.

110   Davidsohn, *Geschichte von Florenz*, IV, iii, p. 67; Mazzi, "Alcune leggi suntuarie senesi", p. 143; A.S.G., San Giorgio, Institutiones Cabellarum, carte 170 (anno 1402); Newett, "Sumptuary Laws of Venice", p. 259.

111   Belgrano, *Della vita privata*, pp. 395–404.

system stressed patrilineal distinctions at a time when rising dowries were exaggerating them. If hungry husbands were the villains of sumptuary laws which set limits on dowries, the wealth they gained did not keep the wives who brought them from being distinguished, ever more clearly, as their fathers' daughters.

By the sixteenth century many cities had stopped legislating about women as primarily daughters or wives; for hierarchical considerations had risen to supplant lineal ones. The early laws of most Italian cities made some hierarchical distinctions, but they pertained more frequently to men than to women, and hierarchy was used more as a means of excusing the powerful than of regulating the whole.[113] In its fully hierarchical sumptuary plan, the Bolognese law of 1474 was, however, almost a response to Nicolosa Sanuti's demands. Colour alone would have placed a woman: gold for the wives and daughters of knights, sleeves of gold for those of notaries, bankers and similar grandees, crimson for those of important artisans, but only crimson sleeves for the women whose husbands and fathers belonged to the humbler trades. Although a husband's gifts to his wife were still tied to her dowry, the limit established varied according to his rank: doctors and gentlemen might spend up to two-thirds the value of the dowry; others, no more than one-half. And women, when they married, left behind the rank of their fathers to assume a place in the hierarchy beside their husbands.[114] Given the visible consequences of such a move, daughters must have been increasingly reluctant to marry down. Rich women or the wives of rich husbands might, within the bounds of the law, still dress more splendidly or more eccentrically than their peers; but it was largely rank that distinguished them – rank which for most of their fashionable lives was in the gift of their husbands. In April 1476, Messer Lorenzo di messer Antonio de' Lanti of Siena was called before the office of the *Tre Segreti* because his wife had worn silk velvet. He tried to explain that he was a keen observer of the laws; that the gown had cost less than one of more ordinary material; and that anyway his father had been knighted by the king of Cyprus in Milan.[115] The officials would have none of it. In addition to the doubtful nature of his title, his tax assessment was not high enough to allow him entrance into the highest ranks of Sienese society. He paid the fine; and

112   Casanova, "La donna senese", pp. 79–80.

113   Bologna's law of 1289 let knights and doctors of law go to their graves in cloth of scarlet. Siena's of 1343 also permitted their wives to do the same; but only the men of those professions might wear cloth of gold in their lifetime. Frati, *La vita privata in Bologna*, pp. 236–7; Casanova, "La donna senese", pp. 52–72. The law of Pistoia of 1332, which seems to be modelled on the Florentine law of 1330, lets the wives of knights, judges and doctors wear more gold and silver and precious fur than the wives of other citizens were allowed. Ciampi, *Statuti suntuarii*, p. xi.

114   Frati, *La vita privata in Bologna*, pp. 245–8.

unless he intended to keep paying, his wife had to give up her velvet dress.

Hierarchical solutions created new forms of distinction, which can be most fully delineated in the seventeenth and eighteenth centuries when Italian legislation began more to resemble those codes issued by northern monarchs, who wanted to keep the economy up and upstarts down. Yet the legislation may have had its roots in the same social needs. Renaissance legislators tried to create order at those points in social organization where structure was ambivalent, particularly where social ideology was in conflict with many social practices. Their society had an ideology of orders but was in practice governed by money, which could alter position and rank. Clothes were a visible sign of this conflict: a better tax position would probably have let Messer Lorenzo's wife clothe herself in cloth of gold. Their society had a patrilineal ideology but was governed in everyday life by a confusion of cognatic, patrilineal and conjugal arrangements. This had the effect of splintering women's social identity, while giving them, as status-bearers of their fathers' lineage and their husbands', a position of increasing dominance within the household. High dowries and accompanying marital gifts were a sign of this, diminishing fathers and the economic strength of the patrimony, and at the same time diminishing the power of husbands in the home. These structural inconsistencies, for which there was no real cure, created social tensions which the legislation sought to remedy and which the *process* of legislating may have eased. They became clearly visible in Italian cities in the thirteenth century, as men who rose through money became politically significant and assumed political power and as urban governments, freed from aristocratic control, began in a concerted way to attack lineal bonds and organization. It is not a coincidence that this was when the sumptuary legislation began.

Italian sumptuary legislation was, among other things, an approach to easing tensions caused by structural problems of a local social nature. Though it resembled the legislation of the northern monarchies, and even more closely that of German and Swiss cities, it was far less hierarchical than the one and far more anti-feminist than both. But Europe did in a sense form a sumptuary whole, expressing its frustration over social problems it could not fully solve through legislative control over their outward signs. These signs can be controlled by formal, often religious means in societies where orders attain the rigidity of caste, and they are generally allowed as more legitimate expressions of identity in a society ordered by class. In Renaissance Italy, a society that dreamed of orders while facing the daily consequences of class fluidity, they had to be controlled by legislation.

---

115   Archivio di Stato, Siena, Tre Segreti sulle vesti, n. 1, f. 2, quoted by Casanova, "La donna senese", p. 38, n. 4.

6

The Virgin on the Street Corner: The Place of the Sacred in Italian Cities

Edward Muir

On nearly every street corner in the back alleys of Venice, one can still find the Virgin Mary.[1] She usually presents herself as a modest statue or crude painting, or sometimes only a faded picture postcard set up within a niche or frame (*capitello*) on the outside wall of a house or church. Thousands of images of Mary, the saints, and Christ proliferated throughout the city, encouraged by religious orders and parish priests but most often produced by neighborhood or private devotions. Beginning in 1450 the republic charged a local patrician with responsibility for watching over these images, and in the residential neighborhoods they still flourish. Historians can never recapture all their functions and meanings in the little and great dramas of urban activity, but these Madonnas and saints had many lives. Some depicted the patron of the parish church, extending the sacrality of the church outward through a neighborhood cult; others worked miracles, cured the afflicted, and guarded against plague; some succored the poor, protected against street crime, or discouraged blasphemy; and most reminded the living of their obligations to pray for the dead.[2] Saintly images created a setting where reverential behavior was appropriate, and the

---

1   Portions of this article have been adapted from an article co-authored with Ronald F. E. Weissman, "Social and Symbolic Places in Renaissance Venice and Florence," in *The Power of Place*, ed. John Agnew and James Duncan (London and Boston: Allen & Unwin, 1989).

2   Antonio Niero, "Per la storia della pietà popolare veneziana: Capitelli e immagini di santi a Venezia," *Ateneo Veneto*, n.s., 8 (1970): 262–7 and idem, "Il culto dei santi nell'arte popolare," in A. Niero, G. Musolino, and S. Tramontin, *Sanctità a Venezia* (Venice: Edizioni dello Studium Cattolico Veneziano, 1972), 229–89. Cf. M. Nani Mocenigo, "I capitelli veneziani," *Le Tre Venezie* 17 (1942): 224–7 and Paolo Toschi, "Mostra di arte religiosa popolare," *Lares* 13 (1942): 195–7.

ubiquity of images may point to a social style characterized by formality and the pervasiveness of ritual and theatricality in daily life. Intercessors with the divine permeated urban spaces in many Italian cities to such a degree that rigid distinctions between sacred and profane, so typical of the Reformation, must have seemed alien, even irreligious, to many who lived in towns magically tied together by little shrines. Italian towns, moreover, were themselves mystical bodies, a corporation both in the legal sense and the literal one of a number of persons united in one body, nourished and protected by a civic patron saint.[3] Citizenship was not just a legal distinction but one of the principal social influences in identity formation.

But situating little holy places about the city like fountains hardly guaranteed appropriate behavior. In an attempt to reduce street violence, Udine followed such a strategy by erecting images at the entrances of each quarter and on certain houses and by encouraging neighborhood cults, but the city fathers largely failed to pacify their community.[4] Local context determined the social significance of holy places, and the multiple touchstones of the sacred in Italian cities – street-corner Madonnas, parish churches, monasteries, confraternity chapels, even government buildings – created tangled, overlapping, and conflicted religious commitments among believers which resembled the agonistic character of their social lives.[5] In the relationship between place and the sacred, one finds contradictory tendencies – some that promoted tensions and urban conflicts, others that fostered spiritual community. By focusing on the relationship between social behavior and the character of the holy, one can see both how humans create sacred objects and places and how these influence behavior.

In her essay, "The Sacred and the Body Social in Sixteenth-Century Lyon," Natalie Zemon Davis analyzes the symbolic configurations of urban religion and treats Protestantism and Catholicism as "two languages which, among many uses, could describe, mark and interpret urban life, and in particular urban space, urban time and the urban community."[6] Whether or not the sacred could be localized in space became, after all, a major issue in the theological conflict between Catholics and Protestants, the former

---

3   Hans Conrad Peyer, *Stadt und Stadtpatron im Mittelalterlichen Italien* (Zurich: Europa Verlag, 1955). Ernst H. Kantorowicz, *The King's Two Bodies: A Study in Medieval Political Theology* (Princeton: Princeton University Press, 1957).
4   Antonio Battistella, "Udine nel secolo XVI: La religione e i provvedimenti economico-sociale," *Memorie storiche forogiuliesi* 20 (1924): 5.
5   Ronald F. E. Weissman, "Reconstructing Renaissance Sociology: The 'Chicago School' and the Study of Renaissance Society," in *Persons in Groups: Social Behavior as Identity Formation in Medieval and Renaissance Europe*, ed. Richard C. Trexler (Binghamton, N.Y.: Center for Medieval and Early Renaissance Studies, 1985), 44–5.
6   Natalie Zemon Davis, "The Sacred and the Body Social in Sixteenth-Century Lyon," *Past and Present* 90 (1981): 42.

insisting on the divine presence in the Eucharist and treating relics as special objects of devotion, the latter refusing to acknowledge such an impious mixing of spirit and matter. But the dispute was never purely theological. Relations with the sacred provide an idealized pattern of earthly social relations, and changes in attitudes toward the sacred altered the means by which Renaissance townspeople might form their social identity.[7] Even before the Reformation many Italian cities exhibited religious heteroglossia, to adopt Bakhtin's term, multiple languages through which various social groups approached and understood the location of the sacred.[8] Structured in part by dogma and in part by the relations between clergy and laity, a language of religious symbolism is also the product of the "distinctive experience of the people who use it."[9] It is this peculiarly lay language of the sacred that wants recapturing, an argot discovered in what Angelo Torre calls the "consumption of devotions."[10] Despite many dialectal variants, two forms, I would suggest, dominated in Italian cities.

One might be called the prophetic language, unstable in time and space, appearing, disappearing, and reappearing according to the vicissitudes of events. Prophecies played a major role in lay culture, as Ottavia Niccoli has shown in her analysis of the pamphlets sold by itinerant ballad singers and preachers after piazza performances. During the political disintegration of Italy after 1494, editions of prophecies multiplied, but after the Peace of Bologna in 1530, they virtually disappeared, except perhaps in Venice.[11] The notorious plasticity of prophecies, subject to highly imaginative reinterpretations, made them alluring in unstable times but apt to evanesce after a short time.

The second kind of sacred language, and for our purposes the more important, might be called the iconic, in which holiness tended to adhere

---

7   William A. Christian, Jr., *Apparitions in Late Medieval and Renaissance Spain* (Princeton: Princeton University Press, 1981).

8   Mikhail Bakhtin, *Rabelais and His World* (Cambridge, Mass.: MIT Press, 1968). Katarina Clark and Michael Holquist, *Mikhail Bakhtin* (Cambridge, Mass.: Harvard University Press, 1984). Tzvetan Todorov, *Mikhail Bakhtin: The Dialogical Principle* (Minneapolis: University of Minnesota Press, 1984), 56, 72–3, 77.

9   Davis, "The Sacred and the Body Social," 67.

10   Il consumo di devozioni: rituali e potere nelle campagne Piemontesi nella prima metà del Settecento," *Quaderni storici*, n.s., 58 (1985): 181–2.

11   Ottavia Niccoli, "Profezie in piazza: Note sul profetismo popolare nell'Italia del primo Cinquecento, *Quaderni storici* 41 (1979): 514–15. Cf. idem, "Il re dei morti sul campo di Agnadello," *Quaderni storici* 51 (1982): 929–58. I have not yet been able to consult Niccoli's new book on prophecies. On the survival of a prophetic tradition in Venice after the period Niccoli discusses, see Marion Leathers Kuntz, *Guglielmo Postello e la "Vergine Veneziana": Appunti storici sulla vita spirituale dell'Ospedaletto nel Cinquecento* (Venice: Centro Tedesco di Studi Veneziani, Quaderni no. 21, 1981). John Martin discussed a late sixteenth-century millennialist group of Venetian artisans in "The Sect of Benedetto Corazzaro," a paper presented at the Sixteenth Century Studies Conference, Tempe, Arizona, October 30, 1987.

to an object or a place, sometimes in direct defiance of theological doctrine. The sacred presented itself in temporal cycles rather than with apocalyptic finality and had a more fixed relationship to space than the prophetic language, although all venerated objects were potentially mobile and some actually so, regularly moving about the city in processions. The iconic language offered citizens immediate and personal intimacy with the saints rather than the future collective salvation promised by the prophets, and images and relics had intensely meaningful relationships with urban spaces, not only because the devout wished to see and touch such objects, but also because the moving of images and relics through city streets in processions celebrated *communitas*. The perpetuation of the procession's salubrious effects was one of the objectives in erecting images of the Virgin in public places. Virgins in many locations created a different kind of procession, one actively experienced by citizens as they walked about following their daily affairs.[12]

The meanings conveyed and behaviors evoked by these images, however, could hardly be controlled or predicted. In particular, women may have reacted very differently from men to the Virgin, and since Jews could not be expected to respond as Christians, authorities had to face the reality that their cities were never fully united. In Venice and other cities where ghettos were established, residential segregation created zones free from Catholic notions of sacred spaces, and the movement of non-Christian residents about the rest of the city was carefully restricted, since they would not be influenced toward righteousness by the Virgin Mary or Saint Francis. In a few cases Jews were even allowed to destroy Christian images painted on the walls of their houses, although the reaction of the Christian populace to such perceived defilements might be quite violent.[13] Despite the variety of behavior stimulated by such images, established norms defined appropriate responses.

Most Italian urban laymen and women were likely to seek communion with the saints through a proper self-presentation rather than through an agonized Augustinian self-examination on the issue of sincerity. In his recent historical anthropology of Italy, the "land of façades," Peter Burke proposes what he calls the "sincerity threshold." Higher in the North of Europe than in the South, the sincerity threshold operates on a "kind of sliding scale . . . so that a stress on sincerity in a given culture tends to be associated with a lack of emphasis on other qualities, such as courtesy. . . . Paradoxical as it may seem on the surface, sincerity cultures need a greater

12   Niero counted 406 images of the Virgin in the streets of Venice. "Il culto dei santi," 264–85.

13   Michele Luzzatti, "Ebrei, chiesa locale, 'Principe' e popolo: Due episodi di distruzione di immagini sacre alla fine del Quattrocento," *Quaderni storici* 54 (1983): 847–77.

measure of self-deception than the rest – since we are all actors – while 'theatre cultures', as we may call them, are able to cultivate the self-awareness they value less."[14] Burke seems to mean that it is more important in the North than the South to make statements on intention correspond to overt actions. In the southern theater cultures, norms are more often established in behavioral rather than verbal terms; thus, the issue of intention and sincerity is less likely to arise. The goal of social relations in a theater culture is similar to that of dramatic acting: to create the appearance of effortless, natural behavior even though all may be calculated. Such an emphasis on appearances correlates with the belief, which anthropologists find characteristic of Mediterranean societies, that "seeing" is the only reliable source of knowledge.[15] The Virgin hovering in every street required a performance, and even for the pious the most important thing was to bring it off.

Thus, when approaching the various sacred images and objects, the devout conveyed reverence through a demonstration that one had been properly socialized.[16] To calm a riotous crowd, priests would proceed through the city with a miracle-working image or relic. But there also remained a deep ambiguity about the range of behaviors acceptable in the presence of the sacred. Its separation from the corruption of business activity (seemingly required of Christians by the example of Christ's casting out the money-changers from the Temple) was often transgressed in Renaissance Italy, where the market needed holy objects to facilitate business and where, for many, religious behavior was merely another form of negotiation. Requiring an atmosphere of trust for the extension of credit and the firming of business deals, traders and artisans sought to sanctify their commercial dealings by notarizing, signing, and witnessing their contracts in a church where the parties might be invested with a fear of divine punishment for breaking their word.[17] One of the oldest standing churches in Venice, for example, is in the center of the Rialto market, and elsewhere saints' shrines became the site for market fairs. Such profane uses provoked protests from reforming preachers, such as Bernardino of Siena, but they enjoyed little success in isolating churches from the mundane, at least until the Counter-Reformation.

14   Peter Burke, *The Historical Anthropology of Early Modern Italy: Essays on Perception and Communication* (Cambridge: Cambridge University Press, 1987), 12–13. Cf. David I. Kertzer, *Ritual, Politics, and Power* (New Haven: Yale University Press, 1988).

15   David D. Gilmore, "Anthropology of the Mediterranean Area," *Annual Reviews in Anthropology* 11 (1982): 197–8.

16   Richard C. Trexler, *Public Life in Renaissance Florence* (New York: Academic Press, 1980), 45–128. Cf. Moshe Barasch, *Gestures of Despair in Medieval and Early Renaissance Art* (New York: New York University Press, 1976). Michael Baxandall, *Painting and Experience in Fifteenth-Century Italy: A Primer in the Social History of Pictorial Style* (Oxford: Clarendon Press, 1976), 56–71.

17   Trexler, *Public Life*, 111–12, 263–70.

Ambiguity about the proper use of churches, of course, reached back to the concept of sacred space peculiar to Christianity. Peter Brown has argued that one of the distinguishing characteristics of early Christianity was its belief in the mobility of the sacred.[18] Christians replaced sacred wells, caves, and trees with Christ's eucharistic body and the corpses of martyrs for the faith, objects which could be moved from place to place. Churches and monasteries were holy because of the ceremony of consecration but also because of the activities they permitted and the objects they contained: "The place does not sanctify the man but the man the place," and the church is not essential to the relic but the relic to the church. In devotional practice holiness was revealed in gradations of intensity: some things were more holy than others. Even Saint Bernardino argued that a sacrilege against a holy object was far worse than one simply perpetrated within a holy place.[19]

Such distinctions manifested themselves in numerous ways. *Ex votos* clustered around a reliquary or a miracle-working image reflected a sensitivity to the location and intensity of the holy, and pilgrimages encouraged belief in the efficacy of gaining access to sacred objects.[20] Lay devouts often seem to have considered images as signs that indicated the presence of the saint rather than as symbols that brought the saint's spiritual qualities to mind. The impulse to decorate and embellish churches (especially altars) may have come in part from an underlying anxiety about the mobility of the sacred. A saint who was ill-treated or forced to dwell in shabby surroundings might just allow his or her body to be "translated" elsewhere. And the theft of relics was always a danger. Many of Venice's most important relics, including the body of Saint Mark and the head of Saint George, had in fact been stolen in North Africa or the Near East and brought to Venice by traveling merchants and crusaders.[21] Anxious about such possibilities, Italian citizens' and clerics sought to fix sacred objects in particular places by arguing – often through hagiography, pious legends, and apparitions – that a saint favored" a certain place or church. The emanations of ecclesiastical buildings confused spirit and matter in a manner that would become especially offensive to reformers. Although Catholic theology placed strict limits on sanctified objects and rejected as pagan the notion that places could be sacred by themselves, popular practice tended nonetheless to create sacred places. Leon Battista Alberti, who saw all spaces in the

---

18   Peter Brown, *The Cult of the Saints: Its Rise and Function in Latin Christianity* (Chicago: University of Chicago Press, 1981), 86–105.
19   Quotation from Francesco da Barberino as translated in Trexler, *Public Life*, 52–4.
20   Cf. Burke, *Historical Anthropology*, 209–10.
21   Edward Muir, *Civic Ritual in Renaissance Venice* (Princeton: Princeton University Press, 1981), 78–102. Patrick J. Geary, *Furta Sacra: Thefts of Relics in the Central Middle Ages* (Princeton: Princeton University Press, 1978).

mathematics of proportionality and geometry, was puzzled by the mystic hierarchy of places created, he thought, by popular beliefs. But in recognizing how widespread such attitudes were, he conceded that the architect must prescribe fixed places for religious statues.

> I wonder how most people can so credit the opinions transmitted by our ancestors that it is believed that a certain picture of a god [or saint] situated in one place hears prayers while a statue of the same god a short distance away is unwilling to heed appeals? Not only that but when these same, most venerated images are moved to a different place, the people lose faith in them and quit praying to them. Such statues, therefore, must have permanent, dignified locations set aside for them alone.[22]

Complex social patterns and traditions enmeshed sacred places in a profusion of ambiguities that forced concessions to popular beliefs, which were themselves often highly creative. At the present state of research perhaps all that can be achieved is a very tentative suggestion of the varieties of these relationships. To do so, one might compare Venice, Florence, Naples, and Udine. As often happens in Italian history, systematic comparisons are difficult, especially because research in these cities has concentrated on different periods. Given the diversity of Italian regions, moreover, it would be absurd to argue that these cities are representative or typical, but they do encompass a calculated variety by including two major city-republics and two cities linked by formal feudal ties to the countryside and dominated by a "foreign" power. By the end of the sixteenth century Naples was the largest of these cities, indeed the largest of Christendom. With a population of 280,000, it was twice the size of Venice, three times that of Rome, four times that of Florence, and nearly twenty times the population of Udine.[23] Within each of these cities diverse social groups expressed their devotion in various ways. Diversity seems to have been most dramatic in Naples, least evident in Venice. Particularly before 1530, Florence displayed a range of competing forms, and the laity of Udine lacked a deeply-rooted Christian language of the sacred, at least in comparison to that of other Italian towns.

As a "theater state" Venice, like Counter-Reformation Rome, most effectively interpreted an iconic language for the purposes of maintaining public

---

22   Leon Battista Alberti, *L'Architettura [De Re Aedificatoria]*, ed. Giovanni Orlandi (Milan: Edizioni il Polifilo, 1966), 2: 661–3 (book 7, chap. 17). The translation is mine. The passage is analyzed in Joan Gadol, *Leon Battista Alberti: Universal Man of the Early Renaissance* (Chicago: University of Chicago Press, 1969), 150–1. Also see Lionel Rothkrug, "Holy Shrines, Religious Dissonance and Satan in the Origins of the German Reformation," *Historical Reflections* 14 (1987): 146 and idem, "German Holiness," 161–4.
23   Fernand Braudel, *The Mediterranean and the Mediterranean World in the Age of Philip II*, 2 vols. (New York: Harper & Row, 1972), 1: 345.

order.[24] The doges succeeded in permanently capturing Saint Mark for themselves, and although Mark was the patron of all Venetians, after the fourteenth century he was so surrounded by institutional barriers that he was limited to silent service at the placid center of the state cult. In Venice processional routes included the whole city and tied the neighborhoods to a ceremonial center where a vast architectural frame set apart ritual performances. In Piazza San Marco, as in Rome's Piazza San Pietro, a large public square retained a special character derived from the sacred activities that took place there, and through an escalation of magnificences during the late sixteenth century, these two cities defiantly reasserted the incorporation of the sacred into worldly spaces.[25]

The salient feature of Venice's distinctive cityscape was its center, where the most prestigious and powerful institutions clustered around the Doge's Palace and adjacent Basilica of Saint Mark. Exhibiting weaker forms of neighborhood organization than in other cities and a high level of residential mobility evident as early as the thirteenth century, Venetian parishes played a small role in forming citizens' social identity.[26] Males from patrician families pursued rewards and influence by competing for civic offices and seeking government favors; thus in Venice patronage was more city-wide and less neighborhood-bound than in Florence, Genoa, or probably most other Italian cities.

Venetian patronage, however, may have been peculiarly sex- and class-specific. Dennis Romano has suggested that Venetian patrician women, in contrast to their husbands, developed well-articulated local patronage networks largely because women were secluded in their palaces and seldom appeared in public beyond the parish confines. Romano has found evidence that lower-class women in the fourteenth century frequently chose a patrician woman from their own parish to act as executor of their wills whereas lower-class men almost never designated a male patrician to serve in this delicate capacity. Neighborhood patronage among males in Venice fell to the better-off commoners, especially to the secondary legal elite of *cittadini*, who dominated, for example, the parish-level priesthood. A Venetian priest's influence came less perhaps from his role as confessor, spiritual advisor, and preacher than from his involvement in the secular world.

24   Cf. Clifford Geertz, *Negara: The Theatre State in Nineteenth-Century Bali* (Princeton: Princeton University Press, 1980), and Burke, *Historical Anthropology*, 10, 174.
25   Muir, *Civic Ritual*. Charles Stinger, *The Renaissance in Rome* (Bloomington: Indiana University Press, 1985). Burke, *Historical Anthropology*, 168–82.
26   Stanley Chojnacki, "In Search of the Venetian Patriciate: Families and Factions in the Fourteenth Century," in *Renaissance Venice*, ed. J. R. Hale (London: Faber and Faber, 1973), 59–60. Rona Goffen, *Piety and Patronage in Renaissance Venice: Bellini, Titian, and the Franciscans* (New Haven: Yale University Press, 1986), 27–8.

Parish priests served as executors of wills, held the power of attorney, acted as notaries, invested in commercial ventures, and were particularly valued as sources for small loans.[27] Apparently indifferent to parish affairs, the upper class male Venetian experienced the sacred by joining a city-wide confraternity or by acting as a lay patron for a monastery or mendicant church as did Italians of other cities. In fact, a significant minority of wealthy Venetians sought burial sites outside of their parish and paid for tombs in convents, monasteries, or mendicant churches often located at some distance from the family house or place.[28]

For the various annual feasts the Venetian doge and signoria attended special masses throughout the city, and in comparison to other cities, especially Florence, Venice more often commemorated historical events important for the entire city in its civic liturgy and less often recognized local patrons or important ecclesiastics.[29] Lay officials exemplified their control by dominating sacred places. Unlike Florence, neither parishes, *sestieri* (quarters), nor any other neighborhood division was ever represented after the fourteenth century in a Venetian ritual. The constituent elements of the Corpus Christi rite in Venice, for example, were corporate groups, especially the confraternities, which were carefully regulated by the Council of Ten, and the greatest annual festival, the marriage of the doge to the sea, engaged secular and ecclesiastical hierarchies, arranged according to a rigid protocol precedence, in a mystical union with the watery environment.[30] In comparison to other Italian cities except perhaps Rome, Venice displayed the most precise hierarchy of sacred and profane spaces, a time-bound, sometimes inverted, occasionally subverted hierarchy, but nevertheless a symbolic scheme which organized much of the urban plan. In most other cities the relative strength of private power ensured that private groups would successfully compete with public authority by elevating their private spaces to a high symbolic position.

The goal of the public control of space, to be perhaps too crudely simple, was to influence the loyalties and obligations of individuals. To accomplish this, the sacred was employed iconically to work a miraculous restructur-

27   Dennis Romano, *Patricians and Popolani: The Social Foundations of the Venetian Renaissance State* (Baltimore: Johns Hopkins University Press, 1987), 91–102, 131–40. Romano has further discussed the decline of Venetian parishes after 1297 in a superb paper, "Politics and Parishes in Early Renaissance Venice," presented at the annual conference of the Renaissance Society of America, New York, March 18, 1988. Also see Richard Mackenney, *Tradesmen and Traders: The World of the Guilds in Venice and Europe, c. 1250–c. 1650* (Totowa, N.J.: Barnes & Noble Books, 1987), 47.

28   Romano, *Patricians and Popolani*, 102–18; Mackenney, *Tradesmen and Traders*, 56–61; Brian Pullan, *Rich and Poor in Renaissance Venice: The Social Institutions of a Catholic State, to 1620* (Oxford: Basil Blackwell, 1971), 33–196.

29   Muir, *Civic Ritual*, 212–23.

30   Ibid., 119–34.

ing of social obligations in a way impossible merely through the legal expansion of public domination over urban spaces. In Venice, the necessity of controlling a difficult habitat, that ever recalcitrant space that would disappear into the sea without consistent intervention, led to the subordination of neighborhood-based loyalties in the interest of collective ecologic survival. Only the highly personalized street Virgins and saints had strong neighborhood ties, but the central government encouraged devotion to these images and they never seem to have threatened the hegemony of Saint Mark, who had a greater, more unifying, and more lasting hold on Venetian loyalties than anyone or anything else. The civic triumphed in Venice, not completely, perhaps, but completely enough to allow centrally located institutions to dominate the Venetian social and spatial order.

Multicentered Florence, in contrast, had various sources of social power and a physical geography with several distinct and dominant visual foci.[31] Major institutions were dispersed throughout the city, creating a physical geography that was visually and conceptually chaotic. Up to the end of the fifteenth century Florence was the home of prophetic publications in Italy, a sign of instability furthered by the absence of a single source of the sacred that triumphed over all others.[32] In Florence neighborhood clients were still the base for a political career, and in contrast to Venice there was a greater tendency for patricians to identify with their neighborhood by sponsoring works for the local church, as the Medici did so famously with San Lorenzo.[33]

Outside of the political class, Florentines found their most vital daily contacts in their face-to-face relationships in the neighborhood piazza. These neighborhoods, like those in Venice, did not conform to the stereotype of the medieval city in which members of the same craft lived close together in the same district. Most neighborhoods were socially heterogeneous, containing both the palaces of the rich and the tenements of the poor, and members of many different trades. With a few exceptions, industry was organized on such a small scale that artisans in the same trade had no special incentive to live in close proximity to one another. Apart from ethnic ghettos of

31   My analysis of Florence closely follows Muir and Weissman, "Social and Symbolic Places," and is particularly indebted to Ronald F. E. Weissman, *Ritual Brotherhood in Rinaissance Florence* (New York: Academic Press, 1982), and Trexler, *Public Life*. Also see Giorgio Simoncini, *Città e società nel Rinascimento*, 2 vols. (Turin: Einaudi, 1974), and Richard Goldthwaite, *The Building of Renaissance Florence* (Baltimore: Johns Hopkins University Press, 1980).

32   Donald Weinstein, *Savonarola and Florence: Prophecy and Patriotism in the Renaissance* (Princeton: Princeton University Press, 1970). Niccoli, "Profezie in piazza," 505.

33   Dale Kent and F. W. Kent, *Neighbours and Neighbourhood in Renaissance Florence: The District of the Red Lion in the Fifteenth Century* (New York: J. Augustin, 1982). Cf. Goldthwaite, *Building of Renaissance Florence*, 12–13.

foreign workers, residential segregation was normal only for the artisans in a few specialized crafts, so that the majority lived among and married the daughters of craftsmen in other professions, although during the fifteenth century, as Samuel Cohn has argued, members of the Florentine working class may have begun to experience higher rates of parish, if not occupational, endogamy than before.[34] The extended family, although it had lost its thirteenth-century corporate status, remained a vital social unit, serving as the organizing force behind Florentine commerce, qualifying one for membership in guilds and other corporate groups, continuing as a component of prestige, and influencing one's honor, status, and ability to participate in urban politics.[35]

Neighborhood could also generate strong animosities and jealousies, for the piazza served as a common stage bringing together a citizen's many, sometimes incompatible, roles of kinsman, friend, political ally, tax assessor, business partner, client, parishioner. Managing them and maintaining numerous potentially conflicting loyalties was an arduous task in which the most valuable social commodity of honor could be won or lost.[36] The specific role of neighborhood in social life varied by class, by status, by age, and almost certainly by sex. For the Florentine citizens who were politically eligible and wealthy enough to pay taxes, the *gonfaloni* and quarters of the town had significant meaning. It was, after all, around the banner of the *gonfalon* that each male citizen assembled under threat of fines during the city's chief civic pageant, the feast day of Saint John the Baptist. For the socially marginal – the poor and the working classes, adolescents, and women – neighborhood boundaries were more fluid and amorphous, and could include piazza, street corner, or alley but generally coalesced around the parish. In the fourteenth century and again in the late fifteenth century the *popolo minuto* organized neighborhood festive bands which staged mock and occasionally real turf battles during feast days. By the middle of the sixteenth century, the parish, newly energized by the forces of Catholic reform, was the only remaining source of corporate solidarity, in the wake of the collapse of *gonfaloni* and guilds.[37]

As a counterweight to neighborhood loyalties, Florentine city fathers promoted civism with the cult of Saint John the Baptist, whose popularity

---

34   Samuel Kline Cohn, *The Laboring Classes in Renaissance Florence* (New York: Academic Press, 1980).

35   Francis William Kent, *Household and Lineage in Renaissance Florence: The Family Life of the Capponi, Ginori, and Rucellai* (Princeton: Princeton University Press, 1977). Alfred Doren, *Le arti fiorentine*, 2 vols. (Florence: Le Monnier, 1940). John M. Najemy, *Corporatism and Consensus in Florentine Electoral Politics, 1280–1400* (Chapel Hill: University of North Carolina Press, 1982). Dale Kent, *The Rise of the Medici: Faction in Florence* (Oxford: Oxford University Press, 1978).

36   Weissman, *Ritual Brotherhood*. Kent and Kent, *Neighbours and Neighbourhood*.

37   Weissman, *Ritual Brotherhood*. Trexler, *Public Life*.

spread from the Romanesque baptistry where all of Florence went to be baptized. The baptistry and the adjacent cathedral became the spiritual center of Florence, and the beginning and end for most processions. In addition, government buildings, especially the city hall, represented political salvation through the display of sacred signs and symbols. A raised platform in front of Florence's hall, for example, became an altar during civic ceremonies, thereby directly imputing divine sanction to public authority.[38]

The mobility of the sacred and the annual liturgical cycle conspired to give every major neighborhood and its chief lay patrons a chance to demonstrate their charisma to the entire city, a chance to link the collective honor of its inhabitants to devotion to the city's chief saints. In the Florentine feast of the Magi, the link between space, sacred charisma, and earthly honor was especially obvious. In this Medici-sponsored celebration of the fifteenth century, representatives of each of three quarters of Florence, dressed as Magi kings, paid homage to the fourth quarter, passing the Medici palace and walking on to "Bethlehem," the Medici-dominated convent of San Marco, to adore the Christ Child.[39] In contrast to Venice, private groups in Florence enhanced their charisma and their claims by manipulating sacred spaces. There the sacred was subject to the same particularist forces as was the secular. Among the constants of Florentine history are that every regime laid claim to legitimacy by employing the city's vocabulary of sacred space and that social ties to local places constrained the thoroughgoing expansion of public over private space.

Naples shows even more dramatically the strangely contradictory forces playing upon sacred objects and place names, which were ritually invoked by authorities for social control and adopted by intermittent rebels to legitimate themselves and to cleanse the body politic of evil rulers. One of the distinguishing features of Naples may have been that its central sacred object, the relic of Saint Janarius, recurrently stimulated prophetic enthusiasms through the prognostic capabilities of the triennial liquification of the saint's blood.[40] Since the liquifications only began after Saint Janarius's translation to Naples in 1497, the cult evolved during Naples' domination by foreign powers, principally Spain; and since social strife was manifest through struggles over the control of the cult, its socio-political role was ambiguous.[41]

---

38   Trexler, *Public Life*, 49.

39   Ibid., 424–45.

40   Tommaso Costo, *Giunta di tre libri al compendio dell'Istoria del Regno di Napoli. Ne' quali si contiene quanto di notabile, e ad esso Regno appartiene e accaduto, dal principio dall'anno MDLXIII insino al fine dell'Ottantasei. Con la tavola delle cose memorabili, che in essa si contengono* (Venice: Gio. Battista Cappelli e Gioseffo Peluso, 1588), 120.

41   G. B. Alfano and A. Amitrano, *Il miracolo di S. Gennaro in Napoli* (Naples: Scarpati, 1950), 145. Cf. Giuseppe Galasso, "Ideologia e sociologia del patronato di San Tommaso d'Aquino su Napoli (1605)," in *Per la storia sociale e religiosa del Mezzogiorno d'Italia*, ed. G. Galasso and Carla

Almost every year the archbishop, civic deputies, and the viceroy argued over rights of precedence in the ceremonies. For example, in 1646, the year before the revolution of Masaniello, the archbishop provocatively announced that the relics were his alone and denied the laity any rights to them. During the revolution the following year, the cathedral diarist assigned to describe the liquifications laconically recorded, "there is nothing to note because there was the revolution."[42] But the people saw visions of Saint Janarius and employed his image on rebel coins, stealing his favor, in effect, from the archbishop, who was constrained from presiding over the regular liquification miracle. Additionally, a dark, miracle-working image of the Virgin offered special assistance to the poor of the fruit market; and on several occasions, while the authorities squabbled over the blood of Saint Janarius, her feast days supplied the occasions for piazza uprisings. In 1647, in fact, the market-place church of Santa Maria del Carmine served as the stage for Masaniello's raptured but short-lived revolutionary performance.[43] The great Neapolitan revolution consisted, in large part, of a competition among saints. After Masaniello's death, the archbishop interpreted a dramatically complete liquification as a sign of the saint's pleasure with the suppression of the rebellion: "In particular," reads the cathedral diary, "His Eminence commented more than once about never having seen [the blood] so beautifully [liquified], since after calamitous times [in the past] it had always appeared thus as a happy augury for our city . . . which has in the end been liberated from the tyranny of the mob."[44]

Even more than Florence's, Naples' sacred and political centers were widely dispersed; its cathedral housing the miraculous relics of Janarius lay far from the Castel Nuovo, where thick stone walls protected the viceroys. Large sections of the city were divided among the noble barons, and the packed popular quarters clustered around the marketplace where the Carmelites and other orders provided the spiritual services the parish clergy neglected. Unlike Venetian doges or the Medici of Florence, no Neapolitan authority succeeded in capturing for himself the charisma of Saint Janarius through the sacralization of urban spaces and institutions, a failure that assisted in keeping Naples permanently unstable and politically backward.

Russo, 2 vols. (Naples: Guida Editori, 1982). I wish to thank John Marino for bringing Galasso's article to my attention.
42   Archivio dell'Arcivescovado, Naples (hereafter, AAN), MS titled "I diari dei ceremonieri della cattedrale di Napoli," 3: 165. Franco Strazzullo, *I diari dei cerimonieri della cattedrale di Napoli: Una fonte per la storia napoletana* (Naples: Agar, 1961), xxi.
43   Burke, *Historical Anthropology*, 191–206. Rosario Villari, "Masaniello: Contemporary and Recent Interpretations," *Past and Present* 108 (1985): 117–32. Cf. Rothkrug, "Holy Shrines," 175–6.
44   AAN, "I diari dei cerimonieri della cattedrale di Napoli," 2: 173.

An even more extreme example of such a failure might be Udine, a city where social divisions had clear cultural and linguistic correlates. In the early sixteenth century Udine and the surrounding Friulan countryside witnessed some of the most widespread and violent revolts by artisans and peasants in Renaissance Italy. In 1511 more than twenty palaces in Udine were looted and burned and perhaps two dozen castles beseiged and damaged in the nearby countryside. What is most remarkable about these disturbances, especially when compared to the nearly contemporaneous revolts in the South Tyrol and Upper Swabia, is the absence of any religious content. Even the urban riots of Udine lacked the sensitivity to symbolic places so evident in similar disturbances in Florence and Naples.

This relative poverty of Christian imagery was widespread even though for nearly four centuries the region had been an ecclesiastical principality under the patriarchs of Aquileia and still had an exceptionally large establishment of religious, constituting nearly 4 percent of the population of Udine alone. But this establishment was notoriously neglectful of its pastoral duties. Even after Trent, suburban parish churches were still being used as barns, and the functioning of Udine's cathedral was jeopardized by a lack of liturgical vessels and ill repair. One report noted that the roof leaked so badly that divine offices might as well be said in the open. A visiting cardinal lamented that cathedral canons were infamous street fighters, most parish priests were illiterate and incapable of reciting the Mass, and the monasteries were dangerous places where the monks divided into armed camps. The cathedral chapter and the civil government were forever bickering over the administration of the divine cult, but artisans and suburban peasants were apparently indifferent to the expressive possibilities of religious ritual and sacred places, neither invoking the saints nor following a ritual geography during disturbances.[45] Their models of representation derived from other sources, the vendetta, factional loyalty, magic, and carnival practices, while the populace was far more open to Protestant doctrines than the Venetians, Florentines, or Neapolitans. The Cardinal of San Severina complained in 1535 that monasteries in Udine could barely survive from what charity trickled in from the laity because "this land is close to German places infested with Lutheran lies."[46] Lacking a charismatic center, the extremely agonistic society of Friuli was symbolically atomistic, failing to accept any social bodies larger than family and faction.

The gap between ecclesiastical institutions and popular spiritual life was so vast that the town remained in a semi-feudal, almost clannish environment in which animal totems and heraldic blazons carried greater emotive

---

45 Battistella, "Udine nel secolo XVI," 1–17. The situation in Friuli paralleled the prince-bishoprics in Germany. Rothkrug, "German Holiness," 162.
46 Battistella, "Udine nel secolo XVI," 7.

power than relics and images. Neighborhoods in Udine demarcated factional turfs, and even the images of the Virgin, erected about the city (probably in imitation of Venetian practice) seem to have been largely ignored by the laity. Much as did the Spanish viceroy of Naples, the Venetian *luogotenente* in Udine, who after 1420 was officially in charge, lived as the outsider he was, separated from the citizens on a strongly fortified hill within the city; the cathedral and monasteries, extensions of factional patronage systems, were thoroughly incapable of providing refuge from the recurrent strife.[47] Udine might not represent so much a failure of cognition or of faith as a failure of Christianity and of political institutions to create a civic culture by encouraging the veneration of images in public places.

In all these cities, conflicting forces exerted pressure on the sacred. On the one hand, relations with the sacred presented an idealized pattern for human social relations that emphasized the virtues of hierarchy, deference, and obedience and that encouraged civic concord by investing urban places with a hallowed character. Ecclesiastic and secular authorities cooperated by representing the sacred in ways that would serve desirable social ends, but their effectiveness largely depended on the ability of the civil government to marshal support and suppress opposition. Although all governments appeared to legitimate themselves through divine sanction, only those regimes that built or forced some degree of social consensus succeeded in achieving legitimacy.

On the other hand, agonistic relations among individuals and urban groups – families, neighborhoods, guilds, classes – were projected onto the sacred, creating counter pressures that gave spiritual sanction to civil conflicts. In Venice the Virgin encouraged passivity; in Naples she sponsored rebellion. In all of these cities, sacred places and objects were approached and understood through public performances and rituals, but the meaning of gestures of reverence came not from the form of the performance itself but from what one might call the social script. In the theater states, the authorities made certain that they wrote the script and dominated the stage. The sincerity threshold was quite low because performing well brought rewards even if it masked crude self-interest and significant social conflict. In other cities, sacred performances were competitive – they constituted street fighting by another means – and the sincerity threshold was higher precisely because there was little agreement over the social script or even the most appropriate stage.

Where the sacred was most completely interwoven into the urban fabric, where the spiritual was most readily manifest in objects, where the incandescence of the holy could be found in the most mundane places, such as

47   These comments come from Muir, *Mad Blood Stirring: Vendetta and Faction in Friuli during the Renaissance* (Baltimore, 1993).

in Venice and Florence, one also finds the most effectively institutionalized, most politically sophisticated, the most economically advanced cities. Communities that failed to infuse urban spaces with a spiritual presence or to control their sacred objects were more awkwardly organized, more conflict-ridden, more economically backward, and perhaps more often open to religious reformist ideas. Such a pattern is, of course, the exact inverse of what traditional Durkheimian sociology might lead one to expect and differs, as well, from the more recent revisionist view that all societies are equally ritualized.[48] It is not the amount of ritual that counts but its character and its relationship to social behavior and verbal protestations.

The proper balance between ritual and the word, performance and intention, spirit and objects in representing the sacred was certainly one of the more vexing issues of the sixteenth century. Debated by theologians and humanists, these issues met the hard realities of daily social life in the cities. When one recalls Luther's reaction to his Roman sojourn or Erasmus's complaints about the moral laxity among celebrants of the liturgy and lay believers alike, one wonders how much of the Reformation may have come from misunderstandings of the various dialects of popular devotion, misunderstandings that were stumblings, in effect, upon the threshold of sincerity.

48   Cf. the comments on this issue in Burke, *Historical Anthropology*, 223–4.

Part IV
Gender and Society

Introduction to Part IV

Italian Renaissance society had well-defined expectations of men and women that coalesced around the idea of family. Men collectively shaped the public life of the cities and acted as *patresfamilias* within the home. They represented their family's interests by voting and holding office, and by participating in the varied kinds of fraternal organizations that structured urban life; their activities connected their family to the world. Within the family, men ostensibly made the most important social and financial decisions, though women had much greater agency than we have typically expected in such an early period. Heads of household worked with the other male members of their extended family to preserve their patrimony and increase their wealth. They educated their sons to take their place in the family business – or in other areas of public life that facilitated family interests. They invested their wives' dowries in their business ventures, and hoped that they did not have to withdraw the money prematurely. They decided when and if their children would marry, selecting potential spouses who ideally would further the family fortunes by transforming friendships into strategic alliances of kinship. When marriage did not seem feasible, they sent their daughters to the convents in order to reduce the burden of dowering too many girls, and occasionally had younger sons take religious orders so that they might further the family's honor in the service of God.

Within such a system, we might initially imagine that there was little scope for women's independent activities. The vast majority of women had little choice in the decision to marry or to enter the convent. Those who married had virtually no say in the selection of a husband since marriage was a family decision. Women often married at a much younger age than men in Italian Renaissance society – on average between fourteen and eighteen – while men tended to marry in their late twenties to early thirties. Female virtue was carefully guarded because it was a matter of family honor. The occasions in which women participated in public life were few – ceremonies organized with a local parish, rituals of mourning for kin, and occasionally state rituals that demanded the symbolic presence of women. Such opportunities only seemed to diminish in the course of the fifteenth and sixteenth centuries, as various Italian Renaissance city-states reorganized political and religious ritual to reflect their image of society as a well-ordered family in which women had more clearly delineated roles.

If civic life offered little scope for women's activities, the domestic sphere was the location in which women exercised most of their power and authority. The importance of such activities is underscored in Stanley Chojnacki's essay. Let us consider a famous fictional image of the Italian Renaissance family, Leon Battista Alberti's *Books on the Family* (ca. 1434–7). In the third dialogue, a Tuscan husband shows his new and considerably younger wife around their house as a prelude to giving her the keys. It is quite apparent that virtually all of the household is hers to command since Alberti only singled out one room – the husband's study filled with his account books and family papers – as a place that she cannot enter. Even fictional accounts of patriarchy, in other words, acknowledged women's command of the domestic sphere. What, then, was a woman's place within the home?

Domestic life encompassed a broad range of activities, from the daily management of the household and care of younger children to many tasks that facilitated a family's business. Too often we have taken patrician families as the model of an Italian Renaissance family because we know considerably more about them. Yet elite families do not provide us with a comprehensive portrait of the experiences of men and women in this society. Artisanal families, for example, involved women much more directly in the family business which often occurred within the home and were more creative about family arrangements. Imagine a Renaissance *palazzo* with the shops below and the family quarters above. It is hard to divide easily the worlds of work and family, at which point we have to revise our image of women confined to a strictly domestic sphere. Or let us take the case of an elite merchant and banking family in which fathers and sons frequently spent months, even years, out of the city in pursuit of business (or, more often than not, in political exile). Who managed affairs at home? Merchants' letters provide us with noteworthy examples of wives who participated in their husband's affairs, paid taxes, and worked with male relatives to arrange their sons' and daughters' marriages. Finally, we should not forget the age difference between husbands and wives, which made the widow an important figure in Italian Renaissance society. In an artisanal family, she might manage the shop with her male relatives and enjoy membership in a guild. In a patrician family, she would guide her sons into adulthood, unless she was widowed so early that her own family pressured her to remarry.

Gender relations in Renaissance Italy, in other words, created a dynamic balance between the patriarchal structure of public life and the powerful social and economic roles that women could create for themselves within the domestic economy. Yet to say that women were disinterested in, or utterly removed from public life would undervalue the ways in which family and state informed each other. The Florentine patrician Alessandra Strozzi watched carefully the comings and goings of the *signoria*. She did not hesitate to allude to perceived deficiencies in government in her letters to her sons. Similarly, we can point to a series of Venetian women writers, among them the seventeenth-century nun Arcangela Tarabotti, who did not hesitate to critique the Venetian Republic for creating a highly limited definition of freedom that favored the desires of men over those of women. It is quite evident that women with property in many Italian cities understood that the first step to power was economic and the second step was cultural. Having property to use in one's own lifetime and to pass on to heirs, and having the power to wield a pen, represented two fundamental avenues towards giving women a certain sense of autonomy that they otherwise might not have.

One area in which women had considerably less autonomy than men concerned their sexuality. As Michael Rocke notes, patrician males chose their sexual partners at many different stages in their lives, suggesting that social status as much as gender defined sexual behavior. For every patrician girl whose family guarded her honor scrupulously, there were others whose sexual identity was defined by a system of marriage in which adult males remained single until well into adulthood, and who in the meantime took multiple sexual partners from the lower classes. The young boys and girls who served as prostitutes to men had little choice in their place in the sexual hierarchy. Often children of poor immigrants, artisans, and domestic slaves, they sold sexual favors to survive or to cover the shame of what initially began as a forced encounter. Their experience of the sexual marketplace was entirely different from that of a high-class courtesan such as the sixteenth-century writer Veronica Franco, celebrated in Venice for her poetry as well as her beauty. Yet Franco, too, condemned the life of a prostitute with great bitterness despite the intellectual freedoms that she enjoyed as a woman who moved easily among men in her society. Sexual freedom was an elite, largely male prerogative in Renaissance Italy. To the extent that women could and did make choices about the expression of their sexuality, they did so within a highly circumscribed system that placed a premium upon female sexuality as an expression of a family's honor. The two essays in this section by Stanley Chojnacki and Michael Rocke allow us to consider how gender and sexuality shaped public and private life in the Italian Renaissance.

Plate 7 Lavinia Fontana, *Portrait of a Family* (ca. 1600). *Source:* Pinacoteca Nazionale di Brera, Milan.

Lavinia Fontana (1552–1614) was one of a handful of female artists, many of them Bolognese, to make a living as a painter in the sixteenth and early seventeenth century. Most of her work was done in her native city of Bologna, where she often depicted the urban elite in her portraits. This particular image is of an unknown family. It captures key aspects of the dynamics of family life in the late Renaissance. Fontana groups the male and female members of this extended household to reflect the divisions between men's and women's worlds in domestic life and inheritance practices. Within every household, there were two lineages: a patrilineage in which property and name descended through sons, and a matrilineage in which the women within the family constantly made connections for their male relatives through marriage into other families. Women's property typically lay in their dowry which came to their husband for his use during marriage, but returned to the woman and her family upon her husband's death. At her death, she could pass it on as she pleased. Fontana's family portrait is probably an image of a widow and her children portrayed with their recently deceased father. The son in the center, now head of the household, gestures to his father, while the oldest daughter gestures to heaven. Note the literacy of the youngest daughter who holds a book in her hand.

7

"The Most Serious Duty": Motherhood, Gender, and Patrician Culture in Renaissance Venice

Stanley Chojnacki

"Educatio liberorum, pars uxorii muneris fructuosa et longe gravissima" ("the upbringing of children, which is surely a rewarding and by far the most serious of a wife's duties").[1] When the young Venetian patrician Francesco Barbaro wrote these words in his erudite treatise on marriage of 1415–16, he likely did not have in mind the complex implications that they would have over the next century for the private and public culture of the ruling elite to which he belonged. Although convinced of the importance for family well-being of a wife's breeding and character, Barbaro fully shared Venice's time-honored subscription to the patriarchal principles of Roman law, encapsulated in the *patria potestas*.[2] For him, as for most commentators then and later, mothers contributed but fathers commanded; as Barbaro wrote, "Let the husband give the orders and let the wife carry them out with a cheerful temper."[3] Indeed, for the Venetian patriciate the patriarchal ideal covered both private and public life. Husbandly dominion within the palazzo paralleled the central place of fathers in the functioning of the patrician

---

1 *Francisci Barbari de re uxoria liber in partes duas*, ed. Attilio Gnesotto (Padua: Randi, 1915), p. 92. The translation is based on that of Benjamin G. Kohl, *The Earthly Republic: Italian Humanists on Government and Society*, ed. Benjamin G. Kohl and Ronald G. Witt (Philadelphia: University of Pennsylvania Press, 1978), p. 220. Barbaro's discussion makes clear that he uses *educatio* in the sense that includes general upbringing as well as pedagogy. On Barbaro, see Margaret L. King, "Caldiera and the Barbaros on Marriage and the Family," *Journal of Medieval and Renaissance Studies* 6 (1976): 19–50, esp. 31–5.

2 On Venice's uninterrupted subscription to family principles of Roman law, see Giorgio Zordan, "I vari aspetti della comunione familiare dei beni nella Venezia dei secoli XI–XII," *Studi veneziani* 8 (1966): 127–94.

3 *De re uxoria*, p. 63; Kohl's translation, p. 193.

regime. A man's membership in the elite rested on his documented descent from generations of patrician fathers, and the benefits he gained from patrician status depended on his paternal legacy: not just material assets but also the friendships, esteem, and social and political credit acquired by his father through involvement in the activity of his class.[4]

These traits made up the gender triptych of patriarchal, patrilineal, and patrimonial principles that formally governed family and regime. They give the strong impression that if any women had a Renaissance, it was not patrician women in Renaissance Venice. Yet gender and the relations between the sexes are complex matters with many dimensions and embracing both precept and practice. For a historian the insights offered by attention to gender come not just from ascertaining society's gender principles, but also from exploring the relationship between these and the practical activity of men acting as men and women acting as women. It is in this dialectical dynamic between gender norms and gender-interpretable behavior that much of what we think of as cultural change takes place – change of the kind implied in the complex question of a Renaissance for women.[5] Gender as an analytical concept is still in lively evolution, with no fixed consensus about its dimensions yet in place. This encourages exploration of varied configurations, mining its many rich veins in the interest of achieving an enhanced, more nuanced historical discourse.[6]

4   The fullest discussion of patrician political practice is in Robert Finlay, *Politics in Renaissance Venice* (New Brunswick, N.J.: Rutgers University Press, 1980). On the establishment of the hereditary principle in the patriciate, see Frederic C. Lane, "The Enlargement of the Great Council of Venice," in *Florilegium Historiale: Essays Presented to Wallace K. Ferguson*, ed. J. G. Rowe and W. H. Stockdale (Toronto: University of Toronto Press, 1971), pp. 236–74. See also Stanley Chojnacki, "Political Adulthood in Fifteenth-Century Venice," *American Historical Review* 91 (1986): 791–810.

5   See the seminal essay of Joan Kelly, "Did Women Have a Renaissance?" (1977), reprinted in *Becoming Visible: Women in European History*, 2d ed., ed. Renate Bridenthal, Claudia Koonz, and Susan M. Stuard (Boston: Houghton Mifflin, 1987), pp. 175–202. The broad strokes of Kelly's essay are given historical nuance in Susan M. Stuard, "The Dominion of Gender: Women's Fortunes in the High Middle Ages," ibid., pp. 153–74. For other considerations of change in the position of women during the Middle Ages and Renaissance, see Judith M. Bennett, *Women in the Medieval English Countryside* (New York: Oxford University Press, 1987), esp. the introduction; Merry E. Wiesner, *Working Women in Renaissance Germany* (New Brunswick, N.J.: Rutgers University Press, 1986); and Martha C. Howell, "Citizenship and Gender: Women's Political Status in Northern Medieval Cities," in *Women and Power in the Middle Ages*, ed. Mary Erler and Maryanne Kowaleski (Athens: University of Georgia Press, 1988), pp. 37–60.

6   My views of gender in historical analysis have been especially influenced by Sherry B. Ortner and Harriet Whitehead, "Introduction," in *Sexual Meanings: The Cultural Construction of Gender and Sexuality* (Cambridge: Cambridge University Press, 1981); Michelle Zimbalist Rosaldo, "Woman, Culture, and Society: A Theoretical Overview," in *Woman, Culture, and Society*, ed. Michelle Zimbalist Rosaldo and Louise Lamphere (Stanford: Stanford University Press, 1974), pp. 17–42; Rosaldo, "The Use and Abuse of Anthropology: Reflections on

In this essay I would like to venture such an exploration, taking as my point of departure a configuration of gender as involving two sets of relationships, one between men and women, and one between individuals of each sex and the cultural norms governing gender. It seems to me helpful to picture these relationships as played out along the sides of a triangle, with reciprocal dynamics going on along each side. Along the horizontal base, men at one corner and women at the other interact under the influence of various cultural norms, chiefly that of patriarchy, but also according to the peculiar contingencies of individual circumstance, allowing or forcing greater or lesser conformity with those norms. The contingencies also figure in the other two dynamics. Individual men, grouped in this image at one of the bottom corners, and individual women, grouped at the other, both interact with the prevailing gender norms (or culture, or ideology: any term will do), which sit at the apex of the triangle. The action is reciprocal on all sides, for the subordination of individual women to patriarchal dominance depends on, but also influences, their relationships with men. With individual men the situation is the same, but in reverse: their conformity with the patriarchal model is expressed in, but in practice also depends on, their relationships with women. And gender ideology itself is subject to change on the basis of large-scale nonconformity with it in individual experience.

Among Venetian patricians, to ease away from such abstract schemes, the relationship between gender principles, gender in practice, and the direction of change may be observed concretely along three axes. One is influence within the family, and we may pose a focusing question about it: How closely did the legal endurance of the *patria potestas* correspond to a reality of paternal dominance in the home? The second axis runs through gender roles in patrician society at large: Did the deeply rooted patrilineal and patrimonial principles produce in practice male privilege and centrality, female subordination and marginality in the identities, activities, and relationships that made up patrician society? The third axis arrives at the symbolic forms in which patrician culture expressed itself at its broadest: Did the patriciate convey its dominant ideals in a symbolic vocabulary that is recognizably patriarchal? These are big questions, the interrelatedness of which draws attention to the linkage between manifestations of gender in the domestic setting and in the broader social, political, and cultural arenas, and to the dynamic friction of that linkage as it affected individual lives and

Feminism and Cross-Cultural Understanding," *Signs: Journal of Women in Culture and Society* 5 (1980): 389–417; Jean Bethke Elshtain, *Public* Man, Private Woman (Princeton: Princeton University Press, 1981); Jane Flax, "Postmodernism and Gender Relations in Feminist Theory," *Signs: Journal of Women in Culture and Society* 12 (1987): 621–43; and Joan W. Scott, "Gender: A Useful Category of Historical Analysis," *American Historical Review* 91 (1986): 1053–75.

identities.[7] They are too vast to be fully posed, let alone satisfactorily answered, here.[8] But it is possible to pick at them in a limited way. This essay inquires into patriarchy by looking at patrician mothers, and specifically their involvement in the shaping of their children's adult identities.

Just as gender elucidates its social and cultural context, so context is essential to understanding gender. Two matters of context must be kept in view when assessing gender in Venetian patrician culture. One is the paramount place of marriage.[9] From the late fourteenth century, patricians deepened their class's exclusivism, enacting a steady stream of laws that built an iron curtain of pedigree between themselves and the populace, with the patrician antecedents of a man's mother coming to be regarded as almost as important as those of his father in making valid his claim to patrician status.[10] This increased the stakes of matrimonial choice, making it more desirable than ever to marry within the class, but also to marry well within it, leading patricians to seek the richest, most influential and socially lustrous spouses possible for their children.[11] The concern with status was inseparable from concrete interest. The material advantages of membership in the elite were of pressing concern to patricians, and an elaborate business of patron–client relations, friendship cultivating, favor exchange, alliance forging, and bloc voting, all directed toward gaining or apportioning the remunerative government jobs and other privileges on which patrician families depended, was the main stuff of patrician politics.[12] In this

7   The complex interaction between gender, social placement, and individual identity is variously explored by Stephen Greenblatt, "Fiction and Friction," and Natalie Zemon Davis, "Boundaries and the Sense of Self in Sixteenth-Century France," both in *Reconstructing Individualism: Autonomy, Individuality, and the Self in Western Thought*, ed. Thomas C. Heller et al. (Stanford: Stanford University Press, 1986), pp. 30–52 and 53–63, respectively.

8   This essay is part of a larger project exploring patrician politics, society, and culture, with special attention to gender, especially as it related to the liminal groups of women and young men. See, preliminarily, my "Patrician Adulthood," and also "The Power of Love: Wives and Husbands in Late Medieval Venice," in Erler and Kowaleski, *Women and Power in the Middle Ages*, pp. 126–48.

9   On marriage in the patriciate, see Finlay, *Politics*, esp. pp. 81–96; Bianca Betto, "Linee di politica matrimoniale nella nobiltà veneziana fino al XV secolo: Alcune note genealogiche e l'esempio della famiglia Mocenigo," *Archivio storico italiano* 139 (1981): 3–64; Stanley Chojnacki, "Marriage Legislation and Patrician Society in Fifteenth-Century Venice," in *Law, Custom, and the Social Fabric in Medieval Europe: Essays in Honor of Bryce Lyon*, ed. Bernard Bachrach and David Nicholas (Kalamazoo: Medieval Institute Publications, 1990), pp. 163–84.

10   See Chojnacki, "Marriage Legislation," on governmental definitions of the status requirements of patrician wives. Barbaro ranked the pedigree of the mother at least as high as that of the father in producing worthy offspring; *De re uxoria*, p. 41.

11   Chojnacki, "Marriage Legislation."

12   Finlay, *Politics*; on patrician dependence on political office, see Donald E. Queller, *The Venetian Patriciate: Reality versus Myth* (Urbana: University of Illinois Press, 1986).

high-stakes social world matrimony was the chief means of forging the associations through which families ensured their status and promoted their interests. Matrimony involved marriage portions; good marriages required big portions; and assembling these entailed the commitment of great chunks of family resources.[13]

The zeal for good marriages is tied to the second component of the context of patrician gender. The currency of matrimony, dowries, were the property of the women whose marriages they brought about. Husbands could invest their wives' dowries, and in fifteenth-century Venice one-third of the total marriage portion normally became the husband's property to keep.[14] But the bulk of these growing marriage portions belonged to the wives themselves, to spend, save, or distribute as they pleased during widowhood, and to bequeath to the heirs of their choice, whether they predeceased their husbands or not.[15] Wifely dowry wealth, growing in lockstep with families' matrimonial ambitions and safeguarded by statute and court, is central to gender in patrician family, society, and culture. It is the key to the way women discharged their "most serious duty," the launching of their children into the complex world of patrician adulthood.

Formally and prescriptively, fathers as patresfamilias had the principal responsibility for and authority over family strategy, including the planning of children's destinies.[16] In the pedigree-conscious climate of the fifteenth

13 On assembling dowries, see Stanley Chojnacki, "Dowries and Kinsmen in Early Renaissance Venice," *Journal of Interdisciplinary History* 5 (1975): 571–600. For non-Venetian perspectives, see Diane Owen Hughes, "From Brideprice to Dowry in Mediterranean Europe, "*Journal of Family History* 3 (1978): 262–96; Julius Kirshner and Anthony Molho, "The Dowry Fund and the Marriage Market in Early *Quattrocento* Florence," *Journal of Modern History* 50 (1978): 403–38; and Christiane Klapisch-Zuber, "The Griselda Complex: Dowry and Marriage Gifts in the Quattrocento," in Klapisch-Zuber, *Women, Family, and Ritual in Renaissance Italy,* trans. Lydia G. Cochrane (Chicago: University of Chicago Press, 1985), pp. 213–46.

14 In the fifteenth century, marriage portions usually consisted of two-thirds strict dowry, to be returned to the wife, and one-third *corredum,* at that time an outright gift to the husband. The complex and evolving relationship of dowry to *corredum* (the latter in its twin dimensions as trousseau and as gift to the husband) is addressed in my larger study (see note 8). See, meanwhile, Chojnacki, "Marriage Legislation."

15 The mechanisms guaranteeing women's rights to their dowries at marriage's end are too elaborate to discuss here; they are treated in my larger study (see note 8). The principal evidence is in the Venetian statutes, especially Book 4, chaps. 53–61, *Volumen statutorum legum, ac iurium D. Venetorum* (Venice, 1564), pp. 24v–29v; and Archivio di Stato, Venice (hereafter abbreviated ASV), Giudici del Proprio, Diiudicatum, Reg. 1, 2 (1468–77); and innumerable notarial acts securing wives' rights to their husband's property against restitution of their dowries. See also Julius Kirshner, "Wives' Claims against Insolvent Husbands in Late Medieval Italy," in *Women of the Medieval World,* ed. Julius Kirshner and Suzanne F. Wemple (Oxford: Basil Blackwell, 1985), pp. 256–93; and Thomas Kuehn, "Some Ambiguities of Female Inheritance Ideology in the Renaissance," *Continuity and Change* 2 (1987): 11–36.

16 On the authority of fathers, see Thomas Kuehn, *Emancipation in Late Medieval Florence* (New Brunswick, N.J.: Rutgers University Press, 1982).

century, fathers exercising this authority merged the interests of family with those of lineage, the matrix of membership in patrician society, and the operating environment of the patriarchal triptych. The influence and motivations of fathers in the concentric settings of family and lineage are illustrated in the 1401 will of Gasparino Morosini.[17] Widowed three times, Gasparino had, among other kin, three living sons and a married daughter, a widowed daughter-in-law with two sons (Gasparino's grandsons), and an orphaned granddaughter by another deceased son. To each of these persons he had something to give, but he commanded as he gave. Setting up a generous investment fund for his youngest, underage son, Antonio, he declared that his two adult sons (Antonio's half-brothers) were not to complain, because they had already been provided for; indeed, of one of them, Nicolò, Gasparino said, "non digo niente" ("I say nothing"), because Nicolò had been so well set up at his emancipation.[18] Gasparino's strictures had added force because, beyond his own wealth, he had administrative control over the legacies that the elder sons had received from their respective mothers. And he flatly asserted that if they failed to treat the underage Antonio well, they would lose half their bequest from him, which would then go to Antonio.

Gasparino's authoritative largesse extended beyond his sons to the women in his life. To his widowed daughter-in-law, Maria, he bequeathed several properties, including the house where she was living, and he declared that his estate should bear the expenses of the upbringing of his two grandsons, who were also to share one-quarter of Gasparino's residuary estate (the other three-quarters going to his sons). He even bequeathed two hundred ducats toward Maria's dowry, should she decide to remarry: this is remarkable, since a remarriage might produce children who would compete for Maria's beneficence with her present offspring, Gasparino's grandsons. He further declared that if any of his sons should oppose his generosity toward Maria, he was to be disinherited.[19] Finally, to his

---

17   ASV, Archivio Notarile, Testamenti (hereafter abbreviated NT, followed by *busta* number and notary's name) 575, Gibellino, no. 675, 9 May 1401.

18   On the continuing relationships between fathers and their emancipated sons, see Kuehn, *Emancipation.*

19   Gasparino's unusual generosity toward Maria runs exactly counter to the remarrying "cruel mother" syndrome analyzed in the Florentine context by Christiane Klapisch-Zuber in her influential essay "The 'Cruel Mother': Maternity, Widowhood, and Dowry in Florence in the Fourteenth and Fifteenth Centuries," in *Women, Family, and Ritual*, pp. 117–31. Whereas the cruelty of the mother in Klapisch-Zuber's formulation consisted in her willing or coerced abandonment of her children after remarriage, Gasparino, though solicitous of his grandchildren by Maria, nevertheless benignly supported the prospect of her remarriage. It remains to be demonstrated that a remarrying Venetian mother was more likely than her Florentine counterpart to continue caring for the children of her first marriage. Gasparino himself was accustomed to cherish ties to in-laws even after remarriage; in an earlier will of 1374, written

orphaned granddaughter Franceschina he left the conspicuous sum of two thousand ducats in state bonds, to be used for her marriage, at age thirteen, to a "Venetian patrician worthy of her rank and acceptable to my sons Nicolò, Benedetto, and Antonio, and also to my cousins Bernardo and Barbon Morosini and my cousin-german Zanin Morosini."[20]

He enlisted the involvement of his sisters as well. One, a nun, he asked to care for Franceschina, keeping her in the convent until the girl was eleven, at which point his other, married sister was to take over, presumably to prepare Franceschina for her marriage. Gasparino also provided for Franceschina's living expenses; but despite his wide-ranging generosity in substance, the tone of the will, in this as in its other arrangements, is one of command. He was head of the extended family, mobilizer of its human resources, committed molder of the lineage's destiny. In short, he was the very model of a patriarch, solicitous of his living kin, mindful of the dead, but especially concerned with the young, both children and grandchildren, whose upbringing and future prospects he attended to in detail, applying moral and material leverage to ensure equity among his heirs, especially his sons by different mothers.[21] And as he made explicit in his instructions for his granddaughter, his authoritative concern extended to the enduring dignity of his lineage, to be secured by "worthy" marriages in which an array of agnatic kinsmen were to interest themselves. Gasparino resembles the patriarch ruling over what F. W. Kent calls in a Florentine context the "grand family."[22] As such he fills a quintessentially conventional male role. Yet virtually every one of his will's provisions (and those of other patrician patriarchs) can be found, though with significant differences, in the wills of wealthy, influential, self-confident patrician mothers.

during his second marriage, he had bequeathed fifty ducats to each of the brothers of his deceased first wife, "per grande amor e raxion chio o portado sempre a quella caxa" ("because of the great love and interest I have always had for that house"). NT 1062, Della Torre, no. 300, 14 April 1374.

20   "Vojo la se dia a quelo zentilomo venizian che sia dexevele ala so condizion e che sia de conttentto e azetto a mi fiuoli Nicolò Benedetto e Antuonio. E semelmentre sia azeto a miy cosini Barbon e Bernardo Morexini e mio coxin german Zanin Morexini, hover a la plu parte de questi." NT 571, "carte varie," 18 April 1401. (The May 9 will added codicils to the basic text of the April 18 will.)

21   The example of a father mediating equitably the legacies to his sons by their different pre-deceased mothers represents another alternative to the child-abandoning widow discussed as a model of Florentine wifehood by Klapisch-Zuber in "Cruel Mother." The remarrying widow was only one of several maternal typologies; in addition to women who, like Gasparino's three wives, preceded their husbands to the grave, many mothers remained head of household after their husband's death, giving a distinctive cast to their discharge of that role. See my discussion later in this chapter.

22   F. W. Kent, *Household and Lineage in Renaissance Florence: The Family Life of the Capponi, Ginori, and Rucellai* (Princeton: Princeton University Press, 1977), pp. 29–36, 58–60.

Gasparino's solicitude over the needs of individual kin is a useful reminder that men did not mechanically follow a blinkered lineage interest. Nevertheless, male patricians were constantly reminded that their very social identity, to say nothing of their enjoyment of the benefits of elite status, was rooted in a title tied to the male line of descent. From the ritual at age eighteen that ascertained and registered their paternal descent to the mobilization of lineage loyalties and associations that gained them remunerative government posts and other privileges, men of the patriciate were labeled as their fathers' sons, and indeed had every reason to brandish the label and, like Gasparino, to transfer it, and the lineage orientation to which it was the key, to their own progeny.[23]

The case of patrician women was different. As Christiane Klapisch-Zuber, Diane Owen Hughes, and Sharon Strocchia have emphasized, women's membership in the patrilineage was tenuous and temporary.[24] All married women belonged to two families, and most to two lineages, in some respects sequentially, moving from the natal to the marital *casa*, but in another sense simultaneously, retaining ties to each.[25] The complementary, countervailing, complexly interwoven lineage ties of married patrician women affected their relations with their variously aligned kin. Especially toward their children and grandchildren, dowry-possessing women pro-

---

23   On the Balla d'Oro exercise establishing patrician adulthood, see Chojnacki, "Political Adulthood," and also "Kinship Ties and Young Patricians in Fifteenth-Century Venice," *Renaissance Quarterly* 38 (1985): 240–70. In 1405 the Venetian Great Council passed a law requiring candidates for office to be identified not only by given name and surname but by patronymic as well. ASV, Maggior Consiglio, Reg. (hereafter abbreviated MC) 21, Leona, f. 127.
24   Christiane Klapisch-Zuber, "Cruel Mother," and "Kin, Friends, and Neighbors: The Urban Territory of a Merchant Family in 1400," in *Women, Family, and Ritual*, pp. 68–93. Diane Owen Hughes, "From Brideprice to Dowry," and "Representing the Family: Portraits and Purposes in Early Modern Italy," *Journal of Interdisciplinary History* 17 (1986): 7–38. Sharon T. Strocchia, "Remembering the Family: Women, Kin, and Commemorative Masses in Renaissance Florence," *Renaissance Quarterly* 42 (1989): 635–54. See also Ronald F. E. Weissman, *Ritual Brotherhood in Renaissance Florence* (New York: Academic Press, 1982), p. 33.
25   Female testators often advertised their double affiliation: "Ego Victoria filia qd. domini Andree Victuri *ad presens* uxor nobilis viri domini Valerii Geno" ("I Vittoria, daughter of the late Lord Andrea Vitturi, *at present* wife of the noble Lord Valerio Zeno") (NT 857, Rizoto, no. 349, 31 July 1427; emphasis added); "Mi Franceschina fia fo del nobel homo miser Domenego Loredan *al prexente* spoxa del nobel homo miser Nicholo Chapelo" ("I Franceschina, daughter of the late noble messer Domenico Loredan, *at present* spouse of the noble messer Nicolò Capello") (NT 1238, Tomei, Part II, no. 292, 2 December 1464; emphasis added). The allusion to the temporariness of marital ties suggests a more durable natal than marital identification for these women. Other wives, however, emphasized the marital family connection: Briseida Pisani, wife of Nicolò Bragadin, while retaining close ties to her mother and brother (naming them as testamentary executors and leaving them bequests), nevertheless identified herself as "ego Briseida consors viri nobilis domini Nicolai Bragadeno" ("I Briseida, consort of the noble Lord Nicolò Bragadin"). Ibid., no. 17, 10 July 1438.

jected influences that intersected the lineage orientation of men, alloying it with the values of what the anthropologist Meyer Fortes termed the "complementary line of filiation."[26] It is the exercise of the moderating influence of mothers in the discharge of "their most serious duty" of raising children to adulthood that is of interest for our understanding of patrician gender roles. For the participation of mothers, with their distinctive social orientation, in ostensibly patriarchal prerogatives affected the gender identities of their children.

Male identity in patrician culture was essentially public. No sooner did a young man reach age eighteen than he was presented to public officials for an induction ritual, the so-called Balla d'Oro, that began his gradual passage into full adulthood, which was reckoned in terms of governmental activity.[27] The public nature of men's vocational activity and the economic dependence of, as officials noted, a "majority" of patrician families on government programs reinforced lineage discipline.[28] Fathers hurried sons into public life, and young manhood was a period of apprenticeship under the guidance of fathers and male kinsmen, whose political direction and economic support emphasized the benefits to be derived from cultivation of collective virtues: of the family, the lineage, the patriciate as a whole. Personal relations between fathers and sons in so highly structured a family culture make a fascinating subject requiring more study. But they were in any case enfolded within an ideology of mutually advantageous conformity to the requirements of lineage and regime. From this structure it was psychologically and materially difficult for either generation to extricate itself, with the result that the public gave form and substance to the personal, leading fathers to cultivate in their sons a conformist ideal of male adulthood, a male gender model in which, paradoxically, patriarchy dictated a narrow range of individual identity for men.[29]

Fathers' relationships with their daughters were inevitably different from those with their sons. The exclusion of women from the public life where fathers and sons consorted, and the convention that ushered daughters out of the natal household to marry in their mid-teens, make fathers seem

26   Meyer Fortes, "The Structure of Unilineal Descent Groups," *American Anthropologist* 55 (1953): 17–41, at 34. On functional bilaterality in formally unilineal descent groups, see Jack Goody, *The Development of the Family and Marriage in Europe* (Cambridge: Cambridge University Press, 1983), pp. 6, 226; cf. Chojnacki, "Kinship Ties."

27   Chojnacki, "Political Adulthood."

28   Official testimony about the dependence of a majority of patricians on office holding is in MC 34, Stella, f. 109v. The fullest treatment of governmental careerism among the patriciate is in Queller, *Venetian Patriciate*.

29   On the tension between youthful expansiveness and adult conformity, see Chojnacki, "Political Adulthood," especially the references to liminality, pp. 806–10. See also the discussion of Richard C. Trexler, *Public Life in Renaissance Florence* (New York: Academic Press, 1980), chap. 5.

remote figures in their daughters' lives. That helps to explain the apparent coldness with which fathers, or grandfathers such as Gasparino Morosini, negotiated marriages that took girls from the family hearth at a tender age and plunked them willy-nilly into the households and beds of male strangers.[30] It is wise not to universalize paternal stoniness: statements by fathers of warm affection for daughters do appear in the sources.[31] Moreover, fathers were under considerable pressure to forge advantageous family alliances by means of marriage; gathering a competitive dowry and bestowing a young daughter in marriage were two sacrifices that even tenderhearted patriarchs might be obliged to make. Nor were married daughters written off by their fathers or other family members. On the contrary, a father had a powerful practical reason for maintaining close ties to his daughter: the hope that she would return some of her dowry wealth to the natal family that had assembled it. For their part, young wives showed lingering ties to their fathers, for example, by making them executors and legatees of their wills, thereby attesting to the endurance of father–daughter bonds beyond the wedding day.[32]

Nevertheless, practical interest blended with cultural principles to make daughters instruments of the family strategies pursued by their fathers. Prevailing values tied men's honor to control over their womenfolk's sexuality; in practice, that limited women's approved gender roles to wifehood

---

30 Among testating parents in the sample of wills, thirty-four identified specific ages for their daughters' marriages. Their preferences ranged from age eleven or twelve to twenty, with a median age of fourteen to sixteen. See, briefly, note 53.

31 In 1497 Francesco Morosini made a bequest to his daughter, who lived in a convent, "che io amo come lanima mia propria" ("whom I love as my very soul"). He urged the convent authorities (to whom he left a large bequest) to treat her well, "perche la dita mia fia mai non ho lassato haver senestro dapoi che ie [i.e., lei è] li dentro nel dito monastier, per esserli sta bon padre e lei dolcissima fiola et esser el mio cuor proprio" ("because I have allowed no harm to befall her from the time she entered that convent, in order to be a good father to her, who is my most sweet daughter and my very heart"). ASV, Procuratori di San Marco, Commissarie de Ultra, B. 221, fasc. 1, Francesco Morosini, Register, 10 November 1497.

32 Not yet systematically documented, this tendency emerges anecdotally: Isabetta Trevisan, married in 1417 to Filippo Foscari, named as executors of her 1419 will her father and a paternal uncle as well as her husband. Pregnant, she bequeathed to the unborn child six hundred ducats, which, if the child did not reach adulthood, were to go to her father and uncle, who in any case were named her residuary heirs; her husband was to get only one hundred ducats. NT 367, Angeletus, unnumbered, 4 January 1419 (1418 Venetian style); Marco Barbaro, "Libro di nozze patrizie," Biblioteca Nazionale Marciana, Venice, Codici italiani, classe VII, 156 (= 8492) (hereafter abbreviated as Barbaro, Nozze), f. 189 left. Maria Barbarigo, married in 1450, named as executors of the will she drew up during her pregnancy in 1451 her father, a paternal uncle, and her husband. She bequeathed two hundred ducats to her husband, but the same amount each to her father and her mother and one hundred ducats to one of her brothers; her remaining hundred ducats she left to the child she was carrying, but if it died before reaching age fourteen, the money was to go to her brothers. NT 558, Gambaro, no. 220, 17 December 1451; Barbaro, Nozze, f. 368 left.

or enclosure in a convent.[33] Even that restricted vocational choice generally seems to have been made by the father, not the daughter. The large dowries that families were obliged to commit to favorable marriages, and the tender age at which women's vocations were decided, meant that factors other than a girl's preference dominated in her father's assessment of prospective sons-in-law; at the same time, many families simply lacked the wealth to arrange marriages for all their daughters, requiring fathers to force some into convents amid, as the preamble to one legislative act put it, "tears and wailing."[34] The evidence in fathers' wills shows that Gasparino Morosini was following custom in decreeing that the "gentleman" to whom his granddaughter Franceschina was to be married at age thirteen should be chosen by her male kinsmen.[35]

Mothers writing their wills applied the influence of their wealth in ways that both contrasted with and complemented the intentions of fathers, but with the ultimate effect of broadening the range of gender identity for both sons and daughters. Owing to their distinctive placement overlapping two lineages and families, women had greater flexibility in their family and kinship orientation than did men; indeed, such variety is a hallmark of women's wills. Women wrote more wills than men – in a sampling of 614 patrician

33   On male honor and female vocations, see Julius Kirshner, "Pursuing Honor while Avoiding Sin: The *Monte delle Doti* of Florence," *Studi senesi* 89 (1977): 175–258.

34   ASV, Senato, Misti, Reg. 53, f. 70. This act, aimed at restraining dowry inflation, is discussed at length in Chojnacki, "Marriage Legislation." Motives for consigning daughters to convents are discussed in Richard C. Trexler, "Le célibat à la fin du Moyen Age: Les religieuses de Florence," *Annales: Économies, sociétés, civilisations* 27 (1972): 1329–50. Questions about the effectiveness of the religious life in guaranteeing male honor by preserving female chastity are raised by evidence of sexual activity in convents presented in Guido Ruggiero, *The Boundaries of Eros: Sex Crime and Sexuality in Renaissance Venice* (New York: Oxford University Press, 1985), chap. 4, "Sex Crimes against God."

35   Nonetheless, Gasparino was more explicit than most about his lineage ties to the men he charged with arranging Franceschina's marriage. Men usually assigned the responsibility for their daughters' marriages to their executors, who normally included a large proportion of agnates, though by no means agnates alone. For example, Lorenzo Loredan: "Volio che mia fie . . . siano maridade o munegade segondo aparera a dischrezio de mio chommessarii" ("I want my daughters to be married or placed in a convent, at the discretion of my executors"), who were his three brothers, his wife, her father, and his sons when they reached age fourteen. NT 558, Gambaro, no. 86, 10 May 1441. Similarly, Andrea Arimondo provided that when his daughter turned fifteen, "lasso libertas ala maor parte de mii commessarii . . . al suo maridar a uno zentilomo de Veniesia" ("I give liberty to the majority of my executors [to make the appropriate arrangements] at her marriage to a Venetian noble"). ASV, Cancelleria inferiore (hereafter abbreviated CI), Miscellanea testamenti, notai diversi, B. 27, no. 2697, 13 August 1427. His executors were his mother, his four brothers, his wife, her parents, and her brother. On the involvement of wives and their natal kin in the determination of their children's futures, see my discussion later in this chapter.

wills more than twice as many, 431 to 183.[36] This seems chiefly a result of adjustment to the sharp social and thus affective changes in a woman's life as she proceeded through the uxorial cycle from young bridehood to mature wife and motherhood to widowhood. But it also reflects a woman's broader range of choice among potential recipients of her beneficence, a consequence of her more complex network of family ties, and it contrasts with the determinism apparent in men's wills, whose provisions followed a narrower path of family and lineage responsibility.[37] Whereas men's wills usually added a few special touches to the statutory conventions, sticking mainly to the male line, those of women included both greater variety among beneficiaries and less conventional – that is, less masculinely lineage-bound – patterns of bequests, to children and others. These different approaches to testation, revealing concrete differences in gender characteristics and showing women's confidence in institutional responsiveness to their intentions, enlarged the impact of women's dowry wealth beyond the economic to the social and cultural.[38]

To their sons, women offered a more ample social context for lineage affiliation. Husbands themselves frequently recognized the capacity of their wives to contribute to the lineage, enlisting them as collaborators in family strategy, naming them as executors of their estates, and committing to them, with inducements, the upbringing of the children, including control over their children's patrimonies – a mirror image of Gasparino Morosini's administration of the estates of his wives.[39] For their part, mothers appreciated the inseparability of their sons' well-being from the matrix of the lineage. When, as often happened, widows sponsored their eighteen-year-old sons' patrician credentialing, they joined with their husbands' paternal kinsmen in seeing the young men through the ritual.[40] Women recognized the symbolic as well as the practical importance of lineage, for example,

---

36   This sample is not scientific but simply the product of careful study over several years of all the wills I could read. Most but not all were drawn up by members, by birth or marriage, of sixteen patrician clans whose social and political experiences I am reconstructing in detail. I know of no statistical breakdown of surviving Venetian wills; but extensive work with the card index of wills in the ASV, as well as with the testament files of dozens of notaries, gives the overpowering impression that women left wills far more often than men.

37   The Venetian statutes governing inheritance in cases of intestacy reflected patrilineal principles, favoring first children, then ascendants in the male line. Fathers who conformed to those principles could thus entrust their estates to the enforcements of the statutes. *Volumen statutorum*, bk. 4, chaps. 24–7, pp. 70v–74v. Mothers, whose intestacy was governed largely but not completely by the same rules, had reason in their more complex social placement to make their intentions testamentarily explicit. Ibid., chap. 28, p. 74v.

38   For differences in men's and women's patterns of testation, see Chojnacki, "Dowries and Kinsmen," pp. 60–7.

39   See note 35; also Chojnacki, "The Power of Love," p. 132.

40   Chojnacki, "Kinship Ties and Young Patricians."

with regard to real estate: in 1401 the widow Beruzza Soranzo urged her son Girolamo to add one thousand ducats to the dowry of his sister Caterina, in return for which Beruzza would prevail on the girl to consign to Girolamo the share of the family palace that their father had left her. This is a wonderfully neat and revealing arrangement. It fattened the dowry that would enhance Caterina's social placement and, ultimately, her personal wealth, while at the same time giving Girolamo sole possession of the palace that identified him with his father's line. It also displays the contrast between fixed, locked-in male property, literally "immovable," and the more liquid, flexible, "movable" wealth that gave women's social relations greater agility.[41]

Mothers also supplemented their sons' lineage affiliation by strengthening the sons' ties to the mothers' kinsmen. Maternal uncles frequently joined with their widowed sisters in ushering nephews into official patrician adulthood. This practice served both parties. For young men it enlarged the web of friends and patrons whose support was necessary for success in the adult patrician world. To the uncles it offered a friendly vote in the council chamber as well as the prospect of economic cooperation, and through that some tangible benefit from the investment they had committed to their sister's dowry.[42] Young men who entered adulthood in these circumstances had a broader range of social options with which to fashion their identities, enlarging the basic lineage orientation, with the guidance of mothers serving as a key to flexible social placement and the vocational advantages that it promised.[43] Encouraging that filial attitude was mothers' wealth and the capacity it gave them to smooth their sons' way, for example, by providing business capital and – interesting irony here – by pledging their own wealth for the safe restitution of the dowries of their daughters-in-law.[44]

41   NT 575, Giorgio Gibellino, no. 704, 15 November 1401. Beruzza was the married sister whom Gasparino Morosini wanted to prepare his granddaughter Franceschina for marriage. The preference for men as heirs to immovable property and women as heirs to movables was clearly stated in the statutes governing intestacy. *Volumen statutorum*, bk. 4, chap. 15, p. 71v. On similar rules in Florence, see Kuehn, "Some Ambiguities of Female Inheritance," p. 28 n.4.

42   Chojnacki, "Kinship Ties and Young Patricians"; Finlay, *Politics in Renaissance Venice*, pp. 87–9. Hughes, "From Brideprice to Dowry," pp. 284, 290, argues that the dowry regime diminished bilateral ties; she also notes, however, that men retained an interest in the woman to whose dowry they had contributed as well as in the affines it produced.

43   On family and kin boundaries as the frame of adult identity, see Davis, "Boundaries and the Sense of Self."

44   E.g., in 1430 Cristina Falier, widow of Nicolò Barbarigo, invested 1,300 ducats with her son, Andrea, who acknowledged that it was "pro meis utilitatibus" ("for my use"). CI, Busta 122, Marevidi, Protocollo, f. 15v. In a marriage contract of 1451 Marina, widow of Tomaso Donà, "se hobliga la mittade de tuti i suo beni" ("pledges one-half of all her property") as security for repayment of the dowry that her son, Nicolò, was to receive from his wife-to-be, Isabetta Querini; the total dowry to be repaid was 1,200 ducats. ASV, Giudici del Proprio, Vadimoni, Reg. 4, ff. 58v–59v.

Such mother–son associations softened the edges of patriarchy by giving mothers a role in guiding their sons into successful adulthood. This urges nuance in categorizing parental roles by gender, showing as it does that mothers could be directive, not merely supportive, in discharging their upbringing duties – even vis-à-vis their patriarchally privileged male offspring. For patrician social organization, it shows mothers enriching the basic kinship structure, interlacing formal patriliny with practical bilaterality. But dowry wealth had another effect on male gender identity, one with deep cultural and psychological as well as social significance: it narrowed men's chances to fulfill the patriarchal ideal of becoming husbands and fathers. That is, the heavy commitment of family wealth to daughters' dowries effectively deprived many of their brothers of the chance to marry: men from less influential or prestigious families, or members of fraternal groups that lacked the resources to guarantee the dowries of wives for all the brothers, or simply men into whose sisters' dowries had gone the wherewithal for taking on the responsibilities of patrician husbandhood. In the fifteenth century only three in five adult patrician men married.[45] Other reasons contributed, but the premium that high dowries placed on worthy husbands was an important one. In an indirect way, then, wealthy mothers fostered a schism in male gender identity, separating those who would assume the mantle of patriarchy from those who neither ruled families nor propagated their lineage (at least legitimately) nor presided over the integration of sons into patrician government and society. But mothers also had a more direct effect on the options of their sons, by way of their concern for their daughters.

As I have noted, fathers, by preference or necessity, generally treated daughters as prime instruments of family strategy. But, as if in compensation, mothers gave them concern, wealth, and latitude of vocation. A couple of examples convey the texture of this maternal influence. In 1415 Barbarella Contarini declared that her imminent marriage had been made possible by "her most benign and generous mother," who had provided the

---

45 The exact percentage of adult male patricians who married, 62 percent, was gained by comparing marriage lists in Barbaro, Nozze (see note 32), with registrations for the Balla d'Oro (see note 23) among sixteen sample clans for the period 1410–90. This involved 952 registrants, of whom 540 married. ASV, Avogaria di Comun, Balla d'Oro, Reg. 162, 163, 164. To these were added 132 husbands recorded in Barbaro, Nozze, who did not register for the Balla d'Oro, making a total of 1,084 men, of whom 672 (62 percent) married. The practice among patricians of limiting male marriage for purposes of preserving the property of a group of brothers is discussed for the sixteenth through eighteenth centuries in James C. Davis, *A Venetian Family and Its Fortune, 1500–1900: The Donà and the Conservation of Their Wealth* (Philadelphia: American Philosophical Society, 1975). pp. 93–106. Davis cites sources asserting that the practice began in the mid-sixteenth century; the evidence just noted, however, suggests that it was already in effect in the fifteenth century.

entire dowry: a good thing, she went on, "because of the meagerness [*carentium*] of my inheritance from my father."[46] In thus providing for her daughter's vocational destiny, Barbarella's mother was discharging an essential patriarchal responsibility. By supplying the material means that spelled the difference between Barbarella's being able to marry or not, she was also influencing – or, instead and significantly, giving Barbarella herself the chance to shape – the young woman's sexual identity.

A second case further displays this maternal power, here generationally doubled. In 1464 Petronella Falier, wife of Zilio Morosini, ordered in her will that as soon as her daughter Paolina turned fourteen, she was to be immediately married to a patrician ("subito in un zentilom"), to be chosen by her husband and her executors, the procurators of Saint Mark. Paolina's dowry was to consist of a one-third share of Petronella's estate (the other two-thirds to be divided between her son and her unborn child) and one thousand ducats which Paolina's maternal grandmother had bequeathed the girl. Yet, worried that Zilio might prove dilatory or even resistant, Petronella gave primary authority for the marriage arrangements to the procurators, who were to carry out her intentions for Paolina whether Zilio liked it or not.[47] Remarkably, Petronella was asserting that a mother with enough wealth could prevail over her husband in deciding their daughter's marital future. It is impossible to know who would have won in litigation, but in the event, Paolina did get married two years later, at age fifteen or less, to a member of Petronella's natal lineage.[48]

Petronella Falier's influence came from female wealth, specifically her own and her mother's large contributions to her daughter's dowry, which it would have pained her husband to do without. But the dowry wealth of other mothers enabled them to influence their daughters' destinies in even more elaborate ways, by letting them choose their vocations. The 1479 will of Maria Bembo, wife of Girolamo Zane, illustrates this point. Toward the marriage portion of each of her three daughters Maria allocated six hundred ducats.[49] But she also allocated bequests to them if they should decide not to marry but instead elect the religious life ("nolent maritare, sed monacare"). That was not the end of it, however, for she offered them an

---

46 CI 56, Griffon, Protocollo I, f. 76v. In return for this maternal generosity, Barbarella transferred to her mother all her rights of succession to her father's estate. This case shows how, by discharging a paternal responsibility, a mother could lay claim to a child's share of a paternal estate.

47 NT 1239, Tomei, no. 600: "ma tuto quel parera a diti commisarii sia fato in chaxo el padre dilatase el suo maridar" ("but my executors should take whatever action they deem appropriate in the event that her father delays arranging her marriage").

48 Paolina's marriage to Luca Falier in 1466, when she could not have been more than fifteen (calculated from Petronella's will of 1464), is in Barbaro, Nozze, f. 327 right.

49 NT 68, Bonicardi, no. 210, 16 May 1479.

even broader range of choice. If the girls chose neither marriage nor the convent ("nolent maritare nec monacare") but instead wished to remain spinsters, living with their father and brothers, then Maria's estate was to provide their expenses for food and clothing for as long as they lived. Moreover, if for some reason they could not live with their brothers, then each was to get an additional forty ducats yearly for housing expenses, and each who lived to age twenty-four under these circumstances would be able to dispose freely of an additional hundred ducats in her will.

Maria Bembo effectively underwrote for her daughters three different vocational choices, involving three different social situations and gender identities. Nor was she unique. Increasingly in the fifteenth century, mothers were offering daughters vocational choice and the economic means to exercise it.[50] Fathers were restrained from opposing these maternal intentions because to make the good marriage alliances that served family interest, they needed the mothers' contributions to their daughters' marriage portions, most of which were actually paid out to husbands while the mothers, like Petronella Falier, were still alive. Indeed, in a remarkable development, which I believe shows the influence of wives on their husbands' attitudes toward their families, by the late fifteenth century fathers too were beginning to follow their wives' lead and themselves offer their daughters the choice between marriage and the convent, although, not surprisingly, they do not appear to have followed them into an acceptance of lay spinsterhood.[51]

50 Francesca Loredan Capello bequeathed four hundred ducats to each of her daughters; but "ista condicio sit et intelligatur in filiabus meis que maritaverintur. Ille vero que monacaverintur aut *starent honeste in domo* habeant ducatos trecentos" ("this provision should be understood as applying to my daughters who marry. Those indeed who become nuns or *live chastely at home* are to have three hundred ducats"). NT 1238, Tomei, pt. II, no. 292 bis, 6 October 1473; emphasis added. See also the wills of Isabetta Gritti da Lezze (ibid., no. 220, 4 May 1465), Fantina Contarini Morosini (NT 486, Gibellino, no. 204, 11 July 1435), and Isabetta Morosini, who bequeathed one hundred ducats to her granddaughter "o per so maridar, o se lie volese andar munega in monastier de oservancia voio lie i abia e posa far quelo lie vora, *e cusi se la vuol star in nel mondo sença maridarse, o, munegarse*" ("either for her marriage or, if she chooses to become a nun in an observant convent, I want her to have them to use as she wishes; and likewise if she elects to live a secular life without marrying or becoming a nun"). (NT 1156, Croci, no. 517, 23 October 1450; emphasis added).

51 Although I have found no fathers explicitly endorsing spinsterhood for their daughters, Prodocimo Arimondo instructed that his daughter Pellegrina, "que ducit vitam spiritualem" ("who is leading a spiritual life"), was to live not in a convent but with her brothers, "et habeat vitum de bonis meis et vestitum et bene tractetur" ("and she is to have food and clothing from my estate, and be well treated"). NT 1239, Tomei, no. 606, 27 February 1474 (1473 Venetian style). More in line with the growing tendency to allow daughters vocational choice, Lorenzo Loredan left it "in libertade dele do mie fie zoe Chataruza e Ixabela se quelle volesse servir a dio" ("up to my two daughters, namely Cateruzza and Isabella, if they wish to serve God"), in which case each was to receive four hundred ducats; but "se veramente quelle volesse esser maridada, abiano de beni dela mia comessaria ducati 600 per suo dota"

Addressing the issue of female identity in early modern France, Natalie Zemon Davis suggests that giving oneself away in marriage, consciously accepting the imposed vocation, was a means by which women could attain a certain psychological autonomy, could carve out a personal identity, in a patriarchal society.[52] In the case of Venice, the wealth of mothers was permitting some women to go even further, to elect the adult vocational and sexual identity of their choice. To be sure, even young women who could choose marriage rather than be thrust into it still had their husbands selected for them, with family interest, not psychological compatibility, the paramount consideration. Yet, the growing attention to female choice in the matter of marriage, by mothers above all but also by some fathers, is reflected in a gradual rise in the preferred marriage age for women. The evidence is sparse, but by the later Quattrocento the age at which parents wanted their daughters to marry had risen from the early teens – the fourteenth-century fashion – to the middle or late teens.[53] This delay may have been encouraged by fathers, for whom a married daughter's greater maturity made likelier a capacity to resist the influence of husband and father-in-law, thus enabling her to demonstrate tangible loyalty to the natal family. But mothers as well were influential in pushing back their daughters' marriage age.[54] The later a girl married, the more maturely considered her choice of vocation. And we may speculate that mothers may also have eagerly used their influence to spare their daughters the psychological distress, even terror, of coercive youthful marriage to a stranger.

("if indeed they wish to marry, each is to receive six hundred ducats from my estate for her dowry"). NT 1186, Groppi, no. 71, 29 April 1476. More munificently, Alvise Zane left his daughter Michela his entire residuary estate for her marriage portion, unless his wife bore a son, in which case Michela would get only (!) 3,500 ducats; but if Michela "vellet monacare solum habere debeat ducatos 1,500 ("wishes to become a nun, she is to have only 1,500 ducats"). NT 68, Bonicardi, no. 316, 7 April 1485.

52 Davis, "Boundaries and the Sense of Self," p. 61. This essay lays out the components of the complex issue, central to social and cultural history, and especially to the benefits of a gender-sensitive approach to it, of the tension between individual identity and the group membership that both restricts and gives it shape. The conceptual and methodological problems involved in attending to both sociocultural context and the vagaries of individual circumstance and experience require much discussion, but they are helpfully clarified by Davis' essay.

53 Of 361 wills of married patricians, most mentioned the age of majority (conventionally age fourteen) as the preferred marriage age. But among thirty-three parents who specified marriage ages between 1350 and 1500, those testating between 1350 and 1400 ranged in their specifications from eleven to seventeen years, with a median preferred age of thirteen; the preference of those testating between 1401 and 1450 ranged from age thirteen to twenty, with a median of fifteen; and between 1451 and 1500 from fourteen to eighteen, with a median of sixteen.

54 The evidence is mixed on mothers' preferences; some seem to have favored early marriage for their daughters, possibly to free them from their fathers' control; but others favored delaying marriage, to give the daughters greater maturity in choosing and adapting to marriage.

A trend toward later marriage for women, toward a more considered measure of female adulthood and its implications, is one notable effect of the influence that propertied women were having on the upbringing and the adult identities of their children. Later marriages, larger dowries, and the choice of vocations altered the gender balance in patrician society, giving each successive generation of wives greater means of affecting the culture of the ruling class. But the modification of male gender models through the direct and indirect action of mothers was equally significant for patrician culture. Alongside the patriarchal figure shaping the interests of family and lineage, his authority in the household mirroring his patrician entitlement to participate in Venice's government, the irreversible commitment to ever-larger dowries was now producing in increasing numbers alternative male types, notably the patrician bachelor, equally active in political affairs but lacking the titular family authority of his married brothers. As Guido Ruggiero has suggested, these bachelors may also have produced alternative sexual cultures, or subcultures, both heterosexual and homosexual.[55]

Indeed, for all male patricians the broad-ranging social orientation of influential mothers complemented and even displaced the narrow lineage configuration with strong loyalties to and involvements with a broad range of kin, maternal as well as paternal. Young men whose mothers forged close ties between them and their maternal uncles grew into full adulthood with an ampler kinship orientation, embracing a range of close, trusted associations beyond the boundaries of lineage. I have argued that this elaborate network of loyalties combined with shared exclusivism to promote the solidarity for which Venice's patrician regime was noted; I believe that this adds up to an important female impact on patrician politics, the public sphere putatively monopolized by men.[56]

In a sociopolitical elite such as Venice's patriciate the private and public spheres can be only artificially separated. It is therefore no surprise that the influence on patrician society at large of propertied women of clear intention found parallel expression within the private sphere of the conjugal family as well, in ways that caution against easy assumptions about patriarchal authority in practice. An act of the Venetian senate in 1535 noted that many men were no longer engaging in productive economic activity but were instead living off their wives' dowries.[57] Such men were adapting to the fact that patrician liquid wealth was gravitating into female hands, a

55   Ruggiero, *Boundaries of Eros*, pp. 137–40. See also Patricia H. Labalme, "Sodomy and Venetian Justice in the Renaissance," *Tijdschrift voor Rechtsgeschiedenis* 52 (1984): 217–54, at 232–5.

56   Chojnacki, "Kinship Ties and Young Patricians," esp. pp. 259–60.

57   ASV, Senato, Terra, Reg. 28, f. 151r.

consequence of steadily increasing dowries, the commitment by families of large portions of their wealth to their daughters' marriage prospects, and the provision by wealthy mothers for their daughters' adulthood. Without knowing more about individual marriages dominated by wifely wealth, one cannot conclude either that such husbands exploited their wives or, alternatively, that wives called the connubial tune. In either case, however, the inescapable fact is that these husbands were apatriarchally making a vocation of marriage.

Yet the nonconformity of individual men, whether bachelors or husbands, to a generalized model of the authoritative, directive patriarch does not mitigate the wholesale formal dominion of patriarchal institutions in Venice. However dependent on or even subject to this or that woman an individual male patrician might have been in practical matters, his sex gave him a share of the formal stature and prescriptive dominance that belonged exclusively to men as men. Michelle Rosaldo noted some time ago that female *power* does not dislodge male *authority*; no matter what leverage patrician mothers might have been able to exert on their families, the institutional and discursive framework of Venetian society accorded authority only to men – authority that no amount of female influence, wealth, and power could ever dislodge.[58] This asymmetry between firmly lodged principle and fluid, contingent practice reminds us how complex gender was in Venice, and remains in historical discourse about Venice and elsewhere. Indeed, it is the conceptual plasticity of gender, its potential to provide a coherent pattern connecting deeply ingrained patriarchal conventions with the Brownian movement of quotidian social relations guided by but also deviating from these conventions, that makes gender so valuable for a nuanced historical discourse embracing public and private life.

The anecdotal evidence presented herein shows Venetian patrician society as lacking absolute patterns of either patriarchal power or female subversion of it; of either exclusively patrilineal or effectively bilateral kinship orientation; of either paternal or maternal inheritance as the critical element in a child's future. Indicating above all that both sides of each pair constitute essential elements of the picture, the lack of compelling evidence either of sweeping patriarchy or of its absence reveals that patterns of gender identity in the Venetian patriciate were flexible, offering at least a range of choice, for women and for men. Although the possibilities of alternative gender identities were contained within the formal boundaries of patriarchy, their expression in the practical world of patrician adulthood owed much to – and therefore reveals the cultural importance of – propertied, socially influential, self-confident patrician mothers performing their most sacred duty.

58 Rosaldo, "Woman, Culture, and Society," p. 21.

8

Gender and Sexual Culture in Renaissance Italy

Michael Rocke

In February 1496, friar Girolamo Savonarola, campaigning to reform the morals of Florentine society, fulminated against the sexual debauchery that, in his view, had "ruined the world, . . . corrupted men in lust, led women into indecency, and boys into sodomy and filth, and made them become like prostitutes". His condemnation of erotic licence stemmed not merely from its immorality, but also from his conviction that the indulgence of sexual pleasures produced a dangerous confusion of gender boundaries: "Young lads have been made into women. But that's not all: fathers are like daughters, brothers like sisters. There is no distinction between the sexes or anything else anymore."[1]

Savonarola's comment reveals some central assumptions of the culture of sex and gender in Renaissance Italy. Sexual behaviour was in fact a basic component of the complex of cultural and social signifiers that distinguished individuals, beyond their belonging to one biological sex or the other, as gendered beings, as masculine or feminine. His insistence on the transformative capacity of sex to make men into women, and presumably vice versa, indicates an awareness that gender identity was not a natural or fixed quality but was constructed and malleable, and as such it needed to be adequately shaped, reinforced and defended. The friar's remarks also betrayed deep anxiety about establishing and enforcing borders, not only between licit and illicit sexual comportment, but also between related virile and feminine conventions and ideals, for it was in part around such confines that society was properly ordered.

---

1 Girolamo Savonarola, *Prediche sopra Amos e Zaccaria*, P. Ghiglieri, ed., 3 vols (Rome, 1971–2), Vol. I, pp. 194, 200 (23 February 1496).

In recent years, historians have dedicated growing attention to sexual practices, beliefs and attitudes, and to how unauthorized sex was regulated in various regions of late medieval and early modern Italy. Although much remains to be learned about the peninsula's distinctive sexual cultures and about local systems of policing sex, these studies have already deepened our understanding of Italian society and have thrown new light on relationships between sexuality, gender ideology, and masculine and feminine identities. Here I would like to chart some of these connections, beginning with the ideological conventions that shaped and constrained men's and women's sexual comportment in different ways; then examining how gender differences were configured in certain religious and legal prescriptions regarding sex; and finally exploring perspectives on gender that have emerged from unauthorized or illicit sexual behaviours.

Norms and Ideals

In this strongly patriarchal and patrilineal society, the control of women's sexual conduct and reproductive functions was accorded especially high importance. Centuries-old philosophical, medical, legal and religious discourses on sexual difference continued to sustain the notion that women were inferior in all ways to men and subject to their dominion. Medieval understanding of female biology contributed to beliefs that women were passive and receptive in their sexual nature yet possessed a powerful yearning for semen and a more ravenous sexual appetite than that of men – a view reinforced by the Judeo-Christian myth of Eve the temptress, responsible for original sin and the fall from grace. Both religious doctrine and lay society upheld chastity as the supreme virtue of women, whether as young unwed virgins, wives or widows. The purity and modesty of the *donna onesta* was regularly contrasted with the shamelessness and incontinence of the "indecent" woman, embodied especially in the figure of the prostitute.

The defence of female virginity before marriage and chastity thereafter also played an essential role in the pervasive culture of honour, a woman's sexual behaviour largely defining both her own standing and reputation and those of her family and of the males responsible for "governing" her. Such concerns loomed especially large for wealthy and propertied families, for whom the guarantee of paternity determined the transmission of patrimonies and the competition for public honour carried momentous political stakes. This obsession was aptly stated by the Florentine patrician and humanist Matteo Palmieri in his *Vita Civile*:

> Wives must exercise the greatest and most extraordinary guard not only against uniting with another man, but even to avoid all suspicion of such

filthy wickedness. This error is the supreme disgrace to decency, it effaces honour, destroys union, renders paternity uncertain, heaps infamy on families and within them brings dissension and hatred and dissolves every relationship; she no longer deserves to be called a married woman but rather a corrupt wench, worthy only of public humiliation.[2]

It was in part to safeguard both their daughters' virginity and the family's honour that parents rushed their girls into marriage as soon as possible after sexual maturity, usually between the ages of fifteen and eighteen. For the same reason, unmarriageable patrician girls were quickly made nuns and secluded within a convent. To preserve their chastity, women of middle- and upper-class families tended to be isolated in their homes and their contacts with men were carefully controlled. Women at lower social levels, who generally lacked this powerful familial protection, had greater exposure to males and more freedom in their daily lives; for them, the conventions regarding virginity and chastity were probably somewhat less rigid.

Despite religious proscriptions against all extra-marital sex, standards and expectations with regard to male sexual behaviour were generally more flexible than those applied to women. No social ideal compelled men to remain virgins before marriage or demanded fidelity of them afterward. They were supposed to obey laws against rape, adultery, and other illicit acts, but lax enforcement and light penalties for many offences helped dull their dissuasive force. While men were to respect the virtue of women of honourable families, they had a large pool of slaves and servants, poor or immodest women, and prostitutes with whom they could acceptably indulge their desires. This sexual liberty was reinforced by the late age at which men normally married – from their late twenties to early thirties – and by substantial rates of men who never married. Denied economic autonomy under their fathers' patriarchal rule, and forbidden significant civic roles, young men lived in a state of prolonged and powerless adolescence. These footloose bachelors were the main protagonists of the violence and sexual debauchery characteristic of Renaissance Italy. City fathers, themselves once young, viewed their profligacy with some sympathy and indulgence; it also provided an excuse for barring them from the serious business of governing, since "they say youths should not discuss public affairs, but pursue their sexual needs".[3]

2   Matteo Palmieri, *Vila Civile*, F. Battaglia, ed. (Bologna, 1944), p. 133.
3   Donato Giannotti, *Opere politiche e letterarie di Donato Giannotti*, F. Polidori, ed., 2 vols (Florence, 1850), Vol. I, p. 230. On late male marriage and sexual behaviour, see David Herlihy, "Vieillir à Florence au Quattrocento", *Annales, ESC*, 24 (1969), pp. 1346–9; Guido Ruggiero, *The Boundaries of Eros: Sex Crime and Sexuality in Renaissance Venice* (New York, 1985), esp. pp. 159–62; Michael Rocke, *Forbidden Friendships: Homosexuality and Male Culture in Renaissance Florence* (New York, 1996), pp. 113–32.

Masculine identity did not, however, lie only in the double standard that allowed men the sexual freedoms denied to women, but also in conventions that identified manliness solely with a dominant role in sex. In this regard, males' sexual and gendered norms were as rigid as those imposing chastity on females. Potency figured among the constitutive features of masculinity, such that a man's failure to achieve erection was grounds for annulment of his marriage or divorce.[4] The association of virility with dominance was one source of the religious ban against couples engaging in intercourse with the woman on top, an "unnatural" position considered emblematic of woman's usurpation – or man's abdication – of males' superior status.[5] Similar notions pervaded same-sex relations, in which adult men were expected to take an exclusively "active" role in sex with adolescents, behaviour that corresponded fully with masculine ideals, while a mature man's assumption of the receptive role was abhorred as a dangerous transgression of gender norms.

Conjugal Relations and Religious Precepts

The Church, the most authoritative source of moral teachings on sexual behaviour, established guidelines and norms which in principle were equally applicable to men and women. For all, sex was licit only within marriage, with the conscious aim of procreation, in prescribed times and conditions, and in a single position, with the couple facing and the man above. All intercourse outside marriage, as well as conjugal sex for mere pleasure, in forbidden positions, or in a manner that might impede generation, was condemned and prohibited. Although some late medieval theologians began to modify these tenets somewhat, sanctioning sensual pleasure as a reproductive aid and even permitting unconventional positions, the Church's sexual orthodoxy remained restricted.[6] How closely couples observed these prescriptions is another matter and is difficult to ascertain. That moralists continued to vehemently denounce practices such as anal intercourse that could serve contraceptive aims, and the rapid decline in wives' fertility that has been observed in fifteenth-century Tuscany would

4 James A. Brundage, *Law, Sex, and Christian Society in Medieval Europe* (Chicago, 1987), p. 512; Vern Bullough, "On being a male in the Middle Ages", in *Medieval Masculinities: Regarding Men in the Middle Ages*, C. A. Lees, ed. (Minneapolis, MN, 1994), pp. 41–2.

5 Natalie Davis, "Women on top", in her *Society and Culture in Early Modern France: Eight Essays* (Stanford, CA, 1975), pp. 124–51.

6 Nicholas Davidson, "Theology, nature and the law: sexual sin and sexual crime in Italy from the fourteenth to the seventeenth century", in *Crime, Society and the Law in Renaissance Italy*, T. Dean and K. J. P. Lowe, eds (Cambridge, UK, 1994), pp. 77–85.

suggest that many spouses disregarded the sexual guidance of their preachers and confessors.[7]

However its teachings on sexual conduct were received, the Church played an important and perhaps more effective role in forming and transmitting notions of gender. While all were supposed to bear equal liability for their carnal acts, preachers presented sexual doctrines to the faithful in ways that carried considerably different messages for men and women. The sermons of Bernardino of Siena to the Sienese and Florentines in the 1420s offer some pertinent illustrations.[8] Bernardino's preaching on conjugal life fitted well with his culture's growing emphasis on marriage as a form of companionship between spouses who were to treat each other with mutual love and respect.[9] Regarding sex, he maintained that spouses shared responsibility for preventing each other from sinning, stressed that fidelity was a duty of wives and husbands, and reproached both for sexual failings. His teachings were embedded in a framework of values, consistent with Church doctrine and patrician ideals, that endorsed sexual moderation for both sexes, sustained the notion that women's frailty of reason made them more inclined than men to sin, and upheld wives' subjection to their husbands' authority. Within these traditions, however, the emphases and omissions of his remarks, or the shifts depending on the audience addressed, show some ways in which gendered assumptions framed his teachings and how ideal genders were shaped.

This can be seen most clearly in Bernardino's sermons about a basic tenet of Church doctrine, that is, the equality of spouses' rights and duties with regard to the "marriage debt": while carefully observing the proper times, position, devout spirit and procreative aim of sex, husbands and wives possessed an identical right to intercourse, which their spouse was obliged, under penalty of mortal sin, to "render" to them. Bernardino reiterated that this injunction applied indistinctly to both partners, but in developing this egalitarian theme he employed examples and lessons that revealed and reinforced assumptions about gender difference. He normally directed his remarks on rendering the debt to wives, rather than to husbands, as if he

---

7   David Herlihy and Christiane Klapisch-Zuber, *Les Toscans et leurs families: une étude du catasto florentin de 1427* (Paris, 1978), pp. 441–2; Christiane Klapisch-Zuber, "Famille, religion et sexualité à Florence au Moyen Age", *Revue de l'histoire des religions*, 209 (1992), pp. 381–92; Maria Serena Mazzi, *Prostitute e lenoni nella Firenze del Quattrocento* (Milan, 1991), pp. 55–9, 61–86.

8   *Prediche volgari sul campo di Siena 1427*, Carlo Delcorno, ed., 2 vols (Milan, 1989), Vol. I, pp. 538–621 (hereafter, *Siena 1427*); *Le prediche volgari*, C. Cannarozzi, ed., 2 vols (Pistoia, 1934), Vol. I, pp. 380–404 (hereafter, *Florence 1424*), *Le prediche volgari*, C. Cannarozzi, ed., 3 vols (Florence, 1940), Vol. II, pp. 173–90 (hereafter, *Florence 1425*).

9   For example, *Siena 1427*, I, pp. 556, 568–9; *Florence 1424*, I, p. 412; *Florence 1425*, II, p. 177. On increasingly positive evaluations of marriage, see Herlihy and Klapisch-Zuber, *Les Toscans*, pp. 586–8.

assumed that males more commonly importuned their spouses for sex, thus implicitly fortifying notions of man's "active" nature and pressing desire and of woman's "passivity" and, ideally, her modesty.[10] Sexual continence and shame were considered women's crowning virtues, and when he discussed marital sex Bernardino reminded wives to remain as chaste as possible, never allowing their spouses to see them naked, to look at their "shameful parts", or to touch them indecently. On the few occasions he acknowledged wives' prerogative to request intercourse, he in effect disempowered them by insisting on their modesty. So as to reduce a wife's temptation to commit adultery, it was better, he claimed, that the husband anticipate her request and render his carnal obligation voluntarily, rather than for her to voice her longings. While a wife was bound to respond only if asked expressly for sex and was exonerated if her husband's signals were unclear, he was obliged to react to the "smallest sign" of his wife's yearning to protect her from the indelicacy of having to express her desire.[11]

Although Bernardino stressed women's virtue and modesty in carnal relations, he paradoxically also placed on them a greater burden of sexual knowledge and responsibility. He began one discussion on conjugal sex by warning that ignorance of sin exculpated neither partner, but proceeded to address only the wives, mothers and nubile girls in the congregation. Girls about to marry "had to know how to do it", and sinned if they neglected to learn; mothers who failed to impart the facts of life to their daughters committed a serious mortal sin.[12] Rarely, if ever, did he encourage fathers to give their sons lessons in sex education.

Accordingly, Bernardino often instructed wives about the times and conditions when they could and should legitimately refuse their husbands' requests, thereby giving them some control over the frequency and character of intercourse. Although he warned both partners about the evils of unrestrained passion and specific sins, he tended to represent husbands as more inclined to "disorderly affections" and excessive lust, which it was wives' duty to curb and correct. He insisted that, while wives were bound to obey their husbands, this never meant yielding to sinful requests. They were to refuse especially when their spouses wanted, as he implied they often did, to engage in acts *contra naturam* that impeded procreation. He also warned the wife to decline if her husband had imbibed too much wine, was crazed with lust, or desired sex so frequently that it might devitalize his seed, make him lose his senses, or cause illness or death.[13] Repeating an ancient taboo, revived vigorously in the Renaissance, he admonished women to

10   *Florence 1424*, I, pp. 381–404; *Siena 1427*, I, pp. 573–603.
11   *Siena 1427*, pp. 594, 617–18; *Florence 1425*, II, p. 179; *Florence 1424*, I, p. 393.
12   *Siena 1427*, pp. 577–83.
13   *Florence 1424*, I, pp. 388–9, 395–8; *Siena 1427*, I, pp. 588–91, 593, 600, 602–3.

rebuff husbands' requests for coitus during their menstrual period, which according to both popular and learned belief risked generating deformed or leprous children.[14] But in Italy, he conceded, a wife had better conceal her menstruous state and quietly render the debt, because otherwise her husband would demand anal intercourse. Bernardino also instructed wives, not husbands, to assess their mates' age and their physical and spiritual condition when considering whether or how often to consent to intercourse. He more often mentioned husbands' threats to satisfy their desires elsewhere as binding wives to render the debt, a tacit acknowledgment of men's greater opportunities to pursue extra-marital relations. It was only wives, however, whom he urged to grant consent selectively, in order to wean their husbands gradually from sex and convince them to embrace abstinence – for the Church, the "perfect state".[15]

The Law and the Courts

Distinctions in the treatment of men and women also characterized the regulation of illicit sex, both in law and in court practice. Italian governments between 1400 and 1600 took a forceful role in legislating and policing sexual behaviour. Although legal norms, judiciary systems and enforcement of sex laws varied widely, making generalization difficult, these distinctions commonly reflected male assumptions about the sexes' different natures and the need to enforce conventional gender roles and ideals. Laws and courts were influenced by beliefs that women's desires were more ravenous than men's, that women were more prone to sin, and that therefore their sexual behaviour had to be regulated more strictly. "The laws presume that all women are usually bad", according to one commentator, "because they are so full of mischief and vices that are difficult to describe"; a Belluno law of 1428 decreed that no woman over the age of twenty should be presumed to be a virgin, unless her virtue could be convincingly proved.[16]

Frequently, the social status, life-cycle stage or reputed virtue of the woman involved in illicit sex helped determine distinctions in guilt or penalties. This was especially true of rape and fornication, in which women were usually considered victims and absolved, but also of adultery or sodomy, in

---

14 *Florence 1424*, I, pp. 387–8; *Siena 1427*, I, pp. 591–2. On menstruation beliefs, see Joan Cadden, *Meanings of Sex Differences in the Middle Ages: Medicine, Science, and Culture* (Cambridge, UK, 1993), pp. 173–6, 268; Ottavia Niccoli, " 'Menstruum quasi monstruum': monstrous births and menstrual taboo in the sixteenth century", in E. Muir and G. Ruggiero, eds. *Sex & Gender in Historical Perspective* (Baltimore, 1990), pp. 1–25.

15 *Siena 1427*, I, pp. 592, 594–7, 600–1.

16 Brundage, *Law*, p. 492; quote from Giovanni Nevizzani, *Silva nuptialis . . .* (Lyon, 1524), fol. 21va (cited in ibid., pp. 548–9).

which women were often held criminally liable. Generally, the higher the woman's status was the greater the penalty levied on her seducer or lover, but finer distinctions were also drawn. The Florentine statutes of 1415 set a fine of 500 lire for men who had intercourse, whether consensual or forced, with a virgin, a respectable widow or a married woman, and allowed harsher punishment depending on the "condition and quality of the person". For the violation of women "of lesser condition", the fine fell to 100 lire, while sex with a consenting servant or a prostitute carried no penalty at all.[17] Venetian authorities levied progressively milder penalties on rapists according to whether their victims were pre-pubescent girls, wives, widows or, at the bottom of the scale, sexually mature nubile women; the severest penalties were reserved for those who raped women of high status.[18]

The treatment of adultery revealed the sharpest gender discrepancies and bore the most onerous consequences for women. Despite the gender-blind injunction against extra-marital sex, in practical terms adultery was a crime of wives. Husbands' infidelity, unless with a married woman, was considered of little significance, while that of wives was deemed a most serious offence that dishonoured their spouses and undermined the conjugal bond. Courts commonly punished an adulteress more severely than her partner, and her penalty usually included the forfeiture to her husband or children of her dowry – a key commodity in the definition of a woman's honour and often her sole means of subsistence in widowhood. Sometimes adulterous husbands were also legally subject to punishment: in Venice this might mean prison or exile plus the loss of their wife's dowry. But from 1480 to 1550 not a single Venetian husband was convicted for infidelity, unlike scores of wives prosecuted from the 1360s on.[19] This gender disparity concorded fully with religious precepts. According to Bernardino, in addition to her dowry an adulteress's husband had the right to expel her from his house, yet he forbade the wife of a philandering man to abandon him under any circumstances. He once stressed the differently gendered implications of infidelity by asserting that a husband's adultery was a greater sin, since as a man he was more rational and should therefore be more devoted, but a wife's unfaithfulness resulted in her "perpetual shame", for she had "no other virtue to lose" than her sexual honour.[20]

17 *Statuta populi et communis florentiae publica auctoritate collecta castigata et praeposita anno salutis MCCCCVI*, 3 vols (Fribourg, 1778–83), Vol. Ill, rubric 112, p. 318.
18 Ruggiero, *Boundaries of Eros*, pp. 96–108.
19 Ibid., pp. 45–69; Giovanni Scarabello, "Devianza sessuale ed interventi di giustizia a Venezia nella prima metà del XVI secolo", in *Tiziano e Venezia*, exhibition catalogue (Vicenza, 1980), p. 79; Brundage, *Law*, pp. 517–21.
20 *Siena 1427*, I, p. 557; *Florence 1424*, I, p. 413; *Florence 1425*, II, p. 178.

Women's shame also influenced the courts' tendency to punish them with public humiliation. Floggings and mutilations were common penalties for men too, but it appears that women convicted of sex crimes were more frequently exposed to public derision. While male adulterers were usually fined, jailed or exiled, adulteresses (besides losing their dowry) were often whipped along the streets, in various states of undress and sometimes wearing a defamatory mitre on their heads; occasionally their heads were shaved. In Pescia in 1419 an adulteress, half-naked and wearing a "crown of shame", was placed on a donkey and whipped through the countryside.[21] In Florence between 1490 and 1515, more than half of the women convicted of sodomy with men were sentenced to a flogging or the pillory, while only a third of their partners received similar penalties; most of the men, unlike the women, were allowed to avoid the shaming by paying an alternate fine. Since women's honour and reputation were more contingent than men's on community opinion, authorities tended to punish them in precisely that public fashion that would be most defaming.

Unauthorized Sexual Behaviour and Rendered Identities

Social conventions, religious precepts and the policing of sex all played important roles in constructing and transmitting notions of gender ideals and of distinctions between the sexes, but so did sexual behaviour itself. The forms of sexual compartment that are best documented, however, are those that were illicit or occured outside marriage, and it is consequently this realm of unauthorized sex that has proven most fruitful for historians seeking to throw new light on gender relations and identities in Renaissance Italy.

A key figure here was the prostitute, central to the sexual culture and gender system of Renaissance Italy both for the services she provided and for the symbolic functions she performed. Christian society had long considered prostitution a distasteful but necessary evil, a "lesser sin" that was grudgingly tolerated to prevent greater transgressions: "Do you see that in cities prostitutes are tolerated? This is a great evil, but if it were to be removed a great good would be eliminated, because there would be more adultery, more sodomy, which would be much worse."[22] In a sexual regime that prescribed female chastity but tacitly condoned male fornication, the

---

21   Samuel Cohn, Jr, *Women in the Streets: Sex and Power in Renaissance Italy* (Baltimore, 1996), p. 114; see also Brundage, *Law*, p. 520; Ruggiero, *Boundaries of Eros*, pp. 54–5.
22   Giordano da Pisa, *Quaresimale fiorentino 1305–1306*, Carlo Delcorno, ed. (Florence, 1974), p. 210.

prostitute played the dual role of furnishing an outlet for incontinent bachelors and philandering husbands, while also diverting their desires from adolescent males and women of "good" families, whose virtue and honour were thus safeguarded. Prostitutes and their clients were usually exempt from laws against fornication and adultery, though authorities limited the locations and visibility of their debauchery to protect the morality of upright citizens and defend the purity of civic and sacred buildings. During the Renaissance, the notion of the public utility of prostitution underwent a significant evolution, however. From the mid-1300s, governments began to abandon earlier exclusionary policies that relegated prostitutes and brothels outside the city walls and forced the women to wear identifying signs or apparel. Instead, the state became the official sponsor of urban sexual commerce, establishing municipal brothels or designated residential areas where whores could lawfully ply their trade. Dress codes and other norms intended to distinguish prostitutes were relaxed or abandoned. Some cities created magistracies to administer the bordellos or defend whores from assault and other offences, such as the "Officers of Decency" in Florence in 1403 and the "Protectors of the Prostitutes" in Lucca in 1534.[23]

By around 1500, however, this attitude of tolerance was beginning to change again, in Italy as elsewhere. The complexity of the marriage market and the steady escalation in dowries made it increasingly difficult for girls to marry. Convents thrived as patrician families discarded growing numbers of unwed daughters into nunneries, while humbler women slid into situations of solitude and poverty that made them easy recruits to the ranks of occasional and professional whores. The spread of prostitutes from brothel areas into "honest" neighbourhoods, together with the new phenomenon of prosperous courtesans who imitated the fashions and demeanour of patrician women, heightened concerns both about the bad example these unruly females posed to chaste women and about the blurring of social and moral distinctions between the *donna onesta* and the lusty *meretrice*. The sixteenth century consequently saw a return to a more negative assessment of the ancient sexual trade. Brothels remained open, but authorities revived or tightened policies on residence or dress to stigmatize prostitutes – laws that only a few wealthy courtesans could evade by buying licences or exploiting

---

23   Richard C. Trexler, "Florentine prostitution in the fifteenth century: patrons and clients", in idem. *The Women of Renaissance Florence* (Binghamton, NY, 1993), pp. 31–65; Mazzi, *Prostitute*; John Brackett, "The Florentine Onestà and the control of prostitution, 1403–1680", *Sixteenth-Century Journal*, 24 (1993), pp. 273–300; Elisabeth Pavan, "Police des moeurs, société et politique à Venise à la fin du Moyen Age", *Revue historique*, 264 (1980), pp. 241–88; Romano Canosa and Isabella Colonnello, *Storia della prostituzione in Italia dal Quattrocento alla fine del Settecento* (Rome, 1989).

the protection of powerful clients.[24] Influenced also by religious reform movements, institutions proliferated to convert prostitutes and to prevent poor or precarious females from slipping into the profession.[25]

Prostitutes, whether professionals in brothels, courtesans catering to upper-class clients, or women who occasionally sold themselves, undoubtedly played an important role in men's sexual education and experience and thus in the formation of masculine identity. This was precisely one of the criticisms levelled by Catholic reformers after the Council of Trent against the evil influence prostitution had in shaping men's sexual habits and attitudes towards women.[26] In their heyday the brothels were also central institutions of male sociability, especially for young bachelors. They provided a public forum where camaraderie and erotic licence mingled with outbreaks of violence, where men tested and displayed their virility in brawls and sexual conquests. It was in the brothel, an anecdote by the Florentine humanist Poliziano suggests, that youths who were once sodomites' "passive" boyfriends could redeem their reputations by proving their manliness with compliant whores.[27]

Unauthorized sex involving males and females encompassed far more than men's commerce with prostitutes, however. Legal records suggest that fornication, rape and adultery were typical features of the sexual culture, such activities hardly being discouraged by the light penalties usually levied on (male) offenders. But even the serious crimes of sex with nuns and (by the later 1400s) heterosexual sodomy were also commonplace occurrences on the rosters of carnal offences.[28]

Evidence on unauthorized sex tends to confirm that, for women especially, the relationship between sexual behaviour and gender was subtly but

24 Trexler, "Florentine prostitution", pp. 60–5; Mazzi, *Prostitute*, pp. 225–31, 403–7. On rising dowry values, see Anthony Molho, *Marriage Alliance in Late Medieval Florence* (Cambridge, MA, 1994), pp. 298–310. On the growth of monasteries and convent populations, see Richard C. Trexler, "Celibacy in the Renaissance: the nuns of Florence", in idem, *The Women of Renaissance Florence*, pp. 10–19; Judith C. Brown, "Monache a Firenze all'inizio dell'età moderna: un'analisi demografica", *Quaderni storici*, 29 (1994), pp. 117–52. On courtesans, see Brackett, "Onestà", pp. 293–5; *Il gioco dell'amore: le cortigiane di Venezia dal Trecento al Settecento*, exh. cat. (Milan, 1990).

25 Sherill Cohen, *The Evolution of Women's Asylums since 1500: From Refuges for Ex-Prostitutes to Shelters for Battered Women* (New York, 1992); Lucia Ferrante, "Honor regained: women in the Casa del Soccorso di San Paolo in sixteenth-century Bologna", in Muir and Ruggiero, eds, *Sex & Gender*, pp. 46–72.

26 Brackett, "Onestà", p. 293; Guido Ruggiero, "Marriage, love, sex, and Renaissance civic morality", in J. G. Turner, ed., *Sexuality and Gender in Early Modern Europe: Institutions, Texts, Images* (Cambridge, UK, 1993), pp. 25–6.

27 Angelo Poliziano, *Detti piacevoli*, T. Zanato, ed. (Rome, 1983), p. 78, number 211.

28 Rocke, *Forbidden Friendships*, pp. 215–16; Canosa and Colonnello, *Storia*, pp. 67–71; Ruggiero, *Boundaries of Eros*, pp. 70–84, 118–20.

significantly shaped by their social status. This illicit realm involved men from the entire social spectrum, but the women who were implicated were – except for nuns – mainly from the class of artisans, peasants, poor labourers and shopkeepers. Women of higher status were rarely embroiled in sexual scandals or crimes, and if they were, their families had the means to conceal the disgrace, to discipline the fallen or defiant woman privately, or to ensure that their assailants or lovers were severely punished. On the whole, the protective net thrown up by patrician males around their families' females effectively minimized women's perilous liaisons with men outside their kin group. Conscious of their family's status and indoctrinated from childhood that its honour depended on their chastity, genteel women probably tended to assimilate the values and gender ideology of their class, scrupulously avoiding behaviour that could defame them as much as their fathers, husbands and kinsmen.[29] The morality of humbler women was perhaps no less principled, but their circumstances of hardship and work, or their lack of networks of male kin, exposed them to the flattery of dishonest or fickle seducers, to sexual molestation by employers and social superiors, and to assaults by individuals or gangs. Court records are littered with such stories: plebeian girls and women attacked while alone on country roads or in the fields, servants and apprentices exploited sexually by their masters, isolated widows and their daughters powerless to defend their homes and virtue against assailants. Moreover, whether forced or consensual, most sexual relations between socially dominant men and their servants, slaves and other disadvantaged women simply evaded any judiciary control. The abandoned offspring of such unions swelled the overflowing foundling homes of Renaissance Italian cities.[30]

Because the imperatives of status, property and paternity that so heavily constrained patrician women's sexual behaviour carried less force among the less wealthy, working women appear to have had their own sense of proper sexual conduct and illicit activity, implying different customs and norms from those that prevailed among the dominant classes. For both rural and urban young people of the lower classes, for instance, premarital intercourse was evidently accepted and widespread, as long as relations were initiated with an intent to marry, or at least to create a stable bond. Such romances generally came to court as fornication only when the man failed to maintain his promise of marriage and abandoned his lover, often pregnant or with a young child. The loss of virginity impaired a woman's

29   For unchaste women from "good" families, see ibid., pp. 36–9, 55–64; and Mazzi, *Prostitute*, pp. 88–96.
30   Christiane Klapisch-Zuber, "Women servants in Florence during the fourteenth and fifteenth centuries", in B. A. Hanawalt, ed., *Women and Work in Preindustrial Europe* (Bloomington, IN, 1986), pp. 69–70; Philip Gavitt, *Charity and Children in Renaissance Florence: The Ospedale degli Innocenti, 1410–1536* (Ann Arbor, MI, 1990), p. 207.

future chances of marrying, and the tribunals to which these deflowered victims of desertion or rape turned for redress usually sought to redeem their honour and restore their marriage prospects by forcing their seducers or violators to give them a dowry or, alternatively, to marry them. Prosecution of fornication often became embroiled in ambiguities about what constituted a valid marriage, since, according to the pre-Tridentine Church, this required no other formalities than the partners' mutual consent. For this same reason, long-term informal unions and clandestine marriages remained unexceptional outside the upper classes well into the sixteenth century, and even women's extra-marital relations were not uncommon.[31] Facilitated by the contacts that they forged with men through neighbourly ties, work and sociable occasions, these plebeian romances were sometimes the fruit of an intolerable marriage, the evasion from a violent or overbearing husband, and may have been aided by neighbours and relatives. Such affairs typically attracted judicial attention only when they exceeded bounds of discretion or when a wife actually fled with her lover, signalling the open rupture of her conjugal union.[32]

Studies of illicit sex have also begun to illuminate in sharp relief the problem of men's sexual abuse of children, both female and male. In Florence from 1495 to 1515, over one-third of the forty-nine documented victims of convicted rapists were girls between the ages of six and twelve, and at least half were aged fourteen or under; numerous others were seduced without force or were sodomized. One man condemned in 1488 regularly picked up children begging in the market, sodomized them in his home, and then offered them to others to ravish; some of his cronies, conducted before one ten-year-old victim, were reportedly repelled by her tender age and refused to touch her, but others had no such scruples.[33] In a typical year, an average of four boys aged twelve or under would also come before the courts as victims of sodomizers, often having suffered severe anal injury. In Venice, too, pre-pubescent children were common victims of sexual abuse. A Venetian law of 1500, which prohibited pimps from prostituting girls under the age of twelve, revealed that it was regular practice

---

31   Brundage, *Law*, pp. 514–18; Ruggiero, *Boundaries of Eros*, pp. 16–44, 89–108; Sandra Cavallo and Simona Cerruti, "Female honor and the social control of reproduction in Piedmont between 1600 and 1800", in Muir and Ruggiero, eds. *Sex & Gender*, pp. 73–109; Gene Brucker, *Giovanni and Lusanna: Love and Marriage in Renaissance Florence* (Berkeley, CA, 1986); Daniela Lombardi, "Intervention by church and state in marriage disputes in sixteenth- and seventeenth-century Florence", in Dean and Lowe, eds. *Crime, Society and the Law in Renaissance Italy*, pp. 142–56. In Florence, unlike Venice, men condemned for fornication or rape were rarely given the option of marrying their victims, though they commonly had to provide a dowry for the unmarried ones.

32   Ruggiero, *Boundaries of Eros*, pp. 45–69; Mazzi, *Prostitute*, pp. 103–8.

33   ASF, OGBR 79, fols 9v–10r (8 March 1488).

to offer clients girls as young as seven to nine years of age to be sodomized. The abuse of children merits further attention, for this was evidently not merely a problem of individual aberration. The frequent subjugation of impotent juveniles probably reflects a psychosexual immaturity and aggressiveness, and an insecurity about masculine identity that had deep social, cultural and familial roots.[34]

Another prominent, if less explored, aspect of male behaviour were assaults by gangs against women or younger boys. In Florence between 1495 and 1515, nineteen out of forty-nine documented female rape victims were attacked by at least two men, and typically by three to six or more; in 1499, thirteen men abducted a married woman from her home and violated her. Many more men took part in collective ravishings (89) than in single assaults (30), and among the perpetrators, patrician youths figured prominently (34 of 89). Groups of men also brutally sodomized women, such as Costanza, a thirty-year-old servant sodomized and raped by fourteen youths in 1497, or Francesca, a married woman who in 1501 was anally raped by thirty assailants. Gangs attacked adolescent males as well, part of a broader context in which the sexual "possession" of boys by groups of men, whether by force or not, was both common and deeply implicated in the fashioning of manly and social identities. The gangs that terrorized women and boys offered strength in numbers to overpower their victims and guarantee the success of their sordid ventures, but their members also gave one another psychological incentive and support, an incitement to prove their virility before their comrades as, one after the other, they humiliated their helpless prey.[35]

Beside reinforcing an impression of the aggressive and predatory character of masculine behaviour and identity, evidence about illicit sex can also provide glimpses of individuals who implicitly evaded or openly challenged not only the law but also prevailing gender conventions. A few mature men, as will be seen, defied masculine norms by taking the proscribed receptive role in same-sex relations. Women, by contrast, were not always passive victims but instead often assumed an assertive role in seeking to fulfil their sexual desires and in shaping their own affective experiences and sense of identity. Some enterprizing nubile girls apparently engaged calculatingly in pre-marital sex, to circumvent parental objections over their choice of a spouse. In extra-marital affairs wives are commonly found taking the initiative, perhaps to relieve the monotony of a loveless union or escape the

---

34   Rocke, *Forbidden Friendships*, pp. 162–3; Scarabello, "Devianza", p. 80; Patricia Labalme, "Sodomy and Venetian justice in the Renaissance", *Legal History Review*, 52 (1984), pp. 236–7; Ruggiero, *Boundaries of Eros*, pp. 95, 121–5, 149–54.
35   Rocke, *Forbidden Friendships*, pp. 163, 182–9; Ruggiero, "Marriage", pp. 17–18; Mazzi, *Prostitute*, pp. 110–12. Cases cited: ASF, OGBR 113, 78v (6 March 1499); ASF, UN 31, 65r–66v, 119v (21 February–5 April 1497); ibid. 34, 56r (26 August 1501).

brutality of a cruel husband.[36] Especially striking examples of women resisting gender and social conventions to pursue erotic pleasure and male companionship come from what is, at first glance, a most unlikely source – the nunnery. Many of the women who swelled Italy's bulging convents were deposited there, willingly or not, by genteel families unable to place them in suitable marriages; not all were prepared or willing to submit to a regime of chastity or to renounce the world. Not only were nuns often implicated in sexual scandals involving laymen or priests, but some managed to conduct quite rich sexual lives, apparently shielded by a web of complicity within and perhaps outside the convent.[37] Other women confuted the submissive role assigned them in gender ideology by withstanding assailants or by denouncing abusive husbands. A distinct sense of determination and proud identity emerges from the protest that a young Florentine patrician wife, Agnoletta de' Ricci, made to her husband Ardingo, whom she publicly accused in 1497 of having repeatedly sodomized her: "I told him that in no way did I want him to treat me like an animal, but like a woman of perfect character."[38] Such examples serve as reminders that, though the dominant ideology of gender and sexual behaviour was powerfully constraining, it was also contestable – and contested – terrain.

Same-Sex Relations and Masculine Identity

Same-sex relations between males, classified as sodomy, provide an especially revealing perspective on the construction of masculine identity. Ranked among the most nefarious of carnal acts in both Church doctrine and legal rhetoric, sodomy – mainly but not only sex between males – was one of the most frequently prosecuted and heavily penalized crimes in Italy between 1400 and 1600. Reputedly common across the peninsula, sodomy so alarmed the governments of Venice, Florence and Lucca that they created special judiciary commissions to prosecute it (in 1418, 1432 and 1448 respectively). Penalties and patterns of control varied, but in Florence the Office of the Night, as the magistracy there was known, unearthed an exceptionally thriving sodomitical milieu. Between 1432 and 1502 as many as 17,000 males were incriminated and some 3,000 convicted for homosexual relations. Indeed, sodomy was so common and its policing in

36   Elizabeth S. Cohen, "No longer virgins: self-presentation by young women in late Renaissance Rome", in M. Migiel and J. Schiesari, eds, *Refiguring Woman: Perspectives on Gender and the Italian Renaissance* (Ithaca, NY, 1991), pp. 172–4; Ruggiero, *Boundaries of Eros*, pp. 16–69; Mazzi, *Prostitute*, pp. 87, 103–16; Scarabello, "Devianza", p. 78.
37   Ruggiero, *Boundaries of Eros*, pp. 78–84; Scarabello, "Devianza", pp. 78–9.
38   ASF, UN 31, 44v (3 January 1497).

the later fifteenth century so effective that, by the time they reached the age of forty, probably two of every three Florentine men had been officially implicated.[39]

Whether this "vice" was as pervasive elsewhere remains to be seen; nonetheless, the evidence suggests that throughout Italy same-sex relations shared similar forms, contexts and ascribed cultural meanings. Generally, homosexual behaviour had little to do with current notions of sexual orientation or identity, but was organized instead around notions of gender and life stages. For most males, same-sex sodomy was a sporadic or temporary transgression that did not preclude relations with females or imply anything about long-term inclinations.[40]

Some contemporaries saw connections between homoeroticism and the quality of relations between men and women. Bernardino of Siena singled out sodomites for their loathing and paltry esteem of women, while the Sienese *novelliere*, Pietro Fortini, attributed the homoerotic bent of both Florentine and Lucchese men to their universal misogyny, asserting that their "vices are such [referring to sodomy] that they cannot bear to look at women, who they say are their enemies". Acting in part on the belief that making public women accessible would help curtail sodomy, the governments of both Florence and Lucca promoted municipalized prostitution. This sexual equation was given a different twist by Savonarola: Florentine parents, he said, so feared the disgrace of unwed pregnant daughters that they encouraged their sons to engage instead in what they deemed the "lesser evil" of sex with men.[41]

Notions of gender also shaped sex between males in more direct ways, while homosexual behaviour in turn had important implications for masculine identities – implications that were relevant for all males, whether they engaged in sodomy or not. Same-sex relations in Italy corresponded to a hierarchical pattern, very ancient in Mediterranean cultures and long-lasting throughout Europe, in which adult males took the so-called active, usually anally insertive role with "passive" teenage boys or adolescents to the age of about eighteen or twenty. In Florence, the best-documented example, nine out of ten active partners were aged nineteen and above; mainly in their twenties and thirties, their mean age was twenty-seven. Of those who took the passive role, nine out of ten were between the ages of thirteen and twenty, with a mean age of sixteen. Reciprocal or age-reversed

39 Rocke, *Forbidden Friendships*; Ruggiero, *Boundaries of Eros*, pp. 109–45; Labalme, "Sodomy"; Pavan, "Police", pp. 266–88; Canossa and Colonnello, *Storia*, pp. 57–73.

40 Rocke, *Forbidden Friendships*, pp. 87–132.

41 Bernardino of Siena, *Florence 1425*, II, p. 276; *Siena 1427*, I, p. 560; ibid., II, pp. 1158, 1160, 1166; *Novelle di Pietro Fortini*, T. Rughi, ed. (Milan, 1923), p. 64; Girolamo Savonarola, *Prediche sopra i Salmi*, V. Romano, ed., 2 vols (Rome, 1969), Vol. I, p. 164.

relations were rare, and limited to adolescence, while it was rarer still for mature males to have sex together. Indeed, the assumption of the receptive sexual role by adult men constituted a widely respected taboo.[42]

Sex between males thus always embodied oppositions – older and younger, active and passive, penetrator and penetrated. These were far from neutral distinctions, for contrasting values related to gender adhered to them, values such as dominance and submission, honour and shame, and, not least, masculine and feminine. These differences were neatly expressed in fourteenth-century Florentine laws, which blandly designated the active partner either as *pollutus* (morally corrupt) or as someone who committed sodomy with another, but contemptuously branded the passive as one who had dirtied or disgraced himself, or who "willingly suffered the said crime to be inflicted upon him".[43]

The gendered meaning of sexual roles, central to conceptions of same-sex behaviour, emerged most vividly from denunciations accusing men and boys of sodomy. Informers commonly referred to the passive partner, and only to him, with derogatory feminine expressions and metaphors. People derided sodomized boys with the epithets *bardassa*, derived from an Arabic word for slave and designating a debauched boy who offered himself to men, usually for payment; *puttana* (whore); *cagna or cagna in gestra* (bitch or bitch in heat), all evoking the commonplace of voracious female lust. Most often, however, informers referred to them simply as women, stating that a man kept or used a boy "as a woman", or even "as his wife". What turned these boys symbolically into women was not any effeminate appearance or manner, but rather their assumption of the subordinate position in sex, which was construed in this culture as feminine. In contrast, accusers virtually never represented the "active" partner in feminine terms, calling him at most a "sodomite" or "bugger". Neither term bore overt gendered connotations other than indicating the dominant role in sex. Indeed, while passive partners were hardly ever described with these terms, both were regularly used to indicate men who sodomized women.[44] Late medieval and early modern Italians evidently found it difficult to conceive of same-sex relations – whether between males or females – outside the traditional gender dichotomy of masculine and feminine roles.[45]

---

42   Rocke, *Forbidden Friendships*, pp. 94–7, 113–19. Passive partners in Venice appear somewhat younger than in Florence, though this may only reflect poorer reporting of age there; Ruggiero, *Boundaries of Eros*, pp. 118, 121–5; Pavan, "Police", p. 284.

43   R. Caggese, ed., *Statuti della repubblica fiorentina*, 2 vols (Florence, 1910–21), Vol. II, p. 218; ASF, PR 52, 128rv (13 April 1365).

44   Rocke, *Forbidden Friendships*, pp. 105–10.

45   Judith C. Brown, *Immodest Acts: The Life of a Lesbian Nun in Renaissance Italy* (New York, 1986).

These representations suggest that the sodomite, though castigated as a criminal and a sinner, was perceived as conforming to the behaviours and values defined in this culture as masculine. As long as he observed proper conventions, a man's sexual relations with boys did not compromise his status as a "normal" and virile male. Indeed, the act of dominating another male, even if a boy, might well have reinforced it. Since sodomizing someone did not constitute deviation from "manly" norms, and the "womanly" role was in effect limited to very young males, this permitted all mature men to engage in same-sex activity – as very many did – without endangering their masculine identity or being relegated to a distinctive category of deviants.

What was an aberration was, of course, the passive sexual role. But as this was normally restricted to the phase of physical and social immaturity, it marked only a temporary detour from a boy's progress towards manhood. In Florence, virtually all adolescent passives whose later same-sex activity is documented converted with success to a solely dominant role with teenage boys. This helps explain why passive minors usually received much lighter penalties than their companions, or, as in Florence, no punishment whatsoever, no matter how promiscuous they were. If penalties were levied, they often involved corporal punishments of the sort usually applied to women.[46]

This also accounts for the paramount significance attributed to the transition to sexual adulthood, with its expectations of adherence to virile conventions. For Florentine boys up to the age of eighteen or twenty the passive role was considered more or less consonant with their status, but afterward most men carefully avoided the shame of being penetrated "like a woman". This was a crucial experiential and symbolic passage, and the border between passive and active, boyhood and maturity, feminine and masculine, was anxiously patrolled by both community and state. With a combination of embarrassment and derision, informers castigated the rare youth or older man who still "let themselves be sodomized", emphasizing their dishonour and disgrace. The authorities often reinforced these concerns about proper masculine roles by punishing over-aged passives with exemplary penalties of public floggings, exorbitant fines or exile. So powerful was the aversion to older men's sexual receptivity, in particular, that when Salvi Panuzzi, a sixty-three-year-old citizen long notorious for sodomizing boys, publicly admitted in 1496 that he himself had been sodomized by several youths, the Night Officers condemned him to death by burning, one of only three known capital sentences they levied in their seventy-year activity. Yet while they abhorred his acts, they also feared that his execution, by rendering

46   Rocke, *Forbidden Friendships*, pp. 51–2, 61, 99–101, 214–15; Ruggiero, *Boundaries of Eros*, pp. 121–4.

public his womanish "evil ways, . . . might bring shame on the entire city" and make a mockery of Florentine manhood. They therefore commuted his sentence, upon payment of a huge fine, to life imprisonment hidden away in *la pazzeria*, the prison ward for the insane.[47]

The exemplary punishments imposed on adult men for taking the "unmanly" sexual role emphasize that individual erotic behaviour and collective gender norms and identity formed part of a seamless whole. Informers expressed concern that the passivity of older men, a disgrace to themselves, would also implicate and malign the honour – that is, the virility – of the entire male community. By defusing the potential shame of Panuzzi's execution, and by secluding this violator of manhood among the dangerously insane, the Night Officers affirmed both the public nature of gender and the Commune's role to defend the conventions that helped fashion masculine identity. Such worries were hardly limited to Florence. In 1516, Venetian lawmakers, their offended sense of masculine propriety fairly bursting from their words, resolved to stamp out "an absurd and unheard-of thing [that] has recently become known, which can in no way be tolerated, that several most wicked men of 30, 40, 50, 60 years and more have given themselves like prostitutes and public whores to be passives in such a dreadful excess". This revelation scandalized local commentators, in part because it evoked a deep anxiety that the hierarchy of age and gender on which masculine identity was constructed risked being subverted. One nobleman was appalled that "Fathers and Senators", men who were "mature, full of wisdom, with white beards" – the very symbols of patriarchy – would shamelessly allow youths to penetrate them, and he branded this "truly a wicked and abhorrent thing, never before heard of in our times, especially among old men". Equally menacing to their manly sense of self and civic image was the news that informed foreigners were now gleefully ridiculing the virility of all Venetians.[48] Similar concerns about defending Florentine manhood led the government of Duke Cosimo I, in a law of 1542, to single out the adult man who dared allow himself to be sodomized by ordering his public execution by burning, "for his own punishment and as an example to others", as "a wicked and infamous man".[49]

Perhaps more effectively than any other contemporary erotic behaviour, the same-sex practices described here, with their age-, role- and gender-bound conventions, underline the distance that separates the culture of sex and gender in Renaissance Italy from that which prevails in the modern Western world. Little trace, if any, can be found then of the categories that

---

47   Rocke, *Forbidden Friendships*, pp. 101–5.
48   Labalme, "Sodomy", pp. 243 n. 73, 251 n. 160; Scarabello, "Devianza", p. 82.
49   L. Cantini, ed., *Legislazione toscana raccolta e illustrata*, 32 vols (Florence, 1800–8), Vol. I, pp. 211–13.

today largely define sexual experience and personae; it was not, in other words, the biological sex of one's partners in erotic pleasures that significantly distinguished and classified individuals, but rather the extent to which their sexual behaviour conformed to culturally determined gender roles. In different but related ways, the norms and ideology of gender forcefully shaped and constrained the experience of sex for both women and men. And sexual activity, in turn, played important roles in fashioning gendered identities and in reinforcing – or sometimes challenging – traditional gender conventions. As historians and other scholars continue to explore the complex and still relatively uncharted universe of sexual comportments, attitudes and controls throughout the rural and urban communities of the Italian peninsula, their studies promise to further enrich our understanding of the culturally specific modes of the construction of sex and gender in late medieval and early modern Italy.

Part V
The Power of Knowledge

Introduction to Part V

In the late thirteenth and fourteenth centuries, a new kind of scholar could be found in Italy and, to a lesser degree, in other parts of Europe. Educated in Latin and steeped in the writings of ancient philosophers and Christian authorities, the Renaissance humanist was, at first glance, not that different from his predecessors. He saw knowledge as a product of a long tradition of learning that connected the scholastic learning of the Middle Ages, which emphasized critical commentary on and debate about ancient texts, to the intellectual life of ancient Greece and Rome.

While scholastic education provided a framework for Renaissance learning, it also served as a point of departure for a more deeply historical vision of knowledge that moved beyond the traditional academic pursuits of the medieval university and cathedral schools into new domains. Theology and philosophy continued to be important areas of intellectual inquiry during the Renaissance, but they were reinvigorated by their relationship with other subjects that had received considerably less attention prior to the fourteenth century. Borrowing Cicero's term *studia humanitatis*, Renaissance scholars invented a new kind of learning that we now know as humanism. Humanism emphasized grammar, rhetoric, poetry, history, and ethics. It also revived certain aspects of the classical ideal of the seven liberal arts, making the *quadrivium* (arithmetic, geometry, music, and poetry) as important as the *trivium* (grammar, rhetoric, and logic). Cultural pursuits such as painting and architecture that we closely associate with Renaissance intellectual life could not have flourished without the newfound appreciation of mathematical arts and sciences.

Humanism was Renaissance Italy's most important and lasting intellectual contribution and reflects the role of education in this society. But what exactly were its goals? Fundamentally, the majority of humanists exhibited a widespread curiosity about the history of knowledge. They saw learning as a kind of archeology that allowed them to appropriate the past in order to make it meaningful in their own times. As Theodor Mommsen discusses in his classic essay, Petrarch famously saw the distant past as a better place than the present. His concept of the "dark ages" invoked history as a framework for understanding antiquity as a high moment for cultural and intellectual pursuits that had been lost, but not entirely forgotten. Recuperating the languages and learning of the ancient world was the first step towards self-improvement, since history told its Renaissance readers that the past was not unknowable but instead was worthy of emulation. These were lessons that Petrarch learned from at least two previous generations of scholars in the late thirteenth and early fourteenth centuries, who inspired his fascination with the Greek and Roman past.

The fourteenth and early fifteenth centuries spawned a generation of scholars whose greatest delight lay in uncovering forgotten manuscripts in monastic libraries throughout Europe. Poggio Bracciolini had the good fortune to find eight lost speeches of Cicero, Quintilian's *Institutes*, and Vitruvius' *Ten Books on Architecture*. The archeology of knowledge occurred not only in libraries but also amidst the ancient ruins. Scholars such as Flavio Biondo initiated the idea that history could be written from things as well as words, making Roman coins, inscriptions, and ruins crucial evidence in the reconstruction of the past. This new appreciation for the material world produced a different kind of humanist who traveled in search of knowledge, as Ciriaco d'Ancona would do when he went to Greece to gain a richer appreciation of Hellenistic culture. Rather than simply seeing Greece through Roman eyes, it became possible to imagine multiple antiquities. The growing fascination with ancient Egypt and Israel in the late fifteenth and sixteenth centuries further underscored the idea that the cultural heritage that Renaissance humanists valued had emerged from many different pasts. Petrarch's original idea of antiquity was enlarged to accommodate a fuller understanding of the past.

Humanism encompasses such a wide array of practices in relationship to the cultivation of learning that we cannot think of it as a monolithic enterprise. While Petrarch personally chastised Cicero for being too involved in Roman politics because he preferred to imagine him as a contemplative man, Leonardo Bruni saw these political activities as the very model of what he aspired to do in his own times. As a civic humanist, Bruni burnished the image of Florence on numerous occasions by using his eloquence and learning to give his city a history worthy of its significance. He could think of no better way to do this than to connect it to ancient Rome and to celebrate the ancient Etruscans who had given Tuscany its name. Venetian humanists were so desperate to connect their city to the Roman empire that they imported fragments of Roman ruins to Venice in order to build a piece of this past into their aristocratic palaces, much as Roman nobles did more routinely with the materials that surrounded them in the papal city. As this episode illustrates, humanism succeeded not only because it offered a new pedagogy in the classroom but because it provided a powerful and persuasive framework for understanding society.

The libraries of Renaissance humanists reflected many different aspects of the uses of learning in Italian society. Studies became a more significant part of Italian Renaissance palaces in the fifteenth and sixteenth centuries. Often richly decorated with images of illustrious ancients and moderns, these rooms reflected a new appreciation for learning as central to the activities of a Renaissance household. Patricians kept books, precious objects, and family papers in the study. Princes used their studies as places of retreat from public life, much as Machiavelli would describe the process of writing *The Prince* as a secular ritual in which he entered the courts of ancient men to commune with their wisdom. They also used them as highly political spaces, inviting visiting dignitaries to see their collections, as Cosimo de' Medici often did in Florence.

As Anthony Grafton details in his essay, the library epitomized the place of knowledge in this society because it was both solitary and social, removed from worldly cares yet filled with objects that arrived in the study because of the lively marketplace for ideas. Renaissance Italy was a world of active and engaged readers who consumed books with enormous passion, initially because books were the primary means of gaining access to antiquity and ultimately because, by the early sixteenth century, the widespread diffusion of the printing press made it even easier to acquire copies of books, which made them an even more important means of communicating and exchanging new ideas. Public repositories of learning such as the Laurentian Library in Florence and the Vatican Library in Rome in the mid-fifteenth century, and the Library of St. Mark in Venice in the late sixteenth century, emerged because leading citizens of the Italian Renaissance cities considered knowledge to be a civic virtue.

Despite these lofty principles and the eloquence with which they were stated, we should not imagine humanism as a movement that brought education to a broad sector of society. Too many Renaissance schoolboys found the emphasis on grammar and rhetoric restrictive rather than liberating. The struggles of women humanists in fifteenth-century Italy remind us that learning had its social and political boundaries. Knowledge was powerful in Renaissance Italy precisely because it was for the powerful. Others might become learned, as the case of Isotta Nogarola demonstrates in Lisa Jardine's essay, but this did not necessarily mean that they easily found a use for their learning in society if they could not work for a prince or a pope, or enter public life in some way. However, the fact that a significant number of women were humanists suggests that the new learning could be valued on its own terms. Woman humanists used their learning, among other things, to ascertain their place in the historical record. Bruni told Battista Malatesta that women were especially suited to the reading of history. They used this knowledge to begin to suggest a new history that included the history of women's accomplishments, just as Nogarola felt capable of offering her own assessment of the relative sins of Adam and Eve in a series of letters she exchanged with the Venetian humanist Ludovico Foscarini in 1451–53. In this respect, Nogarola's efforts to participate in humanist debates about knowledge was as much a success as it might be perceived to be a failure.

The three essays by Theodor Mommsen, Anthony Grafton, and Lisa Jardine describe some of the fundamental attributes of humanism. Taken together, they remind us that knowledge had its contemplative, pragmatic, and political uses in Renaissance Italy. It was the interaction among these different visions of a new learning that made humanism truly an influential force in this society.

Plate 8 Pedro Berruguete (?), *Portrait of Federico da Montefeltro and His Son Guidobaldo* (1480–1). *Source:* Galleria Nazionale delle Marche, Urbino.

The duke of Urbino, Federico da Montefeltro (1420–82), was one of the great mercenary soldiers of the fifteenth century. He amassed a considerable fortune fighting for rulers of other Italian states. By 1464, the pope had legitimized his family's right to inherit Urbino; in 1474, pope Sixtus IV officially gave him the title of duke. During this period Federico transformed Urbino into "a city in the form of a palace," as Baldassare Castiglione would later describe it, bringing foreign artists such as Berruguete to decorate it. He was not only interested in architecture, but generally in learning and culture, leading many contemporaries to consider him the equal of Cosimo de' Medici in his patronage. In this painting attributed to the Spanish artist Berruguete (1450–1504), Federico is depicted in the study he had built in his palace, reading to his young son, whom Castiglione would celebrate in *The Book of the Courtier* (1528). Federico's library was the envy of many scholars. The Florentine bookseller Vespasiano da Bisticci would praise the duke for not putting any printed volumes on his shelves next to the beautiful copied manuscripts he owned – a reflection of the early distaste for printing as a poor substitute for a beautiful, handwritten copy of a book. This painting captures well the idea that learning was an equivalent form of power to arms. "A military leader who knows Latin has a great advantage over one who does not," observed Bisticci.

9

Petrarch's Conception of the "Dark Ages"

Theodor E. Mommsen

The conception of the Dark Ages originated with the Italian humanists of the Renaissance.[1] In a recent essay on "La coscienza della rinascita negli umanisti,"[2] Franco Simone emphasizes the fact that "the idea of renovation brought with it, in a supplementary way, the idea of a period of absolute ignorance of the classical culture," and that "the humanists, in order to express this double conception of theirs, used another metaphor which was no less common than that of "rebirth"; this other formula was that of light and darkness."[3] The metaphor as such was, of course, not at all new, for throughout the Middle Ages it had been used to contrast the light, which Christ had brought into this world, with the darkness in which the heathen had languished before His time.[4] It was in this sense that Petrarch used the old metaphor when he pitied Cicero who had had to die shortly before "the end of the darkness and the night of error" and before "the dawn of the true light."[5]

But the same Petrarch asserted that "amidst the errors there shone forth men of genius, and no less keen were their eyes, although they were surrounded by darkness and dense gloom; therefore they ought not so much

1 L. Varga, *Das Schlagwort vom "finsteren Mittelalter"* (Vienna–Leipzig, 1932), pp. 36 ff.
2 Published in *La Rinascita*, II (1939), 838–71; III (1940), 163–86.
3 Franco Simone, "La coscienza della rinascita negli umanisti," *La Rinascita*, III, 169 f.
4 Cf. Varga, *Das Schlagwort*, pp. 5 ff.; Simone, "La coscienza della rinascita," III, 177 ff.
5 Petrarca, *De sui ipsius et multorum ignorantia*, ed. M. Capelli (Paris, 1906), p. 45: "paucis enim ante Cristi ortum obierat oculosque clauserat, heu! quibus e proximo noctis erratice ac tenebrarum finis et ueritatis initium, uereque lucis aurora et iustitie sol instabat." Compare Petrarch's remarks on Aristotle, *ibid.*, pp. 40 f.

to be hated for their erring but pitied for their ill fate."[6] These words are a good illustration of the attitude which Petrarch held throughout his life toward the classical poets and thinkers and of the way in which he justified the object of his life's work. But these sentences have an importance beyond this personal aspect. They mark, as Simone says, "the moment at which the metaphor of light and darkness lost its original religious value and came to have a literary connotation."[7] This concept was soon to be developed fully. Men like Boccaccio, Filippo Villani, Ghiberti and others contrasted the "rebirth" of the arts and letters which, they held, had been effected by Dante, Giotto, and Petrarch, with the preceding period of cultural darkness.[8] With this change of emphasis from things religious to things secular, the significance of the old metaphor became reversed: Antiquity, so long considered as the "Dark Age," now became the time of "light" which had to be "restored"; the era following Antiquity, on the other hand, was submerged in obscurity.

The use of the expression "the Dark Ages" was not, however, confined to the circles of artists and writers of the Renaissance. The term was also used, and in an even more comprehensive sense, by the humanist historians who, from a general point of view, attempted to assign to their own time its place in the course of history. This problem of periodization of history, as it appeared to the Renaissance scholars themselves, has recently been studied by Wallace K. Ferguson.[9] Ferguson concludes that "the Humanists . . . are in fairly general agreement that there was a decline of ancient civilization with the decline of Rome and that this decline led to a period of barbaric darkness."[10]

In this connection it is obviously important to find out which humanist first used the expression "the Dark Ages" as a term of periodization, since the figure of speech in itself implies a sharp chronological demarcation. Scholars have pointed to Petrarch as the man whose writings seemed to suggest such a conception.[11] But there is no definite agreement on this particular point.[12] I think, however, that sufficient material can be adduced to

---

6   "Nullo enim modo diuinarum illis uerum ueritas apparere illis poterat, quibus nondum uerus sol iustitiae illuxerat. Elucebant tamen inter errores ingenia, neque ideo minus uiuaces erant oculi quamuis tenebris et densa caligine circumsepti, ut eis non erranti odium, sed indignae sortis miseratio deberetur"; *Apologia contra cuiusdam anonymi Galli calumnias* (in *Opera omnia*, Basel, 1554, p. 1195); quoted by Simone, "La coscienza della rinascita," III, 182.

7   Simone, "La coscienza della rinascita," III, 182 f.

8   Cf. Varga, *Das Schlagwort*, pp. 44 ff.; W. Goetz, "Mittelalter und Renaissance," *Historische Zeitschrift*, CII (1907), pp. 31, 53 f.

9   Wallace K. Ferguson, "Humanist Views of the Renaissance," *The American Historical Review*, XLV (1939), pp. 1–28.

10   Ferguson, "Humanist Views," p. 28.

11   Cf. e.g., W. Rehm, *Der Untergang Roms im abendländischen Denken* (Leipzig, 1930), p. 45; Simone, "La coscienza della rinascita," II, 842 f.; Ferguson, "Humanist Views," p. 7.

12   Cf. Varga, *Das Schlagwort*, p. 41 f.: "Petrarca und . . . Coluccio Salutati . . . bezeichnen im allgemeinen noch nicht das von ihnen abgelehnte Jahrtausend mit der Metapher der Finster-

decide the disputed question. This problem must be approached with an investigation of the development of the conception which Petrarch held with regard to his main historical work, the *De viris illustribus*. This investigation will lead directly to a discussion of Petrarch's historical conceptions in general and the part which the term "Dark Ages" played in them.

In a letter written from Parma in 1349, Petrarch recalls the years full of personal happiness and literary productivity which he once spent in the seclusion of his beloved Vaucluse.[13] In it he enumerates the various poems and works which he began there; then he continues: "No place gave more leisure or offered stronger stimulation. That solitude encouraged me to bring together the illustrious men of all countries and of all times."[14] This composition which Petrarch conceived in the solitude of Vaucluse was to become his work *De viris illustribus*.

It is possible to fix the approximate date of the conception of this plan. The earliest possible date is 1337, when Petrarch took up residence in Vaucluse. We learn moreover from another remark of Petrarch that the design of *De viris illustribus* formed itself in his mind before that of the *Africa*.[15] The date of this latter work is Good Friday 1338.[16] Thus we may conclude that the first plan of *De viris illustribus* dates from 1337/38.

According to his plan to write on "illustrious men of all countries and of all times," Petrarch went to work immediately and started writing "biographies" of Jewish and oriental, Greek and Roman figures, belonging to the realm of both myth and reality. This first version began with the life of Adam and ended with that of Caesar.[17]

A few years later, however, the original program was to undergo a decisive change. In Petrarch's *Secretum*, which was begun about 1342/43,[18] Saint Augustine addresses the poet in the following words: "You have been

nis; wohl aber sprechen sie, trotz aller Verehrung für die Antike, vom 'finsteren Heidentum' ... Bei Petrarca und Salutati ist somit die Verteilung von Licht und Schatten auf die Geschichte fast ausschliesslich vom christlichen Standpunkt aus bestimmt."

13   *Fam.*, VIII, 3 (ed. V. Rossi, *Le Familiari*, II, 158–61). – As to the frequently controversial dates of Petrarch's letters, I refer once and for all to the valuable bibliography gathered by E. H. Wilkins, *Modern discussions of the dates of Petrarch's prose letters* (Chicago, 1929).

14   *Fam.*, VIII, 3 (ed. Rossi, II, 160): "Nullus locus aut plus otii prebuit aut stimulos acriores: ex omnibus terris ac seculis illustres viros in unum contrahendi illa michi solitudo dedit animum."

15   *De contemptu mundi*, Dial. III (in *Opera omnia*, Basel, 1554, p. 411). Cf. P. de Nolhac, "Le 'De viris illustribus' de Pétrarque," *Notices et extraits des Manuscrits de la Bibliothèque Nationale*, XXXIV, 1 (Paris, 1890), 61 f. – On Petrarch's historical conceptions in general cf. G. Koerting, *Petrarca's Leben und Werke* (Leipzig, 1878), pp. 592–617; H. W. Eppelsheimer, *Petrarca* (Bonn, 1926), pp. 77–96; L. Tonelli, *Petrarca* (Milan, 1930), pp. 253–66.

16   N. Festa, *Saggio sull' Africa del Petrarca* (Palermo–Rome, 1926), p. 4 ff.

17   It was only at the end of the nineteenth century that this first text of *De viris illustribus* was discovered by P. de Nolhac, who published extracts from it, " 'De viris illustribus' ", p. 110 ff.; cf. P. de Nolhac, *Pétrarque et l'Humanisme*, II (2nd edit., Paris, 1907), 1 ff.

18   Cf. L. Tonelli, *Petrarca* p. 122 f.

dreaming of becoming renowned to posterity and for this reason . . . you have ventured upon writing the history from King Romulus to Emperor Titus, an immense undertaking that requires much time and work."[19] This sentence shows that in 1342/43 Petrarch no longer intended, as he had done five years earlier, to write on the illustrious men of all ages.[20] By this time he had restricted his theme to the history of a very definite period, stretching from Romulus, the first king, down through the centuries of the Roman Republic to the first hundred years of the Empire.

How are we to account for this alteration of the original design? Must we believe that Petrarch abandoned the initial project because he had come to realize that the task was "too vast and beyond his power"?[21] Surely no mere external difficulties could offer an impulse strong enough to make Petrarch discontinue his original plan and even discard all the lives of biblical and Greek personages which he had already written. It seems more logical to assume that it was a new concept of history which necessitated these alterations. A search for possible causes of this decisive change, which took place in Petrarch's mind between the years 1337 and 1342/43, reveals that one of the most important events in the poet's life fell in this period: his coronation as poet laureate on the Capitol on April 8, 1341. The question, then, arises whether Petrarch's new concept of history as Roman history is to be connected with his Roman coronation?

To answer this question we have to consider Petrarch's relation to Rome.[22] Ever since his childhood his thoughts had centered around "the city

---

19   *Opera omnia* (Basel, 1554), p. 411: "famam inter posteros concepisti, ideoque manum ad maiora iam porrigens, librum historiarum a rege Romulo in Titum Caesarem, opus immensum temporisque et laboris capacissimum aggressus es."

20   R. Tatham, *Francesco Petrarca, the first modern man of letters; his life and letters*, II (London, 1926), p. 66, believes that Petrarch started out with writing "a series of lives of Roman warriors and statesmen from Romulus to Titus," and that "afterwards – at what date is not clear – he extended his design so as to include famous men of all ages and countries." Tatham argues as follows (II, 66, n. 3): "(Petrarch) alludes to the longer design in *Fam.*, VIII, 3, which was written in 1349; and since the *Secret* was written in 1342–1343, the change must have been between these dates." This argument is wrong: Tatham did not notice that in *Fam.*, VIII, 3, Petrarch does not speak of books he was working on in 1349, but of plans which he had conceived in a happy past when he was living in Vaucluse.

21   Cf. P. de Nolhac, in *Notices et extraits* . . . , XXXIV, 1, p. 109, who says that Petrarch "a fini par abandonner un sujet trop vaste et trop au dessus de ses forces, pour se consacrer de préférence à l'histoire romaine. Sur ce terrain, pour lui, les sources abondaient, et il était soutenu dans son œuvre par le sentiment d'un hommage rendu à des aïeux directs, aux ancêtres et aux modèles de la patrie italienne qu'il rêvait." Cf. P. de Nolhac, *Pétrarque et l'Humanisme*, II, 2; E. C. (arrara), Petrarca, in *Enciclopedia Italiana*, XXVII (Rome, 1935), p. 13: "Poi l'audace disegno giovanile gli si venne restringendo ai personaggi romani da Romolo a Tito."

22   On this point compare Tatham, *Francesco Petranca*, I, 328–48; in his text Tatham gives large extracts from a number of Petrarch's letters dealing with Rome, viz. *Fam.*, II, 9, 12, 13, 14; VI, 2; VIII, 1.

to which there is none like, nor ever will be."[23] But when in 1337 he came to Rome for the first time and actually saw the remains of her ancient grandeur, he was so overwhelmed by the impressions he received that he was unable to express his feelings in words.[24] The fact that Petrarch saw himself reduced to an almost complete silence in viewing the city and wonders for which he had longed throughout his life, seems the more remarkable when we remind ourselves that under normal circumstances he was very well able to describe his travelling experiences; we have only to think, for instance, of the two journal-letters, which he wrote during his journey in Germany in 1333, and the brilliant picture which he drew in them of the city of Cologne.[25] The entirely different reactions of Petrarch toward his impressions in Cologne and in Rome is, of course, easily explained. Whereas in Germany he could and did take the attitude of a "tourist" interested in new sights and in the observation of foreign people and strange customs, he went to Rome as to "that queenly city, of which I have read, aye, and written so much and shall perhaps write more, unless death break off my efforts prematurely."[26] This first visit to Rome, therefore, evoked emotions in Petrarch so deep that he was unable immediately to express them in concise words but had first to ponder over them for a long time.[27]

Quite different was the case when in 1341 Petrarch paid his second visit to Rome. On the actual caremony of his coronation as poet laureate, it is true, he left only one – and that rather general – description to posterity in one of his *Epistles*.[28] But this time he was able to render a real account of the impression which Rome had made upon him. Witness the letter which at the end of same year he addressed to his friend, the mendicant friar

---

23 *Fam.*, II, 9 (ed. Rossi I, 96): "de civitate . . . illa, cui nulla similis fuit, nulla futura est"; translat. by Tatham, I, 331.

24 Thus Petrarch wrote in a letter of 1337, dated "Rome, idibus Martii, in Capitolio," to his great patron, the Cardinal Giovanni Colonna: "Ab urbe Roma quid expectet, qui tam multa de montibus acceperit? Putabas me grande aliquid scripturum, cum Romam pervenissem. Ingens michi forsan in posterum scribendi materia oblata est; in presens nichil est quod inchoare ausim, miraculo rerum tantarum et stuporis mole obrutus"; *Fam.*, II, 14 (ed. Rossi, I, 103); translat. by Tatham 1, 338. Cf. *Senil.*, X, 2 (in *Opera omnia*, Basel, 1554, p. 963).

25 *Fam.*, I, 4 and 5 (ed. Rossi, I, 24–31); compare the notes in P. Piur's edition of these letters in K. Burdach, *Vom Mittelalter zur Reformation*, VII (Berlin, 1933), 161–74.

26 *Fam.*, II, 9 (ed. Rossi, I, 96): "hec cursim attigi, ut intelligeres non parvipendere me regine urbis aspectum, de qua infinita perlegi et ipse multa iam scripsi, plura forte scripturus, nisi primordia mea precipitata dies mortis abrumpat"; translat. by Tatham, I, 331.

27 Cf. Tatham, *Francesco Petrarca*, I, 338 ff.

28 *Epist. metr.*, II, 1, ed. D. Rossetti, *F. Petrarchae poëmata minora*, III (Milan, 1834), p. 1 ff.; see also *Fam.*, IV, 7, 8, 9, 13; *Africa*, IX, 237 ff. Cf. Tatham, *Francesco Petrarca*, II, 104–56; A. Marpicati, "L'incoronazione del Petrarca in Campidoglio," *Annali della Cattedra Petrarchesca*, VII (Arezzo, 1937), 1–25.

Giovanni Colonna.[29] Petrarch had first met Giovanni in Avignon and had carried on a correspondence with him, after this scion of the great Colonna family had gone to Rome to conclude his life as a monk. When Petrarch came to Rome in 1341, Giovanni often accompanied him on his promenades around the city. These common wanderings of theirs Petrarch recalls in that letter to Giovanni which begins: "Deambulabamus Rome soli." After a digression on the relative values of the various ancient schools of philosophy Petrarch continues: "We were wandering together in that mighty city, which, though from its extent it seems empty, has an immense population; we were wandering not merely in it but all around it; and at every step we encountered food for musing and for conversation."[30] There follows a long list of the localities which the two friends visited on their walks through Rome. It is to be noted that for the most part Petrarch recalls spots which were connected with the great figures and events of the history of pagan Rome, especially of the time of the Roman Republic, whereas only a very small part of the enumeration is devoted to scenes of Christian Rome: the proportion shows where Petrarch's main interest lay.[31] This is the more noteworthy, since in the beginning of the same letter Petrarch affirms: "We are to read philosophy, poetry, or history in such fashion that the echo of Christ's gospel, by which alone we are wise and happy, may ever be sounding in our hearts, – that gospel, without which the more we have learnt, the more ignorant and wretched shall we be; to which, as the highest citadel of truth, all things must be referred; on which alone, as the firm foundation of sound learning, all human toil is built."[32] Here a strong inconsistency appears: on the one hand Petrarch denies the intrinsic value of secular knowledge and declares that everything must be referred to eternal religious truth; on the other he puts an allmost exclusive emphasis on the

---

29 *Fam.*, VI, 2 (ed. Rossi, II, 55–60); partly translated by Tatham, *Francesco Petrarca*, I, 343–6. The date of the letter was controversial and it was doubtful whether it referred to Petrarch's first or second visit to Rome. However, L. Foresti, *Aneddoti della vita di Petrarca* (Brescia, 1928), pp. 81–4, has proved beyond any doubt that "la lettera fu invero scritta in cammino per la campagna di Parma il 30 Novembre 1341" (p. 82); F. E. H. Wilkins, *A tentative chronology of Petrarch's prose letters* (Chicago, 1929), p. 6 (under November 30).

30 "Vagabamur pariter in illa urbe tam magna, que cum propter spatium vacua videatur, populum habet immensum; nec in illa urbe tantum sed circa urbem bagabamur, aderatque per singulos passus quod linguam atque animum excitaret" (ed. Rossi, II, 56; translat. by Tatham, *Francesca Petrarca*, I, 344).

31 In Rossi's edition of the letter in *Le Familiari*, the ratio is about ten to one: lines 47 to 105 are devoted to the description of pagan Rome, lines 106 to 111 to that of Christian Rome.

32 "Sic philosophica, sic poetica, sic historias legamus, ut semper ad aurem cordis Evangelium Cristi sonet: quo uno satis docti ac felices; sine quo quanto plura didicerimus, tanto indoctiores atque miseriores futuri sumus; ad quod velut ad summam veri arcem referenda sunt omnia; cui, tanquam uni literarum verarum immobili fundamento, tuto superedificat humanus labor." (ed. Rossi, II, 56); translat. by Tatham, *Francesca Petranca*, I, 344.

history of pagan Rome and neglects the Christian aspects of the eternal city.[33]

After enumerating the historical spots, Petrarch complains bitterly that the contemporary Romans know nothing about Rome and things Roman. In his opinion this ignorance is disastrous. For he asks: "Who can doubt that Rome would rise up again if she but began to know herself?"[34] After this emotional outburst, Petrarch continues the reminiscences of his wanderings with Giovanni Colonna: "After the fatigue of walking over the immense circuit of the city, we used often to stop at the Baths of Diocletian; sometimes we even climbed upon the vaulted roof of that once magnificent building, for nowhere is there a healthier air, a wider prospect, or more silence and desirable solitude. There we did not talk of business nor of private or public affairs on which we had shed tears enough. As we walked over the walls of the shattered city or sat there, the fragments of the ruins were under our very eyes. Our conversation often turned on history, which we appeared to have divided up between us in such a fashion that in modern history you, in ancient history I, seemed to be more expert; and ancient were called those events which took place before the name of Christ was celebrated in Rome and adored by the Roman emperors, modern, however, the events from that time to the present."[35]

What strikes the modern reader of this letter is the fact that the poet looked at Rome and the Roman scene primarily from a historical and not from an aesthetic point of view. And even this historical point of view is quite unique. This becomes evident in the climax of the letter where Petrarch recalls the conversations which he had with his old friend on the

33   In this connection it is interesting to contrast this letter of 1341 with a passage in a letter which Petrarch wrote to Barbato da Sulmona in 1352 (*Fam.*, XII, 7; ed. Rossi, III, 28): "Id quidem quod non in ultimis adversitatum numeras, ut me Rome non inveneris, divinitus factum reor, ne si congredi licuisset, non templa Dei devotione catholica sed Urbis ambitum lustraremus curiositate poetica, non anime curam agentes sed negotium literarum, quod licet sit iocundissimum pabulum intellectus, nisi tamen ad unum verum finem redigatur, infinitum quiddam et inane est."

34   *Fam.*, VI, 2 (ed. Rossi, II, 58): "Quis enim dubitare potest quin illico surrectura sit, si ceperit se Roma cognoscere?"

35   "Solebamus ergo, post fatigationem quam nobis immensa urbs ambita pepererat, sepius ad Termas Dioclitianas subsistere, nonnunquam vero supra testudinem illius magnificentissime olim domus ascendere, quod et aer salutaris et prospectus liber et silentium ac votiva solitudo nusquam magis. Ibi de negotiis nichil omnino, nichil de re familiari nichilque de publica, quam semel flevisse satis est. Et euntibus per menia fracte urbis et illic sedentibus, ruinarum fragmenta sub oculis erant. Quid ergo? Multus de historiis sermo erat, quas ita partiti videbamur, ut in novis tu, in antiquis ego viderer expertior, et dicantur antique quecunque ante celebratum Rome et veneratum romanis principibus Cristi nomen, nove autem ex illo usque ad hanc etatem." (ed. Rossi, II, 58); compare Tatham's translation, *Francesco Petrarca*, I, 345. – The rest of the letter deals with the problem of the beginnings of the liberal and mechanical arts.

roof of the Baths of Diocletian, the ruins of the city spread beneath them. The reader of these sentences is immediately reminded of the words with which in his *Memoirs* Gibbon records the conception of his great history: "It was on the fifteenth of October (1764), in the gloom of evening, as I sat musing on the Capitol, while the barefooted fryars were chanting their litanies in the temple of Jupiter, that I conceived the first thought of my history. My original plan was confined to the decay of the City; my reading and reflection pointed to that aim; but several years elapsed, and several avocations intervened, before I grappled with the decline and fall of the Roman Empire.'[36] To Gibbon, true son of the age of *Ruinen-Romantik*,[37] those Roman ruins bore witness to "the greatest, perhaps, and most awful scene in the history of mankind";[38] and thus was he inspired to inquire and to describe the decadence of Rome. Petrarch's reaction as shown by his letter was entirely different. To him those ruins evidently bore witness to the time when Rome and the Romans had been great: "Of minute things," he exclaims, "there are no great ruins; ... he never will fall from a height who already lies in the abyss";[39] thus Petrarch shows his main interest, the rise and greatness of the *Respublica Romana*. In Gibbon's opinion Rome had fallen once and for all; in Petrarch's opinion there was a hope of resurrection, "if Rome but began to know herself."

This interpretation of the letter of 1341 reveals that by this time a new concept of history existed in Petrarch's mind. It would be highly gratifying to our sense of the logical if we were able to prove conclusively that this gravitation toward ancient Rome originated in and resulted directly from Petrarch's coronation which made him a *civis Romanus* both legally and ideally.[40] The material at our disposal, however, is too scanty to show this with absolute certainty.[41] But one conclusion we may safely draw from Petrarch's letter to Giovanni Colonna in 1341: here for the first time he

36   Quoted by D. M. Low, E. Gibbon (London, 1937), p. 184; cf. the similar words at the very end of *The Decline and Fall of the Roman Empire*.

37   Cf. W. Rehm, *Der Untergang Roms im abendländischen Denken* (Leipzig, 1930), pp. 120 ff.

38   E. Gibbon, *The Decline and Fall of the Roman Empire*, last page.

39   "Minutarum rerum ruina magna esse non potest; procul absunt ab hoc metu; nunquam cadet ex alto, qui in imo iacet; Roma igitur ex alto cecidit, non cadet Auinio"; *Apologia contra cuiusdam anonymi Galli calumnias* (in *Opera omnia*, Basel, 1554, p. 1180).

40   In the *Apologia contra cuiusdam anonymi Galli calumnias* (in *Opera omnia*, Basel, 1554, p. 1185) Petrarch proudly proclaims: "Sum uero Italus natione et Romanus ciuis esse glorior." In a letter of January 5, 1342, i.e. shortly after his coronation, Petrarch speaks of Rome as the city, "in qua civis (sum)"; *Fam.*, IV, 12 (ed. Rossi, I, 185). Cola di Rienzo calls Petrarch his "concivis" in a letter of July 28, 1347 (ed. K. Burdach, *Vom Mittelalter zur Reformation*, II, 3 (Berlin, 1912), p. 85.

41   There exists the possibility that Petrarch had conceived of this idea before he went to Rome, and that his laurel crown merely fortified his belief in the focal importance of Roman history.

ventured to state explicitly that his primary interest was in the history of pagan rather than of Christian Rome, thus drawing a sharp boundary-line between "ancient" and "modern" history. As in this letter he spoke almost exclusively of the remains of the classical time in Rome, also shortly afterwards he stated in his *Secretum* that he had confined his work *De viris illustribus* to the time "from Romulus to Titus."

The same demarcation of two clearly separated epochs of history is found in a letter of 1359, which Petrarch addresses to another member of the Colonna family, Agapito Colonna.[42] Petrarch's main purpose in writing this letter is to defend himself against Agapito's reproach of ingratitude and haughtiness and against the accusation that he intended to use Agapito as an example of vanity. Petrarch repudiates these charges and assures Agapito that he never had introduced his name in any of his works, 'not because I lacked affection but because I lacked occasion.'[43] Petrarch continues: "And yet had I touched upon illustrious men of our time, I will not say that I should have introduced your name (lest in my present anger I should seem to flatter you, a thing which is not my habit even when well disposed), but most assuredly I should not have passed over in silence either your uncle or your father. I did not wish for the sake of so few famous names, however, to guide my pen so far and through such darkness. Therefore sparing myself the excess both of subject-matter and of effort, I have determined to fix a limit to my history long before this century."[44]

In accordance with the passages quoted above from the letter of 1341 and from the *Secretum*, Petrarch states in this letter of 1359 that he had resolved to set a precise date limit to his historical studies. At the same time, however, he qualifies his judgment of the epoch following the period to which he was devoting his attention: this epoch was to him an era of "*tenebrae*," of "darkness."

What did Petrarch mean to say by using this word "*tenebrae*"? In his opinion was this period dark simply because the lack of sources prevented the historian to shed light on it? Or was it dark because "the lamps had gone out all over Europe" for a time of more than a thousand years? With this alternative we come to the crucial point in the interpretation of Petrarch's conception of history. For the acceptance of the second assumption would

---

42   *Fam.*, XX, 8 (ed. J. Fracassetti, *Epistolae de rebus familiaribus*, III, 28–34).

43   "Caeterum nusquam ibi, nusquam alibi hactenus tuum nomen inserui, destituente quidem materia, non affectu" (ed. Fracassetti III, 30).

44   "Quamquam si illustres aevi nostri viros attigissem, non dicam te, ne tibi, quod placatus non soleo, iratus adulari videar, at certe nec patruum nec patrem tuum silentio oppressurus fuerim. Nolui autem pro tam paucis nominibus claris, tam procul tantasque per tenebras stilum ferre: ideoque vel materiae vel labori parcens, longe ante hoc saeculum historiae limitem statui ac defixi." (ed. Fracassetti, III, 30 f.).

mean that by the use of the word "darkness" Petrarch passed a very definite judgement of value upon the long era in question.

To solve this problem we turn to statements made by Petrarch elsewhere in his writings. In a famous passage in the second book of the *Africa* he makes the father of the elder Scipio Africanus predict the future of Rome to his son. Lucius Scipio breaks off his prophecy with the reigns of the Emperors Vespasian and Titus. "I cannot bear," he exclaims, "to proceed; for strangers of Spanish and African extraction will steal the sceptre and the glory of the Empire founded by us with great effort. Who can endure the thought of the seizure of supreme control by these dregs of the people, these contemptible remnants, passed over by our sword"?[45]

Similar ideas Petrarch expresses in a letter which he directed to the German King Charles IV in 1351.[46] The second half of this letter is a speech which Roma herself addresses to Charles. She describes in detail the rise of the Roman Republic up to the Augustan era: hundreds of years of effort and struggle, she says, resulted in the foundation of the Empire and in the establishment of eternal peace. At this point Roma suddenly breaks off her narration. She declares emphatically that she does not wish to begin "the lamentable story" of the decline: "where things have retrograded," Charles will see for himself.[47]

In the history of the later Roman emperors of "foreign" extraction Petrarch is no more interested than he is in the history of all those rulers of non-Roman nations, "whose names," as he says in the preface to the second version of *De viris illustribus*, "were always obscure and are now entirely obliterated because of the long lapse of time.[48] In this connection it is noteworthy that in an early letter (written in 1333) Petrarch calls Charlemagne simply 'King Charles whom,' by the cognomen of 'the Great,' barbarous peoples dare to raise to the level of Pompey and Alexander."[49] If in this letter

---

45 Ulterius transire piget; nam sceptra decusque

> Imperii tanto nobis fundata labore
> Externi rapient Hispane stirpis et Afre.
> Quis ferat has hominum sordes nostrique pudendas
> Relliquias gladii fastigia prendere rerum; *Africa*, II, 274–8
> (ed. N. Festa, p. 40); cf. *Africa* II, 255 ff.

46 *Fam.*, X, 1 (ed. Rossi, II, 277–284); cf. P. Piur's edition of this letter in K. Burdach, *Vom Mittelalter zur Reformation*, VII (Berlin, 1933), pp. 1–11.

47 "voti compos, omnia sub pedibus meis vidi. Inde sensim nescio quonammodo, nisi quia mortalium opera decet esse mortalia, in labores meos irrepsit aliena segnities, ac ne lacrimabilem ordiar historiam, quorsum res redierint, vides" (ed. Rossi, II, 282).

48 "Quis enim, queso, Parthorum aut Macedonum, quis Gothorum et Unnorum et Vuandalorum atque aliarum gentium reges ab ultimis repetitos in ordinem digerat, quorum et obscura semper et iam senio deleta sunt nomina?" (ed. P. de Nolhac, in *Notices et extraits de la Bibliothèque Nationale*, XXXIV, 1 (Paris, 1890), p. 112.

49 "Carolum regem quem magni cognomine equare Pompeio et Alexandro audent"; *Fam.*, I, 4 (ed. Rossi, I, 25).

and elsewhere Petrarch denies to Charles both his official and his popular titles,[50] he denies more than the personal greatness of a single individual: he expresses his disregard of the whole institution – the first and greatest representative of which Charlemagne had been – the mediaeval Empire, the self-proclaimed heir and successor of the *Imperium Romanum*. That Petrarch does not contest the imperial idea, according to which the Empire had been transferred from the Romans to the Byzantines, the Franks and eventually the Germans, is shown by the prediction which in the *Africa* he puts in the mouth of Lucius Scipio.[51] But in contradiction to the political theorists and historians of the Middle Ages, Petrarch looks with scorn at this continuity. For in his opinion the Roman Empire "had been impaired, debilitated, and almost consumed at the hands of the barbarians."[52]

From these passages it is clear that Petrarch discarded the whole history of the Roman Empire during late Antiquity and the Middle Ages because within that age, everywhere in the western world, had come into power "barbarous" nations which brought even Rome and the Romans under their domination. Because Petrarch could think of this whole development only with a feeling of scornful grief, he consciously and consistently consigned it to oblivion in all his writings. In his letters time and again he conjures up the great shades of Antiquity, but scarcely ever does he refer to a mediaeval name. In his *Rerum memorandarum libri quatuor*, more than half of the examples are drawn from Roman history, about two-fifths from ancient Greek history, and only the rest from "more recent" times, which in this case meant almost exclusively from the fourteenth century; the Middle Ages proper are passed over in complete silence.[53] Exactly the same is true

---

50   See the canzone "Il successor di Carlo" (in *Le Rime sparse e i trionfi*, ed. E. Chiòrboli, Bari, 1930, n. 27, p. 22), and the first version of the "Trionfo della Fama" (ed. Chiòrboli, *Rime*, p. 376, v. 163). – On Charlemagne's cognomen compare P. Lehmann, "Das literarische Bild Karls des Grossen vornehmlich im lateinischen Schrifttum des Mittelalters," *Sitzungsberichte der Bayerischen Akademie der Wissenschaften, philosoph-histor. Klasse* (Munich, 1934).

51   Vivet honos Latius, semperque vocabitur uno

> Nomine Romanum imperium; sed rector habenas
> Non semper Romanus aget; quin Siria mollis
> Porriget ipsa manum, mox Gallia dura, loquaxque
> Grecia, et Illiricum: tandem cadet ista potestas

In Boream: sic res humanas fata rotabunt; *Africa*, II, 288–93 (ed. Festa, p. 40).

52   In the *Apologia contra cuiusdam anonymi Galli calumnias* Petrarch says of the Empire: "quod licet inter manus barbaricas imminutum atque debilitatum et pene consumptum sit, Romanas inter manus tale fuit, ut omnia mundi illi admota pueriles ludi fuisse videantur et inania nomina" (in *Opera omnia*, Basel, 1554, p. 1187).

53   Compare *Rerum memorandarum libri IV* (in *Opera omnia*, Basel, 1554, pp. 442–550). The work contains 20 chapters, each of which is arranged in the three sections of the history of the Romans, the "externi," and the "recentiores." There are about 350 entries in the work; of these, 30 entries are grouped under the heading of "recentiores," more than 130 under that

of his *Trionfi*, where nearly all of the handful of mediaeval figures mentioned belong to the realm of legend or poetry or to the period close to Petrarch's own time.[54] To realize the peculiarity of Petrarch's standpoint, we have only to think of the entirely different picture of the past in the *Divine Comedy*, where Dante usually couples ancient and mediaeval figures in his representation of the various vices and virtues of man.[55]

Petrarch's conception of history, I think, cannot be better expressed than by the words which he wrote in the *Apologia contra cuiusdam anonymi Galli calumnias*: "What else, then, is all history, if not the praise of Rome?"[56] This peculiar notion of history, very impressive in its Latin succinctness, was formulated by Petrarch only at the end of his life. But evidently he conceived of it much earlier, in the beginning of the 1340s, when he started work on the second version of *De viris illustribus*. When in his historical work Petrarch emphasized everything that was Roman and excluded everything that was outside Rome, he was entirely in accord with all his other writings; both in his letters and in his poetical works he confined himself to the same topic as in *De viris illustribus*.

This consistent restriction to subjects taken from Roman history makes it clear that Petrarch did not narrow down the scope of his historical studies for mere external reasons, but that he rather limited himself on principle. This limitation was based on a very definite judgement of value: the praise of Rome corresponded to the condemnation of the "barbarous" countries and peoples outside Rome. This point of view Petrarch expressed when in 1341 he drew a line of demarcation between "ancient" and "modern" history, and when later on he called the period stretching from the fall of the Roman Empire down to his own age a time of "darkness." In Petrarch's opinion that era was "dark" because it was worthless, not because it was little known. The sooner the period dropped from man's memory, the better. Therefore Petrarch, personally at least, was resolved to bury it in oblivion.

---

of "externi"; the remaining more than 180 stories are from Roman history. – On the general character of this work cf. L. Tonelli, *Petrarca* (Milan, 1930), pp. 261 ff.

54   Out of more than 400 names mentioned in the *Trionfi*, I count only 14 mediaeval names: King Arthur, Charlemagne, Godfrey of Bouillon, Saladin, Admiral Ruggero di Lauria, Duke Henry of Lancaster, King Robert of Sicily, Stefano Colonna, Tristan and Iseult, Lancelot and Guenevere, Paolo and Francesca Malatesta da Rimini; compare the index of names in C. Calcaterra's edition of the *Trionfi* (Turin, 1923).

55   Cf. J. Burckhardt, *The Civilization of the Renaissance in Italy*, b. III, ch. 4: "In the *Divine Comedy* (Dante) treats the ancient and the Christian worlds, not indeed as of equal authority, but as parallel to one another. Just as, at an earlier period of the Middle Ages types and antitypes were sought in the history of the Old and New Testaments, so does Dante constantly bring together a Christian and a pagan illustration of the same fact."

56   "Quid est enim aliud omnis historia quam Romana laus?" (in *Opera omnia*, Basel, 1554, p. 1187); cf. H. W. Eppelsheimer, *Petrarca* (Bonn, 1926), p. 77.

This notion, however, has an importance beyond its relation to the life and works of Petrarch. It offers not only a key to the understanding of Petrarch's personal standards of value, but it deserves attention as well in connection with the problem with which our discussion started, the problem of the humanist periodization of history.

As we have seen, Petrarch divided the course of history into two sharply separated periods and set as a dividing point between them either the time when Christianity became the state religion in the Roman Empire or the time when the Roman Empire began to "decline" under the rule of "barbarian," that is non-Roman emperors. Mediaeval historiography was based on essentially different principles.[57] Whereas after the modification of his original plan Petrarch concerned himself exclusively with the first period and concentrated upon the secular history of Rome "from Romulus to Titus," the mediaeval historians almost without exception wrote universal history, that is, in the words of Benedetto Croce, "a history of the universal, of the universal by excellence, which is history in labor with God and toward God."[58] Even the most meager monastic chroniclers and annalists dealt usually with their particular monasteries within the framework of a history of the world from its creation to the present. In doing so they followed very definite schemes according to which universal history was divided up into the succession either of the four world-monarchies or of the six ages.[59] These two patterns were first drawn up by Jerome in his *Commentaries* on Daniel's famous prophecy on the statue composed of different metals and on the four beasts (*Daniel*, 2, 31 ff. and 7, 1 ff.); and by Augustine in the *City of God* (XXII). Both schemes had in common the conception of the world and its various countries and peoples as a unity. Which implied the notion both of universality and of continuity in history. This idea originated in Hellenistic times,[60] and later on was taken over by the greatest of the early Christian historians, Eusebius of Caesarea. Because of the authority of Jerome and Augustine the patterns of the four world-monarchies and the six ages became the models of almost all the mediae-

---

57   Compare M. Ritter, *Die Entwicklung der Geschichtswissenschaft an den führenden Werken betrachtet* (Munich–Berlin, 1919); B. Croce, *Theory and history of historiography*, translat. by D. Ainslie (London, 1921), pp. 200–23; H. von Eicken, *Geschichte und System der mittelalterlichen Weltanschauung* (4th edition, Stuttgart–Berlin, 1923), pp. 641–71; H. E. Barnes, *A History of historical writing* (Norman, 1937), pp. 41–98.

58   B. Croce, *Theory and history*, p. 206.

59   On these two schemes cf. H. F. Massmann, *Der keiser und der kunige buoch oder die sogenannte Kaiserchronik* (Quedlinburg–Berlin, 1854), III, 353–64; M. Ritter, *Die Entwicklung*, pp. 84 f.; B. Croce, *Theory and history*, pp. 206, 213 f.; H. Spangenberg, "Die Perioden der Weltgeschichte," *Historische Zeitschrift*, CXXVII (1923), pp. 7 f.; G. Falco, *La polemica sul medio evo* (Turin, 1933), pp. 1–6; W. K. Ferguson, "Humanist Views," pp. 5 f.

60   Cf. C. Trieber, "Die Idee der vier Weltreiche," *Hermes*, XXVII (1892), pp. 311–42.

val universal histories, those of Isidore of Seville, Bede, Otto of Freising, Vincent of Beauvais, to mention only the greatest names. As late as in the seventeenth century we find histories of the world organized in accordance with the interpretation of Daniel's prophecy.[61] In these two schemes the beginnings of the last period coincided, since in the one it began with the foundation of the Roman Empire by Caesar or Augustus, in the other with the birth of Christ. "And thus," as Comparetti says, "history was divided into two distinct periods – a long period of error and darkness, and then a period of purification and truth, while midway between the two stood the Cross of Calvary."[62]

Against this background we may now place Petrarch's division of history: he certainly drew an entirely different line of demarcation. Since he concerned himself exclusively with one particular state, Rome, he was not interested in the four world-monarchies. He started out from the very beginnings of Rome and showed her growth under the leadership of the great men of the republican period, whereas the mediaeval historians paid very little attention to the epoch preceding the foundation of the Empire.[63] "The lamentable story of how things retrograded," Petrarch did not want to recount (*Fam.*, X, 1), and therefore he stopped precisely at the point where in his opinion the "decline" of the Empire began. The mediaeval historians, on the other hand, continued the history of the Empire straight through to their own time: in their opinion the *Imperium Romanum* still existed although the rule over it had been "transferred" from the Romans to other peoples.

By setting up the "decline of the Empire" as a dividing point and by passing over the traditional marks either of the foundation of the Empire or of the birth of Christ, Petrarch introduced a new chronological demarcation in history. This scheme has been distinguished from the older mediaeval or "Hellenistic" ones by the name "humanistic,"[64] for it formed the underlying principle of most of the historical works written by Italian humanists.[65] Its most manifest expression is found in the title of Flavio

---

61 Cf. E. Fueter, *Geschichte der neueren Historiographie* (3rd edition, Munich–Berlin, 1936), pp. 187 f., 288, 618.

62 D. Comparetti, *Vergil in the Middle Ages*, translat. by E. F. M. Benecke (London, 1908), p. 174.

63 Cf. A. Graf, *Roma nella memoria e nelle immaginazioni del Medio Evo*, I (Turin, 1882), 230 f.: "Il periodo della storia romana che più sta a cuore al medio evo è il periodo imperiale . . . L'interesse per Roma repubblicana è, generalmente parlando, un frutto del Rinascimento avanzato." Cf. Comparetti, *Vergil in the Middle Ages*, pp. 177 f.

64 Cf. A. Dove, "Der Streit um das Mittelalter," in *Historische Zeitschrift*, CXVI (1916), p. 210.

65 On humanist historiography see P. Joachimsen, *Geschichtsauffassung und Geschichtschreibung in Deutschland unter dem Einfluss des Humanismus* (Leipzig–Berlin, 1910), pp. 15–36; M. Ritter, *Die Entwicktung der Geschichtswissenschaft* (Munich–Berlin, 1919), pp. 125–204; B. Croce, *Theory and history*, pp. 224–42; H. Baron, "Das Erwachen des historischen Denkens im

Biondo's work *Decades historiarum ab inclinatione imperii,* a history of the period stretching from 410 to 1440. The origin of this new chronological demarcation, therefore, has usually been dated hitherto from the middle of the fifteenth century.[66] But, since Petrarch consciously confined his historical studies to the period *"usque ad declinationem imperii,"* if we may say so, we are justified in stating that thereby he implicitly anticipated ideas of the fifteenth-century Italian humanists.

This statement with regard to Petrarch's demarcation of "Antiquity" raises another question. The humanists were to replace the older patterns with a division of history into three periods which, under the names of "ancient," "mediaeval," and "modern" times, live to the present day.[67] Is it possible to connect Petrarch also with the origin of this division? I think that the question can be answered in the affirmative. To be sure, this threefold division we shall nowhere find expressed directly by Petrarch. As we have seen, he speaks only of "ancient" and "modern" history.[68] The use of the word "modern" in this connection cannot be interpreted otherwise than that Petrarch thought of his own time as still a part of the period which had begun with the "decline" of the Empire. His was an age of decadence: this idea Petrarch has expressed time and again in his letters. The feeling of profound pessimism finds perhaps its most impressive wording in an early letter where Petrarch says: "As conditions are, I foresee worse things from day to day; but, although I can fear worse things, I can scarcely imagine them."[69] But like so many men of all ages, Petrarch was a pessimist because he was an idealist at heart. In measuring the actual conditions of his time with the standards of his lofty ideals he could not escape despair, a despair, however, which did not always mean hopelessness. His "Golden Age," it is true, lay in the past but, on occasion at least, he was able to visualize the possibility of its return in the future. Thus, in a letter to Pope Urban V, he expresses his belief that Christ desires the re-establishment of the papal court in Rome *"pro aurei saeculi principio."*[70] In similar, though less religious language

Humanismus des Quattrocento," *Historische Zeitschrift,* CXXXVII (1933), pp. 5–20; E. Fueter, *Geschichte der neueren Historiograptice,* pp. 1-36 (cf. the bibliography pp. 607 ff.); H. E. Barnes, *A History of historical Writing,* pp. 99–111; W. K. Ferguson, "Humanist Views," pp. 1–28.

66 Cf. P. Joachimsen, *Geschichtsauffassung,* pp. 22 ff.

67 On the question of division of history compare K. Heussi, *Altertum, Mittelalter und Neuzeit; ein Beitrag zum Problem der historischen Periodisierung* (Tübingen, 1921); H. Spangenberg, "Die Perioden der Weltgeschichte," *Historische Zeitschrift,* CXXVII (1923), pp. 1–49.

68 *Fam.,* VI, 2 (ed. Rossi, II, 58).

69 *Fam.,* II, 10 (ed. Rossi, I, 98): "Sed, ut res eunt, in dies peiora conicio; quamvis iam peiora VIX possim nedum timere, sed fingere; cf. Tatham, *Petrarca,* II, 72.

70 *Senil.,* VII (in *Opera omnia,* Basel, 1554, p. 903): "Incipit, credo, Christus Deus noster suorum fidelium misereri, uult ut arbitror, finem malis imponere, quae multa per hos annos uidimus, uult pro aurei saeculi principio Ecclesiam suam, quam uagari propter culpas hominum diu sinit, ad antiquas et proprias sedes suas et priscae fidei statum reuocare."

Petrarch phrases his passionate appeals to the Roman Tribune of the People, Cola di Rienzo, and to the German Emperor Charles IV, urging them to take over the legacy of Antiquity and to follow the models of the great men of ancient Rome: by so doing they were to revive the grandeur of times past. It was this same conviction which impelled Petrarch to pursue historical studies.[71] Since he believed that "Rome would rise up again if she but began to know herself," he strove throughout his life and his work to make his contemporaries conscious of the great traditions of the eternal city. In spite of his often expressed pessimism Petrarch evidently was convinced that there existed the chance of a spiritual rebirth which would put an end to the process of decline, and bring about the beginning of a "new time." This ardent hope of his for the future Petrarch voices nowhere more impressively than in the work which he himself considered as his greatest: at the very end of the *Africa* he addresses his own poem as follows: "My fate is to live amid varied and confusing storms. But for you perhaps, if as I hope and wish you will live long after me, there will follow a better age. This sleep of forgetfulness will not last for ever. When the darkness has been dispersed, our descendants can come again in the former pure radiance."[72]

These verses of the *Africa* show clearly Petrarch's views on the periodization of history. He holds that there was an era of "pure radiance" in the past, Antiquity, and that there is an era of "darkness" succeeding this former period and lasting to the poet's own days. Thus, in Petrarch's opinion, there exists, for the time being, only a twofold division of history. But, since he hopes for the coming of "a better time," the conception of a third era is expressed, or at least implied, in his thoughts. This is illustrated most distinctly in one of his *Epistles*, in which he complains against Fate for having decreed his birth in such sad times, and in which he wishes that he had been born either earlier or much later; for he says, "there was a more fortunate age and probably there will be one again; in the middle, in our time, you see the confluence of wretches and ignominy."[73] In these lines

---

71   I shall give this question detailed treatment in a monograph on *Petrarch's historical and political ideas.*

72   *Africa*, IX, 451–7 (ed. Festa, p. 278): . . . Michi degere vitam.

> Impositum varia rerum turbante procella.
> At tibi fortassis, is – quod mens sperat et optat –
> Es post me victura diu, meliora supersunt
> Secula: non omnes veniet Letheus in annos
> Iste sopor! Poterunt discussis forte tenebris
> Ad purum priscumque inbar remeare nepotes.

73   *Epist. metr.*, III, 33 (ed. D. Rossetti, F. *Petrarchae poëmata minora*, II (Milan, 1831), p. 262) begins as follows:

> Vivo, sed indignans, quae nos in tristia fatum
> Saecula dilatos peioribus intulit annis.

Petrarch plainly distinguishes between three eras: the fortunate ages of the past and, possibly, of the future; between them there is a "middle" time which has not yet come to an end. For the humanists of the fifteenth century periodization of history was to be much simpler. In their opinion the "new" era had actually come to" light, because of the work of the great artists and poets of the fourteenth century, among them Petrarch himself. Thus, in their minds, there was no doubt about the reality of three periods: a "middle" period separated the Golden Age of Antiquity from a "modern" time of "renascence."[74] It would be asking too much to expect Petrarch to proclaim himself explicitly the inaugurator of a new era, although occasionally he comes close to making such a claim.[75] But implicitly he certainly paved the way to the idea which was to be set forth by the humanists of following generations. In this sense, then, our modern threefold division of history can be traced back to Petrarch.

The strength of Petrarch's hope for a revival of the Golden Age varied throughout his life, in accordance with general circumstances and his personal moods. But he never vacillated in his firm conviction that the era following the decline of the Roman Empire was a period of "darkness." The fact that we are able to associate this conception with Petrarch, means more than merely the fixation of a late. For the whole idea of the Italian "rinascita," is inseparably connected with the notion of the preceding era as an age of obscurity. The people living in that "renascence" thought of it as a time of revolution. They wanted to break away from the mediaeval past and all its traditions and they were convinced that they had effected such a break. They believed that in their time, to use the words of Petrarch, "the darkness had been dispersed," and that they had "come again in the former pure radiance." Their model was Antiquity, "and the Middle Ages did seem to be a ditch or a declivity."[76]

> Aut prius, aut multo decuit post tempore nasci;
> Nam fuit, et fortassis erit, felicius aevum.
> In medium sordes, in nostrum turpia tempus
> Confluxisse vides; gravium sentina malorum
> Nos habet; ingenium, virtus et gloria mundo
> Cesserunt; regnumque tenent fortuna, voluptas;
> Dedecus ingenti visu! nisi surgimus actum est.

74 The first written proofs of the expression "Middle Ages" used in the technical sense, date from the middle of the fifteenth century; cf. P. Lehmann, "Mittelalter und Küchenlatein," in *Historische Zeitschrift*, CXXXVII (1928), pp. 200–6.

75 Cf. *Rerum memorandarum*, I, 2 (in *Opera omnia*, Basel, 1554, p. 448); "Ego . . . uelut in confinio duorum populorum constitutus, ac simul ante retroque prospiciens . . .' – Cf. N. Sapegno, "Petrarca e l'Umanesimo," in *Annali della Cattedra Petrarchesca*, VIII (Arezzo, 1938), pp. 77–119; F. Simone, "La coscienza, della rinascita," II, 843 f.

76 B. Croce, *Theory and history*, p. 201; cf. *ibid.*, p. 241.

From our modern point of view we may find it impossible to draw such a sharp line of demarcation between the Renaissance and the preceding period. We have, however, to keep in mind one very essential fact which has been expressed by Joachimsen as follows: "If there is one thing that unites the men of the Renaissance, it is the notion of belonging to a new time."[77] It is precisely this notion of a "new time" which distinguishes the Italian Renaissance from all the so-called earlier "Renaissances" in the Carolingian and Ottonian times or in the twelfth century. These times may have experienced a certain revival of classical studies, but the people living in them did not conceive of or wish for a complete break with the traditions of the times immediately preceding.[78] This idea was peculiar to the Italian Renaissance and it found its expression in the condemnation of the mediaeval epoch as an era of "darkness." Petrarch stands at the very fountainhead of Renaissance thought. It is logical that the "Father of Humanism" is also the father of the concept or attitude which regards the Middle Ages as the "Dark Ages."

---

77   P. Joachimsen, *Geschichtsauffassung*, p. 24.

78   On the problem of the earlier "Renaiassances" compare E. Patzelt, *Die karolingische Renaissance; Beiträge zur Geschichte der Kultur des frühen Mittelalters* (Vienna, 1924); H. Naumann, *Karolingische und Ottonische Renaissance* (Frankfurt, 1926); C. H. Haskins, *The Renaissance of the twelfth century* (Cambridge, 1927). Cf. the remarks of F. Simone, "La coscienza della rinascita," II, 867.

10

Commerce with the Classics

Anthony Grafton

A Book for a Pope

On 13 July 1452 the scribe Ioannes Lamperti de Rodenberg finished copying a manuscript of Lorenzo Valla's Latin translation of Thucydides. In a holograph note at the end, Valla explained both how excellent he found the result and what he saw as its purpose: "I, Lorenzo Valla, corrected this codex of Thucydides, of whom I believe that even the Greeks had no more splendidly written or illuminated text, at the command of Pope Nicholas and working with the very Ioannes who wrote it so well. Therefore I have entered this subscription in my own hand, so that this codex would be the official copy of my translation and could be used to correct other copies."[1] Valla deposited the manuscript in the Vatican Library. There, Nicholas and Valla both hoped, it would serve as an official text – the model for all other copies and a resource for the members of "la corte di Roma," for whom Nicholas destined his collection.

At first sight both the manuscript and the text it proffers seem to realize the humanists' boldest claims. Its readers made contact with two of the keenest intellects that the classical tradition can boast. Thucydides, that most darkly analytical and starkly eloquent of historians, had remained unknown in the Western Middle Ages and the early Renaissance. Some of the best-informed readers in the early fifteenth century, such as Coluccio

---

1 MS Vat. lat. 1801, fol. 184 recto. For a description of the MS see B. Nogara, *Codices Vaticani Latini III: Codices 1461–2059* (Vatican City, 1912), 275–6, but his text of the subscription is imperfect. For a critical text and an important discussion see S. Rizzo, *Il lessico filologico degli umanisti* (Rome, 1973), 312.

Salutati – who had parts of book 1 of Diodorus Siculus specially translated by Leonardo Bruni to aid him in his mythological researches – seem not to have read him. A number of Salutati's younger friends, who learned Greek from the Byzantine scholar Manuel Chrysoloras, studied the *Histories* in whole or in part. But the text remained the possession of the tiny group capable of reading the original.[2] To encounter his history, translated in full, for the first time, was surely a great and salutary shock – as if one had come to the top of a roller coaster and then had the full panorama of Athens in prosperity, crisis, and defeat suddenly appear.

Valla, moreover, made the perfect interpreter for his demanding Thucydidean text. A brilliant iconoclast, he demolished the pretensions of medieval lawyers and theologians by showing that they misunderstood their own canonical texts. He destroyed the reputation of a rival humanist, Poggio Braccolini, by writing a dialogue in which the cook and stable-boy of another humanist, Guarino da Verona, exposed Poggio's errors in Latinity.[3] And he dismantled the papal claim to lordship over the Western empire by proving that it rested on a forged text, the *Donation of Constantine*. In this case rhetoric and hermeneutics combined to produce an unreading, rather than a reading – a searing demonstration that the text could not be what its title claimed, could not even have been written in its supposed century of origin.[4] No one was better equipped by temperament than Valla to appreciate Thucydides' clear-eyed unmasking of the springs of victory and defeat in human affairs.

In technique, moreover, no one was better qualified than Valla to translate Thucydides. An expert Greek scholar, he could cope with what he called Thucydides' notoriously "difficult and rocky" style, even when Cardinal Bessarion, who had promised to help him, proved unable to do so.[5] A bril-

---

2   See B. L. Ullman, *The Humanism of Coluccio Salutati* (Padua, 1963), 227; Salutati, *De laboribus Herculis*, ed. Ullman (Zürich, 1951), 2:569–71. For the early spread of interest in Thucydides in the circle of the Greek scholar Manuel Chrysoloras see U. Klee, *Beiträge zur Thukydides-Rezeption während des 15. und 16. Jahrhunderts in Italien und Deutschland* (Bern, New York, and Paris, 1990), 19–23.

3   On this episode see R. Pfeiffer, "Küchenlatein," *Philologus* 86 (1931): 455–9 = *Ausgewählte Schriften*, ed. W. Bühler (Munich, 1960), 183–7.

4   See J. M. Levine, "Reginald Pecock and Lorenzo Valla on the *Donation of Constantine*," *Studies in the Renaissance* 20 (1973): 118–43; W. Setz, *Lorenzo Vallas Schrift gegen die Konstantinische Schenkung* (Tübingen, 1975); V. de Caprio, "Retorica e ideologia nella *Declamatio* di Lorenzo Valla sulla *donazione di Costantino*," *Paragone* 29, no. 338 (1978): 36–56; and G. W. Most, "Rhetorik und Hermeneutik: Zur Konstitution der Neuzeitlichkeit," *Antike und Abendland* 30 (1984): 62–79.

5   Vat. lat. 1801, fol. 1 verso. On the earliest stage in his progress see also his letter to Tortelli of 28 October 1448, *Epistole*, ed. O. Besomi and M. Regoliosi (Padua, 1984), 345. See also the editors' very helpful commentary, ibid., 323–4, and cf. J. Monfasani, "Bessarion, Valla, Agricola, and Erasmus," *Rinascimento*, ser. 2, 28 (1988): 319–20.

liant Latinist, the author of the first systematic modern treatment of Latin syntax and usage, Valla could also devise a fitting Latin dress for his author.[6] But Valla's qualifications went beyond the technical. He had read much and thought hard about history. He knew and quoted, for example, the now famous argument in Aristotle's *Poetica* that "poetry is more akin to philosophy and is a better thing than history; poetry deals with general truths, history with specific events. The latter are, for example, what Alcibiades did or suffered."[7] This passage seemed, at least to an Aristotelian of a somewhat later generation, to prove the superficiality of historical knowledge and the impossibility of constructing an *ars historica*: a systematic and methodical art of historical writing.[8] Valla explained the text as a precise reference to "Thucydides, who records the deeds of Pericles, Lysander, and some other men of his time."[9] And he rebutted Aristotle's argument at length, on grounds to which we will return later in this chapter. Evidently, Valla was a connoisseur of history in general and of Greek history in particular. When he set out to translate Thucydides, he had made a principled decision to do so, one informed by a sense of the pains, as well as the pleasures, of history. His new text, written in classical Latin, not surrounded by a thorny hedge of medieval misinformation, offered the new men of the Curia an orderly Renaissance garden, elegant and symmetrical, sown with the most vivid historical insights.

Valla's manuscript and text were splendid creations. But naturally they did not offer the mid-fifteenth-century reader a crisp, panoramic view of Athens in the late fifth century B.C. The manuscript, in the first place, was a physical object – and one which, as Valla himself said, had enormous sensual appeal. Each book of the text began with a fine miniature. A bearded man, wearing a robe (and sometimes a hat or a tabard), holds a book: presumably this man is Thucydides himself. In book 1 he writes on a scroll, in book 4 he reads one, and in book 8 he holds one; in books 2, 3, 5, 6, and 7 he holds a modern codex bound in red. This series of coordinated images gives the impression, no doubt deliberately, that Thucydides has come back to converse directly with his reader. The scribe's writing rein-

---

6   On Valla's text (and its Greek *Vorlage*) see *Thucydidis Historiae*, ed. G. B. Alberti (Rome, 1972–), 1:cxix–cxxxii; F. Ferlauto, *Il testo di Tucidide e la traduzione latina di Lorenzo Valla* (Palermo, 1979); and N. G. Wilson, *From Byzantium to Italy* (London, 1992), chap. 9.

7   Aristotle *Poetics* (trans. Grube) 1451 b 5–11.

8   See J. Zabarella, *De natura logicae* (1578), *Opera logica* (Hildesheim, 1966), 100–2; quoted by L. Gardiner Janik, "A Renaissance Quarrel: The Origin of Vico's Anti-Cartesianism," *New Vico Studies*, 1983, 49 n. 14.

9   L. Valla, *Gesta Ferdinandi regis Aragonum*, ed. O. Besomi (Padua, 1973), 3. See the full analysis of Valla's work by G. Ferraù, "La concezione storiografica de Valla: I 'Gesta Ferdinandi regis Aragonum,'" *Lorenzo Valla e l'umanesimo italiano*, ed. O. Besomi and M. Regoliosi (Padua, 1986), 265–310.

forced the impression of direct access to classical instruction. Firm, stately epigraphic capitals dramatized the titles of the books, while a round, legible, open minuscule, only lightly peppered with abbreviations, made the body of the text smooth classical sailing. A good deal of gold leaf highlighted the book's significance. Valla himself evidently prized – and very likely chose – this design. As we saw, he described the book as "more splendidly written and illuminated" than any Greek codex.

In fact, the book's design has little to do with ancient precedent, everything with up-to-date humanist tastes. Many of its special features were shaped by its modern situation. The book's lack of extensive marginal apparatus, for example, reflects the taste of its future owner. Nicholas V told Vespasiano that he infinitely preferred Traversari's translation of pseudo-Dionysius the Areopagite, which had no glosses, to "the others with the numberless commentaries they contained."[10]

Valla clearly knew that the material qualities of his book would help to endear it to Nicholas. Among the metaphors of conquest in his dedicatory letter appears an even more revealing metaphor of commerce.[11] Valla compares the translator to the merchant: both make precious things universally available. The comparison was highly charged in the 1440s and 1450s. Fraticelli pounded the streets of Italian cities, preaching a doctrine of total renunciation. Bernardino da Siena hung from the ceiling of the Florentine Duomo, denouncing the city's rampant greed and usury. But he and many Dominicans argued that social life required the existence of commerce and commerce that of merchants. Humanists like Leonardo Bruni, for their part, derived from Greek texts on ethics and household management the thesis that only wealth enabled the citizen to practice the virtues of philanthropy and magnificence.[12] Valla clearly knew these debates, in which his enemy Poggio took an active hand.[13] He occupied a characteristically mocking position, arguing that merchants, by moving goods of all sorts around the world, restored the original golden age, when all things were held in common. Translation did the same for the (naturally more valuable) things of the mind.

Valla thus made clear that he offered his patron a thing of monetary, as well as a text of spiritual, value. Like many of his Italian contemporaries, Valla did not see the desire for gain and that for learning as necessarily contradictory. The same project could please a patron and bring men to the true

10   Vespasiano, *Vite*, ed. A. Greco (Florence, 1970–6), 1:68.

11   On Valla's preface and its context in his work see M. Pade, "The Place of Translation in Valla's Thought," *Classica et Medievalia* 35 (1984): 285–306.

12   See H. Baron, *In Search of Florentine Civic Humanism* (Princeton, N.J., 1988), 1:chaps. vii–ix.

13   J. Oppel, "Poggio, San Bernardino of Siena, and the Dialogue *On Avarice*," *Renaissance Quarterly* 30 (1977): 564–87.

religion. Without translation, after all, the Latins could have no "commerce" – *commercium* – with God himself. Valla's use of a term that had a traditional religious meaning and a prominent place in the mass only sharpened his metaphor.[14] Valla's critical self-awareness and lack of pretense make it easier to appreciate the extent of the sensual, even erotic appeal that the humanist book undoubtedly often held for both its maker and its intended reader. The vivid dreams of Girolamo Cardano included several scenes in which he saw vivid images of books or script – from more than one of which he derived a piercing feeling of pleasure.[15] What Nicholas dreamed we do not know. But there is every reason to think that he took as much interest in the appearance of books as he did in that of buildings – a subject that, as we will see, interested him deeply.

Reading, of course, requires more than a text and an editor; the reader must also play a part and have a stage on which to play it. Valla prepared his Thucydides for Nicholas V, the pope whose subsidies made possible the infusion of so much of classical Greek prose into the Latin mental world of Quattrocento Italy. Valla revealed again and again his desire to please this singular prelate and to use his scholarly work to cement their relations. This desire animated his dedicatory letter, in which he claimed that Nicholas' support for new translations had enhanced the power of Rome as greatly as the conquest of Asia, Macedonia, or the rest of Greece. It lent fire to Vallas' praise of Nicholas' project, which he described as an effort to translate books from Greek, Hebrew, Chaldean, and Punic into Latin.[16] It found concrete embodiment in the miniatures on the first page, which show Valla holding out his book and looking dutifully upward from the first initial, while Nicholas beams down at him from the top margin. It even inspired one of Valla's marginal notes. He picked out from an otherwise uninspired passage on a Greek embassy to Persia a reference to a Corinthian envoy whose name would delight his patron: "NICOLAUS," says Valla's note, in capital letters as revealing as they are unusual.[17]

Valla's patron demanded more than pleasant coincidences. Nicholas V was a very serious consumer of books, with strongly developed tastes and

14   Vat. lat. 1801, fol. 1 recto. My thanks to Charles Fantazzi for pointing out to me the ecclesiastical usage of *commercium*.

15   G. Cardano, *Somniorum Synesiorum omnis generis insomnia explicantes libri iiii* (Basel, 1562), bk. 4, chap. 4, 259 (no. 18), 260–1 (nos. 25–6), 262 (no. 29), 276 (no. 54).

16   Here Valla elided the distance between Nicholas' program for translations of the Greek classics and the program of the Egyptian king Ptolemy Philadelphus to translate just about everything – including the Hebrew Bible. See later in this chapter for a more detailed treatment of Renaissance views of Ptolemy's Alexandrian library. Described in glowing terms in more than one accessible text, it glimmered alluringly before the eyes of patrons and intellectuals, just too far away to see clearly.

17   BAV, Vat. lat. 1801, fol. 42 verso, on 2.67.1.

a personal commitment to the humanist program for direct study of classical texts. Thucydides, even in Valla's Latin, was a tough nut. The reader needed guidance, needed to have the text not only brought over into Latin but also both equipped with explanatory notes where the going became too difficult and set into an interpretative frame that provided perspective and emphasis.

Valla provided the stately arias and choruses of his text with a staccato accompaniment of glosses, sometimes frequent, but often interrupted by rests for several pages at a stretch. These did the donkeywork that glosses always do. Valla cleared up difficulties and offered helpful tips. When Thucydides remarked that it was dark "at the end of the month," for example, Valla explained that "he means a lunar month," of the sort the Greeks had used – one in which new moon, and dark nights, invariably came at the end.[18] When Thucydides mentioned Stagirus (better known as Stagira), Valla noted, "this is the native country of the philosopher Aristotle."[19] More complex glosses pointed out implications that might remain hidden even from a reader who could construe the words of the text. For example, Valla explained that Pericles' praise of the mutability of the Athenian constitution implied a critique of the conservative Spartans, who had never changed the laws Lycurgus gave them.[20] And he suggested that Thucydides spent so much time on the story of Harmodius and Aristogiton's plot against Hippias, the son of Pisistratus, because he himself was descended from Pisistratus.[21] Pointing hands and monograms formed from the word *NOTA*, finally, called attention to especially sententious bits of speech or narrative.

Valla's glosses are for the most part elementary in content, fragmentary in character, and scattered in distribution. Most important, they are unoriginal. Valla translated most of them word for word from the Greek scholia on Thucydides.[22] Many more scholia, as Marianne Pade has shown, found employment, even though Valla did not explicitly translate them as part of his marginal apparatus. Rather, he incorporated them – occasional errors and all – into the Latin text of his translation.[23] Valla's notes and text thus represent, like Ricci's rewriting of Epictetus, moves in an existing game of updating and interpretation. A personal note emerges rarely, and for the

---

18 Ibid., fol. 30 recto, on 2.4.2: "Mensem lunarem intelligit."

19 Ibid., fol. 89 verso, on 4.88.2: "hec est patria Aristotelis philosophi."

20 Ibid., fol. 36 recto, on 2.37.1: "Contra lacedemonios quibus lycurgus scripsit leges, emulatus cretenses atque egyptios."

21 Ibid., fol. 130 recto, on 6.54.1: "Ideo tot verbis de hac re loquitur Thucydides, quia ipse a Pisistrato fuit oriundus."

22 E.g., for the notes on 2.4.2, 4.88.2, and 2.37.1 previously quoted; see *Scholia in Thucydidem*, ed. K. Hude (Leipzig, 1927; repr., New York, 1973), ad locc.

23 M. Pade, "Valla's Thucydides: Theory and Practice in a Renaissance Translation," *Classica et Medievalia* 36 (1985): 275–301.

most part only in contexts peculiar to a translator, as when Valla compares a Greek expression peculiar to Thucydides with the Latin equivalent used by his Roman imitator Sallust.[24] In other cases, Valla compiled his final, commented copies of texts with meticulous care: he had an especially keen eye for chronology and context. To prepare his glosses on Quintilian's *Institutio oratoria*, he wrote, he had tried to read "all extant books, especially those that existed before Quintilian's time." Only the purchase and reading of the complete works of Hippocrates, for example, had enabled him to gloss the word παιδομαθεῖς, which Quintilian used once.[25] When examined in the light of Valla's own standards and practices, his Thucydidean glosses disappoint. They seem to reflect surprisingly little thought about what equipment the Quattrocento reader needed to grapple in detail with Thucydides, crux by crux.

The frame into which Valla set the text as a whole, by contrast, was both coherent and innovative. As we saw, he insisted, against Aristotle, that history was no less philosophical than poetry. His argument was simple. Historians did not simply narrate whatever happened to Lysander or Pericles. Rather, they invented, just as poets did, works of high literature: "Does anyone believe," Valla asked, "that the admirable speeches in the historians are real, and that they were not adapted by those skillful artisans to the persons, times, and events, so that they could teach us eloquence and wisdom?" Historians' speeches, like poems, had artistic unity in conception and execution. Unlike poems, however, they were only partly fictitious, since they accreted around a core of historical fact. The difference was entirely to history's advantage. "The truer history is," Valla contended, "the more powerful it is."[26]

Valla's argument was deft. He converted rhetoric, the art of composing speeches, into hermeneutics, an art of historical reading and reasoning – the art that worked out what sort of speech fitted the needs of a given place, time, and speaker. The whole text of Thucydides became a series of cases in point. A quotation from Quintilian in Valla's dedicatory letter established Thucydides' status as an exemplary writer. Careful headings, in capitals, identified the speeches and speakers in the text. In the Melian dialogue in book 5, for example, headings in red letters set off the Melians from the Athenians throughout. Even the derivative marginal glosses fell most thickly beside the most elaborate rhetorical venture in the work, Pericles' funeral oration for the Athenian dead in book 2. The book that resulted from Valla's efforts, in short, sheds as much light on the needs and interests of a

24   E.g., Vat. lat. 1801, fol. 59 recto, on 3.42.1 (φιλεῖ γίγνεσθαι): "mos suus loquendi Thucydidis. ut Salustius eum imitatus: vulgus amat fieri." On Valla's notes and their diffusion see E. B. Fryde, *Humanism and Renaissance Historiography* (London, 1983), 93–8.
25   Valla, *Epistole*, ed. Besomi and Regoliosi, 306.
26   Valla, *Gesta Ferdinandi*, 5.

fifteenth-century humanist rhetorician as on those of the original Greek author. It looks more like an anthology of speeches than a narrative. Leonardo Bruni, who had read Thucydides before Valla translated the text, also saw the speeches as especially valuable, and he imitated Pericles' funeral oration in his own set-piece funeral speech of 1428 for Nanni degli Strozzi.[27] This way of reading Thucydides has a certain justification: a recent historian of classical rhetoric has suggested that Thucydides meant his work to serve as a coherent collection of set-piece speeches, each of which exhibited the qualities appropriate to its situation and its speaker.[28] But Valla, for all his wit and insight, framed the text in a way that suppressed some of its basic elements – for example, its tragic qualities – as effectively as it emphasized others. The most original, even radical, of Renaissance thinkers wrapped an unconventional Greek text in a Latin toga that made it acceptable by disguising it. Is this what the patrons and first readers of such advanced texts expected of Valla and their other suppliers? We turn now from production to consumption: to the world of the erudite nobles and teachers who read – and paid for – books like Valla's Thucydides.

Into the Library

One natural way to begin watching readers encounter books is to explore the place where the two naturally met: the library. Here, as Roger Chartier has recently shown, the centrifugal and centripetal forces inherent in reading interfere with each other like opposed waves in a tank of water. Librarians arrange books into branches of a coherent system of knowledge; they put related books next to each other; they set limits on the numbers of books one can have, the hours in which one can have them, and the things one can do to them. Readers, by contrast, try to find new connections between apparently unrelated texts and to see more books than the rules allow; they write in the margins and tear out individual pages or steal whole books. Interesting meanings are constructed where the two interact; but their simultaneous presence always implies a struggle.[29]

Of the several humanist libraries that invite and reward inspection, one makes an especially attractive case study: that of the Este family of Ferrara. Many of its original holdings survive in the Biblioteca Estense in Modena. A vivid account of its formative years also survives – one that describes in

---

27 H. Baron, *The Crisis of the Early Italian Renaissance* (Princeton, 1966), chap. 18. Bruni used Thucydides in many other ways as well: see Klee, *Beiträge zur Thukydides-Rezeption*, 23–58.
28 T. Cole, *The Origins of Rhetoric in Ancient Greece* (Baltimore, 1991). Cf. also T. P. Wiseman, *Clio's Cosmetics* (Leicester, 1979) and A. J. Woodman, *Rhetoric in Classical Historiography* (London and Sydney, 1988).
29 R. Chartier, *L'ordre du livre* (Paris, 1992).

detail both the literary debates and decisons that guided it and the creative, quarrelsome readers who used it. This forms the central thread of one of the oddest and most colorful texts ever woven by a humanist: the set of curious dialogues *De politia litteraria* that the Milanese humanist Angelo Decembrio dedicated to Pius II in 1462. These describe the intellectual life of the court of Ferrara in the age of Leonello d'Este, who studied with the great humanist teacher Guarino of Verona during the 1430s and ruled the city, after the death of his father, Niccolò III, from 1441 to 1450.[30] The shifting cast of characters in Decembrio's dialogues includes the court's dominant humanist, Guarino of Verona; Leonello himself; and the young poet Feltrino Boiardo. The settings range from the spectacular Este palaces of Belriguardo and Belfiore, outside the city, to Leonello's private room or *studiolo*. Decembrio's subjects cover the humanist waterfront, from the psychological analysis of Aeneas' behavior toward Helen to the mechanical details of Latin grammar and lexicography. For two reasons, the text has not yet found an editor. First, its Latin style is idiosyncratic, ungrammatical, even difficult to divide into individual sentences. Second, it exists in two recensions, one represented by a famous manuscript in the Vatican Library, the other by two printed editions, both based on a second manuscript stolen from the Vatican during the Sack of 1527.[31] Every page challenges the reader with difficult constructions, obscure references, or simple solecisms. Yet it eminently deserves a critical edition, as one of the richest extant sources for the teaching, the scholarship, and the sociability of the humanists.[32]

---

30   The wider background is laid out by E. G. Gardner, *Dukes and Poets at Ferrara* (London, 1904); W. Gundersheimer, *Ferrara: The Style of a Renaissance Despotism* (Princeton, 1973); and L. Lockwood, *Music in Renaissance Ferrara, 1400–1505* (Cambridge, Mass., 1984). On Decembrio's career see esp. R. Sabbadini, *Classici e umanisti da codici Ambrosiani* (Florence, 1933), 94–103; and *Dizionario biografico degli italiani*, s.v. "Decembrio, Angelo Camillo," by P. Viti. For his manuscripts see P. Scarcia Piacentini, "Angelo Decembrio e la sua scrittura," *Scrittura e civiltà* 4 (1980): 247–77.

31   The manuscript is Vat. lat. 1794; the printed editions appeared at Augsburg in 1540 and at Basel in 1562.

32   Scarcia Piacentini denies that the Vatican manuscript was the one Decembrio prepared for presentation to Pius II, because (among other reasons) it lacks Pius' arms. For a recent and cogent counterargument, arguing that Decembrio intended the manuscript for Pius but left it unfinished after the pope died in August 1464, see E. Fumagalli, *Matteo Maria Boiardo volgarizzatore dell' "Asino d'Oro"* (Padua, 1988), 15–16 n. 24. J. Monfasani and M. Regoliosi both inform me that students working under their supervision have produced more systematic studies of the question: the latter are in course of publication. The most elaborate studies of the content of the *Politia* are M. di Cesare, *Vida's "Cristiad" and Virgilian Epic* (New York, 1964); A. Biondi, "Angelo Decembrio e la cultura del principe," in *La corte e lo spazio: Ferrara estense*, ed. G. Papagno and A. Quondam (Rome, 1982), 2:637–57; L. Balsamo, "La circolazione del libro a corte," in ibid., 659–81; and C. Ross, "Poetics at the Court of Leonello d'Este: Virgil, the Marvelous, and Feltrino Boiardo in the Competing Discourses of Angelo Decembrio's

One central theme links many of the variegated sections of the *Politia*: the question of how a Renaissance prince and his courtiers and scholars should choose and use books.[33] Leonello himself provides such a precise description of the ideal library and its contents that it reads, as he promises, rather like a catalog.[34] An analysis of this text – and of the complementary information preserved in Guarino's rich correspondence, edited by Sabbadini, and in the Este archives, studied by Fava and Bertoni – does not yield simple results.[35] But it does show that large parts of Decembrio's account correspond with the testimony of less artful sources. Taken together, these materials provide some vivid examples of the programs and practices of the humanist library in the decades when princes, patrons, humanists, and librarians were inventing it.

The Este library of the mid-fifteenth century, as Decembrio describes it, not only swarmed with classical texts but embodied classical principles of design. The intellectuals of the Este court had read about and marveled at the scale and splendor of the ancient public libraries. Pier Candido Decembrio – Angelo's older brother – explicitly wrote of Nicholas V in 1451, "He has decided to create a library that, if he has time, will rival even that of Pergamum or the one given by Antony to Cleopatra in both size and elegance."[36] In a passage preserved only in the printed version of the *Politia*, Angelo made Guarino denounce the medieval popes "who, in the belief that they were doing a good deed, destroyed many of the finest monuments of

'De politia literaria,' " in *La corte di Ferrara e il suo mecenatismo, 1441–1598: The Court of Ferrara and Its Patronage*, ed. M. Pade, L. W. Petersen, and D. Quarta (Copenhagen and Ferrara, 1990), 55–69; A. Tissoni Benvenuti, "Guarino, i suoi libri, e le letture della corte estense," *Le muse e il principe: Arte di corte nel Rinascimento padano* (Milan, 1991), 1: 63–82; A. Chiappini, "La biblioteca dello studiolo," ibid., 155–64. For editions of segments of the text with important commentary, see M. Baxandall, "A Dialogue on Art from the Court of Leonello d'Este," *Journal of the Warburg and Courtauld Institutes*, 26 (1963): 304–26; Rizzo, *Il lessico filologico*, 200–2; J. P. Perry, "A Fifteenth-Century Dialogue on Literary Taste: Angelo Decembrio's Account of Playwright Ugolino Pisani at the Court of Leonello d'Este," *Renaissance Quarterly*, 39 (1986): 613–43; and B. Curran and A. Grafton, "A Fifteenth-Century Site Report on the Vatican Obelisk," in *Journal of the Warburg and Courtauld Institutes* 58 (1995).

33 In the dedication to Pius II, Decembrio describes his intentions. See BAV, Vat. lat. 1794 (hereafter *Politia*), fol. 6 verso.

34 Ibid., fol. 13 verso: "in catalogi speciem."

35 *Epistolario di Guarino Veronese*, ed. R. Sabbadini (Venice, 1915–19); G. Bertoni, *La biblioteca Estense e la coltura Perrarese ai tempi del Duca Ercole I (1471–1505)* (Turin, 1903); D. Fava, *La biblioteca Estense nel suo sviluppo storico* (Modena, 1925). Naturally, the text contains certain anachronisms: for example, Decembrio makes Leonello refer to Valla as already hard at work on a translation of Herodotus: this project actually began after Leonello's death, in 1453 (*Politia*, fol. 21 recto).

36 Quoted by L. Gargan, "Gli umanisti e la biblioteca pubblica," in *Le biblioteche nel mondo antico e medievale*, ed. G. Cavallo (Bari, 1989), 183 n. 40. Given the ancient story that Antony gave the library of Pergamum to Cleopatra (Plut. *Ant.* 58.5), I have tried to preserve the ambiguity of Decembrio's Latin in my translation.

the ancients, including their loveliest libraries."[37] Evidently he thought Christian bigotry had polished off the Palatine and Ulpian libraries – where Roman scholars, as he knew from his beloved *Noctes Atticae* of Aulus Gellius, had once applied to see rare manuscripts and argued about the variant readings these provided. To a considerable extent, in fact, Decembrio modeled both the style and the content of the *Politia* – with its extended, polite conversations about rare texts and corrupt passages, carried out in the presence of books and libraries – on those of Gellius.[38] The Este library, which provided the background for so much of Decembrio's book, was clearly meant to appear as a locus classicus: a small corner of the Roman literary world called back to life.

The external evidence of manuscripts confirms the classical origin of the Este library program. The most famous text produced for Leonello is the illustrated manuscript of Caesar that survives in the Biblioteca Estense (α W.1.3). The most revealing point about it, for present purposes, is its closing subscription: "Corrected by Guarino of Verona, with the help of Giovanni Lamola of Bologna, 4 July 1432, at Ferrara."[39] The critical work Guarino and Lamola did in this Caesar is not in fact as distinguished as what they did in other manuscripts.[40] But they represented what they did achieve as the continuation of a classical enterprise: the work of those late antique correctors, or *emendatores*, whose subscriptions appear in manuscripts of Caesar and Livy, to name only two of Decembrio's, and Leonello's, favorite writers.[41] By formulating this message to readers as they did, the Ferrarese humanists asserted their connection to ancient scholarship as well as to the modern court.

At the beginning of the fifteenth century, the Florentine chancellor Coluccio Salutati had lamented the ongoing corruption of classical and vernacular texts. He had also suggested a solution – that the authorities should revive the ancient library, in which the librarians had been textual critics who corrected and stabilized the texts in their care: "Let public libraries be established, as repositories for all texts, and let scholars of the highest quality be put in charge of them, so they may correct the texts by careful comparison. . . . We find that the greatest men used to do this job, thinking it glorious to add subscriptions to the texts they had revised, as can be seen in ancient codices. That is why in the plays of Terence one commonly finds

---

37   Decembrio, *Politia*, chap. 55 (Basel, 1562), 428.
38   On the study of the *Noctes Atticae* in Guarino's circle in Ferrara see H. Baron, *From Petrarch to Leonardo Bruni* (Chicago and London, 1968), chap. 7.
39   "Emendavit Guarinus Veronensis adiuvante Io. Lamola cive bononiensi anno Christi MCCCCXXXII IIII° nonas Iulias Ferrarie."
40   V. Brown, *The Textual Transmission of Caesar's Gallic War* (Leiden, 1972), 46.
41   See L. D. Reynolds and N. G. Wilson, *Scribes and Scholars*, 3d ed. (Oxford, 1991), 39–43.

'Calliopius recensui' at the end."[42] Salutati thus neatly conflated the work of the ancient scholars who emended manuscripts with the practices of the medieval university book trade, in which entrepreneurs stabilized the texts of required books by maintaining official copies of them, from which segments, or *peciae*, were copied over and over again for customers. Like Salutati, and even more literally, Guarino and Lamola set out to imitate ancient scholars and reconstruct ancient libraries as they tried to create a modern textual criticism.

The enterprise Decembrio described was not idiosyncratic. Valla, as we have seen, also tried to make the copy of his Thucydides that he prepared for the Vatican at the orders of Nicholas V an official copy, a standard for all the rest.[43] To that extent at least the Roman and Ferrarese enterprises moved on parallel tracks (and shared an anachronistic vision of ancient scholarship). More generally, as Armando Petrucci has shown, the founders of the public libraries of the humanist republic of letters looked back with passionate interest at the achievements of their ancient predecessors.[44] The great libraries of Alexandria, Pergamum, and republican and imperial Rome, in particular, fascinated them. They collected every detail they could find (in texts that ranged from the letters of Cicero to the so-called letter of Aristeas) about these lost encyclopedias of ancient knowledge – which, they hoped, could still serve as models of enlightened patronage. From Petrarch on, they marveled at Livy's account of the vast public library of Ptolemy Philadelphus in Alexandria and drooled enviously at what the *Scriptores historiae Augustae* had to say about the vast private library of Serenus Sammonicus – even if they also quoted Seneca, at length, about the importance of collecting books for use only, not for ostentation.[45] Imitation took place on every level, down to the minutely technical – as when the Vatican Library followed Roman precedent in dividing its holdings into, among other sections, a Bibliotheca Graeca and a Bibliotheca Latina.

The new libraries, like the books they housed, set out to be classical in more than a general sense. Their owners and librarians read in Plutarch about the grand public library founded by Lucullus, with its porticos and *exedrae*. They read in the *Scriptores historiae Augustae* about the *armaria* (cases) of the Ulpian Library in Rome, where one of the supposed authors of this text, Flavius Vopiscus, claimed to have read a precious book written

---

42   C. Salutati, *De fato et fortuna*, ed. C. Bianca (Florence, 1985), 49 (2.6). See Rizzo, *Il lessico filologico*, 227–8, 341–4.

43   Vat. lat. 1801; see Rizzo, *Il lessico filologico*, 312.

44   A. Petrucci, "Le biblioteche antiche," in *Letteratura italiana*, vol. 2, *Produzione e consumo*, ed. A. Asor Rosa (Turin, 1983), 527–54.

45   See Petrarch *De remediis utriusque fortunae* 1.43: *De librorum copia*; for a Latin text, English translation, and extensive commentary on Petrarch's sources see *Four Dialogues for Scholars*, ed. C. H. Rawski (Cleveland, 1967).

on ivory (unfortunately, he was lying). Above all, they read in Gellius and Cicero that Roman libraries had been centers of conversation and debate – the sort of place where Cicero and his brother Quintus discussed the validity of astrology and haruspication and where Gellius and his friends teased out the intricacies of poetic allusions.[46]

Patrons, architects, and librarians did their best to replicate these ancient machines for learning. They used what they took to be the same library furniture that the Romans described – though they had to ignore the inconvenient fact that modern readers of codices needed desks on which to prop them, while ancient readers of rolls had simply held their books in their laps. They emulated the Roman customs of illuminating the library with large windows and of decorating its walls with portraits and busts of the learned. This updated classical ideal persisted. At the end of the sixteenth century the Salone Sistino in the Vatican and the Library of the University of Leiden in Holland, at the intellectual centers respectively of Catholicism and Calvinism, still shared the same largely Roman vision of what a library should be, though they expressed it in sharply contrasting styles; they also shared the same anachronisms (most vividly apparent in the fresco of a Roman library in the Salone Sistino, with its benches covered with chained books).

The single overriding model for public libraries, the one that continued to reverberate in the European mind as a sort of metaphor for the enchanted palaces of traditional learning, was of course not the Palatine library or its rivals in imperial Rome but the older and more mysterious library of Alexandria. The earliest detailed account in Latin of the Alexandrian library – the so-called *Scholium Plautinum* – was copied down by Giovanni Andrea de' Bussi, an early librarian of the Vatican, in the margins of a manuscript of Plautus. When Giannozzo Manetti wanted to praise the collecting ambitions of Nicholas V, he used the library of the Ptolemies as his standard for comparison. The idea gained some currency. At Nicholas'

---

46   For a full review of the main texts about Roman libraries and their intimate connection with literary and philosophical life see H. Blanck, *Das Buch in der Antike* (Munich, 1992), chap. 8. This account – like that of P. Fedeli, "Biblioteche private e pubbliche a Roma e nel mondo romano," in *Le biblioteche*, ed. G. Cavallo, 29–64 – seems a bit optimistic in the use of certain sources (notably the *Scriptores historiae Augustae*). Both Blanck and Fedeli, however, give a good sense of the textual information that would have lain at a fifteenth-century humanist's disposal and that would have seemed generally reliable; cf. also E. J. Kenney, "Books and Readers in the Roman World," *Cambridge History of Classical Literature*, vol. 2, *Latin Literature*, ed. E. J. Kenney and W. V. Clausen (Cambridge, 1982), 23–7. The information available in classical literary texts about ancient libraries was first fully assembled in the later sixteenth century by Achilles Statius and Justus Lipsius. See, e.g., S. Zurawksi, "Reflections on the Pitti Friendship Portrait of Rubens: In Praise of Lipsius and in Remembrance of Erasmus," *Sixteenth Century Journal* 23 (1992): 727–53. Most of it, however, came from Latin texts that Petrarch and the fifteenth-century humanists knew well.

death, according to the book dealer Vespasiano, he left behind the largest library since that of the Ptolemies.[47]

As always, however, the house of the ancients proved to have many mansions. Moreover, imitation of ancient models and methods was often – perhaps always – governed by prejudices and assumptions that determined what one thought the ancients had done. Thus Bussi or his informant, translating a Byzantine text about the library of the Ptolemies, introduced into his Latin version the erroneous notion that Callimachus had served as librarian in Alexandria. Perhaps Bussi hoped to find himself an illustrious predecessor: certainly he introduced a long-lasting confusion into the history of the Alexandrian library. He also omitted the equally problematic statement of the original Greek text that Ptolemy had employed foreign experts who knew both their own languages and Greek to translate important works for his library. It seems all too likely that Bussi did so because he deprecated the importance of Byzantine emigrés in the Roman book world of his own time and wished to give no leverage to Levantine rivals.[48]

For all its equally classical inspiration, the Ferrarese model of collection and reading evoked by Decembrio differed widely from the project of Nicholas V. Vespasiano described Nicholas as, if not a universal man, at least

47   E. Garin, *Il rinascimento italiano* (Florence, 1980), 56–7. For another reference to the ancient precedents of Pisistratus and Ptolemy, forming part of a poetic compliment to Federigo da Montefeltro's library, see G. Zannoni, "Il Cantalicio alla corte di Urbino," *Rendiconti della Reale Accademia dei Lincei, Classe di scienze, morali, storiche e filologiche*, ser. 5, 3, pt. 2 (1894): 503 (reference kindly supplied by D. Hughes).
48   For the text of the *Scholium*, see W. J. Koster, "Scholium Plautinum plene editum," *Mnemosyne*, ser. 4, 14 (1961): 23–37. A color facsimile appears as the frontispiece of E. A. Parsons, *The Alexandrian Library* (Amsterdam, 1952); a detailed description appears in J. Ruysschaert, *Codices Vaticani latini: Codices 11414–11709* (Vatican City, 1959), 104–5. For Bussi's source (Johannes Tzetzes) see *Comicorum Graecorum Fragmenta*, ed. G. Kaibel (Berlin, 1899–), 1:19–20. On the omissions and interpolations in the Latin see Koster's notes in "Scholium Plautinum" and R. Pfeiffer, *A History of Classical Scholarship from the Beginnings to the End of the Hellenistic Age* (Oxford, 1968), 101. The more normal version of the story – which rested on the letter of Aristeas, either read directly or as abridged and reproduced by Josephus – emphasized the Septuagint. It found much wider circulation. See, e.g., U. Jaitner-Hahner, *Humanismus in Umbrien und Rom: Lilius Tifernas, Kanzler und Gelehrter des Quattrocento* (Baden-Baden, 1993), 1:354 and 2:766; and C. Landino, *Disputationes Camaldulenses*, ed. P. Lobe (Florence, 1980), 53, 191–3. Silvia Rizzo (to whom I owe warm thanks) points out (in a private communication) that the classical scholars who have studied the *Scholium* have taken no interest in the fact that Bussi, a scholar famous in his own right, was the scribe who wrote out the text. See now Rizzo, "Per una tipologia delle tradizioni manoscritte di classici latini in età umanistica," *Formative Stages of Classical Traditions: Latin Texts from Antiquity to the Renaissance*, ed. O. Pecere and M. D. Reeve (Spoleto, 1995), 371–407 at 386–92, which reached me after the present text was written. Yet Ruysschaert (*Codices Vaticani*) identified Bussi long ago, using paleographical evidence, and the nature of Bussi's own scholarly interests and contacts could well help to explain the nature of the text he wrote. This case provides another instance of the unnecessary separation between two different ways of studying the history of reading: one based on textual content, the other on external form.

a universal reader: "There was no Latin writer that he did not know, in any discipline, to such an extent that he knew all the writers, Greek as well as Latin."[49] An expert bibliophile in his own right, Nicholas had drawn up in the 1430s instructions for Cosimo de' Medici to follow in creating an ambitious collection.[50] In building his own library he emulated the grandiosity, as well as the catholicity, of the Ptolemies. "At his death," Vespasiano commented, "it was found by inventory that since the time of Ptolemy, there had never been collected half so great a store of books in every discipline."[51] No more modest project would have slaked what Pier Candido Decembrio described as Nicholas' insatiable thirst for books. Pier Candido's brother Angelo also had a clear sense of Nicholas' plans. He described the libraries of Eugenius IV and Nicholas V above all as huge: "they saw to it that they had, in addition to the sacred scriptures, libraries replete with ancient authors."[52]

By contrast, Leonello and Guarino followed a different vein of ancient commentary, one that insisted on the need to limit one's collection to the good and the useful. When Ugolino Pisani tried to present Leonello with an elegant manuscript of his dire Latin comedy about kitchens, for example, he was deliberately and systematically humiliated.[53] Tito Strozzi began his inquisition by asking if Pisani knew the views of Seneca: "'But doesn't Seneca give you some example of how to read and treat books? You look to me like a sort of third Seneca.' 'But no,' replied Pisani, 'he warns us above all to avoid a large number of books, because it distracts the mind.'"[54] Here, as Decembrio's readers knew, he referred to Seneca's characteristically stern warning against bibliophilia: "A large quantity of books distracts the mind. Therefore, since you cannot read all the books you have, it is better to have only as many as you can read."[55] Seneca – who hated ostentation in the buying and adorning of books – set the prevailing aesthetic tone for Decembrio's discussion. The central intellectual question of the *Politia*, like that of Seneca's discussions of bibliophilia, is how to limit a library to the correct, restricted set of classics, arranged in the proper way. The collector, Guarino explains, must adopt a "modus," to ensure "that he does not buy more books than he needs."[56]

In Decembrio's portrayal, Guarino and Leonello assess the riches of the fifteenth-century stationer's shop with the disdainful air of jewelers looking

49 Vespasiano, *Vite*, ed. Greco, 1:4.
50 L. Balsamo, *Bibliography: History of a Tradition*, trans. W. A. Pettas (Berkeley, 1990), 18–19.
51 Vespasiano, *Vite*, ed. Greco, 1:63–4.
52 Decembrio, *Politia*, fol. 151 recto.
53 See Perry, "Fifteenth-Century Dialogue."
54 Decembrio, *Politia*, fol. 147 verso.
55 Seneca *Epistulae morales* 2.3.
56 Decembrio, *Politia*, fol. 8 verso.

for a few real diamonds amid a heap of paste. They reject the great compendiums of the scholastic world with contempt: "But as to the 'Historiarum maria' as they call them, those very heavy loads for asses, and the three equally huge Vincents, who wrote histories, rather than historically, and made many grammatical errors, we think that these giants, like so many Polyphemuses and Cyclopes, should not be given room and board in our library."[57] They dismiss the standard texts of the fourteenth-century court library – vernacular translations of the classics and vernacular writers, such as Petrarch and Boccaccio – as medieval and inferior, comparable at best to the baroque preciosities of late antique Latin: "We do not dare to admit them into this more refined library that we are seeking to create. They should be given another place, along with the Gualfredi, the Gualteri, and their like, with Cassiodorus and Isidore, glittering with the torch of their imperial style."[58] More solid medieval authors, such as Albertus Magnus and Pietro de' Crescenzi, they damn with faint praise – as informative but unfit, because of their poor style, for a cultivated collection.[59] Even Dante is dismissed; the scholar should read the *Divine Comedy* only with women and children, on long winter nights. Minor Latin classics gain entrance only because the owner can lend them to friends of lower status, "minores amici," without worrying too much about their return.[60] Cicero and Virgil, Sallust and Terence, the classics from whom the best grammarians took their examples, provide all the literary territory that the courtly scholar really needs to explore and settle.[61] Leonello insists more than once that the scholar should not waste much time and attention on those books that seem "more fit to fill a library than to adorn it" – even though one must own some of them.[62] The ideal library thus offers neither an encyclopedia in the style of the Vatican nor a massive historical record of a lost civilization in the manner of Bessarion, who set out to rescue and collect as many of the shattered remains of Greek culture as he could and preserve them in Italy. Rather, it should amount to a modest shelf of canonical texts chosen with meticulous care. Such a collection would embody the same chastely classical aesthetic that led Leonello, elsewhere in the text, to condemn Flemish tapestries for their historical mistakes and anachronisms.[63] Even here, however, as Fumagalli has pointed out, differences of taste appear; Feltrino Boiardo's glorification of Livy and appreciation of Apuleius mark a departure from Guarino's nar-

57   Decembrio, *Politia*, fol. 16 verso.
58   Ibid., fol. 17 verso.
59   Ibid., fol. 19 recto.
60   Ibid., fol. 14 verso.
61   Cf. Leonello's comment, ibid., fol. 13 verso.
62   Decembrio, *Politia*, fol. 14 verso.
63   Baxandall, "Dialogue on Art," 316–19.

rower canon of classic texts.[64] The humanist library had centrifugal elements of a sort even before the first reader trod its tiled floor.

The problems that Guarino and his pupil solved by their self-denying ordinances would persist – would, in fact, grow more serious with time. In the fifteenth century as in the ancient world, collectors had somehow to construct a filter that would stop the mass of worthless texts from entering their collections, while offering a place to genuinely valuable ones. The problem, of course, was where to place the filter and how wide to make its mesh. Some, like Guarino, made a chaste, selective canon of worthwhile texts their instrument of selection; but this, as we will see, was inevitably too fine. If strictly applied it would have kept out far too much. More promising, but more difficult, was the formulation of a systematic art of reading – an art whose practitioners could discriminate between the genuine and the spurious, the historical and the fanciful.[65] But here too, as we will see, grave problems confronted orderly minds. The librarian had to cope not only with the Latin canon, which was complex enough, but also with the more and more bizarre and foreign texts and theses that came to light as Greek codices arrived in Western libraries and were translated into Latin. (These novelties, of course, Guarino wanted in his library, whatever the interpretative conundrums they posed.) Over time, moreover, bizarre but attractive Western texts, such as the influential but forged histories of Berosus and Manetho, continued to arrive on the scene; these particular ones may have conquered a wider market in print than Herodotus or Diodorus.[66] Though the Ferrarese effort to impose order on the dangerous crowd of books proved short-lived, in other words, the dangers it recognized did not. They provoked many creative responses from Renaissance readers.

A library, of course, is a collection of physical objects as well as a set of texts. Decembrio describes the material side of the book collector's task in concrete and revealing detail. Guarino, early in the text, insists that the collection must be ruled by "ordo," "so that you have some books which are more accessible than others, as they are better and more familiar."[67] Later, in a powerful speech, Leonello offers what seems to be the earliest detailed treatment of the qualities that add up to order in the humanist library, public or private:

---

64   Fumagalli, *Matteo Maria Boiardo*, 97–100.
65   See J. Franklin, *John Bodin and the Sixteenth-Century Revolution in the Methodology of Law and History* (New York and London, 1963).
66   For recent discussions see A. Grafton, *Defenders of the Text* (Cambridge, Mass., and London, 1991), chap. 3; V. de Caprio, *La tradizione e la trauma* (Manziana, 1991); and M. Wifstrand Schiebe, *Annius von Viterbo und die schwedische Historiographie des 16. und 17. Jahrhunderts* (Uppsala, 1992).
67   Decembrio, *Politia*, fol. 8 verso.

If you are making diligent enquiry about everything that pertains to creating a polished library (which is the origin of our term *polity*), you will keep your books free from household dust. Some make a habit of keeping them in chests or a cupboard, taking them out only one by one to read them and replacing them. That is to reserve them within a private and secret library, not a public and household one. They become dusty when, as it were, they travel, and the dust sticks all the harder if the floor tiles of the room are often swept. Wetting these in advance prevents that inconvenience. One must provide for this still more carefully if one has the books tied, and as it were chained, to the desks before the shelves, as is the custom in the libraries of monks. But some introduce glass or cloth windows because of that sort of dirt. These serve to keep off the excess brightness of the invading sun and dust that is raised nearby. Odors stick for a long time in such places, which are rather unpleasant to visitors not accustomed to them, just as happens in the dining halls of priests, which they call refectories. Therefore the entrance should be somewhat closed off, and one should provide for this with some form of sweet odors – though not those that hurt the brain, such as white lilies and cypress planks. But this may be trivial. More harmful and entirely poisonous is the practice of using coals for heat without ventilation. Twigs of rosemary and myrrh or bouquets of roses and violets and sweet apples, especially those called crab apples, delight; so do some bitter things, such as wormwood and rue, which are also sensible remedies against maggots, scorpions, and other insects of that kind. When dried, these last for several years, and their juices, when combined in a glue, prevent bookworms in bindings. This is thought useful not only to books but to clothing and all sorts of household possessions. One should not admit playing kittens and birds in cages. For these reasons it is proper to have your library in the more private part of the house; this sort of special room for a collection is seen, in Pliny, and contains, as he says, the books that are to be reread rather than read: it should be proof against noises not only from the household but also from next door. Inside the library it is appropriate to have as well a sundial or sphere of the universe and a lyre, if you find that pleasant at times (it makes no noise unless we want it to); also decent pictures and carvings that represent the records of gods or heroes. There we often see that many find it pleasant to have an image of Jerome writing in his retreat; this teaches us that solitude, silence, and hard work in reading and writing are appropriate to libraries. . . . Therefore let everything in the library be seen to be polished and elegantly laid out – the paving, the wall, the beams. Indeed, you should not even leave spiderwebs under the desks or smearings from the wax of candles and the smelly and sometimes inconvenient remains of night work, which Pliny calls *vulcanalia*. Not to mention that some who have fallen asleep while reading have burned the book even in the midst of letters.[68]

Leonello's imaginary library – its walls decorated with an image of Saint Jerome writing while his lion sleeps, its ceiling painted with the horoscope

68   Decembrio, *Politia*, fols. 8 verso–9 recto.

of its owner, its tiled floors and wooden benches and cupboards immaculately clean – is as vivid and austere as one of Botticelli's paintings of a saint among his books.[69] Revealingly, its classical model is not one of the ancient descriptions of the Alexandrian library but the younger Pliny's brief but appealing evocation of his private collection of his favorite books and Juvenal's description of the rich man's library, with its statues in bronze and marble.[70] The same Roman model reappears in another passage, in which Guarino and Leonello defend the practice of decorating libraries with elaborate classical sculptures.[71]

Decembrio gives precise information on the iconography of Leonello's *studiolo*: "I remember that in the dwelling of Leonello at Ferrara, where he used to spend the winter, separate from his father but in the same palace, I often saw images of Scipio Africanus and Hannibal painted on the wall, addressing one another, as it were, with shared admiration, as in Livy. The Roman was accompanied by a horse and a servant, the Carthaginian by an elephant bearing a seat and a black Ethiopian controlling it. But the generals were there on foot."[72] In the room where only one's favorite classic texts were to be savored, scholarly and precise images of historical characters naturally replaced the chivalrous, armored ancients anachronistically displayed on Flemish tapestries.

Two set pieces about another library offer complementary information. Leonello and his circle leave the palace at one point to visit the suburban house of an older man, Giovanni Gualengo, with the Curia of Eugenius IV and the Florentine ambassadors in attendance. They eat early figs from Giovanni's garden and wash with rose water from a silver vessel. Then they go upstairs to the library – which they find decked out as a celebration of spring, its floor and books strewn with white and purple flowers – and read Terence together.[73] In another passage Giovanni himself describes his modest, orderly holdings: "They include all the works of Cicero, especially in moral philosophy, in one volume. I also have a very correct copy of Terence, surrounded in the more difficult passages by the commentaries of Donatus, and I read it regularly. . . . And clearly if you believe me at all, when I look at and study the ranks of my books – for I have put the name

---

69   In fact, elsewhere Leonello expressly criticizes the collector who has a splendid set of rooms to house a large set of elegant books that he has not read. Decembrio, *Politia*, fol. 10 verso. This position seems in keeping with the Senecan morality of the book as a whole. The widely felt tension between the desire for beauty and that for well-prepared, useful texts call for repeated discussion later in this chapter.

70   See Juvenal 3.216–20 and the commentary of E. Courtney (London, 1980), 184 ad loc. Giorgio Valla remarked in his commentary (which he claimed came from one Probus) that the "forulos" mentioned by Juvenal were "loculos librorum sive armaria"; see *Scholia in Iuvenalem vetustiora*, ed. P. Wessner (Leipzig, 1931), 44.

71   See Baxandall, "Dialogue on Art."

72   Decembrio, *Politia*, fol. 33 verso.

73   Ibid., fol. 49 recto.

of each author on the binding – I feel as if I am looking at the holy graves of those who wrote them."[74]

These charming evocations of *primavera nella biblioteca* refer to real books and collections. Leonello's description of the physical problems of maintaining a library, for example, corresponds exactly to what we know from other sources. Guarino describes himself, in a letter to Leonello, as pathetically trying to work in a small apartment that lacks all the facilities Leonello calls for. The children play and cry; rain streams in when the window is open; but candles must be lit in daytime, and the coal smoke suffocates Guarino, when the window is shut.[75] Leonello's ideal library sets out to preserve not only the books but the scholars who use them. Many of the problems he confronts, such as coal smoke, would remain central for centuries to come.

The two scenes in which Gualengo describes his books are even more realistic. When Gualengo mentions his one-volume Cicero, for example, he refers to a scholar's book, one in which elegance has been sacrificed to compressed script for the sake of convenience and cheapness. He has in mind something like the single codex containing all of Livy, Caesar, Justin, and Sallust that belonged to Decembrio himself.[76] When Gualengo describes his practice of putting authors' names on the spine, he refers to contemporary Ferrarese practice. The first known librarian of the Estensi, Biagio Bussoni, made parchment labels for the bindings of the books in his care.[77] And when Gualengo, in another passage, warns the others never to lend books except to their social inferiors, he clearly refers to the fact that the Este library regularly lent books – sometimes with disastrous results.[78] Aristocratic users are no unmixed blessing for librarians.

Decembrio's programmatic chapters, in short, reflect the specific attention he had given to the two great difficulties, one external and one internal, that tormented a humanist who wished to maintain high standards of order and elegance in a library. The collector had to establish rigorous control over the quality of the books that he bought or copied. But he also had to control the books themselves. A collection of manuscripts on parchment – as librarians know – gives off a powerful smell and attracts pests and rodents of all sorts. Scholars need light and heat; but books need protection from sun and rain. Finally, of course, books also need to be sheltered from users and borrowers, who seek to take them away or leave them in disorder. These long passages, with their descriptions of public and private

---

74   Decembrio, *Politia*, fol. 35 verso.
75   Guarino, *Epistolario*, ed. Sabbadini, no. 557.
76   Laur. Conv. Soppr. 263; see A. De la Mare, "Florentine Manuscripts of Livy in the Fifteenth Century," in *Livy*, ed. T. A. Dorey (London and Toronto, 1971), 186, 194 n. 62.
77   Fava, *La biblioteca Estense*, 27.
78   Decembrio, *Politia*, fol. 37 recto.

library furniture, of methods of keeping order and cleanliness, are the direct ancestor of Gabriel Naudé's *Advis pour dresser une bibliothèque* of 1644, the work often taken as the first detailed manual for librarians.[79]

Even the apparent contradictions within the text are historically revealing. The advice Leonello offers is as confusing as it is specific. Sometimes he describes a large-scale library, with *banchi* and chained books; sometimes a very private collection, held in a single locked press in a *studiolo*. But here too the documents show that Decembrio described the situation in the Ferrara that he knew. For the books of the Estensi, in the time of Niccolò and Leonello, were divided. The official library was housed in two rooms in the palace tower (Buxoni was known as *Ser Biaxio della Torre*). The court eventually employed full-time scribes, illuminators, and binders. But Leonello's books were kept in his *studiolo*, and a constant traffic ran between the two collections, as Leonello and his courtiers borrowed texts that did not figure in his personal collection. The *Politia*, in short, described the practices of the real collections Decembrio and Leonello knew, just as Naudé's *Advis* describes those of the brothers Dupuy, the keepers of the great library assembled by Jacques-Auguste de Thou to serve as a center of historical research. Even more ambitious family libraries – like that of the Medici – led a similarly shady existence, only half formalized. Many humanists did their most important work within the flexible – and sometimes permeable – boundaries of such collections.

The Books on the Benches

Decembrio describes the Ferrarese book stock as vividly as the spaces it occupied. He makes Leonello and his friends condemn those who thought they could assess a book's value from its binding. But Decembrio does not suggest that they completely rejected the notion that books should be physically attractive. Leonello argues, in one careful speech, that the collector should maintain a balance: "One part of the perfection of a library that we surely should not omit, generous sirs, is that the books should be as beautiful as possible and written by the hand of a very deft scribe. Yet we should not become obsessed with this sort of refinement or with shining bosses or ornaments, miniatures, and bindings – as is said to have happened to Aeneas when he fed on an empty image. It is a well-known proverb that

79   See G. Naudé, *Advis pour dresser une bibliothèque* (Paris, 1644; repr., Paris, 1990). Cf. C. Jolly, "L'*Advis*, manifeste de la bibliothèque érudite," in ibid.; J. Revel, "L'*Advis pour dresser une bibliothèque*," in G. Naudé, *Consigli per la formazione di una biblioteca*, trans. and ed. M. Bray (Naples, 1992), vii–xvi; and A. Coron, " 'Ut prosint aliis': Jacques-Auguste de Thou et sa bibliothèque," in *Histoire des bibliothèques françaises*, vol. 2, *Les bibliothèques sous l'Ancien Régime*, ed. C. Jolly (Paris, 1988), 101–25.

ornaments put on an ordinary sort of horse make it prettier but not better."[80] Collectors' tastes vary. Some "deck their books in purple, silk, pearls, and gold, for beauty makes many men more eager to read, just as proper ornaments make a soldier more spirited." Others prefer old script and dust, as severe parents care about their children's characters, not their beauty. Others want virtue, talent, and beauty together.[81] The most important quality of any book is that it be correct.[82] And the ideal library will obviously include both beautiful new texts and reliable old ones.

Leonello – or Decembrio – here takes a position on live issues. Books are physical objects as well as sets of words. Their outward signs tell stories about their inward grace or lack of it. Any Western intellectual of the 1990s can infer volumes from the chaste white cover of a Gallimard monograph or the lurid, moulting colors of a Zone Books dust jacket. This was at least as true in the mid-fifteenth century. Historians of the book and paleographers have shown that the humanists demanded, produced, and consumed new kinds of book as well as a new canon of texts. They objected not only philologically to the content of the medieval scholarly book but also aesthetically to its form.

The authoritative books of the medieval scholarly world were produced by monastic scriptoria and the specialized, efficient stationers of the university towns. The most elaborate of these works – glossed copies of the Bible, theological and legal texts – were laid out in two columns and written in a spiky, formal Gothic script. The texts in question occupied a relatively small space in the center of a large page. Around them a thick hedge of official commentary written in a still smaller, less inviting script repelled unlicensed readers. This was, of course, the very mass of medieval glosses that the humanists so disliked. Even smaller-scale high medieval texts – like the portable two-column Paris Bibles, many of which had little or no marginal commentary – seemed ugly and unreadable to Renaissance readers, who saw their modern script and layout as a distortion of their contents.[83]

Petrarch hated "the tiny and compressed characters" that the scribe himself "would be unable to decipher, while the reader ends up buying not just a book but blindness along with it."[84] And he rejected just as indignantly the more flamboyant scripts that were becoming fashionable in his day. These seemed to him "delightful to the eye from a distance but confus-

---

80 Decembrio, *Politia*, fol. 9 verso.

81 Decembrio, *Politia*, fols. 9 verso –10 recto.

82 Ibid., fol. 9 verso.

83 See in general *La production du livre universitaire au moyen âge: Exemplar et pecia*, ed. L. J. Bataillon et al. (Paris, 1985), esp. the articles by H. V. Schooner ("La production du livre par la pecia," 17–37) and R. H. Rouse and M. A. Rouse ("The Book Trade at the University of Paris, ca. 1250–ca. 1350," 41–114).

84 *Seniles* 6.5, quoted by A. Petrucci, "Libro e scrittura in Francesco Petrarca," in *Libri, scrittura e pubblico nel Rinascimento*, ed. A. Petrucci (Bari and Rome, 1979), 5.

ing and tiresome when seen close by, as if it were intended not for reading but for some other purpose." Petrarch's tastes ran above all to the splendid courtly manuscripts of his time, such as his own famous manuscript of Virgil; but his criticism of other types of book presaged momentous changes.[85]

In the years around 1400 Coluccio Salutati and Poggio Bracciolini devised a new, rounded, elegant minuscule, which they considered more classical than the Gothic of their own day. Scholars and artists – notably Alberti and Mantegna – learned from Roman inscriptions to draw capital letters in a convincingly symmetrical and grandiose style. Others – above all the scholar Niccolò Niccoli and the scribe Bartolomeo Sanvito – invented an elegant cursive, which could be used for less formal purposes, such as the compilation of notebooks, and which fitted more words into less space than the standard, straightforward, humanist script. These new scripts were gradually taught to other scholars and, with difficulty, to professional scribes (whom Poggio, after long experience, described as *faex mundi*, "the excrement of the universe").[86]

The transformation of the classical text only began with the classicizing of its script. Fine binding became a specialty – even an obsession – for producers and consumers alike. Early collectors, such as Federigo of Urbino, favored red velvet with gold clasps. But from the middle of the fifteenth century, as Anthony Hobson has shown, a taste for a different, more austere style took hold. Binders learned how to make and wield delicately patterned stamps. Richly worked leather, more austere than velvet, became the binding preferred by all great collectors, from manuscript hunters, such as Sixtus IV and Matthias Corvinus, to lovers of the printed word, such as Jean Grolier and Jacques Auguste de Thou. They employed famous artists to design intricate traceries for the leather-covered boards that protected their books. Patterns from ancient coins and medals, supplied by antiquarians, such as Felice Feliciano, often gave these a classical patina, and the owner's name or initials or motto, which often figured amid the classicizing ornament, identified the patron whose tastes were on display. The great person's classic book could certainly be told by its cover.[87] And even plain men, paid

85   A. Petrucci, " 'L'antiche e le moderne carte', *imitatio e renovatio* nella riforma grafica umanistica," in *Renaissance- und Humanistenhandschriften*, ed. J. Autenrieth with U. Eigler (Munich, 1988), 1–12.

86   B. L. Ullman, *The Origin and Development of Humanistic Script* (Rome, 1960); J. Wardrop, *The Script of Humanism* (Oxford, 1963); M. Meiss, "Towards a More Comprehensive Renaissance Paleography," in *The Painter's Choice* (New York, 1976), 151–75; *Libri, scrittura e pubblico nel Rinascimento*, ed. Petrucci; A. C. de la Mare, "New Research on Humanistic Scribes in Florence," in *Miniatura fiorentina del Rinascimento*, ed. A. Garzelli (Florence, 1985), 1:393–476. For Poggio see E. Walser, *Poggius Florentinus* (Leipzig, 1914), 104–10.

87   A. Hobson, *Humanists and Bookbinders* (Cambridge, 1989).

scholars, considered it tasteless to keep a book in paper wrappers. "I can't stand to read books unless they're bound," Joseph Scaliger commented soon after 1600, as he made a rare exception to read a polemic against him and a friend by the Jesuit Serarius. The catalog of Scaliger's library, made for its sale by auction on 11 March 1609, confirms his statement. Of the almost 250 books designated as containing his marginal notes, not a single one figures in the section of "libri incompacti."[88]

E. H. Gombrich, in short, was characteristically prescient when he pointed out a generation ago that classical books underwent an aesthetic revolution in the Renaissance. But books do not result from parthenogenesis, or revolutions from the cogitations of detached intellectuals. Entrepreneurs and merchants hired and instructed the scribes, typesetters, and illuminators who produced the books. And those who dominated the economics of publishing also had much to do with the identity and physical form of the books that the humanist public read. Even in the age of the manuscript book, entrepreneurs dominated the trade and shaped the experience of most readers of the classics. The *cartolai* who hired scribes and illuminators and provided texts and materials for them to work with also did much to set the proper styles for classic texts. Vespasiano, the brilliant Florentine bookseller who supplied Federigo da Montefeltro with his famous all-manuscript collection, did as much as any scholar to spread the taste for humanist script and title pages glamorously wrapped with intricately knotted, white grapevines.

However, in the age of manuscripts and even in the later one of print, Renaissance consumers did not buy ready-made books like slabs of pizza and consume them standing up. The well-educated reader knew his duty: he must personalize his texts before reading them. Individual choices of format, script, rubrication, and illustration sharply distinguished one library from another. The heavily illustrated classical texts that went into court libraries in northern and southern Italy, in which isolated classic elements did not transform the medieval appearance of landscapes and costumes, differed radically from the chaste texts manufactured for the Medici library and the library of San Marco. In them only the first page normally bore elaborate decoration – often, a spectacular architectural border, classical in style, around which satyrs or putti sport. The Vatican and the great Roman library of Francesco Gonzaga, in this respect and in others, followed a via media.[89] Bindings, which bristled with classical medallions, owners'

88 See *The Auction Catalogue of the Library of J. J. Scaliger*, ed. H. J. de Jonge (Utrecht, 1977).
89 See esp. de la Mare, 401–6, and J. J. G. Alexander, ed., *The Painted Page* (Munich, 1994). It should be noted that Federigo did own some printed books. For the library of Francesco Gonzaga see D. S. Chambers, *A Renaissance Cardinal and His Worldly Goods: The Will and Inventory of Francesco Gonzaga (1444–83)* (London, 1992).

devices, and elegant mottos, made particularly strong statements about the tastes and values of collectors.[90] In every case, however, one rule holds. The classical text was defined, even before its entrance into a public or an individual library, as both a precious object and a personal possession – the point at which a cultural and an individual style should intersect. Before most books even entered a humanist library, serious thought and substantial resources had been devoted to their appearance.

The documents confirm the general accuracy of this description. The Caesar that Guarino and Lamola emended for Leonello, for example, was profusely illuminated in a handsome, if old-fashioned, way by Giovanni Falcone and Iacopino d'Arezzo. A letter from Falcone to Guarino, published by Sabbadini, shows that Guarino supervised the illustrations personally. Other manuscripts clearly appealed to the reader's eye as well as to his mind. Guarino's translation of Plutarch's *Sulla* and *Lysander*, for example, begins with an illuminated capital *P*. Inside its loop Guarino himself appears on bended knee, handing a copy of his book to Leonello.[91]

The library that Guarino and his noble pupil created, in other words, clearly reflected not just a negative effort to avoid excesses but a positive one to follow the best tastes of the time. As a very young man, just back from his time in Constantinople, Guarino fetched up in Florence. There he became enmeshed in a battle with one of the creators of the new humanist book, Niccolò Niccoli. In a brilliant piece of invective, Guarino lampooned Niccoli's obsession with the fine points of bookmaking – as opposed to the true details of scholarship. Niccoli, Guarino insisted, wasted his time on trivialities – such as the diphthongs that he insisted on restoring to classical texts and the elegant, legible loops and risers of humanistic script.[92] His attack – like the several others provoked by Niccoli, a spiky personality who treated his mistress, Benvenuta, too much as an intellectual and social equal for the comfort of other humanists – need not be taken literally. All of these diatribes, as Martin Davies has shown, reflect in part an inspiration more rhetorical than factual. One of the classical discoveries that Niccoli greedily collected and generously shared, Cicero's *In Pisonem*, which Poggio had discovered in 1417, ironically provided their model. Niccoli served as a popular victim of what became a favorite form of intellectual aggression, the formal invective. A useful surrogate Piso, he found more than one would-be Cicero taking aim against him with a pleasurably bent nib.[93]

90   See E. Diehl, *Bookbinding: Its Background and Technique* (New York, 1980); Hobson, *Humanists and Bookbinders*, and J. B. Trapp's review of Hobson, *TLS*, 17 May 1991.
91   Laur. 65, 27, fol. 1 recto. For Leonello's Caesar see the preceding section of this chapter.
92   Guarino, *Epistolario*, ed. Sabbadini, no. 652.
93   See M. C. Davies, "An Emperor without Clothes? Niccolò Niccoli under Attack," *Italia Medioevale e Umanistica* 30 (1987): 95–148.

For all their stylized quality, several of these texts converge in detail. They describe Niccoli as someone who cared only for the commercial, not the aesthetic or intellectual, value of his library.[94] Evidently the beauty of the humanist's books could prove threatening as well as attractive. The very value of a collection of splendid books like Niccoli's might reveal that the motive behind its collection had been commercial, not intellectual.[95] For all their iconoclasm, many humanists still accepted the old principle that knowledge, as a gift of God, cannot be sold. Valla, who happily admitted that a fine book could properly become a fine commodity, stood against convention in that respect as in others.

By the time Guarino came to Ferrara, more than a generation later, his views had not radically altered, but they had softened. At one point in the *Politia*, Guarino's pupils clamor to know what Livy could possible have meant when he made Philip of Macedon demand "a Romanis equum sibi restitui."[96] Decembrio describes the manuscript of Livy that they used as "a book very prettily written in [or by] the Florentine hand, but without completely correct use of diphthongs."[97] In fact, of course, Philip had demanded not "equum," a horse, but "aequum," fair treatment. Another passage shows that the text in question filled three volumes. Leonello's Livy belonged, in short, to a well-known family – the three-decker manuscripts, equipped with elegant title pages and written in humanistic script, that Vespasiano produced for court libraries from Naples to Ferrara. Decembrio acknowledges this fact when he has Guarino say: "The most beautifully made books are normally bought from Tuscany and Florence. They say that there is one Vespasiano there, an excellent bookseller, with expert knowledge of both books and scribes, to whom all of Italy and foreigners as well resort when they want to find elegant books for sale. Though we think he seeks out good exemplars, with the diligence of Leonardo Bruni and Carlo Marsuppini, nevertheless, as I said, the exemplars read one way, the scribes copy them in another."[98] Guarino's speech reveals much. He now accepted Niccoli's view that the details of a text matter deeply, since they can inter-

---

94   See Leonardo Bruni's *oratio* in G. Zippel, "Niccolò Niccoli, Contributo alla storia dell'umanesimo," in *Storia e cultura del Rinascimento italiano*, ed. Zippel (Padua, 1979), 136; and Zippel, "L'invettiva di Lorenzo di Marco Benvenuti contra Niccolò Niccoli," in ibid., 164–5.
95   In fact, Niccoli lent texts in his collection freely to others and meant them to serve, as they eventually did, as a public library for Florence. For the history of his collection, see B. L. Ullman and P. A. Stadter, *The Public Library of Renaissance Florence* (Padua, 1972).
96   Livy 33.13.9 (on Phaineas).
97   Decembrio, *Politia*, fol. 178 verso. A manuscript of Livy that belonged to Leonello, its opening page splendidly illuminated by Marco dell'Avogaro in 1449, is now in a private library in France. See H. J. Hermann, *La miniatura estense*, ed. F. Toniolo et al. (Modena, 1994), plate 50 and 249–53, and cf. more generally G. Mariani Canova, "La committenza dei codici miniati alla corte estense al tempo di Leonello e di Borso," *Le muse e il principe*, 1: 87–117.
98   Decembrio, *Politia*, fol. 180 recto.

fere with its understanding. He thus acknowledged a fact that recent scholars have rediscovered and underlined: that Niccoli read his books with a sharp eye for content as well as form, stripping them down for historical and bibliographical information that could help him in his lifelong effort to reconstruct the canon of Latin literature.[99]

Yet Guarino's speech also reveals that the pursuit of correct texts and that of elegant ones were not always yoked. Even by his new standard, he held, the elegant copies of texts produced by Vespasiano and other stationers who served the luxury trade must fail, for they did not rest on critical scholarship.[100] But a court library necessarily consisted, at least in part, of the elegant folios Vespasiano and others produced – such as the Caesar whose creation Vespasiano himself supervised in Ferrara. This fact was hardly surprising; stationers and their scribes designed these folio manuscripts of the classics to appeal to noble and princely tastes. As Feltrino Boiardo puts it early in the *Politia*, all princes made a habit of ordering fine copies of Livy from Florence.[101] Evidently Guarino's time in Ferrara changed him as well as his pupils. Exposure to life at court made him see the utility of the Florentine elegances of book production that he had once scorned (even as his experience as a teacher made him insist that they should be accompanied by Florentine niceties of scholarship).[102] For as Leonello himself points out, an attractive appearance makes a text more readable – just as a fine suit of armor may give its wearer new courage.[103] The new court library meant a genuine fusion of courtly and humanist tastes, not a simple victory for the austerity of the early humanist book. At least some of its manuscripts fused the traditional decorations of the traditional aristocratic book with the classicizing mise-en-scène preferred by the innovative humanist pedagogue. Unfortunately, these elegant superstructures sometimes rested on shaky textual foundations.

Vespasiano's folios had plenty of company on Leonello's shelves. Ferrara offered the collector ample opportunities (and dangers). The city had its own stationers and monastic scriptoria, and patronage of the Este made it

---

99   For Niccolio's methods and habits as a reader, see the excellent survey by Stadter, "Niccolò Niccoli: Winning Back the Knowledge of the Ancients," in *Vestigia: Studi in onore di Giuseppe Billanovich*, ed. R. Avesani et al. (Rome, 1984), 2:747–64, with references to the earlier literature.

100   The accuracy of this judgment cannot be definitively tested even now, since no full assessment of the quality of Vespasianio's texts exists.

101   Decembrio, *Politia*, fol. 9 verso.

102   Cf. the views of his son Battista, who praised a friend for amassing a library full of "ubris adeo ornatis et, quos [quod?] praestantius est, adeo emendatis . . . ut plurimos tum vetustatis tum bonitatis causa ad sui spectaculum alliciat." L. Piacente, "Tirocinio ed attività esegetica dell'umanista Battista Guarini," *Giornale italiano di filologia*, n.s., 13 [34] (1982), 70.

103   Decembrio, *Politia*, fol. 9 verso.

one of Italy's centers of lively, lavish manuscript illumination.[104] Books also streamed into its many substantial private libraries, humanistic and legal, Jewish and Christian, from a wide catchment area. One of the greatest humanist collectors, Aurispa, spent the last decades of his life in the Ferrara of the Este. A substantial part of his unique collection – which contained several hundred classical texts, almost all chosen for their contents rather than their luxurious materials – was bought by Borso d'Este in 1461. He gave the books in part to his Carthusian monastery, in part to one of Decembrio's most attractive characters, "that noble and charming student of humane letters, Tito Strozzi."[105]

Decembrio's characters refer to texts of many shapes and sizes – and often, as in the case of Livy, fashionable ones. For at least a century, for example, cultivated Italians had liked to own pocket-size copies of their favorite books, portable texts that they did not have to consult on a lectern but could toss into their rucksacks and consult even while playing the courtier. Leonello describes the pious elders he has seen, "who carried about with them the texts of the Old and New Testaments, bound in a very small volume." He mentions from among his own books a tiny Sallust, "minima forma compactum," and a pocket anthology of verses from the Latin comic poets, "libellus dictorum in Terentio Plautoque notabilium."[106] The last phrase at least describes a book that belonged to the historical Leonello – the "libreto de li fioreti de Terentio de messer Leonello" that the *cartolaio* Nigrisolo dei Nigrisoli bound in April 1433.[107] The library, in short, contained a full range of fashionable types of book – not quite the tiny canon of prim, austere texts that the scene between Pisani and the courtiers might lead one to expect.

Reeling and Writhing

Readers and patrons also shared a sense of what they should do in a library, and the range of permissible activites included, as it had in Rome, a good deal more than silent scrutiny of texts. Pietro Crinito, in his *De honesta disciplina* of 1504, describes the lively discussions held by Pico, Poliziano, and others in what he called both the library of San Marco and the Florentine academy.[108] His reference is clear. Cicero set the *De divinatione* in the library

---

104   See, e.g., D. Diringer, *The Illuminated Book: Its History and Production* (New York and Washington, 1967), 338–42.
105   A. Franceschini, *Giovanni Aurispa e la sua biblioteca* (Padua, 1976). Decembrio describes Strozzi as "generoso et lepidissimo studiorum humanitatis cultore Tito Strozza."
106   Decembrio, *Politia*, fol. 22 recto; fols. 42 verso, 12 verso.
107   Bertoni, *La biblioteca Estense*, 103 n. 2.
108   P. Crinito, *De honesta disciplina*, ed. C. Angeleri (Rome, 1955), 3.2.

in his villa in Tusculum, part of which he called the academy (the other part, eclectic as ever, he called the lyceum; the library was actually there). Crinito and his contemporaries imitated art in life, staging their conversations as the Roman scholars had, in the midst of the great book collections.

Decembrio shows the members of Leonello's circle engaged in a variety of rituals that demonstrate their intimate command of the right texts. One day at Belriguardo, a courtier brings Leonello's Sallust to the young prince just as he wakes from his midday nap. He not only hands over the book but delivers a little appreciative speech about Sallust's brevity. Decembrio explains that this was customary: "For it had become the standard practice that one who offered him a book should deliver a short, appropriate discourse at the same time. This reached such a high level of literary elegance or royal license, in the manner of plays, that the most pleasant of actors, Matotus, though illiterate, still recited speeches in Leonello's presence, both by heart and sometimes in Greek."[109] Books thus provided the occasion for formal, ceremonious exchanges – something like that courtly civil conversation of which *The Book of the Courtier* would give the definitive portrait many years later.

Books also gave Leonello's courtiers opportunities for informal duels of wit, in which they fought politely (or at least without doing one another physical harm) for precedence. This was a matter of besetting interest in the Renaissance court, that world in which new men equipped with spurious genealogies and real swords fought to retain their footing on slippery floors that could at any moment turn into quicksand and engulf them.[110] At one point in Decembrio's text, for example, the courtiers play a game of *sortes Livianae*. Feltrino Boiardo clutches all three volumes of Livy in one arm and reads out passages chosen by chance for discussion. The game ends badly for him, however. A devoted admirer of Hannibal, he opens his book at the passage where Hannibal, forced to leave Italy, appears wailing and complaining in a most unheroic way; like Pisani, he is humiliated in public for his literary error.[111] At another point Tito Strozzi tells the tale of how a schoolmaster had challenged Tito and his friends to give him any verse of Virgil's *Bucolics*. He promised to respond by quoting the next two and more from memory. Tito at once said: "Vrbem quam dicunt Romam Meliboee putavi"(1.20), forcing the schoolmaster to reply with the next line, which begins "Stultus ego" – "I was a fool"(1.21).[112]

---

109   Decembrio, *Politia*, fol. 43 recto.
110   Cf. Leon Battista Alberti's remark, significantly made in Ferrara: "Ferrariensibus ante aedem, ⟨in⟩ qua per Nicolai Estensis tempora maxima iuventutis pars eius urbis deleta est: 'O amici – inquit – quam lubrica erunt proximam per aestatem pavimenta haec, quando sub his tectis multae impluent guttae!' " (R. Fubini and A. N. Gallorini, "L'autobiografia di Leon Battista Alberti: Studio e edizione," *Rinascimento*, n.s., 12 [1972], 21–78, at 76).
111   Decembrio, *Politia*, fol. 57 recto.
112   Ibid., fol. 145 rectc–verso.

Decembrio naturally makes Leonello retain mastery in the game, dominating interpretation as he will the state. Twice courtiers challenge the conduct of ancient heroes, criticizing Aeneas for mistreating Helen in *Aeneid* 2 and Caesar for weeping when he saw the corpse of his enemy Pompey (in Petrarch's poem on the event).[113] In each case Leonello draws on the superior real-life experience of the prince to support the excellence of the ancient hero. Great men, he insists, were certainly prey to strong emotion at certain moments. His own father, Niccolò, had expressed his feelings powerfully in the crisis of his life, when he caught his young wife flagrante delicto with his older son and had to put both of them to death.[114]

Books, in short, permeated everyday life in Leonello's world. They offered entertainment in dull moments and helped to deal with crises. They also moved about Ferrara and its suburbs almost as continually as the peripatetic court itself. Leonello carried his Sallust with him when he and his court moved dramatically out of the city to Belriguardo, "riding at night to avoid the heat."[115] And he discussed literary questions while lying in bed, hunting, hawking, and sitting under the great laurel at Belriguardo. Early in the sixteenth century, in his eloquent praise of Aldo Manuzio, Erasmus described the "library without walls" that the great printer created.[116] In some sense, the humanist library of Estense Ferrara was already a library without walls – a library constantly connected with the big and little dramas of court life. To be sure, many ancient books had to stay on the shelves – such as Juvenal, who, Leonello comments, "should not be the subject of public discussion but should be read privately," because of his frank attacks on the vices.[117]

Decembrio's accounts of reading practices are what one might expect from the pupils and friends of Guarino. He had trained all his pupils, including Leonello, to master every detail of the texts they studied. The good reader would work through his text sentence by sentence, parsing every verb and solving every difficulty, pronouncing the words as he read to promote both memorization and good digestion of food. Then he must enter the results in systematic notebooks, organized by topics – or at least pay a poor young scholar to do it for him.[118] Naturally, young men who had mastered this disciplined way of reading knew their classical texts as the products of a modern yeshiva know the Talmud. Like the library of a yeshiva, that in Ferrara ideally served as a reinforcement to an oral culture, as the basis for a knowledge that was meant to be demonstrated not in silent

113 *Rime* 102 ("Cesare, poi che 1 traditor d'Egitto").
114 Decembrio, *Politia*, fols. 30 verso–31 verso, 34 verso–35 recto.
115 Ibid., fol. 42 verso.
116 *Adagia* 2.1.1 ("Festina lente"); *Ausgewählte Schriften*, 7:464–513, at 488–9.
117 Decembrio, *Politia*, fol. 14 recto.
118 Guarino, *Epistolario*, ed. Sabbadini, no. 679.

reading but in active and ardent debate and writing. Leonello describes how his senior "orator" exulted and wept for sheer joy as he heard his son reciting *Aeneid* 2.[119] Elsewhere in the dialogue, Thomas Rheatinus makes savage fun of a Spaniard who brought his elaborate notebook with him to court so that he could quote appositely from it.[120] These literary evocations of learned conversation that was carried on without reference books at hand correspond well with other documents – for example, a letter from Guarino to Leonello, in which he described, at second hand, a lively discussion about the meaning of the peplum mentioned in book 1 of Virgil's *Aeneid*.[121]

Leonello and his friends never resembled their master more than when they took their books out of the library, risking the books' cleanliness and safety to read them in the open air. In another letter to Leonello, Guarino evoked the beauties of making nature into one's study. Escaping the noise and squalor of the family house, he took a river journey to visit a friend. His description of what he saw and did obviously inspired his young pupil:

> I saw both banks, blooming with fertility, with tall, shady trees in every direction, with furrows, vines, and carefully cultivated fields, which offered a sweet spectacle, since nothing can be more attractive than a well-cultivated field. There were also the villages with their closely clustered farmhouses, stretched out far and wide; a sign of peace and blessedness, a matter of envy to neighbors and of glory to the Este, was that everything rang with the songs and dances of the farmers. Sometimes, to feed my mind as well as my ears and eyes, I let my book rest on my knees, while I read, made notes, and copied out extracts. Thus while my mind profited by reading, my eyes drew great pleasure from looking.[122]

Leonello and his friends knew exactly what Guarino meant.

In another and perhaps more important respect, however, the Ferrarese evidence remains provocative rather than definitive. One wants to know what Guarino's pupils and Leonello's friends made of the texts they used. But the evidence of the *Politia* and the associated documents reveals only one side of the coin. The text shows how closely the Ferrarese studied their books, how strongly they believed that they could wring a coherent and instructive sentiment from every line, and how reluctant they were to believe that a great canonical text could have gaps. Leonello discusses at one point the humanist Maffeo Vegio's addition to the *Aeneid* of a thirteenth

---

119   Decembrio, *Politia*, fol. 11 recto.
120   Ibid., fol. 166 recto.
121   L. Capra, "Nuove lettere di Guarino," *Italia Medioevale e Umanistica* 10 (1967): 165–218, at 212–13. Capra makes the connection with Decembrio in his headnote to the letter (210).
122   Guarino, *Epistolario*, ed. Sabbadini, no. 557.

book that rounds out the plot and arrives, as the original did not, at a happy, moral ending. He tries to show in detail that Virgil's text is complete in itself and needs no description of the funeral of Turnus and the marriage of Lavinia. "After all, by Turnus' own confession, 'Lavinia is your spouse; and let your hatred not continue.' All this, though said as it were in passing, is abundantly clear to the competent."[123]

This attitude seems natural enough in readers schooled by Guarino – and all the more so when one takes into account that he not only trained his pupils to read in a moral, positive way but marked up their texts so they could not avoid reaching the proper conclusions about them. The marginal notes in the Caesar that he prepared for Leonello, as Pade has shown, steer the reader through the *Commentarii*, praising Caesar's actions as clement, benign, and marvelous; labeling the remarks and deeds of his opponents as cruel; and emphasizing the great power of fortune, not to suggest that the cosmos lacks order, but to highlight the virtue that had allowed Caesar to triumph.[124] These tactics marked no exception to Gaurino's normal practices: he had done much the same, as James Hankins has shown in a fascinating study, when he marked up a Latin translation of Plato's *Respublica* so that Francesco Barbaro could strip-mine it for his own treatise on marriage. Guarino's notes on the *Respublica* avoided any confrontation with Plato's philosophical theses on justice and the good, occasionally misrepresented passages he found especially repellent, and they highlighted sententious sayings that Barbaro could lift out of their original contexts for reuse, without regard to the purposes they had originally served.[125]

Even the most striking passages in Decembrio's book – lcertainly those where Leonello argues that ancient heroes did not violate decorum when they showed violent emotion – reflect no shattering of the rules of the game of moral interpretation. After all, Leonello reflects, even the greatest men are not always pitilessly waging war or bitterly attacking their mortal enemies. "'Men act thus,' Leonello held, 'when they are led by ambition, the desire for glory, greed, or anger. But the same men, when the causes of war and hatred have passed away, know that they too were born men, and that nothing of the natural turn of mind is foreign to them.'"[126] In this case Leonello attacked a respectable late antique authority, Servius, in his great commentary on the *Aeneid*, had condemned Aeneas' conduct in book 2. He

123 Decembrio, *Politia*, fol. 26 recto.

124 M. Pade, "Guarino and Caesar at the Court of the Este," in *La corte di Ferrara*, ed. Fade et al., 71–91, at 76–80.

125 J. Hankins, "A Manuscript of Plato's *Republic* in the Translation of Chrysoloras and Uberto Decembrio with Annotations of Guarino Veronese (Reg. lat. 1131)," in *Supplementum festivum: Studies in Honor of Paul Oskar Kristeller*, ed. Hankins et al. (Binghamton, N.Y., 1987), 149–88, at 162–76, 181–8.

126 Decembrio, *Politia*, fols. 34 verso–35 recto.

described Aeneas' furious desire to kill Helen as both inconsistent with the version of events offered in book 6 and shameful for a hero.[127] But, as Decembrio naturally did not say, Leonello found the moral with which he refuted Servius in a older and still more authoritative source, Terence's *Heauton timorumenos*: "I am a human being: I think nothing human foreign to me."[128] The half-quotation of Terence's phrase, the original of which any schoolboy could have supplied, could actually have come from the Terentian anthology that, according to Decembrio, figured among Leonello's favorite books. His twist on the original wording was perhaps meant to prove that he cited from memory. Leonello's memorized Terentian commonplaces merged with the splendid frontispieces and marginal notes in his books, forming a frame that determined what responses to the ancients were acceptable. As Leonello himself puts it, while describing the feelings that come over him when he hears his favorite Terentian sententiae, "I feel as if I am listening not to arguments between slaves or lovers but to an explanation of the nature and ways of thinking of the whole human race."[129] Only this steeping in general principles, concretely stated in the best Latin, gave Leonello a way to assimilate his father's tragic demeanor to the classical rules of conduct that the fictional Aeneas and the real Caesar had obeyed.[130]

For all its lively qualities, in short, the Ferrarese library remained an intellectual, if not a physical, *hortus conclusus*. The new contact with the ancient world that it promoted and sustained followed rules as clear and restrictive as the aesthetic ones that governed the appearance of its contents. In fact, there is a clear relation between the two sets of principles. The clarity and legibility of the script provided a material counterpart to the moral clarity and legibility of the texts. Though the content and organization of the Este library show the interaction of opposing urges that we expected, the actual contact between books and readers often seems disappointingly predetermined. But the constraints of physical form and interpretative tradition did not hem in the interpretative powers of all those who read texts in Ferrara or elsewhere.

---

127   Servius on *Aeneid* 2.592. On the problems in question – above all the authenticity of the so-called Helen episode in *Aeneid* 2 – see the sharply contrasting treatments of G. P. Goold, "Servius and the Helen Episode," *Harvard Studies in Classical Philology* 74 (1970): 101–68, and G. B. Conte, *Vergilio. Il genere e i suoi confini* (Milan, 1984), 109–19. On the importance of Servius for humanistic commentators on Virgil, see C. Kallendorf, *In Praise of Aeneas* (Hanover and London, 1989), esp. chap. 4; for Guarino's use of Servius see Capra, "Nuove lettere."
128   Ter. *Hau.* 77.
129   Decembrio, *Politia*, fol. 12 verso.
130   Here too, external evidence matches Decembrio's testimony. Guarino's son Battista describes his father's use of Terentian sententiae in his school: see his *De ordine docendi et discendi*, in *Il pensiero pedagogico dello umanesimo*. ed. E. Garin (Florence, 1958), 434–71.

Valla and Thucydides: A Reprise

A second look at Valla's dealings with Thucydides may serve as a coda to this chapter. He too read and used his text in more than one way. Valla certainly understood the dark, even tragic side of the *Histories*. His most striking marginal comment in the manuscript of his translation deals with what remains one of the most powerful and disturbing passages in Thucydides, the analysis of the corruption of political language during civil war that forms the core of his description of the revolution in Corcyra. "Note," Valla wrote, "this neatly fits the corruption of our times as well."[131] Evidently Valla experienced the same shock of recognition that many modern readers have felt on reading this profound analysis of the corruption of political language. He saw that Thucydides offered more than neat, appropriate speeches. Thucydides knew that language, like political behavior and society itself, could fall apart; and he embodied that belief in words that retain their power to frighten, like the Melian dialogue and the last speeches of Nicias. One wonders what Valla made of these passages, which he left unadorned with monograms or explicit comments. He might well have connected them, for example, with the pervasive corruption of ecclesiastical rhetoric at every level, which he exposed in his *Declamation on the Donation of Constantine*.[132] Apparently Valla did not wish such messages to emerge as the dominant ones in his Latin Thucydides. But we will see that at least one contemporary proved as deft as Valla himself at making the text yield information of a sort that the translator had not highlighted.[133]

Valla himself, moreover, made clear in the course of the polemics provoked by his history of Ferdinand and his criticism of other humanists in Naples that his own apparently radical and innovative practices as a historian in fact owed much to the classical model of Thucydides. Early in the *Gesta ferdinandi* Valla pointed out that he could not consistently use classical place-names in his Latin, since some names had changed and others had come into being, and he wrote for a modern, not an ancient, world and public. Language, he argued, rested on nothing more or less than custom, and custom changed with time: "Since I am writing for men of the present and the future, I must use not the original names but those widely used in our time and for a long period before it, if I wish all my readers to understand me. I see that this was the general practice of the ancients. For these and other places came repeatedly to be called by different names, and the

---

131   Vat. lat. 1801, fol. 66 verso, on 3.82.2.
132   See S. Camporeale, "Lorenzo Valla e il 'De falso credita donatione': Retorica, libertà ed ecclesiologia nel '400," *Memorie domenicane*, n.s., 19 (1988): 191–293.
133   See chapter 2.

old language is simply an old custom of speaking."[134] The same point held for other "new things," like the mounted scouts whom Valla insisted on calling "caballerii" or "equerii," rather than "equites." The effort to find a classical term for things that had not existed in the ancient world led only to error and confusion: "Anyone can see that new names must be fitted to new things. This was the custom of the ancients, from whom we have our rules and derive our examples."[135] Valla went so far as to dedicate a long essay to developing this point – a piece that became so long and dense that he eventually excised it from his history and passed it on to his friend Giovanni Tortelli, who included it in his own massive reference work on the Latin language, the *De orthographia*.[136]

Valla had infuriated his Neapolitan rival Bartolomeo Facio, undermining his competence as a Latinist and philologist by asking sharp questions at the public discussions of classical texts that their patron, Alfonso of Aragon, liked to stage. When Valla left Naples, Facio attacked him bitterly in writing, both for his supposed departures from classical usage and for the modest digressions on the history of language that remained in his text to justify them. In his discussion of place-names, Facio argued, Valla had confused history with cosmography. In his discussion of the "caballerius" he had simply wandered off into elementary and irrelevant matters: "You seem not to want to write a history but to transmit the rules of the grammarians. Therefore I think this whole disputation about the words *miles* and *eques* particularly bad, as it is superfluous and awkward."[137]

When Valla appealed to "custom" or "usage" to defend his apparent departures from a strictly classical vocabulary, he in fact adapted a classical source, as Vincenzo de Caprio has made clear. Quintilian, in his *Institutio oratorio*, had discussed the role of "consuetudo," custom, in forming a good orator's choice of words. Though wary of the errors with which popular usage swarmed, Quintilian nonetheless admitted that the speaker of real Latin must sometimes follow modern, oral usage rather than the practice of older writers. After all, he asked, "what is the old language but an old custom of speaking?"[138] Valla characteristically put his own twist on his ancient source. He turned Quintilian's question into a statement. He

---

134 Valla, *Gesta*, ed. Besomi, 10–13, at 11 (1.2.1).
135 Ibid., 62–3, at 63 (1.14.7).
136 Ibid., 194–204; see the more detailed treatment, also by Besomi, "Dai 'Gesta Ferdinandi regis Aragonum' del Valla al 'De orthographia' del Tortelli," *Italia medioevale e umanistica* 9 (1966): 75–121.
137 B. Facio, *Invective in Laurentium Vallam*, ed. E. I. Rao (Naples, 1978), 75–6, 81–2, at 82. On this edition see M. Regoliosi, "Per la tradizione delle 'Invective in L. Vallam' di Bartolomeo Facio," *Italia Medioevale e Umanistica* 23 (1980): 389–97.
138 Quintilian *Institutio oratorio* 1.6.43: "Et sane quid est aliud vetus sermo quam vetus loquendi consuetude?" See de Caprio, *La tradizione e la trauma*, 152–62.

did not fully acknowledge that the Roman orator had hedged this loophole in his classicism with many qualifications. And he did not make clear that a modern Latinist must inevitably find it far harder than did an ancient one to walk the tightrope of "usage" without falling off it into barbarism or vulgarity.

Nonetheless, Valla saw his historical method as classical. And he defended it against Facio, as Mariangela Regoliosi has shown in her exemplary edition of his reply. With assurance and superiority, Valla showed that his apparent departures from classical rules for history in fact rested on the best of ancient authorities.[139] Valla naturally cited Thucydides as his predecedent for discussing problems of language in a historical work. Thucydides, after all, had devoted even more space than Valla to subjects that Facio would have condemned as irrelevant to history. He had discussed the cultural development of Greece between Homer's time and his own – providing, perhaps, the inspiration for Valla's analysis of the necessary mutability of culture and language.[140] And he had shown that a historian must address linguistic problems, at least when they reflected substantial changes in the order of society. Valla argued that his digression was "neither a disputation nor long but a very short account" and that it dealt "not with a new word but with a new thing – just as Thucydides did with the word *Greece*, that is, *Hellas*. "[141] Valla's model of how to write history, in short, was Thucydidean – in a complex, carefully considered sense. In Valla's adherence to this classical model lay the key to his ability to write a work not confined within the sterilizing norms of so much humanist historiography. The ancient text helped the modern reader to bend, even to break, what others defined as the restrictive rules of a classical genre. Valla's library – and the Neapolitan court library in the days when he worked there – was no *hortus conclusus*.

We stop here, for now: in the center of the Italian Renaissance, in another of those locations where books of the new kind were most dramatically collected and discussed. Even here the intermediary comes between the ever receding original text and the hungry reader. But here too, without the intermediary the reader would have no text to consume. Valla's translation of Thucydides offered sharp new insights into ancient historiography as well as models for modern speeches; its apparatus contained rigorously established facts as well as imaginatively fabricated constructions. Both its deceptive glamor and its solid scholarship, its classicizing frame and its ancient content, are emblematic of the humanists' new world of the book.

139 L. Valla, *Antidotum in Facium*, ed. M. Regoliosi (Padua, 1981), introduction, liii–lxvii.
140 Ibid., 211 (3.1.6).
141 Ibid., 235 (3.4.8).

11

Isotta Nogarola: Women Humanists – Education for What?

Lisa Jardine

Somewhere between 1443 and 1448, the distinguished teacher Lauro Quirini,[1] a former pupil of Guarino's, addressed a letter of advice to the humanist Isotta Nogarola of Verona.[2] He was responding to a request from her brother for guidance on appropriate reading for an advanced student of the *studia humanitatis* in the technical disciplines of dialectic and philosophy:

> Your brother Leonardo . . . asked me some time ago if I would write something to you, seeing that at this time you are devoting yourself to the "bitter" study (as he terms it) of dialectic and philosophy. He was anxious for me to impress upon you, in most solid and friendly fashion, which masters above all you ought to follow in these higher disciplines. (Abel II, 10)[3]

1 On Quirini see V. Branca (ed.), *Lauro Quirini umanista* (Florence, 1977); E. Abel, *Isotae Nogarolae Veronensis opera quae supersunt omnia* (Budapest, 1886) I, xliv, cxxxii; R. Sabbadini, "Briciole umanistiche", *Giornale storico della letteratura italiana*, XLIII (1904), 247–50; L. Martines, *The Social World of the Florentine Humanists* (Princeton, 1963), 97–8.

2 On Isotta Nogarola see most recently M. L. King, "The religious retreat of Isotta Nogarola (1418–66): Sexism and its consequences in the fifteenth century", *Signs*, 3 (1978), 807–22, which contains a full bibliography in an appendix. See also Abel's introductory essay in the *Opera*; M. L. King, "Book-lined cells: Women and humanism in the early Italian Renaissance", in P. H. Labalme (ed.), *Beyond Their Sex: Learned Women of the European Past* (New York and London, 1980), 66–90; P. O. Kristeller, "Learned women of early modern Italy: Humanists and university scholars", *ibid.*, 91–116; D. M. Robathan, "A fifteenth-century bluestocking", *Medievalia e Humanistica*, fasc. 2 (1944), 106–11.

3 All references are to Abel's edition of Isotta Nogarola's works (as above). "Leonardus germanus tuus . . . iam pridem me rogarat, ut nonnihil ad te scriberem, nam quoniam hoc tempore dialecticae et philosophiae acrem ut is aiebat, operam das, voluit, ut ipse fidelissime ac amicissime te commonerem, quos praecipue magistros in his altioribus disciplinis sequi deberes."

Quirini prefaces his detailed suggestions for study with an elaborately dismissive paragraph in which he is at pains to point out that to the learned humanist with a real command of classical Latin (amongst whom he numbers Isotta, some of whose writing he has been shown), all study of dialectic and philosophy must appear uncouth and clumsy:

> For you, who have been thoroughly instructed in the most polished and excellent art of discourse, and who find elegance in orating and suavity of speech comes naturally, you are able of your own accord to expect the greatest perfection in eloquent speech. But we semi-orators and petty philosophers have most of the time to be content with mean speech – generally inelegant. (Abel II, 11)[4]

He insists, however, that Isotta Nogarola should not therefore be misled by difficulty for its own sake, even though "now especially we pursue that philosophy which in no way concerns itself with felicity of expression" – "Eam enim hoc potissimum tempore philosophiam sequimur, quae nullum sequitur florem orationis" (Abel II, 11). Technical scholastic dialectic is to be vigorously avoided:

> I absolutely insist, and I place the weight of my authority behind this, that you avoid and shun the new philosophers and new dialecticians as men minimally schooled in true philosophy and true dialectic, and that furthermore you harden your heart against all their writings. For they do not teach the approach of the old tried and tested discipline of dialectic, but they obscure the clear and lucid path of this study with goodness knows what childish quibbles, inextricable circuities and pedantic ambiguities. And while seeming to know a great deal, they distort the most readily intelligible matters with a kind of futile subtlety. So that, as the comedian would say, "they find a knot in a bullrush" ["make difficulties where there are none" (Plautus, Terence)]. On which account, having been diverted by these obstacles, they are unable to aspire to the true philosophy, in which indeed, although they wish to seem sagacious debaters, they let slip the truth, as the old saying goes, with excessive cross-examination. (Abel II, 13–14)[5]

---

4 "Tu enim, quae politissima et exquisitissima arte dicendi edocta es assueta in eleganti oratione suavitateque dicendi, tuo iure perornatissimum exposcere potes eloquium, at nos semioratores minutique philosophi parvo et illo ineleganti persaepe contenti sumus."

5 "Cupio, inquam, idque meo iure iubeo, ut novos hos philosophos novosque dialecticos tamquam homines minime verae philosophiae veraeque dialecticae instructos non modo evites et fugias, verum etiam omnia eorum scripta stomacheris, nam dialecticae quidem non viam disciplinae veteris iam probatae docent, sed nescio quibus puerilibus captionibus, inextricabilibus circuitibus et scrupulosis ambagibus huiusce disciplinae claram et dilucidam semitam obfuscarunt. Nam ut multa scire videantur, omnia etiam planissima futili quadam subtilitate corrumpunt et, ut inquit comicus, "nodum in scirpo quaerunt". Quapropter his impedimentis detenti nequent ad veram et solidam aspirare philosophiam, in qua etiam dum acuti disputatores videri cupiunt, veritatem nimium altercando, ut vetus sententia dicit, amiserunt."

According to Quirini, the source of genuine understanding of dialectic and philosophy remains Aristotle (whose texts "veram et elegantem philosophiam continent"). And for a clear grasp of the sense of Aristotle's philosophical works, he directs Isotta away from the new-fangled, towards less pretentious expositors:

> Let me now instruct you which authors you *should* follow. Read studiously the celebrated works of learned Boethius, easily the most acute of men, and fully the most knowledgeable. Read, that is, all those treatises which he composed with erudition on the art of dialectic, and the dual commentaries he published on Aristotle's *Categories* and *De interpretatione*, the first for understanding the texts, the second as an examination of the higher art. In which you will be able to find the pronouncements of almost all the most relevant and reliable of the Greek commentators. (Abel II, 15–16)[6]

Having mastered dialectic with Boethius, Isotta is to proceed to Aristotle's moral philosophy, and thence to mathematics, natural philosophy and metaphysics. Since she has no Greek, Quirini suggests the Arab commentators (in their Latin versions) as providing the best access to the nuances of Aristotle's texts. In spite of their "barbarity", Averroes and Avicenna are preferable in this respect to any of the "new" philosophers – a sign, incidentally, that Quirini takes Isotta's intellectual aspirations entirely seriously.[7] To these he adds Thomas Aquinas. However, Quirini concludes, in the end it will be the Roman historians and moralists, and supremely Cicero himself, who will add the final gloss and lustre to Isotta's grasp of higher learning, and the lessons in life it provides.

This leads Quirini to round off his letter with a eulogy to philosophy as the supreme guide to virtuous conduct. *Bonae artes* and right living go hand in hand:

> For nothing is more seemly than philosophy, nothing more lively, nothing more beautiful, as our Cicero was wont to say; and I may perhaps add, more

---

6   "[His ergo explosis] quos sequi debeas, breviter edocebo. Lege igitur studiose Boetii Severini, viri facile acutissimi abundeque doctissimi praeclara monumenta, id est tractatus omnes, quos in arte dialectica erudite confecit, et eius commentarios, quos in Aristotelis Cathegoriis et Periermenias duplices edidit, primos ad litterae intelligentiam, secundos ad altioris artis indaginem. In quibus cunctorum fere probatissimorum Graecorum commentatorum sententias videre poteris."

7   For an account of the serious use of Averroes's commentaries on Aristotle's texts in the Renaissance which is entirely compatible with Quirini's advice to Isotta, see C. B. Schmitt, "Renaissance Averroism studied through Venetian editions of Aristotle-Averroes (with particular reference to the Giunta edition of 1550–2)", *Convegno internazionale: l' Averroismo in Italia, Atti dei convegni Lincei*, 40 (Rome, 1979), 121–42. Schmitt is, of course, concentrating largely on a later period.

properly, nothing more divine in matters human. For this is the single, most sacred discipline, which teaches true wisdom and instructs in the right manner of living. Whence it comes about that to be ignorant of philosophy is not simply to go through life basely, but also ruinously. Accordingly, throw yourself wholeheartedly, as they say, into this one matter. For I wish you to be not semi-learned, but skilled in all the liberal arts [*bonae disciplinae*], that is, to be schooled in the art of discourse, and in the study of right debating, and in the science of things divine and human. (Abel II, 21–2)[8]

Quirini's letter articulates a mature humanistic position on the type of rigorous study of language and *scientia* appropriate to *eloquentia*. But although the advice is standard, even commonplace, the circumstances of its being given are unusual. It was not usual for a woman to pursue *advanced* humanistic studies. Indeed, Leonardo Bruni's well-known letter to Battista Malatesta some 40 years earlier explicitly states that whilst the *bonae artes* are an appropriate leisure occupation for a noble woman (the favourite analogy is that it keeps their fingers out of mischief, like spinning and needlework),[9] public proficiency in advanced studies is indecorous:

There are certain disciplines which, whilst it is not altogether seemly to be entirely ignorant of, nevertheless to ascend to the utmost heights of them is not at all admirable. Such are geometry and arithmetic, on which if too much time and energy is expended, and every subtlety and obscurity pursued to the utmost, I shall withdraw and cut off my support from you. And I shall do the same in the case of Astronomy, and perhaps in the case of Rhetoric. I have said this more reluctantly in the case of this last, since if ever there was anyone who has bestowed labour on that study I profess myself to be of their number. But I am obliged to consider many aspects of the matter, and above all I have to bear in mind who it is I am addressing here. For why exhaust a

---

8   "Nihil enim philosophia formosius, nihil pulchrius, nihil amabilius, ut Cicero noster dicebat, ego vero forsan rectius, nihil philosophia in rebus humanis divinius. Haec enim unica, sanctissima disciplina est, quae veram sapientiam edocet et rectum vivendi modum instruit, ex quo fit, ut ignari huius non modo turpiter sed etiam perniciose per vitam obirent. Proinde huic uni rei, toto, ut aiunt, pectore incumbe, volo enim te non semidoctam esse, sed cunctarum bonarum disciplinarum peritiam habere, id est et bene dicendi artem et recte disputandi disciplinam et humanarum atque divinarum rerum scientiam noscere."

9   See, for example, Erasmus: "The distaff and spindle are in truth the tools of all women and suitable for avoiding idleness. . . . Even people of wealth and birth train their daughters to weave tapestries or silken cloths. . . . It would be better if they taught them to study, for study busies the whole soul. . . . It is not only a weapon against idleness but also a means of impressing the best precepts upon a girl's mind and of leading her to virtue". *Christiani matrimonii institutio* (Basle, 1526), ch. 17, unpaginated, cited in J. O'Faolain and L. Martines (eds). *Not in God's Image: Women in History* (London, 1979), 194. Politian, writing in praise of another woman humanist, Cassandra Fedele, commends her for having exchanged "her spinning wool for her books, her rouge for a reed pen, her needle for a quill pen". See I. P. Tomasinus (ed.), *Clarissimae feminae Cassandrae Fidelis Venetae epistolae et orationes* . . . (Padua, 1636), 156.

woman with the concerns of *status* and *epicheremata*, and with what they call *crinomena* and a thousand difficulties of rhetorical art, when she will never be seen in the forum? And indeed that artificial performance which the Greeks call *hypocrisis*, and we call *pronuntiatio* (which Demosthenes maintained to rank first, second and third, such was its importance), as it is essential to performers, so it ought not to be pursued by women at all. For if a woman throws her arms around whilst speaking, or if she increases the volume of her speech with greater forcefulness, she will appear threateningly insane and requiring restraint. These matters belong to men; as war, or battles, and also contests and public controversies. A woman will not, therefore, study any further what to speak either for or against witnesses, either for or against torture, either for or against hearsay evidence, nor will she busy herself with *loci communes*, or devote her attention to dilemmatic questions or to cunning answers; she will leave, finally, all public severity to men.[10]

"Cultivation" is in order for a noblewoman; formal competence is positively unbecoming. I take it that it is because encouraging her higher studies might be considered improper that Quirini insists at the beginning of his letter of advice to Isotta that it is specifically at the request of her brother (her father being dead) that he offers such advice.

So in the case of Quirini's letter to Isotta Nogarola we have familiar sentiments about the moral desirability of humanistic education, addressed to an unusual student, of whom it can be said with certainty that full competence as a humanist would be likely to be construed as unbecoming, if not *immoral*. It is because this particular conjunction must concentrate our minds so remarkably well on the question of what "moral" might possibly mean in the context of humanistic education that I choose it as the focus

---

10 "Sunt enim disciplinarum quaedam, in quibus ut rudem omnino esse non satis decorum, sic etiam ad cacumina illarum evadere nequaquam gloriosum; ut geometria et arithmetica, in quibus, si multum temporis consumere pergat et subtilitates omnes obscuritateque rimari, retraham manu atque divellam. Quod idem faciam in astrologiam, idem fortasse et in arte rhetorica. Invitior de hac postrema dixi, quoniam, si quisquam viventium illi affectus fuit, me unum ex eo numero esse profiteor. Sed multarum rerum habenda mihi ratio est et in primis, cui scribam, videndum. Quid enim *statuum* subtilitates et *epicherematum* curae et illa, quae appellantur *crinomena*, et mille in ea arte difficultates mulierem conterant, quae forum numquam sit aspectura? Iam vero actio illa artificiosa, quam Graeci *hypocrisim*, nostri *pronuntiationem* dixere, cui Demosthenes primas et secundas et tertias tribuit, ut actori necessaria, ita mulieri nequaquam laboranda, quae, si brachium iactabit loquens aut si clamorem vehementius attollet, vesana coercendaque videatur. Ista quidem virorum sunt; ut bella, ut pugnae, sic etiam fori contentiones atque certamina. Non igitur pro testibus neque contra testes dicere addiscet mulier, neque pro tormentis aut contra tormenta, neque pro rumoribus aut contra rumores, nec se communibus locis exercebit, neque interrogationes bicipites neque responsiones veteratorias meditabitur; totam denique fori asperitatem viris relinquet". H. Baron (ed.), *Leonardo Bruni Aretino Humanistische–Philosophische Schriften mit einer Chronologie seiner Werke und Briefe* (Leipzig, 1928), 11–12. In spite of Bruni's warning, Battista Malatesta delivered a public oration in Latin to the Emperor Sigismund. See Kristeller. "Learned women", 93–4.

for this paper. It gives us, I believe, a striking way of approaching the general question (in relation to students of either gender), "What was humanist education envisaged as an education *for?*" – a question posed in the second part of my title.

As historians of education, we regularly scan those familiar propaganda documents issued by humanists on behalf of their emerging educational programme (epistles of advice, introductions and prefaces to texts and translations, epideictic orations for deceased humanist pedagogues, and so forth), and our eye runs smoothly over passages, like Quirini's above, which make the identity of humanistic eloquence and moral integrity – right living – automatic and self-evident. Ludovico Carbone's funeral oration for Guarino Veronese is a masterly example of the form, and one which is pertinent to our present discussion, which moves very much in the shadow of the great teacher's influence:[11]

> It was shameful how little the men of Ferrara knew of letters before the arrival of Guarino. There was no one who even understood the basic principles of grammar, who understood the propriety and impact of words, who was able to interpret the poets, let alone who was learned in the art of oratory, who professed rhetoric, who was competent to speak gravely and elegantly and dared to do so in public. Priscian was lost in oblivion, Servius was unheard of, the works of Cicero were unknown, and it was considered miraculous if someone mentioned Sallust, or Caesar, or Livy, or if anyone aspired to understand the ancient authors. At forty our citizens were still occupied with childish studies, still struggling and embroiled with the rudiments, until the liberal arts had been reduced entirely to ruins. But after a propitious star had brought this divine individual to Ferrara, there followed an extraordinary transformation in competence . . . From all quarters they came to listen to that most felicitous voice, so that one might call him another Theophrastus (of whom it is said that his teaching produced at least two thousand scholars). No one was considered noble, no one as leading a blameless life, unless he had followed Guarino's courses. So that in a short space of time our citizens were led out of the deepest shadows into a true and brilliant light, and all suddenly became eloquent, learned, elegant and felicitous of speech.[12]

11 The Nogarola sisters were tutored in humanistic studies by Martino Rizzoni, one of Guarino's old pupils. This allows Sabbadini to claim the sisters as members of Guarino's "school". In addition to corresponding with Guarino himself, Isotta exchanged letters with a number of humanists of his circle, and received scholarly advice from Quirini, another graduate of Guarino's school.

12 *Ludovico Carbonis Ferrariensis, artium doctoris et comitis palatini apostolici, oratio habita in funere praestantissimi oratoris et poetae Guarini Veronensis,* in E. Garin (ed.), *Prosatori latini del quattrocento* (Milan and Naples, 1952), 381–417; 390–2. "Pudendum erat quam parumper litterarum sciebant nostri [Ferrarienses] homines ante Guarini adventum. Nemo erat, non dicam qui oratoriam facultatem nosceret, qui rhetoricam profiteretur, qui graviter et ornate diceret et in publico aliquo conventu verba facere auderet, sed qui veram grammaticae

Here the equation is unashamedly explicit: Guarino brought literary studies to Ferrara; literary studies transformed men overnight into paragons of virtue. All the detail is about grammar and oratory, all the evaluations concern "leading a blameless life". Good grammarians lead blameless lives.

As I have argued elsewhere,[13] the moment in this century at which intellectual historians turned their attention most singlemindedly to the achievements of the humanist educators was also a moment of passionate commitment to the prospect of a new "Renaissance" of morals in Western Europe through a revival of humane letters. It is hardly surprising, therefore, to find that these modern scholars reinforced, and continue to reinforce, the humanist affirmation of the identity of proficiency in the *bonae artes* and right living. The classic formulation of this position is Garin's,[14] but recent Italian scholars are, if anything, more dogmatic in their view that the study of literature *necessarily entails* improved human values. Writing recently on the school of Vittorino da Feltre, Cesare Vasoli puts the case as follows:

> It is true . . . that the school of Vittorino, in common with those of all the other humanist masters, insisted above all on literary development, or at least, gave pride of place to the acquisition of specific linguistic and oratorical abilities, considered indispensible to further development in studies. But even the most determined upholders of the "pure intellectual pursuit" model of education have surely to admit that Vittorino operated in a society in which word and discourse represented the fundamental strand in "civil" relations, and in which the drilling in linguistic arts not only opened the way to social success, but also provided the means of controlling the most delicate instruments of power . . . For him, as for the majority of his humanistic colleagues, word and culture, language and civilization, grammar and knowledge were, in fact, inseparable concepts.[15]

rationem cognosceret, qui vocabulorum proprietatem vimque intelligeret, qui poetas interpretari posset. Iacebat Priscianus, ignorabatur Servius, incognita erant opera Ciceronis, miraculi loco habebatur, si quis Crispum Sallustium, si quis C. Caesarem, si quis T. Livium nominaret, si quis ad veterum scriptorum intelligentiam aspiraret. Quadragesimus fere annus cives nostros in ludo puerili occupatos inveniebat in iisdem elementis semper laborantes, semper convolutos. Usque adeo bonarum litterarum ruina facta erat. Postea vero quam divinus hic vir dextro sidere Ferrariam ingressus est, secuta est mirabilis quaedam ingeniorum commutatio . . . Currebatur undique ad vocem iucundissimam, ut alterum Theophrastum diceres, ad quem audiendum legimus perrexisse discipulos ad duo milia. Nemo putabatur ingenuus, nemo in lauta vitae parte, nisi Guarini esset auditor. Unde brevi de oscurissimis tenebris educti sunt nostri homines in veram et clarissimam lucem, omnes repente diserti, omnes eruditi, omnes limati, omnes in dicendo suaves extiterunt".

13   See A. T. Grafton and L. Jardine, "Humanism and the school of Guarino: a problem of evaluation", *Past and Present*, 96 (1982), 51–80.

14   See e.g., E. Garin, *L'Educazione umanistica in Italia*, 7, cit. Grafton and Jardine, "Humanism", 77.

15   C. Vasoli, "Vittorino da Feltre e la formazione umanistica dell'uomo", in N. Giannetto (ed.), *Vittorino da Feltre e la sua scuola: umanesimo, pedagogia, arti* (Florence, 1981), 13–33; 26–7.

"Even the most determined [critics] . . . have surely to admit . . ." shows, I think, the strain of this position as it is carried into the 1980s. Do they have to admit any such thing? The fact is, a number of recent English-speaking historians of humanism have drawn attention to the obvious *gap* in the scholarly argument which makes education in grammar and textual exegesis the obvious grooming for an individual destined for high office and public service (and in this sense self-evidently a *moral*, socially-validated, training).[16] And these historians have also pointed out that the concealed premises in such an argument are shared by the fifteenth-century humanists and by the twentieth-century promoters of a socially-reforming liberal arts revival who make the humanist educational texts their study.[17]

Quirini's letter of advice to Isotta Nogarola is heavily ornamented with this assumed equivalence of proficiency in humane letters and personal virtue. What makes his insistence on this conventional humanist equation interesting is that, as applied to advanced studies in relation to a *woman's* life, it lacks the comfortably self-evident quality which traditional historians have found so seductive. Leonardo Bruni's view, in the passage I cited above, that the virtuous woman should not pursue indecorously advanced studies, is typical not just of the humanist educators, but equally of the historians of humanism themselves – the very people who find the equation of letters and virtue inescapable when applied to a man. Garin's footnote to this passage in his Italian abridgement of the text states firmly that "the exaltation of ethico-political studies (which are concerned with the *vita civile*) evidenced in Bruni's treatise is the keynote in all early humanist pedagogy". He then adds that Bruni would obviously not advocate rhetorical studies to a noble *woman*, since she clearly ought not to be concerned with its "excessive use, above all in a practical sphere".[18]

The Latin letters which make up the two volumes of Isotta Nogarola's *Opera* testify eloquently to the intriguing social and practical difficulties which arise when it comes to extolling the virtue inseparable from eloquence of a female humanist. In 1436 Guarino was sent some of the Nogarola sisters' compositions (Isotta's and her sister Ginevra's) by Jacopo Foscari. Guarino replied with a letter of studied and effusive praise for their scholarly achievement and their manifest virtuousness (a letter entirely

---

16   See J. E. Seigel, " 'Civic Humanism' or Ciceronian Rhetoric?", *Past and Present*, 34 (1966), 3–48; L. Jardine, "Lorenzo Valla and the intellectual origins of humanist dialectic", *Journal of the History of Philosophy*, XV (1977), 143–64; D. Robey, "Humanism and education in the early quattrocento: the *De ingenuis moribus* of P. P. Vergerio", *Bibliothèque d'Humanisme et Renaissance* XLII (1980), 27–58; "Vittorino da Feltre e Vergerio", in N. Giannetto (ed.), *Vittorino da Feltre* 241–53. See also L. Martines, *Power and Imagination: City-States in Renaissance Italy* (New York, 1979; London, 1980), 262–300.
17   See e.g., Robey, "Humanism and education", 38.

within the tradition I have been discussing). Their learning and their virtue brought glory to their native city, Verona (which happened also to be Guarino's):

> On this above all I bestow my admiration: such is the likeness of each sister's expression, such the similarity of style, such the sisterhood of writing and indeed the splendour on both their parts, that if you were to remove the names Ginevra and Isotta you would not easily be able to judge which name you should place before which; so that whoever is acquainted with either knows both together. Thus they are not simply sisters in birth and nobility of stock, but also in style and readiness of speech.
>
> Oh the glory indeed of our State and our Age! Oh how rare a bird upon earth, like nothing so much as a black swan! If earlier ages had borne these proven virgins, with how many verses would their praises have been sung, how many deserved praises by truly unstinting authors would have consigned them to immortality! We single out Penelope because she wove so well, Arachne because she spun a most fine thread, Camilla and Penthesilea because they were female warriors, all consecrated in the verses of poets. Why then do they not honour these so modest, so noble, so erudite, so eloquent women, why do they not sing their praises to the skies, why do they not rescue them from the clutches of oblivion, by whatever means they please, and preserve them for posterity? (Abel I, 58–9)[19]

Here the virtue of the Nogarola sisters is characterized in two ways, neither of them "civic": first, the sisters are indubitably virgins (Ginevra in fact fades from the scene when she marries);[20] secondly, they are represented as sisters

---

18 Garin, *L'Educazione umanistica*, 32.

19 There is in fact a better text of this exchange of letters in Sabbadini, *Epistolario di Guarino Veronese*, vol. II (Venice, 1916), 292–309, and I have taken the Latin text from there. Sabbadini wrote a magisterial review of Abel's edition of Isotta Nogarola's works, in which he helpfully points out a large number of discrepancies between his versions of the letters and Abel's: "Isotta Nogarola", *Archivio storico italiano*, 18 (1886), 435–43. He also redates some of the letters. "Quodque praecipua admiratione prosequor, tanta est in intriusque dictione paritas, tanta stili similtudo, tanta scribendi germanitas et quidem utrobique magnifica, ut si Zinebrae nomen auferas et Isotae, non facile utri utram anteponas iudicare queas, adeo ut "qui utramvis norit, ambas noverit" [Terence]: ita sunt non modo creatione et sanguinis nobilitate sorores, sed etiam stilo atque facundia. O civitatis, immo et aetatis nostrae decus! O "rara avis in terris nigroque simillima cygno!" [Juvenal]. Si superiora saecula hasce probandas creassent virgines, quantis versibus decantatae, quantas, modo non malignis scriptoribus, laudes assecutae immortalitati traditae fuissent. Penelopen quia optime textuit, Aragnen quia tenuissima fila deduxit, Camillam et Penthesileam quia bellatrices erant, poetarum carminibus consecratas cernimus; has tam pudicas, tam generosas, tam eruditas, tam eloquentes non colerent, in astra laudibus non eveherent, non ab oblivionis morsibus quavis ratione vendicarent et sempiterno donarent aevo?"

20 There is a striking letter from Damiano Borgo to Isotta describing how much changed Ginevra is for the worse since her marriage. The entire letter is preoccupied with virginity and

in spirit to various magnificent women of classical antiquity. In praising the Nogarola sisters it is almost obligatory apparently for male humanists to liken them routinely to Sappho, Cornelia, Aspasia, Portia[21] – figures also invoked in defence of the education of women by Bruni in his epistle to Battista Malatesta.[22] Guarino's figurative selection of "active" virtuous women is a particularly elegant literary ploy: Penelope and Arachne, spinners of exquisitely fine yarns, Camilla and Penthesilea, seductive Amazons and conquerors of entire male armies, deflect his compliments from any awkwardness over public visibility of (real) women! The strategy of all such compliments is the same: they shift the focus of praise away from the engaged and civic (women speaking publicly), making figurative purity and iconic Amazon valour the object of attention. These are what brings glory to humanism and to Verona for nurturing such distinction.

This method of extolling the Nogarolas' virtue is essentially an evasion of the conventional humanist tactic of identifying the virtue of humanism with morality in the market place. And as before, this evasion is carried over into the scholarly secondary literature. In his *Vita di Guarino Veronese*, Sabbadini describes how Guarino chose to send Leonello d'Este copies of the pieces he had been sent by Foscari, during an absence from Ferrara, as follows:[23]

> How should he spend his time away? In correspondence. But Guarino did not want to send an empty vessel, so he included some fruits of the Verona school – not those which nourish the body, but rather those which provide fruit for the soul. And those fruits issued from the intellects of two Veronese virgins, the Nogarola sisters, Isotta and Ginevra . . . These two women are amongst the most characteristic products of the Renaissance. In them for the first time, humanism was married with feminine gentility, especially in the case of

defloration, and one can only take as the sense of the letter that Isotta's purity preserves for her a transcendent beauty which could not survive loss of virginity. Abel takes this quite naturally as an indication that Ginevra had lost her "flair" with humanist letters. See Abel I, 261–7 for the letter, dated the last day of November 1440; Abel I, xxxi–iii for Abel's verdict on Ginevra s "Fall".

21   See D. M. Robathan, "A fifteenth-century bluestocking", for some references to such compliments: Abel I, 114, 125, 160, 180. Isotta also uses them of herself, e.g. Abel I, 256; I, 76.
22   Baron (ed.), *Leonardo Bruni . . . Schriften*, 5–6. There is a comparable letter from Politian to Cassandra Fidele, written in 1494, which opens with Virgil's "O decus Italiae virgo . . .". See I. P. Thomasino, *Cassandrae Fidelis epistolae*, 155.
23   Guarino's noble pupil replied exactly as he knew he was expected to. He praised the two sisters' works in the same figurative terms as his master: "Hos igitur ingenii et studiorum fructus quos e duabus civitatis virginibus collegisti collectosque ad me misisti non admirari non possum et summis prosequi laudibus eoque magis quod abs et, qui huiusce rei non negligendus testis es, mirum in modum probantur extollunturque. . . . Illud equidem non parvi facio quod id mulierum genus etsi antea perrarum fuit, hoc tamen tempore perrarissimum esse consuevit." (Sabbadini, *Epistolario*, 298).

Isotta, who remained in this respect unsurpassed. With the Nogarola sisters the Guarinian strain of humanist pedagogy reached its culmination.[24]

That Sabbadini sees the glory bestowed by Isotta and Ginevra on the school of Guarino as strictly *figurative* (emblems of virtue rather than performers on the public and professional stage) is touchingly revealed in a comment of Sabbadini's a couple of pages later. Discussing abusive attacks on Isotta (which I will come to in a moment), he says that these were probably the work of jealous women, rather than of men, since "envy is a peculiarly feminine passion".[25]

It proved almost impossible in practice, as it turns out, to sustain the identity of Isotta Nogarola's humanistic competence and her supreme virtue as a woman. Two exchanges of letters make this clear. The first is the exchange between Isotta and Guarino, preluded by the letter of praise from which I have just quoted (the exchange for which Isotta is remembered in histories of humanist education). Guarino's enthusiasm for Isotta's and Ginevra's compositions, expressed in a number of letters to male humanist colleagues and pupils, encouraged Isotta to write to him directly. Guarino failed to answer the letter.[26] At this point the social precariousness of Isotta's position as a humanist scholar becomes evident. Isotta was driven to write a second letter to Guarino, in which she positively begged for a response from the master. And the reason she gives is that her unanswered letter (publicly sent, publicly unanswered) compromises her as a woman. A woman of marriageable age has written an articulate (even pushy) letter, unsolicited, to a man of distinction. He has ignored her, and by so doing has exposed as illusory the notional "equality" and "free scholarly exchange" between them. In her first letter Isotta had expressed in entirely conventional terms her anxiety that, coming from a woman, her writing might be considered presumptuous, garrulous, a woman speaking out of turn:

> Do not hold it against me, if I have transgressed those rules of silence especially imposed on women, and seem scarcely to have read that precept of Vergerio's, which warns against encouraging articulateness in the young, since in plentiful speech there is always that which may be censured. And Sophocles too called silence a woman's greatest ornament. (Abel I, 77)[27]

24 R. Sabbadini, *Vita di Guarino Veronese* (Genoa, 1891), 122.

25 *Ibid.*, 126.

26 For Sabbadini's observations on the dating of this series of letters, as Abel presents it, see Sabbadini, "Isotta Nogarola", *Vita di Guarino Veronese*, 440.

27 "Neque hoc mihi vitio dare, si tacendi leges mulieribus praesertim impositas praegressa sum illudque Vergerii praeceptum haud legisse videar, qui adolescentibus monet parum loqui prodesse, cum in multo sermone semper sit quod reprehendi possit. Et Sophocles quoque taciturnitatem in feminis singularem ornatum appellavit." (Not in Sabbadini.)

In the absence of a reply from Guarino, convention has become a reality. Guarino's silence confirms Isotta's immodesty, her forwardness:

> "You have treated me wretchedly, and have shown as little consideration for me as if I had never been born. For I am ridiculed throughout the city, those of my own condition deride me. I am attacked on all sides: the asses inflict their bites on me, the oxen attack me with their horns" [Plautus]. Even if I am most deserving of this outrage, it is unworthy of you to inflict it. What have I done to be thus despised by you, revered Guarino? (Abel I, 80–1)[28]

"S[a]epissime . . . venit in mentem queri fortunam meam, quoniam femina nata sum" – "How often . . . does it occur to me to lament my fortune, because I was born a woman", exclaims Isotta.[29]

The second epistolary exchange of interest to us here is one between Isotta and Damiano Borgo.[30] Borgo had apparently challenged Isotta with the familiar claim that women outdo men above all in talkativeness. Isotta responded by claiming that to make such an accusation was to condemn all women on the strength of a few, and she challenged Borgo to maintain the view once he had considered the many examples of women who outdo both other women and all men "in every kind of virtue and distinction":

> Consider Cornelia, mother of the Gracchi, for eloquence; Amesia, who publicly pleaded to packed assemblies with most prudent speech; Affrania, wife of the senator Lucinius Buco, who argued the same kind of cases in public. Did not Hortensia do the same? Did not Sappho inspire wonder with the perfection of her verses? Portia, Fannia, and the rest are celebrated in the verses of countless most learned men. Take note of Camilla, who Turnus, so the poet tells, supported with such honour. Did not Tamyris, Queen of the Scythians, massacre Cyrus, King of the Persians, and his entire army, so that indeed no witness survived to tell of so great a defeat? Did not the Amazons subdue the major part of Europe, with Marpesia, Lampedus and Orithyia, and without men to augment the State? Did not others overrun the states of Asia without men? For they were so strongly endowed with *virtus* [valour/virtue] and with knowledge of single combat, that to Hercules and Theseus it seemed impossible to bring the forces of the Amazons under their rule. Penthesilea fought

---

28 " 'Usa sum te nequiore meque magis haud respectus es quam si nunquam gnata essem. Per urbem enim irrideor, meus me ordo deridet, neutrubi habeo stabile stabulum, asini me mordicus scindunt, boves me incursant cornibus' [Plautus]. Nam si ego hac contumelia digna eram maxime, tu tamen indignus qui faceres. Quodnam ob factum ita abs et contemnor, Guarine pater?"

29 Abel I, 79. Eventually Guarino replied at length, and rebuked Isotta for panicking. A strikingly similar incident occurrs in the correspondence between Politian and Cassandra Fidele. See Thomasino, 155–61.

manfully in the Trojan wars in amongst the strongest Greeks, as the poet testifies:

> "Penthesilea in fury in the midst of her thousands, rages."

Since this is so, I ask you whether you will grant that rather than women exceeding men in talkativeness, in fact they exceed them in eloquence and virtue? (Abel I, 256–7)[31]

Here improper talkativeness is replaced by proper "eloquence and virtue", and Isotta maintains that it is in these latter that women outdo men. But the rhetorical means to this end is an appeal once again to ancient female figurative *virtus* to replace social improprieties. Once again also, it is the actual precariousness of Isotta's own position that is the most obvious feature of such an argument. "Virile" argumentative ability and "Amazon-like" independence of men may make nice points in arguing for the appropriateness of female humanistic education. But they are all too readily to be seen in a "real-life" context as a socially indecorous absence of modesty and due deference, if not as a real social threat – the proverbial husband-beating shrew.[32] Isotta's Amazon citations are taken almost verbatim from Justinus, and it is striking that in incorporating Tamyris she herself acknowledges the awkwardly-threatening possibilities of such illustrations. She stops short where Justinus embellishes the story of Cyrus's defeat (exacted by Tamyris to avenge the death of her only son at Cyrus's hands):

> Having hacked off Cyrus' head, Queen Tamyris hurled it into a vat filled with human blood, at the same time exclaiming with cruel venom: "sate yourself with blood, you who were always thirsty and insatiable for it".[33]

---

30   On Borgo see Sabbadini, "Briciole umanistiche", *Vita di Guarino Veronese*, pp. 250–1.

31.   "Volumus in eloquentia aspice Corneliam Grachorum matrem; Amesiam, quae Romano coram populo frequenti concursu prudentissima oratione causam dixit; Affraniam Lucinii Buconis senatoris coniugem, quae easdem causas in foro agitavit. Hortensia nonne hoc idem factitavit? Nonne Sapho mira carminis suavitate manavit? Portiam, Fanniam et reliquas quantis doctissimorum virorum versibus decantatas legimus? Volumus in bello aspice Camillam, quam Turnus, ut ait poeta, tanto honore prosequebatur. Nonne Thomiris regina Scytarum Cirum Persarum regem cum universo exercitu trucidavit, ut ne nuntius quidem tantae cladis superfuerit? Amazones nonne sine viris auxere rem publicam, Marpesia, Lampedo, Orithia maiorem partem Europae subiecerunt, nonnullas quoque sine viris Asiae civitates occupaverunt? Tantum enim virtute et singulari belli scientia pollebant, ut Herculi et Theseo impossibile videretur Amazonum arma regi suo afferre. Pantasilea bello Troiano inter fortissimos Graecos viriliter dimicavit; testis est poeta: "Pantasilea furens mediisque in milibus ardet" [Vigil]. Quod cum ita sit, te rogo, ut me certiorem reddas, si mulieres loquacitate vel potius eloquentia et virtue viros superent?"

32   For a general discussion of the way in which Renaissance literature transformed the "forward" woman into insatiate man-eater and indomitable shrew see my *Still Harping on Daughters: Women and Drama in the Age of Shakespeare* (Brighton, 1983), chapter 4.

Triumphant warrior-women all too easily become voracious, man-eating monsters.

As it happens, Isotta's own fortunes poignantly illustrate the awkward "moral" predicament of the unusually-able, educated woman. (And once again, that awkwardness is common to her personal history and to the secondary literature upon it.) In 1438, a year after Isotta's difficult exchange of letters with Guarino, an anonymous pamphleteer addressed an invective against the vices of Veronese women (a popular brand of formal *vituperatio*).

In it, having lashed out in conventionally-Juvenalian fashion at female immodesty, vanity and promiscuity, he singled out the women of the Nogarola family for special blame. In a passage now much-quoted by feminist historians, he imputes to Isotta a sexual deviancy to match (according to his account) the grotesqueness of her public intellectual self-aggrandizement:

> She who has acquired for herself such praise for her eloquence behaves in ways utterly inconsistent with so much erudition and such a high opinion of herself: although I have long believed the saying of numerous wise men, "the woman of fluent speech [*eloquentem*] is never chaste", which can be supported by the example of the greatest number of learned women ... And lest you are inclined to condone even in the slightest degree this exceedingly loathsome and obscene misconduct, let me explain that before she made her body generally available for uninterrupted intercourse she had first submitted to, and indeed earnestly desired, that the seal of her virginity should be broken by none other than her brother, to make yet tighter her relationship with him. By God! ... [What inversions will the world tolerate], when that woman, whose most filthy lust knows no bounds, dares to boast of her abilities in the finest literary studies.[34]

The charge of incest is, of course, pure libellous invention, although, unfortunately, male scholars since the contemporary Veronese humanist Barbo have seen fit to leap to Isotta's defence as if the accusations were in earnest. The charge that she is *unchaste* challenges the view that as a woman she

---

33   Justinus, *Epitome of Trogus*, I.8.
34   For the text of this invective see A. Segarizzi, "Niccolò Barbo patrizio veneziano del sec. xv e le accuse contro Isotta Nogarola", *Giornale storico della letteratura italiana* XLIII (1904), 39–54; 50–4. "[Ea] que sibi tantam ex dicendi facultate laudem acquisierit, ea agat, que minime cum tanta eruditione et tanta sui existimatione conveniant, quamvis hoc a multis longe sapientissimis viris acceperim: nullam eloquentem esse castam, idque etiam multarum doctissimarum mulierum exemplo comprobari posse. ... Nisi vero hoc nimium sane tetrum atque obscenum scelus sit aliquantulum a te comprobatum quod ante quam corpus suum assiduis connubiis divulgaret primo fuerit passa atque etiam omnino voluerit virginitatis sue specimen non ab alio nisi a fratre eripi hocque modo vincio propiore ligari. Proh deum atque hominum fidem, "quis celum terris non misceat et mare celo" [Juvenal], cum illa, que in tam spurcissima libidine modum sibi non inveniat, audeat se tantum in optimis litterarum studiis iactare." (53) See also Jardine, *Still Harping on Daughters*, 57.

can be a prominent humanist and remain a right living person ("the woman of fluent tongue is never chaste"). It is a studied part of the writer's contention that in Verona women regularly step out of line (are domineering), and that this is evidence of Verona's general decadence and erosion of morals. When Sabbadini maintains, in his account of the Nogarola sisters' importance, that "the fruits of the Verona school . . . issued from the intellects of two Veronese virgins . . . In them for the first time, humanism was married with feminine gentility, especially in the case of Isotta, who remained in this respect unsurpassed", I cannot help thinking that he too bonds Isotta's *chastity* with her acceptability as a humanist. Isotta is "unsurpassed", her hymen intact till death; the bastions of Ginevra's humanist competence were penetrated at her marriage.

When a woman becomes socially visible – visible within the power structure – Renaissance literary convention makes her a sexual predator. One need only compare, for example, Boccaccio's influential Renaissance rendering of Semiramis, the ancient Queen of the Assyrians. Boccaccio celebrates Semiramis amongst "illustrious" women for successfully ruling in her son's place during his minority, thus preserving his patrimony:

> It was almost as if she wanted to show that in order to govern it is not necessary to be a man, but to have courage. This fact heightened that woman's glorious majesty as much as it gave rise to admiration in those who looked upon her.[35]

Then he deftly topples her manly valour into predatory sexuality:

> But with one wicked sin this woman stained all these accomplishments worthy of perpetual memory, which are not only praiseworthy for a woman but would be marvellous even for a vigorous man. It is believed that this unhappy woman, constantly burning with carnal desire, gave herself to many men.[36]

As in the case of Isotta, the heinousness of the sexual offence is intensified by its involving incest. Semiramis, it is claimed, had sexual intercourse with that very son whose power interests she had substituted for (one might remark that as Semiramis seized priority over her first-in-line son, so Isotta publicly obtrudes over her technically "prior" brother).

So the charge against Isotta Nogarola is conventional. But that charge – and the public humiliation of Isotta it effected – does direct our attention to the *problem* of a mature woman who obtrudes herself, in her own right, beyond the bounds of social decorum. Her rank might have entitled her to

35 *De Claris mulieribus*, transl. G. A. Guarino (New Brunswick, 1963), cit. Jardine, *Still Harping on Daughters*, 182.
36 *De claris mulieribus*, Jardine, 99.

be a modest *patron* of learning; it did not entitle her to participate actively within the public sphere.[37] When female patrons of this period write to female humanists it is striking how insistently they dwell on the purely-decorative nature of their scholarly aptitude. Female patron and female scholar alike add lustre (they argue) to male achievement.[38]

Isotta and her family were away from Verona for three years from 1439 to 1441. After their return, Isotta no longer corresponds with other scholars as brilliant student of secular learning ("virilis animi", learned "beyond her sex"). Instead she is "most learned and most religious" (Abel II, 181); "doctissima" becomes "sancta virgo" (Abel II, 96), "dignissima virgo" (Abel II, 39), "pia virgo" (Abel II, 105). Her correspondents extol her for her Christian piety, her deep commitment to sacred letters. And they celebrate her *celibacy* rather than her chaste purity. Not surprisingly, the "illustrious" women with whom she is now compared are Mary and her mother Anna, and the loved woman of the Song of Songs ("Pulchra es amica mea et macula non est in te") (Abel II, 25). There is, indeed, an almost unhealthy insistence, in my view, on the part of Isotta's later male correspondents on the special importance in God's (or their own) eyes of her celibate state as confirmation of the admirable nature of her studiousness (Abel II, 23–7; 96–7; 98–100). Isotta withdrew entirely from public view and became a virtual recluse in her family home (there are signs that her brothers were not entirely delighted with being obliged to support a deliberately celibate sister as well as an aged mother [Abel II, 73–87]).

According to her nineteenth-century biographer Abel, Isotta totally renounced her secular studies, became a mystic and a saint, and devoted the remainder of her life to God. This is a version of events which feminist historians embrace, because it suggests "thwarted ambitions", and the poignancy of a potentially-brilliant career stifled by oppressive patriarchal intervention. But we need to be just as cautious at this point in Isotta's

---

37 The issue of female patrons is an interesting one, and in my view is ripe for investigation. Where women were accidentally in control of *wealth* (through quirks in inheritance law), there appears to have been considerable social encouragement for their directing that wealth towards culture rather than towards power. On the unexpected prominence of noble women with charge of their own wealth in this period, see Jardine, *Still Harping on Daughters*, chapter 3.

38 W. L. Gundersheimer is wrong in thinking that a patron like Eleanora of Aragon did not correspond with female humanists ("her surviving correspondence with nonrelatives is with men", Labalme (ed.), *Beyond Their Sex*, 56). Cassandra Fedele made a point of corresponding with a number of female heads of state, including Eleanora, and the letters received are to be found in Thomasino's edition of her letters. However, the letter from Eleanora to Cassandra (*Epistolae*, 161–2), dated 1488, is conventionally celebratory of Cassandra's chastity/virtue as exemplified by her scholarly abilities. Eleanora associates her own prominence as female patron of learning with Cassandra's as prominent female learned humanist on the grounds that both symbolically ornament the civilized world of Italian (male) city states.

history as at earlier points at which critical prejudice obviously biased its telling. The letter of advice on advanced (secular) logic and philosophy from Quirini with which I opened this paper dates from well after the return to Verona. The letters testifying to Isotta's asceticism, on the other hand, are all those of her "mentor" Ludovico Foscarini (Isotta's letters to him do not survive (Abel I, lvii)). Foscarini's correspondence with Isotta certainly depended for its propriety on the assumption that there could be no carnal involvement intended, so his insistence on Isotta's saintliness and spirituality are part of the strategy for "coping" with a female scholar which it is our business to unravel (even so, Abel claims a passionate love affair between the two (Abel I, lvii–lviii)).[39] The point is, whatever her continuing interest in the *studia humanitatis*, there was no public outlet for Isotta's secular training once she became a mature woman, and there never had been, even before the libel of 1438.

Let me return, now, to my general theme: whether virtue and right living were the direct products of fifteenth-century humanist studies. As I said earlier, the current view of the English-speaking scholarly community is that they were not, that a work like Vergerio's *De ingenuis moribus* "does not lend itself readily to a civic interpretation as formulated by Saitta and Garin, and followed by many recent historians of humanism."[40] But the critics of

---

39   Isotta Nogarola's one major published work was an epistolary dialogue between herself and Ludovico Foscarini entitled *De pari aut impari Evae atque Adae peccato* (a set-piece debate on whether Adam or Eve was the more culpable in the Fall). This, however, does not mean that the case for Isotta's later spirituality and asceticism is proven, since the letters of Heloise and Abelard provide an impeccable model for an exchange of letters between a senior man and a secluded woman strenuously debating the relative culpability of man and woman. It is therefore an eminently suitable form for the single public appearance of the work of a female scholar otherwise debarred from (decorous) public display of her intellectual virtuosity. Although the Renaissance *fortuna* of the Abelard and Heloise letters is cloudy, we do know that Petrarch owned a copy of the medieval "canon" of their exchange. Abel takes it for granted (*a*) that the dialogue between Isotta and Ludovico testifies to the repressed passion between them and (*b*) that it represents the core of Isotta's later preoccupation with spiritual as opposed to secular learning. But it is just as easy to regard the exchange as a virtuoso exercise by an exceptionally talented female debater, in an appropriate "literary" context. For a discussion of some of these problems of "reading" the exchange between Heloise and Abelard see P. Dronke, *Abelard and Heloise in Medieval Testimonies* (Glasgow, 1976), "Heloise and Marianne: Some reconsiderations", *Romanische Forschungen*, 72 (1960), 223–56; Mary Martin McLaughlin, "Peter Abelard and the dignity of women: Twelfth-century 'feminism' in theory and practice", in *Peter Abelard: Pierre le Vénérable* (Paris, 1975). On Isotta's dialogue see P. Gothein, "L'amicizia fra Lodovico Foscarini e l'umanista Isotta Nogarola", *La Rinascita*, 6 (1943), 394–413. As well as describing some of the central arguments of the Adam and Eve dialogue and the further exchanges of letters between Isotta and Ludovico to be found in Abel, Gothein also provides a perfect example of how readily a traditional critic can read spirituality and intense emotional involvement into every line of an exchange between a distinguished public man and a vulnerable secluded woman!

40   D. Robey, "Vittorino da Feltre e Vergerio", in N. Giannetto (ed.), *Vittorino da Feltre e la sua scuola: umanesimo, pedagogia, arti* (Florence, 1981), 241–53; 252.

Saitta and Garin go on to say that if humanism provided an education in grammar and rhetoric which did *not* morally prepare its students for civic life, then it must have been a "pure" intellectual training. When Vergerio writes that liberal studies are a preparation "for every life" and "for every kind of man", they argue, he means that studies are an end in themselves, a way of each individual's realizing his full potential as a human being.

I think that Isotta Nogarola's life shows us that this is not in fact the case. Certainly educators like Vergerio (and it will be remembered that Isotta showed knowledge of Vergerio's treatise in one other letters I used above) insist on the general civilizing effect of the *bonae artes* without specifying either a moral or a civil context to which their training is attached. In other words, the educational programme of the humanist pedagogues is *not* job-specific. But the *value* attached to humanist studies does depend upon a particular ideology, and in this important sense it is firmly tied to its civic context. It is for precisely this reason that Isotta Nogarola failed to "achieve", in spite of having access to humanist studies, as did others who failed to notice the tight interconnectedness between the status of the *bonae artes* as a training and the political establishment and its institutions (other women, and those of inappropriate rank).[41] "Ad omne genus hominum" has to be read out as "for every kind of appropriately well-placed individual of the male gender". "Opportunity", that is, is a good deal more than having ability, and access to a desirable programme of study. It is also being a good social and political *fit* for the society's assumptions about the purpose of "cultivation" as a qualifying requirement for power.

If humanism had been of its nature as tightly "civic" as Garin and his school maintain, then as a woman Isotta Nogarola would never have had the support of the community of distinguished humanist scholars and teachers in her pursuit of humanist studies. But equally, if humanism had really set as its highest goal the pursuit of learning for its own sake, she would not have disappeared so decisively from secular view in the mature years of her life, years in which she continued to excel in those studies. She could continue as excellent student of humanism in private, but she could not be publicly supported as "virtuous" in doing so.

What I am stressing is that the independence of liberal arts education from establishment values is an illusion. The individual humanist is defined in terms of his relation to the power structure, and he is praised or blamed, promoted or ignored, to just the extent that he fulfills or fails to fulfill those terms. It is, that is, a condition of the prestige of humanism in the fifteenth

41   Lauro Martines has been at particular pains to point out the close correlation between social rank and public prominence of the Florentine humanists. See *The Social World of the Florentine Humanists* (Princeton, 1963); *Power and Imagination, passim*. See also Grafton and Jardine, "Humanism", and *From Humanism to the Humanities* (Cambridge, MA, 1986).

century, as Lauro Martines stresses, that "the humanists, whether professionals or noblemen born, were ready to serve [the ruling] class. The most
apolitical of them could be drawn into the political fray".[42]

I have argued that the fortunes of a gifted woman embarked on the
humanist training show vividly how a programme with no explicit employment goals nevertheless presupposes those goals, and how the enterprise of
pursuing secular humanist studies can be regarded as morally laudable (a
"virtuous" undertaking) only where *achieving* that goal is socially acceptable. A woman, as Bruni so eloquently stressed, was not available to be
drawn into the public fray to marshall the morality of humanism in the
service of the state in the fifteenth century. She could not argue politically
in public without appearing indecorous; she could not even *pronounce*
publicly without risking appearing "threateningly insane and requiring
restraint".[43] Study, for her, consigned her to marginality, relegated her to
the cloister. Because she could not enter the public arena, by virtue of her
sex, Isotta Nogarola withdrew, figuratively and emotionally, from public
intellectual intercourse to the nearest thing she could contrive to a secular
cloister, her "book-lined cell".[44]

---

42   Martines, *Power and Imagination*, 295.
43   Having looked at the careers of a number of fifteenth-century educated women, including Cassandra Fedele and Laura Cereta, it is my opinion that *all* celebrated public performances
by female humanists (orations before Emperors and prelates, once-off disputations in the universities, invited lectures, and so forth) are "occasional" rather than professional. That is, an
able woman might be afforded the unusual honour of a public appearance to "show off" her
talent, on the strict understanding that this would not become a regular event. It is striking in
this respect that I have not come across a *single* scholar of the fifteenth century (or of the nineteenth or twentieth) who has suggested that any of these performances by exceptional women
were *not very good* (and some of them are certainly banal). *That* the woman performs is remarkable in itself; *what* they perform is apparently beside the point. For Fedele's orations see
Thomasino, *Cassandrae Fidelis* For Laura Cereta's formal pieces see I. P. Thomasino (ed.),
Laurae Ceretae Brixiensis feminae clarissimae epistolae . . . (Padua, 1640). For a fuller discussion
of humanist education of women and the individual learned women it produced, see Grafton
and Jardine, *From Humanism to the Humanities*.
44   See King, "Book-lined cells", for references to both Matteo Bosso's and Ludovico Foscarini's representation of Isotta Nogarola's study as a "cell", "The religious retreat", 74.

Part VI
Patronage, Art, and Culture

Introduction to Part VI

One of the most distinctive and lasting legacies of Renaissance Italy is its artistic production. Between the fourteenth and sixteenth centuries, painting, sculpture, and architecture transformed the appearance of the Italian cities and created a new visual culture that encompassed both public and private life. While art historians look closely at the iconography of Renaissance works of art, making the world inside the canvas the focal point of analysis, historians are more interested in why artistic endeavors were so fundamental to this society. How did works of art express some of the most fundamental social, political, cultural, and religious values of the Italian Renaissance? Why did Renaissance Italians so value works of art?

The changing nature of artistic patronage offers one answer to these questions. Early Renaissance art was largely a product of civic rather than individual commissions. Taking the case of Florence's Duomo as an example, we can say that a significant portion of the city provided the human and financial resources to build this great cathedral over a century and a half. In the fourteenth and early fifteenth centuries the Italian elite seems to have been relatively uninterested in the details of the paintings they occasional displayed in their homes, save to ensure that these paintings fit the space they had available and used costly ingredients such as gold and lapis lazuli to the extent to which they could afford them. Instead, guilds, confraternities, and city governments sponsored great building and decoration projects, as the famous case of the 1401 competition between Lorenzo Ghiberti and Filippo Brunelleschi to decorate the Baptistery Doors in Florence illustrates. Even commissions initiated by single patrons, such as Masaccio's 1426–27 frescoes for the Brancacci Chapel in Santa Maria del Carmine, often appeared in family chapels attached to large churches so that the entire parish could see a patron's contributions to the community. Many early frescoes reinforced the vision of a society as a corporate entity by painting scenes from the public life of the Renaissance cities – meetings of neighbors in the piazza, marriage processions, the death of children, religious ceremonies, tax collection – often in the guise of illustrating religious themes.

If early Renaissance patronage reflected a collective will to embellish the city with great monuments to God and human ingenuity, later Renaissance patronage became a more direct transaction between patrons and artists, reflecting new forms of social and political organization in the Italian city-states. We can discern this shift even in acts of civic patronage. Cosimo de' Medici may have underwritten the cost of restoring and expanding key churches in Florence such as San Lorenzo, but he did so in relation to his plans to build a lavish family palace in the center of the city. Palazzo Medici advertised Cosimo's power and magnificence not only through what everyone could see – an imposing building designed by Michelozzo – but also because of what many did not see: the paintings by Benozzo Gozzoli in the Medici chapel and Cosimo's splendid collection of antiquities. While civic patronage continued to be an important aspect of Italian Renaissance art, the second half of the fifteenth century witnessed the emergence of a ruling elite who surrounded themselves with art and culture as a statement of their family's wealth and position. A figure such as Cosimo played an active role in the creation of his own legend because he understood that artists and writers would perpetuate his myth during and beyond his own lifetime.

As Melissa Bullard describes in her account of his grandson Lorenzo's activities, no single individual alone determined the outcome of a patronage relationship. Patronage was the most visible aspect of social relations in Renaissance society. It reflected structures of power, but also practices that emphasized the interconnectedness of many different elements of society. Patrons relied on experts for advice about how to design and decorate their palaces and the city as a whole, which artists to support, and what themes to emphasize in the construction of a visual iconography. Many humanists enjoyed an active collaboration with leading artists. Likewise artists often sought out scholars, or became learned themselves, in order to make their art reflect the cultural themes of the day. Botticelli's *Calumny of Apelles* is a famous example of a painting that brought to life a famous description of an ancient painting that one could only read about until Renaissance artists interpreted it on canvas. Leon Battista Alberti had suggested how important it would be to reconstruct this ancient image in his influential *On Painting*, the first treatise to lay out the science and culture of art for a humanist readership. Botticelli's painting responded directly to the need Alberti perceived.

Neither patrons nor their clients single-handedly created the visual culture of Renaissance Italy. To a large degree, patrons shaped the market for art and antiquities, because they increasingly had a taste for such things. They used portraits to commemorate themselves and their family, encouraging artists to render visible the things they valued: learning, wealth, family, and lineage. They collected antiquities and more interpretive paintings and sculptures because such artifacts expressed their delight in learning and conversations about culture. But humanists, artists, and brokers in cultural goods also played an active role in deciding who possessed the objects they created and what they might look like. The most successful artists increasingly felt they had the right to refuse patrons or to resist their efforts to determine the content of their work. They no longer saw themselves as artisans who worked with their hands but as creative producers of the visual language of their society. Leonardo da Vinci's ambivalent relationship with Isabella d'Este is one of many examples where we can see how artists benefited from their new status in society – and from the fact that every Renaissance patron hoped to have a work by a famous master by the end of the fifteenth century. Few, if any, Renaissance artists produced works of art on their own initiative, but this does not mean that they simply depicted what their patrons wanted to see.

The case of Isabella d'Este, as Rose Marie San Juan reveals in her essay, raises interesting questions about the role of women patrons. Raised in the city of Ferrara and tutored by the famous humanist Guarino, the sixteen-year-old Marchesa arrived in Mantua accustomed to thinking of art and culture as some of the most significant pursuits of a Renaissance courtier. But unlike the women described in Castiglione's *Book of the Courtier*, Isabella did not simply manage conversations about culture but took an active role in shaping the cultural life of the Gonzaga court. She carved out a distinct space of her own in the Castello that reflected her desire to become a patron, autonomous of any activities that her husband Francesco Gonzaga might pursue. Inspired by the *studioli* – small, highly decorated retreats of learning and contemplation for rulers – that she had seen created by her great-uncle Leonello in Ferrara and by Federigo da Montefeltro in his palaces in Urbino and Gubbio, Isabella created her own Studiolo and Grotta (a ground level room beneath the Studiolo) and filled them with art and antiquities.

Isabella's aggressive bid to become the leading female patron in Renaissance Italy suggests how powerful this role was within her society. We should certainly compare her with the Medici and other rulers who transformed their palaces and cities into works of art. The fact that she could tell Titian how to paint her portrait suggests a mutual understanding at work in their relationship. Patrons did not exist in the cultural universe of the Renaissance unless their image had been immortalized in painting, commemorative coins, and large statuary. At the same time, artists lacked the means to establish themselves without patronage. The very identity of the Renaissance artist depended upon his or her ability to negotiate with the leading political and cultural figures of Renaissance Italy. The two essays in this section by Melissa Bullard and Rose Marie San Juan offers us excellent case studies of how patronage worked and of the decisions different patrons made in the establishment of "workshops" of culture.

Plate 9 Sandro Botticelli, *Adoration of the Magi* (ca. 1470–5). *Source*: Uffizi Gallery, Florence.

Sandro Botticelli (1445–1510) painted his most famous version of the *Adoration of the Magi* only six years after the death of Cosimo de' Medici (1389–1464) and at the beginning of his grandson Lorenzo's (1449–92) rise to power in Florence in 1469. The Adoration of the Magi was a favorite theme among fifteenth-century Florentines who publicly celebrated the Feast of the Magi; the city government officially recognized the cult of the Magi in 1408. Cosimo was a member of the confraternity of the Magi and often appeared dressed as one the Magi, bearing gifts to the infant Jesus in the ceremonial procession that marked the journey from Jerusalem (either the Baptistery or Palazzo della Signoria) to Bethlehem (the convent of San Marco). Cosimo commissioned Benozzo Gozzoli to depict the Adoration of the Magi on the east wall of the Medici chapel (Palazzo Medici), completed around 1459. The faces of key family members and important political allies looked out at viewers. Botticelli surely must have seen this fresco and decided to renew its significance for a younger generation. In his version, Cosimo presents himself as the oldest king, kneeling before the infant Jesus, while his son Piero appears, clad in a rich red robe, at the front, and his grandson Lorenzo stands to the right of Piero looking down at him. In all likelihood, the robed figure to the far right looking out at the viewers is a self-portrait of Botticelli.

12

Heroes and Their Workshops: Medici Patronage and the Problem of Shared Agency

Melissa Meriam Bullard

Few historical figures have been so mythologized for their cultural patronage as the fifteenth-century Medici, especially Cosimo and his grandson Lorenzo the Magnificent. Contemporaries and near-contemporaries such as Vespasiano da Bisticci in his *Lives of Illustrious Men*, Filarete in his treatise on architecture, Condivi in his biography of Michelangelo, and most notably Vasari in his sixteenth-century *Lives* of the artists, established the verbal *imago* of Medici munificence that has been subsequently enlarged and embellished over the centuries.[1] Vasari's impact has been particularly potent, for both as a wordsmith and as a painter he established images of the early Medici as great patrons of art. Vasari popularized and perhaps originated the familiar legend of how Lorenzo established a school for young sculptors in his garden overseen by master Bertoldo, where the young Michelangelo learned his art while he lodged in the Medici palace.[2]

---

1   Vespasiano da Bisticci, *Lives of Illustrious Men of the XVth Century*, trans. William George and Emily Waters (New York: Harper and Row, 1963), esp. 219–34; Filarete, *Trattato di Archittetura*, ed. Anna Maria Finoli and Liliana Grassi, 2 vols. (Milan: Il Polifilo, 1972), esp. 1:3–4, 2:683–5, 696–8; Ascanio Condivi, *Vita di Michelangelo Buonarotti* (Florence: Rinascimento del Libro, 1927); Giorgio Vasari, *Opere*, ed. Gaetano Milanesi, 9 vols. (Florence: Sansoni, 1878–85).
2   Vasari, *Opere*, 7:141–4. For a critique of Vasari's account, see André Chastel, "Vasari et la légende médicéenne." *Studi Vasariani* (Florence: Sansoni, 1952), 159–67. Recently Caroline Elam has given new credence to the Medici sculpture garden by suggesting its location, but it is altogether another thing to assert, as Vasari does, that Lorenzo had a special school there for young artists. See Elam's paper "Lorenzo's Architectural and Urban Policies," presented at Villa I Tatti, Florence, for the conference "Lorenzo il Magnifico e il suo mondo," June 1992, to be published in the conference acts.

Over time, Medici patronage came to symbolize the remarkable increase in private consumption of the arts in the fifteenth century.[3]

Fascination with Medici patronage continued into the nineteenth century. The tradition was reformulated notably by William Roscoe, who embedded contemporary aristocratic and heroic notions of enlightened despotism in his portrait of Lorenzo as a dedicated promoter of Renaissance culture.[4] Burckhardt knew Roscoe's work, and similar resonances can be found in his *Civilization of the Renaissance*, where Lorenzo figures as an exemplar of the Renaissance individual as a work of art.[5] Burckhardt's emphasis on individualism as a key characteristic of Renaissance culture shaped the following century of interpretation and still retains currency today.

This focus on the centrality of individual Medici in the cultural affairs of the quattrocento has coursed through five hundred years of Renaissance historiography.[6] From the viewpoint of Medici myth, Cosimo and Lorenzo emerge as megapatrons, personally responsible for shaping Florentine culture. That the golden age of the Renaissance in Florence was subsequently identified with the age of Lorenzo the Magnificent demonstrates the power the Medici myth has had in supplying the organizing frame for viewing the history of the period. In addition, Vasari, Roscoe, and Burckhardt, whose writings span more than three centuries, illustrate the persistence of the heroic mode of historiography, which, in regard to patronage, spotlighted great men living in great times and promoting great art and culture.

3   In a series of important articles, Richard A. Goldthwaite has discussed Renaissance art as an aspect of the economics of consumption: "The Empire of Things: Consumer Demand in Renaissance Italy," in F. W. Kent and Patricia Simons, eds., *Patronage, Art, and Society in Renaissance Italy* (Canberra: Humanities Research Centre, and Oxford: Clarendon, 1987), 153–75; "The Economy of Renaissance Italy: The Preconditions for Luxury Consumption," *I Tatti Studies* 2 (1987): 15–39; and now his *Wealth and the Demand for Art in Italy 1300–1600* (Baltimore: Johns Hopkins University Press, 1993).

4   William Roscoe, *The Life of Lorenzo de' Medici Called the Magnificent*, 5th ed. (London: T. Cadell and W. Davies, 1806), 2:237–311.

5   Jacob Burckhardt, *The Civilization of the Renaissance in Italy*, trans. S. G. C. Middlemore (New York: Harper and Row, 1958), 2:319, 381, 425, 491, 515–16.

6   For discussions of the vicissitudes in the posthumous reputation of Lorenzo, see Nicolai Rubinstein, "The Formation of the Posthumous Image of Lorenzo de' Medici," in Edward Chaney and Neil Ritchie, eds., *Oxford, China and Italy: Writings in Honour of Sir Harold Acton on his Eightieth Birthday* (Florence: Passigli, 1984), 94–106; and M. M. Bullard, "The Magnificent Lorenzo de' Medici: Between Myth and History," in Phyllis Mack and Margaret C. Jacob, eds., *Politics and Culture in Early Modern Europe: Essays in Honour of H. G. Koenigsberger* (Cambridge: Cambridge University Press, 1987), 25–58. On Cosimo's image see A. Brown, "The Humanist Portrait of Cosimo de' Medici, Pater Patriae," *Journal of the Warburg and Courtauld Institutes* 24 (1961): 186–221; also A. Fraser Jenkins, "Cosimo de' Medici's Patronage of Architecture and the Theory of Magnificence," *Journal of the Warburg and Courtauld Institutes* 33 (1970): 162–70.

I wish to reexamine the appropriateness of this emphasis on the heroic individual as it relates to our understanding of the role of the Medici as patrons and of Renaissance patronage in general. My approach will be two-pronged, first looking at the problem from the standpoint of recent literature on patronage, and second, considering it in the light of documents from the late fifteenth century. Examination of the historical evidence leads me to propose a workshop, or *bottega*, model for understanding Medici patronage rather than the traditional mythicized, "heroic" one.

I   The Literature on Patronage

Until Ernst Gombrich wrote his provocative, now classic article "The Early Medici as Patrons of Art: A Survey of Primary Sources,"[7] no one had substantially challenged the iconic role of Medici patronage in the history of the period. Gombrich pointed the way toward a more careful assessment of the Medici as patrons based on documentary evidence. He contrasted the rhetorical *amplificatio* of praise showered on the Medici to actual documented commissions and found that Cosimo had been seemingly a more active Maecenas than his more famous grandson Lorenzo: "It comes as a shock of surprise to realize how few works of art there are in existence which can be proved to have been commissioned by Lorenzo."[8] He also suggested that the patronage by all the early Medici had been much more occasional and unplanned and consequently much less monolithic than legend recalls. Thus one of Gombrich's notable contributions was to scale back the accepted range of Medici commissions.

More importantly for present concerns, in his analysis of the language contemporary historians used to describe the Medici as patrons and their relations with artists, Gombrich posited a linguistic explanation for the difference between Cosimo's active support of the arts and Lorenzo's seemingly reduced level of patronage. He suggested that the way contemporaries described commissions changed as the professional status of the artist increased and as his creative authority became more recognized.[9] Thus, for

7   Erust Gombrich, "The Early Medici as Patrons of Art," in E. F. Jacob, ed., *Italian Renaissance Studies* (London: Faber and Faber, 1960), 279–311.

8   Ibid., 304. This realization led Gombrich to suggest that Lorenzo thought of himself more importantly as a connoisseur than as an active patron who commissioned and paid for major works of art (306). Caroline Elam has subsequently argued that, if not in painting and sculpture, at least in the area of architecture, Lorenzo had ambitious plans for urban renewal, which, had he lived longer, might have been executed and thus substantiated his reputation as one of the great patrons of the Renaissance. See her "Lorenzo de' Medici and the Urban Development of Renaissance Florence," *Art History* 1 (1978): 43–66.

9   "The Early Medici as Patrons of Art," 287–311.

example, Michelozzo's role as Cosimo's principal architect was obliterated in the contemporary fifteenth-century literature in which Cosimo stands out as principal *genitor*,[10] whereas by Lorenzo's time at the end of the century, artists such as Michelangelo were accorded more recognition for their independent, artistic genius. Thus, according to this line of reasoning, as artistic genius became valued and praised, the patron was cast more into the role of enabler and less as creator. In the literature that reflected these changes, then, Cosimo figures more directly and prominently as a patron of culture than does Lorenzo. The indirectness of Lorenzo's patronage role, which Gombrich characterized as that of "an arbiter of taste,"[11] appears less surprising when viewed in the context of changes in how artists and patrons were discussed. As I will argue, this problem of language is central to our understanding of all types of Renaissance patronage, although I will be approaching it from a different direction.

Gombrich contended that over the course of the fifteenth century the language used to describe artists and patrons reflected an increase in the professional standing of artists. But was the changing role of the artist the only variable in the patronage equation of the quattrocento? What about the patron? Might the same opacity of language and myth that could hide a Michelozzo beneath Cosimo's cloak, or place Michelangelo as a student in Lorenzo's mythical school, also be obscuring other facets of quattrocento patronage practice? Gombrich did not pursue these implications of his argument, perhaps because the role of the patron is much more difficult to decipher – all the more so since the image of the influential patron accords so neatly with the heroic mode of writing history prevalent since the Renaissance. In Gombrich's own case, despite his critical approach to the language associated with Medici patronage and his call for new accountability based on documentary evidence, the heroic patron still dominated his vision. The actions or absence of action by the principal Medici family members in relation to artists, architects, and writers remained central to his concept of agency in Florentine patronage. And still today, for many students of the period, Florentine culture of the later quattrocento is best described as "Medicean," because they see that culture as reflecting the tastes and personalities of individual Medici.

Today there is much that can be added to Gombrich's critique, for in the years since 1960, when his article was published, we have have the benefit of a whole generation of archival research into patronage questions, plus the findings of historians regarding the larger social context in which both patrons and artists operated. As a result, students of art patronage have been drawn into the debates on social history and the family that raged in

---

10   Ibid., 289. Harriet Caplow has elaborated on this point in her study *Michelozzo* (New York: Garland, 1977), 1:52–9.
11   "The Early Medici as Patrons of Art," 306.

the 1970s and 1980s, and more recently into discussions of political patronage and clientage, or *clientalismo*, a concept that has all but replaced the older terminology of social and economic class as the preferred lens through which to view political, social and economic processes in the Renaissance and their impact on culture.[12] My purpose here is not to rehearse those findings, many of which appear in the publications of recent conferences devoted to patronage at the Folger Library, in Melbourne, and in Hamburg.[13] Rather, it is to consider more specifically how recent research has influenced our understanding of Medici patronage.

One of the notable results of archival digging has been the recognition of significant cultural patronage by members of the wider Medici family other than Cosimo, his son Piero, or Lorenzo. In some cases commissions previously attributed to the major Medici have had to be reassigned. Back in 1908 Herbert Horne was the first to challenge the widely held belief that Lorenzo il Magnifico was the patron of Botticelli's *Primavera*.[14] But despite the evidence, Horne's argument that the painting had belonged instead to the Magnificent's younger cousin, Lorenzo di Pierfrancesco, was not widely accepted until John Pope-Hennessy republished Horne's text with a new introduction.[15] More recently, John Spencer has brought out of the shadows two other Medici from collateral lines who figure prominently as patrons of Andrea del Castagno; one of them, if we may believe Vasari, may have brought the artist as a poor youth to Florence from the Mugello.[16] They are Bernardo d'Antonio (Bernardetto) and Orlando di Guccio de' Medici, six generations remote both from each other and from Cosimo's line.[17] Today, the term Medici patronage is no longer restricted to Cosimo and his direct

12   It is helpful to bear in mind the distinction in Italian between *mecenatismo* and *clientalismo*, or between patronage of the arts and political patronage, both of which are loosely covered in the English term patronage. See Gary Ianziti's helpful discussion, "Patronage and the Production of History: The Case of Quattrocento Milan," in *Patronage, Art, and Society*, 299–311.

13   For the Folger conference, see Guy Fitch Lytle and Stephen Orgel, eds., *Patronage in the Renaissance* (Princeton: Princeton University Press, 1981); for the Melbourne conference, see *Patronage, Art and Society*; for the Hamburg conference, see Bruce T. Moran, ed., *Patronage and Institutions: Science, Technology, and Medicine at the European Court 1500–1750* (Rochester, NY: Boydell, 1991).

14   The original title published by George Bell and Sons in 1908 was *Alessandro Filipepi, Commonly Called Sandro Botticelli, Painter of Florence*. It was republished with a new introduction by John Pope-Hennessy under the title *Botticelli, Painter of Florence* (Princeton: Princeton University Press, 1980). See especially pp. 49–51; 148–52.

15   Ibid. Also instrumental was John Shearman's publication of the inventories of Lorenzo and Giovanni di Pierfrancesco in "The Collections of the Younger Branch of the Medici," *Burlington Magazine* 117 (1975): 12–27. My thanks to Caroline Elam for information on this point.

16   John R. Spencer, *Andrea del Castagno and His Patrons* (Durham, NC: Duke University Press, 1991), 2–3.

17   Ibid., appendix 3, 138–9.

descendants, but must be understood to involve other family members, including Medici women, who actively promoted contemporary culture.

Consanguinity, even that as remote as Bernardo's and Guccio's from Cosimo, has also been revalued in recent discussions of the Renaissance notion of the family. Florentine *ricordanze* from the quattrocento reveal a highly developed sense of lineage and family that reached back to distant ancestors and extended forward into future generations.[18] In regard to artistic patronage, this valency of family expressed itself most clearly in family chapels. Patricia Simon's masterful study of the Tornabuoni Chapel in Santa Maria Novella shows how Ghirlandaio's frescoes were intended to celebrate the whole Tornaquinci *consorteria*, not just the patron Giovanni Tornabuoni and his immediate kin.[19] In another study, Caroline Elam has contrasted the nature of Cosimo de' Medici's patronage in the church of San Lorenzo with that of his father, Giovanni di Bicci. Giovanni initiated the family's involvement as one among a number of chapel patrons in the church. Cosimo, however, took unprecedented de facto control of the financing and reconstruction of the whole church.[20] The high-profile, individualistic character of Cosimo de' Medici's role at San Lorenzo could be interpreted as appropriate to the "heroic" type of patron, intent upon securing his personal fame for eternity. This impression lessens, however, when Cosimo's actions are considered within the larger context of his desire to continue a family tradition of patronage in the church and to memorialize thereby not only himself but his broader kin group, past, present, and future. Social history has thus modified the heroic view of history and of Renaissance patronage by emphasizing the importance of dense, overlapping social networks made up of kinship, friendship, and neighborhood, which circumscribed and informed the actions of individuals, even the Medici.[21] In that close atmosphere, how Renaissance patronage operated becomes a more complex problem.

18   On the importance of *ricordanze* for developing a sense of intergenerational kinship, see Christiane Klapisch-Zuber, " 'Parenti, amici, vicini': Il territorio urbano d'una famiglia mercantile nel XV secolo," *Quaderni storici* 33 (1976): 953–82, republished as " 'Kin, Friends, and Neighbors': The Urban Territory of a Merchant Family in 1400," in *Women, Family, and Ritual in Renaissance Italy* (Chicago: University of Chicago Press, 1985), 68–93. On special regard for ancestors, see F. W. Kent, *Household and Lineage in Renaissance Florence* (Princeton: Princeton University Press, 1977) 252–78.
19   "Patronage in the Tornaquinci Chapel, Santa Maria Novella, Florence," in *Patronage, Art, and Society*, 221–50.
20   Caroline Elam, "Cosimo de' Medici and San Lorenzo," in Francis Ames-Lewis, ed., *Cosimo 'il Vecchio' de' Medici, 1389–1464* (Oxford: Clarendon, 1992), 157–50. Elam also notes a further evolution under Cosimo's son Piero, who exercised complete *ius patronatus* over the remaining patronage rights inside the church (176).
21   See n. 18 above. See also F. W. Kent and Dale Kent, *Neighbours and Neighbourhood in Renaissance Florence* (Locust Valley, NY: J. J. Augustin, 1982); Ronald F. E. Weissman, "The

Paradoxically, while social historians have been deemphasizing the heroic by articulating the wider social context of patronage, other historians, concerned primarily with questions of power, have reintroduced a variant of the heroic. These scholars point out that contemporary culture sustains patterns of dominance, especially when skilled political operators and image crafters such as the Medici use it deliberately as an instrument of power. Ritual as a method of social control and art for the sake of politics are all themes that have been developed in relationship to Florence under the Medici.[22] Studies of political patronage and clientage, borrowing methods and terminology from anthropology to explicate systems of control, have subsumed artistic patronage or *mecenatismo* under the notion of power highly centralized at the top in the hands of a *signore* or prince.[23] Werner Gundersheimer found in the "big man" system described by Mary Douglas a model for Renaissance patronage that seemed to fit the situation in Ferrara under the Este.[24] Others have applied variations of the "big man" theory to Florence under the Medici, likening Cosimo and Lorenzo to city bosses, who, by operating vast patronage networks and manipulating communal institutions, maintain their dominance in the city.[25]

But the implication inherent in such an approach is that it defines patronage and culture solely in terms of the "big man" himself and encourages a top-down view of society. Viewed from the top in this way, all Florentine culture becomes either Medicean or, by extension, anti-Medicean;

Importance of Being Ambiguous: Social Relations, Individualism, and Identity in Renaissance Florence," in Susan Zimmerman and Ronald F. E. Weissman, eds., *Urban Life in the Renaissance* (Newark: University of Delaware Press, 1989), 269–80; and F. W. Kent with Patricia Simons, "Renaissance Patronage: An Introductory Essay," in *Patronage, Art and Society*, 1–21.

22   For a general discussion of Florentine ritual and its political uses, see Richard C. Trexler, *Public Life in Renaissance Florence* (New York: Academic Press, 1980). On Lorenzo's political use of image and culture, see my "Lorenzo de' Medici: Anxiety, Image Making, and Political Reality in the Renaissance," in Gian Carlo Garfagnini, ed., *Lorenzo de' Medici Studi* (Florence: Olschki, 1992), 3–40. For the sixteenth-century Medici, see Janet Cox-Rearick, *Dynasty and Destiny in Medici Art* (Princeton: Princeton University Press, 1984).

23   See Ianziti, "Patronage and the Production of History."

24   Gundersheimer, "Patronage in the Renaissance: An Exploratory Approach," in *Patronage in the Renaissance*, 3–23. esp. 13.

25   Nicolai Rubinstein, *The Government of Florence under the Medici, 1434–1494* (Oxford: Clarendon, 1966); Anthony Molho, "Cosimo de' Medici: *Pater Patriae* or *Padrino?*" *Stanford Italian Review* 1 (1979):5–33; Dale Kent, "The Dynamic of Power in Cosimo de' Medici's Florence," in *Patronage, Art and Society*, 63–77; Alison Brown, "Public and Private Interest: Lorenzo, the Monte and the Seventeen Reformers," in *Lorenzo de' Medici Studi*, 103–65; F. W. Kent, "Palaces, Politics, and Society in Fifteenth-Century Florence," *I Tatti Studies* 2 (1987); 41–70. More recently, Kent has discussed the nature of Lorenzo's patronage powers in "Patron–Client Networks in Renaissance Florence and the Emergence of Lorenzo as '*Maestro' della Bottega*," in Bernard Toscani, ed., *Lorenzo de' Medici: New Perspectives*, Studies in Italian Culture: Literature in History, 13 (New York: Peter Lang, 1994), 279–314.

the art and literature of the day become vast repositories of Medici emblems and propaganda; older civic traditions are seen to have been taken over and molded to serve Medici purposes; and so on. Florence becomes truly "Medicean" when viewed from the top of a Medici patronage system, and I suggest that such a view point does not significantly enlarge our understanding of the complexities of quattrocento society. It merely outfits the traditional mythicized patron/hero in the new garb of anthropology.

We have now reached the heart of the matter. What happens if we abandon the top-down view and the "big man" perspective and look from the bottom up? How does our understanding of Medici patronage change if viewed from the bottom or the side? What other facets of the workings of Medici patronage, both artistic and political, are revealed by inverting our perspective? Let us return to the sources and see what evidence exists for a different reading.

II The Documentary Evidence

The Medici correspondence, which contains thousands of letters written to members of the family, many expressing devotion, offers an excellent testing ground for what a bottom-up perspective can reveal about the workings of patronage. Letters requesting influence and positions offer prime evidence of how gifts were traded for favors, political support exchanged for offices, and so forth. Dale Kent, in her study of Cosimo's rise to power, relied heavily upon such letters to establish who belonged to the Medici "party." F. W. Kent has used similar kinds of evidence in analyzing Lorenzo's position, which he has characterized as boss or *maestro* of Florence.[26] In their letters to Lorenzo, people would often refer to themselves as his "faithful servant" or even "slave." One man went so far as to declare, "I have God in Heaven, and Your Magnificence on earth."[27] Viewed from the top and taken at face value, the obsequious language in some of these letters, comparing Lorenzo to the sun or to a god, would seem to indicate that contemporaries did indeed see

---

26   Dale Kent, *The Rise of the Medici: Faction in Florence 1426–1434* (Oxford: Oxford University Press, 1978); F. W. Kent, "Patron–Client Networks."
27   "Sono vostro fattore et vostro fedele servitore," Nofri Tornabuoni to Lorenzo, 4 March 1490, Archivio di Stato, Firenze, Mediceo avanti il Principato (hereafter ASF, MAP), 41, no. 116; "El Ciampolini vi resta schiavo per quelle lettere vi schrivesti e fate chonto che tutto quello le chapiterà di bono sarà vostro e un dì v'a salterà chon farvi un presente di qualche iacciera," Nofri Tornabuoni to Lorenzo, 3 March 1487, ASF, MAP, 52, no. 32; "perché io' o iddio in celo et Vostra Magnificentia in terra, et benché la qualità mia non sia di poterlo mostrare, almeno con la buona volontà et ll'opera siano quelle l'anno a dimostrare," Giovanni Tornabuoni to Lorenzo, 20 November 1487, ASF, MAP, 40, no. 180. For similar expressions of devotion addressed to Cosimo, see Dale Kent, *The Rise of the Medici*, 84–7.

themselves embedded within a hierarchy as links on a vertical chain leading up to the Medici.[28]

But the language of deference is not transparent and can be misleading. It does not ipso facto substantiate the view that contemporary social reality was structured according to a clear hierarchy. As John Pocock has argued, deferential forms of address were quite common in republican cultures, where at the same time citizens were jealously defensive of their prerogatives and rights vis-à-vis authority.[29] The idiom of deference also conforms to contemporary practices of supplication and prayer, where the petitioner verbally humbles himself before God or a saint in order to attract attention and gain assistance.[30] Such linguistic practices in church ritual probably date back to language associated in Roman times with the *patria potestas* and to feudal law.[31] By the fifteenth century, however, this language did not accurately reflect the more limited prerogatives of Renaissance patrons, no matter how august.[32]

The fact that persons addressed the Medici in fawning language does not mean that they necessarily regarded themselves as lifelong inferiors. Many times deferential forms of address were adopted for a particular occasion. Lorenzo's correspondence contains many examples of such occasionality wherein some of the most slavish expressions of devotion emerge from the pens of men who had little need to use such language. Take for example Giovanni Tornabuoni, author of one of the above-mentioned examples of deferential address. Here was a man who was himself from an old and important Florentine family, fully Lorenzo's social equal. Moreover, he was

28   F. W. Kent has summarized this view by characterizing the Medici's role as follows: "In Florence, members of the Medici family became the biggest of Big Men, around whom, in the analyses of Dale Kent and others, lesser lights shone and moved, and chains of 'satellites' formed"; "Renaissance Patronage," in *Patronage, Art and Society*, 5.

29   J. G. A. Pocock, "The Classical Theory of Deference." *American Historical Review* 81 (1976): 516–23. See also Richard W. Davis, "Deference and Aristocracy in the Time of the Great Reform Act." *American Historical Review* 81 (1976): 532–9. On a "deference community" and the interpretive problems inherent in taking historical information too much at face value, see D. C. Moore, "Social Structure, Political Structure, and Public Opinion in Mid-Victorian England," in Robert Robson, ed., *Ideas and Institutions of Victorian Britain: Essays in Honour of George Kitson Clark* (London: Bell, 1967), 20–57.

30   On the origins of saints' cults and their intercessory power, see Peter Brown, *The Cult of the Saints: Its Rise and Function in Latin Christianity* (Chicago: University of Chicago Press, 1981).

31   See W. K. Lacey, "*Patria Potestas*," in Beryl Rawson, ed., *The Family in Ancient Rome: New Perspectives* (London: Croom Helm, 1986), 121–44. On ties between Roman practices and Renaissance patronage, see Ronald Weissman, "Taking Patronage Seriously: Mediterranean Values and Renaissance Society," in *Patronage, Art, and Society*, 25–46, esp. 33–7.

32   On the difficulties of using legal documents and terminology to write social history, see Thomas Kuehn, *Law, Family and Women: Toward a Legal Anthropology of Renaissance Italy* (Chicago: University of Chicago Press, 1991), 1–12 and passim.

the brother of Lucrezia Tornabuoni, and hence Lorenzo's maternal uncle. In addition, he was Lorenzo's longtime business partner in Rome, who in fact had more of his own money invested in the Rome bank than did Lorenzo, and to whom Lorenzo owed a great deal personally as well as financially.[33] Yet despite these multiple ties of family, social position, and business interests, on this occasion, Tornabuoni still compared Lorenzo to his god on earth, "I have God in heaven and Your Magnificence on earth." Clearly, given their personal relationship, Tornabuoni would hardly think of Lorenzo as near divinity or even as vastly superior to himself. Also, he did not always use this kind of flattering language with his nephew. Here the context is important. In this letter, written in 1487, Tornabuoni was expressing his delight at the news that Lorenzo had signed the contract they negotiated renewing their business partnership in terms very favorable to Tornabuoni, Lorenzo's signature on the contract also reaffirmed his commitment to the Rome company and enhanced its prospects for success.[34] Deference was the available idiom in which Tornabuoni could disclose his considerable emotion at the good news.[35] Language expressing affinity or devotion could, in fact, be used quite flexibly, even in describing feelings for one's relatives. As Bernardo Rucellai once wittily remarked regarding a cousin, "I am a kinsman to Piero di Cardinale [only] when it is necessary."[36]

The other two examples of deferential language cited above were drawn from letters in which the writers were thanking Lorenzo for honoring certain patronage requests, in one case for selecting his name for high office, in the second at receipt of a flattering letter. Seen from the bottom up, these instances, among countless others, show petitioners who had managed to instrumentalize their Medici patron to get what they wanted. In patronage

---

33 In a proposal to reorganize the Medici bank dating from the mid 1480's, of the total capital of 24,000 ducats, Lorenzo's share is 9,000 ducats, whereas that of Giovanni Tornabuoni is 15,000 ducats; ASF, MAP, 83, no. 19.

34 For Giovanni Tornabuoni's role as manager of the Medici bank in Rome, see Raymond de Roover, *The Rise and Decline of the Medici Bank 1397–1494* (New York: Norton, 1966), 218–24. Tornabuoni's profits from his years in Rome allowed him, among other things, to commission the Ghirlandaio frescoes in the altar chapel of Santa Maria Novella in Florence.

35 The fuller context of the passage in question is as follows: "Et veramente non ne siate chanbiato perché io o iddio in celo et Vostra Magnificentia in terra et benché la qualità mia non sia dì poterlo mostrare, almeno con la buona volontà et Il'opera siano quelle l'anno a dimostrare"; ASF, MAP, 40, no. 180. In November 1487, when this letter was written, Lorenzo's wife Clarice and son Piero had accompanied his daughter Maddalena to Rome to meet her new husband. Francescherro Cibo, son of Pope Innocent VIII. The Medici *brigati* was making a very favorable impression at the papal court, and Tornabuoni expected the bank to benefit from the newly cemented ties between Lorenzo and the pope. For a discussion of the significance of the Medici *parentado* with the pope, see my "In Pursuit of *Honore et Utile*: Lorenzo de' Medici and Rome." in Gian Carlo Garfagnini, ed., *Lorenzo il Magnifico e il suo mondo* (Florence: Olschki, 1993), 73–85.

36 ASF, MAP, 48, no. 254, as cited by F. W. Kent, *Household and Lineage*, 297.

letters, even those containing the most sycophantic expressions, the initiative typically belonged with the supplicant, who by the very act of petitioning his chosen patron was structuring and defining the terms of their relationship and seeking to control its outcome in the form of favors granted or an office obtained.

Part of the art of supplication entailed convincing the patron of his or her obligation to help the client and creating a sense of shared expectation for the successful outcome of the appeal. This might be done through rehearsing a history of patronage connections between them or their families, reference to particular services rendered, flattery, or a bald appeal to the emotions. When the humanist Alessandro Cortesi sought Lorenzo's help in obtaining a benefice, he incorporated most of these elements in his appeal: "Having been born and brought up under his [Lorenzo's] protection and having seen how His Excellency elevated the estate of my brother in the secular world, it does not seem unreasonable to ask him to elevate me in the ecclesiastical sphere, especially if I go to Naples where benefices abound and where it is customary to distribute them on the recommendations of such *signori*."[37]

Verbally, Cortesi located himself under Lorenzo's lifelong protection with its implicit obligations of assistance; he appealed to the precedent of Lorenzo's patronage of his brother; he flattered Lorenzo with appropriate terms of deference; and even compared his influence to those great Neapolitan barons and *signori* elsewhere, whose personal control of the ecclesiastical *ius patronatus* was legendary. Lorenzo had few of the actual powers attributed to him by Cortesi, and his influence in church appointments outside of Tuscany was at best indirect. But by creating a verbal fiction of those powers in his letter, Cortesi hoped to prod Lorenzo to act in his behalf.

The language of deference and the rhetoric of implied obligation are closely linked. Even someone like Marsilio Ficino, who in his later years kept an ethical distance from Lorenzo,[38] was not above using the tactic of the emotional appeal in requesting aid for the orphaned children of his deceased brother under his care. "Indeed, Lorenzo, philosophy bids me to be content to live on that which I once received from you. But the nephews in my house truly cannot be satisfied with so little."[39] Once again the request was artfully structured to appeal to Lorenzo's sense of duty to help an old

37   Cited in M. M. Bullard, "Marsilio Ficino and the Medici," in Timothy Verdon and John Henderson, eds., *Christianity and the Renaissance: Image and Religious Imagination in the Quattrocento* (Syracuse, NY: Syracuse University Press, 1990), 483 and 491, n. 59.

38   R. Fubini, "Ficino e il Medici all'avvento di Lorenzo il Magnifico," *Rinascimento*, ser. 2, 24 (1984): 3–52.

39   *Supplementum Ficinianum*, ed. Paul Oskar Kristeller, 2 vols. (Florence: Olschki, 1973), 1:57.

family friend, in this case by supplementing the small stipend Ficino received from the church of San Cristoforo.

A more modern and humorous example can illustrate further the point that in a patronage relationship, agency resides not solely with the patron, but also with the client. In a recent "Blondie" cartoon Dagwood and his boss, Mr. Dithers, are having lunch in a restaurant. Dagwood says, "Boss, it's good for us to have lunch like this. For the moment at least we're not boss and employee. We're just two men hanging out together." Mr. Dithers replies, "By golly, you're right!" Dithers then turns to the waiter and says, "Separate checks, please."[40] By ceasing to use the conventional deferential language appropriate to the employee–boss hierarchy and adopting instead a language of equality, Dagwood unintentionally releases Mr. Dithers from his patronal obligation to pay for his lunch. The unwelcome results of Dagwood's action notwithstanding, the primary agency in this cartoon sketch of a patron–client encounter belongs to Dagwood, the client, and not Dithers, the boss.

Read in this way, petitions demonstrate how agency is initiated and defined by the client and only subsequently shared with the patron who thereafter does or does not act as solicited. Letters of request, viewed from the standpoint of the petitioner, cast the patron more in the role of enabler and less in that of autonomous creator in a way parallel to that suggested by Gombrich in characterizing Cosimo's and Lorenzo's art patronage against the background of the increasing status of artists as reflected in the contemporary rhetoric associated with artistic professionalization.

As these examples of the rhetorical aspects of petitions illustrate, language does not always accurately reflect experience. Rather, it constructs and molds perception. Language can also obscure aspects of existence. The language of deference creates an overstated impression of hierarchy and submission to the "big man." And in so doing it obscures an actuality that was undoubtedly more tangled and complex. Rather than conceiving of Renaissance patronage as a vertical social configuration, we might more accurately describe it, like language itself, as a very flexible medium of negotiation in which agency was shared among various participants.

III   The Workshop

These two ideas of patronage as negotiation and patronage involving shared agency provide the keys to what I would like to propose as an alternate way of regarding Medici patronage, whether in the arts or in the realm of politics. My interpretation centers around the concept of the workshop,

---

40   This syndicated episode of "Blondie" by Young and Drake appeared in the *Durham (NC) Herald-Sun* on 13 October 1992.

or *bottega*, a common enough contemporary term whose roots go back to artisan tradition and corporate guild practices of medieval cities.[41] In fifteenth-century Florence, *botteghe* continued to have a lively existence, particularly among artists and sculptors, most of whom learned their skills as apprentices in a master's shop before setting up their own ateliers. The workshop organization promoted both collaboration and communication, or in other words, shared agency and negotiation.

The importance of the workshop has been seriously underplayed in the historiography of the Renaissance in general and in all aspects of patronage in particular. Very few studies spring to mind that have had collaboration as their focus. Notable exceptions are the volume of studies that Wendy Sheard and John Paoletti edited in 1978 in memory of Charles Seymour, which emphasized "patterns of group functioning" in the production of art as opposed to competition among artists; Margaret Haines's investigation of corporate patronage in the Florentine *duomo*; and a recent exhibition in Florence, part of the fifth centenary celebrations of Lorenzo de' Medici's death, entitled *Maestri e botteghe*.[42]

This neglect of collaboration has resulted from the overemphasis on the heroic individual that has characterized centuries of Renaissance historiography, but that especially grew out of the nineteenth-century notion of individualism and single agency. One brief example, which happily underscores the affinities between fifteenth- and nineteenth-century treatments of patrons and artists, was pointed out by Harriet Caplow in her study of Michelozzo, referred to above as the designer of many of Cosimo de' Medici's architectural commissions. As previously noted, fifteenth-century accounts of Cosimo's patronage fail to mention who his architect was, and Michelozzo's name emerges only in Vasari's *Lives* a century later. But in the nineteenth century, the high-water mark of the heroic, Michelozzo was again obscured by the figure of Cosimo, and was only resurrected, hopefully to stay, in the later twentieth century.[43] The same nineteenth-century heroic mindset automatically assigned the patronage of Botticelli's *Primavera* and *Birth of Venus* to Lorenzo the Magnificent.[44]

---

41   See John Najemy, *Corporatism and Consensus in Florentine Electoral Politics, 1280–1400* (Chapel Hill: University of North Carolina Press, 1982), 15–16 on how normative vocabulary drawn from everyday experience helps shape political behavior and ideas, so that "the meaning of events was built into the language and structure of the institutions themselves."

42   Wendy Stedman Sheard and John T. Paoletti, eds., *Collaboration in Italian Renaissance Art* (New Haven: Yale University Press, 1978); Margaret Haines, "Brunelleschi and Bureaucracy: The Tradition of Public Patronage at the Florence Cathedral," *I Tatti Studies* 3 (1989): 89–126 (in this same volume, pp. 235–79, see also William E. Wallace, "Michelangelo at Work: Bernardino Basso, Friend, Scoundrel and Capomaestro"); Mina Gregori et al., eds., *Maestri e botteghe: Pittura a Firenze alla fine del Quattrocento* (Florence: Silvana, 1992).

43   Caplow, *Michelozzo*, 52–9.

44   The earliest reference Horne found to those erroneous attributions was in an 1886 article by Sir Joseph Crowe in the *Gazette des Beaux Arts*; *Botticelli*, 49.

As I have argued earlier, part of the legacy of the heroic includes the practice of highlighting the contributions of individual patrons or master artists in shaping the culture of the day. This emphasis shades out the many other persons who materially contributed to what the patron or master has received credit for in the literature. How many works of art presently attributed exclusively to a famous artist also incorporate other workshop hands? How many scholars have been so absorbed by the difficult task of identifying the various hands present in a painting or altarpiece that they have lost sight of the collaborative nature of the work? To be sure, a few artists' contracts in the fifteenth century stipulated that only the master was to execute a commission, but that in itself is evidence of how prevalent the workshop mode of production was in the Renaissance and an indication that we need to take it much more seriously.[45]

The *bottega* as a metaphor for collaboration in the creation of culture finds its clearest illustration in the arts, where workshops produced tangible products such as paintings, sculptures, or buildings. But I would like to use the metaphor more broadly to enlarge our understanding of Medici patronage in general, and especially in areas not traditionally associated with workshop organization such as diplomacy, policymaking, and even letter writing.

One might well wonder how someone like Cosimo de' Medici, or particularly Lorenzo the Magnificent, managed to accomplish all that he did in a given day and still find time to sleep. How did Lorenzo oversee the government of Florence, act as arbiter among the states of Italy, entertain foreign dignitaries and ambassadors, field the crush of petitioners who crowded around him wherever he went; spend four or five hours a day on his correspondence, write poetry, hold his own in highbrow exchanges with the leading intellectuals of his day, design buildings, put together an exceptional collection of antiquities and rare manuscripts, enjoy the country air at his villa retreats and spas far away from the press of urban affairs, suffer debilitating attacks of gout in intense pain for days at a time, run a huge household and stable, and oversee a troubled international banking empire that required his constant attention? Certainly Lorenzo was a man of rare intelligence and ability, for which his reputation is well deserved. But the answer to how he accomplished all the activities attributed to him is simply that he had a lot of help, a kind of workshop, in fact, in which secretaries, friends, and agents collaborated with him. Together they generated many of the attributes upon which the historical reputation of the multitalented Lorenzo the Magnificent rests.

---

45   On the *sua mano* stipulation found in a number of Renaissance artists' contracts and its uncertain significance, see Hannelore Glasser, *Artists' Contracts of the Early Renaissance* (New York: Garland, 1977), 73–9.

The writing of Lorenzo's letters dramatically illustrates how the concept of shared agency, already discussed in terms of petitions, can also be applied to other areas of his activities as patron, as politician, and as statesman. One of the ironies of the emerging edition of Lorenzo's letters is how few of the nearly two thousand extant letters were actually written or even signed in Lorenzo's own hand.[46] The overwhelming majority of Lorenzo's personal letters was composed by secretaries, sometimes on the basis of a verbal outline or dictated sketch. Other times Lorenzo delegated the task entirely, and the resulting letter carrying Lorenzo's name was drawn from a secretary's own understanding of Medici policy.[47] An example of how the secretaries' workshop functioned is contained in the postscript to a letter Lorenzo, or more accurately, his secretary Piero Dovizi, composed at Poggio a Caiano and sent to another secretary, Niccolò Michelozzi, in Florence. The body of the letter contains a policy analysis of a pending alliance between Milan and Genoa and gives suggestions as to how the Otto di Pratica, the Florentine foreign office, might respond to Milan so as to ensure that Florentine interests in Liguria were not compromised. In the postscript, which Dovizi signed in his own name, he wrote the following. "Ser Nic[c]olò. I have written this [letter] along the lines Lorenzo instructed me, which however, I cannot express exactly as he would. The effect is the same [however], and you will understand it completely. Make sure the Otto comprehends it, and, if they so please, they can explain and amplify it to Stefano [Taverna Milanese ambassador]. Using your [customary] prudence, you can do the same with the members of the Otto. [Signed,] Ser Piero."[48]

---

46   To date, six volumes of Lorenzo's letters have been published in a critical edition with historical commentary: Lorenzo de' Medici, *Lettere*, ed. R. Fubini et al. (Florence: Giunti Barbera, 1977–90).

47   Lorenzo frequently delegated responsibility for decisionmaking to his secretary Niccolò Michelozzi, as illustrated in two brief letters he wrote on 12 September 1487 from his villa at Spedaletto: "Questo da Montepulciano è stato qui a me richiedendomi di favore costì per potere ribandire alcuni. . . . Voleva da me lettere alla Signoria, et a me è parso dirizarle a te acciò che tu intenda se la cosa è factibile, et secondo che s'è consiglato ti governa," Biblioteca Nazionale di Firenze (hereafter BNF), Ginori Conti, 29, 129, III, 17; "Tu intenderai questi hebrei che sono venuti insino qui per avere lettere da me in beneficio loro; et perché mi pare la cosa di che mi hanno parlato um poco rematicha, non ho voluto scrivere ad altri che a te perché et discretamente te ne governi et secondo la natura della cosa vegha di satisfare a costoro, purché in qualche parte di te restino contenti,"Sotheby sale, 1978, lot 265. Both letters were written and signed by another secretary, Piero Dovizi.

48   "Ser Nic[c]olò. Io ho scripto questa in su l'argine secondo la commissione di Lorenzo, la quale non posso havere expressa come harebbe dectato lui. Lo effecto è certo, el quale so che intenderete benissimo. Fatelo intendere agli Octo, et piacendo loro come intendete, lo distendino poi a Stefano nel parlare più largamente. Voi anchora per la prudentia vostra farete il medesimo a cotesti 8. Ser Piero," postscript to letter of Lorenzo to Niccolò Michelozzi, 18 January 1487, BNF, Ginori Conti, 29, 129, II, 9.

The involvement of the secretaries went beyond elaborating verbal outlines or sketches provided by Lorenzo. They seem to have been closely
engaged in formulating the content of many of his letters as well. Most
likely, Lorenzo was in the habit of discussing issues with them. Obviously,
given the sheer volume of his correspondence, he could not attend to every
detail personally.[49] Sometimes he delegated responsibility entirely, as in the
case when he left to Niccolò Michelozzi the sticky task of sorting out a solution to a dispute in which both parties had appealed separately to him.[50]
Early drafts of Lorenzo's letters that exist in chancery copies reveal considerable rewriting, strikeouts and emendations, sometimes in different hands,
which is further indication of the collaborative character of the enterprise
that engaged Lorenzo and his secretaries in handling his copious correspondence.[51] Similarly, I have argued elsewhere that a characteristically
Florentine approach to diplomacy evolved in the same *bottega* fashion
through frequent conversations and exchanges of letters among Lorenzo,
his secretaries, Florentine officials, and the ambassadors.[52]

The fact that Lorenzo had secretaries and helpers to whom he delegated
tasks is no news to anyone. Most people in positions of great responsibility
do. My point is, however, to draw attention to the extent to which these
helpers themselves formulated plans and policies attributed historically
to Lorenzo alone. At the risk of overdrawing the argument to clarify it,
Lorenzo the Magnificent, hero of history and "big man" in the historiography of patronage, was, in part, a committee.

49   In a letter to Michelozzi dated 20 June 1487, Lorenzo commented that he was stupified
("mi sbigottì") by the huge bundle of letters Michelozzi has forwarded to him; BNF, Ginori Conti,
19, 129, III, 14.

50   "Quello che desidero in effecto è [che né] all'uno né all'altro sia facto torto, et se bene cias-
cuno dirà a proposito suo, è bene inten [dere] la verità da altri et rapportarsi a quelli. Tu farai
intendere quello che giudicherai essere bene a proposito della compositione di questa cosa, et
governatene discretamente," Lorenzo to N. Michelozzi, 14 June 1487, BNF, Ginori Conti, 129,
III, 12.

51   Sometimes parts of letters were penned by different secretaries. Both Piero Dovizi and
Niccolò Michelozzi wrote Lorenzo's letter to G. Lanfredini of 21 August 1487, Nantes, Bibliothèque Municipale, Ms. 670, n. 134. Another letter to Lanfredini, dated 22 July 1487, which
exists in a chancery copy, shows considerable rewriting in Piero Dovizi's hand; ASF, MAP, 89,
no. 327. Photographs of selected Medici letters illustrating different secretaries' hands can be
found at the end of each volume of the *Lettere*. For example, the *minuta* of Lorenzo's autograph
letter in Latin to Ficino of 22 September 1474, *Lettere*, 2:35–40, contains numerous corrections in the hand of Niccolò Michelozzi, which can be seen in the photograph in plate 3 of the
volume.

52   See my articles "The Language of Diplomacy in the Renaissance," in *Lorenzo de' Medici:
New Perspectives*, 263–78, and "Lorenzo de' Medici and Patterns of Diplomatic Discourse
in the Late Fifteenth Century," to be published by the University of London in a volume from
the 1992 conference at the Warburg Institute and Warwick University entitled "Lorenzo the
Magnificent: Culture and Politics in Medicean Florence."

To illustrate the point further, let us consider the collections of antiquities and gems for which Lorenzo is deservedly famous. Into some of these rarities he had his own name engraved, as if to underscore complete personal possession. These objects, however, came into his hands through the mediacy of agents and friends who acted as connoisseurs on his behalf. One of his bank representatives in Rome, Nofri Tornabuoni, and Giovanni Ciampolini, a local merchant and collector, worked together to obtain Roman antiques for him.[53] Nofri exhibited a degree of aesthetic judgment that might seem surprising in a bank agent. It was his task, after all, to send only the best items to Florence for Lorenzo's delectation. Tornabuoni's letters mentioning such matters often contain assessments of who was knowledgeable about antiques[54] and his own appraisals of the quality and prices of various pieces. For example, he dismissed certain objects in the collection of Cardinal de Foix as less than mediocre.[55] Regarding an incised carnelian he made the following statement: "The engraving is lovely and masterfully done, something you will definitely have reason to want."[56] Another time when Nofri came to Florence to discuss bank business with Lorenzo, the two of them conferred at length about some marble statues Nofri had located.[57] Those objects that ended up in the Medici collection had been culled first by men like Nofri and Ciampolini.

Lorenzo's library was built up in a similar fashion. Poliziano, friend and expert, travelled about Italy looking for exceptional Greek manuscripts for Lorenzo to acquire.[58] Lorenzo exercised his judgment only at the very end of the search. Furthermore, he probably developed his own exquisite taste through this very process of consultation and collaboration with agents and friends. Insofar as collecting is an aspect of patronage, here too Lorenzo relied heavily upon an informal *bottega* system.

The contemporary chronicler Benedetto Dei characterized Lorenzo as *maestro della bottega*, master of the workshop. F. W. Kent has very convincingly argued that Dei's description is emblematic of Lorenzo's role as political boss of Florence.[59] But the expression "master of the workshop" can be read and interpreted several ways. If we use a "top-down" approach,

53   Laurie Fusco and Gino Corti, "Giovanni Ciampolini (d. 1505), a Renaissance Dealer in Rome and His Collection of Antiquities," *Xenia* 21 (1991): 7–47.

54   Ibid., 8.

55   He called them "certe medagliaccie" and "alcuni intagliacci," Nofri Tornabuoni to Lorenzo, 14 October 1490, ASF, MAP, 42, no. 158.

56   "Lo intaglio sia molto gentile et artificioso et veramente avete ragione di volerla," Nofri Tornabuoni to Lorenzo, 4 June 1491, ASF, MAP, 42, no. 85.

57   Nofri Tornabuoni to Lorenzo, 31 August 1490, ASF, MAP, 42, no. 140.

58   Angelo Fabroni, *Laurentii Medicis Magnifici vita* (Pisa: J. Gratiolius, 1784), 2:286.

59   F. W. Kent, "Renaissance Patronage: An Introductory Essay," *Patronage, Art, and Society*, 4–5; idem, "Palaces, Politics, and Society," 61; and most extensively in "Patron–Client Networks."

emphasizing the *maestro* part of the phrase and reading all of Florence as the *bottega*, the resulting interpretation accords with the "big man" system of power. We see Lorenzo essentially as puppet master of Florence, pulling the patronage strings. An alternate reading stressing the *bottega* side of things places a higher value on the cooperative nature of the enterprise and recognizes that Lorenzo is inseparable from his workshop. According to the argument presented here, Lorenzo and his patronage can best be understood in the context of collaboration and shared agency, or more simply, as a *maestro* working within a *bottega*. Viewed from the context of the workshop, perhaps Vasari's painting in the Palazzo Vecchio in Florence of Lorenzo seated among the leading literati of his day takes on a new collaborative significance.

IV   Conclusion

This analysis of the language and practices associated with Medici patronage owes much to Gombrich's sensitivity to Renaissance discourse on the arts. Among other things, I have attempted to show how ideas and paradigms drawn from art history can be applicable to other areas of Renaissance studies. The artist's workshop, though nearly obscured in the positivistic historiography of the heroic Renaissance, still remains a potent metaphor for understanding Renaissance culture, which, like patronage and language itself, incorporated strong collaborative features.

In his own way Gombrich was beginning to question the dramatic role Western historiography has given to the patron as autonomous hero, a role that can now be challenged as a historical construction. The heroic patron had begun to emerge in the fifteenth century in relation to the evolving professionalization of the arts and contemporary petitioning behavior with its kindred language of deference. But his figure was redrawn dramatically in the nineteenth century as part of an aesthetic of individualism that focused on single rather than shared agency. As the idealized vision of Renaissance patrons formed, the *maestri* were decontextualized and removed from their workshops. The heroic gloss given to the figure of the patron helped obscure one of the most fundamental and dynamic characteristics of all culture, namely collaboration.

Long before the Medici emerged as first citizens of Florence, the city had enjoyed a lengthy tradition of communal patronage of the arts and of participatory government by the *ottimati* and citizens at large. How ironic that in historical tradition and myth, the Florentine Renaissance should have been made a monument to individual rather than collective genius.

13

The Court Lady's Dilemma: Isabella d'Este and Art Collecting in the Renaissance

Rose Marie San Juan

Isabella d'Este, Marchesa of Mantua, avid collector of art, and always a woman acutely concerned with her public image, has suffered a highly ironic fate at the hands of art historians. Unlike other female collectors who have virtually disappeared from discussions of Renaissance art patronage, Isabella d'Este survives, but in representations strikingly at odds with those constructed in the Renaissance. While "that friend of illustrious deeds and fine studies, liberal, magnanimous Isabella", in Ariosto's *Orlando Furioso* (1512), is acknowledged as a biased topos of praise, the undiscerning, tyrannical and greedy Marchesa in recent histories of Renaissance art retains credibility as a scholarly evaluation.[1] Most of these negative repre-

---

1 Ariosto, *Orlando Funoso*, XIII. 59, (eds.) S. Debenedetti and C. Segre (Bologna, 1960), p. 373:

> De la tua chiara stirpe uscira quella
> d'opere illustri e di bei scudii amica,
> ch'io non so ben se piu saggia e pudica,
> liberale e magnanima Isabella,
> che del bel lume suo di e notte aprica
> fara la terra che sul Menzo siede,
> a cui la madre d'Ocno il nome diede.

J. Aslop, *The Rare Art Traditions. The History of Art Collecting and its linked Phenomena wherever these have appeared* (New York, 1982), is an example of how Isabella d'Este features in general discussions of Renaissance patronage: "Although it is now risky to be unflattering about any leading lady in the long drama of the past. I have to confess that I have never found the celebrated Marchioness of Mantua really likeable. Her humanist culture, although famous in its own day, gives the impression of having been more for show than use. She could be remarkably cold-blooded in getting what she wanted, not least in her art collecting, as will be shown. Her priorities were also just a mite odd for a serious art collector" (p. 430). In P. Burke's *Tradi-*

sentations of Isabella d'Este owe their particulars, and even their existence, to the survival of an unusually voluminous and vivid correspondence.[2] In their scrutiny of these letters, historians have not always agreed on the choice of anecdotes or their interpretation, but what they invariably keep to is the basic framework of a particular personality.[3] It is the very process of elaborating Isabella d'Este's personality, whether to attack or defend her, that has led to the marginalisation of her activities as an art collector. Certainly few steps have been taken to locate these activities within Renaissance patronage patterns, or to define Isabella d'Este's own prescribed social position and patronage options.

The most elaborate representation of Isabella d'Este remains the Renaissance heroine of Julia Cartwright's 1904 biography who fully conforms to Edwardian norms of desirable middle-class female behaviour:

> In her aims and aspirations Isabella was a typical child of the Renaissance, and her thoughts and actions faithfully reflected the best traditions of the age. Her own conduct was blameless. As a wife and mother, as a daughter and sister, she was beyond reproach . . . She had a strong sense of family affections and would have risked her life for the sake of advancing the interests of her husband and children or brothers.[4]

Removed from the broader political and social concerns in which nineteenth-century historians such as Burckhardt had placed her contri-

---

tion and Innovation in Renaissance Italy (London, 1974), Isabella d'Este appears among collectors whose activities were motivated by pleasure rather than external signification (see p. 108). Studies of Isabella d'Este which criticise her collecting choices in terms of a female personality include: A. Martindale, "The Patronage of Isabella d"Este at Mantua", *Apollo*, LXXIX, 1964, pp. 183–91; J. M. Fletcher, "Isabella d"Este, Patron and Collector" in *Splendours of the Gonzaga*, D. S. Chambers and J. Martineau (eds.) (London, Victoria and Albert Museum, 1981), pp. 51–63; C. Hope, "Artists, Patrons, and Advisers in the Italian Renaissance", in *Patronage in the Renaissance*, G. F. Lytle and S. Orgel (eds.) (Princeton, 1981), pp. 293–343. S. Kolsky, "Images of Isabella d'Este", *Italian Studies*, XXXIX, 1984, pp. 47–62. argues that recent critiques of Isabella d'Este are attempts to revise the nineteenth-century bias towards this patron, and that these attempts have been thwarted by "old prejudices" and a recent trend to turn her into a protofeminist. Kolsky ignores the misogynist tendencies of the art historical literature and does not question the process of reconstructing a personality itself.

2   About 12,000 letters by Isabella d'Este survive; see C. M. Brown, "The Grotta of Isabella d'Este", *Gazette des Beaux-Arts*, LXXXIX, 1877, p. 156. For a selection which pertains to her activities as a patron of painting, see D. S. Chambers, *Patrons and Artists in the Italian Renaissance* (London, 1971), pp. 124–50.

3   Male patrons are also discussed in terms of personality but, as I will show, the implications for female patrons are more problematic.

4   J. Cartwright, *Isabella d'Este* (London, 1904). I, p. x. On nineteenth-century notions of middle-class female behaviour, see L. Nead, *Myths of Sexuality. Representations of Women in Victorian England* (Oxford, 1988), pp. 12–47.

bution, here Isabella d'Este is ensconced in family life.[5] Her art patronage, acknowledged as exceptional amongst her sex, becomes a way of defining a private space appropriate to her virtuous, nurturing character:

> It was Isabella's dream to make this Grotta a place of retreat from the world, where she could enjoy the pleasures of solitude or the company of a few chosen friends, surrounded by beautiful paintings and exquisite works of art . . . In this sanctuary, from which the cares and the noise of the outer world were banished, it was Isabella's dream that the walls should be adorned with paintings giving expression to her ideals of culture and disposing the mind to pure and noble thoughts.[6]

While a number of Renaissance female patrons of art served the conventions of the late Victorian biography, only Isabella d'Este has been of interest to recent art historians.[7] One reason for this is that Isabella d'Este, unlike the others, collected mythological panel painting. This, at least, is the one aspect of her activities that has received most attention, particularly her dealings with painters such as Mantegna, Bellini and Perugino. Another incentive has been the wealth of documentation on this patron which includes a detailed inventory of her collection and its manner of display, as well as the correspondence already mentioned.[8] But since these written sources do not concur with the art historical tendency to privilege panel painting over other arts, they have been used to define Isabella d'Este as an anomaly among Renaissance patrons.

When considering the marchesa's overall collecting tactics, scholars have deduced, correctly, that she was more interested in the acquisition of small scale decorative objects than large scale paintings. In 1964, Andrew Martindale aligned this preference to a female personality:

> Isabella herself was a determined collector and, in a typically feminine way, her enthusiasm was especially aroused by *objets d'art*. At first sight, the Mantuan archives, which are rich in information about the paintings, might not suggest this was so; yet, on closer inspection, we soon realize that the bulk of the collection consisted of bronzes, medals, gems and the like: the paintings play, as it were, a supporting role. Moreover, the amount of money which

---

5   Nineteenth and early twentieth-century historians emphasise Isabella d'Este's political rather than cultural contribution. Jacob Burckhardt characterised her as an Italian patriot in his 1860 *The Civilization of the Renaissance in Italy* (Oxford, 1944), pp. 28–9. See also A. Luzio, *Isabella d'Este e i Borgia* (Milan, 1915).
6   Cartwright, *Isabella d'Este*, I, pp. 159–60.
7   J. Cartwright's *Beatrice d'Este, Duchess of Milan* (London, 1903), is another example of a Renaissance female patron who is represented as a virtuous, nurturing mother and wife.
8   On the content of the 1542 inventory, see Brown, "The Grotta", pp. 155–71.

Isabella paid, and was prepared to pay, for these pieces was certainly greater than it was for her paintings.[9]

Yet Isabella d'Este's desire for antique medals and gems, as well as her willingness to spend more money on these objects than on paintings, is in no way inconsistent with the attitudes and practices of other Renaissance collectors.[10] The most celebrated case is that of Lorenzo de' Medici whose apparent lack of interest in painting has always been rationalised by linking his enthusiasm for gems and cameos to humanistic endeavours.[11] An ahistorical assumption – a hierarchy of collectible objects that adheres more to modernism than to Renaissance court society – underlies discussions of both of these patrons, but only in Isabella d'Este's case is this sustained by notions of a stereotypical female personality. In the 1980s, an article by J. M. Fletcher reinserts Isabella d'Este into the traditional female domain of bourgeois domesticity:

> Her motivation was aesthetic and social rather than scholarly and antiquarian . . . [H]er crowded yet calculated display . . . suggests that her collecting, like so much of her patronage, was directed by her highly developed sense of interior decoration.[12]

In addition to anachronisms, the assessment of Isabella d'Este's patronage as atypical is based on, and reinforced by, shifting definitions of the "norm". The representation of the marchesa as old-fashioned and undiscerning was first elaborated by iconographers who privileged intellectual content in painting. Isabella d'Este is renowned for the detailed literary inventions which she instructed painters to follow, and this has served the case of iconographers and their view that humanist advisors were involved in the invention of mythological paintings. Even so, such iconographical studies as Egon Verheyen's *The Paintings in the Studiolo of Isabella d'Este in Mantua* published in 1970, invariably stumble on the fact that the marchesa's inventions draw on moralised reworkings of classical myths rather

9   Martindale, "The Patronage", p. 183.
10   E. H. Gombrich, "The Early Medici as Patrons of Art. A Survey of Primary Sources", in *Italian Renaissance Studies*, E. F. Jacob (ed.) (London, 1960), pp. 303–4, 309. On the preference in the Renaissance for gems instead of painting see Alsop, pp. 376–95, and L. C. Alloisi, "Note sul collezionismo di Paolo II Barbo" in *Da Pisanello alla nascita dei Musei Capitolini. L'Antico a Roma alla viglia del Rinascimento* (Rome, Capitoline Museums, 1988), pp. 239–40.
11   On Lorenzo de'Medici's collection of gems and other small precious objects, see N. Dacos, A. Giuliano, and U. Panniut (eds.), *Il tesoro di Lorenzo il Magnifico*, vol. 1 (Florence, 1973); J. Hook, *Lorenzo de'Medici. An Historical Biography* (London, 1984), pp. 118–37, and especially pp. 125,131–3.
12   Fletcher, "Isabella d'Este, Patron", pp. 55–6.

than on the original texts favoured by iconographers.[13] Verheyen extricates Mantegna – painter of the first two of five mythological paintings commissioned by the marchesa – from the implications of questionable literary sources, but reads the allegorical content of the other paintings in relation to Isabella d'Este's personality:

> The importance of Perugino's painting (*The Combat of Love and Chastity*, the third in the series) within the total decoration is based on the fact that it fulfills two functions. It links the later works to Mantegna's and at the same time introduces a new aspect which is strictly personal and cannot be separated from Isabella's personality. Isabella . . . turned to literary sources which celebrated the world of chivalry, and it may be appropriate to recall here once again Isabella's lasting interest in this world commemorated by Bojardo, whose works she adored. In his paintings, Mantegna contrasts the basic powers in man's life: reason and sensuality. Even more he implies that man's feelings strive with reason, he does not insist that one will ultimately triumph. Thus Mantegna's concept reflects the conviction that man has the liberty to choose one way or the other. Perugino's picture, with its emplicit moral, does not offer a similar choice.[14]

Initially, the critique of Verheyen's interpretation of this group of mythological paintings was directed not at iconography but at the wisdom of applying a rational methodology to an irrational collector:

> No one will envy Professor Verheyen his task, for Isabella's aims are not easy to define. She was an exceptionally difficult patron. She changed her rooms, her artists, her mind . . . Professor Verheyen is methodical but Isabella is unpredictable.[15]

Yet even when scholars challenged the literary focus of iconography, Isabella d'Este's role as patron continued to be reduced, only now in a different way. In a 1981 study of patronage by Charles Hope, the Marchesa of Mantua serves as a foil to the progressive Renaissance collector whose aesthetic interests dovetail into the increasing autonomy of the Renaissance

13   E. Verheyen, *The Paintings in the "Studiolo" of Isabella d'Este at Mantua* (New York, 1971), p. 43.

14   Ibid., p. 50. Matteo Maria Boiardo wrote *Orlando Innamorato* (published in 1495), a chivalric romance in the vernacular, while in the service of the Este family in Ferrara; Ludovico Ariosto's *Orlando Furioso* was intended in part to complete Boiardo's poem left unfinished at his death in 1494.

15   J. Fletcher, review of E. Verheyen's *The Paintings in the "Studiolo" of Isabella d'Este at Mantua*, *Burlington Magazine*, 118, 1976, pp. 426–7.

artist;[16] compared to her brother, the Duke of Ferrara, who supposedly encouraged Titian's initiative and appreciated the aesthetic and erotic components of his mythological paintings, Isabella d'Este's preferences are deemed deviant, and once again her female personality is seen as the most plausible explanation:

> The *Combat of Love and Chastity* illustrates only too clearly what she had in mind – the pedantic elaboration of a banal allegory, conceived with little or no regard for the distinction between a painting and a text. This attitude seems entirely typical of Isabella's pretentious personality; but whether it reflects the normal outlook of contemporary patrons remains to be seen.[17]

The tactic of contrasting Isabella d'Este with such male counterparts as her brother and son is not new, and neither is the explanation of difference in terms of personality; Verheyen himself accounts for the marchesa's preference for moralised classical stories in this way.[18] But now the comparison is based on the supposition that the duke's choices represented objective judgements of artistic quality and therefore did not hinder Titian's talents, while the marchesa's were the consequence of a manipulative personality and served to curtail the artistic process.[19] In fact evidence suggests that while these patrons adhered to different criteria, each permitted certain liberties and disallowed others. Isabella d'Este is said to be unusual in providing painters with detailed literary programmes for mythological pictures yet scholars acknowledge that Alfonso d'Este gave Titian a text to follow.[20] So what does distinguish the duke's dissatisfaction with Bellini's *Feast of the Gods* (due to the fact that the painter relied on a moralised text and represented the gods as peasants),[21] from Isabella d'Este's displeasure with Perugino, who, ignoring her instructions, painted a nude figure of Venus in

16   Hope, "Artists", pp. 293–6, 307–15.
17   Ibid., p. 310.
18   Verheyen contrasts Isabella and her son: "Both Isabella d'Este and her son Federigo II Gonzaga commissioned paintings in which love affairs of the gods were illustrated. In both cases the literary source was the same, namely Ovid's account of the adventures of the gods, especially Zeus, as woven into Arachne's tapestry. Nevertheless, the two representations have entirely different meanings, and this divergence can only be explained by the basic difference in the personalities of Isabella and Federigo" (*The Paintings in the "Studiolo"*, p. 5).
19   This conclusion is also reached by Alsop, *The Rare Art Traditions*, pp. 436–9.
20   Isabella d'Este's most celebrated mythological invention was written into the contract with Perugino for the *Combat of Love and Chastity*, see Chambers, pp. 135–8; on the Duke's instructions to Titian and his motives, see C. Hope. "*Poesie* and Painted Allegories", in *The Genius of Venice 1500–1600*. J. Martineau and C. Hope (eds.) (London, Royal Academy, 1983), p. 36; Hope, "Artists, Patrons and Advisors", pp. 313–15.
21   On the changes made to Bellini's *Feast of the Gods*, see P. Fehl. "The Worship of Bacchus and Venus in Bellini's and Titian's Bacchanals for Alfonso d'Este", *Studies in the History of Art* (Washington, National Gallery of Art), VI, 1974, pp. 37–95.

the *Combat of Love and Chastity?*[22] Evidently different priorities: he adhered to a notion of classical authenticity, while she wanted to ensure a moralising allegorical message.

Isabella d'Este does not demonstrate the "normal outlook" if this is defined as a preference for mythological painting which privileges classical authenticity and an eroticised presentation. Unlike her male counterparts, she was primarily concerned with depictions of mythology which explicitly encouraged a didactic interpretation, what she called a "beautiful meaning".[23] Yet instead of addressing why someone in her position should insist on this, art historians persist in judging Isabella d'Este's collecting activities as if she held a similar position to her brother and son. In other words, they have refused to acknowledge the significance of gender as a factor in social positioning. Isabella d'Este's patronage of mythological painting emerges as unusual in its context, but only by defining the specific role which she occupied can one establish in what ways these activities were exceptional, as well as the implications of such departures from the norm.

Part of the problem is that most art historical studies on collecting remain at the level of defining the preferences of individual collectors.[24] Inevitably this approach tends to skirt such fundamental questions as the social implications of collecting as well as the collectors' links to a particular hierarchy of collectible objects. During the Renaissance the practices of collecting art and the attitudes that gave such practices social significance evolved in relation to an emergent courtly social structure. As with other court collectors, Isabella d'Este's activities register more than the unconstrained actions of an erratic individual, and must be considered in relation to the particular social constraints and expectations which this context imposed on someone of her rank and gender. My intention here is not to justify Isabella d'Este's tactics and attitudes, but to explain the role that collecting played in defining and, I would argue, successfully redefining her prescribed position as the Marchesa of Mantua. By examining her collecting practices within Renaissance social structures and patronage patterns, I hope to show that these functioned very differently in the sixteenth-century Italian court than they do in recent art history.

Baldassare Castiglione's *Il Cortegiano* is a useful source for my purposes, as it attempts to articulate the ideal that underlies courtly life in early

22   Isabella d'Este complained about the nude Venus in a letter to Agostino Strozzi, Abbot of Fiesole, who was acting on her behalf in Florence; her worry was that "by altering one figure he will pervert the whole sentiment of the fable"; see Chambers, *Patrons and Artists*, pp. 140–1.

23   See for example Isabella d'Este's letter to Michele Vianello, Chambers, *Patrons and Artists*, p. 127.

24   For two examples, see Gombrich, no. 8 above and Alsop, no. 1 above.

sixteenth-century Italian despotic city-states such as Mantua;[25] it is set in the comparable court of Urbino, where Isabella d'Este's position was occupied by her sister-in-law Elisabetta Gonzaga. The Gonzaga family, into which Isabella d'Este married, had taken control of Mantua by force, having divested an aristocratic class of its claims and land holdings.[26] Like most despotic rulers, however, the Gonzaga remained dependent on tenuous alliances with larger Italian states and foreign monarchs, who employed them as professional soldiers – *condottieri* – and who offered the titles needed to validate their rights to signorial power. In his book, Castiglione reveals a complex social structure in which dependency – of the nobility and professional courtiers on the ruling family, of the Lady of the court on the prince, of the ruler himself on those he served as military leader – was worked out through rigidly codified behaviour and ritual. The development of a cultivated persona and the acquisition of luxury objects provided ways of negotiating an advantageous position within the court, and in turn a way of life which assured exclusivity and, therefore, some sense of control.

Renaissance collecting practices and their social significations were closely connected to the promotion of antiquity by humanist scholars who endowed classical remnants with an intellectual and ethical framework that proved flexible and assured exclusivity.[27] Collecting became the concern of a larger sector of society when humanism itself was appropriated by the ruling classes, primarily through the employment of humanists in city-republics and small northern courts. The social conflicts that arose from lavish spending on private possessions, an outgrowth of more elaborate family residences, were soon offset with humanist arguments which aligned cultural possession – both physical and intellectual – with moral values.[28] By the second half of the fifteenth century, when powerful families competed in their acquisition of enormous collections, modes of justification were established which not only validated such activities but also gave

---

25   On Castiglione's *Il Cortegiano*, see *Castiglione. The Ideal and the Real in Renaissance Culture*, R. W. Hanning and D. Rosand (eds.) (New Haven, 1983); especially T. M. Greene, "*Il Cortegiano* and the Choice of the Game", pp. 1–15; and D. Javitch, "*Il Cortegiano* and the constraints of Despotism", pp. 17–28. On Renaissance despotic courts, see L. Martines, *Power and Imagination. City-States in Renaissance Italy* (New York, 1979), pp. 218–40.

26   D. S. Chambers, "Mantua and the Gonzaga", in *Splendours of the Gonzaga*, n. 1 above, pp. 17–23. On signorial rule and the position of women, see J. Kelly, "Did Women Have a Renaissance?", in *Women, History and Theory. The Essays of Joan Kelly* (Chicago, 1986), pp. 30–6.

27   A. Grafton, and L. Jardine, *From Humanism to the Humanities. Education and the Liberal Arts in Fifteenth- and Sixteenth-Century Europe* (London, 1986). R. Weiss, *The Rediscovery of Antiquity in the Renaissance* (London, 1978); see also Martines, *Power and Imagination*, pp. 191–217.

28   On attitudes to private spending see, R. Goldthwaite, *The Building of Renaissance Florence. An Economic and Social History* (Baltimore, 1980), pp. 77–83; on the relation between collecting and the family residence, see R. Goldthwaite, "The Empire of Things" in F. W. Kent and P. Simons (eds.), *Patronage, Art, and Society in Renaissance Italy* (Oxford, 1987), pp. 166–9.

further social resonance to the collecting process. For the northern despot, the decoration of a public palace with luxury goods was an opportunity to reaffirm his right to rule by implying, among other things, cultural and moral superiority.[29] It is significant that Alfonso d'Este's set of mythological paintings by Titian, based on Philostratus's description of classical paintings, were – following the example of his sister – kept in his *studiolo*. This type of chamber, originally associated with scholarly pursuits, became a visible component of prominent courts, devoted to the accumulation of objects and facilitating the opportunity to display refinement of taste and learning.[30]

What we know of learned court discussions prompted by collectible objects suggests that these tended to privilege distinctions of artistic skill over the appreciation of precious materials,[31] deflecting criticism of excessive wealth and reinforcing distinctions of education and class. Yet forms of value established through the process of market exchange were very much in place, and served to distinguish the prince not only from his courtiers – the courtier could have intellectual access to a work of art yet the prince usually owned it – but also from his consort. The consort, who, as will emerge below, was more restricted than courtiers in verbal discussions of art, was also limited to forms of art patronage which did not require public competition. One can account for the greater prestige of antique statues over modern painting by their ability to signify the most exclusive form of ownership, precisely because they were scarce, the competition public and increasingly fierce, and undertaken only by the most influential collectors. Such collecting activities, including the emerging hierarchy of collectible objects, presented opportunities to forge links of interdependence between participants while drawing distinctions of rank and gender.

While cultural acumen and the cultivation of personal charm was required of most members of the court, regardless of rank or sex, Castiglione makes clear that only for women was this the primary occupation.[32] The social life of the court centred around the prince's consort who was the orchestrator of much cultural activity, and whose physical presence

29   On the use of culture to legitimise northern despots, see W. L. Gundersheimer, *Ferrara: The Style of a Renaissance Despotism* (Princeton, 1973).
30   On the function of the *studiolo*, see C. Elam, *Studioli and Renaissance Court Patronage*, M.A. thesis, London University 1970; L. Cheles, *The Studiolo of Urbino. An Iconographic Investigation* (University Park, 1986), pp. 22–5; Goldthwaite, "Empire", p. 171.
31   For an early fifteenth-century example of the kinds of interests picked out by courtly collectors, see M. Baxandall, "A Dialogue on Art from the Court of Leonello d'Este. Angelo Decembrio's *De Politia Litteraria Pars LXVIII*", *Journal of the Warburg and Courtauld Institutes*, XXVI, 1963, pp. 304–26.
32   Men's first duty was to serve as military leaders; see B. Castiglione, *The Book of the Courtier*, I, xvii, (trans) C. S. Singleton (Garden City, N.Y. 1959), pp. 32–4. See also Kelly, "Did Women Have a Renaissance?", p. 33.

was the focus of court ritual. Women from the small ruling class of northern Italian city-states were trained exclusively to fulfil this role. Their instruction focused on religious and moralising literature, music, and dance, and prepared them for marriages arranged at a young age with members of other ruling families.[33]

The practice of negotiating advantageous marriage unions put women in the role of cultural possessions whose acquisition required competition in the small but public sphere of Italian courts.[34] At the same time the specific options and limitations faced by these women once married depended on the relative social and political status of the two families in question. For example, the marriage of Isabella d'Este's parents – Eleonora of Aragon, daughter of the King of Naples, and Ercole d'Este, Duke of Ferrara – represented a social leap for the Este family, and served to offset the appearance of sexual ambiguity and dynastic instability that the lack of a consort during the reign of the previous duke had brought to their court.[35] It was no coincidence that the new duchess was encouraged to occupy an unusually visible place in the court of Ferrara. Unlike most court consorts who depended on an allowance from the family into which they married, Eleonora of Aragon had her own inherited income and spent much of this money on religious and charity projects; she collected religious books and funded humanists who produced works which promoted the edifying potential of classical literature. In addition, the duchess commissioned tapestries to embellish the public chambers of the court and was a collector of small precious metal objects.[36] Eleonora of Aragon's presence and patronage not only assured a well-orchestrated social and cultural life for the court, but she also represented its moral underpinnings and by implication contributed to the respectable image of its ruler.

While the role of the consort as patron of the arts served interests more directly embodied by the prince, her physical person and cultivated persona came to function as a catalyst for the cultural life of the court. In this way, she was not distinguished from other Court Ladies who, Castiglione, keeping to the chivalric tradition, views as the courtier's physical source of inspiration:

33   On education of patrician women, see Lionardo Bruni's letter to Baptista di Montefeltro in W. H. Woodward. *Vittorino da Feltre and Other Humanist Educators*(New York, 1963), pp. 123–33.

34   The Duke of Milan, for instance, negotiated for Isabella d'Este, but eventually accepted her sister Beatrice since she was promised to the Gonzaga heir.

35   W. L. Gundersheimer, "Women, Learning and Power: Eleonora of Aragon and the Court of Ferrara", in *Beyond their Sex. Learned Women of the European Past*. P. H. Labalme (ed.) (New York, 1980), pp. 43–65, especially p. 56.

36   Cartwright, *Beatrice d'Este*, pp. 33–4.

no court however great, can have adornment or splendour or gaiety in it without ladies, neither can any Courtier be graceful or pleasing or brave, or do any gallant deed of chivalry, unless he is moved by the society and by the love and charm of ladies.[37]

In Castiglione's idealised Urbino court, the lady at the centre of cultivated discussions is Elisabetta Gonzaga who invariably remains a passive source of inspiration for eloquent courtiers. Apparently the Duchess of Ferrara's youngest daughter, Beatrice d'Este, who was married to the powerful Duke Ludovico Sforza, occupied this kind of space in the court of Milan. Beatrice d'Este presided over a court much richer and culturally more active than the courts of either her mother or sister, but her own achievements were read primarily in terms of her physical person and her ability to inspire her husband and the court at large. Unlike her mother, Beatrice d'Este's patronage was limited to courtly entertainments, particularly to supporting musicians and poets who wrote in the vernacular.[38] Lacking any focus other than her person, the duchess's position was more central but not essentially different from that of other noble women in the court of Milan. Beatrice d'Este as an embodiment of virtue – manifested primarily by her physical beauty, her lavish wardrobe and expensive jewellery – is a recurrent theme in court poetry.[39] It is revealing to compare the references to Beatrice and her sister Isabella in Ariosto's *Orlando Furioso*; while the former is praised for imparting strength and virtue on her husband, the latter is said to have challenged her husband in patronage and achievements.[40]

Isabella d'Este's marriage to Francesco Gonzaga aligned the Gonzaga with a court that superceded them in titles, wealth and even the potential to produce a healthy family dynasty.[41] If the Mantuan court had none the less managed to become a significant presence among northern city-states, it was by making much of its adherence to humanism and its credited cultural pursuits, even supporting a humanist school for children from other courts.[42] Recasting the court in the prestigious humanist vocabulary did not exclude Gonzaga women, who presumably became, more desirable as

---

37 Castiglione, *Il Cortegiano*, III, iii, pp. 204–5.
38 Cartwright, *Beatrice d'Este*, pp. 142–4.
39 G. Visconti, *I Canzonieri per Beatrice d'Este e per Bianca Maria Sforza*. P. Bongrani (ed.) (Milan, 1979), especially pp. 133–4, 150.
40 Ariosto, *Orlando Furioso*, XIII (59–63), p. 373.
41 Gundersheimer, p. 56. Isabella d'Este did not receive an income from her family, although she frequently appealed to her father to supplement her Gonzaga allowance. Gonzaga health problems and their impact on marriage arrangements are discussed by R. Signorini. "Lettura storica degli affreschi della *Camera degli Sposi* di Andrea Mantegna", *Journal of the Warburg and Courtauld Institutes*, XXXVIII, 1975, pp. 109–35.
42 On the humanist school at Mantua, see Woodward, *Vittorino da Feltre*, pp. 24–92.

marriage candidates by the distinction of a humanist education. While a humanist education purported to cultivate personal virtue, for women such education brought virtue into question.[43] As the well known case of Cecilia Gonzaga – sister of Francesco Gonzaga's father – demonstrates, humanist concerns had to be circumscribed within gender expectations if they were to serve the court hierarchy.[44] For Cecilia Gonzaga to pursue humanist studies as an end in itself, she was compelled to withdraw from the life of the court and retire to a convent.[45]

In 1490, Isabella d'Este arrived in Mantua with an established reputation for learned interests, and this reputation – as well as her family connections – well suited a court that relied on its cultural identity. Initially she received an annual allowance of 6,000 gold ducats, and to some extent she and Francesco Gonzaga kept to the expected practice of patronising different kinds of arts – he funding the building and decoration of a palace, she arranging the cultural and social activities of the court.[46] By collecting poets, composers and musicians, the marchesa was able to orchestrate courtly musical entertainments as well as festivities within the city of Mantua which proclaimed state visits, marriage alliances and the family's political accolades.[47] She contributed to festivals staged in other courts, such as the celebrations that marked the marriage of her brother Alfonso d'Este to Lucrezia Borgia in Ferrara, and used these opportunities to gain political favours for the Gonzaga court.[48] The cultural distinction of the court over which she presided buttressed the position of its ruler, certainly more than Francesco Gonzaga's military achievements or family origins did. At the same time, complications in the marchesa's political alliances and military duties distanced him from the court, and this vacuum permitted his wife greater room to establish an independent presence.

In fact, Isabella d'Este's position in Mantua did not adhere to the role of the Court Lady – even the one at the centre of the court – described by Castiglione. Nor can it be explained simply as the readjustment of the ideal to the particular needs of the Gonzaga. From the beginning, her presence

43 Grafton and Jardine, *From Humanism*, pp. 29–57.
44 On Cecilia Gonzaga see Woodward, p. 29; M. L. King. "Book-Lined Cells: Women and Humanism in the Early Italian Renaissance", in *Beyond their Sex* (n. 35 above), pp. 66–90.
45 King, "Book-Lined Cells", p. 69.
46 Isabella d'Este's income is discussed in a 1502 letter to her father; for the full text see Cartwright, *Isabella d'Este*, p. 226.
47 On musical entertainments see W. Prizer, "Isabella d'Este and Lucrezia Borgia as Patrons of Music: The Frottola at Mantua and Ferrara". *Journal of the American Musicological Society*, 38, 1985, pp. 1–33, and I. Felon, "The Gonzaga and Music", in *Splendours of the Gonzaga*, no. 1 above, pp. 87–94; an example of city celebrations is the lavish procession proclaiming Francesco Gonzaga's victory as commander of the League army over the French at the Taro valley July 6th, 1494; Cartwright, *Isabella d'Este*, pp. 126–7.
48 Cartwright, *Isabella d'Este*, pp. 198–214.

in the court came to be represented in terms of physical spaces and tangible external achievements, certainly much more so than those of her sister or even her mother. Her dedication to the acquisition of antique gems, cameos, medals and other precious small objects, fits within collecting practices of the Mantuan court, although previously only pursued on such a scale by male members of the Gonzaga family.[49] Isabella d'Este's original allowance proved inadequate for such pursuits, particularly since she was expected to contribute to the expenses of her large household, including the dowries of the unmarried women.[50] She negotiated an additional 2,000 ducats by assuming full responsibility for one hundred or so people in her service; since she now took charge of employing people, she reduced the numbers, imposed a strict budget, and was able to save about 1,000 ducats with which she bought lands that earned her 2,500 ducats a year in rents.

Not long after her arrival in Mantua, the marchesa devised an elaborate scheme to display her growing collection in rooms devoted exclusively to that purpose.[51] While this idea was a reworking of the humanist *studiolo*, this is the first known case of a court consort arranging such a space as part of her apartments in the palace, as well as one of the first instances in which this kind of space was devoted to the display of an art collection.[52] Evidence suggests that these rooms – known as the *studiolo* and *grotta* – became a focal point of social intercourse in the court, and served as the setting for musical entertainments as well as a showpiece for important visitors.[53]

Isabella d'Este's collecting activities were instrumental in departing from the prescribed activities of the consort, and in inserting herself in spaces traditionally allotted to men. Not only did she collect on a much larger scale than other consorts, but more to the point she departed from the types of objects – religious painting, decorative arts – usually patronised by women in her position. In acquiring mythological paintings and antique statuary, Isabella d'Este seems to have been quite exceptional among Renaissance court women.

---

49 Martindale, pp. 183–91. The major Gonzaga collectors of small precious objects were Cardinal Francesco Gonzaga and his brothers Gianfrancesco and Ludovico (Bishop of Mantua); see Alsop, *The Rare Art Traditions*, p. 392; A. Radcliffe. "Antico and the Mantuan Bronze", in *Splendours of the Gonzaga*, pp. 46–7.
50 In the 1502 letter to her father. Isabella d'Este explains the sources of this income: toll from various mills, excise duties and duties on lands of Letopalidano; in addition to her allowance she was given some houses by her husband but she complains that their expenses supercede their income; Cartwright, *Isabella d'Este*, p. 226.
51 On the grotta, see Brown, no. 8 above, and the second part of this article, *Gazette des Beaux-Arts*, XCI, 1978, pp. 72–82.
52 *Splendours of the Gonzaga* (n. 1 above), pp. 164–72.
53 On musical performances in these rooms, see Fenlon, pp. 87–8. Visits by political envoys are discussed by Kolsky, p. 54.

➤

Plate 10   Titian, *Portrait of Isabella d'Este* (ca. 1536). *Source:* Kunsthistorische Museum, Vienna.

The Venetian artist Titian (ca. 1488–1576) was one of handful of painters, like Leonardo da Vinci and Lorenzo Lotto, known for his portraits of women. During the 1530s he painted two portraits of Isabella d'Este. The marchesa of Mantua, then in her early sixties, had very strong ideas about how she wanted her image to appear. She indicated to various artists that she preferred to be portrayed from descriptions of her rather than from life, believing that words often captured the true essence of someone's character better than one's appearance. To inspire Titian, she had the Ferrarese noble Giovanni Francesco Zaninello lend him a portrait of Isabella done by Francesco Francia in 1511, because it portrayed her as she still wanted to be: a young woman. This image, now lost, provided the inspiration for Titian's portrait of Isabella as a serene, and richly attired court lady holding a book in hand. Even the face seems to have been idealized, since it bears no relation to profiles of Isabella on coins. Like Queen Elizabeth I of England, Isabella had no desire to contemplate the vicissitudes of age. Shortly after Titian's painting arrived in Mantua in 1536, Isabella wrote of the image: "The portrait by Titian's hand is of such a pleasing type that we doubt that we were ever, at the age he represents, of such beauty that is contained in it." Art indeed could improve on life.

But why precisely did activities such as these place Isabella d'Este in a position that was not only unusually visible but also highly exposed? The ruler's consort, obliged to forego any direct action within the court, could distinguish herself only through her ability to influence its male members. Isabella d'Este herself eagerly embraced visual imagery which cast her in the passive role of inspirational body and, as her attitude towards her portraits shows, she was keen to adhere to expected courtly ideals of physical feminine beauty.[54] In relation to artistic endeavours, she even adopted the Muse as a personal insigna.[55] It was commonplace for court poets who wished to please the marchesa to refer to her as the tenth Muse.[56]

Yet the role personified by the Muse (or Titian's idealised portrait of the marchesa (Plate 10)) should not be confused with the actual role of social and cultural catalyst, which obliged women to meet complicated and conflicting expectations. Court women, and particularly the ruler's consort, were on public display, and had to please with physical beauty, personal

54   Discussions of Isabella d'Este's portraits, particularly Titian's 1516 portrait (Plate 10), tend to focus on the Marchesa's vanity; see Fletcher, p. 56.

55   This is a recurring theme in the *studiolo* where the muses appear on the reliefs on the door frames, as well as in Mantegna's *Mars and Venus* and in Costa's *Coronation of a Lady* in which apparently the marchesa is shown as the facilitator of the arts; see Verheyen. *The Paintings in the "Studiolo"*, pp. 44–6. On Isabella's adoption of the Muse as her personal insigna see Fletcher, "Isabella d'Este, Patron", p. 51; R. Lightbown, *Mantegna* (Berkeley, 1986), pp. 197–200.

56   A. Luzio, *I precettori d'Isabella d'Este*. Ancona 1887, p. 25; quoted by Fletcher. p. 51.

charm, and intellectual skills, while simultaneously conveying all the obvious signs of a modest character and chaste body.[57] Castiglione acknowledges that these two sets of demands – public visibility and private chastity – were regarded as contradictory conditions and as such obliged women to balance and offset a number of conflicting impressions:

---

57   On the contradictory demands faced by court women, see two articles by A. R. Jones: "Surprising Fame: Renaissance Gender Ideologies and Women's Lyric", in *The Poetics of Gender*, (ed.) N. K. Miller (New York, 1986), pp. 76–8; "Nets and Bridles: Early Modern Conduct Books

beauty is more necessary to her than to the Courtier, for truly that woman lacks much who lacks beauty. Also she must be more circumspect, and more careful not to give occasion for evil being said of her, and conduct herself so that she may not only escape being sullied by guilt but even by the suspicion of it, for a woman has not so many ways of defending herself against false calumnies as a man has. . . . [I]n a lady who lives at court a certain pleasing affability is becoming above all else, whereby she will be agreeable and comely conversation suited to the time and place and to the station of the person with whom she speaks, joining to serene and modest manners, and to that comeliness that ought to inform all her actions, a quick vivacity of spirit whereby she will show herself a stranger to all boorishness; but with such a kind manner as to cause her to be thought no less chaste, prudent, and gentle than she is agreeable, witty, and discreet: thus, she must observe a certain mean (difficult to achieve and, as it were, composed of contraries) and must strictly observe certain limits and not exceed them.[58]

The emphasis on chastity for women is of course not unique to the courtly situation, and in fact was articulated in humanist literature in relation to bourgeois city-states where the roles of men and women were rigidly confined to the public and private spheres respectively.[59] Castiglione is explicit on why it was adopted in the courtly situation:

we ourselves have set a rule that a dissolute life in us is not a vice, or fault, or disgrace, while in women it means such utter approbrium and shame that any woman of whom ill is once spoken is disgraced forever, whether what is said be calumny or not . . . [C]hastity seemed more needful for them than any other quality, in order for us to be certain of our offspring.[60]

But unlike a woman from the merchant class, the Court Lady had to maintain a reputation for being constant and chaste, while enacting a highly visible and articulate role in the public sphere.

The ideal prescribed by Castiglione and the working out of courtly behaviour were bound in an uneasy relationship which manifests itself in the complex process of cultural representation. Verbal eloquence as defined by the humanistic education programme was at the centre of self-presentation in the court and consequently at the centre of this dilemma.[61] Essential and unqualified to the demonstration of virtue on the part of prince and courtier, verbal proficiency was regarded as being at odds with the most

and Sixteenth-Century Women's Lyrics", in *The Ideology of Conduct. Essays in Literature and the History of Sexuality*, N. Armstrong and L. Tennenhouse (eds.) (London, 1987), pp. 42–8.

58   Castiglione, *Il Cortegiano*, III, iv, pp. 206–7.
59   Kelly, "Did Women Have a Renaissance?" pp. 36–47.
60   Castiglione, *Il Cortegiano*, p. 189.
61   Grafton and Jardine, *From Humanism*, pp. 58–98.

crucial virtue of the Court Lady, namely chastity. For women humanists, such skills led to charges of sexual deviancy or at least sexual ambiguity, and inevitably forced them to choose between a social existence or their scholarly pursuits.[62] The Court Lady was expected to have well enough developed verbal skills, at least to facilitate learned courtly discussion, and court consorts are frequently praised for their appreciation of the achievements of learned men;[63] but the implication is that their access to culture was virtuously innate, rather than the result of a learned mind.

Isabella d'Este departed from this norm and, like many women humanists, was successful in building a reputation for herself as someone with skills and tastes grounded in the classical tradition. Her attempts to continue her study of Latin and read original classical texts, and her efforts to participate with court poets in their demonstrations of verbal and written skills, were visible enough to receive attention inside and outside the court.[64] The Renaissance readings of these activities which survive, although biased towards Isabella d'Este, address any potential charges of excessive worldliness by using tactics frequently employed in the praise of female humanists.[65] Ariosto, while employed by the Este family, praised the marchesa's learning by declaring her an exception among her sex.[66] On the other hand, the celebrated Virgil scholar, Pontanus, was also working from the premise of social deviation when he praised the marchesa for her campaign to raise a statue to Virgil, Mantua's native son, and added that she deserved all the more credit since as a woman she could not appreciate the Roman poet in the original.[67]

But the issue of verbal fluency, central to the ways in which classical culture became a social signifier, as well as to the Court Lady's ability to draw subtle yet clear distinctions between visibility and accessibility, is for these very reasons also pertinent to the marchesa's patronage of mythological painting. In spite of what scholars have suggested, Isabella d'Este was not unique in using mythological painting to show off her leaning; the function of this kind of painting was to facilitate learned witty discussion, and the presence of such images in the court became – like antique gems and cameos – the focus of social exchange. By insisting on elaborate moralised inventions, the marchesa, rather than unwittingly revealing outdated attitudes, was attentive to the fact that established forms of learned courtly wit invariably raised serious problems for the consort's image. This

62 King, "Book-lined Cells", pp. 75–9.
63 Castiglione, *Il Cortegiano*, pp. 208–9.
64 Kolsky, "Images", pp. 59–60.
65 See for example Poliziano's correspondence with Cassandra Fedele. Grafton and Jardine, *From Humanism*, pp. 45–57.
66 Ariosto, *Orlando Furioso*, p. 373.
67 *Splendours of the Gonzaga* (n. 1 above), cat. n. 92, pp. 152–3; Kolsky, "Images", pp. 59–60.

is substantiated by a much self-publicised incident in which the marchesa forbade her unmarried ladies to attend a performance of the comedy *Cassaria* held at the Ferrarese court on account of its lascivious language.[68]

The recorded responses to the marchesa's paintings, all produced within the controlled circle of the Mantuan court, reveal underlying conflicts between the chaste female ideal and the conventional associations of courtly mythology. Court poetry which addresses these paintings, and in the process attempts to be both clever and complimentary to the patron, invariably represents Isabella d'Este in ambiguous ways.[69] In particular Mantegna's *Mars and Venus* (Plate 11), led to implicit suggestions that the nude Venus depicted Isabella d'Este.[70] When poets claimed for the marchesa the courtly expectation of an idealised physical appearance, they were simply following convention. The nude was after all one of the interests promoted by humanist discourse and while it permitted the male patron to display his ability to make learned visual distinctions,[71] erotic interests – and implications – were never far from the surface. When this kind of interest was associated with Isabella d'Este, it incited other court poets to come to the defense of the marchesa's chastity. By the same token, the very ambiguity of mythological images enabled the marchesa to challenge the established notion that classical learning was at odds with female chastity. Ronald Lightbown has noted that in the second picture by Mantegna, *Pallas expelling the Vices from the Garden of Virtue* (Plate 12), the didactic inscriptions – in Greek, Latin and Hebrew – call for Pallas, the goddess of learning and the arts, and Daphne, who represents chastity, to expel vices that threaten a life of chastity, thus explicitly associating learning with chastity.[72]

Perhaps a relevant parallel is provided by the painted female portrait which gave tangible form to the unattainable ideal which court women were compelled to pursue. In fact this type of configuration (Plate 10) had the potential to shift in signification, even within the courtly context, due to the emergence of a type of painting in which depictions of women came to be regarded only as signifying physical beauty. In an article on Renaissance female portraiture, Elizabeth Cropper argues that identity becomes a problem for women when "the portrayal of a beautiful woman also came to function as a synecdoche for the beauty of painting itself".[73] Since physical idealisation is used to represent both the chaste court consort and an

---

68 Cartwright, *Isabella d'Este*, pp. 211–14.

69 On responses to Mantegna's *Mars and Venus*, see Lightbown, Mantegna, pp. 200–3.

70 See example mentioned by Elam, *Splendours of the Gonzaga*, p. 24, of Battista Fiera's comparison between Isabella and Venus.

71 Baxandall, "A Dialogue on Art", pp. 307–8.   72 Lightbown, *Mantegna*, p. 202.

73 E. Cropper, "The Beauty of Woman: Problems of the Rhetoric of Renaissance Portraiture", in *Rewriting the Renaissance. The Discourses of Sexual Difference in Early Modern Europe*. M. W. Ferguson, M. Quilligan and N. J. Vickers (eds.) (Chicago, 1986), pp. 175–90, especially p. 176.

Plate 11 Andrea Mantegna, *Mars and Venus* (ca. 1497). *Source*: Musée du Louvre, Paris.

There is a certain irony in the fact that a son of a carpenter would become one of the most erudite painters of his generation. Andrea Mantegna (1431–1506) grew up in Padua where he benefited from the scholarly world of a university town. Mantegna painted Leonello d'Este in Ferrara in 1449. Within a decade, he had become a court artist in Mantua, where he painted the Camera Picta for Ludovico Gonzaga between 1465 and 1474. He enjoyed the company of such noteworthy humanists as Leon Battista Alberti, who stayed in Mantua on three separate occasions, and later Baldassare Castiglione. In 1490, after spending two years in Rome, he returned to Mantua just as Isabella d'Este settled into the Castello as the wife of the young duke Francesco. In the mid-1490s Isabella commissioned him to do a series of paintings for her Studiolo, the first of which was *Mars and Venus*, also known as *Parnassus*. This image first was displayed in the southeast tower of the Castello where Isabella created her Studiolo. By 1497 it had become a showpiece and Mantegna's image was one of the most important works on display. Isabella took offense at the suggestion that she was Venus and her husband Mars, presiding over an Olympian idyll, because she did not consider it decorous to imagine herself portrayed in the nude.

Plate 12 Andrea Mantegna, *Pallas Expelling the Vices from the Garden of Virtue* (ca. 1502). *Source:* Musée du Louvre, Paris.

In 1484, as the new marchese of Mantua Francesco Gonzaga took charge of his state, Mantegna wrote to Lorenzo de' Medici that he was optimistic about the chances for improving his standing at court. "The disposition of this new lord renews my hopes, seeing him all inclined towards *virtù*." As it turns out, Mantegna was right about Francesco's court but wrong about who would patronize him. Francesco's wife Isabella became his most important and demanding patron in the last sixteen years of his life. Around 1500, Isabella asked him to do the *Pallas*. In this painting the Greek goddess of wisdom with the help of Diana, goddess of chastity, expels the vices from the garden of the mind. Idleness is led away by Sloth, Ignorance carried off by Ingratitude and Avarice. The images of dancing muses and of Mercury were inspired by drawings made by the antiquary Ciriaco d'Ancona. In all likelihood, one of Isabella's humanist advisors, Paride de Ceresara, suggested the theme. We should certainly imagine that this was an allegory of Isabella's image of herself as a learned Athena. At the end of his life, Mantegna found himself forced to part with his most precious antiquities simply to please the marchesa, who described herself as having an "insatiable desire for antique things."

anonymous image where beauty remains, but both chastity and specific identity are removed, what has to be considered is how idealisation impinges on women of specific social rank. It would seem that female portraiture, like conventional female court patronage, served to collapse any distinctions of achievements or access to power between women in the court, and thus distinctions of rank came to be determined primarily by their relations to men.[74]

What is remarkable about Isabella d'Este's patronage of mythological painting, is precisely that it proved a way out of this dilemma. In other words, it gave her a highly visible position within her exclusive courtly circle, while managing to retain a precarious balance between eloquence and a respectable sexual identity. One must consider how the presence of these paintings – as well as other objects in her collection – made her chambers in the court the centre of social exchange, as well as how much of this discussion served to assert her presence rather than that of the prince. Collecting tactics such as the marchesa's novel idea of juxtaposing mythological paintings by different artists, encouraged comparisons of artistic styles, as well as learned discussions on mythological invention.[75] The marchesa, then, unlike women who attempted to pursue humanist studies, was able to occupy a visible place in the cultural life of the court. One obvious reward was the strengthening of her political position when, during her husband's absences and after his death, she eagerly undertook duties as regent of Mantua.[76] For this to be possible, her learning had to be defined in very different terms than those open to and expected from her brother and son. It should come as no surprise that Isabella d'Este's mythological inventions did not address the hedonistic interests favoured by Alfonso d'Este and Federico Gonzaga, but were directed to moralising allegories, and usually revolved around the theme of the battle between chastity and love in which the former invariably emerged triumphant.

But Isabella d'Este's departures from her prescribed role are not limited to her active and externalised position in the court of Mantua. One would be underestimating the social importance of collecting if the acquisition of desirable objects, or even their power to signify and establish a hierarchy within the court, were seen as the only aims; more crucially, the process itself presented a striking opportunity to assert one's position in the social order, particularly outside the court, and even alter it to advantage. Perhaps

74   Cropper considers Titian's portrait of Isabella d'Este in relation to Parmagianino's *Antea* to illustrate the problem of identity. Titian also produced a number of eroticised representations of anonymous women; see C. Cagli and F. Valcanover, *L'Opera completa di Tiziano* (Milan, 1969), cat. ns. 178, 179, 374, 383, 386.
75   This tactic is discussed in a number of Isabella d'Este's letters; see Chambers, *Patrons and Artists*, pp. 130, 134.
76   Kolsky, "Images", pp. 55–7; Fletcher, "Isabella d'Este, Patron", p. 51.

more than any other type of collectible object, antique statuary offered not only the pleasures of physical acquisition but also the symbolic value of this acquisition in social terms; as suggested above, the public visibility and acknowledgement of such acquisitions were particularly rewarding. In other words it took place on an international public arena, and success, even more than money, which northern despots always lacked, depended on a network of contacts, on the strength of one's position in the social order, and one's skills in manipulating that position.[77]

But a woman's access to social rank was indirect and invariably depended on the achievements of male members of her family; any course of action, including collecting, which involved direct public competition, was an avenue that society tacitly considered closed to women. It is here that it seems appropriate to turn to the marchesa's correspondence which in itself is not unusual since letter-writing was a traditional means of communication for Renaissance court women. What is unusual about Isabella d'Este's letters, and what has made them the focus of so much scholarly attention, is their incessant discourse on the patronage of the arts. In her letters Isabella d'Este claims to favour, above all other objects, antique statuary, and in its pursuit, she entered into a highly competitive male domain.[78] With less money than most prominent collectors, she was able to amass a remarkable collection of antiquities. Among the rare and desirable objects the marchesa acquired were a Cupid attributed to Praxiteles, statues from Rhodes and Naxos, and fragments from the Mausoleum of Halicarnassus.[79] She became the acknowledged family expert on various arts, including antique sculpture, so that both her husband, and later her son, were anxious for her approval in their own acquisitions.[80]

How these activities – as well as lengthy negotiations for mythological paintings – feature in Isabella d'Este's correspondence is an indication of the way collecting served as a pretext for building and maintaining a network of contacts outside as well as inside the court.[81] Her tactics are hardly out of keeping within a courtly society in which personal and state

77 By international I mean encompassing different Italian city states. On the relative importance of money and influence to Renaissance collecting see R. Weissman, "Taking Patronage Seriously", in F. W. Kent and P. Simons (eds.), *Patronage, Art, and Society in Renaissance Italy* (Oxford, 1987), pp. 35–6.

78 An example of the letters concerned with the acquisition of antiquities is that addressed to her brother Ippolito d'Este, dated June 30th 1502; Cartwright, pp. 230–1. See also C. Brown, "*Lo Insaciabile Desiderio Nostro De Cose Antique:* New Documents on Isabella d'Este's Collection of Antiquities' in *Cultural Aspects of the Italian Renaissance*, C. Clough (ed.) (Manchester, 1976), pp. 324–53, and Kolsky, "Images", p. 52.

79 Fletcher, "Patrons and Artists", p. 53; Martindale "The Patronage", pp. 188–9; Brown and Lorenzoni, pp. 76–7.

80 Fletcher, "Patrons and Artists", p. 61.

81 Letters, which were also used by women humanists to establish professional contacts, became an accepted means of building up social contacts; see Grafton and Jardine, *From*

interests were not differentiated, and it was expected that personal relationships would enter into the official workings of the court.[82] Isabella
d'Este displays, above all, an acute awareness of her position relative to particular individuals, and assumes drastically different tones, ranging from
the reverential to the disdainful. As someone who depended on others to
serve her interests, she well understood that it was not simply a question of
tyrannising those decidedly beneath her, but of convincing those above that
it was worth having the Marchesa of Mantua beholden to them. Isabella
d'Este is in fact one of the few women who emerge at this time as facilita-
tors and dispensers of political and social patronage.[83]

Yet this correspondence reveals the importance of forms of mediation
when Isabella d'Este was participating in the public sphere. Other Renaissance collectors relied on agents and contacts in metropolitan centres, but
a male representative was particularly crucial for a woman who could not
move about freely, nor to deal directly with other collectors or dealers.[84] For
example, Lorenzo di Pavia, who made musical instruments for Isabella
d'Este and her sister, served as her agent for many years; the exchange of
letters between the two shows the marchesa actively competing for desirable antique pieces while retaining the appearance of a protected courtly
situation.[85]

Of course, much of Isabella d'Este's correspondence is to family and
friends, but these too seem preoccupied with collecting activities, particularly with the acquisition of antiquities. Apparently letter-writing was not
only a means to collecting and its social rewards but, as a traditional form
of communication for educated women, one of the most visible public
voices open to Isabella d'Este. Collecting enabled the marchesa to define a
more credible identity within a traditional female sphere. Instead of limiting discussion to issues of family, these letters show the writer to be someone
with access to the most exclusive forms of culture. In other words, an interest in antiquities and mythological paintings, regarded as exclusive and
prestigious in her social situation, provided the marchesa with a sure way
to be taken more seriously, to be more effective in building contacts and to
endow her with a successful public image.

Renaissance discussions of Isabella d'Este's patronage of art reveal a constant tension between the ideal of the court Lady articulated by Castiglione
and the marchesa's actual ways of operating in the court. At stake was an

---

Humanism, p. 52. On networks based on obligation in Italian city sates, see F. W. Kent and
P. Simons, "Renaissance Patronage: An Introductory Essay", in *Patronage, Art and Society*
(n. 77 above), pp. 1–21.

82   N. Elias, *The Court Society*, (trans) E. Jephcott (Oxford, 1983), pp. 1–2.

83   Kent and Simons, "Renaissance Patronage", pp. 7–8.

84   On the importance of agents and representatives, see ibid., p. 19.

85   C. Brown, *Isabella d'Este and Lorenzo da Pavia*, Documents for the History of Art and
Culture in Renaissance Mantua (Geneva, 1982).

emergent hierarchy of objects and its connection to social positioning. Apparently, it was not the possession of objects usually acquired by men that raised problems for Isabella d'Este as much as the social significations and spaces occupied by these objects. The significances and spaces associated with antiquities and mythological paintings were at odds with the ideal of the Lady of the court, but they brought with them greater opportunity to manoeuvre in the court hierarchy. Thus Isabella d'Este's activities as a collector must be regarded as part of an expansion of prescribed boundaries while also presenting ways of addressing the difficulties that such departures from the norm may have posed to her public image.

In the literature of art history, however, Isabella d'Este occupies a more uncomfortable position, remaining the exception (not only among Renaissance women but also among Renaissance patrons) and all too vulnerable to periodic reassessments of her character. The virtuous nurturing wife and mother in late Victorian biographies, the champion of popular chivalric stories in iconographic readings, and the undiscerning, wilful patron in more recent revisions of iconography are not only the products of gender bias, and diminish Isabella d'Este's contribution, but in different ways have served established patterns of Renaissance art history. In a field concerned with the construction of individual personalities, Isabella d'Este's unusual correspondence has provided more than ample material for such interpretations. But these letters, like other forms of Isabella d'Este's social and cultural activities, must be considered within the intricate network of options and constraints which placed court women in a difficult and problematic relation to cultural representation. Unfortunately, when female patronage in the Renaissance is left largely unexplored, her case remains too much the exception. It would seem that aspects of Isabella d'Este's collecting activities were unusual among court women and opened up certain opportunities for her, but only a fuller account of patronage patterns will forward the question of art collecting as an enabling strategy for Renaissance women.

Index

Page numbers in bold type indicate a main or detailed reference. Page numbers in italic indicate illustrations. Continuous page numbers ignore any intervening illustrations.

Abel, E., 281n, 282n, **288–9**
Abelard, Peter, 289n
Academia Florentina, 59
Acciaioli family, 81, 88
Acciaioli, Agnolo, 78
Acciaioli, Angelo, 74n
Acciaioli, Donato, 77–8
Accolti, Benedetto, 88–9n
Accolti, Bernardo, 35
Adoration of the Magi (Botticelli), *298*
adultery, 198, **199–200**, 202
Aeneid (Virgil), 266, 267–8, 268–9
affines, **110–17**, 122
Africa (Petrarch), 221, 228, 229, 234
age at marriage, 116
    men, 146, 169, 171, 194
    women, 169, 181–2, **189–90**,
        194
agency
    Lorenzo de' Medici and, 313–16
    in patron–client relations, **308–10**,
        316
Agnadello, battle of, 31
Alamanni, Lodovico, 33–4, 57

Alberti, Leon Battista, 18, 20, 21n, 24,
        106, 259, 335
    Books on the Family, 169–70
    on friendship, 53
    On Painting, 296
    on sacred places, 156–7
Albizi family, 140
Albizzi, Rinaldo degli, 64
Alexander VI, pope, 29
Alexandria library, 241, 248, **249–50**
Alfonso of Aragon, 271
Alighieri, Dante *see* Dante
Allegory of Good and Bad Government
        (Lorenzetti), 8, *9*
Andrea del Castagno, 303
*Apologia contra cuiusdam anonymi Galli
        calumnias* (Petrarch), 229n, 230
arbitration, **115–16**, 119n
arbitrio, 52
architecture, **18–21**, 24, 28, 295,
        301n, 311
Aretino, Pietro, 35, 37
Arienti, Sabadino degli, 139
Arimondo, Andrea, 183n

Arimondo, Prodocimo, 188n
Ariosto, Ludovico, 32, 317, 321n,
    327, 333
Aristotle, 239, 242, 243, 275
Arlotto, Piovano, 69, 75, 90n
Arquà, 5, 6
art collecting, 296, 323, **324–5**, 338
    Isabella d'Este, **319–20**, 329–30,
        340
    Lorenzo de' Medici, 315, 320
Art of War, The (Machiavelli), 32
artisans, 20–1, 170
artistic patronage, 65, 218,
    295–301
    correspondence on, 306–10
    literature on, 301–6
artists, professional status, 301–2
Aslop, J., 317n
Augustine of Hippo, St., 5, 231
Aurispa, Giovanni, 264
Averroes, 275
Avicenna, 275
Avignon, 4, 10, 224

bachelors, 190, 194, 202
Baduario, Ziani, 125
Bakhtin, Mikhail, 153
Balla d'Oro, 181
banking, 10, 16, 65, 87–8
Barbarigo, Maria, 182n
Barbaro, Francesco, 19, 173, 268
Barbato da Sulmona, 225n
Bardi family, 111, 113
Bartolomeo, Benedetto di, 22
beauty, 330–2, 334–7
Bec, C., 98n
Bellandi, Donato, 77–8
Bellini, Giovanni, 322
Belluno, 198
Bembo, Maria, 187–8
Bembo, Pietro, 35
Bentivoglio, Sante, 139
Bergamo, 11
Bern, 137
Bernardino of Siena, St., 22, 133–4,
    155, 156, 207
    on commerce, 8, 240

on marriage, **196–8**, 199
on wealth and poverty, 69
Berruguete, Pedro, 218
Bertoni, G., 246
Bessarion, Cardinal, 23, 135, 137,
    139, 238, 252
"big man" theory, 305–6, 310
Biondo, Flavio, 216, 232–3
Bisticci, Vespasiano da, 21, 218, 240,
    250–1, 260, 262, 263, 299
Boccaccio, Giovanni, 5–6, 8, 22, 37,
    252, 287
Boccino da Verçaia, Antonio di Piero,
    71–2
Boethius, 275
Boiardo, Feltrino, 252, 263, 265
Boiardo, Matteo Maria, 321
Boissevain, Jeremy, 76–7
Bologna, 14n, 33, 172
    dress restrictions, 127, 131, 132,
        135, 137, 138, 145, 149
    funeral restrictions, 128
    Nicolosa Sanuti's protest, **139–40**,
        149
    Peace of, 153
Book of the Courtier (Castiglione),
    35–7, 218, 323–4
books, 21, 23, 217, 248
    appearance of, 218, 239–40, 241,
        257–64
    care of, **254**, 256
    choice of texts, 251–3
    church and, 37
Books on the Family (Alberti), 169–70
Bouwsma, William, 39
Borgia, Cesare, 15, 29–31
Borgia, Lucrezia, 328
Borgo, Damiano, 281n, 284
Botero, Giovanni, 34
botteghe see workshops
Botticelli, Sandro, 28, 296, 298, 303,
    311
Bracciolini, Poggio, 216, 238, 240,
    259, 261
Brescia, 144
Bronzino, Agnolo, 36
Brown, Allison, 66

Brown, Peter, 156
Brucker, Gene, 44, 65, 66, 70, 78
Brunelleschi, Filippo, 93, 295
Bruni, Leonardo, 238, 240, 244, 262
    on Florence, 18–19, 24, 48, 216
    on women's education, 217, **276–7**,
        280, 291
Bugliasso, Cristofano del, 119
Bullard, Melissa, 296
Buonarotti, Michelangelo see
        Michelangelo
Buondelmonti family, 111, 113
Buondelmonti, Piero, 52–3
Burckhardt, Jacob, 3, 6–7, 8, 43, 47,
        230n, 300, 318
bureaucracy, 25, **60–1**
Burke, Peter, 154–5, 317–18n
Bussi, Giovanni Andrea de', 249, 250
Bussoni, Biagio, 256

Calderoni, Anselmo, 66–7n
Cambini, Bernardo, 53
Cambrai, League of, 126, 141
Canigiani family, 80–1
Canzona del Popolo (dell'Ottonaio), 69
Capello, Francesca Loredan, 188n
Caplow, Harriet, 311
Capponi, Giovanni, 52
Carbone, Ludovico, 278–9
Cardano, Girolamo, 241
Carpaccio, Vittore, 18, 19, 96
Cartwright, Julia, 318–19
Casolo, Pietro, 143
Castiglione, Baldassare, 335
    Book of the Courtier, **35–7**, 218,
        323–4
    on women's role, 325, 326–7,
        331–2
catasto, 49–50, 52, 80, 88, 101, 102,
        109n, 112n, 118n
Catholic church, 34, 59, 161, 249
    Index of Prohibited Books, **37**, 62
    Jesuits, 38
    Medici influence, 54, 86, 87, 309 see
        also Clement VII, pope; Leo X,
        pope
    sacred objects and, 152–3, 156

sexual behavior and, **195–8**, 202,
        204, 206
    state and, 61–2
    sumptuary laws and, 133–9
Cecchi, Piero di ser Marianno, 82
Cederni, Bartolomeo, 82–3
Cellini, Benevenuto, 33
Ceresara, Paride de, 336
Certaldo, 6
Charlemagne, 228–9
Charles IV, emperor, 228, 234
Charles V, emperor, 33
Charles VIII, king of France, 29
Chartier, Roger, 244
chastity
    court life and, **331–3**, 337
    family honor and, 169, **193–4**, 203
    learning and, 281, **286–9**, 333,
        334
child prostitutes, 171, 204–5
children, 173, **177–80**
    sexual abuse of, 204–5
Chojnacki, Stanley, 169
Christian I, king of Denmark, vii
Chrysoloras, Manuel, 23, 238
churches, 151, 156
    family chapels, 99, 104, 109, **304**
    gonfalons and, 79, 84–5
    Medici patronage, 54, **84–5**, 160,
        304
Ciampolini, Giovanni, 315
Cicero, 215, 249, 252, 255, 261,
        264–5, 275
    Petrarch and, 5, 216, 219
Cimabue, 6
Ciompi revolt, Florence, 44, 51
Ciriaco d'Ancona, 216, 336
cities, 8, **16–21** see also individual cities
citizenship, 10, 13, 14, 26, 43, 93–4,
        152
city-states, 9, 10–11, **13–16**, 19, 25,
        43, 60 see also individual cities
civil society, 58, **63**
Clement VII, pope, 32, 33, 44, 46, 57
clientage, 52–3, 57, 62, 76, 77, 78,
        89, 176, 303, 305
Cohn, Samuel, 70n, 73–4, 89, 161

Cola di Jacopo, 78
Cola di Rienzo, 226n, 234
Colonna, Agapito, 227
Colonna, Giovanni, 223–4, 225, 226
Combat of Love and Chastity, (Perugino), 322–3
communal government, 9, 10, **13–15**, 43–4, 47–8 *see also* Florentine Republic
Commynes, Philippe de, 13
Compagni, Dino, 76
Comparetti, D., 232
compari see godparents
condottieri, 15, 86, 324
confraternities, 54, 59, 93
consorti, **105–6**
Constantine, emperor, 24
Contarini, Barbarella, 186–7
convents, 182n, 183, 201, 206
Corbinelli, Giovanni, 49
Corner, Cristina, 135
Cortegiano, Il (Castiglione), **35–7**, 218, 323–4
Cortesi, Alessandro, 309
costume, 36, 59
    restrictions *see* sumptuary laws
Costa, Lorenzo, 330n
court life
    art collecting and, 323, **324–5**
    Book of the Courtier, **35–7**, 218, 323–4
    consort's role, **325–6**, 327, 330, 333–4
    duels of wit, 265–6
    Florence, **57**, 59
    Mantua, 297, **327–30**, 333–4, 337, 338–9
    women and, 325, 326–7, **330–3**, 334–7, 338
Crinito, Pietro, 264–5
Croce, Benedetto, 231
Cropper, Elizabeth, 334–7

dancing, 147
Dante, 5, 141, 230, 252
Dark Ages, 40, 215, 219–21, **227–31**, 235, 236

Datini, Francesco, 10, 22, 94
Datini, Margherita, 22, 25
Davies, Martin, 261
Davis, Natalie Zemon, 152, 189
de Caprio, Vincenzo, 271
De honesta disciplina (Crinito), 264
De Mussis, Iohannes, 135
De orthographia (Tortelli), 271
De politia litteraria (Decembrio), 244–7
    on books as objects, **257–8**, 262, 263
    on choice of texts, **251–3**, 255–6, 264
    on libraries, **253–5**, 256–7
De Roover, Raymond, 65, 88
De viris illustribus (Petrarch), **221–2**, 227, 228, 230
Decades historiarum ab inclinatione imperii (Biondo), 232–3
Decembrio, Angelo, 245 *see also De politia litteraria*
Decembrio, Pier Candido, 246, 251
Declamation on the Forged Donation of Constantine (Valla), 24, 238, 270
décolletage, 135–7
Dei, Benedetto, 66n, 315
Delille, Gerard, 61
Della Casa, Giovanni, 35
Della Marca, Jacopo, 134, 137
Della Stufa family, 88
Dell'Ottonaio, Giovambattista, 69
dialectic, 273–6
Diodorus Siculus, 130, 238
Discourses on the First Ten Books of Titus Livy (Machiavelli), 29, 32
Divine Comedy (Dante), 230, 252
Douglas, Mary, 305
Dovizi, Piero, 313, 314
dowries, 53, 70, 132, 169, 178, 182
    effect on gender roles, 146–7, 172, 177, 184, **185–8**, 190–1
    forfeiture for adultery, 99
    legislation on, 146, 148–9
    Niccolini family, 106n, 111, 112, **113–14**, 115
    public funding, 17
Dupuy brothers, 257

economy, 8, 10–11, 13, **39**
  sumptuary laws and, 130–3
Elam, Caroline, 299n, 301n, 304
Eleanora of Aragon, 288n, 326
Eleanora of Toledo, 36
Erasmus, 266, 276n
Este family, 8, 45, 305
Este, Alfonso d', 322–3, 325, 328, 337
Este, Beatrice d', 326n, **327**
Este, Borso d', 264
Este, Ercole I d', duke of Ferrara, 19,
  326
Este, Isabella d', 25, 31, **317–19**, 324,
  326, *330*
  art historians' view, **317–23**, 340
  artists and, 296, 297, 322–3, 330,
    335, 336
  correspondence, 318, 319, **338–9**,
    340
  court role, 297, **327–30**, 337–8,
    338–9, 339–40
  learning, 297, 328, 333–4, 337
  mythological paintings and, 319,
    320–3, 329, 333, 334, 337, 338
  objets d'art collection, **319–20**, 329
Este, Leonello d', 245, 264, 335
  books belonging to, 247, 261, 262,
    264, 268
  correspondence with Guarino, 256,
    267, 282
  studiolo, 245, **255**, 257, 297
  see also De politia litteraria
Este, Niccolò d', 266
Eugenius IV, pope, 251
Eusebius of Caesarea, 231

Facio, Bartolomeo, 271, 272
Falcone, Giovanni, 261
Falier, Cristina, 185n
Falier, Petronella, 187
family *see* kinship
fashion, 141–2 *see also* sumptuary
  laws
Fava, D., 246
Feast of the Gods (Bellini), 322
Fedele, Cassandra, 25, 276n, 284n,
  288n

Ferdinand of Aragon, 29
Ferguson, Wallace K., 220
Ferrante of Aragon, 27
Ferrara, 8, 19, 45, 144–5, 297, 305,
  328, 335
  center for books, 263–4
  court, 265n, **326**, 334
  Este library, 244–5, 246, 247, 256,
    263, 266–7
  school of Guarino, 23, 263, **278–9**
feudalism, 10, 15, 43, 47–8, 60, 157
Fiamma, Galvano, 136
Ficino, Marsilio, 309–10, 314n
Fidele, Cassandra *see* Fedele
Fletcher, J. M., 320
Florence, 8, 16, 25, 36, 124, 240,
  261, 263
  Boccaccio and, 5, 6
  Bruni and, 18–19, 24, 48, 216
  civic buildings, 8, 14, *28*, 93, 162,
    295
  class divisions, **68–76**, 89–90
  communal government *see*
    Florentine Republic
  gonfalons, **78–81**, 83, 84–5, 161
  Medici principate, 33, 44, 57,
    58–60, 62
  neighborhood loyalties, 73–4, 76,
    160–1
  pater patriae, **66–8**, 89, 90, 94
  patronage, 76, 77–8, **81–8**, 90, 160
  religion, 157, 159, 160, **161–2**,
    166, *298*
  sexual behavior, 199, 200, 201,
    204, 205, 206–7, 207–8,
    209–10
  sumptuary laws, 127, 129, 130,
    134, 136, 148, 149n
  territorial expansion, 11
  women's costume, 140
Florentine Histories (Machiavelli), 32
Florentine Republic, 13, 24, 44,
  48–51
  Machiavelli and, 26, 27, 31, **32–3**
  Medici domination (1434–94), 14,
    44, **51–5**, 64–5, 66, 300,
    305–6

Florentine Republic *cont.*
  Medici expulsion (1494–1512), 26–7, 28, **55–7**
  Medici restoration (1512–27), 31, 32–3, 57
  Second Republic, 33, 129
Foix, Cardinal de, 315
Fontana, Lavinia, *172*
Fortebracci, Niccolò de', 87n
Fortes, Meyer, 181
Fortini, Pietro, 207
Foscari, Francesco, doge of Venice, 86
Foscari, Jacopo, 280, 282
Foscarini, Ludovico, 217, 289
France, 6, 8, 27, 29, 31, 40, 45, 55, 128
Francesco, Savese di, 86–7
Francia, Francesco, 330
Franco, Veronica, 171
Fraticelli, 240
Frederick III, emperor, vii, 139
friendship, 53, 94, 97, **117–22**
Fumagalli, Edoardo, 252–3
funerals, 128, 137, 138

Gagliano, Roberto da, 88
Gagliano, Piero da, 84
Galateo (Della Casa), 35
Galeazzo, Gian, duke of Milan, 129
Galileo Galilei, 40
gang rape, 205
Garin, E., 279, 280, 289, 290
Garzoni, Giovanni, 146
Gellius, Aulus, 247, 249
gender roles
  dowry wealth and, 146–7, 172, 177, 184, **185–8**, 190–1
  men, 169, 173–4, **177–80**, 181–3, 190–1
  women, 169–71, 173, 180–1, **183–91**
Genoa, 10–11, 144, 313
  sumptuary laws, 125, 126, 127, 131, 132–3, 136, 143n, 145–6, 148
Germany, 33, 223

Gesta ferdinandi (Valla), 270
Gherardini, Niccolò, 78
Ghiberti, Lorenzo, 295
Ghirlandaio, Domenico, 304
Gibbon, Edward, 6, 226
Giotto, 5, 6
Giovanni, Francesco di Tommaso, 71–3, 120n
godparents, 115, 118, **119–21**, 122
gold, 132–3
Golden Book (*Libro d'oro*), Venice, 13
Gombrich, Ernst, 260, 301–2, 310, 316
gonfalons, 49, **78–83**, 110, 161
  Medici and, 83–5
Gonzaga family, 45, 324, 327–8, 329
Gonzaga, Cecilia, 328
Gonzaga, Elisabetta, 35, 324, 327
Gonzaga, Federigo II, 322n, 337
Gonzaga, Francesco, 260, 297, 327, 328, 336
Gonzaga, Ludovico, duke of Mantua, vii, 335
Good City-Republic, The (Lorenzetti), 9
Gothein, P., 289n
Gozzoli, Benozzo, 298
Grafton, Anthony, 217
Grand Tour, 40
Great Council, Florence, 27, 55, 56
Great Schism, 20
Greece, 216, 252, 272
Gritti, Andrea, doge of Venice, 148
Gualengo, Giovanni, 255–6
Guarini, Battista, 263n, 269n
Guarino da Verona, 23, 24, 238, 245, 246, 248, 266, 273, 297
  funeral oration for, 278–9
  letters to Leonello d'Este, 256, 267
  Niccoli and, 261, 262–3
  Nogarola sisters and, 280–4
  texts emended by, 247, 261, 268
  see also De politia litteraria
Guicciardini, Francesco, 34–5, 38, 57
Guicciardini, Piero, 88–9n
guilds, 13, 39, 43–4, 48, 54, 59, 93
Gundersheimer, Werner, 305

Haines, Margaret, 311
Hankins, James, 268
Healing of the Possessed Man
 (Carpaccio), *96*
Heers, Jacques, 128
Heloise, 289n
history, 3, 217, 239, 243
 divisions of, 231–6
History of Italy, The (Guicciardini),
 34–5
Hobson, Anthony, 259
homosexuality, 190, 195, 205,
 206–11
Hope, Charles, 321–2
Horne, Herbert, 303
house ownership, 99, **108–10**, 118
Hughes, Diane Owen, 94, 180
humanism, 3, 4–5, 6, 7, **215–17**,
 324, 332, 334
 church and, 38
 Dark Ages concept, 215, **219–21**
 learning, **23–6**, 216
 periodization of history, 232–3
 virtue and, 282, **289–91**, 328
 women and, 25–6, 217, 327–8, 333
 see also Nogarola, Isotta

Iacopino d'Arezzo, 261
iconic language, 153–4, 157–8
illustrations, 260–1
immovable property, 185
incest, 286, 287
Index of Prohibited Books, **37**, 62
Inquisition, 62
intestacy, 109n, 184n, 185n
Italian League, 27, 29
Italian Wars, 26, **29**, 31, 33
Italy, 7, 8, 11–13, **15–16**, 29, 34–5,
 39, 40, 45

Jardine, Lisa, 217
Jerome, St., 231
Jesuits, 38
jewellery, **132–3**, 148
Jews, 50, 154
Joachimsen, P., 236

Julius II, pope, 20, 46
Justinus, 285
Juvenal, 255, 266

Kent, Dale, 65–6, 80, 83, 306
Kent, F. W., 179, 306, 307n, 315
kinship, 61, 94, 97, **99–108**, 122–3,
 161, 169, 190, 191, 304
 affines, **110–17**, 122
 house ownership and, 99, **108–10**,
 118
Klapisch-Zuber, Christiane, 94, 178n,
 180
Kolsky, S., 318n

Lamola, Giovanni, 247, 248, 261
Landucci, Luca, 87n
Lane, Frederic C., 47
Lanfredini, G., 314n
language, 5, 11–13, 32, 35, 311n
 change in, 270–2
 of deference, **306–10**, 316
 of patronage, 301–2
 of the sacred, **152–4**, 157
Lanti, Lorenzo di messer Antonio de',
 149
law, sexual behavior and, **198–200**,
 201, 208
Latino, Cardinal, 134, 135, 144
Leo X, pope, 20, 32, 35, 44, *46*, 57
Leonardo da Vinci, 21, 29, 31, 32,
 296, 330
Leonora of Portugal, 139
libraries, 5, 21, 23, **216–17**, 244, 315
 choice of texts, 251–3
 classical, 246–7, **248–50**, 255
 Este library, 244–5, 246, 247,
 266–7, 269
 of Federico da Montefeltro, *218*
 ideal, **253–5**, 256–7
 Salutati on, 247–8
 Vatican, 24, 217, 237, 246, 248,
 249–50, 250–1
 see also De politia litteraria
lineage, 13–14, 99–100, 104, 172,
 184–6, 190

literacy, 22–3
literature, 7, **320–1**, 322
Littlewood, Paul, 77
Lives of the Artists, (Vasari), 38, 299
Livorno (Leghorn), 38
Livy, 26, 248, 252, 262, 263, 265
Loredan, Franceschina, 180n
Loredan, Lorenzo, 183n, 188–9n
Lorenzetti, Ambrogio, 8, *9*
Lotto, Lorenzo, 330
Louis VIII, king of France, 128
Louis XII, king of France, 29
Luca di Cino, 50
Lucca, 64, 68, 145, 201, 206, 207
Luther, Martin, 46

Machiavelli, Niccolò, 10, 15, 26, 27,
    28, 34, 59
  admiration for Cesare Borgia, 29–31
  on Italy, **16**, 29, 45
  literary works, 10n, 16, 29, 31, **32**,
    37, 45, 216
  Medici and, 31, 32–3
  political career, 27, 31, 33
magnates, 14
Malatesta, Battista, 217, 276, 282
Malpiglio (Tasso), 37
Mandrake, The (Machiavelli), 32
Manetti, Giannozzo, 249
Mantegna, Andrea, vii, 259, 321,
    330n, 334, *335, 336*
Mantua, 8, 23, 24, 45, 324, 327–9,
    335, 337
Manutius, Aldus (Aldo Manuzzio), 21,
    266
Manzoni, Alessandro, 62
Mapheo, Andrea, 86
marriage, 17, 53, 201
  age at, 116, 146, 169, 171, 181–2,
    189–90, 194
  alliance strategies, **110–17**, 169,
    176–7, 182, 326
  Bernardino da Siena on, 196–8
  lower classes, 73–4, 203–4
  maternal influence and, 170,
    186–90
  paternal authority and, 169, **181–3**

  remarriage, 104, 178
  sumptuary laws and, **145–7**, 182
  women's kinship status and, **103–4**,
    145, 180–1, 182, 189
marriage debt, 196–7
Mars and Venus (Mantegna), 330n,
    334, *335*
Martelli, Ugolino, *36*
Martindale, Andrew, 319–20
Martines, Lauro, 290n, 291
Masaccio, 295
Masaniello, 163
Mazzei, Ser Lapo, 22
Medici family, 16, 33, 36, 44–5, 51–2,
    57, 160, 162, 257
  artistic patronage, 32, **299–304**,
    312
  political patronage, 83–4, **305–10**
Medici, Bernardo d'Antonio
    (Bernardetto) de', 303
Medici, Cosimo de' (il Vecchio), 14, 44,
    54, **64–5**
  artistic patronage, 295–6, *298*, 299,
    300, 301–2, 311
  church of San Lorenzo and, 84, 85,
    297, 304
  library of, 21, 217, 251
  pater patriae, **66–8**, 88, 90, 94
  political patronage, 52, 76, 83–4,
    85–8, 305
  studies on, **65–6**, 306
  workers and, 67, 70–1, 74n
Medici, Cosimo I de', duke of Florence,
    36, 57, 58–9, 60, 62, 210
Medici, Francesco di Giuliano de', 87n
Medici, Giovanni de' *see* Leo X, pope
Medici, Giovanni di Bicci de', 64, 71n,
    83, 84, 304
Medici, Giulio de' *see* Clement VII, pope
Medici, Lorenzo de' (Il Magnifico), 19,
    20, 27, 28, 32, 33–4, *298*
  artistic patronage, 299, 300, 301–2,
    303, 311, 320
  delegation of tasks, 312–16
  letters to, 52–3, **307–10**, 336
  political patronage, **52–5**, 305, 306
Medici, Lorenzo de', 33–4

Medici, Lorenzo di Pierfrancesco de', 303
Medici, Orlando di Guccio de', 303
Medici, Piero de' 27, 52, 54, 67n, 84, 89, 90, *298*, 304n
men, 181
    family role *see* patriarchal system
    same-sex relations, 205, **206–11**
    sexuality, **194–5**
merchants, **8–11**, 94, 170, 240–1
Michelangelo, 6, 32, 38, 40, 46, 299, 302
Michelet, Jules, 6
Michelozzi, Niccolò, 313, 314
Michelozzo, 302, 311
Milan, 5, 13–14, 25, 29, 34, 45, 65, 134, 313, 327
    sumptuary laws, 127, **129–30**, 131, 136, 144
Milo, Yoram, 70n
Molho, Anthony, 44
Mommsen, Theodor, 215
Montaigne, Michel de, 130
Montefeltro, Federico da, 19, *218*, 259, 260, 297
Montefeltro, Guidobaldo da, 35, *218*
Montpellier, Council of, 128
Morelli, Giovanni di Pagolo
    on marriage strategy, **110–11**, 112
    on Romans, 23
    on social relationships, 81, 97, 119, 122
    on trust, 17, 106, 107n
    on uncloistered nuns, 104n
Morexini, Vetor, 147
Morosini, Francesco, 182n
Morosini, Gasparino, **178–80**, 183, 185n
Morosini, Isabetta, 188n
motherhood, 173
    mother–daughter relationships, **186–8**, 189
    mother–son relationships, **184–6**
movable property, 185
Muir, Edward, 93
Muntz, E., 89n

mythological painting, 319, **320–3**, 329, 333, 337, 338

Najemy, John, 49, 311n
Naples, 5, 27–9, 157, **162–3**, 165, 309
Nardi family, 81
Naudé, Gabriel, 257
neighbors, 97, **122**
Neroni, Dietisalvi, 90
Newton, Jeffrey, 70n
Niccoli, Niccolò, 259, **261–2**, 262–3
Niccoli, Ottavia, 153
Niccolini dei Sirigatti, Lapo de' Giovanni, 97–8
    blood relatives, **99–108**, 115
    family houses, 108–10
    friendships, 117–23
    marriage alliances, 110–17
Nicholas V, pope, 20, 27
    Valla's Thucydides and, 237, 240, 241–2, 248
    Vatican Library and, 24, 237, 246, 249–50, 250–1
Nicola, Bernardo di, 53
Nigrisoli, Nigrisolo dei, 264
Nogarola, Ginevra, 278n, **280–3**
Nogarola, Isotta, 217, 290
    Borgo and, 284–6
    Guarino and, 278n, **280–4**
    incest accusation, 286–7
    Quirini's advice to, **273–6**, 277, 280, 289
    studies abandoned, **288–9**, 291
Nolan, Mary, 63
Nolhac, P. de, 222n
nuns, 104, 202, 206
Nuremberg, 130

On Painting (Alberti), 296
On Wifely Duties (Barbaro), 19
Orlando Furioso (Ariosto), 32, 317, 327
Orpheus de Cancellariis, 133, 136
Orsini, Giovanni Antonio di Blazo, 15
Orsini, Rinaldo, 54
Ottoman Empire, 27
ottomati, 51, 60

Pade, Marianne, 242, 268
Padua, 5, 335
   sumptuary laws, 125, 126, 134,
     137, 138, 139, 147
*Pallas expelling the Vices from the
   Garden of Virtue* (Mantegna), 334,
   336
palleschi, 83
Palmieri, Matteo, 193–4
Panciatichi, Giovanni, 78
Panegyric to the City of Florence (Bruni),
   18–19
Panuzzi, Salvi, 209–10
Paoletti, John, 311
Paolino, Fra, 133
papacy, 4, 8, 20, 29, 34, 45, 46, 62,
   134, 238, 246
Papal States, 8, 20, 46, 59n
Passerini, Luigi, 105
pater patriae, **66–8**, 89, 90, 94
patriarchal system, 169, 170, 173–4,
   175–6, 186, 190, 191
patronage, 52–3, 57, 62, **295–340**
   Boissevain's definition, 76–7
   Venice, **158–9**, 176
   by women, 287–8
Paul III, pope, 38
Pavia, Lorenzo di, 339
Perugia, 135
Perugino, 321, 322–3
Pescia, 200
Petrarch, **4–5**, 6, 8, 16, 22, 216, 252,
   266, 289n
   Africa, 221, 228, 229, 234
   Dark Ages concept, 40, 215,
     219–20, **227–31**, 235, 236
   De viris illustribus, **221–2**, 227, 228,
     230
   periodization of history, 226–7, 230,
     231, **232–5**
   on script, 258–9
   Secretum, 221–2, 227
   visits to Rome, 4, **222–6**
Petrucci, Armando, 248
Petrucci, Battista, 139
Philip II, king of Spain, 29

Philip IV (the Fair), king of France,
   128
philosophy, 215, **273–6**
Pietribuoni, Pietro, 72n, 88n
Pisa, 11, 55
Pisani, Briseida, 180n
Pisano, Andrea, 8
Pisano, Ugolino, 251
Pistoia, sumptuary laws, 131, 141,
   149n
Pius II, pope, 11, 14, 15, 27, 245
Placentini, Scarcia, 245n
plague, 8, 16, 68, 101, 103, 104, 105,
   109, 127
Plato, 268
Pliny the Younger, 254, 255
Pocock, John, 307
Poetica (Aristotle), 239
political patronage, 52–3, 90, 303,
   305
   Florence, **77–83**, 160
   language of, 306–10
   Medici, 83–8
Poliziano, Angelo (Politian), 70–1,
   74–5, 202, 264, 278n, 284n,
   315
Polo, Jacomo Donado fu di Messer, 87n
Pontanus, 333
Pope Leo X with Two Cardinals
   (Raphael), *46*
Pope-Hennessy, John, 303
population levels, 8, 16–17, 157
Portrait of a Family (Fontana), *172*
*Portrait of Federico da Montefeltro and
   His Son Guidobaldo* (Berruguete),
   218
Portrait of Isabella d'Este (Titian), 330,
   331
Portrait of Ugolino Martelli (Bronzino),
   36
Prato, 10, 11, 94
Prato, Baldassare di Luigi da, 84
precious metals, 132–3
priests, 158–9
Prince, The (Machiavelli), 16, 29, 31,
   32, 45, 216

Promessi sposi, I, (Manzoni), 62
prophecies, 153, 160
prosecution under sumptuary laws, 137
prostitutes, 19, 35, 129, 143n, 144–5, 147, 193, **200–2**
  children, 171
protectionism, economic, 131–2
Protestantism, 34, 152–3, 164

Quarata family, 80–1
Quintilian, 216, 243, 271–2
Quirini, Lauro, **273–7**, 289

rape, 198, 199, 202, 204, 205
Raphael, 46
reading, art of, 253, **254–9**
Reason of State, The (Botero), 34
Reformation, 34, 166
Regoliosi, Mariangela, 272
relics, 162–3
religious dissent, 62
remarriage, 104, 178
Renaissance, 3, **6–7**, 235–6
  ending, 33–40
republics *see* communal government
Rerum memorandarum libri (Petrarch), 229
Respublica (Plato), 268
revolts, 164
Rheatinus, Thomas, 267
Ricasoli, Bettino, 62–3n
Ricci, Agnoletta de', 206
Ricci, Uguccione de', 50
Riccobaldo of Ferrara, 141
Rinuccini, Filippo di Cino, 67n, 68n
Rizzo, Silvia, 250n
Rizzoni, Martino, 278n
Robert, Count of Arras, 129, 143
Rocke, Michael, 171
Rodenberg, Ioannes Lamperti de, 237
Romano, Dennis, 158
Rome, 5, 8, 16, 20, 23, 32, 33, 34, 38, 46, 157, 216
  libraries, 248–9
  Petrarch and, 4, **222–7**

Rosaldo, Michelle, 191
Roscoe, William, 300
Rossi, Luigi de' 46
Rossi, Matteo di ser Giovanni de', 68, 70n
Rosso, Franco di, 90
Rubinstein, Nicolai, 65, 66
Rucellai family, 113
Rucellai, Bernardo, 32, 308
Rucellai, Giovanni, 20, 53, 68, 71, 72n, 81, 87n
Ruggiero, Guido, 190
Ruysschaert, J., 250n

Sabbadini, R., 246, 261, 278n, 281n, **282–3**, 287
Sacchetti, Franco, 124–5, 137
sacred images, 151–4
Saitta, Armando, 289
Salimbene, 134, 135
Salutati, Coluccio, 24–5, 237–8, 247–8, 259
Salviati, Alamanno, 86
same-sex relations, 190, 195, 205, **206–11**
San Juan, Rose Marie, 297
San Severina, Cardinal of, 164
Sanuti, Nicolosa, **139–40**, 145, 148, 149
Sanvito, Bartolomeo, 259
Savona, 136
Savonarola, Girolamo, 26–7, 28, 56, 129, 136, 192, 207
Scali, Manetto, 76
Scaliger, Joseph, 260
Scholium Plautinum, 249, 250
Scipio, Lucius, **228**, 229
script, 240, **258–9**, 261
Scriptores historiae Augustae, 248
secretaries, 25, 313–14
Secretum (Petrarch), 221–2, 227
Seneca, 248, 251
Servius, 268–9
sexuality, 192–3
  Church's view, 195–8
  illicit, 200–6

sexuality *cont.*
  law and, 198–200
  of men, 171, **194–5**
  same-sex relations, 195, **206–11**
  of women, 146, 171, **193–4**
Seymour, Charles, 311
Sforza, Francesco, duke of Milan, vii, 14, 45, 65, 86, 87–8
Sforza, Ludovico, duke of Milan, 29, 327
Sheard, Wendy, 311
Siena, 16, 142, 148
  Allegory of Good and Bad Government, 8, 9
  dress restrictions, 127, 128, 131, 135n, 143, 144
  jewellery restrictions, 128, 129, 132, 145
  prosecutions, 147, 149–50
  silk industry, 131
  sumptuary law relaxations, 129, 139, 143
silver, 132
Simmel, Georg, 141
Simon, Patricia, 304
Simone, Domenico di Guasparre, 82–3
Simone, Franco, 219, 220
sincerity threshold, 154–5, 165
Sirigatti, Niccolò, 106, 109
Sixtus IV, pope, 24, 218
Sixtus V, pope, 20
slaves, 13, 101, 102n, 171
Society of Jesus, 38
Soderini family, 80, 82
Soderini, Tommaso, 82–3
Soranzo, Beruzza, 185
Spain, 27, 29, 33, 34, 129, 162
Spencer, John, 303
spinsterhood, 188
spiritual kinship *see* godparents
sprezzatura, 35
state, 43, **60–3** *see also* city-states; communal government
Strocchia, Sharon, 180
Strozzi, Agostino, 323n
Strozzi, Alessandra, 10, 25–6, 170

Strozzi, Nanni degli, 244
Strozzi, Tito, 251, 264, 265
studioli, 325
  of Isabella d'Este, 297, 329, 330n, 335
  of Leonello d'Este, 245, **255**, 257, 297
sumptuary laws, 19, 21, 94–5, **124–8**
  church influence, **133–6**, 137–9
  economic motives, 130–3
  fashion and, 125, **141–2**
  hierarchical distinctions, **128–30**, 149, 150
  Nicolosa Sanuti's protest, **139–40**, 148
  social function, 142–7
  women and, 135–41
Supreme Council of Italy, 29, 32
Sylvester I, pope, 24

Tagliamillo, Alexander, 87
Tagliamillo, Niccola, 87
Tarabotti, Arcangela, 170
Tasso, Torquato, 37
Tatham, R., 222n
taxation, 49–50, 52, 60, 62, 75, 80, 84–5, 144
Terence, 247–8, 252, 255, 269
territorial expansion, **11**, 20
theater cultures, 155, 165
third order, 104
Thirty Years' War, 39
Thomas, St., 133
Thou, Jacques-Auguste de, 257, 259
Thucydides, 237–8, 248, 270, 272
Titian, 297, 322, 325, 330, *331*, 337n
Tornabuoni, Giovanni, 304, 306n, 307–8
Tornabuoni, Nofri, 306n, 315
Torre, Angelo, 153
Tortelli, Giovanni, 271
trade, **8–11**, 39
Traversari, Ambrogio, 240
Trent, Council of, 34, 37, 164, 202
Trevisan, Isabetta, 182n
Treviso, 11

Trionfi (Petrarch), 229–30
Turks, 27, 126
Tuscan dialect, 5, 11–12, 32, 35
Two Venetian Ladies on a Terrace
   (Carpaccio), *18*, 19

Udine, 152, 157, **164–5**
Urban V, pope, 233
Urbino, 19, 35, 36, 46, 218, 324, 327
Uzzano, Niccolò da, 64

Vaglienti, Piero, 57–8
Valla, Giorgio, 255n
Valla, Lorenzo, 24, 37, 246n, 262
   on linguistic change, 270–2
   translation of Thucydides, 237,
     238–44, 248, 270
Varga, L., 220–1n
Vasari, Giorgio, 6, 38, 40, 299, 300,
   303, 311, 316
Vasoli, Cesare, 279
Vatican Library, 24, 217, 237, 245,
   248, 249, 260
Vaucluse, 221, 222n
Vecellio, Cesare, 141
Vegio, Maffeo, 267–8
Venice, 8, 16, 23, 37, 93, 153, 155,
   216
   defeat at Agnadello, 31
   dowry restrictions, 146
   dress restrictions, 125, 130, 132,
     134, 136, 137, **141–2**, 143, 144
   foreign population, 13, 154
   government, 11, 13, 14, 44
   marriage, 176–7
   papacy and, 27, 31, 37
   patriarchy, 173–4, 175–6, **177–80**,
     181–3, 191
   patronage, **158–9**, 176
   ritual, *96*, 157–8, 159
   sacred images/objects, 151–2, 154,
     156, 165
   sexual behavior, 199, 204–5, 206,
     208n, 210
   sumptuary legislation, **126**, 130,
     131, 148
   territorial expansion, 11

trade, 10–11, 27, 39, 155
women, *18*, 19, 147, 158, 170,
   171, 174, **180–91**
Vergerio, Pietro Paolo, 289, 290
Verheyen, Egon, 320–1, 322
Verona, 5, 281
Vettori, Giovanni, 50
Villani, Giovanni, 141
Virgil, 252, 265, 267–8, 333
Virgin Mary, statues of, 151, 154, 155,
   163, 165
virtue
   humanism and, 282, **289–91**, 328
   women and, **281–3**, 284–5, 327,
     328 *see also* chastity
Visconti family, 8, 13, 14, 45
Vita Civile (Palmieri), 193–4
Vitelleschi, Giovanni, 86
Vitruvius, 216
Vittorino da Feltre, 23, 279
Vitturi, Vittoria, 180n
Voltaire, 124

Wacquet, Jean Claude, 61n
weddings, 128, 135, 137, 138
Weissman, Ronald, 70n
widowhood, 103, 179n, 199
wills, 99n, 103–4, 109, **178–80**,
   189
   of women, 158, 179, 182, 183–4,
     187–8
wine consumption, 75
women, 190–1
   age at marriage, 169, 181–2,
     189–90, 194
   church's view, 133–4, 195,
     196–8
   family role, 169–70
   father–daughter relationships,
     181–3, 186, 188, 189
   kinship status, **103–4**, 145, 150,
     180–1
   law and, 198–200
   learning and, 22, **25–6**, 217, 333
     see also Nogarola, Isotta
   mother–daughter relationships,
     186–8, 189

women *cont.*
   mother–son relationships, **184–6**
   as patrons, 287–8 *see also* Este,
     Isabella d'
   sexuality, **193–4**, 203–4, 205–6
   sumptuary laws and, 135–41
   wills, 158, 179, 182, 183–4,
     187–8

worker–employer relationships, 62–3n,
   68–76, 89–90
workshops, 301, **310–16**

Zaleucus, 130, 144
Zane, Alvise, 189n
Zaninello, Giovanni Francesco, 330
Zustinian, Lorenzo, 134